The Henry Drummond Reader

by Henry Drummond

Natural Law in the Spiritual World
Stones Rolled Away and Other Addresses
The Ascent of Man
The Greatest Thing in the World and Other Addresses
A Life for A Life and Other Addresses
The Changed Life
The City Without a Church
Beautiful Thoughts From Henry Drummond
The Program of Christianity

©2008 Wilder Publications

Wilder Publications, LLC.
PO Box 3005
Radford VA 24143-3005

ISBN 10: 1-60459-186-2
ISBN 13: 978-1-60459-186-6

Natural Law in the Spiritual World

Table of Contents

Preface

No class of works is received with more suspicion, I had almost said derision, than those which deal with Science and Religion. Science is tired of reconciliations between two things which never should have been contrasted; Religion is offended by the patronage of an ally which it professes not to need; and the critics have rightly discovered that, in most cases where Science is either pitted against Religion or fused with it, there is some fatal misconception to begin with as to the scope and province of either. But although no initial protest, probably, will save this work from the unhappy reputation of its class, the thoughtful mind will perceive that the fact of its subject-matter being Law—a property peculiar neither to Science nor to Religion—at once places it on a somewhat different footing.

The real problem I have set myself may be stated in a sentence. Is there not reason to believe that many of the Laws of the Spiritual World, hitherto regarded as occupying an entirely separate province, are simply the Laws of the Natural World? Can we identify the Natural Laws, or any one of them, in the Spiritual sphere? That vague lines everywhere run through the Spiritual World is already beginning to be recognized. Is it possible to link them with those great lines running through the visible universe which we call the Natural Laws, or are they fundamentally distinct? In a word, Is the Supernatural natural or unnatural?

I may, perhaps, be allowed to answer these questions in the form in which they have answered themselves to myself. And I must apologize at the outset for personal references which, but for the clearness they may lend to the statement, I would surely avoid.

It has been my privilege for some years to address regularly two very different audiences on two very different themes. On week days I have lectured to a class of students on the Natural Sciences, and on Sundays to an audience consisting for the most part of working men on subjects of a moral and religious character. I cannot say that this collocation ever appeared as a difficulty to myself, but to certain of my friends it was more than a problem. It was solved to me, however, at first, by what then seemed the necessities of the case—I must keep the two departments entirely by themselves. They lay at opposite poles of thought; and for a time I succeeded in keeping the Science and the Religion shut off from one another in two separate compartments of my mind. But gradually the wall of partition showed symptoms of giving way. The two fountains of knowledge also slowly began to overflow, and finally their waters met and mingled. The great change was in the compartment which held the Religion. It was not that the well there was dried; still less that the fermenting waters were washed away by the flood of Science. The actual contents remained the same. But the crystals of former doctrine were dissolved; and as they precipitated themselves once more in definite forms, I observed that the Crystalline System was changed. New channels also for outward expression opened, and some of the old closed up; and I found the truth running out to my audience on the Sundays by the week-day outlets. In other words, the subject-matter Religion had taken on the method of expression of Science, and I discovered myself enunciating Spiritual Law in the exact terms of Biology and Physics.

Now this was not simply a scientific coloring given to Religion, the mere freshening of the theological air with natural facts and illustrations. It was an entire re-casting of truth. And when I came seriously to consider what it involved, I saw, or seemed to see, that it meant essentially the introduction of Natural Law into the Spiritual World. It was not, I repeat, that new and detailed analogies of *Phenomena* rose into view—although material for Parable lies unnoticed and unused on the field of recent Science in inexhaustible profusion. But Law has a still grander function to discharge toward Religion than Parable. There is a deeper unity between the two Kingdoms than the analogy of their Phenomena—a unity which the poet's vision, more quick than the theologian's, has already dimly seen:—

> "And verily many thinkers of this age,
> Aye, many Christian teachers, half in heaven,
> Are wrong in just my sense, who understood
> Our natural world too insularly, as if
> No spiritual counterpart completed it,
> Consummating its meaning, rounding all
> To justice and perfection, *line by line,*
> *Form by form, nothing single nor alone,*
> The great below clenched by the great above."

The function of Parable in religion is to exhibit "form by form." Law undertakes the profounder task of comparing "line by line." Thus Natural Phenomena serve mainly an illustrative function in Religion. Natural Law, on the other hand, could it be traced in the Spiritual World, would have an important scientific value—it would offer Religion a new credential. The effect of the introduction of Law among the scattered Phenomena of Nature has simply been to make Science, to transform knowledge into eternal truth. The same crystallizing touch is needed in Religion. Can it be said that the Phenomena of the Spiritual World are other than scattered? Can we shut our eyes to the fact that the religious opinions of mankind are in a state of flux? And when we regard the uncertainty of current beliefs, the war of creeds, the havoc of inevitable as well as of idle doubt, the reluctant abandonment of early faith by those who would cherish it longer if they could, is it not plain that the one thing thinking men are waiting for is the introduction of Law among the Phenomena of the Spiritual World? When that comes we shall offer to such men a truly scientific theology. And the Reign of Law will transform the whole Spiritual World as it has already transformed the Natural World.

I confess that even when in the first dim vision, the organizing hand of Law moved among the unordered truths of my Spiritual World, poor and scantily-furnished as it was, there seemed to come over it the beauty of a transfiguration. The change was as great as from the old chaotic world of Pythagoras to the symmetrical and harmonious universe of Newton. My Spiritual World before was a chaos of facts; my Theology, a Pythagorean system trying to make the best of Phenomena apart from the idea of Law. I make no charge against Theology in general. I speak of my own. And I say that I saw it to be in many essential respects centuries behind every department of Science I knew. It was the one region still unpossessed by Law. I saw then why men of Science distrust Theology; why those who have learned to look upon Law as Authority grow cold to it—it was the Great Exception.

I have alluded to the genesis of the idea in my own mind partly for another reason—to show its naturalness. Certainly I never premeditated anything to myself so objectionable and so unwarrantable in itself, as either to read Theology into Science or Science into Theology. Nothing could be more artificial than to attempt this on the speculative side; and it has been a substantial relief to me throughout that the idea rose up thus in the course of practical work and shaped itself day by day unconsciously. It might be charged, nevertheless, that I was all the time, whether consciously or unconsciously, simply reading my Theology into my Science. And as this would hopelessly vitiate the conclusions arrived at, I must acquit myself at least of the intention. Of nothing have I been more fearful throughout than of making Nature parallel with my own or with any creed. The only legitimate questions one dare put to Nature are those which concern universal human good and the Divine interpretation of things. These I conceive may be there actually studied at first-hand, and before their purity is soiled by human touch. We have Truth in Nature as it came from God. And it has to be read with the same unbiased mind, the same open eye, the same faith, and the same reverence as all other Revelation. All that is found there, whatever its place in Theology, whatever its orthodoxy or heterodoxy, whatever its narrowness or its breadth, we are bound to accept as Doctrine from which on the lines of Science there is no escape.

When this presented itself to me as a method, I felt it to be due to it—were it only to secure, so far as that was possible, that no former bias should interfere with the integrity of the results—to begin again at the beginning and reconstruct my Spiritual World step by step. The result of that inquiry, so far as its expression in systematic form is concerned, I have not given in this book. To reconstruct a Spiritual Religion, or a department of Spiritual Religion—for this is all the method can pretend to—on the lines of Nature would be an attempt from which one better equipped in both directions might well be pardoned if he shrank. My object at present is the humbler one of venturing a simple contribution to practical Religion along the lines indicated. What Bacon predicates of the Natural World, *Natura enim non nisi parendo vincitur*, is also true, as Christ had already told us, of the Spiritual World. And I present a few samples of the religious teaching referred to formerly as having been prepared under the influence of scientific ideas in the hope that they may be useful first of all in this direction.

I would, however, carefully point out that though their unsystematic arrangement here may create the impression that these papers are merely isolated readings in Religion pointed by casual scientific truths, they are organically connected by a single principle. Nothing could be more false both to Science and to Religion than attempts to adjust the two spheres by making out ingenious points of contact in detail. The solution of this great question of conciliation, if one may still refer to a problem so gratuitous, must be general rather than particular. The basis in a common principle—the Continuity of Law—can alone save specific applications from ranking as mere coincidences, or exempt them from the reproach of being a hybrid between two things which must be related by the deepest affinities or remain forever separate.

To the objection that even a basis in Law is no warrant for so great a trespass as the intrusion into another field of thought of the principles of Natural Science, I would reply that in this I find I am following a lead which in other departments has not only been allowed but has achieved results as rich as they were unexpected. What is the Physical Politic of Mr. Walter Bagehot but the extension of Natural Law to the Political World? What is the Biological Sociology of Mr. Herbert Spencer but the application of Natural Law to the Social World? Will it be charged that the splendid achievements of such thinkers are hybrids between things which Nature has meant to remain apart? Nature usually solves such problems for herself. Inappropriate hybridism is checked by the Law of Sterility. Judged by this great Law these modern developments of our knowledge stand uncondemned. Within their own sphere the results of Mr. Herbert Spencer are far from sterile—the application of Biology to Political Economy is already revolutionizing the Science. If the introduction of Natural Law into the Social sphere is no violent contradiction but a genuine and permanent contribution, shall its further extension to the Spiritual sphere be counted an extravagance? Does not the Principle of Continuity demand its application in every direction? To carry it as a working principle into so lofty a region may appear impracticable. Difficulties lie on the threshold which may seem, at first sight, insurmountable. But obstacles to a true method only test its validity. And he who honestly faces the task may find relief in feeling that whatever else of crudeness and imperfection mar it, the attempt is at least in harmony with the thought and movement of his time.

That these papers were not designed to appear in a collective form, or indeed to court the more public light at all, needs no disclosure. They are published out of regard to the wish of known and unknown friends by whom, when in a fugitive form, they were received with so curious an interest as to make one feel already that there are minds which such forms of truth may touch. In making the present selection, partly from manuscript, and partly from articles already published, I have been guided less by the wish to constitute the papers a connected series than to exhibit the application of the principle in various directions. They will be found, therefore, of unequal interest and value, according to the standpoint from which they are regarded. Thus some are designed with a directly practical and popular bearing, others being more expository, and slightly apologetic in tone. The risk of combining two objects so very different is somewhat serious. But, for the reason named, having taken this responsibility, the only compensation I can offer is to indicate which of the papers incline to the one side or to the other. "Degeneration," "Growth," "Mortification," "Conformity to Type," "Semi-Parasitism," and "Parasitism" belong to the more practical order; and while one or two are intermediate, "Biogenesis," "Death," and "Eternal Life" may be offered to those who find the atmosphere of the former uncongenial. It will not disguise itself, however, that, owing to the circumstances in which they were prepared, all the papers are more or less practical in their aim; so that to the merely philosophical reader there is little to be offered except—and that only with the greatest diffidence—the Introductory chapter.

In the Introduction, which the general reader may do well to ignore, I have briefly stated the case for Natural Law in the Spiritual World. The extension of Analogy to Laws, or rather the extension of the Laws themselves so far as known to me, is new; and I cannot hope to have escaped the mistakes and misadventures of a first exploration in an unsurveyed land. So general has been the survey that I have not even paused to define specially to what departments of the Spiritual

World exclusively the principle is to be applied. The danger of making a new principle apply too widely inculcates here the utmost caution. One thing is certain, and I state it pointedly, the application of Natural Law to the Spiritual World has decided and necessary limits. And if elsewhere with undue enthusiasm I seem to magnify the principle at stake, the exaggeration—like the extreme amplification of the moon's disc when near the horizon—must be charged to that almost necessary aberration of light which distorts every new idea while it is yet slowly climbing to its zenith.

In what follows the Introduction, except in the setting there is nothing new. I trust there is nothing new. When I began to follow out these lines, I had no idea where they would lead me. I was prepared, nevertheless, at least for the time, to be loyal to the method throughout, and share with nature whatever consequences might ensue. But in almost every case, after stating what appeared to be the truth in words gathered directly from the lips of Nature, I was sooner or later startled by a certain similarity in the general idea to something I had heard before, and this often developed in a moment, and when I was least expecting it, into recognition of some familiar article of faith. I was not watching for this result. I did not begin by tabulating the doctrines, as I did the Laws of Nature, and then proceed with the attempt to pair them. The majority of them seemed at first too far removed from the natural world even to suggest this. Still less did I begin with doctrines and work downward to find their relations in the natural sphere. It was the opposite process entirely. I ran up the Natural Law as far as it would go, and the appropriate doctrine seldom even loomed in sight till I had reached the top. Then it burst into view in a single moment.

I can scarcely now say whether in those moments I was more overcome with thankfulness that Nature was so like Revelation, or more filled with wonder that Revelation was so like Nature. Nature, it is true, is a part of Revelation—a much greater part doubtless than is yet believed—and one could have anticipated nothing but harmony here. But that a derived Theology, in spite of the venerable verbiage which has gathered round it, should be at bottom and in all cardinal respects so faithful a transcript of "the truth as it is in Nature" came as a surprise and to me at least as a rebuke. How, under the rigid necessity of incorporating in its system much that seemed nearly unintelligible, and much that was barely credible, Theology has succeeded so perfectly in adhering through good report and ill to what in the main are truly the lines of Nature, awakens a new admiration for those who constructed and kept this faith. But however nobly it has held its ground, Theology must feel to-day that the modern world calls for a further proof. Nor will the best Theology resent this demand; it also demands it. Theology is searching on every hand for another echo of the Voice of which Revelation also is the echo, that out of the mouths of two witnesses its truths should be established. That other echo can only come from Nature. Hitherto its voice has been muffled. But now that Science has made the world around articulate, it speaks to Religion with a twofold purpose. In the first place it offers to corroborate Theology, in the second to purify it.

If the removal of suspicion from Theology is of urgent moment, not less important is the removal of its adulterations. These suspicions, many of them at least, are new; in a sense they mark progress. But the adulterations are the artificial accumulations of centuries of uncontrolled speculation. They are the necessary result of the old method and the warrant for its revision—they mark the impossibility of progress without the guiding and restraining hand of Law.

The felt exhaustion of the former method, the want of corroboration for the old evidence, the protest of reason against the monstrous overgrowths which conceal the real lines of truth, these summon us to the search for a surer and more scientific system. With truths of the theological order, with dogmas which often depend for their existence on a particular exegesis, with propositions which rest for their evidence upon a balance of probabilities, or upon the weight of authority; with doctrines which every age and nation may make or unmake, which each sect may tamper with, and which even the individual may modify for himself, a second court of appeal has become an imperative necessity.

Science, therefore, may yet have to be called upon to arbitrate at some points between conflicting creeds. And while there are some departments of Theology where its jurisdiction cannot be sought, there are others in which Nature may yet have to define the contents as well as the limits of belief.

What I would desire especially is a thoughtful consideration of the method. The applications ventured upon here may be successful or unsuccessful. But they would more than satisfy me if they suggested a method to others whose less clumsy hands might work it out more profitably. For I am convinced of the fertility of such a method at the present time. It is recognized by all that the younger and abler minds of this age find the most serious difficulty in accepting or retaining the ordinary forms or belief. Especially is this true of those whose culture is scientific. And the reason is palpable. No man can study modern Science without a change coming over his view of truth. What impresses him about Nature is its solidity. He is there standing upon actual things, among fixed laws. And the integrity of the scientific method so seizes him that all other forms of truth begins to appear comparatively unstable. He did not know before that any form of truth could so hold him; and the immediate effect is to lessen his interest in all that stands on other bases. This he feels in spite of himself; he struggles against it in vain; and he finds perhaps to his alarm that he is drifting fast into what looks at first like pure Positivism. This is an inevitable result of the scientific training. It is quite erroneous to suppose that science ever overthrows Faith, if by that is implied that any natural truth can oppose successfully any single spiritual truth. Science cannot overthrow Faith; but it shakes it. Its own doctrines, grounded in Nature, are so certain, that the truths of Religion, resting to most men on Authority, are felt to be strangely insecure. The difficulty, therefore, which men of Science feel about Religion is real and inevitable, and in so far as Doubt is a conscientious tribute to the inviolability of Nature it is entitled to respect.

None but those who have passed through it can appreciate the radical nature of the change wrought by Science in the whole mental attitude of its disciples. What they really cry out for in Religion is a new standpoint—a standpoint like their own. The one hope, therefore, for Science is more Science. Again, to quote Bacon—we shall hear enough from the moderns by-and-by—"This I dare affirm in knowledge of Nature, that a little natural philosophy, and the first entrance into it, doth dispose the opinion to atheism; but, on the other side, much natural philosophy, and wading deep into it, will bring about men's minds to religion."

The application of *similia similibus curantur* was never more in point. If this is a disease, it is the disease of Nature, and the cure is more Nature. For what is this disquiet in the breasts of men but the loyal fear that Nature is being violated? Men must oppose with every energy they possess what seems to them to oppose the eternal course of things. And the first step in their deliverance must be not to "reconcile" Nature and Religion, but to exhibit Nature in Religion. Even to convince them that there is no controversy between Religion and Science is insufficient. A mere flag of truce, in the nature of the case, is here impossible; at least, it is only possible so long as neither party is sincere. No man who knows the splendor of scientific achievement or cares for it, no man who feels the solidity of its method or works with it, can remain neutral with regard to Religion. He must either extend his method into it, or, if that is impossible, oppose it to the knife. On the other hand, no one who knows the content of Christianity, or feels the universal need of a Religion, can stand idly by while the intellect of his age is slowly divorcing itself from it. What is required, therefore, to draw Science and Religion together again—for they began the centuries hand in hand—is the disclosure of the naturalness of the supernatural. Then, and not till then, will men see how true it is, that to be loyal to all of Nature, they must be loyal to the part defined as Spiritual. No science contributes to another without receiving a reciprocal benefit. And even as the contribution of Science to Religion is the vindication of the naturalness of the Supernatural, so the gift of Religion to Science is the demonstration of the supernaturalness of the Natural. Thus, as the Supernatural becomes slowly Natural, will also the Natural become slowly Supernatural, until in the impersonal authority of Law men everywhere recognize the Authority of God.

To those who already find themselves fully nourished on the older forms of truth, I do not commend these pages. They will find them superfluous. Nor is there any reason why they should mingle with light which is already clear the distorting rays of a foreign expression.

But to those who are feeling their way to a Christian life, haunted now by a sense of instability in the foundation of their faith, now brought to bay by specific doubt at one point raising, as all doubt does, the question for the whole, I would hold up a light which has often been kind to me. There is a sense of solidity about a Law of Nature which belongs to nothing else in the world. Here, at last, amid all that is shifting, is one thing sure; one thing outside ourselves, unbiased, unprejudiced, uninfluenced by like or dislike, by doubt or fear; one thing that holds on its way to me eternally, incorruptible, and undefiled. This more than anything else, makes one eager to see the Reign of Law traced in the Spiritual Sphere. And should this seem to some to offer only a surer, but not a higher Faith; should the better ordering of the Spiritual World appear to satisfy the intellect at the sacrifice of reverence, simplicity, or love; especially should it seem to substitute a Reign of Law and a Lawgiver for a Kingdom of Grace and a Personal God, I will say, with Browning,—

"I spoke as I saw.
I report, as a man may of God's work—*all's love, yet all's Law*.
Now I lay down the judgeship He lent me. Each faculty tasked,
To perceive Him, has gained an abyss where a dewdrop was asked."

Analysis of Introduction

For the sake of the general reader who may desire to pass at once to the practical applications, the following outline of the Introduction—devoted rather to general principles—is here presented.

Part I: Natural Law in the Spiritual Sphere

1. The growth of the Idea of Law.

2. Its gradual extension throughout every department of Knowledge.

3. Except one. Religion hitherto the Great Exception. Why so?

4. Previous attempts to trace analogies between the Natural and Spiritual spheres. These have been limited to analogies between *Phenomena*; and are useful mainly as illustrations. Analogies of *Law* would also have a Scientific value.

5. Wherein that value would consist. (1) The Scientific demand of the age would be met; (2) Greater clearness would be introduced into Religion practically; (3) Theology, instead of resting on Authority, would rest equally on Nature.

Part Ii: the Law of Continuity

A priori argument for Natural Law in the spiritual world.

1. The Law Discovered.

2. Defined.

3. Applied.

4. The objection answered that the *material* of the Natural and Spiritual worlds being different they must be under different Laws.

5. The existence of Laws in the Spiritual world other than the Natural Laws (1) improbable, (2) unnecessary, (3) unknown. Qualification.

6. The Spiritual not the projection upward of the Natural; but the Natural the projection downward of the Spiritual.

Introduction

"This method turns aside from hypotheses not to be tested by any known logical canon familiar to science, whether the hypothesis claims support from intuition, aspiration or general plausibility.

And, again, this method turns aside from ideal standards which avow themselves to be lawless, which profess to transcend the field of law. We say, life and conduct shall stand for us wholly on a basis of law, and must rest entirely in that region of science (not physical, but moral and social science), where we are free to use our intelligence in the methods known to us as intelligible logic, methods which the intellect can analyze. When you confront us with hypotheses, however sublime and however affecting, if they cannot be stated in terms of the rest of our knowledge, if they are disparate to that world of sequence and sensation which to us is the ultimate base of all our real knowledge, then we shake our heads and turn aside."—*Frederick Harrison.*

"Ethical science is already forever completed, so far as her general outline and main principles are concerned, and has been, as it were, waiting for physical science to come up with her."—*Paradoxical Philosophy.*

Part I

Natural Law is a new word. It is the last and the most magnificent discovery of science. No more telling proof is open to the modern world of the greatness of the idea than the greatness of the attempts which have always been made to justify it. In the earlier centuries, before the birth of science, Phenomena were studied alone. The world then was a chaos, a collection of single, isolated, and independent facts. Deeper thinkers saw, indeed, that relations must subsist between these facts, but the Reign of Law was never more to the ancients than a far-off vision. Their philosophies, conspicuously those of the Stoics and Pythagoreans, heroically sought to marshal the discrete materials of the universe into thinkable form, but from these artificial and fantastic systems nothing remains to us now but an ancient testimony to the grandeur of that harmony which they failed to reach.

With Copernicus, Galileo, and Kepler the first regular lines of the universe began to be discerned. When Nature yielded to Newton her great secret, Gravitation was felt to be not greater as a fact in itself than as a revelation that Law was fact. And thenceforth the search for individual Phenomena gave way before the larger study of their relations. The pursuit of Law became the passion of science.

What that discovery of Law has done for Nature, it is impossible to estimate. As a mere spectacle the universe to-day discloses a beauty so transcendent that he who disciplines himself by scientific work finds it an overwhelming reward simply to behold it. In these Laws one stands face to face with truth, solid and unchangeable. Each single Law is an instrument of scientific research, simple in its adjustments, universal in its application, infallible in its results. And despite the limitations of its sphere on every side Law is still the largest, richest, and surest source of human knowledge.

It is not necessary for the present to more than lightly touch on definitions of Natural Law. The Duke of Argyll indicates five senses in which the word is used, but we may content ourselves here by taking it in its most simple and obvious significance. The fundamental conception of Law is an ascertained working sequence or constant order among the Phenomena of Nature. This impression of Law as order it is important to receive in its simplicity, for the idea is often corrupted by having attached to it erroneous views of cause and effect. In its true sense Natural Law predicates nothing of causes. The Laws of Nature are simply statements of the orderly condition of things in Nature, what is found in Nature by a sufficient number of competent observers. What these Laws are in themselves is not agreed. That they have any absolute existence even is far from certain. They are relative to man in his many limitations, and represent for him the constant expression of what he may always expect to find in the world around him. But that they have any causal connection with the things around him is not to be conceived. The Natural Laws originate nothing, sustain nothing; they are merely responsible for uniformity in sustaining what has been originated and what is being sustained. They are modes of operation, therefore, not operators; processes, not powers. The Law of Gravitation, for instance, speaks to science only of process. It has no light to offer as to itself. Newton did not discover Gravity—that is not discovered yet. He discovered its Law, which is Gravitation, but tells us nothing of its origin, of its nature or of its cause.

The Natural Laws then are great lines running not only through the world, but, as we now know, through the universe, reducing it like parallels of latitude to intelligent order. In themselves, be it once more repeated, they may have no more absolute existence than parallels of latitude. But they exist for us. They are drawn for us to understand the part by some Hand that drew the whole; so drawn, perhaps, that, understanding the part, we too in time may learn to understand the whole. Now the inquiry we propose to ourselves resolves itself into the simple question, Do these lines stop with what we call the Natural sphere? Is it not possible that they may lead further? Is it probable that the Hand which ruled them gave up the work where most of all they were required? Did that Hand divide the world into two, a cosmos and a chaos, the higher being the chaos? With Nature as the symbol of all of harmony and beauty that is known to man, must we still talk of the super-natural, not as a convenient word, but as a different order of world, an unintelligible world, where the Reign of Mystery supersedes the Reign of Law?

This question, let it be carefully observed, applies to Laws not to Phenomena. That the Phenomena of the Spiritual World are in analogy with the Phenomena of the Natural World requires no restatement. Since Plato enunciated his doctrine of the Cave or of the twice-divided line; since Christ spake in parables; since Plotinus wrote of the world as an image; since the mysticism of Swedenborg; since Bacon and Pascal; since "Sartor Resartus" and "In Memoriam," it has been all but a commonplace with thinkers that "the invisible things of God from the creation of the world are clearly seen, being understood by the things that are made." Milton's question—

"What if earth
Be but the shadow of heaven, and things therein
Each to other like more than on earth is thought?"

is now superfluous. "In our doctrine of representations and correspondences," says Swedenborg, "we shall treat of both these symbolical and typical resemblances, and of the astonishing things that occur, I will not say in the living body only, but throughout Nature, and which correspond so entirely to supreme and spiritual things, that one would swear that the physical world was purely symbolical of the spiritual world." And Carlyle: "All visible things are emblems. What thou seest is not there on its own account; strictly speaking is not there at all. Matter exists only spiritually, and to represent some idea and body it forth."

But the analogies of Law are a totally different thing from the analogies of Phenomena and have a very different value. To say generally, with Pascal, that—"La nature est une image de la grace," is merely to be poetical. The function of Hervey's "Meditations in a Flower Garden," or, Flavel's "Husbandry Spiritualized," is mainly homiletical. That such works have an interest is not to be denied. The place of parable in teaching, and especially after the sanction of the greatest of Teachers, must always be recognized. The very necessities of language indeed demand this method of presenting truth. The temporal is the husk and framework of the eternal, and thoughts can be uttered only through things.

But analogies between Phenomena bear the same relation to analogies of Law that Phenomena themselves bear to Law. The light of Law on truth, as we have seen, is an immense advance upon the light of Phenomena. The discovery of Law is simply the discovery of Science. And if the analogies of Natural Law can be extended to the Spiritual World, that whole region at once falls within the domain of science and secures a basis as well as an illumination in the constitution and course of Nature. All, therefore, that has been claimed for parable can be predicated *a fortiori* of this—with the addition that a proof on the basis of Law would want no criterion possessed by the most advanced science.

That the validity of analogy generally has been seriously questioned one must frankly own. Doubtless there is much difficulty and even liability to gross error in attempting to establish analogy in specific cases. The value of the likeness appears differently to different minds, and in discussing an individual instance questions of relevancy will invariably crop up. Of course, in the language of John Stuart Mill, "when the analogy can be proved, the argument founded upon it cannot be resisted." But so great is the difficulty of proof that many are compelled to attach the most inferior weight to analogy as a method of reasoning. "Analogical evidence is generally more successful in silencing objections than in evincing truth. Though it rarely refutes it frequently repels refutation; like those weapons which though they cannot kill the enemy, will ward his blows.... It must be allowed that analogical evidence is at least but a feeble support, and is hardly ever honored with the name of proof." Other authorities on the other hand, such as Sir William Hamilton, admit analogy to a primary place in logic and regard it as the very basis of induction.

But, fortunately, we are spared all discussion on this worn subject, for two cogent reasons. For one thing, we do not demand of Nature directly to prove Religion. That was never its function. Its function is to interpret. And this, after all, is possibly the most fruitful proof. The best proof of a thing is that we *see* it; if we do not see it, perhaps proof will not convince us of it. It is the want of the discerning faculty, the clairvoyant power of seeing the eternal in the temporal, rather than the failure of the reason, that begets the sceptic. But secondly, and more particularly, a significant circumstance has to be taken into account, which, though it will appear more clearly afterward, may be stated here at once. The position we have been led to take up is not that the Spiritual Laws are analogous to the Natural Laws, but that *they are the same Laws.* It is not a question of analogy but of *Identity.* The Natural Laws are not the shadows or images of the Spiritual in the same sense as autumn is emblematical of Decay, or the falling leaf of Death. The Natural Laws, as the Law of Continuity might well warn us, do not stop with the visible and then give place to a new set of Laws bearing a strong similitude to them. The Laws of the invisible are the same Laws, projections of the natural not supernatural. Analogous Phenomena are not the fruit of parallel Laws, but of the same Laws—Laws which at one end, as it were, may be dealing with Matter, at the other end with Spirit. As there will be some inconvenience, however, in dispensing with the word analogy, we shall continue occasionally to employ it. Those who apprehend the real relation will mentally substitute the larger term.

Let us now look for a moment at the present state of the question. Can it be said that the Laws of the Spiritual World are in any sense considered even to have analogies with the Natural World? Here and there certainly one finds an attempt, and a successful attempt, to exhibit on a rational basis one or two of the great Moral Principles of the Spiritual World. But the Physical World has not been appealed to. Its magnificent system of Laws remains outside, and its contribution meanwhile is either silently ignored or purposely set aside. The Physical, it is said, is too remote from the Spiritual. The Moral World may afford a basis for religious truth, but even this is often the baldest concession; while the appeal to the Physical universe is everywhere dismissed as, on the face of it, irrelevant and unfruitful. From the scientific side, again, nothing has been done to court a closer fellowship. Science has taken theology at its own estimate. It is a thing apart. The Spiritual World is not only a different world, but a different kind of world, a world arranged on a totally different principle, under a different governmental scheme.

The Reign of Law has gradually crept into every department of Nature, transforming knowledge everywhere into Science. The process goes on, and Nature slowly appears to us as one great unity, until the borders of the Spiritual World are reached. There the Law of Continuity ceases, and the harmony breaks down. And men who have learned their elementary lessons truly from the alphabet of the lower Laws, going on to seek a higher knowledge, are suddenly confronted with the Great Exception.

Even those who have examined most carefully the relations of the Natural and the Spiritual, seem to have committed themselves deliberately to a final separation in matters of Law. It is a surprise to find such a writer as Horace Bushnell, for instance, describing the Spiritual World as "another system of nature incommunicably separate from ours," and further defining it thus: "God has, in fact, erected another and higher system, that of spiritual being and government for which nature exists; a system not under the law of cause and effect, but ruled and marshaled under other kinds of laws." Few men have shown more insight than Bushnell in illustrating Spiritual truth from the Natural World; but he has not only failed to perceive the analogy with regard to Law, but emphatically denies it.

In the recent literature of this whole region there nowhere seems any advance upon the position of "Nature and the Supernatural." All are agreed in speaking of Nature *and* the Supernatural. Nature *in* the Supernatural, so far as Laws are concerned, is still an unknown truth.

"The Scientific Basis of Faith" is a suggestive title. The accomplished author announces that the object of his investigation is to show that "the world of nature and mind, as made known by science, constitute a basis and a preparation for that highest moral and spiritual life of man, which is evoked by the self-revelation of God." On the whole, Mr. Murphy seems to be more philosophical and more profound in his view of the relation of science and religion than any writer of modern times. His conception of religion is broad and lofty, his acquaintance with science adequate.

He makes constant, admirable, and often original use of analogy; and yet, in spite of the promise of this quotation, he has failed to find any analogy in that department of Law where surely, of all others, it might most reasonably be looked for. In the broad subject even of the analogies of what he defines as "evangelical religion" with Nature, Mr. Murphy discovers nothing. Nor can this be traced either to short-sight or over-sight. The subject occurs to him more than once, and he deliberately dismisses it—dismisses it not merely as unfruitful, but with a distinct denial of its relevancy. The memorable paragraph from Origen which forms the text of Butler's "Analogy," he calls "this shallow and false saying." He says: "The designation of Butler's scheme of religious philosophy ought then to be *the analogy of religion, legal and evangelical, to the constitution of nature*. But does this give altogether a true meaning? Does this double analogy really exist? If justice is natural law among beings having a moral nature, there is the closest analogy between the constitution of nature and merely legal religion. Legal religion is only the extension of natural justice into a future life.... But is this true of evangelical religion? Have the doctrines of Divine grace any similar support in the analogies of nature? I trow not." And with reference to a specific question, speaking of immortality, he asserts that "the analogies of mere nature are opposed to the doctrine of immortality."

With regard to Butler's great work in this department, it is needless at this time of day to point out that his aims did not lie exactly in this direction. He did not seek to indicate analogies *between* religion and the constitution and course of Nature. His theme was, "The Analogy *of* Religion *to* the constitution and course of Nature." And although he pointed out direct analogies of Phenomena, such as those between the metamorphoses of insects and the doctrine of a future state; and although he showed that "the natural and moral constitution and government of the world are so connected as to make up together but one scheme," his real intention was not so much to construct arguments as to repel objections. His emphasis accordingly was laid upon the difficulties of the two schemes rather than on their positive lines; and so thoroughly has he made out this point that as is well known, the effect upon many has been, not to lead them to accept the Spiritual World on the ground of the Natural, but to make them despair of both. Butler lived at a time when defence was more necessary than construction, when the materials for construction were scarce and insecure, and when, besides, some of the things to be defended were quite incapable of defence. Notwithstanding this, his influence over the whole field since has been unparalleled.

After all, then, the Spiritual World, as it appears at this moment, is outside Natural Law. Theology continues to be considered, as it has always been, a thing apart. It remains still a stupendous and splendid construction, but on lines altogether its own. Nor is Theology to be blamed for this. Nature has been long in speaking; even yet its voice is low, sometimes inaudible. Science is the true defaulter, for Theology had to wait patiently for its development. As the highest of the sciences, Theology in the order of evolution should be the last to fall into rank. It is reserved for it to perfect the final harmony. Still, if it continues longer to remain a thing apart, with increasing reason will be such protests as this of the "Unseen Universe," when, in speaking of a view of miracles held by an older Theology, it declares:—"If he submits to be guided by such interpreters, each intelligent being will forever continue to be baffled in any attempt to explain these phenomena, because they are said to have no physical relation to anything that went before or that followed after; in fine, they are made to form a universe within a universe, a portion cut off by an insurmountable barrier from the domain of scientific inquiry."

This is the secret of the present decadence of Religion in the world of Science. For Science can hear nothing of a Great Exception. Constructions on unique lines, "portions cut off by an insurmountable barrier from the domain of scientific inquiry," it dare not recognize. Nature has taught it this lesson, and Nature is right. It is the province of Science to vindicate Nature here at any hazard. But in blaming Theology for its intolerance, it has been betrayed into an intolerance less excusable. It has pronounced upon it too soon. What if Religion be yet brought within the sphere of Law? Law is the revelation of time. One by one slowly through the centuries the Sciences have crystallized into geometrical form, each form not only perfect in itself, but perfect in its relation to all other forms. Many forms had to be perfected before the form of the Spiritual. The Inorganic has to be worked out before the Organic, the Natural before the Spiritual. Theology at present has merely an ancient and provisional philosophic form. By-and-by it will be seen whether it be not susceptible of another. For Theology must pass through the necessary stages of progress, like any other science. The method of science-making is now fully established. In almost all cases the natural history and development are the same. Take, for example, the case of Geology. A century ago there was none. Science went out to look for it, and brought back a Geology which, if Nature were a harmony, had falsehood written almost on its face. It was the Geology of Catastrophism, a Geology so out of line with Nature as revealed by the other sciences, that on *a priori* grounds a thoughtful mind might have been justified in dismissing it as a final form of any science. And its fallacy was soon and thoroughly exposed. The advent of modified uniformitarian principles all but banished the word catastrophe from science, and marked the birth of Geology as we know it now. Geology, that is to say, had fallen at last into the great scheme of Law. Religious doctrines, many of them at least, have been up to this time all but as *catastrophic* as the old Geology. They are not on the lines of Nature as we have learned to decipher her. If any one feel, as Science complains that it feels, that the lie of things in the Spiritual World as arranged by Theology is not in harmony with the world around, is not, in short, scientific, he is entitled to raise the question whether this be really the final form of those departments of Theology to which his complaint refers. He is justified, moreover, in demanding a new investigation with all modern methods and resources; and Science is bound by its principles not less than by the lessons of its own past, to suspend judgment till the last attempt is made. The success of such an attempt will be looked forward to with hopefulness or fearfulness just in proportion to one's confidence in

Nature—in proportion to one's belief in the divinity of man and in the divinity of things. If there is any truth in the unity of Nature, in that supreme principle of Continuity which is growing in splendor with every discovery of science, the conclusion is foregone. If there is any foundation for Theology, if the phenomena of the Spiritual World are real, in the nature of things they ought to come into the sphere of Law. Such is at once the demand of Science upon Religion and the prophecy that it can and shall be fulfilled.

The Botany of Linnæus, a purely artificial system, was a splendid contribution to human knowledge, and did more in its day to enlarge the view of the vegetable kingdom than all that had gone before. But all artificial systems must pass away. None knew better than the great Swedish naturalist himself that his system, being artificial, was but provisional. Nature must be read in its own light. And as the botanical field became more luminous, the system of Jussieu and De Candolle slowly emerged as a native growth, unfolded itself as naturally as the petals of one of its own flowers, and forcing itself upon men's intelligence as the very voice of Nature, banished the Linnæan system forever. It were unjust to say that the present Theology is as artificial as the system of Linnæus; in many particulars it wants but a fresh expression to make it in the most modern sense scientific. But if it has a basis in the constitution and course of Nature, that basis has never been adequately shown. It has depended on Authority rather than on Law; and a new basis must be sought and found if it is to be presented to those with whom Law alone is Authority.

It is not of course to be inferred that the scientific method will ever abolish the radical distinctions of the Spiritual World. True science proposes to itself no such general leveling in any department. Within the unity of the whole there must always be room for the characteristic differences of the parts, and those tendencies of thought at the present time which ignore such distinctions, in their zeal for simplicity really create confusion. As has been well said by Mr. Hutton: "Any attempt to merge the distinctive characteristic of a higher science in a lower—of chemical changes in mechanical—of physiological in chemical—above all, of mental changes in physiological—is a neglect of the radical assumption of all science, because it is an attempt to deduce representations—or rather misrepresentations—of one kind of phenomena from a conception of another kind which does not contain it, and must have it implicitly and illicitly smuggled in before it can be extracted out of it. Hence, instead of increasing our means of representing the universe to ourselves without the detailed examination of particulars, such a procedure leads to misconstructions of fact on the basis of an imported theory, and generally ends in forcibly perverting the least-known science to the type of the better known."

What is wanted is simply a unity of conception, but not such a unity of conception as should be founded on an absolute identity of phenomena. This latter might indeed be a unity, but it would be a very tame one. The perfection of unity is attained where there is infinite variety of phenomena, infinite complexity of relation, but great simplicity of Law. Science will be complete when all known phenomena can be arranged in one vast circle in which a few well known Laws shall form the radii—these radii at once separating and uniting, separating into particular groups, yet uniting all to a common center. To show that the radii for some of the most characteristic phenomena of the Spiritual World are already drawn within that circle by science is the main object of the papers which follow. There will be found an attempt to restate a few of the more elementary facts of the

Spiritual Life in terms of Biology. Any argument for Natural Law in the Spiritual World may be best tested in the *a posteriori* form. And although the succeeding pages are not designed in the first instance to prove a principle, they may yet be entered here as evidence. The practical test is a severe one, but on that account all the more satisfactory.

And what will be gained if the point be made out? Not a few things. For one, as partly indicated already, the scientific demand of the age will be satisfied. That demand is that all that concerns life and conduct shall be placed on a scientific basis. The only great attempt to meet that at present is Positivism.

But what again is a scientific basis? What exactly is this demand of the age? "By Science I understand," says Huxley, "all knowledge which rests upon evidence and reasoning of a like character to that which claims our assent to ordinary scientific propositions; and if any one is able to make good the assertion that his theology rests upon valid evidence and sound reasoning, then it appears to me that such theology must take its place as a part of science." That the assertion has been already made good is claimed by many who deserve to be heard on questions of scientific evidence. But if more is wanted by some minds, more not perhaps of a higher kind but of a different kind, at least the attempt can be made to gratify them. Mr. Frederick Harrison, in name of the Positive method of thought, "turns aside from ideal standards which avow themselves to be *lawless* [the italics are Mr. Harrison's], which profess to transcend the field of law. We say, life and conduct shall stand for us wholly on a basis of law, and must rest entirely in that region of science (not physical, but moral and social science) where we are free to use our intelligence, in the methods known to us as intelligible logic, methods which the intellect can analyze. When you confront us with hypotheses, however sublime and however affecting, if they cannot be stated in terms of the rest of our knowledge, if they are disparate to that world of sequence and sensation which to us is the ultimate base of all our real knowledge, then we shake our heads and turn aside." This is a most reasonable demand, and we humbly accept the challenge. We think religious truth, or at all events certain of the largest facts of the Spiritual Life, can be stated "in terms of the rest of our knowledge."

We do not say, as already hinted, that the proposal includes an attempt to prove the existence of the Spiritual World. Does that need proof? And if so, what sort of evidence would be considered in court? The facts of the Spiritual World are as real to thousands as the facts of the Natural World—and more real to hundreds. But were one asked to prove that the Spiritual World can be discerned by the appropriate faculties, one would do it precisely as one would attempt to prove the Natural World to be an object of recognition to the senses—and with as much or as little success. In either instance probably the fact would be found incapable of demonstration, but not more in the one case than in the other. Were one asked to prove the existence of Spiritual Life, one would also do it exactly as one would seek to prove Natural Life. And this perhaps might be attempted with more hope. But this is not on the immediate programme. Science deals with known facts; and accepting certain known facts in the Spiritual World we proceed to arrange them, to discover their Laws, to inquire if they can be stated "in terms of the rest of our knowledge."

At the same time, although attempting no philosophical proof of the existence of a Spiritual Life and a Spiritual World, we are not without hope that the general line of thought here may be useful to some who are honestly inquiring in these directions. The stumbling-block to most minds is perhaps less the mere existence of the unseen than the want of definition, the apparently hopeless vagueness, and not least, the delight in this vagueness as mere vagueness by some who look upon this as the mark of quality in Spiritual things. It will be at least something to tell earnest seekers that the Spiritual World is not a castle in the air, of an architecture unknown to earth or heaven, but a fair ordered realm furnished with many familiar things and ruled by well-remembered Laws.

It is scarcely necessary to emphasize under a second head the gain in clearness. The Spiritual World as it stands is full of perplexity. One can escape doubt only by escaping thought. With regard to many important articles of religion perhaps the best and the worst course at present open to a doubter is simple credulity. Who is to answer for this state of things? It comes as a necessary tax for improvement on the age in which we live. The old ground of faith, Authority, is given up; the new, Science, has not yet taken its place. Men did not require to *see* truth before; they only needed to believe it. Truth, therefore, had not been put by Theology in a seeing form—which, however, was its original form. But now they ask to see it. And when it is shown them they start back in despair. We shall not say what they see. But we shall say what they might see. If the Natural Laws were run through the Spiritual World, they might see the great lines of religious truth as clearly and simply as the broad lines of science. As they gazed into that Natural-Spiritual World they would say to themselves, "We have seen something like this before. This order is known to us. It is not arbitrary. This Law here is that old Law there, and this Phenomenon here, what can it be but that which stood in precisely the same relation to that Law yonder?" And so gradually from the new form everything assumes new meaning. So the Spiritual World becomes slowly Natural; and, what is of all but equal moment, the Natural World becomes slowly Spiritual. Nature is not a mere image or emblem of the Spiritual. It is a working model of the Spiritual. In the Spiritual World the same wheels revolve—but without the iron. The same figures flit across the stage, the same processes of growth go on, the same functions are discharged, the same biological laws prevail—only with a different quality of {bios}. Plato's prisoner, if not out of the Cave, has at least his face to the light.

"The earth is cram'd with heaven,
And every common bush afire with God."

How much of the Spiritual World is covered by Natural law we do not propose at present to inquire. It is certain, at least, that the whole is not covered. And nothing more lends confidence to the method than this. For one thing, room is still left for mystery. Had no place remained for mystery it had proved itself both unscientific and irreligious. A Science without mystery is unknown; a Religion without mystery is absurd. This is no attempt to reduce Religion to a question of mathematics, or demonstrate God in biological formulæ. The elimination of mystery from the universe is the elimination of Religion. However far the scientific method may penetrate the Spiritual World, there will always remain a region to be explored by a scientific faith. "I shall never rise to the point of view which wishes to 'raise' faith to knowledge. To me, the way of truth is to come through the knowledge of my ignorance to the submissiveness of faith, and then, making that my starting place, to raise my knowledge into faith."

Lest this proclamation of mystery should seem alarming, let us add that this mystery also is scientific. The one subject on which all scientific men are agreed, the one theme on which all alike become eloquent, the one strain of pathos in all their writing and speaking and thinking, concerns that final uncertainty, that utter blackness of darkness bounding their work on every side. If the light of Nature is to illuminate for us the Spiritual Sphere, there may well be a black Unknown, corresponding, at least at some points, to this zone of darkness round the Natural World.

But the final gain would appear in the department of Theology. The establishment of the Spiritual Laws on "the solid ground of Nature," to which the mind trusts "which builds for aye," would offer a new basis for certainty in Religion. It has been indicated that the authority of Authority is waning. This is a plain fact. And it was inevitable. Authority—man's Authority, that is—is for children. And there necessarily comes a time when they add to the question, What shall I do? or, What shall I believe? the adult's interrogation—Why? Now this question is sacred, and must be answered.

"How truly its central position is impregnable," Herbert Spencer has well discerned, "religion has never adequately realized. In the devoutest faith, as we habitually see it, there lies hidden an innermost core of scepticism; and it is this scepticism which causes that dread of inquiry displayed by religion when face to face with science."

True indeed; Religion has never realized how impregnable are many of its positions. It has not yet been placed on that basis which would make them impregnable. And in a transition period like the present, holding Authority with one hand, the other feeling all around in the darkness for some strong new support, Theology is surely to be pitied. Whence this dread when brought face to face with Science? It cannot be dread of scientific fact. No single fact in Science has ever discredited a fact in Religion. The theologian knows that, and admits that he has no fear of facts. What then has Science done to make Theology tremble? It is its method. It is its system. It is its Reign of Law. It is its harmony and continuity. The attack is not specific. No one point is assailed. It is the whole system which when compared with the other and weighed in its balance is found wanting. An eye which has looked at the first cannot look upon this. To do that, and rest in the contemplation, it has first to uncentury itself.

Herbert Spencer points out further, with how much truth need not now be discussed, that the purification of Religion has always come from Science. It is very apparent at all events that an immense debt must soon be contracted. The shifting of the furnishings will be a work of time. But it must be accomplished. And not the least result of the process will be the effect upon Science itself. No department of knowledge ever contributes to another without receiving its own again with usury—witness the reciprocal favors of Biology and Sociology. From the time that Comte defined the analogy between the phenomena exhibited by aggregations of associated men and those of animal colonies, the Science of Life and the Science of Society have been so contributing to one another that their progress since has been all but hand-in-hand. A conception borrowed by the one has been observed in time finding its way back, and always in an enlarged form, to further illuminate and enrich the field it left. So must it be with Science and Religion. If the purification of Religion comes from Science, the purification of Science, in a deeper sense, shall come from Religion. The true ministry of Nature must at last be honored, and Science take its place as the great expositor. To Men of Science, not less than to Theologians,

"Science then
Shall be a precious visitant; and then,
And only then, be worthy of her name;
For then her heart shall kindle, her dull eye,
Dull and inanimate, no more shall hang
Chained to its object in brute slavery;
But taught with patient interest to watch
The process of things, and serve the cause
Of order and distinctness, not for this
Shall it forget that its most noble use,
Its most illustrious province, must be found
In furnishing clear guidance, a support,
Not treacherous, to the mind's *excursive* power."

But the gift of Science to Theology shall be not less rich. With the inspiration of Nature to illuminate what the inspiration of Revelation has left obscure, heresy in certain whole departments shall become impossible. With the demonstration of the naturalness of the supernatural, scepticism even may come to be regarded as unscientific. And those who have wrestled long for a few bare truths to ennoble life and rest their souls in thinking of the future will not be left in doubt.

It is impossible to believe that the amazing succession of revelations in the domain of Nature during the last few centuries, at which the world has all but grown tired wondering, are to yield nothing for the higher life. If the development of doctrine is to have any meaning for the future, Theology must draw upon the further revelation of the seen for the further revelation of the unseen. It need, and can, add nothing to fact; but as the vision of Newton rested on a clearer and richer world than that of Plato, so, though seeing the same things in the Spiritual World as our fathers, we may see them clearer and richer. With the work of the centuries upon it, the mental eye is a finer instrument, and demands a more ordered world. Had the revelation of Law been given sooner, it had been unintelligible. Revelation never volunteers anything that man could discover for himself—on the principle, probably, that it is only when he is capable of discovering it that he is capable of appreciating it. Besides, children do not need Laws, except Laws in the sense of commandments. They repose with simplicity on authority, and ask no questions. But there comes a time, as the world reaches its manhood, when they will ask questions, and stake, moreover, everything on the answers. That time is now. Hence we must exhibit our doctrines, not lying athwart the lines of the world's thinking, in a place reserved, and therefore shunned, for the Great Exception; but in their kinship to all truth and in their Law-relation to the whole of Nature. This is, indeed, simply following out the system of teaching begun by Christ Himself. And what is the search for spiritual truth in the Laws of Nature but an attempt to utter the parables which have been hid so long in the world around without a preacher, and to tell men at once more that the Kingdom of Heaven is like unto this and to that?

Part II

The Law of Continuity having been referred to already as a prominent factor in this inquiry, it may not be out of place to sustain the plea for Natural Law in the Spiritual Sphere by a brief statement and application of this great principle.

The Law of Continuity furnishes an *a priori* argument for the position we are attempting to establish of the most convincing kind—of such a kind, indeed, as to seem to our mind final. Briefly indicated, the ground taken up is this, that if Nature be a harmony, Man in all his relations—physical, mental, moral, and spiritual—falls to be included within its circle. It is altogether unlikely that man spiritual should be violently separated in all the conditions of growth, development, and life, from man physical. It is indeed difficult to conceive that one set of principles should guide the natural life, and these at a certain period—the very point where they are needed—suddenly give place to another set of principles altogether new and unrelated. Nature has never taught us to expect such a catastrophe. She has nowhere prepared us for it. And Man cannot in the nature of things, in the nature of thought, in the nature of language, be separated into two such incoherent halves.

The spiritual man, it is true, is to be studied in a different department of science from the natural man. But the harmony established by science is not a harmony within specific departments. It is the universe that is the harmony, the universe of which these are but parts. And the harmonies of the parts depend for all their weight and interest on the harmony of the whole. While, therefore, there are many harmonies, there is but one harmony. The breaking up of the phenomena of the universe into carefully guarded groups, and the allocation of certain prominent Laws to each, it must never be forgotten, and however much Nature lends herself to it, are artificial. We find an evolution in Botany, another in Geology, and another in Astronomy, and the effect is to lead one insensibly to look upon these as three distinct evolutions. But these sciences, of course, are mere departments created by ourselves to facilitate knowledge—reductions of Nature to the scale of our own intelligence. And we must beware of breaking up Nature except for this purpose. Science has so dissected everything, that it becomes a mental difficulty to put the puzzle together again; and we must keep ourselves in practice by constantly thinking of Nature as a whole, if science is not to be spoiled by its own refinements. Evolution being found in so many different sciences, the likelihood is that it is a universal principle. And there is no presumption whatever against this Law and many others being excluded from the domain of the spiritual life. On the other hand, there are very convincing reasons why the Natural Laws should be continuous through the Spiritual Sphere—not changed in any way to meet the new circumstances, but continuous as they stand.

But to the exposition. One of the most striking generalizations of recent science is that even Laws have their Law. Phenomena first, in the progress of knowledge, were grouped together, and Nature shortly presented the spectacle of a cosmos, the lines of beauty being the great Natural Laws. So long, however, as these Laws were merely great lines running through Nature, so long as they remained isolated from one another, the system of Nature was still incomplete. The principle which sought Law among phenomena had to go further and seek a Law among the Laws. Laws themselves accordingly came to be treated as they treated phenomena, and found themselves finally grouped in a still narrower circle. That inmost circle is governed by one great Law, the Law of Continuity. It is the Law for Laws.

It is perhaps significant that few exact definitions of Continuity are to be found. Even in Sir W. R. Grove's famous paper, the fountain-head of the modern form of this far from modern truth, there is no attempt at definition. In point of fact, its sweep is so magnificent, it appeals so much more to the imagination than to the reason, that men have preferred to exhibit rather than to define it. Its true greatness consists in the final impression it leaves on the mind with regard to the uniformity of Nature. For it was reserved for the Law of Continuity to put the finishing touch to the harmony of the universe.

Probably the most satisfactory way to secure for one's self a just appreciation of the Principle of Continuity is to try to conceive the universe without it. The opposite of a continuous universe would be a discontinuous universe, an incoherent and irrelevant universe—as irrelevant in all its ways of doing things as an irrelevant person. In effect, to withdraw Continuity from the universe would be the same as to withdraw reason from an individual. The universe would run deranged; the world would be a mad world.

There used to be a children's book which bore the fascinating title of "The Chance World." It described a world in which everything happened by chance. The sun might rise or it might not; or it might appear at any hour, or the moon might come up instead. When children were born they might have one head or a dozen heads, and those heads might not be on their shoulders—there might be no shoulders—but arranged about the limbs. If one jumped up in the air it was impossible to predict whether he would ever come down again. That he came down yesterday was no guarantee that he would do it next time. For every day antecedent and consequent varied, and gravitation and everything else changed from hour to hour. To-day a child's body might be so light that it was impossible for it to descend from its chair to the floor; but to-morrow, in attempting the experiment again, the impetus might drive it through a three-story house and dash it to pieces somewhere near the center of the earth. In this chance world cause and effect were abolished. Law was annihilated. And the result to the inhabitants of such a world could only be that reason would be impossible. It would be a lunatic world with a population of lunatics.

Now this is no more than a real picture of what the world would be without Law, or the universe without Continuity. And hence we come in sight of the necessity of some principle of Law according to which Laws shall be, and be "continuous" throughout the system. Man as a rational and moral being demands a pledge that if he depends on Nature for any given result on the ground that Nature has previously led him to expect such a result, his intellect shall not be insulted, nor his confidence in her abused. If he is to trust Nature, in short, it must be guaranteed to him that in doing so he will "never be put to confusion." The authors of the *Unseen Universe* conclude their examination of this principle by saying that "assuming the existence of a supreme Governor of the universe, the Principle of Continuity may be said to be the definite expression in words of our trust that He will not put us to permanent intellectual confusion, and we can easily conceive similar expressions of trust with reference to the other faculties of man." Or, as it has been well put elsewhere, Continuity is the expression of "the Divine Veracity in Nature." The most striking examples of the continuousness of Law are perhaps those furnished by Astronomy, especially in connection with the more recent applications of spectrum analysis. But even in the case of the simpler Laws the demonstration is complete. There is no reason apart from Continuity to expect that gravitation for instance should prevail outside our world. But wherever matter has been detected throughout the entire universe, whether in the form of star or planet, comet or meteorite, it is found to obey that Law. "If there were no other indication of unity than this, it would be almost enough. For the unity which is implied in the mechanism of the heavens is indeed a unity which is all-embracing and complete. The structure of our own bodies, with all that depends upon it, is a structure governed by, and therefore adapted to, the same force of gravitation which has determined the form and the movements of myriads of worlds. Every part of the human organism is fitted to conditions which would all be destroyed in a moment if the forces of gravitation were to change or fail."

But it is unnecessary to multiply illustrations. Having defined the principle we may proceed at once to apply it. And the argument may be summed up in a sentence. As the Natural Laws are continuous through the universe of matter and of space, so will they be continuous through the universe of spirit.

If this be denied, what then? Those who deny it must furnish the disproof. The argument is founded on a principle which is now acknowledged to be universal; and the *onus* of disproof must lie with those who may be bold enough to take up the position that a region exists where at last the Principle of Continuity fails. To do this one would first have to overturn Nature, then science, and last, the human mind.

It may seem an obvious objection that many of the Natural Laws have no connection whatever with the Spiritual World, and as a matter of fact are not continued through it. Gravitation for instance—what direct application has that in the Spiritual World? The reply is threefold. First, there is no proof that it does not hold there. If the spirit be in any sense material it certainly must hold. In the second place, gravitation may hold for the Spiritual Sphere although it cannot be directly proved. The spirit may be armed with powers which enable it to rise superior to gravity. During the action of these powers gravity need be no more suspended than in the case of a plant which rises in the air during the process of growth. It does this in virtue of a higher Law and in apparent defiance of the lower. Thirdly, if the spiritual be not material it still cannot be said that gravitation ceases at that point to be continuous. It is not gravitation that ceases—it is matter.

This point, however, will require development for another reason. In the case of the plant just referred to, there is a principle of growth or vitality at work superseding the attraction of gravity. Why is there no trace of that Law in the Inorganic world? Is not this another instance of the discontinuousness of Law? If the Law of vitality has so little connection with the Inorganic kingdom—less even than gravitation with the Spiritual, what becomes of Continuity? Is it not evident that each kingdom of Nature has its own set of Laws which continue possibly untouched for the specific kingdom but never extend beyond it?

It is quite true that when we pass from the Inorganic to the Organic, we come upon a new set of Laws. But the reason why the lower set do not seem to act in the higher sphere is not that they are annihilated, but that they are overruled. And the reason why the higher Laws are not found operating in the lower is not because they are not continuous downward, but because there is nothing for them there to act upon. It is not Law that fails, but opportunity. The biological Laws are continuous for life. Wherever there is life, that is to say, they will be found acting, just as gravitation acts wherever there is matter.

We have purposely, in the last paragraph, indulged in a fallacy. We have said that the biological Laws would certainly be continuous in the lower or mineral sphere were there anything there for them to act upon. Now Laws do not act upon anything. It has been stated already, although apparently it cannot be too abundantly emphasized, that Laws are only modes of operation, not themselves operators. The accurate statement, therefore, would be that the biological Laws would be continuous in the lower sphere were there anything there for them, not to act upon, but to keep in order. If there is no acting going on, if there is nothing being kept in order, the responsibility does not lie with Continuity. The Law will always be at its post, not only when its services are required, but wherever they are possible.

Attention is drawn to this, for it is a correction one will find one's self compelled often to make in his thinking. It is so difficult to keep out of mind the idea of substance in connection with the Natural Laws, the idea that they are the movers, the essences, the energies, that one is constantly on the verge of falling into false conclusions. Thus a hasty glance at the present argument on the part of any one ill-furnished enough to confound Law with substance or with cause would probably lead to its immediate rejection. For, to continue the same line of illustration, it might next be urged that such a Law as Biogenesis, which, as we hope to show afterward, is the fundamental Law of life for both the natural and spiritual worlds, can have no application whatsoever in the latter sphere. The *life* with which it deals in the Natural World does not enter at all into the Spiritual World, and therefore, it might be argued, the Law of Biogenesis cannot be capable of extension into it. The Law of Continuity seems to be snapped at the point where the natural passes into the spiritual. The vital principle of the body is a different thing from the vital principle of the spiritual life. Biogenesis deals with bios, with the natural life, with cells and germs, and as there are no exactly similar cells and germs in the Spiritual World, the Law cannot therefore apply. All which is as true as if one were to say that the fifth proposition of the First Book of Euclid applies when the figures are drawn with chalk upon a blackboard, but fails with regard to structures of wood or stone.

The proposition is continuous for the whole world, and, doubtless, likewise for the sun and moon and stars. The same universality may be predicated likewise for the Law of life. Wherever there is life we may expect to find it arranged, ordered, governed according to the same Law. At the beginning of the natural life we find the Law that natural life can only come from preëxisting natural life; and at the beginning of the spiritual life we find that the spiritual life can only come from preëxisting spiritual life. But there are not two Laws; there is one—Biogenesis. At one end the Law is dealing with matter, at the other with spirit. The qualitative terms natural and spiritual make no difference. Biogenesis is the Law for all life and for all kinds of life, and the particular substance with which it is associated is as indifferent to Biogenesis as it is to Gravitation. Gravitation will act whether the substance be suns and stars, or grains of sand, or raindrops. Biogenesis, in like manner, will act wherever there is life.

The conclusion finally is, that from the nature of Law in general, and from the scope of the Principle of Continuity in particular, the Laws of the natural life must be those of the spiritual life. This does not exclude, observe, the possibility of there being new Laws in addition within the Spiritual Sphere; nor does it even include the supposition that the old Laws will be the conspicuous Laws of the Spiritual World, both which points will be dealt with presently. It simply asserts that whatever else may be found, these must be found there; that they must be there though they may not be seen there; and that they must project beyond there if there be anything beyond there. If the Law of Continuity is true, the only way to escape the conclusion that the Laws of the natural life are the Laws, or at least are

Laws, of the spiritual life, is to say that there is no spiritual life. It is really easier to give up the phenomena than to give up the Law.

Two questions now remain for further consideration—one bearing on the possibility of new Law in the spiritual; the other, on the assumed invisibility or inconspicuousness of the old Laws on account of their subordination to the new.

Let us begin by conceding that there may be new Laws. The argument might then be advanced that since, in Nature generally, we come upon new Laws as we pass from lower to higher kingdoms, the old still remaining in force, the newer Laws which one would expect to meet in the Spiritual World would so transcend and overwhelm the older as to make the analogy or identity, even if traced, of no practical use. The new Laws would represent operations and energies so different, and so much more elevated, that they would afford the true keys to the Spiritual World. As Gravitation is practically lost sight of when we pass into the domain of life, so Biogenesis would be lost sight of as we enter the Spiritual Sphere.

We must first separate in this statement the old confusion of Law and energy. Gravitation is not lost sight of in the organic world. Gravity may be, to a certain extent, but not Gravitation; and gravity only where a higher power counteracts its action. At the same time it is not to be denied that the conspicuous thing in Organic Nature is not the great Inorganic Law.

But the objection turns upon the statement that reasoning from analogy we should expect, in turn, to lose sight of Biogenesis as we enter the Spiritual Sphere. One answer to which is that, as a matter of fact, we do not lose sight of it. So far from being invisible, it lies across the very threshold of the Spiritual World, and, as we shall see, pervades it everywhere. What we lose sight of, to a certain extent, is the natural bios. In the Spiritual World that is not the conspicuous thing, and it is obscure there just as gravity becomes obscure in the Organic, because something higher, more potent, more characteristic of the higher plane, comes in. That there are higher energies, so to speak, in the Spiritual World is, of course, to be affirmed alike on the ground of analogy and of experience; but it does not follow that these necessitate other Laws. A Law has nothing to do with potency. We may lose sight of a substance, or of an energy, but it is an abuse of language to talk of losing sight of Laws.

Are there, then, no other Laws in the Spiritual World except those which are the projections or extensions of Natural Laws? From the number of Natural Laws which are found in the higher sphere, from the large territory actually embraced by them, and from their special prominence throughout the whole region, it may at least be answered that the margin left for them is small. But if the objection is pressed that it is contrary to the analogy, and unreasonable in itself, that there should not be new Laws for this higher sphere, the reply is obvious. Let these Laws be produced. If the spiritual nature, in inception, growth, and development, does not follow natural principles, let the true principles be stated and explained. We have not denied that there may be new Laws. One would almost be surprised if there were not. The mass of material handed over from the natural to the spiritual, continuous, apparently, from the natural to the spiritual, is so great that till that is worked out it will be impossible to say what space is still left unembraced by Laws that are known. At present it is impossible even approximately to estimate the size of that supposed *terra incognita*. From one point of view it ought to be vast, from another extremely small. But however large the region governed by the suspected new Laws may be that cannot diminish by a hair's-breadth the size of the territory where the old Laws still prevail. That territory itself, relatively to us though perhaps not absolutely, must be of great extent. The size of the key which is to open it, that is, the size of all the Natural Laws which can be found to apply, is a guarantee that the region of the knowable in the Spiritual World is at least as wide as these regions of the Natural World which by the help of these Laws have been explored. No doubt also there yet remain some Natural Laws to be discovered, and these in time may have a further light to shed on the spiritual field. Then we may know all that is? By no means. We may only know all that may be known. And that may be very little. The Sovereign Will which sways the scepter of that invisible empire must be granted a right of freedom—that freedom which by putting it into our wills He surely teaches us to honor in His. In much of His dealing with us also, in what may be called the paternal relation, there may seem no special Law—no Law except the highest of all, that Law of which all other Laws are parts, that Law which neither Nature can wholly reflect nor the mind begin to fathom—the Law of Love. He adds nothing to that, however, who loses sight of all other Laws in that, nor does he take from it who finds specific Laws everywhere radiating from it.

With regard to the supposed new Laws of the Spiritual World—those Laws, that is, which are found for the first time in the Spiritual World, and have no analogies lower down—there is this to be said, that there is one strong reason against exaggerating either their number or importance—their importance at least for our immediate needs. The connection between language and the Law of Continuity has been referred to incidentally already. It is clear that we can only express the Spiritual Laws in language borrowed from the visible universe. Being dependent for our vocabulary on images, if an altogether new and foreign set of Laws existed in the Spiritual World, they could never take shape as definite ideas from mere want of words. The hypothetical new Laws which may remain to be discovered in the domain of Natural or Mental Science may afford some index of these hypothetical higher Laws, but this would of course mean that the latter were no longer foreign but in analogy, or, likelier still, identical. If, on the other hand, the Natural Laws of the future have nothing to say of these higher Laws, what can be said of them? Where is the language to come from in which to frame them? If their disclosure could be of any practical use to us, we may be sure the clue to them, the revelation of them, in some way would have been put into Nature. If, on the contrary, they are not to be of immediate use to man, it is better they should not embarrass him. After all, then, our knowledge of higher Law must be limited by our knowledge of the lower. The Natural Laws as at present known, whatever additions may yet be made to them, give a fair rendering of the facts of Nature. And their analogies or their projections in the Spiritual sphere may also be said to offer a fair account of that sphere, or of one or two conspicuous departments of it. The time has come for that account to be given. The greatest among the theological Laws are the Laws of Nature in disguise. It will be the splendid task of the theology of the future to take off the mask and disclose to a waning scepticism the naturalness of the supernatural.

It is almost singular that the identification of the Laws of the Spiritual World with the Laws of Nature should so long have escaped recognition. For apart from the probability on *a priori* grounds, it is involved in the whole structure of Parable. When any two Phenomena in the two spheres are seen to be analogous, the parallelism must depend upon the fact that the Laws governing them are not analogous but identical. And yet this basis for Parable seems to have been overlooked. Thus Principal Shairp:—"This seeing of Spiritual truths mirrored in the face of Nature rests not on any fancied, but in a real analogy between the natural and the spiritual worlds. They are *in some sense which science has not ascertained*, but which the vital and religious imagination can perceive, counterparts one of the other." But is not this the explanation, that parallel Phenomena depend upon identical Laws? It is a question indeed whether one can speak of Laws at all as being analogous. Phenomena are parallel, Laws which make them so are themselves one.

In discussing the relations of the Natural and Spiritual kingdom, it has been all but implied hitherto that the Spiritual Laws were framed originally on the plan of the Natural; and the impression one might receive in studying the two worlds for the first time from the side of analogy would naturally be that the lower world was formed first, as a kind of scaffolding on which the higher and Spiritual should be afterward raised. Now the exact opposite has been the case. The first in the field was the Spiritual World.

It is not necessary to reproduce here in detail the argument which has been stated recently with so much force in the "Unseen Universe." The conclusion of that work remains still unassailed, that the visible universe has been developed from the unseen. Apart from the general proof from the Law of Continuity, the more special grounds of such a conclusion are, first, the fact insisted upon by Herschel and Clerk-Maxwell that the atoms of which the visible universe is built up bear distinct marks of being manufactured articles; and, secondly, the origin in time of the visible universe is implied from known facts with regard to the dissipation of energy. With the gradual aggregation of mass the energy of the universe has been slowly disappearing, and this loss of energy must go on until none remains. There is, therefore, a point in time when the energy of the universe must come to an end; and that which has its end in time cannot be infinite, it must also have had a beginning in time. Hence the unseen existed before the seen.

There is nothing so especially exalted therefore in the Natural Laws in themselves as to make one anxious to find them blood relations of the Spiritual. It is not only because these Laws are on the ground, more accessible therefore to us who are but groundlings; not only, as the "Unseen Universe" points out in another connection, "because they are at the bottom of the list—are in fact the simplest and lowest—that they are capable of being most readily grasped by the finite intelligences of the universe." But their true significance lies in the fact that they are on the list at all, and especially in that the list is the same list. Their dignity is not as Natural Laws, but as Spiritual Laws, Laws which, as already said, at one end are dealing with Matter, and at the other with Spirit. "The physical properties of matter form the alphabet which is put into our hands by God, the study of which, if properly conducted, will enable us more perfectly to read that great book which we call the 'Universe.'" But, over and above this, the Natural Laws will enable us to read that great duplicate which we call the "Unseen Universe," and to think and live in fuller harmony with it. After all, the true greatness of Law lies in its vision of the Unseen. Law in the visible is the Invisible in the visible. And to speak of Laws as Natural is to define them in their application to a part of the universe, the sense-part, whereas a wider survey would lead us to regard all Law as essentially Spiritual. To magnify the Laws of Nature, as Laws of this small world of ours, is to take a provincial view of the universe. Law is great not because the phenomenal world is great, but because these vanishing lines are the avenues into the eternal Order. "It is less reverent to regard the universe as an illimitable avenue which leads up to God, than to look upon it as a limited area bounded by an impenetrable wall, which, if we could only pierce it would admit us at once into the presence of the Eternal?" Indeed the authors of the "Unseen Universe" demur even to the expression *material universe*, since, as they tell us "Matter is (though it may seem paradoxical to say so) the less important half of the material of the physical universe." And even Mr. Huxley, though in a different sense, assures us, with Descartes, "that we know more of mind than we do of body; that the immaterial world is a firmer reality than the material."

How the priority of the Spiritual improves the strength and meaning of the whole argument will be seen at once. The lines of the Spiritual existed first, and it was natural to expect that when the "Intelligence resident in the 'Unseen'" proceeded to frame the material universe He should go upon the lines already laid down. He would, in short, simply project the higher Laws downward, so that the Natural World would become an incarnation, a visible representation, a working model of the spiritual. The whole function of the material world lies here. The world is only a thing that is; it is not. It is a thing that teaches, yet not even a thing—a show that shows, a teaching shadow. However useless the demonstration otherwise, philosophy does well in proving that matter is a non-entity. We work with it as the mathematician with an x. The reality is alone the Spiritual. "It is very well for physicists to speak of 'matter,' but for men generally to call this 'a material world' is an absurdity. Should we call it an x-world it would mean as much, viz., that we do not know what it is." When shall we learn the true mysticism of one who was yet far from being a mystic—"We look not at the things which are seen, but at the things which are not seen; for the things which are seen are temporal, but the things which are not seen are eternal?" The visible is the ladder up to the invisible; the temporal is but the scaffolding of the eternal. And when the last immaterial souls have climbed through this material to God, the scaffolding shall be taken down, and the earth dissolved with fervent heat—not because it was base, but because its work is done.

Biogenesis

"What we require is no new Revelation, but simply an adequate conception of the true essence of Christianity. And I believe that, as time goes on, the work of the Holy Spirit will be continuously shown in the gradual insight which the human race will attain into the true essence of the Christian religion. I am thus of opinion that a standing miracle exists, and that it has ever existed—a direct and continued influence exerted by the supernatural on the natural."—*Paradoxical Philosophy.*

"He that hath the Son hath Life, and he that hath not the Son of God hath not Life."—*John.*

"*Omne vivum ex vivo.*"—*Harvey.*

For two hundred years the scientific world has been rent with discussions upon the Origin of Life. Two great schools have defended exactly opposite views—one that matter can spontaneously generate life, the other that life can only come from preëxisting life. The doctrine of Spontaneous Generation, as the first is called, has been revived within recent years by Dr. Bastian, after a series of elaborate experiments on the Beginnings of Life. Stated in his own words, his conclusion is this: "Both observation and experiment unmistakably testify to the fact that living matter is constantly being formed *de novo*, in obedience to the same laws and tendencies which determined all the more simple chemical combinations." Life, that is to say, is not the Gift of Life. It is capable of springing into being of itself. It can be Spontaneously Generated.

This announcement called into the field a phalanx of observers, and the highest authorities in biological science engaged themselves afresh upon the problem. The experiments necessary to test the matter can be followed or repeated by any one possessing the slightest manipulative skill. Glass vessels are three-parts filled with infusions of hay or any organic matter. They are boiled to kill all germs of life, and hermetically sealed to exclude the outer air. The air inside, having been exposed to the boiling temperature for many hours, is supposed to be likewise dead; so that any life which may subsequently appear in the closed flasks must have sprung into being of itself. In Bastian's experiments, after every expedient to secure sterility, life did appear inside in myriad quantity. Therefore, he argued, it was spontaneously generated.

But the phalanx of observers found two errors in this calculation. Professor Tyndall repeated the same experiment, only with a precaution to insure absolute sterility suggested by the most recent science—a discovery of his own. After every care, he conceived there might still be undestroyed germs in the air inside the flasks. If the air were absolutely germless and pure, would the myriad-life appear? He manipulated his experimental vessels in an atmosphere which under the high test of optical purity—the most delicate known test—was absolutely germless. Here not a vestige of life appeared. He varied the experiment in every direction, but matter in the germless air never yielded life.

The other error was detected by Mr. Dallinger. He found among the lower forms of life the most surprising and indestructible vitality. Many animals could survive much higher temperatures than Dr. Bastian had applied to annihilate them. Some germs almost refused to be annihilated—they were all but fire-proof.

These experiments have practically closed the question. A decided and authoritative conclusion has now taken its place in science. So far as science can settle anything, this question is settled. The attempt to get the living out of the dead has failed. Spontaneous Generation has had to be given up. And it is now recognized on every hand that Life can only come from the touch of Life. Huxley categorically announces that the doctrine of Biogenesis, or life only from life, is "victorious along the whole line at the present day." And even while confessing that he wishes the evidence were the other way, Tyndall is compelled to say, "I affirm that no shred of trustworthy experimental testimony exists to prove that life in our day has ever appeared independently of antecedent life."

For much more than two hundred years a similar discussion has dragged its length through the religious world. Two great schools here also have defended exactly opposite views—one that the Spiritual Life in man can only come from preëxisting Life, the other that it can Spontaneously Generate itself. Taking its stand upon the initial statement of the Author of the Spiritual Life, one small school, in the face of derision and opposition, has persistently maintained the doctrine of Biogenesis. Another, larger and with greater pretension to philosophic form, has defended Spontaneous Generation. The weakness of the former school consists—though this has been much exaggerated—in its more or less general adherence to the extreme view that religion had nothing to do with the natural life; the weakness of the latter lay in yielding to the more fatal extreme that it had nothing to do with anything else. That man, being a worshiping animal by nature, ought to maintain certain relations to the Supreme Being, was indeed to some extent conceded by the naturalistic school, but religion itself we looked upon as a thing to be spontaneously generated by the evolution of character in the laboratory of common life.

The difference between the two positions is radical. Translating from the language of Science into that of Religion, the theory of Spontaneous Generation is simply that a man may become gradually better and better until in course of the process he reaches that quantity of religious nature known as Spiritual Life. This Life is not something added *ab extra* to the natural man; it is the normal and appropriate development of the natural man. Biogenesis opposes to this the whole doctrine of Regeneration. The Spiritual Life is the gift of the Living Spirit. The spiritual man is no mere development of the natural man. He is a New Creation born from Above. As well expect a hay infusion to become gradually more and more living until in course of the process it reached Vitality, as expect a man by becoming better and better to attain the Eternal Life.

The advocates of Biogenesis in Religion have founded their argument hitherto all but exclusively on Scripture. The relation of the doctrine to the constitution and course of Nature was not disclosed. Its importance, therefore, was solely as a dogma; and being directly concerned with the Supernatural, it was valid for those alone who chose to accept the Supernatural.

Yet it has been keenly felt by those who attempt to defend this doctrine of the origin of the Spiritual Life, that they have nothing more to oppose to the rationalistic view than the *ipse dixit* of Revelation. The argument from experience, in the nature of the case, is seldom easy to apply, and Christianity has always found at this point a genuine difficulty in meeting the challenge of Natural Religions. The direct authority of Nature, using Nature in its limited sense, was not here to be sought for. On such a question its voice was necessarily silent; and all that the apologist could look for lower down was a distant echo or analogy. All that is really possible, indeed, is such an analogy; and if that can now be found in Biogenesis, Christianity in its most central position secures at length a support and basis in the Laws of Nature.

Up to the present time the analogy required has not been forthcoming. There was no known parallel in Nature for the spiritual phenomena in question. But now the case is altered. With the elevation of Biogenesis to the rank of a scientific fact, all problems concerning the Origin of Life are placed on a different footing. And it remains to be seen whether Religion cannot at once reaffirm and re-shape its argument in the light of this modern truth.

If the doctrine of the Spontaneous Generation of Spiritual Life can be met on scientific grounds, it will mean the removal of the most serious enemy Christianity has to deal with, and especially within its own borders, at the present day. The religion of Jesus has probably always suffered more from those who have misunderstood than from those who have opposed it. Of the multitudes who confess Christianity at this hour how many have clear in their minds the cardinal distinction established by its Founder between "born of the flesh" and "born of the Spirit?" By how many teachers of Christianity even is not this fundamental postulate persistently ignored? A thousand modern pulpits every seventh day are preaching the doctrine of Spontaneous Generation. The finest and best of recent poetry is colored with this same error. Spontaneous Generation is the leading theology of the modern religious or irreligious novel; and much of the most serious and cultured writing of the day devotes itself to earnest preaching of this impossible gospel. The current conception of the Christian religion in short—the conception which is held not only popularly but by men of culture—is founded upon a view of its origin which, if it were true, would render the whole scheme abortive.

Let us first place vividly in our imagination the picture of the two great Kingdoms of Nature, the inorganic and organic, as these now stand in the light of the Law of Biogenesis. What essentially is involved in saying that there is no Spontaneous Generation of Life? It is meant that the passage from the mineral world to the plant or animal world is hermetically sealed on the mineral side. This inorganic world is staked off from the living world by barriers which have never yet been crossed from within. No change of substance, no modification of environment, no chemistry, no electricity, nor any form of energy, nor any evolution can endow any single atom of the mineral world with the attribute of Life. Only by the bending down into this dead world of some living form can these dead atoms be gifted with the properties of vitality, without this preliminary contact with Life they remain fixed in the inorganic sphere forever. It is a very mysterious Law which guards in this way the portals of the living world. And if there is one thing in Nature more worth pondering for its strangeness it is the spectacle of this vast helpless world of the dead cut off from the living by the Law of Biogenesis and denied forever the possibility of resurrection within itself. So very strange a thing, indeed, is this broad line in Nature, that Science has long and urgently sought to obliterate it. Biogenesis stands in the way of some forms of Evolution with such stern persistency that the assaults upon this Law for number and thoroughness have been unparalleled. But, as we have seen, it has stood the test. Nature, to the modern eye, stands broken in two. The physical Laws may explain the inorganic world; the biological Laws may account for the development of the organic. But of the point where they meet, of that strange borderland between the dead and the living, Science is silent. It is as if God had placed everything in earth and heaven in the hands of Nature, but reserved a point at the genesis of Life for His direct appearing.

The power of the analogy, for which we are laying the foundations, to seize and impress the mind, will largely depend on the vividness with which one realizes the gulf which Nature places between the living and the dead. But those who, in contemplating Nature, have found their attention arrested by this extraordinary dividing-line severing the visible universe eternally into two; those who in watching the progress of science have seen barrier after barrier disappear—barrier between plant and plant, between animal and animal, and even between animal and plant—but this gulf yawn more hopelessly wide with every advance of knowledge, will be prepared to attach a significance to the Law of Biogenesis and its analogies more profound perhaps than to any other fact or law in Nature. If, as Pascal says, Nature is an image of grace; if the things that are seen are in any sense the images of the unseen, there must lie in this great gulf fixed, this most unique and startling of all natural phenomena, a meaning of peculiar moment.

Where now in the Spiritual spheres shall we meet a companion phenomena to this? What in the Unseen shall be likened to this deep dividing-line, or where in human experience is another barrier which never can be crossed?

There is such a barrier. In the dim but not inadequate vision of the Spiritual World presented in the Word of God, the first thing that strikes the eye is a great gulf fixed. The passage from the Natural World to the Spiritual World is hermetically sealed on the natural side. The door from the inorganic to the organic is shut, no mineral can open it; so the door from the natural to the spiritual is shut, and no man can open it. This world of natural men is staked off from the Spiritual World by barriers which have never yet been crossed from within. No organic change, no modification of environment, no mental energy, no moral effort, no evolution of character, no progress of civilization can endow any single human soul with the attribute of Spiritual Life. The Spiritual World is guarded from the world next in order beneath it by a law of Biogenesis—*except a man be born again ... except a man be born of water and of the Spirit, he cannot enter the Kingdom of God.*

It is not said, in this enunciation of the law, that if the condition be not fulfilled the natural man *will not* enter the Kingdom of God. The word is *cannot.* For the exclusion of the spiritually inorganic from the Kingdom of the spiritually organic is not arbitrary. Nor is the natural man refused admission on unexplained grounds. His admission is a scientific impossibility. Except a mineral be born "from above"—from the Kingdom just *above* it—it cannot enter the Kingdom just above it. And except a man be born "from above," by the same law, he cannot enter the Kingdom just above him. There being no passage from one Kingdom to another, whether from inorganic to organic, or from organic to spiritual, the intervention of Life is a scientific necessity if a stone or a plant or an animal or a man is to pass from a lower to a higher sphere. The plant stretches down to the dead world beneath it, touches its minerals and gases with its mystery of Life, and brings them up ennobled and transformed to the living sphere. The breath of God, blowing where it listeth, touches with its mystery of Life the dead souls of men, bears them across the bridgeless gulf between the natural and the spiritual, between the spiritually inorganic and the spiritually organic, endows them with its own high qualities, and develops within them these new and secret faculties, by which those who are born again are said to *see the Kingdom of God.*

What is the evidence for this great gulf fixed at the portals of the Spiritual World? Does Science close this gate, or Reason, or Experience, or Revelation? We reply, all four. The initial statement, it is not to be denied, reaches us from Revelation. But is not this evidence here in court? Or shall it be said that any argument deduced from this is a transparent circle—that after all we simply come back to the unsubstantiality of the *ipse dixit?* Not altogether, for the analogy lends an altogether new authority to the *ipse dixit.* How substantial that argument really is, is seldom realized. We yield the point here much too easily. The right of the Spiritual World to speak of its own phenomena is as secure as the right of the Natural World to speak of itself. What is Science but what the Natural World has said to natural men? What is Revelation but what the Spiritual World has said to Spiritual men? Let us at least ask what Revelation has announced with reference to this Spiritual Law of Biogenesis; afterward we shall inquire whether Science, while indorsing the verdict, may not also have some further vindication of its title to be heard.

The words of Scripture which preface this inquiry contain an explicit and original statement of the Law of Biogenesis for the Spiritual Life. "He that hath the Son hath Life, and he that hath not the Son of God hath not Life." Life, that is to say, depends upon contact with Life. It cannot spring up of itself. It cannot develop out of anything that is not Life. There is no Spontaneous Generation in religion any more than in Nature. Christ is the source of Life in the Spiritual World; and he that hath the Son hath Life, and he that hath not the Son, whatever else he may have, hath not Life. Here, in short, is the categorical denial of Abiogenesis and the establishment in this high field of the classical formula *Omne vivum ex vivo*—no Life without antecedent Life. In this mystical theory of the Origin of Life the whole of the New Testament writers are agreed. And, as we have already seen, Christ Himself founds Christianity upon Biogenesis stated in its most literal form. "Except a man be born of water and of the Spirit he cannot enter into the Kingdom of God. That which is born of the flesh is flesh; and that which is born of the Spirit is Spirit. Marvel not that I said unto you, ye must be born again." Why did He add *Marvel not?* Did He seek to allay the fear in the bewildered ruler's mind that there was more in this novel doctrine than a simple analogy from the first to the second birth?

The attitude of the natural man, again, with reference to the Spiritual, is a subject on which the New Testament is equally pronounced. Not only in his relation to the spiritual man, but to the whole Spiritual World, the natural man is regarded as *dead.* He is as a crystal to an organism. The natural world is to the Spiritual as the inorganic to the organic. "To be carnally minded is *Death.*" "Thou hast a name to live, but art *Dead.*" "She that liveth in pleasure is *Dead* while she liveth." "To you he Hath given Life which were *Dead* in trespasses and sins."

It is clear that a remarkable harmony exists here between the Organic World as arranged by Science and the Spiritual World as arranged by Scripture. We find one great Law guarding the thresholds of both worlds, securing that entrance from a lower sphere shall only take place by a direct regenerating act, and that emanating from the world next in order above. There are not two laws of Biogenesis, one for the natural, the other for the Spiritual; one law is for both.

Wherever there is Life, Life of any kind, this same law holds. The analogy, therefore, is only among the phenomena; between laws there is no analogy—there is Continuity. In either case, the first step in peopling these worlds with the appropriate living forms is virtually miracle. Nor in one case is there less of mystery in the act than in the other. The second birth is scarcely less perplexing to the theologian than the first to the embryologist.

A moment's reflection ought now to make it clear why in the Spiritual World there had to be added to this mystery the further mystery of its proclamation through the medium of Revelation. This is the point at which the scientific man is apt to part company with the theologian. He insists on having all things materialized before his eyes in Nature. If Nature cannot discuss this with him, there is nothing to discuss. But Nature can discuss this with him—only she cannot open the discussion or supply all the material to begin with. If Science averred that she could do this, the theologian this time must part company with such Science. For any Science which makes such a demand is false to the doctrines of Biogenesis. What is this but the demand that a lower world, hermetically sealed against all communication with a world above it, should have a mature and intelligent acquaintance with its phenomena and laws? Can the mineral discourse to me of animal Life? Can it tell me what lies beyond the narrow boundary of its inert being? Knowing nothing of other than the chemical and physical laws, what is its criticism worth of the principles of Biology? And even when some visitor from the upper world, for example some root from a living tree, penetrating its dark recess, honors it with a touch, will it presume to define the form and purpose of its patron, or until the bioplasm has done its gracious work can it even know that it is being touched? The barrier which separates Kingdoms from one another restricts mind not less than matter. Any information of the Kingdoms above it that could come to the mineral world could only come by a communication from above. An analogy from the lower world might make such communication intelligible as well as credible, but the information in the first instance must be vouchsafed as a *revelation*. Similarly if those in the organic Kingdom are to know anything of the Spiritual World, that knowledge must at least begin as Revelation. Men who reject this source of information, by the Law of Biogenesis, can have no other. It is no spell of ignorance arbitrarily laid upon certain members of the Organic Kingdom that prevents them reading the secrets of the Spiritual World. It is a scientific necessity. No exposition of the case could be more truly scientific than this: "The natural man receiveth not the things of the Spirit of God; for they are foolishness unto him: *neither can he know them*, because they are spiritually discerned." The verb here, it will be again observed, is potential. This is not a dogma of theology, but a necessity of Science. And Science, for the most part, has consistently accepted the situation. It has always proclaimed its ignorance of the Spiritual World. When Mr. Herbert Spencer affirms, "Regarding Science as a gradually increasing sphere we may say that every addition to its surface does but bring it into wider contact with surrounding nescience," from his standpoint he is quite correct. The endeavors of well-meaning persons to show that the Agnostic's position, when he asserts his ignorance of the Spiritual World, is only a pretense; the attempts to prove that he really knows a great deal about it if he would only admit it, are quite misplaced. He really does not know. The verdict that the natural man receiveth not the things of the Spirit of God, that they are foolishness unto him, that *neither can he* know them, is final as a statement of scientific truth—a statement on which the entire Agnostic literature is simply one long commentary.

We are now in a better position to follow out the more practical bearings of Biogenesis. There is an immense region surrounding Regeneration, a dark and perplexing region where men would be thankful for any light. It may well be that Biogenesis in its many ramifications may yet reach down to some of the deeper mysteries of the Spiritual Life. But meantime there is much to define even on the surface. And for the present we shall content ourselves by turning its light upon one or two points of current interest.

It must long ago have appeared how decisive is the answer of Science to the practical question with which we set out as to the possibility of a Spontaneous Development of Spiritual Life in the individual soul. The inquiry into the Origin of Life is the fundamental question alike of Biology and Christianity. We can afford to enlarge upon it, therefore, even at the risk of repetition. When men are offering us a Christianity without a living Spirit, and a personal religion without *conversion*, no emphasis or reiteration can be extreme. Besides, the clearness as well as the definiteness of the Testimony of Nature to any Spiritual truth is of immense importance. Regeneration has not merely been an outstanding difficulty, but an overwhelming obscurity. Even to earnest minds the difficulty of grasping the truth at all has always proved extreme. Philosophically one scarcely sees either the necessity or the possibility of being born again. Why a virtuous man should not simply grow better and better until in his own right he enter the Kingdom of God is what thousands honestly and seriously fail to understand. Now Philosophy cannot help us here. Her arguments are, if anything, against us. But Science answers to the appeal at once. If it be simply pointed out that this is the same absurdity as to ask why a stone should not grow more and more living till it enters the Organic World, the point is clear in an instant.

What now, let us ask specifically, distinguishes a Christian man from a non-Christian man? Is it that he has certain mental characteristics not possessed by the other? Is it that certain faculties have been trained in him, that morality assumes special and higher manifestations, and character a nobler form? Is the Christian merely an ordinary man who happens from birth to have been surrounded with a peculiar set of ideas? Is his religion merely that peculiar quality of the moral life defined by Mr. Matthew Arnold as "morality touched by emotion?" And does the possession of a high ideal, benevolent sympathies, a reverent spirit, and a favorable environment account for what men call his Spiritual Life?

The distinction between them is the same as that between the Organic and the Inorganic, the living and the dead. What is the difference between a crystal and an organism, a stone and a plant? They have much in common. Both are made of the same atoms. Both display the same properties of matter. Both are subject to the Physical Laws. Both may be very beautiful. But besides possessing all that the crystal has, the plant possesses something more—a mysterious something called Life. This Life is not something which existed in the crystal only in a less developed form. There is nothing at all like it in the crystal. There is nothing like the first beginning of it in the crystal, not a trace or symptom of it. This plant is tenanted by something new, an original and unique possession added over and above all the properties common to both. When from vegetable Life we rise to animal Life, here again we find something original and unique—unique at least as compared with the mineral. From animal Life we ascend again to Spiritual

Life. And here also is something new, something still more unique. He who lives the Spiritual Life has a distinct kind of Life added to all the other phases of Life which he manifests—a kind of Life infinitely more distinct than is the active Life of a plant from the inertia of a stone. The Spiritual man is more distinct in point of fact than is the plant from the stone. This is the one possible comparison in Nature, for it is the widest distinction in Nature; but compared with the difference between the Natural and the Spiritual the gulf which divides the organic from the inorganic is a hair's-breadth. The natural man belongs essentially to this present order of things. He is endowed simply with a high quality of the natural animal Life. But it is Life of so poor a quality that it is not Life at all. He that hath not the Son *hath not Life*; but he that hath the Son hath Life—a new and distinct and supernatural endowment. He is not of this world. He is of the timeless state, of Eternity. *It doth not yet appear what he shall be.*

The difference between the Spiritual man and the Natural man is not a difference of development, but of generation. It is a distinction of quality not of quantity. A man cannot rise by any natural development from "morality touched by emotion," to "morality touched by Life." Were we to construct a scientific classification, Science would compel us to arrange all natural men, moral or immoral, educated or vulgar, as one family. One might be high in the family group, another low; yet, practically, they are marked by the same set of characteristics—they eat, sleep, work, think, live, die. But the Spiritual man is removed from this family so utterly by the possession of an additional characteristic that a biologist, fully informed of the whole circumstances, would not hesitate a moment to classify him elsewhere. And if he really entered into these circumstances it would not be in another family but in another Kingdom. It is an old-fashioned theology which divides the world in this way—which speaks of men as Living and Dead, Lost and Saved—a stern theology all but fallen into disuse. This difference between the Living and the Dead in souls is so unproved by casual observation, so impalpable in itself, so startling as a doctrine, that schools of culture have ridiculed or denied the grim distinction. Nevertheless the grim distinction must be retained. It is a scientific distinction. "He that hath not the Son hath not Life."

Now it is this great Law which finally distinguishes Christianity from all other religions. It places the religion of Christ upon a footing altogether unique. There is no analogy between the Christian religion and, say, Buddhism or the Mohammedan religion. There is no true sense in which a man can say, He that hath Buddha hath Life. Buddha has nothing to do with Life. He may have something to do with morality. He may stimulate, impress, teach, guide, but there is no distinct new thing added to the souls of those who profess Buddhism. These religions *may* be developments of the natural, mental, or moral man. But Christianity professes to be more. It is the mental or moral man *plus* something else or some One else. It is the infusion into the Spiritual man of a New Life, of a quality unlike anything else in Nature. This constitutes the separate Kingdom of Christ, and gives to Christianity alone of all the religions of mankind the strange mark of Divinity.

Shall we next inquire more precisely what is this something extra which constitutes Spiritual Life? What is this strange and new endowment in its nature and vital essence? And the answer is brief—it is Christ. He that hath *the Son* hath Life.

Are we forsaking the lines of Science in saying so? Yes and No. Science has drawn for us the distinction. It has no voice as to the nature of the distinction except this—that the new endowment is a something different from anything else with which it deals. It is not ordinary Vitality, it is not intellectual, it is not moral, but something beyond. And Revelation steps in and names what it is—it is Christ. Out of the multitude of sentences where this announcement is made, these few may be selected: "Know ye not your own selves how that *Jesus Christ is in you?*" "Your bodies are the members of Christ." "At that day ye shall know that I am in the Father, and ye in Me, and I in you." "We will come unto him and make our abode with him." "I am the Vine, ye are the branches." "I am crucified with Christ, nevertheless I live, yet not I, but Christ liveth in me."

Three things are clear from these statements: First, they are not mere figures of rhetoric. They are explicit declarations. If language means anything these words announce a literal fact. In some of Christ's own statements the literalism is if possible still more impressive. For instance, "Except ye eat the flesh of the Son of man and drink His blood, ye have no life in you. Whoso eateth My flesh and drinketh My blood hath eternal life; and I will raise him up at the last day. For My flesh is meat indeed, and My blood is drink indeed. He that eateth My flesh and drinketh My blood *dwelleth in Me and I in him.*"

In the second place, Spiritual Life is not something outside ourselves. The idea is not that Christ is in heaven and that we can stretch out some mysterious faculty and deal with Him there. This is the vague form in which many conceive the truth, but it is contrary to Christ's teaching and to the analogy of nature. Vegetable Life is not contained in a reservoir somewhere in the skies, and measured out spasmodically at certain seasons. The Life is *in* every plant and tree, inside its own substance and tissue, and continues there until it dies. This localization of Life in the individual is precisely the point where Vitality differs from the other forces of nature, such as magnetism and electricity. Vitality has much in common with such forces as magnetism and electricity, but there is one inviolable distinction between them—that Life is permanently fixed and rooted in the organism. The doctrines of conservation and transformation of energy, that is to say, do not hold for Vitality. The electrician can demagnetize a bar of iron, that is, he can transform its energy of magnetism into something else—heat, or motion, or light—and then re-form these back into magnetism. For magnetism has no root, no individuality, no fixed indwelling. But the biologist cannot devitalize a plant or an animal and revivify it again. Life is not one of the homeless forces which promiscuously inhabit space, or which can be gathered like electricity from the clouds and dissipated back again into space. Life is definite and resident; and Spiritual Life is not a visit from a force, but a resident tenant in the soul.

This is, however, to formulate the statement of the third point, that Spiritual Life is not an ordinary form of energy or force. The analogy from Nature indorses this, but here Nature stops. It cannot say what Spiritual Life is. Indeed what natural Life is remains unknown, and the word Life still wanders through Science without a definition. Nature is silent, therefore, and must be as to Spiritual Life. But in the absence of natural light we fall back upon that complementary revelation which always shines, when truth is necessary and where Nature fails. We ask with Paul when this Life first visited him on the Damascus road, What is this? "Who art Thou, Lord?" And we hear, "I am Jesus."

We must expect to find this denied. Besides a proof from Revelation, this is an argument from experience. And yet we shall still be told that this Spiritual Life is a force. But let it be remembered what this means in Science, it means the heresy of confounding Force with Vitality. We must also expect to be told that this Spiritual Life is simply a development of ordinary Life—just as Dr. Bastian tells us that natural Life is formed according to the same laws which determine the more simple chemical combinations. But remember what this means in Science. It is the heresy of Spontaneous Generation, a heresy so thoroughly discredited now that scarcely an authority in Europe will lend his name to it. Who art Thou, Lord? Unless we are to be allowed to hold Spontaneous Generation there is no alternative: Life can only come from Life: "I am Jesus."

A hundred other questions now rush into the mind about this Life: How does it come? Why does it come? How is it manifested? What faculty does it employ? Where does it reside? Is it communicable? What are its conditions? One or two of these questions may be vaguely answered, the rest bring us face to face with mystery. Let it not be thought that the scientific treatment of a Spiritual subject has reduced religion to a problem of physics, or demonstrated God by the laws of biology. A religion without mystery is an absurdity. Even Science has its mysteries, none more inscrutable than around this Science of Life. It taught us sooner or later to expect mystery, and now we enter its domain. Let it be carefully marked, however, that the cloud does not fall and cover us till we have ascertained the most momentous truth of Religion—that Christ is in the Christian.

Not that there is anything new in this. The Churches have always held that Christ was the source of Life. No spiritual man ever claims that his spirituality is his own. "I live," he will tell you; "nevertheless it is not I, but Christ liveth in me." Christ our Life has indeed been the only doctrine in the Christian Church from Paul to Augustine, from Calvin to Newman. Yet, when the Spiritual man is cross-examined upon this confession it is astonishing to find what uncertain hold it has upon his mind. Doctrinally he states it adequately and holds it unhesitatingly. But when pressed with the literal question he shrinks from the answer. We do not really believe that the Living Christ has touched us, that He makes His abode in us. Spiritual Life is not as real to us as natural Life. And we cover our retreat into unbelieving vagueness with a plea of reverence, justified, as we think, by the "Thus far and no farther" of ancient Scriptures. There is often a great deal of intellectual sin concealed under this old aphorism. When men do not really wish to go farther they find it an honorable convenience sometimes to sit down on the outermost edge of the Holy Ground on the pretext of taking off their shoes. Yet we must be certain that, making a virtue of reverence, we are not merely excusing ignorance; or, under the plea of mystery, evading a truth which has been stated in the New Testament a hundred times, in the most literal form, and with all but monotonous repetition. The greatest truths are always the most loosely held. And not the least of the advantages of taking up this question from the present standpoint is that we may see how a confused doctrine can really bear the luminous definition of Science and force itself upon us with all the weight of Natural Law.

What is mystery to many men, what feeds their worship, and at the same time spoils it, is that area round all great truth which is really capable of illumination, and into which every earnest mind is permitted and commanded to go with a light. We cry mystery long before the region of mystery comes. True mystery casts no shadows around. It is a sudden and awful gulf yawning across the field of knowledge; its form is irregular, but its lips are clean cut and sharp, and the mind can go to the very verge and look down the precipice into the dim abyss—

> "Where writhing clouds unroll,
> Striving to utter themselves in shapes."

We have gone with a light to the very verge of this truth. We have seen that the Spiritual Life is an endowment from the Spiritual World, and that the Living Spirit of Christ dwells in the Christian. But now the gulf yawns black before us. What more does Science know of life? Nothing. It knows nothing further about its origin in detail. It knows nothing about its ultimate nature. It cannot even define it. There is a helplessness in scientific books here, and a continual confession of it which to thoughtful minds is almost touching. Science, therefore, has not eliminated the true mysteries from our faith, but only the false. And it has done more. It has made true mystery scientific. Religion in having mystery is in analogy with all around it. Where there is exceptional mystery in the Spiritual world it will generally be found that there is a corresponding mystery in the natural world. And, as Origen centuries ago insisted, the difficulties of Religion are simply the difficulties of Nature.

One question more we may look at for a moment. What can be gathered on the surface as to the process of Regeneration in the individual soul? From the analogies of Biology we should expect three things: First, that the New Life should dawn suddenly; Second, that it should come "without observation;" Third, that it should develop gradually. On two of these points there can be little controversy. The gradualness of growth is a characteristic which strikes the simplest observer. Long before the word Evolution was coined Christ applied it in this very connection—"First the blade, then the ear, then the full corn in the ear." It is well known also to those who study the parables of Nature that there is an ascending scale of slowness as we rise in the scale of Life. Growth is most gradual in the highest forms. Man attains his maturity after a score of years; the monad completes its humble cycle in a day. What wonder if development be tardy in the Creature of Eternity? A Christian's sun has sometimes set, and a critical world has seen as yet no corn in the ear. As yet? "As yet," in this long Life, has not begun. Grant him the years proportionate to his place in the scale of Life. "The time of harvest is *not yet*."

Again, in addition to being slow, the phenomena of growth are secret. Life is invisible. When the New Life manifests itself it is a surprise. *Thou canst not tell whence it cometh or whither it goeth.* When the plant lives whence has the Life come? When it dies whither has it gone? *Thou canst not tell ... so is every one that is born of the Spirit. For the kingdom of God cometh without observation.*

Yet once more—and this is a point of strange and frivolous dispute—this Life comes suddenly. This is the only way in which Life can come. Life cannot come gradually—health can, structure can, but not Life. A new theology has laughed at the Doctrine of Conversion. Sudden Conversion especially has been ridiculed as untrue to philosophy and impossible to human nature. We may not be concerned in buttressing any theology because it is old. But we find that this old theology is scientific. There may be cases—they are probably in the majority—where the moment of contact with the Living Spirit though sudden has been obscure. But the real moment and the conscious moment are two different things. Science pronounces nothing as to the conscious moment. If it did it would probably say that that was seldom the real moment—just as in the natural Life the conscious moment is not the real moment. The moment of birth in the natural world is not a conscious moment—we do not know we are born till long afterward. Yet there are men to whom the Origin of the New Life in time has been no difficulty. To Paul, for instance, Christ seems to have come at a definite period of time, the exact moment and second of which could have been known. And this is certainly, in theory at least, the normal Origin of Life, according to the principles of Biology. The line between the living and the dead is a sharp line. When the dead atoms of Carbon, Hydrogen, Oxygen, Nitrogen, are seized upon by Life, the organism at first is very lowly. It possesses few functions. It has little beauty. Growth is the work of time. But Life is not. That comes in a moment. At one moment it was dead; the next it lived. This is conversion, the "passing," as the Bible calls it, "from Death unto Life." Those who have stood by another's side at the solemn hour of this dread possession have been conscious sometimes of an experience which words are not allowed to utter—a something like the sudden snapping of a chain, the waking from a dream.

Degeneration

"I went by the field of the slothful, and by the vineyard of the man void of understanding; and lo, it was all grown over with thorns, and nettles had covered the face thereof, and the stone wall thereof was broken down. Then I saw and considered it well; I looked upon it and received instruction."—*Solomon*.

"How shall we escape if we neglect so great salvation?"—*Hebrews*.

"We have as possibilities either Balance, or Elaboration, or Degeneration."—*E. Ray Lankester*.

In one of his best known books, Mr. Darwin brings out a fact which may be illustrated in some such way as this: Suppose a bird fancier collects a flock of tame pigeons distinguished by all the infinite ornamentations of their race. They are of all kinds, of every shade of color, and adorned with every variety of marking. He takes them to an uninhabited island and allows them to fly off wild into the woods. They found a colony there, and after the lapse of many years the owner returns to the spot. He will find that a remarkable change has taken place in the interval. The birds, or their descendants rather, have all become changed into the same color. The black, the white and the dun, the striped, the spotted, and the ringed, are all metamorphosed into one—a dark slaty blue. Two plain black bands monotonously repeat themselves upon the wings of each, and the loins beneath are white; but all the variety, all the beautiful colors, all the old graces of form it may be, have disappeared. These improvements were the result of care and nature, of domestication, of civilization; and now that these influences are removed, the birds themselves undo the past and lose what they had gained. The attempt to elevate the race has been mysteriously thwarted. It is as if the original bird, the far remote ancestor of all doves, had been blue, and these had been compelled by some strange law to discard the badges of their civilization and conform to the ruder image of the first. The natural law by which such a change occurs is called *The Principle of Reversion to Type*.

It is a proof of the universality of this law that the same thing will happen with a plant. A garden is planted, let us say, with strawberries and roses, and for a number of years is left alone. In process of time it will run to waste. But this does not mean that the plants will really waste away, but that they will change into something else, and, as it invariably appears, into something worse; in the one case, namely, into the small, wild strawberry of the woods, and in the other into the primitive dog-rose of the hedges.

If we neglect a garden plant, then, a natural principle of deterioration comes in, and changes it into a worse plant. And if we neglect a bird, by the same imperious law it will be gradually changed into an uglier bird. Or if we neglect almost any of the domestic animals, they will rapidly revert to wild and worthless forms again.

Now the same thing exactly would happen in the case of you or me. Why should Man be an exception to any of the laws of Nature? Nature knows him simply as an animal—Sub-kingdom *Vertebrata*, Class *Mammalia*, Order *Bimana*. And the law of Reversion to Type runs through all creation. If a man neglect himself for a few years he will change into a worse man and a lower man. If it is his body that he neglects, he will deteriorate into a wild and bestial savage—like the de-humanized men who are discovered sometimes upon desert islands. If it is his mind, it will degenerate into imbecility and madness—solitary confinement has the power to unmake men's minds and leave them idiots. If he neglect his conscience, it will run off into lawlessness and vice. Or, lastly, if it is his soul, it must inevitably atrophy, drop off in ruin and decay.

We have here, then, a thoroughly natural basis for the question before us. If we neglect, with this universal principle staring us in the face, how shall we escape? If we neglect the ordinary means of keeping a garden in order, how shall it escape running to weeds and waste? Or, if we neglect the opportunities for cultivating the mind, how shall it escape ignorance and feebleness? So, if we neglect the soul, how shall it escape the natural retrograde movement, the inevitable relapse into barrenness and death?

It is not necessary, surely, to pause for proof that there is such a retrograde principle in the being of every man. It is demonstrated by facts, and by the analogy of all Nature. Three possibilities of life, according to Science, are open to all living organisms—Balance, Evolution, and Degeneration. The first denotes the precarious persistence of a life along what looks like a level path, a character which seems to hold its own alike against the attacks of evil and the appeals of good. It implies a set of circumstances so balanced by choice or fortune that they neither influence for better nor for worse. But except in theory this state of equilibrium, normal in the inorganic kingdom, is really foreign to the world of life; and what seems inertia may be a true Evolution unnoticed from its slowness, or likelier still a movement of Degeneration subtly obliterating as it falls the very traces of its former height. From this state of apparent Balance, Evolution is the escape in the upward direction, Degeneration in the lower. But Degeneration, rather than Balance or Elaboration, is the possibility of life embraced by the majority of mankind. And the choice is determined by man's own nature. The life of Balance is difficult. It lies on the verge of continual temptation, its perpetual adjustments become fatiguing, its measured virtue is monotonous and uninspiring. More difficult still, apparently, is the life of ever upward growth. Most men attempt it for a time, but growth is slow; and despair overtakes them while the goal is far away. Yet none of these reasons fully explains the fact that the alternative which remains is adopted by the majority of men. That Degeneration is easy only half accounts for it. Why is it easy? Why but that already in each man's very nature this principle is supreme? He feels within his soul a silent drifting motion impelling him downward with irresistible force. Instead of aspiring to Conversion to a higher Type he submits by a law of his nature to Reversion to a lower. This is Degeneration—that principle by which the organism, failing to develop itself, failing even to keep what it has got, deteriorates, and becomes more and more adapted to a degraded form of life.

All men who know themselves are conscious that this tendency, deep-rooted and active, exists within their nature. Theologically it is described as a gravitation, a bias toward evil. The Bible view is that man is conceived in sin and shapen in iniquity. And experience tells him that he will shape himself into further sin and ever deepening iniquity without the smallest effort, without in the least intending it, and in the most natural way in the world if he simply let his life run. It is on this principle that, completing the conception, the wicked are said further in the Bible to be lost. They are not really lost as yet, but they are on the sure way to it. The bias of their lives is in full action. There is no drag on anywhere. The natural tendencies are having it all their own way; and although the victims may be quite unconscious that all this is going on, it is patent to every one who considers even the natural bearings of the case that "the end of these things is Death." When we see a man fall from the top of a five-story house, we say the man is lost. We say that before he has fallen a foot; for the same principle that made him fall the one foot will undoubtedly make him complete the descent by falling another eighty or ninety feet. So that he is a dead man, or a lost man from the very first. The gravitation of sin in a human soul acts precisely in the same way. Gradually, with gathering momentum it sinks a man further and further from God and righteousness, and lands him, by the sheer action of a natural law, in the hell of a neglected life.

But the lesson is not less clear from analogy. Apart even from the law of Degeneration, apart from Reversion to Type, there is in every living organism a law of Death. We are wont to imagine that Nature is full of Life. In reality it is full of Death. One cannot say it is natural for a plant to live. Examine its nature fully, and you have to admit that its natural tendency is to die. It is kept from dying by a mere temporary endowment which gives it an ephemeral dominion over the elements—gives it power to utilize for a brief span the rain, the sunshine, and the air. Withdraw this temporary endowment for a moment and its true nature is revealed. Instead of overcoming Nature it is overcome. The very things which appeared to minister to its growth and beauty now turn against it and make it decay and die. The sun which warmed it, withers it; the air and rain which nourished it, rot it. It is the very forces which we associate with life which, when their true nature appears, are discovered to be really the ministers of death.

This law, which is true for the whole plant-world, is also valid for the animal and for man. Air is not life, but corruption—so literally corruption that the only way to keep out corruption, when life has ebbed, is to keep out air. Life is merely a temporary suspension of these destructive powers; and this is truly one of the most accurate definitions of life we have yet received—"the sum total of the functions which resist death."

Spiritual life, in like manner, is the sum total of the functions which resist sin. The soul's atmosphere is the daily trial, circumstance, and temptation of the world. And as it is life alone which gives the plant power to utilize the elements, and as, without it, they utilize it, so it is the spiritual life alone which gives the soul power to utilize temptation and trial; and without it they destroy the soul. How shall we escape if we refuse to exercise these functions—in other words, if we neglect?

This destroying process, observe, goes on quite independently of God's judgment on sin. God's judgment on sin is another and a more awful fact of which this may be a part. But it is a distinct fact by itself, which we can hold and examine separately, that on purely natural principles the soul that is left to itself unwatched, uncultivated, unredeemed, must fall away into death by its own nature. The soul that sinneth "it shall die." It shall die, not necessarily because God passes sentence of death upon it, but because it cannot help dying. It has neglected "the functions which resist death" and has always been dying. The punishment is in its very nature, and the sentence is being gradually carried out all along the path of life by ordinary processes which enforce the verdict with the appalling faithfulness of law.

There is an affectation that religious truths lie beyond the sphere of the comprehension which serves men in ordinary things. This question at least must be an exception. It lies as near the natural as the spiritual. If it makes no impression on a man to know that God will visit his iniquities upon him, he cannot blind himself to the fact that Nature will. Do we not all know what it is to be punished by Nature for disobeying her? We have looked round the wards of a hospital, a prison, or a madhouse, and seen there Nature at work squaring her accounts with sin. And we knew as we looked that if no Judge sat on the throne of heaven at all there was a Judgment there, where an inexorable Nature was crying aloud for justice, and carrying out her heavy sentences for violated laws.

When God gave Nature the law into her own hands in this way, He seems to have given her two rules upon which her sentences were to be based. The one is formally enunciated in this sentence, "*Whatsoever a man soweth that shall he also reap.*" The other is informally expressed in this, "*If we neglect how shall we escape?*"

The first is the positive law, and deals with sins of commission. The other, which we are now discussing, is the negative, and deals with sins of omission. It does not say anything about sowing but about not sowing. It takes up the case of souls which are lying fallow. It does not say, if we sow corruption we shall reap corruption. Perhaps we would not be so unwise, so regardless of ourselves, of public opinion, as to sow corruption. It does not say, if we sow tares we shall reap tares. We might never do anything so foolish as sow tares. But if we sow nothing, it says, we shall reap nothing. If we put nothing into the field, we shall take nothing out. If we neglect to cultivate in summer, how shall we escape starving in winter?

Now the Bible raises this question, but does not answer it—because it is too obvious to need answering. How shall we escape if we neglect? The answer is, we cannot. In the nature of things we cannot. We cannot escape any more than a man can escape drowning who falls into the sea and has neglected to learn to swim. In the nature of things he cannot escape—nor can he escape who has neglected the great salvation.

Now why should such fatal consequences follow a simple process like neglect? The popular impression is that a man, to be what is called lost, must be an open and notorious sinner. He must be one who has abandoned all that is good and pure in life, and sown to the flesh with all his might and main. But this principle goes further. It says simply, "If we neglect." Any one may see the reason why a notoriously wicked person should not escape; but why should not all the rest of us escape? What is to hinder people who are not notoriously wicked escaping—people who never sowed anything in particular? Why is it such a sin to sow nothing in particular?

There must be some hidden and vital relation between these three words, Salvation, Neglect, and Escape—some reasonable, essential, and indissoluble connection. Why are these words so linked together as to weight this clause with all the authority and solemnity of a sentence of death?

The explanation has partly been given already. It lies still further, however, in the meaning of the word Salvation. And this, of course, is not at all Salvation in the ordinary sense of forgiveness of sin. This is one great meaning of Salvation, the first and the greatest. But this is spoken to people who are supposed to have had this. It is the broader word, therefore, and includes not only forgiveness of sin but salvation or deliverance from the downward bias of the soul. It takes in that whole process of rescue from the power of sin and selfishness that should be going on from day to day in every human life. We have seen that there is a natural principle in man lowering him, deadening him, pulling him down by inches to the mere animal plane, blinding reason, searing conscience, paralyzing will. This is the active destroying principle, or Sin. Now to counteract this, God has discovered to us another principle which will stop this drifting process in the soul, steer it round, and make it drift the other way. This is the active saving principle, or Salvation. If a man find the first of these powers furiously at work within him, dragging his whole life downward to destruction, there is only one way to escape his fate—to take resolute hold of the upward power, and be borne by it to the opposite goal. And as this second power is the only one in the universe which has the slightest real effect upon the first, how shall a man escape if he neglect it? To neglect it is to cut off the only possible chance of escape. In declining this he is simply abandoning himself with his eyes open to that other and terrible energy which is already there, and which, in the natural course of things, is bearing him every moment further and further from escape.

From the very nature of Salvation, therefore, it is plain that the only thing necessary to make it of no effect is neglect. Hence the Bible could not fail to lay strong emphasis on a word so vital. It was not necessary for it to say, how shall we escape if we trample upon the great salvation, or doubt, or despise, or reject it. A man who has been poisoned only need neglect the antidote and he will die. It makes no difference whether he dashes it on the ground, or pours it out of the window, or sets it down by his bedside, and stares at it all the time he is dying. He will die just the same, whether he destroys it in a passion, or coolly refuses to have anything to do with it. And as a matter of fact probably most deaths, spiritually, are gradual dissolutions of the last class rather than rash suicides of the first.

This, then, is the effect of neglecting salvation from the side of salvation itself; and the conclusion is that from the very nature of salvation escape is out of the question. Salvation is a definite process. If a man refuse to submit himself to that process, clearly he cannot have the benefits of it. *As many as received Him to them gave He* power *to become the sons of God.* He does not avail himself of this power. It may be mere carelessness or apathy. Nevertheless the neglect is fatal. He cannot escape because he will not.

Turn now to another aspect of the case—to the effect upon the soul itself. Neglect does more for the soul than make it miss salvation. It despoils it of its capacity for salvation. Degeneration in the spiritual sphere involves primarily the impairing of the faculties of salvation and ultimately the loss of them. It really means that the very soul itself becomes piecemeal destroyed until the very capacity for God and righteousness is gone.

The soul, in its highest sense, is a vast capacity for God. It is like a curious chamber added on to being, and somehow involving being, a chamber with elastic and contractile walls, which can be expanded, with God as its guest, illimitably, but which without God shrinks and shrivels until every vestige of the Divine is gone, and God's image is left without God's Spirit. One cannot call what is left a soul; it is a shrunken, useless organ, a capacity sentenced to death by disuse, which droops as a withered hand by the side, and cumbers nature like a rotted branch. Nature has her revenge upon neglect as well as upon extravagance. Misuse, with her, is as mortal a sin as abuse.

There are certain burrowing animals—the mole for instance—which have taken to spending their lives beneath the surface of the ground. And Nature has taken her revenge upon them in a thoroughly natural way—she has closed up their eyes. If they mean to live in darkness, she argues, eyes are obviously a superfluous function. By neglecting them these animals made it clear they do not want them. And as one of Nature's fixed principles is that nothing shall exist in vain, the eyes are presently taken away, or reduced to a rudimentary state. There are fishes also which have had to pay the same terrible forfeit for having made their abode in dark caverns where eyes can never be required. And in exactly the same way the spiritual eye must die and lose its power by purely natural law if the soul choose to walk in darkness rather than in light.

This is the meaning of the favorite paradox of Christ, "From him that hath not shall be taken away even that which he hath;" "take therefore the talent from him." The religious faculty is a talent, the most splendid and sacred talent we possess. Yet it is subject to the natural conditions and laws. If any man take his talent and hide it in a napkin, although it is doing him neither harm nor good apparently, God will not allow him to have it. Although it is lying there rolled up in the darkness, not conspicuously affecting any one, still God will not allow him to keep it. He will not allow him to keep it any more than Nature would allow the fish to keep their eyes. Therefore, He says, "take the talent from him." And Nature does it.

This man's crime was simply neglect—"thou wicked and *slothful* servant." It was a wasted life—a life which failed in the holy stewardship of itself. Such a life is a peril to all who cross its path. Degeneration compasses Degeneration. It is only a character which is itself developing that can aid the Evolution of the world and so fulfill the end of life. For this high usury each of our lives, however small may seem our capital, was given us by God. And it is just the men whose capital seems small who need to choose the best investments. It is significant that it was the man who had only one talent who was guilty of neglecting it. Men with ten talents, men of large gifts and burning energies, either direct their powers nobly and usefully, or misdirect them irretrievably. It is those who belong to the rank and file of life who need this warning most. Others have an abundant store and sow to the spirit or the flesh with a lavish hand. But we, with our small gift, what boots our sowing? Our temptation as ordinary men is to neglect to sow at all. The interest on our talent would be so small that we excuse ourselves with the reflection that it is not worth while.

It is no objection to all this to say that we are unconscious of this neglect or misdirection of our powers. That is the darkest feature in the case. If there were uneasiness there might be hope. If there were, somewhere about our soul, a something which was not gone to sleep like all the rest; if there were a contending force anywhere; if we would let even that work instead of neglecting it, it would gain strength from hour to hour, and waken up one at a time each torpid and dishonored faculty till our whole nature became alive with strivings against self, and every avenue was open wide for God. But the apathy, the numbness of the soul, what can be said of such a symptom but that it means the creeping on of death? There are accidents in which the victims feel no pain. They are well and strong they think. But they are dying. And if you ask the surgeon by their side what makes him give this verdict, he will say it is this numbness over the frame which tells how some of the parts have lost already the very capacity for life.

Nor is it the least tragic accompaniment of this process that its effects may even be concealed from others. The soul undergoing Degeneration, surely by some arrangement with Temptation planned in the uttermost hell, possesses the power of absolute secrecy. When all within is festering decay and rottenness, a Judas, without anomaly, may kiss his Lord. This invisible consumption, like its fell analogue in the natural world, may even keep its victim beautiful while slowly slaying it. When one examines the little *Crustacea* which have inhabited for centuries the lakes of the Mammoth Cave of Kentucky, one is at first astonished to find these animals apparently endowed with perfect eyes. The pallor of the head is broken by two black pigment specks, conspicuous indeed as the only bits of color on the whole blanched body; and these, even to the casual observer, certainly represent well-defined organs of vision. But what do they with eyes in these Stygian waters? There reigns an everlasting night. Is the law for once at fault? A swift incision with the scalpel, a glance with a lens, and their secret is betrayed. The eyes are a mockery. Externally they are organs of vision—the front of the eye is perfect; behind, there is nothing but a mass of ruins. The optic nerve is a shrunken, atrophied and insensate thread. These animals have organs of vision, and yet they have no vision. They have eyes, but they see not.

Exactly what Christ said of men: They had eyes, but no vision. And the reason is the same. It is the simplest problem of natural history. The *Crustacea* of the Mammoth Cave have chosen to abide in darkness. Therefore they have become fitted for it. By refusing to see they have waived the right to see. And Nature has grimly humored them. Nature had to do it by her very constitution. It is her defence against waste that decay of faculty should immediately follow disuse of function. He that hath ears to hear, he whose ears have not degenerated, let him hear.

Men tell us sometimes there is no such thing as an atheist. There must be. There are some men to whom it is true that there is no God. They cannot see God because they have no eye. They have only an abortive organ, atrophied by neglect.

All this, it is commonplace again to insist, is not the effect of neglect when we die, but while we live. The process is in full career and operation now. It is useless projecting consequences into the future when the effects may be measured now. We are always practicing these little deceptions upon ourselves, postponing the consequences of our misdeeds as if they were to culminate some other day about the time of death. It makes us sin with a lighter hand to run an account with retribution, as it were, and delay the reckoning time with God. But every day is a reckoning day. Every soul is a Book of Judgment and Nature, as a recording angel, marks there every sin. As all will be judged by the great Judge some day, all are judged by Nature now. The sin of yesterday, as part of its penalty, has the sin of to-day. All follow us in silent retribution on our past, and go with us to the grave. We cannot cheat Nature. No sleight-of-heart can rob religion of *a present*, the immortal nature of a *now*. The poet sings—

"I looked behind to find my past,
And lo, it had gone before."

But no, not all. The unforgiven sins are not away in keeping somewhere to be let loose upon us when we die; they are here, within us, now. To-day brings the resurrection of their past, to-morrow of to-day. And the powers of sin, to the exact strength that we have developed them, nearing their dreadful culmination with every breath we draw, are here, within us, now. The souls of some men are already honey-combed through and through with the eternal consequences of neglect, so that taking the natural and rational view of their case *just now*, it is simply inconceivable that there is any escape *just now*. What a fearful thing it is to fall into the hands of the living God! A fearful thing even if, as the philosopher tells us, "the hands of the Living God are the Laws of Nature."

Whatever hopes of a "heaven" a neglected soul may have, can be shown to be an ignorant and delusive dream. How is the soul to escape to heaven if it has neglected for a lifetime the means of escape from the world and self? And where is the capacity for heaven to come from if it be not developed on earth? Where, indeed, is even the smallest spiritual appreciation of God and heaven to come from when so little of spirituality has ever been known or manifested here? If every Godward aspiration of the soul has been allowed to become extinct, and every inlet that was open to heaven to be choked, and every talent for religious love and trust to have been persistently neglected and ignored, where are the faculties to come from that would ever find the faintest relish in such things as God and heaven give?

These three words, Salvation, Escape, and Neglect, then, are not casually, but organically and necessarily connected. Their doctrine is scientific, not arbitrary. Escape means nothing more than the gradual emergence of the higher being from the lower, and nothing less. It means the gradual putting off of all that cannot enter the higher state, or heaven, and simultaneously the putting on of Christ. It involves the slow completing of the soul and the development of the capacity for God.

Should any one object that from this scientific standpoint the opposite of salvation is annihilation, the answer is at hand. From this standpoint there is no such word.

If, then, escape is to be open to us, it is not to come to us somehow, vaguely. We are not to hope for anything startling or mysterious. It is a definite opening along certain lines which are definitely marked by God, which begin at the Cross of Christ, and lead direct to Him. Each man in the silence of his own soul must work out this salvation for himself with fear and trembling—with fear, realizing the momentous issues of his task; with trembling, lest before the tardy work be done the voice of Death should summon him to stop.

What these lines are may, in closing, be indicated in a word. The true problem of the spiritual life may be said to be, do the opposite of Neglect. Whatever this is, do it, and you shall escape. It will just mean that you are so to cultivate the soul that all its powers will open out to God, and in beholding God be drawn away from sin. The idea really is to develop among the ruins of the old a new "creature"—a new creature which, while the old is suffering Degeneration from Neglect, is gradually to unfold, to escape away and develop on spiritual lines to spiritual beauty and strength. And as our conception of spiritual being must be taken simply from natural being, our ideas of the lines along which the new religious nature is to run must be borrowed from the known lines of the old.

There is, for example, a Sense of Sight in the religious nature. Neglect this, leave it undeveloped and you never miss it. You simply see nothing. But develop it and you see God. And the line along which to develop it is known to us. Become pure in heart. The pure in heart shall see God. Here, then, is one opening for soul-culture—the avenue through purity of heart to the spiritual seeing of God.

Then there is a Sense of Sound. Neglect this, leave it undeveloped, and you never miss it. You simply hear nothing. Develop it, and you hear God. And the line along which to develop it is known to us. Obey Christ. Become one of Christ's flock. "The sheep hear His voice, and He calleth them by name." Here, then, is another opportunity for the culture of the soul—a gateway through the Shepherd's fold to hear the Shepherd's voice.

And there is a Sense of Touch to be acquired—such a sense as the woman had who touched the hem of Christ's garment, that wonderful electric touch called faith, which moves the very heart of God.

And there is a Sense of Taste—a spiritual hunger after God; a something within which tastes and sees that He is good. And there is the Talent for Inspiration. Neglect that, and all the scenery of the spiritual world is flat and frozen. But cultivate it, and it penetrates the whole soul with sacred fire, and illuminates creation with God. And last of all there is the great capacity for Love, even for the love of God—the expanding capacity for feeling more and more its height and depth, its length and breadth. Till that is felt no man can really understand that word, "so great salvation," for what is its measure but that other "so" of Christ—God so loved the world that He gave His only begotten Son? Verily, how shall we escape if we neglect that?

Growth

"Is not the evidence of Ease on the very front of all the greatest works in existence? Do they not say plainly to us, not 'there has been a great *effort* here,' but 'there has been a great *power* here?' It is not the weariness of mortality but the strength of divinity, which we have to recognize in all mighty things; and that is just what we now never recognize, but think that we are to do great things by help of iron bars and perspiration; alas! we shall do nothing that way, but lose some pounds of our own weight."—*Ruskin.*

"Consider the lilies of the field how they grow."—*The Sermon on the Mount.*

"Nunquam aliud natura, aliud sapientia dicit."—*Juvenal.*

What gives the peculiar point to this object-lesson from the lips of Jesus is, that He not only made the illustration, but made the lilies. It is like an inventor describing his own machine. He made the lilies and He made me—both on the same broad principle. Both together, man and flower, He planted deep in the Providence of God; but as men are dull at studying themselves He points to this companion-phenomenon to teach us how to live a free and natural life, a life which God will unfold for us, without our anxiety, as He unfolds the flower. For Christ's words are not a general appeal to consider nature. Men are not to consider the lilies simply to admire their beauty, to dream over the delicate strength and grace of stem and leaf. The point they were to consider was *how they grew*—how without anxiety or care the flower woke into loveliness, how without weaving these leaves were woven, how without toiling these complex tissues spun themselves, and how without any effort or friction the whole slowly came ready-made from the loom of God in its more than Solomon-like glory. "So," He says, making the application beyond dispute, "you care-worn, anxious men must grow. You, too, need take no thought for your life, what ye shall eat or what ye shall drink or what ye shall put on. For if God so clothe the grass of the field, which to-day is, and to-morrow is cast into the oven, shall He not much more clothe you, O ye of little faith?"

This nature-lesson was a great novelty in its day; but all men now who have even a "little faith" have learned this Christian secret of a composed life. Apart even from the parable of the lily, the failures of the past have taught most of us the folly of disquieting ourselves in vain, and we have given up the idea that by taking thought we can add a cubit to our stature.

But no sooner has our life settled down to this calm trust in God than a new and graver anxiety begins. This time it is not for the body we are in travail, but for the soul. For the temporal life we have considered the lilies, but how is the spiritual life to grow. How are we to become better men? How are we to grow in grace? By what thought shall we add the cubits to the spiritual stature and reach the fullness of the Perfect Man? And because we know ill how to do this, the old anxiety comes back again and our inner life is once more an agony of conflict and remorse. After all, we have but transferred our anxious thoughts from the body to the soul. Our efforts after Christian growth seem only a succession of failures, and instead of rising into the beauty of holiness our life is a daily heartbreak and humiliation.

Now the reason of this is very plain. We have forgotten the parable of the lily. Violent efforts to grow are right in earnestness, but wholly wrong in principle. There is but one principle of growth both for the natural and spiritual, for animal and plant, for body and soul. For all growth is an organic thing. And the principle of growing in grace is once more this, "Consider the lilies *how they grow*."

In seeking to extend the analogy from the body to the soul there are two things about the lilies' growth, two characteristics of all growth, on which one must fix attention. These are—

First, Spontaneousness.

Second, Mysteriousness.

I. Spontaneousness. There are three lines along which one may seek for evidence of the spontaneousness of growth. The first is Science. And the argument here could not be summed up better than in the words of Jesus. The lilies grow, He says, of themselves; they toil not, neither do they spin. They grow, that is, automatically, spontaneously, without trying, without fretting, without thinking. Applied in any direction, to plant, to animal, to the body or to the soul this law holds. A boy grows, for example, without trying. One or two simple conditions are fulfilled, and the growth goes on. He thinks probably as little about the condition as about the result; he fulfills the conditions by habit, the result follows by nature. Both processes go steadily on from year to year apart from himself and all but in spite of himself. One would never think of *telling* a boy to grow. A doctor has no prescription for growth. He can tell me how growth may be stunted or impaired, but the process itself is recognized as beyond control—one of the few, and therefore very significant, things which Nature keeps in her own hands. No physician of souls, in like manner, has any prescription for spiritual growth. It is the question he is most often asked and most often answers wrongly. He may prescribe more earnestness, more prayer, more self-denial, or more Christian work. These are prescriptions for something, but not for growth. Not that they may not encourage growth; but the soul grows as the lily grows, without trying, without fretting, without ever thinking. Manuals of devotion, with complicated rules for getting on in the Christian life, would do well sometimes to return to the simplicity of nature; and earnest souls who are attempting sanctification by struggle instead of sanctification by faith might be spared much humiliation by learning the botany of the Sermon on the Mount. There *can* indeed be no other principle of growth than this. It is a vital act. And to try to *make* a thing grow is as absurd as to help the tide to come in or the sun rise.

Another argument for the spontaneousness of growth is universal experience. A boy not only grows without trying, but he cannot grow if he tries. No man by taking thought has ever added a cubit to his stature; nor has any man by mere working at his soul ever approached nearer to the stature of the Lord Jesus. The stature of the Lord Jesus was not itself reached by work, and he who thinks to approach its mystical height by anxious effort is really receding from it. Christ's life unfolded itself from a divine germ, planted centrally in His nature, which grew as naturally as a flower from a bud. This flower may be imitated; but one can always tell an artificial flower. The human form may be copied in wax, yet somehow one never fails to detect the difference. And this precisely is the difference between a native growth of Christian principle and the moral copy of it. The one is natural, the other mechanical. The one is a growth, the other an accretion. Now this, according to modern biology, is the fundamental distinction between the living and the not living, between an organism and a crystal. The living organism grows, the dead crystal increases. The first grows vitally from within, the last adds new particles from the outside. The whole difference between the Christian and the moralist lies here. The Christian works from the center, the moralist from the circumference. The one is an organism, in the center of which is planted by the living God a living germ. The other is a crystal, very beautiful it may be; but only a crystal—it wants the vital principle of growth.

And one sees here also, what is sometimes very difficult to see, why salvation in the first instance is never connected directly with morality. The reason is not that salvation does not demand morality, but that it demands so much of it that the moralist can never reach up to it. The end of Salvation is perfection, the Christ-like mind, character and life. Morality is on the way to this perfection; it may go a considerable distance toward it, but it can never reach it. Only Life can do that. It requires something with enormous power of movement, of growth, of overcoming obstacles, to attain the perfect. Therefore the man who has within himself this great formative agent, Life, is nearer the end than the man who has morality alone. The latter can never reach perfection; the former *must*. For the Life must develop out according to its type; and being a germ of the Christ-life, it must unfold into *a Christ*. Morality, at the utmost, only develops the character in one or two directions. It may perfect a single virtue here and there, but it cannot perfect all. And especially it fails always to give that rounded harmony of parts, that perfect tune to the whole orchestra, which is the marked characteristic of life. Perfect life is not merely the possessing of perfect functions, but of perfect functions perfectly adjusted to each other and all conspiring to a single result, the perfect working of the whole organism. It is not said that the character will develop in all its fullness in this life. That were a time too short for an Evolution so magnificent. In this world only the cornless ear is seen; sometimes only the small yet still prophetic blade. The sneer at the godly man for his imperfections is ill-judged. A blade is a small thing. At first it grows very near the earth. It is often soiled and crushed and downtrodden. But it is a living thing. That great dead stone beside it is more imposing; only it will never be anything else than a stone. But this small blade—*it doth not yet appear what it shall be.*

Seeing now that Growth can only be synonymous with a living automatic process, it is all but superfluous to seek a third line of argument from Scripture. Growth there is always described in the language of physiology. The regenerate soul is a new creature. The Christian is a new man in Christ Jesus. He adds the cubits to his stature just as the old man does. He is rooted and built up in Christ; he abides in the vine, and so abiding, not toiling or spinning, brings forth fruit. The Christian in short, like the poet, is born not made; and the fruits of his character are not manufactured things but living things, things which have grown from the secret germ, the fruits of the living Spirit. They are not the produce of this climate, but exotics from a sunnier land.

II. But, secondly, besides this Spontaneousness there is this other great characteristic of Growth—Mysteriousness. Upon this quality depends the fact, probably, that so few men ever fathom its real character. We are most unspiritual always in dealing with the simplest spiritual things. A lily grows mysteriously, pushing up its solid weight of stem and leaf in the teeth of gravity. Shaped into beauty by secret and invisible fingers, the flower develops we know not how. But we do not wonder at it. Every day the thing is done; it is Nature, it is God. We are spiritual enough at least to understand that. But when the soul rises slowly above the world, pushing up its delicate virtues in the teeth of sin, shaping itself mysteriously into the image of Christ, we deny that the power is not of man. A strong will, we say, a high ideal, the reward of virtue, Christian influence—these will account for it. Spiritual character is merely the product of anxious work, self-command, and self-denial. We allow, that is to say, a miracle to the lily, but none to the man. The lily may grow; the man must fret and toil and spin.

Now grant for a moment that by hard work and self-restraint a man may attain to a very high character. It is not denied that this can be done. But what is denied is that this is growth, and that this process is Christianity. The fact that you can account for it proves that it is not growth. For growth is mysterious; the peculiarity of it is that you cannot account for it. Mysteriousness, as Mozley has well observed, is "the test of spiritual birth." And this was Christ's test. "The wind bloweth where it listeth. Thou hearest the sound thereof, but canst not tell whence it cometh or whither it goeth, *so is every one that is born of the Spirit.*" The test of spirituality is that you cannot tell whence it cometh or whither it goeth. If you can tell, if you can account for it on philosophical principles, on the doctrine of influence, on strength of will, on a favorable environment, it is not growth. It may be so far a success, it may be a perfectly honest, even remarkable, and praiseworthy imitation, but it is not the real thing. The fruits are wax, the flowers artificial—you can tell whence it cometh and whither it goeth.

The conclusion is, then, that the Christian is a unique phenomenon. You cannot account for him. And if you could he would not be a Christian. Mozley has drawn the two characters for us in graphic words: "Take an ordinary man of the world—what he thinks and what he does, his whole standard of duty is taken from the society in which he lives. It is a borrowed standard: he is as good as other people are; he does, in the way of duty, what is generally considered proper and becoming among those with whom his lot is thrown. He reflects established opinion on such points. He follows its lead. His aims and objects in life again are taken from the world around him, and from its dictation. What it considers honorable, worth having, advantageous and good, he thinks so too and pursues it. His motives all come from a visible quarter. It would be absurd to say that there is any mystery in such a character as this, because it is formed from a known external influence—the influence of social opinion and the voice of the world. 'Whence such a character cometh' we see; we venture to say that the source and origin of it is open and palpable, and we know it just as we know the physical causes of many common facts."

Then there is the other. "There is a certain character and disposition of mind of which it is true to say that 'thou canst not tell whence it cometh or whither it goeth.' ... There are those who stand out from among the crowd, which reflects merely the atmosphere of feeling and standard of society around it, with an impress upon them which bespeaks a heavenly birth.... Now, when we see one of those characters, it is a question which we ask ourselves. How has the person become possessed of it? Has he caught it from society around him? That cannot be, because it is wholly different from that of the world around him. Has he caught it from the inoculation of crowds and masses, as the mere religious zealot catches his character? That cannot be either, for the type is altogether different from that which masses of men, under enthusiastic impulses, exhibit. There is nothing gregarious in this character; it is the individual's own; it is not borrowed, it is not a reflection of any fashion or tone of the world outside; it rises up from some fount within, and it is a creation of which the text says, We know not whence it cometh."

Now we have all met these two characters—the one eminently respectable, upright, virtuous, a trifle cold perhaps, and generally, when critically examined, revealing somehow the mark of the tool; the other with God's breath still upon it, an inspiration; not more virtuous, but differently virtuous; not more humble, but different, wearing the meek and quiet spirit artlessly as to the manner born. The other-worldliness of such a character is the thing that strikes you; you are not prepared for what it will do or say or become next, for it moves from a far-off center, and in spite of its transparency and sweetness that presence fills you always with awe. A man never feels the discord of his own life, never hears the jar of the machinery by which he tries to manufacture his own good points, till he has stood in the stillness of such a presence. Then he discerns the difference between growth and work. He has considered the lilies, how they grow.

We have now seen that spiritual growth is a process maintained and secured by a spontaneous and mysterious inward principle. It is a spontaneous principle even in its origin, for it bloweth where it listeth; mysterious in its operation, for we can never tell whence it cometh; obscure in its destination, for we cannot tell whence it goeth. The whole process therefore transcends us; we do not work, we are taken in hand—"it is God which worketh in us, both to will and to do of His good pleasure." We do not plan—we are "created in Christ Jesus unto good works, which God hath before ordained that we should walk in them."

There may be an obvious objection to all this. It takes away all conflict from the Christian life? It makes man, does it not, mere clay in the hands of the potter? It crushes the old character to make a new one, and destroys man's responsibility for his own soul?

Now we are not concerned here in once more striking the time-honored "balance between faith and works." We are considering how lilies grow, and in a specific connection, namely, to discover the attitude of mind which the Christian should preserve regarding his spiritual growth. That attitude, primarily, is to be free from care. We are not lodging a plea for inactivity of the spiritual energies, but for the tranquillity of the spiritual mind. Christ's protest is not against work, but against anxious thought; and rather, therefore, than complement the lesson by showing the other side, we take the risk of still further extending the plea in the original direction.

What is the relation, to recur again to analogy, between growth and work in a boy? Consciously, there is no relation at all. The boy never thinks of connecting his work with his growth. Work in fact is one thing and growth another, and it is so in the spiritual life. If it be asked therefore, Is the Christian wrong in these ceaseless and agonizing efforts after growth? the answer is, Yes, he is quite wrong, or at least, he is quite mistaken. When a boy takes a meal or denies himself indigestible things, he does not say, "All this will minister to my growth;" or when he runs a race he does not say, "This will help the next cubit of my stature." It may or it may not be true that these things will help his stature, but, if he thinks of this, his idea of growth is morbid. And this is the point we are dealing with. His anxiety here is altogether irrelevant and superfluous. Nature is far more bountiful than we think. When she gives us energy she asks none of it back to expend on our own growth. She will attend to that. "Give your work," she says, "and your anxiety to others; trust me to add the cubits to your stature." If God is adding to our spiritual stature, unfolding the new nature within us, it is a mistake to keep twitching at the petals with our coarse fingers. We must seek to let the Creative Hand alone. "It is God which giveth the increase." Yet we never know how little we have learned of the fundamental principle of Christianity till we discover how much we are all bent on supplementing God's free grace. If God is spending work upon a Christian, let him be still and know that it is God. And if he wants work, he will find it there—in the being still.

Not that there is no work for him who would grow, to do. There is work, and severe work—work so great that the worker deserves to have himself relieved of all that is superfluous during his task. If the amount of energy lost in trying to grow were spent in fulfilling rather the conditions of growth, we should have many more cubits to show for our stature. It is with these conditions that the personal work of the Christian is chiefly concerned. Observe for a moment what they are, and their exact relation. For its growth the plant needs heat, light, air, and moisture. A man, therefore, must go in search of these, or their spiritual equivalents, and this is his work? By no means. The Christian's work is not yet. Does the plant go in search of its conditions? Nay, the conditions come to the plant. It no more manufactures the heat, light, air, and moisture, than it manufactures its own stem. It finds them all around it in Nature. It simply stands still with its leaves spread out in unconscious prayer, and Nature lavishes upon it these and all other bounties, bathing it in sunshine, pouring the nourishing air over and over it, reviving it graciously with its nightly dew. Grace, too, is as free as the air. The Lord God is a Sun. He is as the Dew to Israel. A man has no more to manufacture these than he has to manufacture his own soul. He stands surrounded by them, bathed in them, beset behind and before by them. He lives and moves and has his being in them. How then shall he go in search of them? Do not they rather go in search of him? Does he not feel how they press themselves upon him? Does he not know how unweariedly they appeal to him? Has he not heard how they are sorrowful when he will not have them? His work, therefore, is not yet. The voice still says, "Be still."

The conditions of growth, then, and the inward principle of growth being both supplied by Nature, the thing man has to do, the little junction left for him to complete, is to apply the one to the other. He manufactures nothing; he earns nothing; he need be anxious for nothing; his one duty is *to be in* these conditions, to abide in them, to allow grace to play over him, to be still therein and know that this is God.

The conflict begins and prevails in all its life-long agony the moment a man forgets this. He struggles to grow himself instead of struggling to get back again into position. He makes the church into a workshop when God meant it to be a beautiful garden. And even in his closet, where only should reign silence—a silence as of the mountains whereon the lilies grow—is heard the roar and tumult of machinery. True, a man will often have to wrestle with his God—but not for growth. The Christian life is a composed life. The Gospel is Peace. Yet the most anxious people in the world are Christians—Christians who misunderstand the nature of growth. Life is a perpetual self-condemning because they are not growing. And the effect is not only the loss of tranquillity to the individual. The energies which are meant to be spent on the work of Christ are consumed in the soul's own fever. So long as the Church's activities are spent on growing there is nothing to spare for the world. A soldier's time is not spent in earning the money to buy his armor, in finding food and raiment, in seeking shelter. His king provides these things that he may be the more at liberty to fight his battles. So, for the soldier of the Cross all is provided. His Government has planned to leave him free for the Kingdom's work.

The problem of the Christian life finally is simplified to this—man has but to preserve the right attitude. To abide in Christ, to be in position, that is all. Much work is done on board a ship crossing the Atlantic. Yet none of it is spent on making the ship go. The sailor but harnesses his vessel to the wind. He puts his sail and rudder in position, and lo, the miracle is wrought. So everywhere God creates, man utilizes. All the work of the world is merely a taking advantage of energies already there. God gives the wind, and the water, and the heat; man but puts himself in the way of the wind, fixes his water-wheel in the way of the river, puts his piston in the way of the steam; and so holding himself in position before God's Spirit, all the energies of Omnipotence course within his soul. He is like a tree planted by a river whose leaf is green and whose fruits fail not. Such is the deeper lesson to be learned from considering the lily. It is the voice of Nature echoing the whole evangel of Jesus, "Come unto Me, and I will give you rest."

Death

"What could be easier than to form a catena of the most philosophical defenders of Christianity, who have exhausted language in declaring the impotence of the unassisted intellect? Comte has not more explicitly enounced the incapacity of man to deal with the Absolute and the Infinite than the whole series of orthodox writers. Trust your reason, we have been told till we are tired of the phrase, and you will become Atheists or Agnostics. We take you at your word; we become Agnostics."—*Leslie Stephen*.

"To be carnally minded is Death."—*Paul*.

"I do not wonder at what men suffer, but I wonder often at what they lose."—*Ruskin*.

"Death," wrote Faber, "is an unsurveyed land, an unarranged Science." Poetry draws near Death only to hover over it for a moment and withdraw in terror. History knows it simply as a universal fact. Philosophy finds it among the mysteries of being, the one great mystery of being not. All contributions to this dead theme are marked by an essential vagueness, and every avenue of approach seems darkened by impenetrable shadow.

But modern Biology has found it part of its work to push its way into this silent land, and at last the world is confronted with a scientific treatment of Death. Not that much is added to the old conception, or much taken from it. What it is, this certain Death with its uncertain issues, we know as little as before. But we can define more clearly and attach a narrower meaning to the momentous symbol.

The interest of the investigation here lies in the fact that Death is one of the outstanding things in Nature which has an acknowledged spiritual equivalent. The prominence of the word in the vocabulary of Revelation cannot be exaggerated. Next to Life the most pregnant symbol in religion is its antithesis, Death. And from the time that "If thou eatest thereof thou shalt surely die" was heard in Paradise, this solemn word has been linked with human interests of eternal moment.

Notwithstanding the unparalleled emphasis upon this term in the Christian system, there is none more feebly expressive to the ordinary mind. That mystery which surrounds the word in the natural world shrouds only too completely its spiritual import. The reluctance which prevents men from investigating the secrets of the King of Terrors is for a certain length entitled to respect. But it has left theology with only the vaguest materials to construct a doctrine which, intelligently enforced, ought to appeal to all men with convincing power and lend the most effective argument to Christianity. Whatever may have been its influence in the past, its threat is gone for the modern world. The word has grown weak. Ignorance has robbed the Grave of all its terror, and platitude despoiled Death of its sting. Death itself is ethically dead. Which of us, for example, enters fully into the meaning of words like these: "She that liveth in pleasure is *dead* while she liveth?" Who allows adequate weight to the metaphor in the Pauline phrase, "To be carnally minded is *Death;*" or in this, "The wages of sin is *Death?*" Or what theology has translated into the language of human life the terrific practical import of "Dead in trespasses and sins?" To seek to make these phrases once more real and burning; to clothe time-worn formulæ with living truth; to put the deepest ethical meaning into the gravest symbol of Nature, and fill up with its full consequence the darkest threat of Revelation—these are the objects before us now.

What, then, is Death? Is it possible to define it and embody its essential meaning in an intelligible proposition?

The most recent and the most scientific attempt to investigate Death we owe to the biological studies of Mr. Herbert Spencer. In his search for the meaning of Life the word Death crosses his path, and he turns aside for a moment to define it. Of course what Death is depends upon what Life is. Mr. Herbert Spencer's definition of Life, it is well known, has been subjected to serious criticism. While it has shed much light on many of the phenomena of Life, it cannot be affirmed that it has taken its place in science as the final solution of the fundamental problem of biology. No definition of Life, indeed, that has yet appeared can be said to be even approximately correct. Its mysterious quality evades us; and we have to be content with outward characteristics and accompaniments, leaving the thing itself an unsolved riddle. At the same time Mr. Herbert Spencer's masterly elucidation of the chief phenomena of Life has placed philosophy and science under many obligations, and in the paragraphs which follow we shall have to incur a further debt on behalf of religion.

The meaning of Death depending, as has been said, on the meaning of Life, we must first set ourselves to grasp the leading characteristics which distinguish living things. To a physiologist the living organism is distinguished from the not-living by the performance of certain functions. These functions are four in number—Assimilation, Waste, Reproduction, and Growth. Nothing could be a more interesting task than to point out the co-relatives of these in the spiritual sphere, to show in what ways the discharge of these functions represent the true manifestations of spiritual life, and how the failure to perform them constitutes spiritual Death. But it will bring us more directly to the specific subject before us if we follow rather the newer biological lines of Mr. Herbert Spencer. According to his definition, Life is "The definite combination of heterogeneous changes, both simultaneous and successive, in correspondence with external co-existences and sequences," or more shortly "The continuous adjustment of internal relations to external relations." An example or two will render these important statements at once intelligible.

The essential characteristic of a living organism, according to these definitions, is that it is in vital connection with its general surroundings. A human being, for instance, is in direct contact with the earth and air, with all surrounding things, with the warmth of the sun, with the music of birds, with the countless influences and activities of nature and of his fellow-men. In biological language he is said thus to be "in correspondence with his environment." He is, that is to say, in active and vital connection with them, influencing them possibly, but especially being influenced by them. Now it is in virtue of this correspondence that he is entitled to be called alive. So long as he is in correspondence with any given point of his environment, he lives. To keep up this correspondence is to keep up life. If his environment changes he must instantly adjust himself to the change. And he continues living only as long as he succeeds in adjusting himself to the "simultaneous and successive changes in his environment" as these occur. What is meant by a change in his environment may be understood from an example, which will at the same time define more clearly the intimacy of the relation between environment and organism. Let us take the case of a civil-servant whose environment is a district in India. It is a region subject to occasional and prolonged droughts resulting in periodical famines. When such a period of scarcity arises, he proceeds immediately to adjust himself to this external change. Having the power of locomotion, he may remove himself to a more fertile district, or, possessing the means of purchase, he may add to his old environment by importation the "external relations" necessary to continued life. But if from any cause he fails to adjust himself to the altered circumstances, his body is thrown out of correspondence with his environment, his "internal relations" are no longer adjusted to his "external relations," and his life must cease.

In ordinary circumstances, and in health, the human organism is in thorough correspondence with its surroundings; but when any part of the organism by disease or accident is thrown out of correspondence, it is in that relation dead.

This Death, this want of correspondence, may be either partial or complete. Part of the organism may be dead to a part of the environment, or the whole to the whole. Thus the victim of famine may have a certain number of his correspondences arrested by the change in his environment, but not all. Luxuries which he once enjoyed no longer enter the country, animals which once furnished his table are driven from it. These still exist, but they are beyond the limit of his correspondence. In relation to these things therefore he is dead. In one sense it might be said that it was the environment which played him false; in another, that it was his own organization—that he was unable to adjust himself, or did not. But, however caused, he pays the penalty with partial Death.

Suppose next the case of a man who is thrown out of correspondence with a part of his environment by some physical infirmity. Let it be that by disease or accident he has been deprived of the use of his ears. The deaf man, in virtue of this imperfection, is thrown out of *rapport* with a large and well-defined part of the environment, namely, its sounds. With regard to that "external relation," therefore, he is no longer living. Part of him may truly be held to be insensible or "Dead." A man who is also blind is thrown out of correspondence with another large part of his environment. The beauty of sea and sky, the forms of cloud and mountain, the features and gestures of friends, are to him as if they were not. They are there, solid and real, but not to him; he is still further "Dead." Next, let it be conceived, the subtle finger of cerebral disease lays hold of him. His whole brain is affected, and the sensory nerves, the medium of communication with the environment, cease altogether to acquaint him with what is doing in the outside world. The outside world is still there, but not to him; he is still further "Dead." And so the death of parts goes on. He becomes less and less alive. "Were the animal frame not the complicated machine we have seen it to be, death might come as a simple and gradual dissolution, the 'sans everything' being the last stage of the successive loss of fundamental powers." But finally some important part of the mere animal framework that remains breaks down. The correlation with the other parts is very intimate, and the stoppage of correspondence with one means an interference with the work of the rest. Something central has snapped, and all are thrown out of work. The lungs refuse to correspond with the air, the heart with the blood. There is now no correspondence whatever with environment—the thing, for it is now a thing, is Dead.

This then is Death; "part of the framework breaks down," "something has snapped"—these phrases by which we describe the phases of death yield their full meaning. They are different ways of saying that "correspondence" has ceased. And the scientific meaning of Death now becomes clearly intelligible. Dying is that breakdown in an organism which throws it out of correspondence with some necessary part of the environment. Death is the result produced, the want of correspondence. We do not say that this is all that is involved. But this is the root idea of Death—Failure to adjust internal relations to external relations, failure to repair the broken inward connection sufficiently to enable it to correspond again with the old surroundings. These preliminary statements may be fitly closed with the words of Mr. Herbert Spencer: "Death by natural decay occurs because in old age the relations between assimilation, oxidation, and genesis of force going on in the organism gradually fall out of correspondence with the relations between oxygen and food and absorption of heat by the environment. Death from disease arises either when the organism is congenitally defective in its power to balance the ordinary external actions by the ordinary internal actions, or when there has taken place some unusual external action to which there was no answering internal action. Death by accident implies some neighboring mechanical changes of which the causes are either unnoticed from inattention, or are so intricate that their results cannot be foreseen, and consequently certain relations in the organism are not adjusted to the relations in the environment."

With the help of these plain biological terms we may now proceed to examine the parallel phenomenon of Death in the spiritual world. The factors with which we have to deal are two in number as before—Organism and Environment. The relation between them may once more be denominated by "correspondence." And the truth to be emphasized resolves itself into this, that Spiritual Death is a want of correspondence between the organism and the spiritual environment.

What is the spiritual environment? This term obviously demands some further definition. For Death is a relative term. And before we can define Death in the spiritual world we must first apprehend the particular relation with reference to which the expression is to be employed. We shall best reach the nature of this relation by considering for a moment the subject of environment generally. By the natural environment we mean the entire surroundings of the natural man, the entire external world in which he lives and moves and has his being. It is not involved in the idea that either with all or part of the environment he is in immediate correspondence. Whether he correspond with it or not, it is there. There is in fact a conscious environment and an environment of which he is not conscious; and it must be borne in mind that the conscious environment is not all the environment that is. All that surrounds him, all that environs him, conscious or unconscious, is environment. The moon and stars are part of it, though in the daytime he may not see them. The polar regions are parts of it, though he is seldom aware of their influence. In its widest sense environment simply means all else that is.

Now it will next be manifest that different organisms correspond with this environment in varying degrees of completeness or incompleteness. At the bottom of the biological scale we find organisms which have only the most limited correspondence with their surroundings. A tree, for example, corresponds with the soil about its stem, with the sunlight, and with the air in contact with its leaves.

But it is shut off by its comparatively low development from a whole world to which higher forms of life have additional access. The want of locomotion alone circumscribes most seriously its area of correspondence, so that to a large part of surrounding nature it may truly be said to be dead. So far as consciousness is concerned, we should be justified indeed in saying that it was not alive at all. The murmur of the stream which bathes its roots affects it not. The marvelous insect-life beneath its shadow excites in it no wonder. The tender maternity of the bird which has its nest among its leaves stirs no responsive sympathy. It cannot correspond with those things. To stream and insect and bird it is insensible, torpid, dead. For this is Death, this irresponsiveness.

The bird, again, which is higher in the scale of life, corresponds with a wider environment. The stream is real to it, and the insect. It knows what lies behind the hill; it listens to the love-song of its mate. And to much besides beyond the simple world of the tree this higher organism is alive. The bird we should say is more living than the tree; it has a correspondence with a larger area of environment. But this bird-life is not yet the highest life. Even within the immediate bird-environment there is much to which the bird must still be held to be dead. Introduce a higher organism, place man himself within this same environment, and see how much more living he is. A hundred things which the bird never saw in insect, stream, and tree appeal to him. Each single sense has something to correspond with. Each faculty finds an appropriate exercise. Man is a mass of correspondences, and because of these, because he is alive to countless objects and influences to which lower organisms are dead, he is the most living of all creatures.

The relativity of Death will now have become sufficiently obvious. Man being left out of account, all organisms are seen as it were to be partly living and partly dead. The tree, in correspondence with a narrow area of environment, is to that extent alive; to all beyond, to the all but infinite area beyond, it is dead. A still wider portion of this vast area is the possession of the insect and the bird. Their's also, nevertheless, is but a little world, and to an immense further area insect and bird are dead. All organisms likewise are living and dead—living to all within the circumference of their correspondences, dead to all beyond. As we rise in the scale of life, however, it will be observed that the sway of Death is gradually weakened. More and more of the environment becomes accessible as we ascend, and the domain of life in this way slowly extends in ever-widening circles. But until man appears there is no organism to correspond with the whole environment. Till then the outermost circles have no correspondents. To the inhabitants of the innermost spheres they are as if they were not.

Now follows a momentous question. Is man in correspondence with the whole environment? When we reach the highest living organism, is the final blow dealt to the kingdom of Death? Has the last acre of the infinite area been taken in by his finite faculties? Is his conscious environment the whole environment? Or is there, among these outermost circles, one which with his multitudinous correspondences he fails to reach? If so, this is Death. The question of Life or Death to him is the question of the amount of remaining environment he is able to compass. If there be one circle or one segment of a circle which he yet fails to reach, to correspond with, to know, to be influenced by, he is, with regard to that circle or segment, dead.

What then, practically, is the state of the case? Is man in correspondence with the whole environment or is he not? There is but one answer. He is not. Of men generally it cannot be said that they are in living contact with that part of the environment which is called the spiritual world. In introducing this new term spiritual world, observe, we are not interpolating a new factor. This is an essential part of the old idea. We have been following out an ever-widening environment from point to point, and now we reach the outermost zones. The spiritual world is simply the outermost segment, circle, or circles of the natural world. For purposes of convenience we separate the two just as we separate the animal world from the plant. But the animal world and the plant world are the same world. They are different parts of one environment. And the natural and spiritual are likewise one. The inner circles are called the natural, the outer the spiritual. And we call them spiritual simply because they are beyond us or beyond a part of us. What we have correspondence with, that we call natural; what we have little or no correspondence with, that we call spiritual. But when the appropriate corresponding organism appears, the organism, that is, which can freely communicate with these outer circles, the distinction necessarily disappears. The spiritual to it becomes the outer circle of the natural.

Now of the great mass of living organisms, of the great mass of men, is it not to be affirmed that they are out of correspondence with this outer circle? Suppose, to make the final issue more real, we give this outermost circle of environment a name. Suppose we call it God. Suppose also we substitute a word for "correspondence" to express more intimately the personal relation. Let us call it Communion. We can now determine accurately the spiritual relation of different sections of mankind. Those who are in communion with God live, those who are not are dead.

The extent or depth of this communion, the varying degrees of correspondence in different individuals, and the less or more abundant life which these result in, need not concern us for the present. The task we have set ourselves is to investigate the essential nature of Spiritual Death. And we have found it to consist in a want of communion with God. The unspiritual man is he who lives in the circumscribed environment of this present world. "She that liveth in pleasure is Dead while she liveth." "To be carnally minded is Death." To be carnally minded, translated into the language of science, is to be limited in one's correspondences to the environment of the natural man. It is no necessary part of the conception that the mind should be either purposely irreligious, or directly vicious. The mind of the flesh, {phronêma tês sarkos}, by its very nature, limited capacity, and time-ward tendency, is {thanatos}, Death. This earthly mind may be of noble caliber, enriched by culture, high toned, virtuous and pure. But if it know not God? What though its correspondences reach to the stars of heaven or grasp the magnitudes of Time and Space? The stars of heaven are not heaven. Space is not God. This mind certainly, has life, life up to its level. There is no trace of Death. Possibly, too, it carries its deprivation lightly, and, up to its level, lies content. We do not picture the possessor of this carnal mind as in any sense a monster. We have said he may be high-toned, virtuous, and pure. The plant is not a monster because it is dead to the voice of the bird; nor is he a monster who is dead to the voice of God. The contention at present simply is that he is *Dead*.

We do not need to go to Revelation for the proof of this. That has been rendered unnecessary by the testimony of the Dead themselves. Thousands have uttered themselves upon their relation to the Spiritual World, and from their own lips we have the proclamation of their Death. The language of theology in describing the state of the natural man is often regarded as severe. The Pauline anthropology has been challenged as an insult to human nature. Culture has opposed the doctrine that "The natural man receiveth not the things of the Spirit of God, for they are foolishness unto him: neither can he know them, because they are spiritually discerned." And even some modern theologies have refused to accept the most plain of the aphorisms of Jesus, that "Except a man be born again he cannot see the Kingdom of God." But this stern doctrine of the spiritual deadness of humanity is no mere dogma of a past theology. The history of thought during the present century proves that the world has come round spontaneously to the position of the first. One of the ablest philosophical schools of the day erects a whole antichristian system on this very doctrine. Seeking by means of it to sap the foundation of spiritual religion, it stands unconsciously as the most significant witness for its truth. What is the creed of the Agnostic, but the confession of the spiritual numbness of humanity? The negative doctrine which it reiterates with such sad persistency, what is it but the echo of the oldest of scientific and religious truths? And what are all these gloomy and rebellious infidelities, these touching, and too sincere confessions of universal nescience, but a protest against this ancient law of Death?

The Christian apologist never further misses the mark than when he refuses the testimony of the Agnostic to himself. When the Agnostic tells me he is blind and deaf, dumb, torpid and dead to the spiritual world, I must believe him. Jesus tells me that. Paul tells me that. Science tells me that. He knows nothing of this outermost circle; and we are compelled to trust his sincerity as readily when he deplores it as if, being a man without an ear, he professed to know nothing of a musical world, or being without taste, of a world of art. The nescience of the Agnostic philosophy is the proof from experience that to be carnally minded is Death. Let the theological value of the concession be duly recognized. It brings no solace to the unspiritual man to be told he is mistaken. To say he is self-deceived is neither to compliment him nor Christianity. He builds in all sincerity who raises his altar to the *Unknown* God. He does not know God. With all his marvelous and complex correspondences, he is still one correspondence short.

It is a point worthy of special note that the proclamation of this truth has always come from science rather than from religion. Its general acceptance by thinkers is based upon the universal failure of a universal experiment. The statement, therefore, that the natural man discerneth not the things of the spirit, is never to be charged against the intolerance of theology. There is no point at which theology has been more modest than here. It has left the preaching of a great fundamental truth almost entirely to philosophy and science. And so very moderate has been its tone, so slight has been the emphasis placed upon the paralysis of the natural with regard to the spiritual, that it may seem to some to have been intolerant. No harm certainly could come now, no offence could be given to science, if religion asserted more clearly its right to the spiritual world. Science has paved the way for the reception of one of the most revolutionary doctrines of Christianity; and if Christianity refuses to take advantage of the opening it will manifest a culpable want of confidence in itself. There never was a time when its fundamental doctrines could more boldly be proclaimed, or when they could better secure the respect and arrest the interest of Science.

To all this, and apparently with force, it may, however, be objected that to every man who truly studies Nature there is a God. Call Him by whatever name—a Creator, a Supreme Being, a Great First Cause, a Power that makes for Righteousness—Science has a God; and he who believes in this, in spite of all protest, possesses a theology. "If we will look at things, and not merely at words, we shall soon see that the scientific man has a theology and a God, a most impressive theology, a most awful and glorious God. I say that man believes in a God who feels himself in the presence of a Power which is not himself, and is immeasurably above himself, a Power in the contemplation of which he is absorbed, in the knowledge of which he finds safety and happiness. And such now is Nature to the scientific man." Such now, we humbly submit, is Nature to the very few. Their own confession is against it. That they are "absorbed" in the contemplation we can well believe. That they might "find safety and happiness" in the knowledge of Him is also possible—if they had it. But this is just what they tell us they have not. What they deny is not a God. It is the correspondence. The very confession of the Unknowable is itself the dull recognition of an Environment beyond themselves, and for which they feel they lack the correspondence. It is this want that makes their God the Unknown God. And it is this that makes them *dead*.

We have not said, or implied, that there is not a God of Nature. We have not affirmed that there is no Natural Religion. We are assured there is. We are even assured that without a Religion of Nature Religion is only half complete; that without a God of Nature the God of Revelation is only half intelligible and only partially known. God is not confined to the outermost circle of environment, He lives and moves and has His being in the whole. Those who only seek Him in the further zone can only find a part. The Christian who knows not God in Nature, who does not, that is to say, correspond with the whole environment, most certainly is partially dead. The author of "Ecce Homo" may be partially right when he says: "I think a bystander would say that though Christianity had in it something far higher and deeper and more ennobling, yet the average scientific man worships just at present a more awful, and, as it were, a greater Deity than the average Christian. In so many Christians the idea of God has been degraded by childish and little-minded teaching; the Eternal and the Infinite and the All-embracing has been represented as the head of the clerical interest, as a sort of clergyman, as a sort of schoolmaster, as a sort of philanthropist. But the scientific man knows Him to be eternal; in astronomy, in geology, he becomes familiar with the countless millenniums of His lifetime. The scientific man strains his mind actually to realize God's infinity. As far off as the fixed stars he traces Him, 'distance inexpressible by numbers that have name.' Meanwhile, to the theologian, infinity and eternity are very much of empty words when applied to the object of his worship. He does not realize them in actual facts and definite computations." Let us accept this rebuke. The principle that want of correspondence is Death applies all round. He who knows not God in Nature only partially lives. The converse of this, however, is not true; and that is the point we are insisting on. He who knows God only in Nature lives not. There is no "correspondence" with an Unknown God, no "continuous adjustment" to a fixed First Cause. There is no "assimilation" of Natural Law; no growth in the Image of "the All-embracing." To correspond with the God of Science assuredly is not to live. "This is Life Eternal, to know Thee, *the true God*, and *Jesus Christ* Whom Thou hast sent."

From the service we have tried to make natural science render to our religion, we might be expected possibly to take up the position that the absolute contribution of Science to Revelation was very great. On the contrary, it is very small. The *absolute* contribution, that is, is very small. The contribution on the whole is immense, vaster than we have yet any idea of. But without the aid of the higher Revelation this many-toned and far-reaching voice had been forever dumb. The light of Nature, say the most for it, is dim—how dim we ourselves, with the glare of other Light upon the modern world, can only realize when we seek among the pagan records of the past for the groupings after truth of those whose only light was this. Powerfully significant and touching as these efforts were in their success, they are far more significant and touching in their failure. For they did fail. It requires no philosophy now to speculate on the adequacy or inadequacy of the Religion of Nature. For us who could never weigh it rightly in the scales of Truth it has been tried in the balance of experience and found wanting. Theism is the easiest of all religions to get, but the most difficult to keep. Individuals have kept it, but nations never. Socrates and Aristotle, Cicero and Epictetus had a theistic religion; Greece and Rome had none. And even after getting what seems like a firm place in the minds of men, its unstable equilibrium sooner or later betrays itself. On the one hand theism has always fallen into the wildest polytheism, or on the other into the blankest atheism. "It is an indubitable historical fact that, outside of the sphere of special revelation, man has never obtained such a knowledge of God as a responsible and religious being plainly requires. The wisdom of the heathen world, at its very best, was utterly inadequate to the accomplishment of such a task as creating a due abhorrence of sin, controlling the passions, purifying the heart, and ennobling the conduct."

What is the inference? That this poor rush-light by itself was never meant to lend the ray by which man should read the riddle of the universe. The mystery is too impenetrable and remote for its uncertain flicker to more than make the darkness deeper. What indeed if this were not a light at all, but only part of a light—the carbon point, the fragment of calcium, the reflector in the great Lantern which contains the Light of the World?

This is one inference. But the most important is that the absence of the true Light means moral Death. The darkness of the natural world to the intellect is not all. What history testifies to is, first the partial, and then the total eclipse of virtue that always follows the abandonment of belief in a personal God. It is not, as has been pointed out a hundred times, that morality in the abstract disappears, but the motive and sanction are gone. There is nothing to raise it from the dead. Man's attitude to it is left to himself. Grant that morals have their own base in human life; grant that Nature has a Religion whose creed is Science; there is yet nothing apart from God to save the world from moral Death. Morality has the power to dictate but none to move. Nature directs but cannot control. As was wisely expressed in one of many pregnant utterances during a recent *Symposium*, "Though the decay of religion may leave the institutes of morality intact, it drains off their inward power. The devout faith of men expresses and measures the intensity of their moral nature, and it cannot be lost without a remission of enthusiasm, and under this low pressure, the successful reëntrance of importunate desires and clamorous passions which had been driven back. To believe in an ever-living and perfect Mind, supreme over the universe, is to invest moral distinctions with immensity and eternity, and lift them from the provincial stage of human society to the imperishable theater of all being. When planted thus in the very substance of things, they justify and support the ideal estimates of the conscience; they deepen every guilty shame; they guarantee every righteous hope; and they help the will with a Divine casting-vote in every balance of temptation." That morality has a basis in human society, that Nature has a Religion, surely makes the Death of the soul when left to itself all the more appalling. It means that, between them, Nature and morality provide all for virtue—except the Life to live it.

It is at this point accordingly that our subject comes into intimate contact with Religion. The proposition that "to be carnally minded is Death" even the moralist will assent to. But when it is further announced that "the carnal mind is *enmity against God*" we find ourselves in a different region. And when we find it also stated that "the wages of *sin* is Death," we are in the heart of the profoundest questions of theology. What before was merely "enmity against society" becomes "enmity against God;" and what was "vice" is "sin." The conception of a God gives an altogether new color to worldliness and vice. Worldliness it changes into heathenism, vice into blasphemy. The carnal mind, the mind which is turned away from God, which will not correspond with God—this is not moral only but spiritual Death. And Sin, that which separates from God, which disobeys God, which *can* not in that state correspond with God—this is hell.

To the estrangement of the soul from God the best of theology traces the ultimate cause of sin. Sin is simply apostasy from God, unbelief in God. "Sin is manifest in its true character when the demand of holiness in the conscience, presenting itself to the man as one of loving submission to God, is put from him with aversion. Here sin appears as it really is, a turning away from God; and while the man's guilt is enhanced, there ensues a benumbing of the heart resulting from the crushing of those higher impulses. This is what is meant by the reprobate state of those who reject Christ and will not believe the Gospel, so often spoken of in the New Testament; this unbelief is just the closing of the heart against the highest love." The other view of sin, probably the more popular at present, that sin consists in selfishness, is merely this from another aspect. Obviously if the mind turns away from one part of the environment it will only do so under some temptation to correspond with another. This temptation, at bottom, can only come from one source—the love of self. The irreligious man's correspondences are concentrated upon himself. He worships himself. Self-gratification rather than self-denial; independence rather than submission—these are the rules of life. And this is at once the poorest and the commonest form of idolatry.

But whichever of these views of sin we emphasize, we find both equally connected with Death. If sin is estrangement from God, this very estrangement is Death. It is a want of correspondence. If sin is selfishness, it is conducted at the expense of life. Its wages are Death—"he that loveth his life," said Christ, "shall lose it."

Yet the paralysis of the moral nature apart from God does not only depend for its evidence upon theology or even upon history. From the analogies of Nature one would expect this result as a necessary consequence. The development of any organism in any direction is dependent on its environment. A living cell cut off from air will die. A seed-germ apart from moisture and an appropriate temperature will make the ground its grave for centuries. Human nature, likewise, is subject to similar conditions. It can only develop in presence of its environment. No matter what its possibilities may be, no matter what seeds of thought or virtue, what germs of genius or of art, lie latent in its breast, until the appropriate environment present itself the correspondence is denied, the development discouraged, the most splendid possibilities of life remain unrealized, and thought and virtue, genius and art, are dead. The true environment of the moral life is God. Here conscience wakes. Here kindles love. Duty here becomes heroic; and that righteousness begins to live which alone is to live forever. But if this Atmosphere is not, the dwarfed soul must perish for mere want of its native air. And its Death is a strictly natural Death. It is not an exceptional judgment upon Atheism. In the same circumstances, in the same averted relation to their environment, the poet, the musician, the artist, would alike perish to poetry, to music, and to art. Every environment is a cause. Its effect upon me is exactly proportionate to my correspondence with it. If I correspond with part of it, part of myself is influenced. If I correspond with more, more of myself is influenced; if with all, all is influenced. If I correspond with the world, I become worldly; if with God, I become Divine. As without correspondence of the scientific man with the natural environment there could be no Science and no action founded on the knowledge of Nature, so without communion with the spiritual Environment there can be no Religion. To refuse to cultivate the religious relation is to deny to the soul its highest right—the right to a further evolution. We have already admitted that he who knows not God may not be a monster; we cannot say he will not be a dwarf. This precisely, and on perfectly natural principles, is what he must be. You can dwarf a soul just as you can dwarf a plant, by depriving it of a full environment. Such a soul for a time may have "a name to live." Its character may betray no sign of atrophy. But its very virtue somehow has the pallor of a flower that is grown in darkness, or as the herb which has never seen the sun, no fragrance breathes from its spirit. To morality, possibly, this organism offers the example of an irreproachable life; but to science it is an instance of arrested development; and to religion it presents the spectacle of a corpse—a living Death. With Ruskin, "I do not wonder at what men suffer, but I wonder often at what they lose."

Mortification

"If, by tying its main artery, we stop most of the blood going to a limb, then, for as long as the limb performs its functions, those parts which are called into play must be wasted faster than they are repaired: whence eventual disablement. The relation between due receipt of nutritive matters through its arteries, and due discharge of its duties by the limb, is a part of the physical order. If instead of cutting off the supply to a particular limb, we bleed the patient largely, so drafting away the materials needed for repairing not one limb but all limbs, and not limbs only but viscera, there results both a muscular debility and an enfeeblement of the vital functions. Here, again, cause and effect are necessarily related.... Pass now to those actions more commonly thought of as the occasions for rules of conduct."—*Herbert Spencer.*

"Mortify therefore your members which are upon earth."—*Paul.*

"O Star-eyed Science! hast thou wandered there
To waft us home the message of despair?"—*Campbell.*

The definition of Death which science has given us is this: *A falling out of correspondence with environment.* When, for example, a man loses the sight of his eyes, his correspondence with the environing world is curtailed. His life is limited in an important direction; he is less living than he was before. If, in addition, he loses the senses of touch and hearing, his correspondences are still further limited; he is therefore still further dead. And when all possible correspondences have ceased, when the nerves decline to respond to any stimulus, when the lungs close their gates against the air, when the heart refuses to correspond with the blood by so much as another beat, the insensate corpse is wholly and forever dead. The soul, in like manner, which has no correspondence with the spiritual environment is spiritually dead. It may be that it never possessed the spiritual eye or the spiritual ear, or a heart which throbbed in response to the love of God. If so, having never lived, it cannot be said to have died. But not to have these correspondences is to be in the state of Death. To the spiritual world, to the Divine Environment, it is dead—as a stone which has never lived is dead to the environment of the organic world.

Having already abundantly illustrated this use of the symbol Death, we may proceed to deal with another class of expressions where the same term is employed in an exactly opposite connection. It is a proof of the radical nature of religion that a word so extreme should have to be used again and again in Christian teaching, to define in different directions the true spiritual relations of mankind. Hitherto we have concerned ourselves with the condition of the natural man with regard to the spiritual world. We have now to speak of the relations of the spiritual man with regard to the natural world. Carrying with us the same essential principle—want of correspondence—underlying the meaning of Death, we shall find that the relation of the spiritual man to the natural world, or at least to part of it, is to be that of Death.

When the natural man becomes the spiritual man, the great change is described by Christ as a passing from Death unto Life. Before the transition occurred, the practical difficulty was this, how to get into correspondence with the new Environment? But no sooner is this correspondence established than the problem is reversed. The question now is, how to get out of correspondence with the old environment? The moment the new life is begun there comes a genuine anxiety to break with the old. For the former environment has now become embarrassing. It refuses its dismissal from consciousness. It competes doggedly with the new Environment for a share of the correspondences. And in a hundred ways the former traditions, the memories and passions of the past, the fixed associations and habits of the earlier life, now complicate the new relation. The complex and bewildered soul, in fact, finds itself in correspondence with two environments, each with urgent but yet incompatible claims. It is a dual soul living in a double world, a world whose inhabitants are deadly enemies, and engaged in perpetual civil-war.

The position of things is perplexing. It is clear that no man can attempt to live both lives. To walk both in the flesh and in the spirit is morally impossible. "No man," as Christ so often emphasized, "can serve two masters." And yet, as matter of fact, here is the new-born being in communication with both environments? With sin and purity, light and darkness, time and Eternity, God and Devil, the confused and undecided soul is now in correspondence. What is to be done in such an emergency? How can the New Life deliver itself from the still-persistent past?

A ready solution of the difficulty would be *to die*. Were one to die organically, to die and "go to heaven," all correspondence with the lower environment would be arrested at a stroke. For Physical Death of course simply means the final stoppage of all natural correspondences with this sinful world.

But this alternative, fortunately or unfortunately, is not open. The detention here of body and spirit for a given period is determined for us, and we are morally bound to accept the situation. We must look then for a further alternative.

Actual Death being denied us, we must ask ourselves if there is nothing else resembling it—no artificial relation, no imitation or semblance of Death which would serve our purpose. If we cannot yet die absolutely, surely the next best thing will be to find a temporary substitute. If we cannot die altogether, in short, the most we can do is to die as much as we can. And we now know this is open to us, and how. To die to any environment is to withdraw correspondence with it, to cut ourselves off, so far as possible, from all communication with it. So that the solution of the problem will simply be this, for the spiritual life to reverse continuously the processes of the natural life. The spiritual man having passed from Death unto Life, the natural man must next proceed to pass from Life unto Death. Having opened the new set of correspondences, he must deliberately close up the old. Regeneration in short must be accompanied by Degeneration.

Now it is no surprise to find that this is the process everywhere described and recommended by the founders of the Christian system. Their proposal to the natural man, or rather to the natural part of the spiritual man, with regard to a whole series of inimical relations, is precisely this. If he cannot really die, he must make an adequate approach to it by "reckoning himself dead." Seeing that, until the cycle of his organic life is complete he cannot die physically, he must meantime die morally, reckoning himself morally dead to that environment which, by competing for his correspondences, has now become an obstacle to his spiritual life.

The variety of ways in which the New Testament writers insist upon this somewhat extraordinary method is sufficiently remarkable. And although the idea involved is essentially the same throughout, it will clearly illustrate the nature of the act if we examine separately three different modes of expression employed in the later Scriptures in this connection. The methods by which the spiritual man is to withdraw himself from the old environment—or from that part of it which will directly hinder the spiritual life—are three in number:—

First, Suicide.
Second, Mortification.
Third, Limitation.

It will be found in practice that these different methods are adapted, respectively, to meet three different forms of temptation; so that we possess a sufficient warrant for giving a brief separate treatment to each.

First, Suicide. Stated in undisguised phraseology, the advice of Paul to the Christian, with regard to a part of his nature, is to commit suicide. If the Christian is to "live unto God," he must "die unto sin." If he does not kill sin, sin will inevitably kill him. Recognizing this, he must set himself to reduce the number of his correspondences—retaining and developing those which lead to a fuller life, unconditionally withdrawing those which in any way tend in an opposite direction. This stoppage of correspondences is a voluntary act, a crucifixion of the flesh, a suicide.

Now the least experience of life will make it evident that a large class of sins can only be met, as it were, by Suicide. The peculiar feature of Death by Suicide is that it is not only self-inflicted but sudden. And there are many sins which must either be dealt with suddenly or not at all. Under this category, for instance, are to be included generally all sins of the appetites and passions. Other sins, from their peculiar nature, can only be treated by methods less abrupt, but the sudden operation of the knife is the only successful means of dealing with fleshly sins. For example, the correspondence of the drunkard with his wine is a thing which can be broken off by degrees only in the rarest cases. To attempt it gradually may in an isolated case succeed, but even then the slightly prolonged gratification is no compensation for the slow torture of a gradually diminishing indulgence. "If thine appetite offend thee cut it off," may seem at first but a harsh remedy; but when we contemplate on the one hand the lingering pain of the gradual process, on the other its constant peril, we are compelled to admit that the principle is as kind as it is wise. The expression "total abstinence" in such a case is a strictly biological formula. It implies the sudden destruction of a definite portion of environment by the total withdrawal of all the connecting links. Obviously of course total abstinence ought thus to be allowed a much wider application than to cases of "intemperance." It's the only decisive method of dealing with any sin of the flesh; The very nature of the relations makes it absolutely imperative that every victim of unlawful appetite, in whatever direction, shall totally abstain. Hence Christ's apparently extreme and peremptory language defines the only possible, as well as the only charitable, expedient: "If thy right eye offend thee, pluck it out, and cast it from thee. And if thy right hand offend thee, cut it off, and cast it from thee."

The humanity of what is called "sudden conversion" has never been insisted on as it deserves. In discussing "Biogenesis" it has been already pointed out that while growth is a slow and gradual process, the change from Death to Life alike in the natural and spiritual spheres is the work of a moment. Whatever the conscious hour of the second birth may be—in the case of an adult it is probably defined by the first real victory over sin—it is certain that on biological principles the real turning-point is literally a moment. But on moral and humane grounds this misunderstood, perverted, and therefore despised doctrine is equally capable of defence. Were any reformer, with an adequate knowledge of human life, to sit down and plan a scheme for the salvation of sinful men, he would probably come to the conclusion that the best way after all, perhaps indeed the only way, to turn a sinner from the error of his ways would be to do it suddenly.

Suppose a drunkard were advised to take off one portion from his usual allowance the first week, another the second, and so on! Or suppose at first, he only allowed himself to become intoxicated in the evenings, then every second evening, then only on Saturday nights, and finally only every Christmas? How would a thief be reformed if he slowly reduced the number of his burglaries, or a wife-beater by gradually diminishing the number of his blows? The argument ends with an *ad absurdum*. "Let him that stole *steal no more*," is the only feasible, the only moral, and the only humane way. This may not apply to every case, but when any part of man's sinful life can be dealt with by immediate Suicide, to make him reach the end, even were it possible, by a lingering death, would be a monstrous cruelty. And yet it is this very thing in "sudden conversion," that men object to—the sudden change, the decisive stand, the uncompromising rupture with the past, the precipitate flight from sin as of one escaping for his life. Men surely forget that this is an escaping for one's life. Let the poor prisoner run—madly and blindly if he like, for the terror of Death is upon him. God knows, when the pause comes, how the chains will gall him still.

It is a peculiarity of the sinful state, that as a general rule men are linked to evil mainly by a single correspondence. Few men break the whole law. Our natures, fortunately, are not large enough to make us guilty of all, and the restraints of circumstances are usually such as to leave a loophole in the life of each individual for only a single habitual sin. But it is very easy to see how this reduction of our intercourse with evil to a single correspondence blinds us to our true position. Our correspondences, as a whole, are not with evil, and in our calculations as to our spiritual condition we emphasize the many negatives rather than the single positive. One little weakness, we are apt to fancy, all men must be allowed, and we even claim a certain indulgence for that apparent necessity of nature which we call our besetting sin. Yet to break with the lower environment at all, to many, is to break at this single point. It is the only important point at which they touch it, circumstances or natural disposition making habitual contact at other places impossible. The sinful environment, in short, to them means a small but well-defined area. Now if contact at this point be not broken off, they are virtually in contact still with the whole environment. There may be only one avenue between the new life and the old, it may be but a small and *subterranean passage*, but this is sufficient to keep the old life in. So long as that remains the victim is not "dead unto sin," and therefore he cannot "live unto God." Hence the reasonableness of the words, "Whatsoever shall keep the whole law, and yet offend at one point, he is guilty of all." In the natural world it only requires a single vital correspondence of the body to be out of order to insure Death. It is not necessary to have consumption, diabetes, and an aneurism to bring the body to the grave if it have heart-disease. He who is fatally diseased in one organ necessarily pays the penalty with his life, though all the others be in perfect health. And such, likewise, are the mysterious unity and correlation of functions in the spiritual organism that the disease of one member may involve the ruin of the whole. The reason, therefore, with which Christ follows up the announcement of His Doctrine of Mutilation, or local Suicide, finds here at once its justification and interpretation: "If thy right eye offend thee, pluck it out, and cast it from thee: *for* it is profitable for thee that *one* of thy members should perish, and not that thy *whole body* should be cast into hell. And if thy right hand offend thee, cut it off, and cast it from thee: *for* it is profitable for thee that *one* of thy members should perish, and not that thy *whole body* should be cast into hell."

Secondly, Mortification. The warrant for the use of this expression is found in the well-known phrases of Paul, "If ye through the Spirit do mortify the deeds of the body ye shall live," and "Mortify therefore your members which are upon earth." The word mortify here is, literally, to make to die. It is used, of course, in no specially technical sense; and to attempt to draw a detailed moral from the pathology of mortification would be equally fantastic and irrelevant. But without in any way straining the meaning it is obvious that we have here a slight addition to our conception of dying to sin. In contrast with Suicide, Mortification implies a gradual rather than a sudden process. The contexts in which the passages occur will make this meaning so clear, and are otherwise so instructive in the general connection, that we may quote them, from the New Version, at length: "They that are after the flesh do mind the things of the flesh; but they that are after the Spirit the things of the Spirit. For the mind of the flesh is death; but the mind of the Spirit is life and peace: because the mind of the flesh is enmity against God; for it is not subject to the law of God, neither indeed can it be: and they that are in the flesh cannot please God. But ye are not in the flesh, but in the Spirit, if so be that the Spirit of God dwell in you. But if any man hath not the Spirit of Christ, he is none of His. And if Christ is in you, the body is dead because of sin; but the Spirit is life because of righteousness. But if the Spirit of Him that raised up Jesus from the dead dwelleth in you, He that raised up Christ Jesus from the dead shall quicken also your mortal bodies through His Spirit that dwelleth in you. So then, brethren, we are debtors not to the flesh, to live after the flesh: for if ye live after the flesh ye must die; but if by the Spirit ye mortify the doings (marg.) of the body, ye shall live."

And again, "If then ye were raised together with Christ, seek the things that are above, where Christ is seated on the right hand of God. Set your mind on the things that are above, not on the things that are upon the earth. For ye died, and your life is hid with Christ in God. When Christ, who is our life, shall be manifested, then shall ye also with Him be manifested in glory. Mortify therefore your members which are upon the earth; fornication, uncleanness, passion, evil desire, and covetousness, the which is idolatry; for which things' sake cometh the wrath of God upon the sons of disobedience; in the which ye also walked aforetime, when ye lived in these things. But now put ye also away all these; anger, wrath, malice, railing, shameful speaking out of your mouth: lie not one to another; seeing that ye have put off the old man with his doings, and have put on the new man, which is being renewed unto knowledge after the image of Him that created him."

From the nature of the case as here stated it is evident that no sudden process could entirely transfer a man from the old into the new relation. To break altogether, and at every point, with the old environment, is a simple impossibility. So long as the regenerate man is kept in this world, he must find the old environment at many points a severe temptation. Power over very many of the commonest temptations is only to be won by degrees, and however anxious one might be to apply the summary method to every case, he soon finds it impossible in practice. The difficulty in these cases arises from a peculiar feature of the temptation. The difference between a sin of drunkenness, and, let us say, a sin of temper, is that in the former case the victim who would reform has mainly to deal with the environment, but in the latter with the correspondence. The drunkard's temptation is a known and definite quantity. His safety lies in avoiding some external and material substance. Of course, at bottom, he is really dealing with the correspondence every time he resists; he is distinctly controlling appetite. Nevertheless it is less the appetite that absorbs his mind than the environment. And so long as he can keep himself clear of the "external relation," to use Mr. Herbert Spencer's phraseology, he has much less difficulty with the "internal relation." The ill-tempered person, on the other hand, can make very little of his environment. However he may attempt to circumscribe it in certain directions, there will always remain a wide and ever-changing area to stimulate his irascibility. His environment, in short, is an inconstant quantity, and his most elaborate calculations and precautions must often and suddenly fail him.

What he has to deal with, then, mainly is the correspondence, the temper itself. And that, he well knows, involves a long and humiliating discipline. The case now is not at all a surgical but a medical one, and the knife is here of no more use than in a fever. A specific irritant has poisoned his veins. And the acrid humors that are breaking out all over the surface of his life are only to be subdued by a gradual sweetening of the inward spirit. It is now known that the human body acts toward certain fever-germs as a sort of soil. The man whose blood is pure has nothing to fear. So he whose spirit is purified and sweetened becomes proof against these germs of sin. "Anger, wrath, malice and railing" in such a soil can find no root.

The difference between this and the former method of dealing with sin may be illustrated by another analogy. The two processes depend upon two different natural principles. The Mutilation of a member, for instance, finds its analogue in the horticultural operation of *pruning*, where the object is to divert life from a useless into a useful channel. A part of a plant which previously monopolized a large share of the vigor of the total organism, but without yielding any adequate return, is suddenly cut off, so that the vital processes may proceed more actively in some fruitful parts. Christ's use of this figure is well-known: "Every branch in Me that beareth not fruit He purgeth it that it may bring forth more fruit." The strength of the plant, that is, being given to the formation of mere wood, a number of useless correspondences have to be abruptly closed while the useful connections are allowed to remain. The Mortification of a member, again, is based on the Law of Degeneration. The useless member here is not cut off, but simply relieved as much as possible of all exercise. This encourages the gradual decay of the parts, and as it is more and more neglected it ceases to be a channel for life at all. So an organism "mortifies" its members.

Thirdly, Limitation. While a large number of correspondences between man and his environment can be stopped in these ways, there are many more which neither can be reduced by a gradual Mortification nor cut short by sudden Death.

One reason for this is that to tamper with these correspondences might involve injury to closely related vital parts. Or, again, there are organs which are really essential to the normal life of the organism, and which therefore the organism cannot afford to lose even though at times they act prejudicially. Not a few correspondences, for instance, are not wrong in themselves but only in their extremes. Up to a certain point they are lawful and necessary; beyond that point they may become not only unnecessary but sinful. The appropriate treatment in these and similar cases consists in a process of Limitation. The performance of this operation, it must be confessed, requires a most delicate hand. It is an art, moreover, which no one can teach another. And yet, if it is not learned by all who are trying to lead the Christian life, it cannot be for want of practice. For, as we shall see, the Christian is called upon to exercise few things more frequently.

An easy illustration of a correspondence which is only wrong when carried to an extreme, is the love of money. The love of money up to a certain point is a necessity; beyond that it may become one of the worst of sins. Christ said: "Ye cannot serve God and Mammon." The two services, at a definite point, become incompatible, and hence correspondence with one must cease. At what point, however, it must cease each man has to determine for himself. And in this consists at once the difficulty and the dignity of Limitation.

There is another class of cases where the adjustments are still more difficult to determine. Innumerable points exist in our surroundings with which it is perfectly legitimate to enjoy, and even to cultivate, correspondence, but which privilege, at the same time, it were better on the whole that we did not use. Circumstances are occasionally such—the demands of others upon us, for example, may be so clamant—that we have voluntarily to reduce the area of legitimate pleasure. Or, instead of it coming from others, the claim may come from a still higher direction. Man's spiritual life consists in the number and fullness of his correspondences with God. In order to develop these he may be constrained to insulate them, to inclose them from the other correspondences, to shut himself in with them. In many ways the limitation of the natural life is the necessary condition of the full enjoyment of the spiritual life.

In this principle lies the true philosophy of self-denial. No man is called to a life of self-denial for its own sake. It is in order to a compensation which, though sometimes difficult to see, is always real and always proportionate. No truth, perhaps, in practical religion is more lost sight of. We cherish somehow a lingering rebellion against the doctrine of self-denial—as if our nature, or our circumstances, or our conscience, dealt with us severely in loading us with the daily cross. But is it not plain after all that the life of self-denial is the more abundant life—more abundant just in proportion to the ampler crucifixion of the narrower life? Is it not a clear case of exchange—an exchange however where the advantage is entirely on our side? We give up a correspondence in which there is a little life to enjoy a correspondence in which there is an abundant life. What though we sacrifice a hundred such correspondences? We make but the more room for the great one that is left. The lesson of self-denial, that is to say of Limitation, is *concentration*. Do not spoil your life, it says, at the outset with unworthy and impoverishing correspondences; and if it is growing truly rich and abundant, be very jealous of ever diluting its high eternal quality with anything of earth. To concentrate upon a few great correspondences, to oppose to the death the perpetual petty larceny of our life by trifles—these are the conditions for the highest and happiest life. It is only Limitation which can secure the Illimitable.

The penalty of evading self-denial also is just that we get the lesser instead of the larger good. The punishment of sin is inseparably bound up with itself. To refuse to deny one's self is just to be left with the self undenied. When the balance of life is struck, the self will be found still there. The discipline of life was meant to destroy this self, but that discipline having been evaded—and we all to some extent have opportunities, and too often exercise them, of taking the narrow path by the shortest cuts—its purpose is balked. But the soul is the loser. In seeking to gain its life it has really lost it. This is what Christ meant when He said: "He that loveth his life shall lose it, and he that hateth his life in this world shall keep it unto life eternal."

Why does Christ say: "Hate Life?" Does He mean that life is a sin? No. Life is not a sin. Still, He says we must hate it. But we must live. Why should we hate what we must do? For this reason: Life is not a sin, but the love of life may be a sin. And the best way not to love life is to hate it. Is it a sin then to love life? Not a sin exactly, but a mistake. It is a sin to love some life, a mistake to love the rest. Because that love is lost. All that is lavished on it is lost. Christ does not say it is wrong to love life. He simply says it is *loss*. Each man has only a certain amount of life, of time, of attention—a definite measurable quantity. If he gives any of it to this life solely it is wasted. Therefore Christ says, Hate life, limit life, lest you steal your love for it from something that deserves it more.

Now this does not apply to all life. It is "life in this world" that is to be hated. For life in this world implies conformity to this world. It may not mean pursuing worldly pleasures, or mixing with worldly sets; but a subtler thing than that—a silent deference to worldly opinion; an almost unconscious lowering of religious tone to the level of the worldly-religious world around; a subdued resistance to the soul's delicate promptings to greater consecration, out of deference to "breadth" or fear of ridicule. These, and such things, are what Christ tells us we must hate. For these things are of the very essence of worldliness. "If any man love the world," even in this sense, "the love of the Father is not in him."

There are two ways of hating life, a true and a false. Some men hate life because it hates them. They have seen through it, and it has turned round upon them. They have drunk it, and come to the dregs; therefore they hate it. This is one of the ways in which the man who loves his life literally loses it. He loves it till he loses it, then he hates it because it has fooled him. The other way is the religious. For religious reasons a man deliberately braces himself to the systematic hating of his life. "No man can serve two masters, for either he must hate the one and love the other, or else he must hold to the one and despise the other." Despising the other—this is hating life, limiting life. It is not misanthropy, but Christianity.

This principle, as has been said, contains the true philosophy of self-denial. It also holds the secret by which self-denial may be most easily borne. A common conception of self-denial is that there are a multitude of things about life which are to be put down with a high hand the moment they make their appearance. They are temptations which are not to be tolerated, but must be instantly crushed out of being with pang and effort.

So life comes to be a constant and sore cutting off of things which we love as our right hand. But now suppose one tried boldly to hate these things? Suppose we deliberately made up our minds as to what things we were henceforth to allow to become our life? Suppose we selected a given area of our environment and determined once for all that our correspondences should go to that alone, fencing in this area all round with a morally impassable wall? True, to others, we should seem to live a poorer life; they would see that our environment was circumscribed, and call us narrow because it was narrow. But, well-chosen, this limited life would be really the fullest life; it would be rich in the highest and worthiest, and poor in the smallest and basest correspondences. The well-defined spiritual life is not only the highest life, but it is also the most easily lived. The whole cross is more easily carried than the half. It is the man who tries to make the best of both worlds who makes nothing of either. And he who seeks to serve two masters misses the benediction of both. But he who has taken his stand, who has drawn a boundary line, sharp and deep about his religious life, who has marked off all beyond as forever forbidden ground to him, finds the yoke easy and the burden light. For this forbidden environment comes to be as if it were not. His faculties falling out of correspondence, slowly lose their sensibilities. And the balm of Death numbing his lower nature releases him for the scarce disturbed communion of a higher life. So even here to die is gain.

Eternal life

"Supposing that man, in some form, is permitted to remain on the earth for a long series of years, we merely lengthen out the period, but we cannot escape the final catastrophe. The earth will gradually lose its energy of relation, as well as that of revolution round the sun. The sun himself will wax dim and become useless as a source of energy, until at last the favorable conditions of the present solar system will have quite disappeared.

"But what happens to our system will happen likewise to the whole visible universe, which will, if finite, become a lifeless mass, if indeed it be not doomed to utter dissolution. In fine, it will become old and effete, no less truly than the individual. It is a glorious garment, this visible universe, but not an immortal one. We must look elsewhere if we are to be clothed with immortality as with a garment."—*The Unseen Universe.*

"This is Life Eternal—that they might know Thee, the True God, and Jesus Christ whom Thou hast sent."—*Jesus Christ.*

"Perfect correspondence would be perfect life. Were there no changes in the environment but such as the organism had adapted changes to meet, and were it never to fail in the efficiency with which it met them, there would be eternal existence and eternal knowledge."—*Herbert Spencer.*

One of the most startling achievements of recent science is a definition of Eternal Life. To the religious mind this is a contribution of immense moment. For eighteen hundred years only one definition of Life Eternal was before the world. Now there are two.

Through all these centuries revealed religion had this doctrine to itself. Ethics had a voice, as well as Christianity, on the question of the *summum bonum*; Philosophy ventured to speculate on the Being of a God. But no source outside Christianity contributed anything to the doctrine of Eternal Life. Apart from Revelation, this great truth was unguaranteed. It was the one thing in the Christian system that most needed verification from without, yet none was forthcoming. And never has any further light been thrown upon the question why in its very nature the Christian Life should be Eternal. Christianity itself even upon this point has been obscure. Its decision upon the bare fact is authoritative and specific. But as to what there is in the Spiritual Life necessarily endowing it with the element of Eternity, the maturest theology is all but silent.

It has been reserved for modern biology at once to defend and illuminate this central truth of the Christian faith. And hence in the interests of religion, practical and evidential, this second and scientific definition of Eternal Life is to be hailed as an announcement of commanding interest. Why it should not yet have received the recognition of religious thinkers—for already it has lain some years unnoticed—is not difficult to understand. The belief in Science as an aid to faith is not yet ripe enough to warrant men in searching there for witnesses to the highest Christian truths. The inspiration of Nature, it is thought, extends to the humbler doctrines alone. And yet the reverent inquirer who guides his steps in the right direction may find even now in the still dim twilight of the scientific world much that will illuminate and intensify his sublimest faith. Here, at least, comes, and comes unbidden, the opportunity of testing the most vital point of the Christian system. Hitherto the Christian philosopher has remained content with the scientific evidence against Annihilation. Or, with Butler, he has reasoned from the Metamorphoses of Insects to a future life. Or again, with the authors of "The Unseen Universe," the apologist has constructed elaborate, and certainly impressive, arguments upon the Law of Continuity. But now we may draw nearer. For the first time Science touches Christianity *positively* on the doctrine of Immortality. It confronts us with an actual definition of an Eternal Life, based on a full and rigidly accurate examination of the necessary conditions. Science does not pretend that it can fulfill these conditions. Its votaries make no claim to possess the Eternal Life. It simply postulates the requisite conditions without concerning itself whether any organism should ever appear, or does now exist, which might fulfill them. The claim of religion, on the other hand, is that there are organisms which possess Eternal Life. And the problem for us to solve is this: Do those who profess to possess Eternal Life fulfill the conditions required by Science, or are they different conditions? In a word, Is the Christian conception of Eternal Life scientific?

It may be unnecessary to notice at the outset that the definition of Eternal Life drawn up by Science was framed without reference to religion. It must indeed have been the last thought with the thinker to whom we chiefly owe it, that in unfolding the conception of a Life in its very nature necessarily eternal, he was contributing to Theology.

Mr. Herbert Spencer—for it is to him we owe it—would be the first to admit the impartiality of his definition; and from the connection in which it occurs in his writings, it is obvious that religion was not even present to his mind. He is analyzing with minute care the relations between Environment and Life. He unfolds the principle according to which Life is high or low, long or short. He shows why organisms live and why they die. And finally he defines a condition of things in which an organism would never die—in which it would enjoy a perpetual and perfect Life. This to him is, of course, but a speculation. Life Eternal is a biological conceit. The conditions necessary to an Eternal Life do not exist in the natural world. So that the definition is altogether impartial and independent. A Perfect Life, to Science, is simply a thing which is theoretically possible—like a Perfect Vacuum.

Before giving, in so many words, the definition of Mr. Herbert Spencer, it will render it fully intelligible if we gradually lead up to it by a brief rehearsal of the few and simple biological facts on which it is based. In considering the subject of Death, we have formerly seen that there are degrees of Life. By this is meant that some lives have more and fuller correspondence with Environment than others. The amount of correspondence, again, is determined by the greater or less complexity of the organism. Thus a simple organism like the Amoeba is possessed of very few correspondences. It is a mere sac of transparent structureless jelly for which organization has done almost nothing, and hence it can only communicate with the smallest possible area of Environment. An insect, in virtue of its more complex structure, corresponds with a wider area. Nature has endowed it with special faculties for reaching out to the Environment on many sides; it has more life than the Amoeba. In other words, it is a higher animal. Man again, whose body is still further differentiated, or broken up into different correspondences, finds himself *en rapport* with his surroundings to a further extent. And therefore he is higher still, more living still. And this law, that the degree of Life varies with the degree of correspondence, holds to the minutest detail throughout the entire range of living things. Life becomes fuller and fuller, richer and richer, more and more sensitive and responsive to an ever-widening Environment as we arise in the chain of being.

Now it will speedily appear that a distinct relation exists, and must exist, between complexity and longevity. Death being brought about by the failure of an organism to adjust itself to some change in the Environment, it follows that those organisms which are able to adjust themselves most readily and successfully will live the longest. They will continue time after time to effect the appropriate adjustment, and their power of doing so will be exactly proportionate to their complexity—that is, to the amount of Environment they can control with their correspondences. There are, for example, in the Environment of every animal certain things which are directly or indirectly dangerous to Life. If its equipment of correspondences is not complete enough to enable it to avoid these dangers in all possible circumstances, it must sooner or later succumb. The organism then with the most perfect set of correspondences, that is, the highest and most complex organism, has an obvious advantage over less complex forms. It can adjust itself more perfectly and frequently. But this is just the biological way of saying that it can live the longest. And hence the relation between complexity and longevity may be expressed thus—the most complex organisms are the longest lived.

To state and illustrate the proposition conversely may the point still further clear. The less highly organized an animal is, the less will be its chance of remaining in lengthened correspondence with its Environment. At some time or other in its career circumstances are sure to occur to which the comparatively immobile organism finds itself structurally unable to respond. Thus a *Medusa* tossed ashore by a wave, finds itself so out of correspondence with its new surroundings that its life must pay the forfeit. Had it been able by internal change to adapt itself to external change—to correspond sufficiently with the new environment, as for example to crawl, as an eel would have done, back into that environment with which it had completer correspondence—its life might have been spared. But had this happened it would continue to live henceforth only so long as it could continue in correspondence with all the circumstances in which it might find itself. Even if, however, it became complex enough to resist the ordinary and direct dangers of its environment, it might still be out of correspondence with others. A naturalist for instance, might take advantage of its want of correspondence with particular sights and sounds to capture it for his cabinet, or the sudden dropping of a yacht's anchor or the turn of a screw might cause its untimely death.

Again, in the case of a bird, in virtue of its more complex organization, there is command over a much larger area of environment. It can take precautions such as the *Medusa* could not; it has increased facilities for securing food; its adjustments all round are more complex; and therefore it ought to be able to maintain its Life for a longer period. There is still a large area, however, over which it has no control. Its power of internal change is not complete enough to afford it perfect correspondence with all external changes, and its tenure of Life is to that extent insecure. Its correspondence, moreover, is limited even with regard to those external conditions with which it has been partially established. Thus a bird in ordinary circumstances has no difficulty in adapting itself to changes of temperature, but if these are varied beyond the point at which its capacity of adjustment begins to fail—for example, during an extreme winter—the organism being unable to meet the condition must perish. The human organism, on the other hand, can respond to this external condition, as well as to countless other vicissitudes under which lower forms would inevitably succumb. Man's adjustments are to the largest known area of Environment, and hence he ought to be able furthest to prolong his Life.

It becomes evident, then, that as we ascend in the scale of Life we rise also in the scale of longevity. The lowest organisms are, as a rule, short-lived, and the rate of mortality diminishes more or less regularly as we ascend in the animal scale. So extraordinary indeed is the mortality among lowly-organized forms that in most cases a compensation is actually provided, nature endowing them with a marvelously increased fertility in order to guard against absolute extinction. Almost all lower forms are furnished not only with great reproductive powers, but with different methods of propagation, by which, in various circumstances, and in an incredibly short time, the species can be indefinitely multiplied. Ehrenberg found that by the repeated subdivisions of a single *Paramecium*, no fewer than 268,000,000 similar organisms might be produced in one month. This power steadily decreases as we rise higher in the scale, until forms are reached in which one, two, or at most three, come into being at a birth. It decreases, however, because it is no longer needed. These forms have a much longer lease of Life. And it may be taken as a rule, although it has exceptions, that complexity in animal organisms is always associated with longevity.

It may be objected that these illustrations are taken merely from morbid conditions. But whether the Life be cut short by accident or by disease the principle is the same. All dissolution is brought about practically in the same way. A certain condition in the Environment fails to be met by a corresponding condition in the organism, and this is death. And conversely the more an organism in virtue of its complexity can adapt itself to all the parts of its Environment, the longer it will live. "It is manifest *a priori*," says Mr. Herbert Spencer, "that since changes in the physical state of the environment, as also those mechanical actions and those variations of available food which occur in it, are liable to stop the processes going on in the organism; and since the adaptive changes in the organism have the effects of directly or indirectly counterbalancing these changes in the environment, it follows that the life of the organism will be short or long, low or high, according to the extent to which changes in the environment are met by corresponding changes in the organism. Allowing a margin for perturbations, the life will continue only while the correspondence continues; the completeness of the life will be proportionate to the completeness of the correspondence; and the life will be perfect only when the correspondence is perfect."

We are now all but in sight of our scientific definitions of Eternal Life. The desideratum is an organism with a correspondence of a very exceptional kind. It must lie beyond the reach of those "mechanical actions" and those "variations of available food," which are "liable to stop the processes going on in the organism." Before we reach an Eternal Life we must pass beyond that point at which all ordinary correspondences inevitably cease. We must find an organism so high and complex, that at some point in its development it shall have added a correspondence which organic death is powerless to arrest. We must in short pass beyond that definite region where the correspondences depend on evanescent and material media, and enter a further region where the Environment corresponded with is itself Eternal. Such an Environment exists. The Environment of the Spiritual world is outside the influence of these "mechanical actions," which sooner or later interrupt the processes going on in all finite organisms. If then we can find an organism which has established a correspondence with the spiritual world, that correspondence will possess the elements of eternity—provided only one other condition be fulfilled.

That condition is that the Environment be perfect. If it is not perfect, if it is not the highest, if it is endowed with the finite quality of change, there can be no guarantee that the Life of its correspondents will be eternal. Some change might occur in it which the correspondents had no adaptive changes to meet, and Life would cease. But grant a spiritual organism in perfect correspondence with a perfect spiritual Environment, and the conditions necessary to Eternal Life are satisfied.

The exact terms of Mr. Herbert Spencer's definition of Eternal Life may now be given. And it will be seen that they include essentially the conditions here laid down. "Perfect correspondence would be perfect life. Were there no changes in the environment but such as the organism had adapted changes to meet, and were it never to fail in the efficiency with which it met them, there would be eternal existence and eternal knowledge." Reserving the question as to the possible fulfillment of these conditions, let us turn for a moment to the definition of Eternal Life laid down by Christ. Let us place it alongside the definition of Science, and mark the points of contact. Uninterrupted correspondence with a perfect Environment is Eternal Life according to Science. "This is Life Eternal," said Christ, "that they may know Thee, the only true God, and Jesus Christ whom Thou hast sent." Life Eternal is to know God. To know God is to "correspond" with God. To correspond with God is to correspond with a Perfect Environment. And the organism which attains to this, in the nature of things must live forever. Here is "eternal existence and eternal knowledge."

The main point of agreement between the scientific and the religious definition is that Life consists in a peculiar and personal relation defined as a "correspondence." This conception, that Life consists in correspondences, has been so abundantly illustrated already that it is now unnecessary to discuss it further. All Life indeed consists essentially in correspondences with various Environments. The artist's life is a correspondence with art; the musician's with music. To cut them off from these Environments is in that relation to cut off their Life. To be cut off from all Environment is death. To find a new Environment again and cultivate relation with it is to find a new Life. To live is to correspond, and to correspond is to live. So much is true in Science. But it is also true in Religion. And it is of great importance to observe that to Religion also the conception of Life is a correspondence. No truth of Christianity has been more ignorantly or willfully travestied than the doctrine of Immortality. The popular idea, in spite of a hundred protests, is that Eternal Life is to live forever. A single glance at the *locus classicus* might have made this error impossible. There we are told that Life Eternal is not to live. This is Life Eternal—*to know*. And yet—and it is a notorious instance of the fact that men who are opposed to Religion will take their conceptions of its profoundest truths from mere vulgar perversions—this view still represents to many cultivated men the Scriptural doctrine of Eternal Life. From time to time the taunt is thrown at Religion, not unseldom from lips which Science ought to have taught more caution, that the Future Life of Christianity is simply a prolonged existence, an eternal monotony, a blind and indefinite continuance of being. The Bible never could commit itself to any such empty platitudes; nor could Christianity ever offer to the world a hope so colorless. Not that Eternal Life has nothing to do with everlastingness. That is part of the conception. And it is this aspect of the question that first arrests us in the field of Science. But even Science has more in its definition than longevity. It has a correspondence and an Environment; and although it cannot fill up these terms for Religion, it can indicate at least the nature of the relation, the kind of thing that is meant by Life. Science speaks to us indeed of much more than numbers of years. It defines degrees of Life. It explains a widening Environment. It unfolds the relation between a widening Environment and increasing complexity in organisms. And if it has no absolute contribution to the content of Religion, its analogies are not limited to a point. It yields to Immortality, and this is the most that Science can do in any case, the board framework for a doctrine.

The further definition, moreover, of this correspondence as *knowing* is in the highest degree significant. Is not this the precise quality in an Eternal correspondence which the analogies of Science would prepare us to look for? Longevity is associated with complexity. And complexity in organisms is manifested by the successive addition of correspondences, each richer and larger than those which have gone before. The differentiation, therefore, of the spiritual organism ought to be signalized by the addition of the highest possible correspondence. It is not essential to the idea that the correspondence should be altogether novel; it is necessary rather that it should not. An altogether new correspondence appearing suddenly without shadow or prophecy would be a violation of continuity. What we should expect would be something new, and yet something that we were already prepared for. We should look for a further development in harmony with current developments; the extension of the last and highest correspondence in a new and higher direction. And this is exactly what we have. In the world with which biology deals, Evolution culminates in Knowledge.

At whatever point in the zoological scale this correspondence, or set of correspondences, begins, it is certain there is nothing higher. In its stunted infancy merely, when we meet with its rudest beginnings in animal intelligence, it is a thing so wonderful, as to strike every thoughtful and reverent observer with awe. Even among the invertebrates so marvelously are these or kindred powers displayed, that naturalists do not hesitate now, on the ground of intelligence at least, to classify some of the humblest creatures next to man himself. Nothing in nature, indeed, is so unlike the rest of nature, so prophetic of what is beyond it, so supernatural. And as manifested in Man who crowns creation with his all-embracing consciousness, there is but one word to describe his knowledge: it is Divine. If then from this point there is to be any further Evolution, this surely must be the correspondence in which it shall take place? This correspondence is great enough to demand development; and yet it is little enough to need it. The magnificence of what it has achieved relatively, is the pledge of the possibility of more; the insignificance of its conquest absolutely involves the probability of still richer triumphs. If anything, in short, in humanity is to go on it must be this. Other correspondences may continue likewise; others, again, we can well afford to leave behind. But this cannot cease. This correspondence—or this set of correspondences, for it is very complex—is it not that to which men with one consent would attach Eternal Life? Is there anything else to which they would attach it? Is anything better conceivable, anything worthier, fuller, nobler, anything which would represent a higher form of Evolution or offer a more perfect ideal for an Eternal Life?

But these are questions of quality; and the moment we pass from quantity to quality we leave Science behind. In the vocabulary of Science, Eternity is only the fraction of a word. It means mere everlastingness. To Religion, on the other hand, Eternity has little to do with time. To correspond with the God of Science, the Eternal Unknowable, would be everlasting existence; to correspond with "the true God and Jesus Christ," is Eternal Life. The quality of the Eternal Life alone makes the heaven; mere everlastingness might be no boon. Even the brief span of the temporal life is too long for those who spend its years in sorrow. Time itself, let alone Eternity, is all but excruciating to Doubt. And many besides Schopenhauer have secretly regarded consciousness as the hideous mistake and malady of Nature. Therefore we must not only have quantity of years, to speak in the language of the present, but quality of correspondence. When we leave Science behind, this correspondence also receives a higher name. It becomes communion. Other names there are for it, religious and theological. It may be included in a general expression, Faith; or we may call it by a personal and specific term, Love. For the knowing of a Whole so great involves the co-operation of many parts.

Communion with God—can it be demonstrated in terms of Science that this is a correspondence which will never break? We do not appeal to Science for such a testimony. We have asked for its conception of an Eternal Life; and we have received for answer that Eternal Life would consist in a correspondence which should never cease, with an Environment which should never pass away. And yet what would Science demand of a perfect correspondence that is not met by this, *the knowing of God*? There is no other correspondence which could satisfy one at least of the conditions. Not one could be named which would not bear on the face of it the mark and pledge of its mortality. But this, to know God, stands alone. To know God, to be linked with God, to be linked with Eternity—if this is not the "eternal existence" of biology, what can more nearly approach it? And yet we are still a great way off—to establish a communication with the Eternal is not to secure Eternal Life. It must be assumed that the communication could be sustained. And to assume this would be to beg the question. So that we have still to prove Eternal Life. But let it be again repeated, we are not here seeking proofs. We are seeking light. We are merely reconnoitring from the furthest promontory of Science if so be that through the haze we may discern the outline of a distant coast and come to some conclusion as to the possibility of landing.

But, it may be replied, it is not open to any one handling the question of Immortality from the side of Science to remain neutral as to the question of fact. It is not enough to announce that he has no addition to make to the positive argument. This may be permitted with reference to other points of contact between Science and Religion, but not with this. We are told this question is settled—that there is no positive side. Science meets the entire conception of Immortality with a direct negative. In the face of a powerful consensus against even the possibility of a Future Life, to content one's self with saying that Science pretended to no argument in favor of it would be at once impertinent and dishonest. We must therefore devote ourselves for a moment to the question of possibility.

The problem is, with a material body and a mental organization inseparably connected with it, to bridge the grave. Emotion, volition, thought itself, are functions of the brain. When the brain is impaired, they are impaired. When the brain is not, they are not. Everything ceases with the dissolution of the material fabric; muscular activity and mental activity perish alike. With the pronounced positive statements on this point from many departments of modern Science we are all familiar. The fatal verdict is recorded by a hundred hands and with scarcely a shadow of qualification. "Unprejudiced philosophy is compelled to reject the idea of an individual immortality and of a personal continuance after death. With the decay and dissolution of its material substratum, through which alone it has acquired a conscious existence and become a person, and upon which it was dependent, the spirit must cease to exist." To the same effect Vogt: "Physiology decides definitely and categorically against individual immortality, as against any special existence of the soul. The soul does not enter the foetus like the evil spirit into persons possessed, but is a product of the development of the brain, just as muscular activity is a product of muscular development, and secretion a product of glandular development." After a careful review of the position of recent Science with regard to the whole doctrine, Mr. Graham sums up thus: "Such is the argument of Science, seemingly decisive against a future life. As we listen to her array of syllogisms, our hearts die within us. The hopes of men, placed in one scale to be weighed, seem to fly up against the massive weight of her evidence, placed in the other. It seems as if all our arguments were vain and unsubstantial, as if our future expectations were the foolish dreams of children, as if there could not be any other possible verdict arrived at upon the evidence brought forward."

Can we go on in the teeth of so real an obstruction? Has not our own weapon turned against us, Science abolishing with authoritative hand the very truth we are asking it to define?

What the philosopher has to throw into the other scale can be easily indicated. Generally speaking, he demurs to the dogmatism of the conclusion. That mind and brain react, that the mental and the physiological processes are related, and very intimately related, is beyond controversy. But how they are related, he submits, is still altogether unknown. The correlation of mind and brain do not involve their identity. And not a few authorities accordingly have consistently hesitated to draw any conclusion at all. Even Büchner's statement turns out, on close examination, to be tentative in the extreme. In prefacing his chapter on Personal Continuance, after a single sentence on the dependence of the soul and its manifestations upon a material substratum, he remarks, "Though we are unable to form a definite idea as to the *how* of this connection, we are still by these facts justified in asserting, that the mode of this connection renders it *apparently* impossible that they should continue to exist separately." There is, therefore, a flaw at this point in the argument for materialism. It may not help the spiritualist in the least degree positively. He may be as far as ever from a theory of how consciousness could continue without the material tissue. But his contention secures for him the right of speculation. The path beyond may lie in hopeless gloom; but it is not barred. He may bring forward his theory if he will. And this is something. For a permission to go on is often the most that Science can grant to Religion.

Men have taken advantage of this loophole in various ways. And though it cannot be said that these speculations offer us more than a probability, this is still enough to combine with the deep-seated expectation in the bosom of mankind and give fresh luster to the hope of a future life. Whether we find relief in the theory of a simple dualism; whether with Ulrici we further define the soul as an invisible enswathement of the body, material yet non-atomic; whether, with the "Unseen Universe," we are helped by the spectacle of known forms of matter shading off into an ever-growing subtilty, mobility, and immateriality; or whether, with Wundt, we regard the soul as "the ordered unity of many elements," it is certain that shapes can be given to the conception of a correspondence which shall bridge the grave such as to satisfy minds too much accustomed to weigh evidence to put themselves off with fancies.

But whether the possibilities of physiology or the theories of philosophy do or do not substantially assist us in realizing Immortality, is to Religion, to Religion at least regarded from the present point of view, of inferior moment. The fact of Immortality rests for us on a different basis. Probably, indeed, after all the Christian philosopher never engaged himself in a more superfluous task than in seeking along physiological lines to find room for a soul. The theory of Christianity has only to be fairly stated to make manifest its thorough independence of all the usual speculations on Immortality. The theory is not that thought, volition, or emotion, as such are to survive the grave. The difficulty of holding a doctrine in this form, in spite of what has been advanced to the contrary, in spite of the hopes and wishes of mankind, in spite of all the scientific and philosophical attempts to make it tenable, is still profound. No secular theory of personal continuance, as even Butler acknowledged, does not equally demand the eternity of the brute. No secular theory defines the point in the chain of Evolution at which organisms became endowed with Immortality. No secular theory explains the condition of the endowment, nor indicates its goal. And if we have nothing more to fan hope than the unexplored mystery of the whole region, or the unknown remainders among the potencies of Life, then, as those who have "hope only in this world," we are "of all men the most miserable."

When we turn, on the other hand, to the doctrine as it came from the lips of Christ, we find ourselves in an entirely different region. He makes no attempt to project the material into the immaterial. The old elements, however refined and subtle as to their matter, are not in themselves to inherit the Kingdom of God. That which is flesh is flesh. Instead of attaching Immortality to the natural organism, He introduces a new and original factor which none of the secular, and few even of the theological theories, seem to take sufficiently into account. To Christianity, "he that hath the Son of God hath Life, and he that hath not the Son hath not Life." This, as we take it, defines the correspondence which is to bridge the grave. This is the clue to the nature of the Life that lies at the back of the spiritual organism. And this is the true solution of the mystery of Eternal Life.

There lies a something at the back of the correspondences of the spiritual organism—just as there lies a something at the back of the natural correspondences. To say that Life is a correspondence is only to express the partial truth. There is something behind. Life manifests itself in correspondences. But what determines them? The organism exhibits a variety of correspondences. What organizes them? As in the natural, so in the spiritual, there is a Principle of Life. We cannot get rid of that term. However clumsy, however provisional, however much a mere cloak for ignorance, Science as yet is unable to dispense with the idea of a Principle of Life. We must work with the word till we get a better. Now that which determines the correspondence of the spiritual organism is a Principle of Spiritual Life. It is a new and Divine Possession. He that hath the Son hath Life; conversely, he that hath Life hath the Son. And this indicates at once the quality and the quantity of the correspondence which is to bridge the grave. He that hath Life hath *the Son*. He possesses the Spirit of a Son. That spirit is, so to speak, organized within him by the Son. It is the manifestation of the new nature—of which more anon. The fact to note at present is that this is not an organic correspondence, but a spiritual correspondence. It comes not from generation, but from regeneration. The relation between the spiritual man and his Environment is, in theological language, a filial relation. With the new Spirit, the filial correspondence, he knows the Father—and this is Life Eternal. This is not only the real relation, but the only possible relation: "Neither knoweth any man the Father save the Son, and he to whomsoever the Son will reveal Him." And this on purely natural grounds. It takes the Divine to know the Divine—but in no more mysterious sense than it takes the human to understand the human. The analogy, indeed, for the whole field here has been finely expressed already by Paul: "What man," he asks, "knoweth the things of a man, save the spirit of man which is in him? even so the things of God knoweth no man, but the Spirit of God. Now we have received, not the spirit of the world, but the Spirit which is of God; that we might know the things that are freely given to us of God."

It were idle, such being the quality of the new relation, to add that this also contains the guarantee of its eternity. Here at last is a correspondence which will never cease. Its powers in bridging the grave have been tried. The correspondence of the spiritual man possesses the supernatural virtues of the Resurrection and the Life. It is known by former experiment to have survived the "changes in the physical state of the environment," and those "mechanical actions" and "variations of available food," which Mr. Herbert Spencer tells us are "liable to stop the processes going on in the organism." In short, this is a correspondence which at once satisfies the demands of Science and Religion. In mere quantity it is different from every other correspondence known. Setting aside everything else in Religion, everything adventitious, local, and provisional; dissecting in to the bone and marrow we find this—a correspondence which can never break with an Environment which can never change. Here is a relation established with Eternity. The passing years lay no limiting hand on it. Corruption injures it not. It survives Death. It, and it only, will stretch beyond the grave and be found inviolate—

"When the moon is old,
And the stars are cold,
And the books of the Judgment-day unfold."

The misgiving which will creep sometimes over the brightest faith has already received its expression and its rebuke: "Who shall separate us from the love of Christ? Shall tribulation, or distress, or persecution, or famine, or nakedness, or peril, or sword?" Shall these "changes in the physical state of the environment" which threaten death to the natural man destroy the spiritual? Shall death, or life, or angels, or principalities, or powers, arrest or tamper with his eternal correspondences? "Nay, in all these things we are more than conquerors through Him that loved us. For I am persuaded that neither death, nor life, nor angels, nor principalities, nor powers, nor things present, nor things to come, nor height, nor depth, nor any other creature, shall be able to separate us from the love of God, which is in Christ Jesus our Lord."

It may seem an objection to some that the "perfect correspondence" should come to man in so extraordinary a way. The earlier stages in the doctrine are promising enough; they are entirely in line with Nature. And if Nature had also furnished the "perfect correspondence" demanded for an Eternal Life the position might be unassailable. But this sudden reference to a something outside the natural Environment destroys the continuity, and discovers a permanent weakness in the whole theory?

To which there is a twofold reply. In the first place, to go outside what we call Nature is not to go outside Environment. Nature, the natural Environment, is only a part of Environment. There is another large part which, though some profess to have no correspondence with it, is not on that account unreal, or even unnatural. The mental and moral world is unknown to the plant. But it is real. It cannot be affirmed either that it is unnatural to the plant; although it might be said that from the point of view of the Vegetable Kingdom it was *supernatural*. Things are natural or supernatural simply according to where one stands. Man is supernatural to the mineral; God is supernatural to the man. When a mineral is seized upon by the living plant and elevated to the organic kingdom, no trespass against Nature is committed. It merely enters a larger Environment, which before was supernatural to it, but which now is entirely natural. When the heart of a man, again, is seized upon by the quickening Spirit of God, no further violence is done to natural law. It is another case of the inorganic, so to speak, passing into the organic.

But in the second place, it is complained as if it were an enormity in itself that the spiritual correspondence should be furnished from the spiritual world. And to this the answer lies in the same direction. Correspondence in any case is the gift of Environment. The natural Environment gives men their natural faculties; the spiritual affords them their spiritual faculties. It is natural for the spiritual Environment to supply the spiritual faculties; it would be quite unnatural for the natural Environment to do it. The natural law of Biogenesis forbids it; the moral fact that the finite cannot comprehend the Infinite is against it; the spiritual principle that flesh and blood cannot inherit the kingdom of God renders it absurd. Not, however, that the spiritual faculties are, as it were, manufactured in the spiritual world and supplied ready-made to the spiritual organism—forced upon it as an external equipment. This certainly is not involved in saying that the spiritual faculties are furnished by the spiritual world. Organisms are not added to by accretion, as in the case of minerals, but by growth. And the spiritual faculties are organized in the spiritual protoplasm of the soul, just as other faculties are organized in the protoplasm of the body. The plant is made of materials which have once been inorganic. An organizing principle not belonging to their kingdom lays hold of them and elaborates them until they have correspondences with the kingdom to which the organizing principle belonged. Their original organizing principle, if it can be called by this name, was Crystallization; so that we have now a distinctly foreign power organizing in totally new and higher directions. In the spiritual world, similarly, we find an organizing principle at work among the materials of the organic kingdom, performing a further miracle, but not a different kind of miracle, producing organizations of a novel kind, but not by a novel method. The second process, in fact, is simply what an enlightened evolutionist would have expected from the first. It marks the natural and legitimate progress of the development. And this in the line of the true Evolution—not the *linear* Evolution, which would look for the development of the natural man through powers already inherent, as if one were to look to Crystallization to accomplish the development of the mineral into the plant—but that larger form of Evolution which includes among its factors the double Law of Biogenesis and the immense further truth that this involves.

What is further included in this complex correspondence we shall have opportunity to illustrate afterward. Meantime let it be noted on what the Christian argument for Immortality really rests. It stands upon the pedestal on which the theologian rests the whole of historical Christianity—the Resurrection of Jesus Christ.

It ought to be placed in the forefront of all Christian teaching that Christ's mission on earth was to give men Life. "I am come," He said, "that ye might have Life, and that ye might have it more abundantly." And that He meant literal Life, literal spiritual and Eternal Life, is clear from the whole course of His teaching and acting. To impose a metaphorical meaning on the commonest word of the New Testament is to violate every canon of interpretation, and at the same time to charge the greatest of teachers with persistently mystifying His hearers by an unusual use of so exact a vehicle for expressing definite thought as the Greek language, and that on the most momentous subject of which He ever spoke to men. It is a canon of interpretation, according to Alford, that "a figurative sense of words is never admissible except when required by the context." The context, in most cases, is not only directly unfavorable to a figurative meaning, but in innumerable instances in Christ's teaching Life is broadly contrasted with Death. In the teaching of the apostles, again, we find that, without exception, they accepted the term in its simple literal sense. Reuss defines the apostolic belief with his usual impartiality when—and the quotation is doubly pertinent here—he discovers in the apostle's conception of Life, first, "the idea of a real existence, an existence such as is proper to God and to the Word; an imperishable existence—that is to say, not subject to the vicissitudes and imperfections of the finite world. This primary idea is repeatedly expressed, at least in a negative form; it leads to a doctrine of immortality, or, to speak more correctly, of life, far surpassing any that had been expressed in the formulas of the current philosophy or theology, and resting upon premises and conceptions altogether different. In fact, it can dispense both with the philosophical thesis of the immateriality or indestructibility of the human soul, and with the theological thesis of a miraculous corporeal reconstruction of our person; theses, the first of which is altogether foreign to the religion of the Bible, and the second absolutely opposed to reason." Second, "the idea of life, as it is conceived in this system, implies the idea of a power, an operation, a communication, since this life no longer remains, so to speak, latent or passive in God and in the Word, but through them reaches the believer. It is not a mental somnolent thing; it is not a plant without fruit; it is a germ which is to find fullest development."

If we are asked to define more clearly what is meant by this mysterious endowment of Life, we again hand over the difficulty to Science. When Science can define the Natural Life and the Physical Force we may hope for further clearness on the nature and action of the Spiritual Powers. The effort to detect the living Spirit must be at least as idle as the attempt to subject protoplasm to microscopic examination in the hope of discovering Life. We are warned, also, not to expect too much. "Thou canst not tell whence it cometh or whither it goeth." This being its quality, when the Spiritual Life is discovered in the laboratory it will possibly be time to give it up altogether. It may say, as Socrates of his soul, "You may bury me—if you can catch me."

Science never corroborates a spiritual truth without illuminating it. The threshold of Eternity is a place where many shadows meet. And the light of Science here, where everything is so dark, is welcome a thousand times. Many men would be religious if they knew where to begin; many would be more religious if they were sure where it would end. It is not indifference that keeps some men from God, but ignorance. "Good Master, what must I do to inherit Eternal Life?" is still the deepest question of the age. What is Religion? What am I to believe? What seek with all my heart and soul and mind?—this is the imperious question sent up to consciousness from the depths of being in all earnest hours; sent down again, alas, with many of us, time after time, unanswered. Into all our thought and work and reading this question pursues us. But the theories are rejected one by one; the great books are returned sadly to their shelves, the years pass, and the problem remains unsolved. The confusion of tongues here is terrible. Every day a new authority announces himself. Poets, philosophers, preachers try their hand on us in turn. New prophets arise, and beseech us for our soul's sake to give ear to them—at last in an hour of inspiration they have discovered the final truth. Yet the doctrine of yesterday is challenged by a fresh philosophy to-day: and the creed of to-day will fall in turn before the criticism of to-morrow. Increase of knowledge increaseth sorrow. And at length the conflicting truths, like the beams of light in the laboratory experiment, combine in the mind to make total darkness.

But here are two outstanding authorities agreed—not men, not philosophers, not creeds. Here is the voice of God and the voice of Nature. I cannot be wrong if I listen to them. Sometimes when uncertain of a voice from its very loudness, we catch the missing syllable in the echo. In God and Nature we have Voice and Echo. When I hear both, I am assured. My sense of hearing does not betray me twice. I recognize the Voice in the Echo, the Echo makes me certain of the Voice; I listen and I know. The question of a Future Life is a biological question. Nature may be silent on other problems of Religion; but here she has a right to speak. The whole confusion around the doctrine of Eternal Life has arisen from making it a question of Philosophy. We shall do ill to refuse a hearing to any speculation of Philosophy; the ethical relations here especially are intimate and real. But in the first instance Eternal Life, as a question of *Life*, is a problem for Biology. The soul is a living organism. And for any question as to the soul's Life we must appeal to Life-science. And what does the Life-science teach? That if I am to inherit Eternal Life, I must cultivate a correspondence with the Eternal. This is a simple proposition, for Nature is always simple. I take this proposition, and, leaving Nature, proceed to fill it in. I search everywhere for a clue to the Eternal. I ransack literature for a definition of a correspondence between man and God. Obviously that can only come from one source. And the analogies of Science permits us to apply to it. All knowledge lies in Environment. When I want to know about minerals I go to minerals. When I want to know about flowers I go to flowers. And they tell me. In their own way they speak to me, each in its own way, and each for itself—not the mineral for the flower, which is impossible, nor the flower for the mineral, which is also impossible. So if I want to know about Man, I go to his part of the Environment. And he tells me about himself, not as the plant or the mineral, for he is neither, but in his own way. And if I want to know about God, I go to His part of the Environment. And He tells me about Himself, not as a Man, for He is not Man, but in His own way. And just as naturally as the flower and the mineral and the Man, each in their own way, tell me about themselves, He tells me about Himself. He very strangely condescends indeed in making things plain to me, actually assuming for a time the Form of a Man that I at my poor level may better see Him. This is my opportunity to know Him. This incarnation is God making Himself accessible to human thought—God opening to man the possibility of correspondence through Jesus Christ. And this correspondence and this Environment are those I seek. He Himself assures me, "This is Life Eternal, that they might know Thee, the only true God, and Jesus Christ whom Thou hast sent."

Do I not now discern the deeper meaning in "*Jesus Christ whom Thou hast sent?*" Do I not better understand with what vision and rapture the profoundest of the disciples exclaims, "The Son of God is come, and hath given us an understanding that we might know Him that is True?"

Having opened correspondence with the Eternal Environment, the subsequent stages are in the line of all other normal development. We have but to continue, to deepen, to extend, and to enrich the correspondence that has been begun. And we shall soon find to our surprise that this is accompanied by another and parallel process. The action is not all upon our side. The Environment also will be found to correspond. The influence of Environment is one of the greatest and most substantial of modern biological doctrines. Of the power of Environment to form or transform organisms, of its ability to develop or suppress function, of its potency in determining growth, and generally of its immense influence in Evolution, there is no need now to speak. But Environment is now acknowledged to be one of the most potent factors in the Evolution of Life. The influence of Environment too seems to increase rather than diminish as we approach the higher forms of being. The highest forms are the most mobile; their capacity of change is the greatest; they are, in short, most easily acted on by Environment. And not only are the highest organisms the most mobile, but the highest part of the highest organisms are more mobile than the lower. Environment can do little, comparatively, in the direction of inducing variation in the body of a child: but how plastic is its mind! How infinitely sensitive is its soul! How infallibly can it be turned to music or to dissonance by the moral harmony or discord of its outward lot! How decisively indeed are we not all formed and moulded, made or unmade, by external circumstance! Might we not all confess with Ulysses—

"I am a part of all that I have met."

Much more, then, shall we look for the influence of Environment on the spiritual nature of him who has opened correspondence with God. Reaching out his eager and quickened faculties to the spiritual world around him, shall he not become spiritual? In vital contact with Holiness, shall he not become holy? Breathing now an atmosphere of ineffable Purity, shall he miss becoming pure? Walking with God from day to day, shall he fail to be taught of God?

Growth in grace is sometimes described as a strange, mystical, and unintelligible process. It is mystical, but neither strange nor unintelligible. It proceeds according to Natural Law, and the leading factor in sanctification is Influence of Environment. The possibility of it depends upon the mobility of the organism; the result, on the extent and frequency of certain correspondences. These facts insensibly lead on to a further suggestion. Is it not possible that these biological truths may carry with them the clue to still profounder philosophy—even that of Regeneration?

Evolutionists tell us that by the influence of environment certain aquatic animals have become adapted to a terrestrial mode of life. Breathing normally by gills, as the result and reward of a continued effort carried on from generation to generation to inspire the air of heaven direct, they have slowly acquired the lung-function. In the young organism, true to the ancestral type, the gill still persists—as in the tadpole of the common frog. But as maturity approaches the true lung appears; the gill gradually transfers its task to the higher organ. It then becomes atrophied and disappears, and finally respiration in the adult is conducted by lungs alone. We may be far, in the meantime, from saying that this is proved. It is for those who accept it to deny the justice of the spiritual analogy. Is religion to them unscientific in its doctrine of Regeneration? Will the evolutionist who admits the regeneration of the frog under the modifying influence of a continued correspondence with a new environment, care to question the possibility of the soul acquiring such a faculty as that of Prayer, the marvelous breathing-function of the new creature, when in contact with the atmosphere of a besetting God? Is the change from the earthly to the heavenly more mysterious than the change from the aquatic to the terrestrial mode of life? Is Evolution to stop with the organic? If it be objected that it has taken ages to perfect the function in the batrachian, the reply is, that it will take ages to perfect the function in the Christian. For every thousand years the natural evolution will allow for the development of its organism, the Higher Biology will grant its product millions. We have indeed spoken of the spiritual correspondence as already perfect—but it is perfect only as the bud is perfect. "It doth not yet appear what it shall be," any more than it appeared a million years ago what the evolving batrachian would be.

But to return. We have been dealing with the scientific aspects of communion with God. Insensibly, from quantity we have been led to speak of quality. And enough has now been advanced to indicate generally the nature of that correspondence with which is necessarily associated Eternal Life. There remain but one or two details to which we must lastly, and very briefly, address ourselves.

The quality of everlastingness belongs, as we have seen, to a single correspondence, or rather to a single set of correspondences. But it is apparent that before this correspondence can take full and final effect a further process is necessary. By some means it must be separated from all the other correspondences of the organism which do not share its peculiar quality. In this life it is restrained by these other correspondences. They may contribute to it, or hinder it; but they are essentially of a different order. They belong not to Eternity but to Time, and to this present world; and, unless some provision is made for dealing with them, they will detain the aspiring organism in this present world till Time is ended. Of course, in a sense, all that belongs to Time belongs also to Eternity; but these lower correspondences are in their nature unfitted for an Eternal Life. Even if they were perfect in their relation to their Environment, they would still not be Eternal. However opposed, apparently, to the scientific definition of Eternal Life, it is yet true that perfect correspondence with Environment is not Eternal Life. A very important word in the complete definition is, in this sentence, omitted. On that word it has not been necessary hitherto, and for obvious reasons, to place any emphasis, but when we come to deal with false pretenders to Immortality we must return to it. Were the definition complete as it stands, it might, with the permission of the psycho-physiologist, guarantee the Immortality of every living thing. In the dog, for instance, the material framework giving way at death might leave the released canine spirit still free to inhabit the old Environment. And so with every creature which had ever established a conscious relation with surrounding things. Now the difficulty in framing a theory of Eternal Life has been to construct one which will exclude the brute creation, drawing the line rigidly at man, or at least, somewhere within the human race. Not that we need object to the Immortality of the dog, or of the whole inferior creation. Nor that we need refuse a place to any intelligible speculation which would people the earth to-day with the invisible forms of all things that have ever lived. Only we still insist that this is not Eternal Life. And why? Because their Environment is not Eternal. Their correspondence, however firmly established, is established with that which shall pass away. An Eternal Life demands an Eternal Environment.

The demand for a perfect Environment as well as for a perfect correspondence is less clear in Mr. Herbert Spencer's definition than it might be. But it is an essential factor. An organism might remain true to its Environment, but what if the Environment played it false? If the organism possessed the power to change, it could adapt itself to successive changes in the Environment. And if this were guaranteed we should also have the conditions for Eternal Life fulfilled. But what if the Environment passed away altogether? What if the earth swept suddenly into the sun? This is a change of Environment against which there could be no precaution and for which there could be as little provision. With a changing Environment even, there must always remain the dread and possibility of a falling out of correspondence. At the best, Life would be uncertain. But with a changeless Environment—such as that possessed by the spiritual organism—the perpetuity of the correspondence, so far as the external relation is concerned, is guaranteed. This quality of permanence in the Environment distinguishes the religious relation from every other. Why should not the musician's life be an Eternal Life? Because, for one thing, the musical world, the Environment with which he corresponds, is not eternal. Even if his correspondence in itself could last, eternally, the environing material things with which he corresponds must pass away. His soul might last forever—but not his violin. So the man of the world might last forever—but not the world. His Environment is not eternal; nor are even his correspondences—the world passeth away *and the lust thereof.*

We find then that man, or the spiritual man, is equipped with two sets of correspondences. One set possesses the quality of everlastingness, the other is temporal. But unless these are separated by some means the temporal will continue to impair and hinder the eternal. The final preparation, therefore, for the inheriting of Eternal Life must consist in the abandonment of the non-eternal elements. These must be unloosed and dissociated from the higher elements. And this is effected by a closing catastrophe—Death.

Death ensues because certain relations in the organism are not adjusted to certain relations in the Environment. There will come a time in each history when the imperfect correspondences of the organism will betray themselves by a failure to compass some necessary adjustment. This is why Death is associated with Imperfection. Death is the necessary result of Imperfection, and the necessary end of it. Imperfect correspondence gives imperfect and uncertain Life. "Perfect correspondence," on the other hand, according to Mr. Herbert Spencer, would be "perfect Life." To abolish Death, therefore, all that would be necessary would be to abolish Imperfection. But it is the claim of Christianity that it can abolish Death. And it is significant to notice that it does so by meeting this very demand of Science—it abolishes Imperfection.

The part of the organism which begins to get out of correspondence with the Organic Environment is the only part which is in vital correspondence with it. Though a fatal disadvantage to the natural man to be thrown out of correspondence with this Environment, it is of inestimable importance to the spiritual man. For so long as it is maintained the way is barred for a further Evolution. And hence the condition necessary for the further Evolution is that the spiritual be released from the natural. That is to say, the condition of the further Evolution is Death. *Mors janua Vitæ*, therefore, becomes a scientific formula. Death, being the final shifting of all the correspondences, is the indispensable factor of the higher Life. In the language of Science, not less than of Scripture, "To die is gain."

The shifting of the correspondences is done by Nature. This is its last and greatest contribution to mankind. Over the mouth of the grave the perfect and the imperfect submit to their final separation. Each goes to its own—earth to earth, ashes to ashes, dust to dust, Spirit to Spirit. "The dust shall return to the earth as it was; and the Spirit shall return unto God who gave it."

Environment

"When I talked with an ardent missionary and pointed out to him that his creed found no support in my experience, he replied: 'It is not so in your experience, but is so in the other world.' I answered: 'Other world! There is no other world. God is one and omnipresent; here or nowhere is the whole fact.'"—*Emerson.*

"Ye are complete in Him."—*Paul.*

"Whatever amount of power an organism expends in any shape is the correlate and equivalent of a power that was taken into it from without."—*Herbert Spencer.*

Students of Biography will observe that in all well-written Lives attention is concentrated for the first few chapters upon two points. We are first introduced to the family to which the subject of memoir belonged. The grandparents, or even the more remote ancestors, are briefly sketched and their chief characteristics brought prominently into view. Then the parents themselves are photographed in detail. Their appearance and physique, their character, their disposition, their mental qualities, are set before us in a critical analysis. And finally we are asked to observe how much the father and the mother respectively have transmitted of their peculiar nature to their offspring. How faithfully the ancestral lines have met in the latest product, how mysteriously the joint characteristics of body and mind have blended, and how unexpected yet how entirely natural a recombination is the result—these points are elaborated with cumulative effect until we realize at last how little we are dealing with an independent unit, how much with a survival and reorganization of what seemed buried in the grave.

In the second place, we are invited to consider more external influences—schools and schoolmasters, neighbors, home, pecuniary circumstances, scenery, and, by-and-by, the religious and political atmosphere of the time. These also we are assured have played their part in making the individual what he is. We can estimate these early influences in any particular case with but small imagination if we fail to see how powerfully they also have moulded mind and character, and in what subtle ways they have determined the course of the future life.

This twofold relation of the individual, first, to his parents, and second, to his circumstances, is not peculiar to human beings. These two factors are responsible for making all living organisms what they are. When a naturalist attempts to unfold the life-history of any animal, he proceeds precisely on these same lines. Biography is really a branch of Natural History; and the biographer who discusses his hero as the resultant of these two tendencies, follows the scientific method as rigidly as Mr. Darwin in studying "Animals and Plants under Domestication."

Mr. Darwin, following Weismann, long ago pointed out that there are two main factors in all Evolution—the nature of the organism and the nature of the conditions. We have chosen our illustration from the highest or human species in order to define the meaning of these factors in the clearest way; but it must be remembered that the development of man under these directive influences is essentially the same as that of any other organism in the hands of Nature. We are dealing therefore with universal Law. It will still further serve to complete the conception of the general principle if we now substitute for the casual phrases by which the factors have been described the more accurate terminology of Science. Thus what Biography describes as parental influences, Biology would speak of as Heredity; and all that is involved in the second factor—the action of external circumstances and surroundings—the naturalist would include under the single term Environment. These two, Heredity and Environment, are the master-influences of the organic world. These have made all of us what we are. These forces are still ceaselessly playing upon all our lives. And he who truly understands these influences; he who has decided how much to allow to each; he who can regulate new forces as they arise, or adjust them to the old, so directing them as at one moment to make them coöperate, at another to counteract one another, understands the rationale of personal development. To seize continuously the opportunity of more and more perfect adjustment to better and higher conditions, to balance some inward evil with some purer influence acting from without, in a word to make our Environment at the same time that it is making us—these are the secrets of a well-ordered and successful life.

In the spiritual world, also, the subtle influences which form and transform the soul are Heredity and Environment. And here especially where all is invisible, where much that we feel to be real is yet so ill-defined, it becomes of vital practical moment to clarify the atmosphere as far as possible with conceptions borrowed from the natural life. Few things are less understood than the conditions of the spiritual life. The distressing incompetence of which most of us are conscious in trying to work out our spiritual experience is due perhaps less to the diseased will which we commonly blame for it than to imperfect knowledge of the right conditions. It does not occur to us how natural the spiritual is. We still strive for some strange transcendent thing; we seek to promote life by methods as unnatural as they prove unsuccessful; and only the utter incomprehensibility of the whole region prevents us seeing fully—what we already half-suspect—how completely we are missing the road. Living in the spiritual world, nevertheless, is just as simple as living in the natural world; and it is the same kind of simplicity. It is the same kind of simplicity for it is the same kind of world—there are not two kinds of worlds. The conditions of life in the one are the conditions of life in the other. And till these conditions are sensibly grasped, as the conditions of all life, it is impossible that the personal effort after the highest life should be other than a blind struggle carried on in fruitless sorrow and humiliation.

Of these two universal factors, Heredity and Environment, it is unnecessary to balance the relative importance here. The main influence, unquestionably, must be assigned to the former. In practice, however, and for an obvious reason, we are chiefly concerned with the latter. What Heredity has to do for us is determined outside ourselves. No man can select his own parents. But every man to some extent can choose his own Environment. His relation to it, however largely determined by Heredity in the first instance, is always open to alteration. And so great is his control over Environment and so radical its influence over him, that he can so direct it as either to undo, modify, perpetuate or intensify the earlier hereditary influence within certain limits. But the aspects of Environment which we have now to consider do not involve us in questions of such complexity. In what high and mystical sense, also, Heredity applies to the spiritual organism we need not just now inquire. In the simpler relations of the more external factor we shall find a large and fruitful field for study.

The influence of Environment may be investigated in two main aspects. First, one might discuss the modern and very interesting question as to the power of Environment to induce what is known to recent science as Variation. A change in the surroundings of any animal, it is now well-known, can so react upon it as to cause it to change. By the attempt, conscious or unconscious, to adjust itself to the new conditions, a true physiological change is gradually wrought within the organism. Hunter, for example, in a classical experiment, so changed the Environment of a sea-gull by keeping it in captivity that it could only secure a grain diet. The effect was to modify the stomach of the bird, normally adapted to a fish diet, until in time it came to resemble in structure the gizzard of an ordinary grain-feeder such as the pigeon. Holmgrén again reversed this experiment by feeding pigeons for a lengthened period on a meat-diet, with the result that the gizzard became transformed into the carnivorous stomach. Mr. Alfred Russel Wallace mentions the case of a Brazilian parrot which changes its color from green to red or yellow when fed on the fat of certain fishes. Not only changes of food, however, but changes of climate and of temperature, changes in surrounding organisms, in the case of marine animals even changes of pressure, of ocean currents, of light, and of many other circumstances, are known to exert a powerful modifying influence upon living organisms. These relations are still being worked out in many directions, but the influence of Environment as a prime factor in Variation is now a recognized doctrine of science.

Even the popular mind has been struck with the curious adaptation of nearly all animals to their *habitat*, for example in the matter of color. The sandy hue of the sole and flounder, the white of the polar bear with its suggestion of Arctic snows, the stripes of the Bengal tiger—as if the actual reeds of its native jungle had nature-printed themselves on its hide;—these, and a hundred others which will occur to every one, are marked instances of adaptation to Environment, induced by Natural Selection or otherwise, for the purpose, obviously in these cases at least, of protection.

To continue the investigation of the modifying action of Environment into the moral and spiritual spheres, would be to open a fascinating and suggestive inquiry. One might show how the moral man is acted upon and changed continuously by the influences, secret and open, of his surroundings, by the tone of society, by the company he keeps, by his occupation, by the books he reads, by Nature, by all, in short, that constitutes the habitual atmosphere of his thoughts and the little world of his daily choice. Or one might go deeper still and prove how the spiritual life also is modified from outside sources—its health or disease, its growth or decay, all its changes for better or for worse being determined by the varying and successive circumstances in which the religious habits are cultivated. But we must rather transfer our attention to a second aspect of Environment, not perhaps so fascinating but yet more important.

So much of the modern discussion of Environment revolves round the mere question of Variation that one is apt to overlook a previous question. Environment as a factor in life is not exhausted when we have realized its modifying influence. Its significance is scarcely touched. The great function of Environment is not to modify but to *sustain*. In sustaining life, it is true, it modifies. But the latter influence is incidental, the former essential. Our Environment is that in which we live and move and have our being. Without it we should neither live or move nor have any being. In the organism lies the principle of life; in the Environment are the conditions of life. Without the fulfillment of these conditions, which are wholly supplied by Environment, there can be no life. An organism in itself is but a part; Nature is its complement. Alone, cut off from its surroundings, it is not. Alone, cut off from my surroundings, I am not—physically I am not. I am, only as I am sustained. I continue only as I receive. My Environment may modify me, but it has first to keep me. And all the time its secret transforming power is indirectly moulding body and mind it is directly active in the more open task of ministering to my myriad wants and from hour to hour sustaining life itself.

To understand the sustaining influence of Environment in the animal world, one has only to recall what the biologist terms the extrinsic or subsidiary conditions of vitality. Every living thing normally requires for its development an Environment containing air, light, heat, and water. In addition to these, if vitality is to be prolonged for any length of time, and if it is to be accompanied with growth and the expenditure of energy, there must be a constant supply of food. When we simply remember how indispensable food is to growth and work, and when we further bear in mind that the food-supply is solely contributed by the Environment, we shall realize at once the meaning and the truth of the proposition that without Environment there can be no life. Seventy per cent. at least of the human body is made of pure water, the rest of gases and earth. These have all come from Environment. Through the secret pores of the skin two pounds of water are exhaled daily from every healthy adult. The supply is kept up by Environment. The Environment is really an unappropriated part of ourselves. Definite portions are continuously abstracted from it and added to the organism. And so long as the organism continues to grow, act, think, speak, work, or perform any other function demanding a supply of energy, there is a constant, simultaneous, and proportionate drain upon its surroundings.

This is a truth in the physical, and therefore in the spiritual, world of so great importance that we shall not mis-spend time if we follow it, for further confirmation, into another department of nature. Its significance in Biology is self-evident; let us appeal to Chemistry.

When a piece of coal is thrown on the fire, we say that it will radiate into the room a certain quantity of heat. This heat, in the popular conception, is supposed to reside in the coal and to be set free during the process of combustion. In reality, however, the heat energy is only in part contained in the coal. It is contained just as truly in the coal's Environment—that is to say, in the oxygen of the air. The atoms of carbon which compose the coal have a powerful affinity for the oxygen of the air. Whenever they are made to approach within a certain distance of one another, by the initial application of heat, they rush together with inconceivable velocity. The heat which appears at this moment, comes neither from the carbon alone, nor from the oxygen alone. These two substances are really inconsumable, and continue to exist, after they meet in a combined form, as carbonic acid gas. The heat is due to the energy developed by the chemical embrace, the precipitate rushing together of the molecules of carbon and the molecules of oxygen. It comes, therefore, partly from the coal and partly from the Environment. Coal alone never could produce heat, neither alone could Environment. The two are mutually dependent. And although in nearly all the arts we credit everything to the substance which we can weigh and handle, it is certain that in the most cases the larger debt is due to an invisible Environment.

This is one of those great commonplaces which slip out of general reckoning by reason of their very largeness and simplicity. How profound, nevertheless, are the issues which hang on this elementary truth, we shall discover immediately. Nothing in this age is more needed in every department of knowledge than the rejuvenescence of the commonplace. In the spiritual world especially, he will be wise who courts acquaintance with the most ordinary and transparent facts of Nature; and in laying the foundations for a religious life he will make no unworthy beginning who carries with him an impressive sense of so obvious a truth as that without Environment there can be no life.

For what does this amount to in the spiritual world? Is it not merely the scientific re-statement of the reiterated aphorism of Christ, "Without Me ye can do nothing?" There is in the spiritual organism a principle of life; but that is not self-existent. It requires a second factor, a something in which to live and move and have its being, an Environment. Without this it cannot live or move or have any being. Without Environment the soul is as the carbon without the oxygen, as the fish without the water, as the animal frame without the extrinsic conditions of vitality.

And what is the spiritual Environment? It is God. Without this, therefore, there is no life, no thought, no energy, nothing—"without Me ye can do nothing."

The cardinal error in the religious life is to attempt to live without an Environment. Spiritual experience occupies itself, not too much, but too exclusively, with one factor—the soul. We delight in dissecting this much tortured faculty, from time to time, in search of a certain something which we call our faith—forgetting that faith is but an attitude, an empty hand for grasping an environing Presence. And when we feel the need of a power by which to overcome the world, how often do we not seek to generate it within ourselves by some forced process, some fresh girding of the will, some strained activity which only leaves the soul in further exhaustion? To examine ourselves is good; but useless unless we also examine Environment. To bewail our weakness is right, but not remedial. The cause must be investigated as well as the result. And yet, because we never see the other half of the problem, our failures even fail to instruct us. After each new collapse we begin our life anew, but on the old conditions; and the attempt ends as usual in the repetition—in the circumstances the inevitable repetition—of the old disaster. Not that at times we do not obtain glimpses of the true state of the case. After seasons of much discouragement, with the sore sense upon us of our abject feebleness, we do confer with ourselves, insisting for the thousandth time, "My soul, wait thou only upon God." But the lesson is soon forgotten. The strength supplied we speedily credit to our own achievement; and even the temporary success is mistaken for a symptom of improved inward vitality. Once more we become self-existent. Once more we go on living without an Environment. And once more, after days of wasting without repairing, of spending without replenishing, we begin to perish with hunger, only returning to God again, as a last resort, when we have reached starvation point.

Now why do we do this? Why do we seek to breathe without an atmosphere, to drink without a well? Why this unscientific attempt to sustain life for weeks at a time without an Environment? It is because we have never truly seen the necessity for an Environment. We have not been working with a principle. We are told to "wait only upon God," but we do not know why. It has never been as clear to us that without God the soul will die as that without food the body will perish.

In short, we have never comprehended the doctrine of the Persistence of Force. Instead of being content to transform energy we have tried to create it.

The Law of Nature here is as clear as Science can make it. In the words of Mr. Herbert Spencer, "It is a corollary from that primordial truth which, as we have seen, underlies all other truths, that whatever amount of power an organism expends in any shape is the correlate and equivalent of a power that was taken into it from without," We are dealing here with a simple question of dynamics. Whatever energy the soul expends must first be "taken into it from without." We are not Creators, but creatures; God is our refuge *and strength*. Communion with God, therefore, is a scientific necessity; and nothing will more help the defeated spirit which is struggling in the wreck of its religious life than a common-sense hold of this plain biological principle that without Environment he can do nothing. What he wants is not an occasional view, but a principle—a basal principle like this, broad as the universe, solid as nature. In the natural world we act upon this law unconsciously. We absorb heat, breathe air, draw on Environment all but automatically for meat and drink, for the nourishment of the senses, for mental stimulus, for all that, penetrating us from without, can prolong, enrich, and elevate life. But in the spiritual world we have all this to learn. We are new creatures, and even the bare living has to be acquired.

Now the great point in learning to live is to live naturally. As closely as possible we must follow the broad, clear lines of the natural life. And there are three things especially which it is necessary for us to keep continually in view. The first is that the organism contains within itself only one-half of what is essential to life; the second is that the other half is contained in the Environment; the third, that the condition of receptivity is simple union between the organism and the Environment.

Translated into the language of religion these propositions yield, and place on a scientific basis, truths of immense practical interest. To say, first, that the organism contains within itself only one-half of what is essential to life, is to repeat the evangelical confession, so worn and yet so true to universal experience, of the utter helplessness of man. Who has not come to the conclusion that he is but a part, a fraction of some larger whole? Who does not miss at every turn of his life an absent God? That man is but a part, he knows, for there is room in him for more. That God is the other part, he feels, because at times He satisfies his need. Who does not tremble often under that sicklier symptom of his incompleteness, his want of spiritual energy, his helplessness with sin? But now he understands both—the void in his life, the powerlessness of his will. He understands that, like all other energy, spiritual power is contained in Environment. He finds here at last the true root of all human frailty, emptiness, nothingness, sin. This is why "without Me ye can do nothing." Powerlessness is the normal state not only of this but of every organism—of every organism apart from its Environment.

The entire dependence of the soul upon God is not an exceptional mystery, nor is man's helplessness an arbitrary and unprecedented phenomenon. It is the law of all Nature. The spiritual man is not taxed beyond the natural. He is not purposely handicapped by singular limitations or unusual incapacities. God has not designedly made the religious life as hard as possible. The arrangements for the spiritual life are the same as for the natural life. When in their hours of unbelief men challenge their Creator for placing the obstacle of human frailty in the way of their highest development, their protest is against the order of nature. They object to the sun for being the source of energy and not the engine, to the carbonic acid being in the air and not in the plant. They would equip each organism with a personal atmosphere, each brain with a private store of energy; they would grow corn in the interior of the body, and make bread by a special apparatus in the digestive organs. They must, in short, have the creature transformed into a Creator. The organism must either depend on his environment, or be self-sufficient. But who will not rather approve the arrangement by which man in his creatural life may have unbroken access to an Infinite Power? What soul will seek to remain self-luminous when it knows that "The Lord God is a *Sun*?" Who will not willingly exchange his shallow vessel for Christ's well of living water? Even if the organism, launched into being like a ship putting out to sea, possessed a full equipment, its little store must soon come to an end. But in contact with a large and bounteous Environment its supply is limitless. In every direction its resources are infinite.

There is a modern school which protests against the doctrine of man's inability as the heartless fiction of a past theology. While some forms of that dogma, to any one who knows man, are incapable of defence, there are others which, to any one who knows Nature, are incapable of denial. Those who oppose it, in their jealousy for humanity, credit the organism with the properties of Environment. All true theology, on the other hand, has remained loyal to at least the root-idea in this truth. The New Testament is nowhere more impressive than where it insists on the fact of man's dependence. In its view the first step in religion is for man to feel his helplessness. Christ's first beatitude is to the poor in spirit. The condition of entrance into the spiritual kingdom is to possess the child-spirit—that state of mind combining at once the profoundest helplessness with the most artless feeling of dependence. Substantially the same idea underlies the countless passages in which Christ affirms that He has not come to call the righteous, but sinners to repentance. And in that farewell discourse into which the Great Teacher poured the most burning convictions of His life, He gives to this doctrine an ever increasing emphasis. No words could be more solemn or arresting than the sentence in the last great allegory devoted to this theme, "As the branch cannot bear fruit of itself except it abide in the vine, no more can ye except ye abide in Me." The word here, it will be observed again, is *cannot*. It is the imperative of natural law. Fruit-bearing without Christ is not an improbability, but an impossibility. As well expect the natural fruit to flourish without air and heat, without soil and sunshine. How thoroughly also Paul grasped this truth is apparent from a hundred pregnant passages in which he echoes his Master's teaching. To him life was hid with Christ in God. And that he embraced this not as a theory but as an experimental truth we gather from his constant confession, "When I am weak, then am I strong."

This leads by a natural transition to the second of the three points we are seeking to illustrate. We have seen that the organism contains within itself only one half of what is essential to life. We have next to observe, as the complement of this, how the second half is contained in the Environment.

One result of the due apprehension of our personal helplessness will be that we shall no longer waste our time over the impossible task of manufacturing energy for ourselves. Our science will bring to an abrupt end the long series of severe experiments in which we have indulged in the hope of finding a perpetual motion. And having decided upon this once for all, our first step in seeking a more satisfactory state of things must be to find a new source of energy. Following Nature, only one course is open to us. We must refer to Environment. The natural life owes all to Environment, so must the spiritual. Now the Environment of the spiritual life is God. As Nature therefore forms the complement of the natural life, God is the complement of the spiritual.

The proof of this? That Nature is not more natural to my body than God is to my soul. Every animal and plant has its own Environment. And the further one inquires into the relations of the one to the other, the more one sees the marvelous intricacy and beauty of the adjustments. These wonderful adaptations of each organism to its surroundings—of the fish to the water, of the eagle to the air, of the insect to the forest bed; and of each part of every organism—the fish's swim-bladder, the eagle's eye, the insect's breathing tubes—which the old argument from design brought home to us with such enthusiasm, inspire us still with a sense of the boundless resources and skill of Nature in perfecting her arrangements for each single life. Down to the last detail the world is made for what is in it; and by whatever process things are as they are, all organisms find in surrounding Nature the ample complement of themselves. Man, too, finds in his Environment provision for all capacities, scope for the exercise of every faculty, room for the indulgence of each appetite, a just supply for every want. So the spiritual man at the apex of the pyramid of life finds in the vaster range of his Environment a provision, as much higher, it is true, as he is higher, but as delicately adjusted to his varying needs. And all this is supplied to him just as the lower organisms are ministered to by the lower environment, in the same simple ways, in the same constant sequence, as appropriately and as lavishly. We fail to praise the ceaseless ministry of the great inanimate world around us only because its kindness is unobtrusive. Nature is always noiseless. All her greatest gifts are given in secret. And we forget how truly every good and perfect gift comes from without, and from above, because no pause in her changeless beneficence teaches us the sad lesson of deprivation.

It is not a strange thing, then, for the soul to find its life in God. This is its native air. God as the Environment of the soul has been from the remotest age the doctrine of all the deepest thinkers in religion. How profoundly Hebrew poetry is saturated with this high thought will appear when we try to conceive of it with this left out. True poetry is only science in another form. And long before it was possible for religion to give scientific expression to its greatest truths, men of insight uttered themselves in psalms which could not have been truer to Nature had the most modern light controlled the inspiration. "As the hart panteth after the water-brooks, so panteth my soul after Thee, O God." What fine sense of the analogy of the natural and the spiritual does not underlie these words. As the hart after its Environment, so man after his; as the water-brooks are fitly designed to meet the natural wants, so fitly does God implement the spiritual need of man. It will be noticed that in the Hebrew poets the longing for God never strikes one as morbid, or unnatural to the men who utter it. It is as natural to them to long for God as for the swallow to seek her nest. Throughout all their images no suspicion rises within us that they are exaggerating. We feel how truly they are reading themselves, their deepest selves. No false note occurs in all their aspiration. There is no weariness even in their ceaseless sighing, except the lover's weariness for the absent—if they would fly away, it is only to be at rest. Men who have no soul can only wonder at this. Men who have a soul, but with little faith, can only envy it. How joyous a thing it was to the Hebrews to seek their God! How artlessly they call upon Him to entertain them in His pavilion, to cover them with His feathers, to hide them in His secret place, to hold them in the hollow of His hand or stretch around them the everlasting arms! These men were true children of Nature. As the humming-bird among its own palm-trees, as the ephemera in the sunshine of a summer evening, so they lived their joyous lives. And even the full share of the sadder experience of life which came to all of them but drove them the further into the Secret Place, and led them with more consecration to make, as they expressed it, "the Lord their portion." All that has been said since from Marcus Aurelius to Swedenborg, from Augustine to Schleiermacher of a besetting God as the final complement of humanity is but a repetition of the Hebrew poets' faith. And even the New Testament has nothing higher to offer man than this. The psalmist's "God is our refuge and strength" is only the earlier form, less defined, less practicable, but not less noble, of Christ's "Come unto Me, and I will give you rest."

There is a brief phrase of Paul's which defines the relation with almost scientific accuracy—"Ye are complete in Him." In this is summed up the whole of the Bible anthropology—the completeness of man in God, his incompleteness apart from God.

If it be asked, In what is man incomplete, or, In what does God complete him? the question is a wide one. But it may serve to show at least the direction in which the Divine Environment forms the complement of human life if we ask ourselves once more what it is in life that needs complementing. And to this question we receive the significant answer that it is in the higher departments alone, or mainly, that the incompleteness of our life appears. The lower departments of Nature are already complete enough. The world itself is about as good a world as might be. It has been long in the making, its furniture is all in, its laws are in perfect working order; and although wise men at various times have suggested improvements, there is on the whole a tolerably unanimous vote of confidence in things as they exist. The Divine Environment has little more to do for this planet so far as we can see, and so far as the existing generation is concerned. Then the lower organic life of the world is also so far complete. God, through Evolution or otherwise, may still have finishing touches to add here and there, but already it is "all very good." It is difficult to conceive anything better of its kind than a lily or a cedar, an ant or an ant-eater. These organisms, so far as we can judge, lack nothing. It might be said of them, "they are complete in Nature." Of man also, of man the animal, it may be affirmed that his Environment satisfies him. He has food and drink, and good food and good drink. And there is in him no purely animal want which is not really provided for, and that apparently in the happiest possible way.

But the moment we pass beyond the mere animal life we begin to come upon an incompleteness. The symptoms at first are slight, and betray themselves only by an unexplained restlessness or a dull sense of want. Then the feverishness increases, becomes more defined, and passes slowly into abiding pain. To some come darker moments when the unrest deepens into a mental agony of which all the other woes of earth are mockeries—moments when the forsaken soul can only cry in terror for the Living God. Up to a point the natural Environment supplies man's wants, beyond that it only derides him. How much in man lies beyond that point? Very much—almost all, all that makes man man. The first suspicion of the terrible truth—so for the time let us call it—wakens with the dawn of the intellectual life. It is a solemn moment when the slow-moving mind reaches at length the verge of its mental horizon, and, looking over, sees nothing more. Its straining makes the abyss but more profound. Its cry comes back without an echo. Where is the Environment to complete this rational soul? Men either find one—*One*—or spend the rest of their days in trying to shut their eyes. The alternatives of the intellectual life are Christianity or Agnosticism. The Agnostic is right when he trumpets his incompleteness. He who is not complete in Him must be forever incomplete. Still more grave becomes man's case when he begins further to explore his moral and social nature. The problems of the heart and conscience are infinitely more perplexing than those of the intellect. Has love no future? Has right no triumph? Is the unfinished self to remain unfinished? Again, the alternatives are two, Christianity or Pessimism. But when we ascend the further height of the religious nature, the crisis comes. There, without Environment, the darkness is unutterable. So maddening now becomes the mystery that men are compelled to construct an Environment for themselves. No Environment here is unthinkable. An altar of some sort men must have—God, or Nature, or Law. But the anguish of Atheism is only a negative proof of man's incompleteness. A witness more overwhelming is the prayer of the Christian. What a very strange thing, is it not, for man to pray? It is the symbol at once of his littleness and of his greatness. Here the sense of imperfection, controlled and silenced in the narrower reaches of his being, becomes audible. Now he must utter himself. The sense of need is so real, and the sense of Environment, that he calls out to it, addressing it articulately, and imploring it to satisfy his need. Surely there is nothing more touching in Nature than this? Man could never so expose himself, so break through all constraint, except from a dire necessity. It is the suddenness and unpremeditatedness of Prayer that gives it a unique value as an apologetic.

Man has three questions to put to his Environment, three symbols of his incompleteness. They come from three different centers of his being. The first is the question of the intellect, What is Truth? The natural Environment answers, "Increase of Knowledge increaseth Sorrow," and "much study is a Weariness." Christ replies, "Learn of Me, and ye shall find Rest." Contrast the world's word "Weariness" with Christ's word "Rest." No other teacher since the world began has ever associated "learn" with "Rest." Learn of me, says the philosopher, and you shall find Restlessness. Learn of Me, says Christ, and ye shall find Rest. Thought, which the godless man has cursed, that eternally starved yet ever living specter, finds at last its imperishable glory; Thought is complete in Him. The second question is sent up from the moral nature, Who will show us any good? And again we have a contrast: the world's verdict, "There is none that doeth good, no, not one;" and Christ's, "There is none good but God only." And finally, there is the lonely cry of the spirit, most pathetic and most deep of all, Where is he whom my soul seeketh? And the yearning is met as before, "I looked on my right hand, and beheld, but there was no man that would know me; refuge failed me; no man cared for my soul. I cried unto Thee, O Lord: I said, Thou are my refuge and my portion in the land of the living."

Are these the directions in which men in these days are seeking to complete their lives? The completion of Life is just now a supreme question. It is important to observe how it is being answered. If we ask Science or Philosophy they will refer us to Evolution. The struggle for Life, they assure us, is steadily eliminating imperfect forms, and as the fittest continue to survive we shall have a gradual perfecting of being. That is to say, that completeness is to be sought for in the organism—we are to be complete in Nature and in ourselves. To Evolution, certainly, all men will look for a further perfecting of Life. But it must be an Evolution which includes all the factors. Civilization, it may be said, will deal with the second factor. It will improve the Environment step by step as it improves the organism, or the organism as it improves the Environment. This is well, and it will perfect Life up to a point. But beyond that it cannot carry us. As the possibilities of the natural Life become more defined, its impossibilities will become the more appalling. The most perfect civilization would leave the best part of us still incomplete. Men will have to give up the experiment of attempting to live in half an Environment. Half an Environment will give but half a Life. Half an Environment? He whose correspondences are with this world alone has only a thousandth part, a fraction, the mere rim and shade of an Environment, and only the fraction of a Life. How long will it take Science to believe its own creed, that the material universe we see around us is only a fragment of the universe we do not see? The very retention of the phrase "Material Universe," we are told, is the confession of our unbelief and ignorance; since "matter is the less important half of the material of the physical universe."

The thing to be aimed at is not an organism self-contained and self-sufficient, however high in the scale of being, but an organism complete in the whole Environment. It is open to any one to aim at a self-sufficient Life, but he will find no encouragement in Nature. The Life of the body may complete itself in the physical world; that is its legitimate Environment. The Life of the senses, high and low, may perfect itself in Nature. Even the Life of thought may find a large complement in surrounding things. But the higher thought, and the conscience, and the religious Life, can only perfect themselves in God. To make the influence of Environment stop with the natural world is to doom the spiritual nature to death. For the soul, like the body, can never perfect itself in isolation. The law for both is to be complete in the appropriate Environment. And the perfection to be sought in the spiritual world is a perfection of relation, a perfect adjustment of that which is becoming perfect to that which is perfect.

The third problem, now simplified to a point, finally presents itself. Where do organism and Environment meet? How does that which is becoming perfect avail itself of its perfecting Environment? And the answer is, just as in Nature. The condition is simple receptivity. And yet this is perhaps the least simple of all conditions. It is so simple that we will not act upon it. But there is no other condition. Christ has condensed the whole truth into one memorable sentence, "As the branch cannot bear fruit of itself except it abide in the vine, no more can ye except ye abide in Me." And on the positive side, "He that abideth in Me the same bringeth forth much fruit."

Conformity to Type

"'So careful of the type?' but no.

From scarpèd cliff and quarried stone
She cries, 'A thousand types are gone:
I care for nothing, all shall go.

'Thou makest thine appeal to me;
I bring to life, I bring to death:
The spirit does but mean thy breath:
I know no more.' And he, shall he,

Man, her last work, who seem'd so fair,
Such splendid purpose in his eyes,
Who roll'd the psalm to wintry skies,
Who built him fanes of fruitless prayer,

Who trusted God was love indeed
And love Creation's final law—
Tho' Nature, red in tooth and claw
With ravine, shriek'd against his creed—

Who loved, who suffer'd countless ills,
Who battled for the True, the Just,
Be blown about the desert dust
Or seal'd within the iron hills?"—*In Memoriam*.

"Until Christ be formed in you."—*Paul*.

"The one end to which, in all living beings, the formative impulse is tending—the one scheme which the Archæus of the old speculators strives to carry out, seems to be to mould the offspring into the likeness of the parent. It is the first great law of reproduction, that the offspring tends to resemble its parent or parents more closely than anything else."—*Huxley*.

If a botanist be asked the difference between an oak, a palm-tree and a lichen, he will declare that they are separated from one another by the broadest line known to classification. Without taking into account the outward differences of size and form, the variety of flower and fruit, the peculiarities of leaf and branch, he sees even in their general architecture types of structure as distinct as Norman, Gothic and Egyptian. But if the first young germs of these three plants are placed before him and he is called upon to define the difference, he finds it impossible. He cannot even say which is which. Examined under the highest powers of the microscope they yield no clue. Analyzed by the chemist with all the appliances of his laboratory they keep their secret.

The same experiment can be tried with the embryos of animals. Take the ovule of the worm, the eagle, the elephant, and of man himself. Let the most skilled observer apply the most searching tests to distinguish one from the other and he will fail. But there is something more surprising still. Compare next the two sets of germs, the vegetable and the animal. And there is still no shade of difference. Oak and palm, worm and man all start in life together. No matter into what strangely different forms they may afterward develop, no matter whether they are to live on sea or land, creep or fly, swim or walk, think or vegetate, in the embryo as it first meets the eye of Science they are indistinguishable. The apple which fell in Newton's garden, Newton's dog Diamond, and Newton himself, began life at the same point.

If we analyze this material point at which all life starts, we shall find it to consist of a clear structureless jelly-like substance resembling albumen or white of egg. It is made of Carbon, Hydrogen, Oxygen and Nitrogen. Its name is protoplasm. And it is not only the structural unit with which all living bodies start in life, but with which they are subsequently built up. "Protoplasm," says Huxley, "simple or nucleated, is the formal basis of all life. It is the clay of the Potter." "Beast and fowl, reptile and fish, mollusk, worm and polype are all composed of structural units of the same character, namely, masses of protoplasm with a nucleus."

What then determines the difference between different animals? What makes one little speck of protoplasm grow into Newton's dog Diamond, and another, exactly the same, into Newton himself? It is a mysterious something which has entered into this protoplasm. No eye can see it. No science can define it. There is a different something for Newton's dog and a different something for Newton; so that though both use the same matter they build it up in these widely different ways. Protoplasm being the clay, this something is the Potter. And as there is only one clay and yet all these curious forms are developed out of it, it follows necessarily that the difference lies in the potters. There must in short be as many potters as there are forms. There is the potter who segments the worm, and the potter who builds up the form of the dog, and the potter who moulds the man. To understand unmistakably that it is really the potter who does the work, let us follow for a moment a description of the process by a trained eye-witness. The observer is Mr. Huxley. Through the tube of his microscope he is watching the development, out of a speck of protoplasm, of one of the commonest animals: "Strange possibilities," he says, "lie dormant in that semi-fluid globule. Let a moderate supply of warmth reach its watery cradle and the plastic matter undergoes changes so rapid and yet so steady and purposelike in their succession that one can only compare them to those operated by a skilled modeler upon a formless lump of clay. As with an invisible trowel the mass is divided and subdivided into smaller and smaller portions, until it is reduced to an aggregation of granules not too large to build withal the finest fabrics of the nascent organism. And, then, it is as if a delicate finger traced out the line to be occupied by the spinal column, and moulded the contour of the body; pinching up the head at one end, the tail at the other, and fashioning flank and limb into due proportions in so artistic a way, that, after watching the process hour by hour, one is almost involuntarily possessed by the notion, that some more subtle aid to vision than an achromatic would show the hidden artist, with his plan before him, striving with skillful manipulation to perfect his work."

Besides the fact, so luminously brought out here, that the artist is distinct from the "semi-fluid globule" of protoplasm in which he works, there is this other essential point to notice, that in all his "skillful manipulation" the artist is not working at random, but according to law. He has "his plan before him." In the zoological laboratory of Nature it is not as in a workshop where a skilled artisan can turn his hand to anything—where the same potter one day moulds a dog, the next a bird, and the next a man. In Nature one potter is set apart to make each. It is a more complete system of division of labor. One artist makes all the dogs, another makes all the birds, a third makes all the men. Moreover, each artist confines himself exclusively to working out his own plan. He appears to have his own plan somehow stamped upon himself, and his work is rigidly to reproduce himself.

The Scientific Law by which this takes place is the Law of Conformity to Type. It is contained, to a large extent, in the ordinary Law of Inheritance; or it may be considered as simply another way of stating what Darwin calls the Laws of Unity of Type. Darwin defines it thus: "By Unity of Type is meant that fundamental agreement in structure which we see in organic beings of the same class, and which is quite independent of their habits of life." According to this law every living thing that comes into the world is compelled to stamp upon its offspring the image of itself. The dog, according to its type, produces a dog; the bird a bird.

The artist who operates upon matter in this subtle way and carries out this law is Life. There are a great many different kinds of Life. If one might give the broader meaning to the words of the apostle: "All life is not the same life. There is one kind of life of men, another life of beasts, another of fishes, and another of birds." There is the Life, or the Artist, or the Potter who segments the worm, the potter who forms the dog, the potter who moulds the man.

What goes on then in the animal kingdom is this—the Bird-Life seizes upon the bird-germ and builds it up into a bird, the image of itself. The Reptile Life seizes upon another germinal speck, assimilates surrounding matter, and fashions it into a reptile. The Reptile-Life thus simply makes an incarnation of itself. The visible bird is simply an incarnation of the invisible Bird-Life.

Now we are nearing the point where the spiritual analogy appears. It is a very wonderful analogy, so wonderful that one almost hesitates to put it into words. Yet Nature is reverent; and it is her voice to which we listen. These lower phenomena of life, she says, are but an allegory. There is another kind of Life of which Science as yet has taken little cognizance. It obeys the same laws. It builds up an organism into its own form. It is the Christ-Life. As the Bird-Life builds up a bird, the image of itself, so the Christ-Life builds up a Christ, the image of Himself, in the inward nature of man. When a man becomes a Christian the natural process is this: The Living Christ enters into his soul. Development begins. The quickening Life seizes upon the soul, assimilates surrounding elements, and begins to fashion it. According to the great Law of Conformity to Type this fashioning takes a specific form. It is that of the Artist who fashions. And all through Life this wonderful, mystical, glorious, yet perfectly definite process, goes on "until Christ be formed" in it.

The Christian Life is not a vague effort after righteousness—an ill-defined pointless struggle for an ill-defined pointless end. Religion is no dishevelled mass of aspiration, prayer, and faith. There is no more mystery in Religion as to its processes than in Biology. There is much mystery in Biology. We know all but nothing of Life yet, nothing of development. There is the same mystery in the spiritual Life. But the great lines are the same, as decided, as luminous; and the laws of natural and spiritual are the same, as unerring, as simple. Will everything else in the natural world unfold its order, and yield to Science more and more a vision of harmony, and Religion, which should complement and perfect all, remain a chaos? From the standpoint of Revelation no truth is more obscure than Conformity to Type. If Science can furnish a companion phenomenon from an every-day process of the natural life, it may at least throw this most mystical doctrine of Christianity into thinkable form. Is there any fallacy in speaking of the Embryology of the New Life? Is the analogy invalid? Are there not vital processes in the Spiritual as well as in the Natural world? The Bird being an incarnation of the Bird-Life, may not the Christian be a spiritual incarnation of the Christ-Life? And is here not a real justification in the processes of the New-Birth for such a parallel?

Let us appeal to the record of these processes.

In what terms does the New Testament describe them? The answer is sufficiently striking. It uses everywhere the language of Biology. It is impossible that the New Testament writers should have been familiar with these biological facts. It is impossible that their views of this great truth should have been as clear as Science can make them now. But they had no alternative. There was no other way of expressing this truth. It was a biological question. So they struck out unhesitatingly into the new fields of words, and, with an originality which commands both reverence and surprise, stated their truth with such light, or darkness, as they had. They did not mean to be scientific, only to be accurate, and their fearless accuracy has made them scientific.

What could be more original, for instance, than the Apostle's reiteration that the Christian was a new creature, a new man, a babe? Or that this new man was "begotten of God," God's workmanship? And what could be a more accurate expression of the law of Conformity to Type than this: "Put on the new man, which is renewed in knowledge after the image of Him that created him?" Or this, "We are changed into the same image from glory to glory?" And elsewhere we are expressly told by the same writer that this Conformity is the end and goal of the Christian life. To work this Type in us is the whole purpose of God for man. "Whom He did foreknow He also did predestinate to be conformed to the image of His Son."

One must confess that the originality of this entire New Testament conception is most startling. Even for the nineteenth century it is the most startling. But when one remembers that such an idea took form in the first, one cannot fail to be impressed with a deepening wonder at the system which begat and cherished it. Men seek the origin of Christianity among philosophies of that age. Scholars contrast it still with these philosophies, and scheme to fit it in to those of later growth. Has it never occurred to them how much more it is than a philosophy, that it includes a science, a Biology pure and simple? As well might naturalists contrast zoology with chemistry, or seek to incorporate geology with botany—the living with the dead—as try to explain the spiritual life in terms of mind alone. When will it be seen that the characteristic of the Christian Religion is its Life, that a true theology must begin with a Biology? Theology is the Science of God. Why will men treat God as inorganic?

If this analogy is capable of being worked out, we should expect answers to at least three questions.

First: What corresponds to the protoplasm in the spiritual sphere?

Second: What is the Life, the Hidden Artist who fashions it?

Third: What do we know of the process and the plan?

First: The Protoplasm.

We should be forsaking the lines of nature were we to imagine for a moment that the new creature was to be found out of nothing. *Ex nihilo nihil*—nothing can be made out of nothing. Matter is uncreatable and indestructible; Nature and man can only form and transform. Hence when a new animal is made, no new clay is made. Life merely enters into already existing matter, assimilates more of the same sort and re-builds it. The spiritual Artist works in the same way. He must have a peculiar kind of protoplasm, a basis of life, and that must be already existing.

Now we find this in the materials of character with which the natural man is previously provided. Mind and character, the will and the affections, the moral nature—these form the bases of spiritual life. To look in this direction for the protoplasm of the spiritual life is consistent with all analogy. The lowest or mineral world mainly supplies the material—and this is true even for insectivorous species—for the vegetable kingdom. The vegetable supplies the material for the animal. Next in turn, the animal furnishes material for the mental, and lastly the mental for the spiritual. Each member of the series is complete only when the steps below it are complete; the highest demands all. It is not necessary for the immediate purpose to go so far into the psychology either of the new creature or of the old as to define more clearly what these moral bases are. It is enough to discover that in this womb the new creature is to be born, fashioned out of the mental and moral parts, substance, or essence of the natural man. The only thing to be insisted upon is that in the natural man this mental and moral substance or basis is spiritually lifeless. However active the intellectual or moral life may be, from the point of view of this other Life it is dead. That which is flesh is flesh. It wants, that is to say, the kind of Life which constitutes the difference between the Christian and the not-a-Christian. It has not yet been "born of the Spirit."

To show further that this protoplasm possesses the necessary properties of a normal protoplasm it will be necessary to examine in passing what these properties are. They are two in number, the capacity for life and plasticity. Consider first the capacity for life. It is not enough to find an adequate supply of material. That must be of the right kind. For all kinds of matter have not the power to be the vehicle of life—all kinds of matter are not even fitted to be the vehicle of electricity. What peculiarity there is in Carbon, Hydrogen, Oxygen, and Nitrogen, when combined in a certain way, to receive life, we cannot tell. We only know that life is always associated in Nature with this particular physical basis and never with any other. But we are not in the same darkness with regard to the moral protoplasm. When we look at this complex combination which we have predicted as the basis of spiritual life, we do find something which gives it a peculiar qualification for being the protoplasm of the Christ-Life. We discover one strong reason at least, not only why this kind of life should be associated with this kind of protoplasm, but why it should never be associated with other kinds which seem to resemble it—why, for instance, this spiritual life should not be engrafted upon the intelligence of a dog or the instincts of an ant.

The protoplasm in man has a something in addition to its instincts or its habits. It has a capacity for God. In this capacity for God lies its receptivity; it is the very protoplasm that was necessary. The chamber is not only ready to receive the new Life, but the Guest is expected, and, till He comes, is missed. Till then the soul longs and yearns, wastes and pines, waving its tentacles piteously in the empty air, feeling after God if so be that it may find Him. This is not peculiar to the protoplasm of the Christian's soul. In every land and in every age there have been altars to the Known or Unknown God. It is now agreed as a mere question of anthropology that the universal language of the human soul has always been "I perish with hunger." This is what fits it for Christ. There is a grandeur in this cry from the depths which makes its very unhappiness sublime.

The other quality we are to look for in the soul is mouldableness, plasticity. Conformity demands conformability. Now plasticity is not only a marked characteristic of all forms of life, but in a special sense of the highest forms. It increases steadily as we rise in the scale. The inorganic world, to begin with, is rigid. A crystal of silica dissolved and redissolved a thousand times will never assume any other form than the hexagonal. The plant next, though plastic in its elements, is comparatively insusceptible of change. The very fixity of its sphere, the imprisonment for life in a single spot of earth, is the symbol of a certain degradation. The animal in all parts is mobile, sensitive, free; the highest animal, man, is the most mobile, the most at leisure from routine, the most impressionable, the most open for change. And when we reach the mind and soul, this mobility is found in its most developed form. Whether we regard its susceptibility to impressions, its lightning-like response even to influences the most impalpable and subtle, its power of instantaneous adjustment, or whether we regard the delicacy and variety of its moods, or its vast powers of growth, we are forced to recognize in this the most perfect capacity for change. This marvellous plasticity of mind contains at once the possibility and prophecy of its transformation. The soul, in a word, is made to be *converted*.

Second: The Life.

The main reason for giving the Life, the agent of this change, a separate treatment, is to emphasize the distinction between it and the natural man on the one hand, and the spiritual man on the other. The natural man is its basis, the spiritual man is its product, the Life itself is something different. Just as in an organism we have these three things—formative matter, formed matter, and the forming principle or life; so in the soul we have the old nature, the renewed nature, and the transforming Life.

This being made evident, little remains here to be added. No man has ever seen this Life. It cannot be analyzed, or weighed, or traced in its essential nature. But this is just what we expected. This invisibility is the same property which we found to be peculiar to the natural life. We saw no life in the first embryos, in oak, in palm, or in bird. In the adult it likewise escapes us. We shall not wonder if we cannot see it in the Christian. We shall not expect to see it. *A fortiori* we shall not expect to see it, for we are further removed from the coarser matter—moving now among ethereal and spiritual things. It is because it conforms to the law of this analogy so well that men, not seeing it, have denied its being. Is it hopeless to point out that one of the most recognizable characteristics of life is its unrecognizableness, and that the very token of its spiritual nature lies in its being beyond the grossness of our eyes?

We do not pretend that Science can define this Life to be Christ. It has no definition to give even of its own life, much less of this. But there are converging lines which point, at least, in the direction that it is Christ. There was One whom history acknowledges to have been the Truth. One of His claims was this, "I am the Life." According to the doctrine of Biogenesis, life can only come from life. It was His additional claim that His function in the world was to give men Life. "I am come that ye might have Life, and that ye might have it more abundantly." This could not refer to the natural life, for men had that already. He that hath the Son hath another Life. "Know ye not your own selves how that Jesus Christ is in you."

Again, there are men whose characters assume a strange resemblance to Him who was the Life. When we see the bird-character appear in an organism we assume that the Bird-Life has been there at work. And when we behold Conformity to Type in a Christian, and know moreover that the type-organization can be produced by the type-life alone does this not lend support to the hypothesis that the Type-Life also has been here at work? If every effect demands a cause, what other cause is there for the Christian? When we have a cause, and an adequate cause, and no other adequate cause; when we have the express statement of that Cause that he is that cause, what more is possible? Let not Science, knowing nothing of its own life, go further than to say it knows nothing of this Life. We shall not dissent from its silence. But till it tells us what it is, we wait for evidence that it is not this.

Third: The Process.

It is impossible to enter at length into any details of the great miracle by which this protoplasm is to be conformed to the Image of the Son. We enter that province now only so far as this Law of Conformity compels us. Nor is it so much the nature of the process we have to consider as its general direction and results. We are dealing with a question of morphology rather than of physiology.

It must occur to one on reaching this point, that a new element here comes in which compels us, for the moment, to part company with zoology. That element is the conscious power of choice. The animal in following the type is blind. It does not only follow the type involuntarily and compulsorily, but does not know that it is following it. We might certainly have been made to conform to the Type in the higher sphere with no more knowledge or power of choice than animals or automata. But then we should not have been men. It is a possible case, but not possible to the kind of protoplasm with which men are furnished. Owing to the peculiar characteristics of this protoplasm an additional and exceptional provision is essential.

The first demand is that being conscious and having this power of choice, the mind should have an adequate knowledge of what it is to choose. Some revelation of the Type, that is to say, is necessary. And as that revelation can only come from the Type, we must look there for it.

We are confronted at once with the Incarnation. There we find how the Christ-Life has clothed Himself with matter, taken literal flesh, and dwelt among us. The Incarnation is the Life revealing the Type. Men are long since agreed that this is the end of the Incarnation—the revealing of God. But why should God be revealed? Why, indeed, but for man? Why but that "beholding as in a glass the glory of the only begotten we should be changed into the same image?"

To meet the power of choice, however, something more was necessary than the mere revelation of the Type—it was necessary that the Type should be the highest conceivable Type. In other words, the Type must be an Ideal. For all true human growth, effort, and achievement, an ideal is acknowledged to be indispensable. And all men accordingly whose lives are based on principle, have set themselves an ideal, more or less perfect. It is this which first deflects the will from what is based, and turns the wayward life to what is holy. So much is true as mere philosophy. But philosophy failed to present men with their ideal. It has never been suggested that Christianity has failed. Believers and unbelievers have been compelled to acknowledge that Christianity holds up to the world the missing Type, the Perfect Man.

The recognition of the Ideal is the first step in the direction of Conformity. But let it be clearly observed that it is but a step. There is no vital connection between merely seeing the Ideal and being conformed to it. Thousands admire Christ who never become Christians.

But the great question still remains, How is the Christian to be conformed to the Type, or as we should now say, dealing with consciousness, to the Ideal? The mere knowledge of the Ideal is no more than a motive. How is the process to be practically accomplished? Who is to do it? Where, when, how? This is the test question of Christianity. It is here that all theories of Christianity, all attempts to explain it on natural principles, all reductions of it to philosophy, inevitably break down. It is here that all imitations of Christianity perish. It is here, also, that personal religion finds its most fatal obstacle. Men are all quite clear about the Ideal. We are all convinced of the duty of mankind regarding it. But how to secure that willing men shall attain it—that is the problem of religion. It is the failure to understand the dynamics of Christianity that has most seriously and most pitifully hindered its growth both in the individual and in the race.

From the standpoint of biology this practical difficulty vanishes in a moment. It is probably the very simplicity of the law regarding it that has made men stumble. For nothing is so invisible to most men as transparency. The law here is the same biological law that exists in the natural world. For centuries men have striven to find out ways and means to conform themselves to this type. Impressive motives have been pictured, the proper circumstances arranged, the direction of effort defined, and men have toiled, struggled, and agonized to conform themselves to the Image of the Son. Can the protoplasm *conform itself* to its type? Can the embryo *fashion itself*? Is Conformity to Type produced by the matter *or by the life*, by the protoplasm or by the Type? Is organization the cause of life or the effect of it? It is the effect of it. Conformity to Type, therefore, is secured by the type. Christ makes the Christian.

Men need only reflect on the automatic processes of their natural body to discover that this is the universal law of Life. What does any man consciously do, for instance, in the matter of breathing? What part does he take in circulating the blood, in keeping up the rhythm of his heart? What control has he over growth? What man by taking thought can add a cubit to his stature? What part voluntarily does man take in secretion, in digestion, in the reflex actions? In point of fact is he not after all the veriest automaton, every organ of his body given him, every function arranged for him, brain and nerve, thought and sensation, will and conscience, all provided for him ready made? And yet he turns upon his soul and wishes to organize that himself! O preposterous and vain man, thou who couldest not make a finger-nail of thy body, thinkest thou to fashion this wonderful, mysterious, subtle soul of thine after the ineffable Image? Wilt thou ever permit thyself *to be* conformed to the Image of the Son? Wilt thou, who canst not add a cubit to thy stature, submit *to be* raised by the Type-Life within thee to the perfect stature of Christ?

This is a humbling conclusion. And therefore men will resent it. Men will still experiment "by works of righteousness which they have done" to earn the Ideal life. The doctrine of Human Inability, as the Church calls it, has always been objectionable to men who do not know themselves. The doctrine itself, perhaps, has been partly to blame. While it has been often affirmed in such language as rightly to humble men, it has also been stated and cast in their teeth with words which could only insult them. Merely to assert dogmatically that man has no power to move hand or foot to help himself toward Christ, carries no real conviction. The weight of human authority is always powerless, and ought to be, where the intelligence is denied a rationale. In the light of modern science when men seek a reason for every thought of God or man, this old doctrine with its severe and almost inhuman aspect—till rightly understood—must presently have succumbed. But to the biologist it cannot die. It stands to him on the solid ground of Nature. It has a reason in the laws of life which must resuscitate it and give it another lease of years. Bird-Life makes the Bird. Christ-Life makes the Christian. No man by taking thought can add a cubit to his stature.

So much for the scientific evidence. Here is the corresponding statement of the truth from Scripture. Observe the passive voice in these sentences: "*Begotten* of God;" "The new man which *is renewed* in knowledge after the Image of Him that created him;" or this, "We *are changed* into the same Image;" or this, "Predestinate *to be conformed* to the Image of His Son;" or again, "Until Christ *be formed* in you;" or "Except a man *be born again* he cannot see the Kingdom of God;" "Except a man *be born* of water and of the Spirit he cannot enter the Kingdom of God." There is one outstanding verse which seems at first sight on the other side: "Work out your own salvation with fear and trembling;" but as one reads on he finds, as if the writer dreaded the very misconception, the complement, "For it is God which worketh in you both to will and to do of His good pleasure."

It will be noticed in these passages, and in others which might be named, that the process of transformation is referred indifferently to the agency of each Person of the Trinity in turn. We are not concerned to take up this question of detail. It is sufficient that the transformation is wrought. Theologians, however, distinguish thus: the indirect agent is Christ, the direct influence is the Holy Spirit. In other words, Christ by his Spirit renews the souls of men.

Is man, then, out of the arena altogether? Is he mere clay in the hands of the potter, a machine, a tool, an automaton? Yes and No. If he were a tool he would not be a man. If he were a man he would have something to do. One need not seek to balance what God does here, and what man does. But we shall attain to a sufficient measure of truth on a most delicate problem if we make a final appeal to the natural life. We find that in maintaining this natural life Nature has a share and man has a share. By far the larger part is done for us—the breathing, the secreting, the circulating of the blood, the building up of the organism. And although the part which man plays is a minor part, yet, strange to say, it is not less essential to the well being, and even to the being, of the whole. For instance, man has to take food. He has nothing to do with it after he has once taken it, for the moment it passes his lips it is taken in hand by reflex actions and handed on from one organ to another, his control over it, in the natural course of things, being completely lost. But the initial act was his. And without that nothing could have been done. Now whether there be an exact analogy between the voluntary and involuntary functions in the body, and the corresponding processes in the soul, we do not at present inquire. But this will indicate, at least, that man has his own part to play. Let him choose Life; let him daily nourish his soul; let him forever starve the old life; let him abide continuously as a living branch in the Vine, and the True-Vine Life will flow into his soul, assimilating, renewing, conforming to Type, till Christ, pledged by His own law, be formed in him.

We have been dealing with Christianity at its most mystical point. Mark here once more its absolute naturalness. The pursuit of the Type is just what all Nature is engaged in. Plant and insect, fish and reptile, bird and mammal—these in their several spheres are striving after the Type. To prevent its extinction, to ennoble it, to people earth and sea and sky with it; this is the meaning of the Struggle for Life. And this is our life—to pursue the Type, to populate the world with it.

Our religion is not all a mistake. We are not visionaries. We are not "unpractical," as men pronounce us, when we worship. To try to follow Christ is not to be "righteous overmuch." True men are not rhapsodizing when they preach; nor do those waste their lives who waste themselves in striving to extend the Kingdom of God on earth. This is what life is for. The Christian in his life-aim is in strict line with Nature. What men call his supernatural is quite natural.

Mark well also the splendor of this idea of salvation. It is not merely final "safety," to be forgiven sin, to evade the curse. It is not, vaguely, "to get to heaven." It is to be conformed to the Image of the Son. It is for these poor elements to attain to the Supreme Beauty. The organizing Life being Eternal, so must this Beauty be immortal. Its progress toward the Immaculate is already guaranteed. And more than all there is here fulfilled the sublimest of all prophecies; not Beauty alone but Unity is secured by the Type—Unity of man and man, God and man, God and Christ and man till "all shall be one."

Could Science in its most brilliant anticipations for the future of its highest organism ever have foreshadowed a development like this? Now that the revelation is made to it, it surely recognizes it as the missing point in Evolution, the climax to which all Creation tends. Hitherto Evolution had no future. It was a pillar with marvelous carving, growing richer and finer toward the top, but without a capital; a pyramid, the vast base buried in the inorganic, towering higher and higher, tier above tier, life above life, mind above mind, ever more perfect in its workmanship, more noble in its symmetry, and yet withal so much the more mysterious in its aspiration. The most curious eye, following it upward, saw nothing. The cloud fell and covered it. Just what men wanted to see was hid. The work of the ages had no apex. But the work begun by Nature is finished by the Supernatural—as we are wont to call the higher natural. And as the veil is lifted by Christianity it strikes men dumb with wonder. For the goal of Evolution is Jesus Christ.

The Christian life is the only life that will ever be completed. Apart from Christ the life of man is a broken pillar, the race of men an unfinished pyramid. One by one in sight of Eternity all human Ideals fall short, one by one before the open grave all human hopes dissolve. The Laureate sees a moment's light in Nature's jealousy for the Type; but that too vanishes.

"'So careful of the type?' but no.
From scarpèd cliff and quarried stone
She cries, 'A thousand types are gone:
I care for nothing, all shall go.'"

All shall go? No, one Type remains. "Whom He did foreknow He also did predestinate to be conformed to the Image of His Son." And "when Christ who is our life shall appear, then shall ye also appear with Him in glory."

Semi-Parasitism

"The Situation that has not its Duty, its Ideal, was never yet occupied by man. Yes, here, in this poor, miserable, hampered, despicable Actual, wherein thou even now standest, here or nowhere is thy Ideal: work it out therefrom; and working, believe, live, be free."—*Carlyle.*

"Work out your own salvation."—*Paul.*

"Any new set of conditions occurring to an animal which render its food and safety very easily attained, seem to lead as a rule to degeneration."—*E. Ray Lankester.*

Parasites are the paupers of Nature. They are forms of life which will not take the trouble to find their own food, but borrow or steal it from the more industrious. So deep-rooted is this tendency in Nature, that plants may become parasitic—it is an acquired habit—as well as animals; and both are found in every state of beggary, some doing a little for themselves, while others, more abject, refuse even to prepare their own food.

There are certain plants—the Dodder, for instance—which begin life with the best intentions, strike true roots into the soil, and really appear as if they meant to be independent for life. But after supporting themselves for a brief period they fix curious sucking discs into the stem and branches of adjacent plants. And after a little experimenting, the epiphyte finally ceases to do anything for its own support, thenceforth drawing all its supplies ready-made from the sap of its host. In this parasitic state it has no need for organs of nutrition of its own, and Nature therefore takes them away. Henceforth, to the botanist, the adult Dodder presents the degraded spectacle of a plant without a root, without a twig, without a leaf, and having a stem so useless as to be inadequate to bear its own weight.

In the Mistletoe the parasitic habit has reached a stage in some respects lower still. It has persisted in the downward course for so many generations that the young forms even have acquired the habit and usually begin life at once as parasites. The Mistletoe berries, which contain the seed of the future plant, are developed especially to minister to this degeneracy, for they glue themselves to the branches of some neighboring oak or apple, and there the young Mistletoe starts as a dependent from the first.

Among animals these *lazzaroni* are more largely represented still. Almost every animal is a living poor-house, and harbors one or more species of *epizoa* or *entozoa*, supplying them gratis, not only with a permanent home, but with all the necessaries and luxuries of life.

Why does the naturalist think hardly of the parasites? Why does he speak of them as degraded, and despise them as the most ignoble creatures in Nature? What more can an animal do than eat, drink, and die to-morrow? If under the fostering care and protection of a higher organism it can eat better, drink more easily, live more merrily, and die, perhaps, not till the day after, why should it not do so? Is parasitism, after all, not a somewhat clever *ruse*? Is it not an ingenious way of securing the benefits of life while evading its responsibilities? And although this mode of livelihood is selfish, and possibly undignified, can it be said that it is immoral?

The naturalist's reply to this is brief. Parasitism, he will say, is one of the gravest crimes in Nature. It is a breach of the law of Evolution. Thou shalt evolve, thou shalt develop all thy faculties to the full, thou shalt attain to the highest conceivable perfection of thy race—and so perfect thy race—this is the first and greatest commandment of nature. But the parasite has no thought for its race, or for perfection in any shape or form. It wants two things—food and shelter. How it gets them is of no moment. Each member lives exclusively on its own account, an isolated, indolent, selfish, and backsliding life.

The remarkable thing is that Nature permits the community to be taxed in this way apparently without protest. For the parasite is a consumer pure and simple. And the "Perfect Economy of Nature" is surely for once at fault when it encourages species numbered by thousands which produce nothing for their own or for the general good, but live, and live luxuriously, at the expense of others?

Now when we look into the matter, we very soon perceive that instead of secretly countenancing this ingenious device by which parasitic animals and plants evade the great law of the Struggle for Life, Nature sets her face most sternly against it. And, instead of allowing the transgressors to slip through her fingers, as one might at first suppose, she visits upon them the most severe and terrible penalties. The parasite, she argues, not only injures itself, but wrongs others. It disobeys the fundamental law of its own being, and taxes the innocent to contribute to its disgrace. So that if Nature is just, if Nature has an avenging hand, if she holds one vial of wrath more full and bitter than another, it shall surely be poured out upon those who are guilty of this double sin. Let us see what form this punishment takes.

Observant visitors to the sea-side, or let us say to an aquarium, are familiar with those curious little creatures known as Hermit-crabs. The peculiarity of the Hermits is that they take up their abode in the cast-off shell of some other animal, not unusually the whelk; and here, like Diogenes in his tub, the creature lives a solitary, but by no means an inactive life.

The *Pagurus*, however, is not a parasite. And yet although in no sense of the word a parasite, this way of inhabiting throughout life a house built by another animal approaches so closely the parasitic habit, that we shall find it instructive as a preliminary illustration, to consider the effect of this free-house policy on the occupant. There is no doubt, to begin with, that, as has been already indicated, the habit is an acquired one. In its general anatomy the Hermit is essentially a crab. Now the crab is an animal which, from the nature of its environment, has to lead a somewhat rough and perilous life. Its days are spent among jagged rocks and boulders. Dashed about by every wave, attacked on every side by monsters of the deep, the crustacean has to protect itself by developing a strong and serviceable coat of mail.

How best to protect themselves has been the problem to which the whole crab family have addressed themselves; and, in considering the matter, the ancestors of the Hermit-crab hit on the happy device of re-utilizing the habitations of the molluscs which lay around them in plenty, well-built, and ready for immediate occupation. For generations and generations accordingly, the Hermit-crab has ceased to exercise itself upon questions of safety, and dwells in its little shell as proudly and securely as if its second-hand house were a fortress erected especially for its private use.

Wherein, then, has the Hermit suffered for this cheap, but real solution of a practical difficulty? Whether its laziness costs it any moral qualms, or whether its cleverness becomes to it a source of congratulation, we do not know; but judged from the appearance the animal makes under the searching gaze of the zoologist, its expedient is certainly not one to be commended. To the eye of Science its sin is written in the plainest characters on its very organization. It has suffered in its own anatomical structure just by as much as it has borrowed from an external source. Instead of being a perfect crustacean it has allowed certain important parts of its body to deteriorate. And several vital organs are partially or wholly atrophied.

Its sphere of life also is now seriously limited; and by a cheap expedient to secure safety, it has fatally lost its independence. It is plain from its anatomy that the Hermit-crab was not always a Hermit-crab. It was meant for higher things. Its ancestors doubtless were more or less perfect crustaceans, though what exact stage of development was reached before the hermit habit became fixed in the species we cannot tell. But from the moment the creature took to relying on an external source, it began to fall. It slowly lost in its own person all that it now draws from external aid.

As an important item in the day's work, namely, the securing of safety and shelter, was now guaranteed to it, one of the chief inducements to a life of high and vigilant effort was at the same time withdrawn. A number of functions, in fact, struck work. The whole of the parts, therefore, of the complex organism which ministered to these functions, from lack of exercise, or total disuse, became gradually feeble; and ultimately, by the stern law that an unused organ must suffer a slow but inevitable atrophy, the creature not only lost all power of motion in these parts, but lost the parts themselves, and otherwise sank into a relatively degenerate condition.

Every normal crustacean, on the other hand, has the abdominal region of the body covered by a thick chitinous shell. In the Hermits this is represented only by a thin and delicate membrane—of which the sorry figure the creature cuts when drawn from its foreign hiding-place is sufficient evidence. Any one who now examines further this half-naked and woe-begone object, will perceive also that the fourth and fifth pair of limbs are either so small and wasted as to be quite useless or altogether rudimentary; and, although certainly the additional development of the extremity of the tail into an organ for holding on to its extemporized retreat may be regarded as a slight compensation, it is clear from the whole structure of the animal that it has allowed itself to undergo severe Degeneration.

In dealing with the Hermit-crab, in short, we are dealing with a case of physiological backsliding. That the creature has lost anything by this process from a practical point of view is not now argued. It might fairly be shown, as already indicated, that its freedom is impaired by its cumbrous exoskeleton, and that, in contrast with other crabs, who lead a free and roving life, its independence generally is greatly limited. But from the physiological standpoint, there is no question that the Hermit tribe have neither discharged their responsibilities to Nature nor to themselves. If the end of life is merely to escape death, and serve themselves, possibly they have done well; but if it is to attain an ever increasing perfection, then are they backsliders indeed.

A zoologist's verdict would be that by this act they have forfeited to some extent their place in the animal scale. An animal is classed as a low or high according as it is adapted to less or more complex conditions of life. This is the true standpoint from which to judge all living organisms. Were perfection merely a matter of continual eating and drinking, the Amoeba—the lowest known organism—might take rank with the highest, Man, for the one nourishes itself and saves its skin almost as completely as the other. But judged by the higher standard of Complexity, that is, by greater or lesser adaption to more or less complex conditions, the gulf between them is infinite.

We have now received a preliminary idea, although not from the study of a true parasite, of the essential principles involved in parasitism. And we may proceed to point out the correlative in the moral and spiritual spheres. We confine ourselves for the present to one point. The difference between the Hermit-crab and a true parasite is, that the former has acquired a semi-parasitic habit only with reference to *safety*. It may be that the Hermit devours as a preliminary the accommodating mollusc whose tenement it covets; but it would become a real parasite only on the supposition that the whelk was of such size as to keep providing for it throughout life, and that the external and internal organs of the crab should disappear, while it lived henceforth, by simple imbibition, upon the elaborated juices of its host. All the mollusc provides, however, for the crustacean in this instance is safety, and, accordingly in the meantime we limit our application to this. The true parasite presents us with an organism so much more degraded in all its parts, that its lessons may well be reserved until we have paved the way to understand the deeper bearings of the subject.

The spiritual principle to be illustrated in the meantime stands thus: *Any principle which secures the safety of the individual without personal effort or the vital exercise of faculty is disastrous to moral character.* We do not begin by attempting to define words. Were we to define truly what is meant by safety or salvation, we should be spared further elaboration, and the law would stand out as a sententious common-place. But we have to deal with the ideas of safety as these are popularly held, and the chief purpose at this stage is to expose what may be called the Parasitic Doctrine of Salvation. The phases of religious experience about to be described may be unknown to many. It remains for those who are familiar with the religious conceptions of the masses to determine whether or not we are wasting words.

What is meant by the Parasitic Doctrine of Salvation one may, perhaps, best explain by sketching two of its leading types. The first is the doctrine of the Church of Rome; the second, that represented by the narrower Evangelical Religion. We take these religions, however, not in their ideal form, with which possibly we should have little quarrel, but in their practical working, or in the form in which they are held especially by the rank and file of those who belong respectively to these communions. For the strength or weakness of any religious system is best judged from the form in which it presents itself to, and influences the common mind.

No more perfect or more sad example of semi-parasitism exists than in the case of those illiterate thousands who, scattered everywhere throughout the habitable globe, swell the lower ranks of the Church of Rome. Had an organization been specially designed, indeed, to induce the parasitic habit in the souls of men, nothing better fitted to its disastrous end could be established than the system of Roman Catholicism. Roman Catholicism offers to the masses a molluscan shell. They have simply to shelter themselves within its pale, and they are "safe." But what is this "safe?" It is an external safety—the safety of an institution. It is a salvation recommended to men by all that appeals to the motives in most common use with the vulgar and the superstitious, but which has as little vital connection with the individual soul as the dead whelk's shell with the living Hermit. Salvation is a relation at once vital, personal, and spiritual. This is mechanical and purely external. And this is of course the final secret of its marvelous success and world-wide power. A cheap religion is the desideratum of the human heart; and an assurance of salvation at the smallest possible cost forms the tempting bait held out to a conscience-stricken world by the Romish Church. Thousands, therefore, who have never been taught to use their faculties in "working out their own salvation," thousands who will not exercise themselves religiously, and who yet cannot be without the exercise of religion, intrust themselves in idle faith to that venerable house of refuge which for centuries has stood between God and man. A Church which has harbored generations of the elect, whose archives enshrine the names of saints whose foundations are consecrated with martyrs' blood—shall it not afford a sure asylum still for any soul which would make its peace with God? So, as the Hermit into the molluscan shell, creeps the poor soul within the pale of Rome, seeking, like Adam in the garden, to hide its nakedness from God.

Why does the true lover of men restrain not his lips in warning his fellows against this and all other priestly religions? It is not because he fails to see the prodigious energy of the Papal See, or to appreciate the many noble types of Christian manhood nurtured within its pale. Nor is it because its teachers are often corrupt and its system of doctrine inadequate as a representation of the Truth—charges which have to be made more or less against all religions. But it is because it ministers falsely to the deepest need of man, reduces the end of religion to selfishness, and offers safety without spirituality. That these, theoretically, are its pretensions, we do not affirm; but that its practical working is to induce in man, and in its worst forms, the parasitic habit, is testified by results. No one who has studied the religion of the Continent upon the spot, has failed to be impressed with the appalling spectacle of tens of thousands of unregenerated men sheltering themselves, as they conceive it for Eternity, behind the Sacraments of Rome.

There is no stronger evidence of the inborn parasitic tendency in man in things religious than the absolute complacency with which even cultured men will hand over their eternal interests to the care of a Church. We can never dismiss from memory the sadness with which we once listened to the confession of a certain foreign professor: "I used to be concerned about religion," he said in substance, "but religion is a great subject. I was very busy; there was little time to settle it for myself. A protestant, my attention was called to the Roman Catholic religion. It suited my case. And instead of dabbling in religion for myself I put myself in its hands. Once a year," he concluded, "I go to mass." These were the words of one whose work will live in the history of his country, one, too, who knew all about parasitism. Yet, though he thought it not, this is parasitism in its worst and most degrading form. Nor, in spite of its intellectual, not to say moral sin, is this an extreme or exceptional case. It is a case, which is being duplicated every day in our own country, only here the confessing is expressed with a candor which is rare in company with actions betraying so signally the want of it.

The form of parasitism exhibited by a certain section of the narrower Evangelical school is altogether different from that of the Church of Rome. The parasite in this case seeks its shelter, not in a Church, but in a Doctrine or a Creed. Let it be observed again that we are not dealing with the Evangelical Religion, but only with one of its parasitic forms—a form which will at once be recognized by all who know the popular Protestantism of this country. We confine ourselves also at present to that form which finds its encouragement in a single doctrine, that doctrine being the Doctrine of the Atonement—let us say, rather, a perverted form of this central truth.

The perverted Doctrine of the Atonement, which tends to beget the parasitic habit, may be defined in a single sentence—it is very much because it can be defined in a single sentence that it is a perversion. Let us state it in a concrete form. It is put to the individual in the following syllogism: "You believe Christ died for sinners; you are a sinner; therefore Christ died for you; *and hence you are saved.*" Now what is this but another species of molluscan shell? Could any trap for a benighted soul be more ingeniously planned? It is not superstition that is appealed to this time; it is reason. The agitated soul is invited to creep into the convolutions of a syllogism, and entrench itself behind a Doctrine more venerable even than the Church. But words are mere chitin. Doctrines may have no more vital contact with the soul than priest or sacrament, no further influence on life and character than stone and lime. And yet the apostles of parasitism pick a blackguard from the streets, pass him through this plausible formula, and turn him out a convert in the space of as many minutes as it takes to tell it.

The zeal of these men, assuredly, is not to be questioned: their instincts are right, and their work is often not in vain. It is possible, too, up to a certain point, to defend this Salvation by Formula. Are these not the very words of Scripture? Did not Christ Himself say, "It is finished?" And is it not written, "By grace are ye saved through faith," "Not of works, lest any man should boast," and "He that believeth on the Son hath everlasting life?" To which, however, one might also answer in the words of Scripture, "The Devils also believe," and "Except a man be born again he cannot see the Kingdom of God." But without seeming to make text refute text, let us ask rather what the supposed convert possesses at the end of the process. That Christ saves sinners, even blackguards from the streets, is a great fact; and that the simple words of the street evangelist do sometimes bring this home to man with convincing power is also a fact. But in ordinary circumstances, when the inquirer's mind is rapidly urged through the various stages of the above piece of logic, he is left to face the future and blot out the past with a formula of words.

To be sure these words may already convey a germ of truth, they may yet be filled in with a wealth of meaning and become a life-long power. But we would state the case against Salvation by Formula with ignorant and unwarranted clemency did we for a moment convey the idea that this is always the actual result. The doctrine plays too well into the hands of the parasitic tendency to make it possible that in more than a minority of cases the result is anything but disastrous. And it is disastrous not in that, sooner or later, after losing half their lives, those who rely on the naked syllogism come to see their mistake, but in that thousands never come to see it all. Are there not men who can prove to you and to the world, by the irresistible logic of texts, that they are saved, whom you know to be not only unworthy of the Kingdom of God—which we all are—but absolutely incapable of entering it? The condition of membership in the Kingdom of God is well known; who fulfill this condition and who do not, is not well known. And yet the moral test, in spite of the difficulty of its applications, will always, and rightly, be preferred by the world to the theological. Nevertheless, in spite of the world's verdict, the parasite is content. He is "safe." Years ago his mind worked through a certain chain of phrases in which the words "believe" and "saved" were the conspicuous terms. And from that moment, by all Scriptures, by all logic, and by all theology, his future was guaranteed. He took out, in short, an insurance policy, by which he was infallibly secured eternal life at death. This is not a matter to make light of. We wish we were caricaturing instead of representing things as they are. But we carry with us all who intimately know the spiritual condition of the Narrow Church in asserting that in some cases at least its members have nothing more to show for their religion than a formula, a syllogism, a cant phrase or an experience of some kind which happened long ago, and which men told them at the time was called Salvation. Need we proceed to formulate objections to the parasitism of Evangelicism? Between it and the Religion of the Church of Rome there is an affinity as real as it is unsuspected. For one thing these religions are spiritually disastrous as well as theologically erroneous in propagating a false conception of Christianity. The fundamental idea alike of the extreme Roman Catholic and extreme Evangelical Religions is Escape. Man's chief end is to "get off." And all factors in religion, the highest and most sacred, are degraded to this level. God, for example, is a Great Lawyer. Or He is the Almighty Enemy; it is from Him we have to "get off." Jesus Christ is the One who gets us off—a theological figure who contrives so to adjust matters federally that the way is clear. The Church in the one instance is a kind of conveyancing office where the transaction is duly concluded, each party accepting the others' terms; in the other case, a species of sheep-pen where the flock awaits impatiently and indolently the final consummation. Generally, the means are mistaken for the end, and the opening-up of the possibility of spiritual growth becomes the signal to stop growing.

Second, these being cheap religions, are inevitably accompanied by a cheap life. Safety being guaranteed from the first, there remains nothing else to be done. The mechanical way in which the transaction is effected, leaves the soul without stimulus, and the character remains untouched by the moral aspects of the sacrifice of Christ. He who is unjust is unjust still; he who is unholy is unholy still. Thus the whole scheme ministers to the Degeneration of Organs. For here, again, by just as much as the organism borrows mechanically from an external source, by so much exactly does it lose in its own organization. Whatever rest is provided by Christianity for the children of God, it is certainly never contemplated that it should supersede personal effort. And any rest which ministers to indifference is immoral and unreal—it makes parasites and not men. Just because God worketh in him, as the evidence and triumph of it, the true child of God works out his own salvation—works it out having really received it—not as a light thing, a superfluous labor, but with fear and trembling as a reasonable and indispensable service.

If it be asked, then, shall the parasite be saved or shall he not, the answer is that the idea of salvation conveyed by the question makes a reply all but hopeless. But if by salvation is meant, a trusting in Christ *in order to likeness to Christ*, in order to that *holiness* without which no man shall see the Lord, the reply is that the parasite's hope is absolutely vain. So far from ministering to growth, parasitism ministers to decay. So far from ministering to holiness, that is to *wholeness*, parasitism ministers to exactly the opposite. One by one the spiritual faculties droop and die, one by one from lack of exercise the muscles of the soul grow weak and flaccid, one by one the moral activities cease. So from him that hath not, is taken away that which he hath, and after a few years of parasitism there is nothing left to save.

If our meaning up to this point has been sufficiently obscure to make the objection now possible that this protest against Parasitism is opposed to the doctrines of Free Grace, we cannot hope in a closing sentence to free the argument from a suspicion so ill-judged. The adjustment between Faith and Works does not fall within our province now. Salvation truly is the free gift of God, but he who really knows how much this means knows—and just because it means so much—how much of consequent action it involves. With the central doctrines of grace the whole scientific argument is in too wonderful harmony to be found wanting here. The natural life, not less than the eternal, is the gift of God. But life in either case is the beginning of growth and not the end of grace. To pause where we should begin, to retrograde where we should advance, to seek a mechanical security that we may cover inertia and find a wholesale salvation in which there is no personal sanctification—this is Parasitism.

Parasitism

"And so I live, you see,
Go through the world, try, prove, reject,
Prefer, still struggling to effect
My warfare; happy that I can
Be crossed and thwarted as a man,
Not left in God's contempt apart,
With ghastly smooth life, dead at heart,
Tame in earth's paddock as her prize.

Thank God, no paradise stands barred
To entry, and I find it hard
To be a Christian, as I said."—*Browning.*

"Work out your own salvation."—*Paul.*

"Be no longer a chaos, but a World, or even Worldkin. Produce!
Produce! Were it but the pitifullest infinitesimal fraction of a
Product, produce it, in God's name!"—*Carlyle.*

From a study of the habits and organization of the family of Hermit-crabs we have already gained some insight into the nature and effects of parasitism. But the Hermit-crab, be it remembered, is in no real sense a parasite. And before we can apply the general principle further we must address ourselves briefly to the examination of a true case of parasitism.

We have not far to seek. Within the body of the Hermit-crab a minute organism may frequently be discovered resembling, when magnified, a miniature kidney-bean. A bunch of root-like processes hangs from one side, and the extremities of these are seen to ramify in delicate films through the living tissues of the crab. This simple organism is known to the naturalist as a Sacculina; and though a full-grown animal, it consists of no more parts than those just named. Not a trace of structure is to be detected within this rude and all but inanimate frame; it possesses neither legs, nor eyes, nor mouth, nor throat, nor stomach, nor any other organs, external or internal. This Sacculina is a typical parasite. By means of its twining and theftuous roots it imbibes automatically its nourishment ready-prepared from the body of the crab. It boards indeed entirely at the expense of its host, who supplies it liberally with food and shelter and everything else it wants. So far as the result to itself is concerned this arrangement may seem at first sight satisfactory enough; but when we inquire into the life history of this small creature we unearth a career of degeneracy all but unparalleled in nature.

The most certain clue to what nature meant any animal to become is to be learned from its embryology. Let us, therefore, examine for a moment the earliest positive stage in the development of the Sacculina. When the embryo first makes its appearance it bears not the remotest resemblance to the adult animal. A different name even is given to it by the biologist, who knows it at this period as a Nauplius. This minute organism has an oval body, supplied with six well-jointed feet by means of which it paddles briskly through the water. For a time it leads an active and independent life, industriously securing its own food and escaping enemies by its own gallantry. But soon a change takes place. The hereditary taint of parasitism is in its blood, and it proceeds to adapt itself to the pauper habits of its race. The tiny body first doubles in upon itself, and from the two front limbs elongated filaments protrude. Its four hind limbs entirely disappear, and twelve short-forked swimming organs temporarily take their place. Thus strangely metamorphosed the Sacculina sets out in search of a suitable host, and in an evil hour, by that fate which is always ready to accommodate the transgressor, is thrown into the company of the Hermit-crab. With its two filamentary processes—which afterward develop into the root-like organs—it penetrates the body; the sac-like form is gradually assumed; the whole of the swimming feet drop off—they will never be needed again—and the animal settles down for the rest of its life as a parasite.

One reason which makes a zoologist certain that the Sacculina is a degenerate type is, that in almost all other instances of animals which begin life in the Nauplius-form—and there are several—the Nauplius develops through higher and higher stages, and arrives finally at the high perfection displayed by the shrimp, lobster, crab, and other crustaceans. But instead of rising to its opportunities, the sacculine Nauplius having reached a certain point turned back. It shrunk from the struggle for life, and beginning probably by seeking shelter from its host went on to demand its food; and so falling from bad to worse, became in time an entire dependant.

In the eyes of Nature this was a twofold crime. It was first a disregard of evolution, and second, which is practically the same thing, an evasion of the great law of work. And the revenge of Nature was therefore necessary. It could not help punishing the Sacculina for violated law, and the punishment, according to the strange and noteworthy way in which Nature usually punishes, was meted but by natural processes, carried on within its own organization. Its punishment was simply that it was a Sacculina—that it was a Sacculina when it might have been a Crustacean. Instead of being a free and independent organism high in structure, original in action, vital with energy, it deteriorated into a torpid and all but amorphous sac confined to perpetual imprisonment and doomed to a living death. "Any new set of conditions," says Ray Lankester, "occurring to an animal which render its food and safety very easily attained, seem to lead as a rule to degeneration; just as an active healthy man sometimes degenerates when he becomes suddenly possessed of a fortune; or as Rome degenerated when possessed of the riches of the ancient world. The habit of parasitism clearly acts upon animal organization in this way. Let the parasitic life once be secured, and away go legs, jaws, eyes, and ears; the active, highly-gifted crab, insect or annelid may become a mere sac, absorbing nourishment and laying eggs."

There could be no more impressive illustration than this of what with entire appropriateness one might call "the physiology of backsliding." We fail to appreciate the meaning of spiritual degeneration or detect the terrible nature of the consequences only because they evade the eye of sense. But could we investigate the spirit as a living organism, or study the soul of the backslider on principles of comparative anatomy, we should have a revelation of the organic effects of sin, even of the mere sin of carelessness as to growth and work, which must revolutionize our ideas of practical religion. There is no room for the doubt even that what goes on in the body does not with equal certainty take place in the spirit under the corresponding conditions.

The penalty of backsliding is not something unreal and vague, some unknown quantity which may be measured out to us disproportionately, or which perchance, since God is good, we may altogether evade. The consequences are already marked within the structure of the soul. So to speak, they are physiological. The thing affected by our indifference or by our indulgence is not the book of final judgment but the present fabric of the soul. The punishment of degeneration is simply degeneration—the loss of functions, the decay of organs, the atrophy of the spiritual nature. It is well known that the recovery of the backslider is one of the hardest problems in spiritual work. To reinvigorate an old organ seems more difficult and hopeless than to develop a new one; and the backslider's terrible lot is to have to retrace with enfeebled feet each step of the way along which he strayed; to make up inch by inch the lee-way he has lost, carrying with him a dead-weight of acquired reluctance, and scarce knowing whether to be stimulated or discouraged by the oppressive memory of the previous fall.

We are not, however, to discuss at present the physiology of backsliding. Nor need we point out at greater length that parasitism is always and indissolubly accompanied by degeneration. We wish rather to examine one or two leading tendencies of the modern religious life which directly or indirectly induce the parasitic habit and bring upon thousands of unsuspecting victims such secret and appalling penalties as have been named.

Two main causes are known to the biologist as tending to induce the parasitic habit. These are, first, the temptation to secure safety without the vital exercise of faculties, and, second, the disposition to find food without earning it. The first, which we have formally considered, is probably the preliminary stage in most cases. The animal, seeking shelter, finds unexpectedly that it can also thereby gain a certain measure of food. Compelled in the first instance, perhaps by stress of circumstances, to rob its host of a meal or perish, it gradually acquires the habit of drawing all its supplies from the same source, and thus becomes in time a confirmed parasite. Whatever be its origin, however, it is certain that the main evil of parasitism is connected with the further question of food. Mere safety with Nature is a secondary, though by no means an insignificant, consideration. And while the organism forfeits a part of its organization by any method of evading enemies which demands no personal effort, the most entire degeneration of the whole system follows the neglect or abuse of the functions of nutrition.

The direction in which we have to seek the wider application of the subject will now appear. We have to look into those cases in the moral and spiritual sphere in which the functions of nutrition are either neglected or abused. To sustain life, physical, mental, moral, or spiritual, some sort of food is essential. To secure an adequate supply each organism also is provided with special and appropriate faculties. But the final gain to the organism does not depend so much on the actual amount of food procured as on the exercise required to obtain it. In one sense the exercise is only a means to an end, namely, the finding food; but in another and equally real sense, the exercise is the end, the food the means to attain that. Neither is of permanent use without the other, but the correlation between them is so intimate that it were idle to say that one is more necessary than the other. Without food exercise is impossible, but without exercise food is useless.

Thus exercise is in order to food, and food is in order to exercise—in order especially to that further progress and maturity which only ceaseless activity can promote. Now food too easily acquired means food without that accompaniment of discipline which is infinitely more valuable than the food itself. It means the possibility of a life which is a mere existence. It leaves the organism *in statu quo*, undeveloped, immature, low in the scale of organization and with a growing tendency to pass from the state of equilibrium to that of increasing degeneration. What an organism is depends upon what it does; its activities make it. And if the stimulus to the exercise of all the innumerable faculties concerned in nutrition be withdrawn by the conditions and circumstances of life becoming, or being made to become, too easy, there is first an arrest of development, and finally a loss of the parts themselves. If, in short, an organism does nothing, in that relation it is nothing.

We may, therefore, formulate the general principle thus: *Any principle which secures food to the individual without the expenditure of work is injurious, and accompanied by the degeneration and loss of parts.*

The social and political analogies of this law, which have been casually referred to already, are sufficiently familiar to render any further development in these directions superfluous. After the eloquent preaching of the Gospel of Work by Thomas Carlyle, this century at least can never plead that one of the most important moral bearings of the subject has not been duly impressed upon it. All that can be said of idleness generally might be fitly urged in support of this great practical truth. All nations which have prematurely passed away, buried in graves dug by their own effeminacy; all those individuals who have secured a hasty wealth by the chances of speculation; all children of fortune; all victims of inheritance; all social sponges; all satellites of the court; all beggars of the market-place—all these are living and unlying witness to the unalterable retributions of the law of parasitism. But it is when we come to study the working of the principle in the religious sphere there we discover the full extent of the ravages which the parasitic habit can make on the souls of men. We can only hope to indicate here one or two of the things in modern Christianity which minister most subtly and widely to this as yet all but unnamed sin.

We begin in what may seem a somewhat unlooked-for quarter. One of the things in the religious world which tends most strongly to induce the parasitic habit is *Going to Church*. Church-going itself every Christian will rightly consider an invaluable aid to the ripe development of the spiritual life. Public worship has a place in the national religious life so firmly established that nothing is ever likely to shake its influence. So supreme indeed, is the ecclesiastical system in all Christian countries that with thousands the religion of the Church and the religion of the individual are one. But just because of its high and unique place in religious regard, does it become men from time to time to inquire how far the Church is really ministering to the spiritual health of the immense religious community which looks to it as its foster-mother. And if it falls to us here reluctantly to expose some secret abuses of this venerable system, let it be well understood that these are abuses, and not that the sacred institution itself is being violated by the attack of an impious hand.

The danger of church-going largely depends on the form of worship, but it may be affirmed that even the most perfect Church affords to all worshipers a greater or less temptation to parasitism. It consists essentially in the deputy-work or deputy-worship inseparable from the church or chapel ministrations. One man is set apart to prepare a certain amount of spiritual truth for the rest. He, if he is a true man, gets all the benefits of original work. He finds the truth, digests it, is nourished and enriched by it before he offers it to his flock. To a large extent it will nourish and enrich in turn a number of his hearers. But still they will lack something. The faculty of selecting truth at first hand and appropriating it for one's self is a lawful possession to every Christian. Rightly exercised it conveys to him truth in its freshest form; it offers him the opportunity of verifying doctrines for himself; it makes religion personal; it deepens and intensifies the only convictions that are worth deepening, those, namely, which are honest; and it supplies the mind with a basis of certainty in religion. But if all one's truth is derived by imbibition from the Church, the faculties for receiving truth are not only undeveloped but one's whole view of truth becomes distorted. He who abandons the personal search for truth, under whatever pretext, abandons truth. The very word truth, by becoming the limited possession of a guild, ceases to have any meaning; and faith, which can only be founded on truth, gives way to credulity, resting on mere opinion.

In those churches especially where all parts of the worship are subordinated to the sermon, this species of parasitism is peculiarly encouraged. What is meant to be a stimulus to thought becomes the substitute for it. The hearer never really learns, he only listens. And while truth and knowledge seem to increase, life and character are left in arrear. Such truth, of course, and such knowledge, are a mere seeming. Having cost nothing, they come to nothing. The organism acquires a growing immobility, and finally exists in a state of entire intellectual helplessness and inertia. So the parasitic Church-member, the literal "adherent," comes not merely to live only within the circle of ideas of his minister, but to be content that his minister has these ideas—like the literary parasite who fancies he knows everything because he has a good library.

Where the worship, again, is largely liturgical the danger assumes an even more serious form, and it acts in some such way as this. Every sincere man who sets out in the Christian race begins by attempting to exercise the spiritual faculties for himself. The young life throbs in his veins, and he sets himself to the further progress with earnest purpose and resolute will. For a time he bids fair to attain a high and original development. But the temptation to relax the always difficult effort at spirituality is greater than he knows. The "carnal mind" itself is "enmity against God," and the antipathy, or the deadlier apathy within, is unexpectedly encouraged from that very outside source from which he anticipates the greatest help. Connecting himself with a Church he is no less interested than surprised to find how rich is the provision there for every part of his spiritual nature. Each service satisfies or surfeits. Twice, or even three times a week, this feast is spread for him. The thoughts are deeper than his own, the faith keener, the worship loftier, the whole ritual more reverent and splendid. What more natural than that he should gradually exchange his personal religion for that of the congregation? What more likely than that a public religion should by insensible stages supplant his individual faith? What more simple than to content himself with the warmth of another's soul. What more tempting than to give up private prayer for the easier worship of the liturgy or of the church? What, in short, more natural than for the independent, free-moving, growing Sacculina to degenerate into the listless, useless, pampered parasite of the pew? The very means he takes to nurse his personal religion often come in time to wean him from it. Hanging admiringly, or even enthusiastically, on the lips of eloquence, his senses now stirred by ceremony, now soothed by music, the parasite of the pew enjoys his weekly worship—his character untouched, his will unbraced, his crude soul unquickened and unimproved. Thus, instead of ministering to the growth of individual members, and very often just in proportion to the superior excellence of the provision made for them by another, does this gigantic system of deputy-nutrition tend to destroy development and arrest the genuine culture of the soul. Our churches overflow with members who are mere consumers. Their interest in religion is purely parasitic. Their only spiritual exercise is the automatic one of imbibition, the clergyman being the faithful Hermit-crab who is to be depended on every Sunday for at least a week's supply.

A physiologist would describe the organism resulting from such a progress as a case of "arrested development." Instead of having learned to pray, the ecclesiastical parasite becomes satisfied with being prayed for. His transactions with the Eternal are effected by commission. His work for Christ is done by a paid deputy. His whole life is a prolonged indulgence in the bounties of the Church; and surely—in some cases at least the crowning irony—he sends for the minister when he lies down to die.

Other signs and consequences of this species of parasitism soon become very apparent. The first symptom is idleness. When a Church is off its true diet it is off its true work. Hence one explanation of the hundreds of large and influential congregations ministered to from week to week by men of eminent learning and earnestness, which yet do little or nothing in the line of these special activities for which all churches exist. An outstanding man at the head of a huge, useless and torpid congregation is always a puzzle. But is the reason not this, that the congregation gets too good food too cheap? Providence has mercifully delivered the Church from too many great men in her pulpits, but there are enough in every country-side to play the host disastrously to a large circle of otherwise able-bodied Christian people, who, thrown on their own resources, might fatten themselves and help others. There are compensations to a flock for a poor minister after all. Where the fare is indifferent those who are really hungry will exert themselves to procure their own supply.

That the Church has indispensable functions to discharge to the individual is not denied; but taking into consideration the universal tendency to parasitism in the human soul it is a grave question whether in some cases it does not really effect more harm than good. A dead church certainly, a church having no reaction on the community, a church without propagative power in the world, cannot be other than a calamity to all within its borders. Such a church is an institution, first for making, then for screening parasites; and instead of representing to the world the Kingdom of God on earth, it is despised alike by godly and by godless men as the refuge for fear and formalism and the nursery of superstition.

And this suggests a second and not less practical evil of a parasitic piety—that it presents to the world a false conception of the religion of Christ. One notices with a frequency which may well excite alarm that the children of church-going parents often break away as they grow in intelligence, not only from church-connection but from the whole system of family religion. In some cases this is doubtless due to natural perversity, but in others it certainly arises from the hollowness of the outward forms which pass current in society and at home for vital Christianity. These spurious forms, fortunately or unfortunately, soon betray themselves. How little there is in them becomes gradually apparent. And rather than indulge in a sham the budding sceptic, as the first step, parts with the form and in nine cases out of ten concerns himself no further to find a substitute. Quite deliberately, quite honestly, sometimes with real regret and even at personal sacrifice he takes up his position, and to his parent's sorrow and his church's dishonor forsakes forever the faith and religion of his fathers. Who will deny that this is a true account of the natural history of much modern scepticism? A formal religion can never hold its own in the nineteenth century. It is better that it should not. We must either be real or cease to be. We must either give up our Parasitism or our sons.

Any one who will take the trouble to investigate a number of cases where whole families of outwardly godly parents have gone astray, will probably find that the household religion had either some palpable defect, or belonged essentially to the parasitic order. The popular belief that the sons of clergymen turn out worse than those of the laity is, of course, without foundation; but it may also probably be verified that in the instances where clergymen's sons notoriously discredit their father's ministry, that ministry in a majority of cases, will be found to be professional and theological rather than human and spiritual. Sequences in the moral and spiritual world follow more closely than we yet discern the great law of Heredity. The Parasite begets the Parasite—only in the second generation the offspring are sometimes sufficiently wise to make the discovery, and honest enough to proclaim it.

We now pass on to the consideration of another form of Parasitism which though closely related to that just discussed, is of sufficient importance to justify a separate reference. Appealing to a somewhat smaller circle, but affecting it not less disastrously, is the Parasitism induced by certain abuses of *Systems of Theology*.

In its own place, of course, Theology is no more to be dispensed with than the Church. In every perfect religious system three great departments must always be represented—criticism, dogmatism, and evangelism. Without the first there is no guarantee of truth, without the second no defence of truth, and without the third no propagation of truth. But when these departments become mixed up, when their separate functions are forgotten, when one is made to do duty for another, or where either is developed by the church or the individual at the expense of the rest, the result is fatal. The particular abuse, however, of which we have now to speak, concerns the tendency in orthodox communities, first to exalt orthodoxy above all other elements in religion, and secondly to make the possession of sound beliefs equivalent to the possession of truth.

Doctrinal preaching, fortunately, as a constant practice is less in vogue than in a former age, but there are still large numbers whose only contact with religion is through theological forms. The method is supported by a plausible defence. What is doctrine but a compressed form of truth, systematized by able and pious men, and sanctioned by the imprimatur of the Church? If the greatest minds of the Church's past, having exercised themselves profoundly upon the problems of religion, formulated as with one voice a system of doctrine, why should the humble inquirer not gratefully accept it? Why go over the ground again? Why with his dim light should he betake himself afresh to Bible study and with so great a body of divinity already compiled, presume himself to be still a seeker after truth? Does not Theology give him Bible truth in reliable, convenient, and moreover, in logical propositions? There it lies extended to the last detail in the tomes of the Fathers, or abridged in a hundred modern compendia, ready-made to his hand, all cut and dry, guaranteed sound and wholesome, why not use it?

Just because it is all cut and dry. Just because it is ready-made. Just because it lies there in reliable, convenient and logical propositions. The moment you appropriate truth in such a shape you appropriate a form. You cannot cut and dry truth. You cannot accept truth ready-made without it ceasing to nourish the soul as the truth. You cannot live on theological forms without becoming a Parasite and ceasing to be a man.

There is no worse enemy to a living Church than a propositional theology, with the latter controlling the former by traditional authority. For one does not then receive the truth for himself, he accepts it bodily. He begins the Christian life set up by his Church with a stock-in-trade which has cost him nothing, and which, though it may serve him all his life, is just exactly worth as much his belief in his Church. This possession of truth, moreover, thus lightly won, is given to him as infallible. It is a system. There is nothing to add to it. At his peril let him question or take from it. To start a convert in life with such a principle is unspeakably degrading. All through life instead of working toward truth he must work from it. An infallible standard is a temptation to a mechanical faith. Infallibility always paralyzes. It gives rest; but it is the rest of stagnation. Men perform one great act of faith at the beginning of their life, then have done with it forever. All moral, intellectual and spiritual effort is over; and a cheap theology ends in a cheap life.

The same thing that makes men take refuge in the Church of Rome makes them take refuge in a set of dogmas. Infallibility meets the deepest desire of man, but meets it in the most fatal form. Men deal with the hunger after truth in two ways. First by Unbelief—which crushes it by blind force; or, secondly, by resorting to some external source credited with Infallibility—which lulls it to sleep by blind faith. The effect of a doctrinal theology is the effect of Infallibility. And the wholesale belief in such a system, however accurate it may be—grant even that it were infallible—is not Faith though it always gets that name. It is mere Credulity. It is a complacent and idle rest upon authority, not a hard-earned, self-obtained, personal possession. The moral responsibility here, besides, is reduced to nothing. Those who framed the Thirty-nine Articles or the Westminster Confession are responsible. And anything which destroys responsibility, or transfers it, cannot be other than injurious in its moral tendency and useless in itself.

It may be objected perhaps that this statement of the paralysis spiritual and mental induced by Infallibility applies also to the Bible. The answer is that though the Bible is infallible, the Infallibility is not in such a form as to become a temptation. There is the widest possible difference between the form of truth in the Bible and the form in theology.

In theology truth is propositional—tied up in neat parcels, systematized, and arranged in logical order. The Trinity is an intricate doctrinal problem. The Supreme Being is discussed in terms of philosophy. The Atonement is a formula which is to be demonstrated like a proposition in Euclid. And Justification is to be worked out as a question of jurisprudence. There is no necessary connection between these doctrines and the life of him who holds them. They make him orthodox, not necessarily righteous. They satisfy the intellect but need not touch the heart. It does not, in short, take a religious man to be a theologian. It simply takes a man with fair reasoning powers. This man happens to apply these powers to theological subjects—but in no other sense than he might apply them to astronomy or physics. But truth in the Bible is a fountain. It is a diffused nutriment, so diffused that no one can put himself off with the form. It is reached not by thinking, but by doing. It is seen, discerned, not demonstrated. It cannot be bolted whole, but must be slowly absorbed into the system. Its vagueness to the mere intellect, its refusal to be packed into portable phrases, its satisfying unsatisfyingness, its vast atmosphere, its finding of us, its mystical hold of us, these are the tokens of its infinity.

Nature never provides for man's wants in any direction, bodily, mental, or spiritual, in such a form as that he can simply accept her gifts automatically. She puts all the mechanical powers at his disposal—but he must make his lever. She gives him corn, but he must grind it. She elaborates coal, but he must dig for it. Corn is perfect, all the products of Nature are perfect, but he has everything to do to them before he can use them. So with truth; it is perfect, infallible. But he cannot use it as it stands. He must work, think, separate, dissolve, absorb, digest; and most of these he must do for himself and within himself. If it be replied that this is exactly what theology does, we answer it is exactly what it does not. It simply does what the green-grocer does when he arranges his apples and plums in his shop window. He may tell me a magnum bonum from a Victoria, or a Baldwin from a Newtown Pippin. But he does not help me to eat it. His information is useful, and for scientific horticulture essential. Should a sceptical pomologist deny that there was such a thing as a Baldwin, or mistake it for a Newtown Pippin, we should be glad to refer to him; but if we were hungry, and an orchard were handy, we should not trouble him. Truth in the Bible is an orchard rather than a museum. Dogmatism will be very valuable to us when scientific necessity makes us go to the museum. Criticism will be very useful in seeing that only fruit-bearers grow in the orchard. But truth in the doctrinal form is not natural, proper, assimilable food for the soul of man.

Is this a plea then for doubt? Yes, for that philosophic doubt which is the evidence of a faculty doing its own work. It is more necessary for us to be active than to be orthodox. To be orthodox is what we wish to be, but we can only truly reach it by being honest, by being original, by seeing with our own eyes, by believing with our own heart. "An idle life," says Goethe, "is death anticipated." Better far be burned at the stake of Public Opinion than die the living death of Parasitism. Better an aberrant theology than a suppressed organization. Better a little faith dearly won, better launched alone on the infinite bewilderment of Truth, than perish on the splendid plenty of the richest creeds. Such Doubt is no self-willed presumption. Nor, truly exercised, will it prove itself, as much doubt does, the synonym for sorrow. It aims at a life-long learning, prepared for any sacrifice of will yet for none of independence; at that high progressive education which yields rest in work and work in rest, and the development of immortal faculties in both; at that deeper faith which believes in the vastness and variety of the revelations of God, and their accessibility to all obedient hearts.

Classification

"I judge of the order of the world, although I know not its end, because to judge of this order I only need mutually to compare the parts, to study their functions, their relations, and to remark their concert. I know not why the universe exists, but I do not desist from seeing how it is modified; I do not cease to see the intimate agreement by which the beings that compose it render a mutual help. I am like a man who should see for the first time an open watch, who should not cease to admire the workmanship of it, although he knows not the use of the machine, and had never seen dials. I do not know, he would say, what all this is for, but I see that each piece is made for the others; I admire the worker in the detail of his work, and I am very sure that all these wheelworks only go thus in concert for a common end which I cannot perceive."—*Rousseau.*

"That which is born of the flesh is flesh; and that which is born of the Spirit is spirit."—*Christ.*

"In early attempts to arrange organic beings in some systematic manner, we see at first a guidance by conspicuous and simple characters, and a tendency toward arrangement in linear order. In successively later attempts, we see more regard paid to combinations of character which are essential but often inconspicuous; and a gradual abandonment of a linear arrangement."—*Herbert Spencer.*

On one of the shelves in a certain museum lie two small boxes filled with earth. A low mountain in Arran has furnished the first; the contents of the second came from the Island of Barbadoes. When examined with a pocket lens, the Arran earth is found to be full of small objects, clear as crystal, fashioned by some mysterious geometry into forms of exquisite symmetry. The substance is silica, a natural glass; and the prevailing shape is a six-sided prism capped at either end by little pyramids modeled with consummate grace.

When the second specimen is examined, the revelation is, if possible, more surprising. Here, also, is a vast assemblage of small glassy or porcelaneous objects built up into curious forms. The material, chemically, remains the same, but the angles of pyramid and prism have given place to curved lines, so that the contour is entirely different. The appearance is that of a vast collection of microscopic urns, goblets, and vases, each richly ornamented with small sculptured discs or perforations which are disposed over the pure white surface in regular belts and rows. Each tiny urn is chiseled into the most faultless proportion, and the whole presents a vision of magic beauty.

Judged by the standard of their loveliness there is little to choose between these two sets of objects. Yet there is one cardinal difference between them. They belong to different worlds. The last belong to the living world, the former to the dead. The first are crystals, the last are shells.

No power on earth can make these little urns of the *Polycystina* except Life. We can melt them down in the laboratory, but no ingenuity of chemistry can reproduce their sculptured forms. We are sure that Life has formed them, however, for tiny creatures allied to those which made the Barbadoes' earth are living still, fashioning their fairy palaces of flint in the same mysterious way. On the other hand, chemistry has no difficulty in making these crystals. We can melt down this Arran earth and reproduce the pyramids and prisms in endless numbers. Nay, if we do melt it down, we cannot help reproducing the pyramid and the prism. There is a six-sidedness, as it were, in the very nature of this substance which will infallibly manifest itself if the crystallizing substance only be allowed fair play. This six-sided tendency is its Law of Crystallization—a law of its nature which it cannot resist. But in the crystal there is nothing at all corresponding to Life. There is simply an inherent force which can be called into action at any moment, and which cannot be separated from the particles in which it resides. The crystal may be ground to pieces, but this force remains intact. And even after being reduced to powder, and running the gauntlet of every process in the chemical laboratory, the moment the substance is left to itself under possible conditions it will proceed to recrystallize anew. But if the Polycystine urn be broken, no inorganic agency can build it up again. So far as any inherent urn-building power, analogous to the crystalline force, is concerned, it might lie there in a shapeless mass forever. That which modeled it at first is gone from it. It was Vital; while the force which built the crystal was only Molecular.

From an artistic point of view this distinction is of small importance. Æsthetically, the Law of Crystallization is probably as useful in ministering to natural beauty as Vitality. What are more beautiful than the crystals of a snowflake? Or what frond of fern or feather of bird can vie with the tracery of the frost upon a window-pane? Can it be said that the lichen is more lovely than the striated crystals of the granite on which it grows, or the moss on the mountain side more satisfying than the hidden amethyst and cairngorm in the rock beneath? Or is the botanist more astonished when his microscope reveals the architecture of spiral tissue in the stem of a plant, or the mineralogist who beholds for the first time the chaos of beauty in the sliced specimen of some common stone? So far as beauty goes the organic world and the inorganic are one.

To the man of science, however, this identity of beauty signifies nothing. His concern, in the first instance, is not with the forms but with the natures of things. It is no valid answer to him, when he asks the difference between the moss and the cairngorm, the frost-work and the fern, to be assured that both are beautiful. For no fundamental distinction in Science depends upon beauty. He wants an answer in terms of chemistry, are they organic or inorganic? or in terms of biology, are they living or dead? But when he is told that the one is living and the other dead, he is in possession of a characteristic and fundamental scientific distinction. From this point of view, however much they may possess in common of material substance and beauty, they are separated from one another by a wide and unbridged gulf. The classification of these forms, therefore, depends upon the standpoint, and we should pronounce them like or unlike, related or unrelated, according as we judged them from the point of view of Art or of Science.

The drift of these introductory paragraphs must already be apparent. We propose to inquire whether among men, clothed apparently with a common beauty of character, there may not yet be distinctions as radical as between the crystal and the shell; and, further, whether the current classification of men, based upon Moral Beauty, is wholly satisfactory either from the standpoint of Science or of Christianity. Here, for example, are two characters, pure and elevated, adorned with conspicuous virtues, stirred by lofty impulses, and commanding a spontaneous admiration from all who look on them—may not this similarity of outward form be accompanied by a total dissimilarity of inward nature? Is the external appearance the truest criterion of the ultimate nature? Or, as in the crystal and the shell, may there not exist distinctions more profound and basal? The distinctions drawn between men, in short, are commonly based on the outward appearance of goodness or badness, on the ground of moral beauty or moral deformity—is this classification scientific? Or is there a deeper distinction between the Christian and the not-a-Christian as fundamental as that between the organic and the inorganic?

There can be little doubt, to begin with, that with the great majority of people religion is regarded as essentially one with morality. Whole schools of philosophy have treated the Christian Religion as a question of beauty, and discussed its place among other systems of ethics. Even those systems of theology which profess to draw a deeper distinction have rarely succeeded in establishing it upon any valid basis, or seem even to have made that distinction perceptible to others. So little, indeed, has the rationale of the science of religion been understood that there is still no more unsatisfactory province in theology than where morality and religion are contrasted, and the adjustment attempted between moral philosophy and what are known as the doctrines of grace.

Examples of this confusion are so numerous that if one were to proceed to proof he would have to cite almost the entire European philosophy of the last three hundred years. From Spinoza downward through the whole naturalistic school, Moral Beauty is persistently regarded as synonymous with religion and the spiritual life. The most earnest thinking of the present day is steeped in the same confusion. We have even the remarkable spectacle presented to us just now of a sublime Morality-Religion divorced from Christianity altogether, and wedded to the baldest form of materialism. It is claimed, moreover, that the moral scheme of this high atheism is loftier and more perfect than that of Christianity, and men are asked to take their choice as if the morality were everything, the Christianity or the atheism which nourished it being neither here nor there. Others, again, studying this moral beauty carefully, have detected a something in its Christian forms which has compelled them to declare that a distinction certainly exists. But in scarcely a single instance is the gravity of the distinction more than dimly apprehended. Few conceive of it as other than a difference of degree, or could give a more definite account of it than Mr. Matthew Arnold's "Religion is morality touched by Emotion"—an utterance significant mainly as the testimony of an acute mind that a distinction of some kind does exist. In a recent Symposium, where the question as to "The influence upon Morality of a decline in Religious Belief," was discussed at length by writers of whom this century is justly proud, there appears scarcely so much as a recognition of the fathomless chasm separating the leading terms of debate.

If beauty is the criterion of religion, this view of the relation of religion to morality is justified. But what if there be the same difference in the beauty of two separate characters that there is between the mineral and the shell? What if there be a moral beauty and a spiritual beauty? What answer shall we get if we demand a more scientific distinction between characters than that based on mere outward form? It is not enough from the standpoint of biological religion to say of two characters that both are beautiful. For, again, no fundamental distinction in Science depends upon beauty. We ask an answer in terms of biology, are they flesh or spirit; are they living or dead?

If this is really a scientific question, if it is a question not of moral philosophy only, but of biology, we are compelled to repudiate beauty as the criterion of spirituality. It is not, of course, meant by this that spirituality is not morally beautiful. Spirituality must be morally very beautiful—so much so that popularly one is justified in judging of religion by its beauty. Nor is it meant that morality is not *a* criterion. All that is contended for is that, from the scientific standpoint, it is not *the* criterion. We can judge of the crystal and the shell from many other standpoints besides those named, each classification having an importance in its own sphere. Thus we might class them according to their size and weight, their percentage of silica, their use in the arts, or their commercial value. Each science or art is entitled to regard them from its own point of view; and when the biologist announces his classification he does not interfere with those based on other grounds. Only, having chosen his standpoint, he is bound to frame his classification in terms of it.

It may be well to state emphatically, that in proposing a new classification—or rather, in reviving the primitive one—in the spiritual sphere we leave untouched, as of supreme value in its own province, the test of morality. Morality is certainly a test of religion—for most practical purposes the very best test. And so far from tending to depreciate morality, the bringing into prominence of the true basis is entirely in its interests—in the interests of a moral beauty, indeed, infinitely surpassing the highest attainable perfection on merely natural lines.

The warrant for seeking a further classification is twofold. It is a principle in science that classification should rest on the most basal characteristics. To determine what these are may not always be easy, but it is at least evident that a classification framed on the ultimate nature of organisms must be more distinctive than one based on external characters. Before the principles of classification were understood, organisms were invariably arranged according to some merely external resemblance. Thus plants were classed according to size as Herbs, Shrubs, and Trees; and animals according to their appearance as Birds, Beasts, and Fishes. The Bat upon this principle was a bird, the Whale a fish; and so thoroughly artificial were these early systems that animals were often tabulated among the plants, and plants among the animals. "In early attempts," says Herbert Spencer, "to arrange organic beings in some systematic matter, we see at first a guidance by conspicuous and simple characters, and a tendency toward arrangement in linear order. In successively later attempts, we see more regard paid to combinations of characters which are essential but often inconspicuous; and a gradual abandonment of a linear arrangement for an arrangement in divergent groups and re-divergent sub-groups." Almost all the natural sciences have already passed through these stages; and one or two which rested entirely on external characters have all but ceased to exist—Conchology, for example, which has yielded its place to Malacology. Following in the wake of the other sciences, the classifications of Theology may have to be remodeled in the same way. The popular classification, whatever its merits from a practical point of view, is essentially a classification based on Morphology. The whole tendency of science now is to include along with morphological considerations the profounder generalizations of Physiology and Embryology. And the contribution of the latter science especially has been found so important that biology henceforth must look for its classification largely to Embryological characters.

But apart from the demand of modern scientific culture it is palpably foreign to Christianity, not merely as a Philosophy but as a Biology, to classify men only in terms of the former. And it is somewhat remarkable that the writers of both the Old and New Testaments seem to have recognized the deeper basis. The favorite classification of the Old Testament was into "the nations which knew God" and "the nations which knew not God"—a distinction which we have formerly seen to be, at bottom, biological. In the New Testament again the ethical characters are more prominent, but the cardinal distinctions based on regeneration, if not always actually referred to, are throughout kept in view, both in the sayings of Christ and in the Epistles.

What then is the deeper distinction drawn by Christianity? What is the essential difference between the Christian and the not-a-Christian, between the spiritual beauty and the moral beauty? It is the distinction between the Organic and the Inorganic. Moral beauty is the product of the natural man, spiritual beauty of the spiritual man. And these two, according to the law of Biogenesis, are separated from one another by the deepest line known to Science. This Law is at once the foundation of Biology and of Spiritual religion. And the whole fabric of Christianity falls into confusion if we attempt to ignore it. The Law of Biogenesis, in fact, is to be regarded as the equivalent in biology of the First Law of motion in physics: *Every body continues in its state of rest or of uniform motion in a straight line, except in so far as it is compelled by force to change that state.* The first Law of biology is: That which is Mineral is Mineral; that which is Flesh is Flesh; that which is Spirit is Spirit. The mineral remains in the inorganic world until it is seized upon by a something called Life outside the inorganic world; the natural man remains the natural man, until a Spiritual Life from without the natural life seizes upon him, regenerates him, changes him into a spiritual man. The peril of the illustration from the law of motion will not be felt at least by those who appreciate the distinction between Physics and biology, between Energy and Life. The change of state here is not as in physics a mere change of direction, the affections directed to a new object, the will into a new channel. The change involves all this, but is something deeper. It is a change of nature, a regeneration, a passing from death into life. Hence relatively to this higher life the natural life is no longer Life, but Death, and the natural man from the standpoint of Christianity is dead. Whatever assent the mind may give to this proposition, however much it has been overlooked in the past, however it compares with casual observation, it is certain that the Founder of the Christian religion intended this to be the keystone of Christianity. In the proposition *That which is flesh is flesh, and that which is spirit is spirit,* Christ formulates the first law of biological religion, and lays the basis for a final classification. He divides men into two classes, the living and the not-living. And Paul afterward carries out the classification consistently, making his entire system depend on it, and throughout arranging men, on the one hand as {pneumatikos}—spiritual, on the other as {psychikos}—carnal, in terms of Christ's distinction.

Suppose now it be granted for a moment that the character of the not-a-Christian is as beautiful as that of the Christian. This is simply to say that the crystal is as beautiful as the organism. One is quite entitled to hold this; but what he is not entitled to hold is that both in the same sense are living. *He that hath the Son hath Life, and he that hath not the Son of God hath not Life.* And in the face of this law, no other conclusion is possible than that that which is flesh remains flesh. No matter how great the development of beauty, that which is flesh is withal flesh. The elaborateness or the perfection of the moral development in any given instance can do nothing to break down this distinction. Man is a moral animal, and can, and ought to, arrive at great natural beauty of character. But this is simply to obey the law of his nature—the law of his flesh; and no progress along that line can project him into the spiritual sphere. If any one choose to claim that the mineral beauty, the fleshly beauty, the natural moral beauty, is all he covets, he is entitled to his claim. To be good and true, pure and benevolent in the moral sphere, are high and, so far, legitimate objects of life. If he deliberately stop here, he is at liberty to do so. But what he is not entitled to do is to call himself a Christian, or to claim to discharge the functions peculiar to the Christian life. His morality is mere crystallization, the crystallizing forces having had fair play in his development. But these forces have no more touched the sphere of Christianity than the frost on the window-pane can do more than simulate the external forms of life. And if he considers that the high development to which he has reached may pass by an insensible transition into spirituality, or that his moral nature of itself may flash into the flame of regenerate Life, he has to be reminded that in spite of the apparent connection of these things from one standpoint, from another there is none at all, or none discoverable by us. On the one hand, there being no such thing as Spontaneous Generation, his moral nature, however it may encourage it, cannot generate Life; while, on the other, his high organization can never in itself result in Life, Life being always the cause of organization and never the effect of it.

The practical question may now be asked, is this distinction palpable? Is it a mere conceit of Science, or what human interests attach to it? If it cannot be proved that the resulting moral or spiritual beauty is higher in the one case than in the other, the biological distinction is useless. And if the objection is pressed that the spiritual man has nothing further to effect in the direction of morality, seeing that the natural man can successfully compete with him, the questions thus raised become of serious significance. That objection would certainly be fatal which could show that the spiritual world was not as high in its demand for a lofty morality as the natural; and that biology would be equally false and dangerous which should in the least encourage the view that "without holiness" a man could "see the Lord." These questions accordingly we must briefly consider. It is necessary to premise, however, that the difficulty is not peculiar to the present position. This is simply the old difficulty of distinguishing spirituality and morality.

In seeking whatever light Science may have to offer as to the difference between the natural and the spiritual man, we first submit the question to Embryology. And if its actual contribution is small, we shall at least be indebted to it for an important reason why the difficulty should exist at all. That there is grave difficulty in deciding between two given characters, the one natural, the other spiritual, is conceded. But if we can find a sufficient justification for so perplexing a circumstance, the fact loses weight as an objection, and the whole problem is placed on a different footing.

The difference on the score of beauty between the crystal and the shell, let us say once more, is imperceptible. But fix attention for a moment, not upon their appearance, but upon their possibilities, upon their relation to the future, and upon their place in evolution. The crystal has reached its ultimate stage of development. It can never be more beautiful than it is now. Take it to pieces and give it the opportunity to beautify itself afresh, and it will just do the same thing over again. It will form itself into a six-sided pyramid, and go on repeating this same form *ad infinitum* as often as it is dissolved and without ever improving by a hair's breadth. Its law of crystallization allows it to reach this limit, and nothing else within its kingdom can do any more for it. In dealing with the crystal, in short, we are dealing with the maximum beauty of the inorganic world. But in dealing with the shell, we are not dealing with the maximum achievement of the organic world. In itself it is one of the humblest forms of the invertebrate sub-kingdom of the organic world; and there are other forms within this kingdom so different from the shell in a hundred respects that to mistake them would simply be impossible.

In dealing with a man of fine moral character, again, we are dealing with the highest achievement of the organic kingdom. But in dealing with a spiritual man we are dealing with *the lowest form of life in the spiritual world*. To contrast the two, therefore, and marvel that the one is apparently so little better than the other, is unscientific and unjust. The spiritual man is a mere unformed embryo, hidden as yet in his earthly chrysalis-case, while the natural man has the breeding and evolution of ages represented in his character. But what are the possibilities of this spiritual organism? What is yet to emerge from this chrysalis-case? The natural character finds its limits within the organic sphere. But who is to define the limits of the spiritual? Even now it is very beautiful. Even as an embryo it contains some prophecy of its future glory. But the point to mark is, that *it doth not yet appear what it shall be*.

The want of organization, thus, does not surprise us. All life begins at the Amoeboid stage. Evolution is from the simple to the complex; and in every case it is some time before organization is advanced enough to admit of exact classification. A naturalist's only serious difficulty in classification is when he comes to deal with low or embryonic forms. It is impossible, for instance, to mistake an oak for an elephant; but at the bottom of the vegetable series, and at the bottom of the animal series, there are organisms of so doubtful a character that it is equally impossible to distinguish them. So formidable, indeed, has been this difficulty that Hæckel has had to propose an intermediate *regnum protisticum* to contain those forms the rudimentary character of which makes it impossible to apply to the determining tests.

We mention this merely to show the difficulty of classification and not for analogy; for the proper analogy is not between vegetal and animal forms, whether high or low, but between the living and the dead. And here the difficulty is certainly not so great. By suitable tests it is generally possible to distinguish the organic from the inorganic. The ordinary eye may fail to detect the difference, and innumerable forms are assigned by the popular judgment to the inorganic world which are nevertheless undoubtedly alive. And it is the same in the spiritual world. To a cursory glance these rudimentary spiritual forms may not seem to exhibit the phenomena of Life, and therefore the living and the dead may be often classed as one. But let the appropriate scientific tests be applied. In the almost amorphous organism, the physiologist ought already to be able to detect the symptoms of a dawning life. And further research might even bring to light some faint indication of the lines along which the future development was to proceed. Now it is not impossible that among the tests for Life there may be some which may fitly be applied to the spiritual organism. We may therefore at this point hand over the problem to Physiology.

The tests for Life are of two kinds. It is remarkable that one of them was proposed, in the spiritual sphere, by Christ. Foreseeing the difficulty of determining the characters and functions of rudimentary organisms, He suggested that the point be decided by a further evolution. Time for development was to be allowed, during which the marks of Life, if any, would become more pronounced, while in the meantime judgment was to be suspended. "Let both grow together," He said, "until the harvest." This is a thoroughly scientific test. Obviously, however, it cannot assist us for the present—except in the way of enforcing extreme caution in attempting any classification at all.

The second test is at least not so manifestly impracticable. It is to apply the ordinary methods by which biology attempts to distinguish the organic from the inorganic. The characteristics of Life, according to Physiology, are four in number—Assimilation, Waste, Reproduction, and Spontaneous Action. If an organism is found to exercise these functions, it is said to be alive. Now these tests, in a spiritual sense, might fairly be applied to the spiritual man. The experiment would be a delicate one. It might not be open to every one to attempt it. This is a scientific question; and the experiment would have to be conducted under proper conditions and by competent persons. But even on the first statement it will be plain to all who are familiar with spiritual diagnosis that the experiment could be made, and especially on one's self, with some hope of success. Biological considerations, however, would warn us not to expect too much. Whatever be the inadequacy of Morphology, Physiology can never be studied apart from it; and the investigation of function merely as function is a task of extreme difficulty. Mr. Herbert Spencer affirms, "We have next to no power of tracing up the genesis of a function considered purely as a function—no opportunity of observing the progressively-increasing quantities of a given action that have arisen in any order of organisms. In nearly all cases we are able only to establish the greater growth of the part which we have found performs the action, and to infer that greater action of the part has accompanied greater growth of it." Such being the case, it would serve no purpose to indicate the details of a barely possible experiment. We are merely showing, at the moment, that the question "How do I know that I am alive" is not, in the spiritual sphere, incapable of solution. One might, nevertheless, single out some distinctively spiritual function and ask himself if he consciously discharged it. The discharging of that function is, upon biological principles, equivalent to being alive, and therefore the subject of the experiment could certainly come to some conclusion as to his place on a biological scale. The real significance of his actions on the moral scale might be less easy to determine, but he could at least tell where he stood as tested by the standard of life—he would know whether he were living or dead. After all, the best test for Life is just *living*. And living consists, as we have formerly seen, in corresponding with Environment. Those therefore who find within themselves, and regularly exercise, the faculties for corresponding with the Divine Environment, may be said to live the Spiritual Life.

That this Life also, even in the embryonic organism, ought already to betray itself to others, is certainly what one would expect. Every organism has its own reaction upon Nature, and the reaction of the spiritual organism upon the community must be looked for. In the absence of any such reactions in the absence of any token that it lived for a higher purpose, or that its real interests were those of the Kingdom to which it professed to belong, we should be entitled to question its being in that Kingdom. It is obvious that each Kingdom has its own ends and interests, its own functions to discharge in Nature. It is also a law that every organism lives for its Kingdom. And man's place in Nature, or his position among the Kingdoms, is to be decided by the characteristic functions habitually discharged by him. Now when the habits of certain individuals are closely observed, when the total effect of their life and work, with regard to the community, is gauged—as carefully observed and gauged as the influence of certain individuals in a colony of ants might be observed and gauged by Sir John Lubbock—there ought to be no difficulty in deciding whether they are living for the Organic or for the Spiritual; in plainer language, for the world or for God. The question of Kingdoms, at least, would be settled without mistake. The place of any given individual in his own Kingdom is a different matter. That is a question possibly for ethics. But from the biological standpoint, if a man is living for the world it is immaterial how well he lives for it. He ought to live well for it. However important it is for his own Kingdom, it does not affect his biological relation to the other Kingdom whether his character is perfect or imperfect. He may even to some extent assume the outward form of organisms belonging to the higher Kingdom; but so long as his reaction upon the world is the reaction of his species, he is to be classed with his species, so long as the bent of his life is in the direction of the world, he remains a worldling.

Recent botanical and entomological researches have made Science familiar with what is termed *Mimicry*. Certain organisms in one Kingdom assume, for purposes of their own, the outward form of organisms belonging to another. This curious hypocrisy is practiced both by plants and animals, the object being to secure some personal advantage, usually safety, which would be denied were the organism always to play its part in Nature *in propria persona*. Thus the *Ceroxylus laceratus* of Borneo has assumed so perfectly the disguise of a moss-covered branch as to evade the attack of insectivorous birds; and others of the walking-stick insects and leaf-butterflies practice similar deceptions with great effrontery and success. It is a startling result of the indirect influence of Christianity or of a spurious Christianity, that the religious world has come to be populated—how largely one can scarce venture to think—with mimetic species. In few cases, probably, is this a conscious deception. In many doubtless it is induced, as in *Ceroxylus*, by the desire for *safety*. But in a majority of instances it is the natural effect of the prestige of a great system upon those who, coveting its benedictions, yet fail to understand its true nature, or decline to bear its profounder responsibilities. It is here that the test of Life becomes of supreme importance. No classification on the ground of form can exclude mimetic species, or discover them to themselves. But if man's place among the Kingdoms is determined by his functions, a careful estimate of his life in itself and in its reaction upon surrounding lives, ought at once to betray his real position. No matter what may be the moral uprightness of his life, the honorableness of his career, or the orthodoxy of his creed, if he exercises the function of loving the world, that defines his world—he belongs to the Organic Kingdom. He cannot in that case belong to the higher Kingdom. "If any man love the world, the love of the Father is not in him." After all, it is by the general bent of a man's life, by his heart-impulses and secret desires, his spontaneous actions and abiding motives, that his generation is declared.

The exclusiveness of Christianity, separation from the world, uncompromising allegiance to the Kingdom of God, entire surrender of body, soul, and spirit to Christ—these are truths which rise into prominence from time to time, become the watch-words of insignificant parties, rouse the church to attention and the world to opposition, and die down ultimately for want of lives to live them. The few enthusiasts who distinguish in these requirements the essential conditions of entrance into the Kingdom of Christ are overpowered by the weight of numbers, who see nothing more in Christianity than a mild religiousness, and who demand nothing more in themselves or in their fellow-Christians than the participation in a conventional worship, the acceptance of traditional beliefs, and the living of an honest life. Yet nothing is more certain than that the enthusiasts are right. Any impartial survey—such as the unique analysis in "Ecce Homo"—of the claims of Christ and of the nature of His society, will convince any one who cares to make the inquiry of the outstanding difference between the system of Christianity in the original contemplation and its representations in modern life. Christianity marks the advent of what is simply a new Kingdom. Its distinctions from the Kingdom below it are fundamental. It demands from its members activities and responses of an altogether novel order. It is, in the conception of its Founder, a Kingdom for which all its adherents must henceforth exclusively live and work, and which opens its gates alone upon those who, having counted the cost, are prepared to follow it if need be to the death. The surrender Christ demanded was absolute. Every aspirant for membership must seek *first* the Kingdom of God. And in order to enforce the demand of allegiance, or rather with an unconsciousness which contains the finest evidence for its justice, He even assumed the title of King—a claim which in other circumstances, and were these not the symbols of a higher royalty, seems so strangely foreign to one who is meek and lowly in heart.

But this imperious claim of a Kingdom upon its members is not peculiar to Christianity. It is the law in all departments of Nature that every organism must live for its Kingdom. And in defining living *for* the higher Kingdom as the condition of living in it, Christ enunciates a principle which all Nature has prepared us to expect. Every province has its peculiar exactions, every Kingdom levies upon its subjects the tax of an exclusive obedience, and punishes disloyalty always with death. It was the neglect of this principle—that every organism must live for its Kingdom if it is to live in it—which first slowly depopulated the spiritual world. The example of its Founder ceased to find imitators, and the consecration of His early followers came to be regarded as a superfluous enthusiasm. And it is this same misconception of the fundamental principle of all Kingdoms that has deprived modern Christianity of its vitality. The failure to regard the exclusive claims of Christ as more than accidental, rhetorical, or ideal; the failure to discern the essential difference between His Kingdom and all other systems based on the lines of natural religion, and therefore merely Organic; in a word, the general neglect of the claims of Christ as the Founder of a new and higher Kingdom—these have taken the very heart from the religion of Christ and left its evangel without power to impress or bless the world. Until even religious men see the uniqueness of Christ's society, until they acknowledge to the full extent its claim to be nothing less than a new Kingdom, they will continue the hopeless attempt to live for two Kingdoms at once. And hence the value of a more explicit Classification. For probably the most of the difficulties of trying to live the Christian life arise from attempting to half-live it.

As a merely verbal matter, this identification of the Spiritual World with what are known to Science as Kingdoms, necessitates an explanation. The suggested relation of the Kingdom of Christ to the Mineral and Animal Kingdoms does not, of course, depend upon the accident that the Spiritual World is named in the sacred writings by the same word. This certainly lends an appearance of fancy to the generalization; and one feels tempted at first to dismiss it with a smile. But, in truth, it is no mere play on the word *Kingdom*. Science demands the classification of every organism. And here is an organism of a unique kind, a living energetic spirit, a new creature which, by an act of generation, has been begotten of God. Starting from the point that the spiritual life is to be studied biologically, we must at once proceed, as the first step in the scientific examination of this organism, to enter it in its appropriate class. Now two Kingdoms, at the present time, are known to Science—the Inorganic and the Organic. It does not belong to the Inorganic Kingdom, because it lives. It does not belong to the Organic Kingdom, because it is endowed with a kind of Life infinitely removed from either the vegetal or animal. Where then shall it be classed? We are left without an alternative. There being no Kingdom known to Science which can contain it, we must construct one. Or rather we must include in the programme of Science a Kingdom already constructed but the place of which in science has not yet been recognized. That Kingdom is the *Kingdom of God*.

Taking now this larger view of the content of science, we may leave the case of the individual and pass on to outline the scheme of nature as a whole. The general conception will be as follows:

First, we find at the bottom of everything the Mineral or Inorganic Kingdom. Its characteristics are, first, that so far as the sphere above it is concerned it is dead; second, that although dead it furnishes the physical basis of life to the Kingdom next in order. It is thus absolutely essential to the Kingdom above it. And the more minutely the detailed structure and ordering of the whole fabric are investigated it becomes increasingly apparent that the Inorganic Kingdom is the preparation for, and the prophecy of, the Organic.

Second, we come to the world next in order, the world containing plant, and animal, and man, the Organic Kingdom. Its characteristics are, first, that so far as the sphere above it is concerned it is dead; and, second, although dead it supplies in turn the basis of life to the Kingdom next in order. And the more minutely the detailed structure and ordering of the whole fabric are investigated, it is obvious, in turn, that the Organic Kingdom is the preparation for, and the prophecy of the Spiritual.

Third, and highest, we reach the Spiritual Kingdom, or the Kingdom of Heaven. What its characteristics are, relatively to any hypothetical higher Kingdom, necessarily remain unknown. That the Spiritual, in turn, may be the preparation for, and the prophecy of, something still higher is not impossible. But the very conception of a Fourth Kingdom transcends us, and if it exists, the Spiritual organism, by the analogy, must remain at present wholly dead to it.

The warrant for adding this Third Kingdom consists, as just stated, in the fact that there are organisms which from their peculiar origin, nature, and destiny cannot be fitly entered in either of the two Kingdoms now known to science. The Second Kingdom is proclaimed by the advent upon the stage of the First, of *once-born* organisms. The Third is ushered in by the appearance, among these once-born organisms, of forms of life which have been born again—*twice-born* organisms. The classification, therefore, is based, from the scientific side on certain facts of embryology and on the Law of Biogenesis; and from the theological side on certain facts of experience and on the doctrine of Regeneration. To those who hold either to Biogenesis or to Regeneration, there is no escape from a Third Kingdom.

There is in this conception of a high and spiritual organism rising out of the highest point of the Organic Kingdom, in the hypothesis of the Spiritual Kingdom itself, a Third Kingdom following the Second in sequence as orderly as the Second follows the First, a Kingdom utilizing the materials of both the Kingdoms beneath it, continuing their laws, and, above all, accounting for these lower Kingdoms in a legitimate way and complementing them in the only known way—there is in all this a suggestion of the greatest of modern scientific doctrines, the Evolution hypothesis, too impressive to pass unnoticed. The strength of the doctrine of Evolution, at least in its broader outlines, is now such that its verdict on any biological question is a consideration of moment. And if any further defence is needed for the idea of a Third Kingdom it may be found in the singular harmony of the whole conception with this great modern truth. It might even be asked whether a complete and consistent theory of Evolution does not really demand such a conception? Why should Evolution stop with the Organic? It is surely obvious that the complement of Evolution is Advolution, and the inquiry, Whence has all this system of things come, is, after all, of minor importance compared with the question, Whither does all this tend? Science, as such, may have little to say on such a question. And it is perhaps impossible, with such faculties as we now possess, to imagine an Evolution with a future as great as its past. So stupendous is the development from the atom to the man that no point can be fixed in the future as distant from what man is now as he is from the atom. But it has been given to Christianity to disclose the lines of a further Evolution. And if Science also professes to offer a further Evolution, not the most sanguine evolutionist will venture to contrast it, either as regards the dignity of its methods, the magnificence of its aims, or the certainty of its hopes, with the prospects of the Spiritual Kingdom. That Science has a prospect of some sort to hold out to man, is not denied. But its limits are already marked. Mr. Herbert Spencer, after investigating its possibilities fully, tells us, "Evolution has an impassable limit." It is the distinct claim of the Third Kingdom that this limit is not final. Christianity opens a way to a further development—a development apart from which the magnificent past of Nature has been in vain, and without which Organic Evolution, in spite of the elaborateness of its processes and the vastness of its achievements, is simply a stupendous *cul de sac*. Far as nature carries on the task, vast as is the distance between the atom and the man, she has to lay down her tools when the work is just begun. Man, her most rich and finished product, marvelous in his complexity, all but Divine in sensibility, is to the Third Kingdom not even a shapeless embryo. The old chain of processes must begin again on the higher plane if there is to be a further Evolution. The highest organism of the Second Kingdom—simple, immobile, dead as the inorganic crystal, toward the sphere above—must be vitalized afresh. Then from a mass of all but homogeneous "protoplasm" the organism must pass through all the stages of differentiation and integration, growing in perfectness and beauty under the unfolding of the higher Evolution, until it reaches the Infinite Complexity, the Infinite Sensibility, God. So the spiritual carries on the marvelous process to which all lower Nature ministers, and perfects it when the ministry of lower Nature fails.

This conception of a further Evolution carries with it the final answer to the charge that, as regards morality, the Spiritual world has nothing to offer man that is not already within his reach. Will it be contended that a perfect morality is already within the reach of the natural man? What product of the organic creation has ever attained to the fullness of the stature of Him who is the Founder and

Type of the Spiritual Kingdom? What do men know of the qualities enjoined in His Beatitudes, or at what value do they estimate them? Proved by results, it is surely already decided that on merely natural lines moral perfection is unattainable. And even Science is beginning to awaken to the momentous truth that Man, the highest product of the Organic Kingdom, is a disappointment. But even were it otherwise, if even in prospect the hopes of the Organic Kingdom could be justified, its standard of beauty is not so high, nor, in spite of the dreams of Evolution, is its guarantee so certain. The goal of the organisms of the Spiritual World is nothing less than this—to be "holy as He is holy, and pure as He is pure." And by the Law of Conformity to Type, their final perfection is secured. The inward nature must develop out according to its Type, until the consummation of oneness with God is reached.

These proposals of the Spiritual Kingdom in the direction of Evolution are at least entitled to be carefully considered by Science. Christianity defines the highest conceivable future for mankind. It satisfies the Law of Continuity. It guarantees the necessary conditions for carrying on the organism successfully, from stage to stage. It provides against the tendency to Degeneration. And finally, instead of limiting the yearning hope of final perfection to the organisms of a future age—an age so remote that the hope for thousands of years must still be hopeless—instead of inflicting this cruelty on intelligences mature enough to know perfection and earnest enough to wish it, Christianity puts the prize within immediate reach of man.

This attempt to incorporate the Spiritual Kingdom in the scheme of Evolution, may be met by what seems at first sight a fatal objection. So far from the idea of a Spiritual Kingdom being in harmony with the doctrine of Evolution, it may be said that it is violently opposed to it. It announces a new Kingdom starting off suddenly on a different plane and in direct violation of the primary principle of development. Instead of carrying the organic evolution further on its own lines, theology at a given point interposes a sudden and hopeless barrier—the barrier between the natural and the spiritual—and insists that the evolutionary process must begin again at the beginning. At this point, in fact, Nature acts *per saltum*. This is no Evolution, but a Catastrophe—such a Catastrophe as must be fatal to any consistent development hypothesis.

On the surface this objection seems final—but it is only on the surface. It arises from taking a too narrow view of what Evolution is. It takes evolution in zoology for Evolution as a whole. Evolution began, let us say, with some primeval nebulous mass in which lay potentially all future worlds. Under the evolutionary hand, the amorphous cloud broke up, condensed, took definite shape, and in the line of true development assumed a gradually increasing complexity. Finally there emerged the cooled and finished earth, highly differentiated, so to speak, complete and fully equipped. And what followed? Let it be well observed—a Catastrophe. Instead of carrying the process further, the Evolution, if this is Evolution, here also abruptly stops. A sudden and hopeless barrier—the barrier between the Inorganic and the Organic—interposes, and the process has to begin again at the beginning with the creation of Life. Here then is a barrier placed by Science at the close of the Inorganic similar to the barrier placed by Theology at the close of the Organic. Science has used every effort to abolish this first barrier, but there it still stands challenging the attention of the modern world, and no consistent theory of Evolution can fail to reckon with it. Any objection, then, to the Catastrophe introduced by Christianity between the Natural and Spiritual Kingdoms applies with equal force against the barrier which Science places between the Inorganic and the Organic. The reserve of Life in either case is a fact, and a fact of exceptional significance.

What then becomes of Evolution? Do these two great barriers destroy it? By no means. But they make it necessary to frame a larger doctrine. And the doctrine gains immeasurably by such an enlargement. For now the case stands thus: Evolution, in harmony with its own law that progress is from the simple to the complex, begins itself to pass toward the complex. The materialistic Evolution, so to speak, is a straight line. Making all else complex, it alone remains simple—unscientifically simple. But, as Evolution unfolds everything else, it is now seen to be itself slowly unfolding. The straight line is coming out gradually in curves. At a given point a new force appears deflecting it; and at another given point a new force appears deflecting that. These points are not unrelated points; these forces are not unrelated forces. The arrangement is still harmonious, and the development throughout obeys the evolutionary law in being from the general to the special, from the lower to the higher. What we are reaching, in short, is nothing less than the *evolution of Evolution.*

Now to both Science and Christianity, and especially to Science, this enrichment of Evolution is important. And, on the part of Christianity, the contribution to the system of Nature of a second barrier is of real scientific value. At first it may seem merely to increase the difficulty. But in reality it abolishes it. However paradoxical it seems, it is nevertheless the case that two barriers are more easy to understand than one—two mysteries are less mysterious than a single mystery. For it requires two to constitute a harmony. One by itself is a Catastrophe. But, just as the recurrence of an eclipse at different periods makes an eclipse no breach of Continuity; just as the fact that the astronomical conditions necessary to cause a Glacial Period will in the remote future again be fulfilled constitutes the Great Ice Age a normal phenomenon; so the recurrence of two periods associated with special phenomena of Life, the second higher, and by the law necessarily higher, is no violation of the principle of Evolution. Thus even in the matter of adding a second to the one barrier of Nature, the Third Kingdom may already claim to complement the Science of the Second. The overthrow of Spontaneous Generation has left a break in Continuity which continues to put Science to confusion. Alone, it is as abnormal and perplexing to the intellect as the first eclipse. But if the Spiritual Kingdom can supply Science with a companion-phenomenon, the most exceptional thing in the scientific sphere falls within the domain of Law. This, however, is no more than might be expected from a Third Kingdom. True to its place as the highest of the Kingdoms, it ought to embrace all that lies beneath and give to the First and Second their final explanation.

How much more in the under-Kingdoms might be explained or illuminated upon this principle, however tempting might be the inquiry, we cannot turn aside to ask. But the rank of the Third Kingdom in the order of Evolution implies that it holds the key to much that is obscure in the world around—much that, apart from it, must always remain obscure. A single obvious instance will serve to illustrate the fertility of the method. What has this Kingdom to contribute to Science with regard to the Problem of the origin of Life itself? Taking this as an isolated phenomenon, neither the Second Kingdom, nor the Third apart from revelation, has anything to pronounce. But when we observe the companion-phenomenon in the higher Kingdom, the question is simplified. It will be disputed by none that the source of Life in the Spiritual World is God. And as the same Law of Biogenesis prevails in both spheres, we may reason from the higher to the lower and affirm it to be at least likely that the origin of life there has been the same.

There remains yet one other objection of a somewhat different order, and which is only referred to because it is certain to be raised by those who fail to appreciate the distinctions of Biology. Those whose sympathies are rather with Philosophy than with Science may incline to dispute the allocation of so high an organism as man to the merely vegetal and animal Kingdom. Recognizing the immense moral and intellectual distinctions between him and even the highest animal, they would introduce a third barrier between man and animal—a barrier even greater than that between the Inorganic and the Organic. Now, no science can be blind to these distinctions. The only question is whether they are of such a kind as to make it necessary to classify man in a separate Kingdom. And to this the answer of Science is in the negative. Modern Science knows only two Kingdoms—the Inorganic and the Organic. A barrier between man and animal there may be, but it is a different barrier from that which separates Inorganic from Organic. But even were this to be denied, and in spite of all science it will be denied, it would make no difference as regards the general question. It would merely interpose another Kingdom between the Organic and the Spiritual, the other relations remaining as before. Any one, therefore, with a theory to support as to the exceptional creation of the Human Race will find the present classification elastic enough for his purpose. Philosophy, of course, may propose another arrangement of the Kingdoms if it chooses. It is only contended that this is the order demanded by Biology. To add another Kingdom mid-way between the Organic and the Spiritual, could that be justified at any future time on scientific grounds, would be a mere question of further detail.

Studies in Classification, beginning with considerations of quality, usually end with a reference to quantity. And though one would willingly terminate the inquiry on the threshold of such a subject, the example of Revelation not less than the analogies of Nature press for at least a general statement.

The broad impression gathered from the utterances of the Founder of the Spiritual Kingdom is that the number of organisms to be included in it is to be comparatively small. The outstanding characteristic of the new Society is to be its selectness. "Many are called," said Christ, "but few are chosen." And when one recalls, on the one hand, the conditions of membership, and, on the other, observes the lives and aspirations of average men, the force of the verdict becomes apparent. In its bearing upon the general question, such a conclusion is not without suggestiveness. Here again is another evidence of the radical nature of Christianity. That "few are chosen" indicates a deeper view of the relation of Christ's Kingdom to the world, and stricter qualifications of membership, than lie on the surface or are allowed for in the ordinary practice of religion.

The analogy of Nature upon this point is not less striking—it may be added, not less solemn. It is an open secret, to be read in a hundred analogies from the world around, that of the millions of possible entrants for advancement in any department of Nature the number ultimately selected for preferment is small. Here also "many are called and few are chosen." The analogies from the waste of seed, of pollen, of human lives, are too familiar to be quoted. In certain details, possibly, these comparisons are inappropriate. But there are other analogies, wider and more just, which strike deeper into the system of Nature. A comprehensive view of the whole field of Nature discloses the fact that the circle of the chosen slowly contracts as we rise in the scale of being. Some mineral, but not all, becomes vegetable; some vegetable, but not all, becomes animal; some animal, but not all, becomes human; some human, but not all, becomes Divine. Thus the area narrows. At the base is the mineral, most broad and simple; the spiritual at the apex, smallest, but most highly differentiated. So form rises above form, Kingdom above Kingdom. *Quantity decreases as quality increases.*

The gravitation of the whole system of nature toward quality is surely a phenomenon of commanding interest. And if among the more recent revelations of Nature there is one thing more significant for religion than another, it is the majestic spectacle of the rise of Kingdoms toward scarcer yet nobler forms, and simpler yet diviner ends. Of the early stage, the first development of the earth from the nebulous matrix of space, Science speaks with reserve. The second, the evolution of each individual from the simple protoplasmic cell to the formed adult, is proved. The still wider evolution, not of solitary individuals, but of all the individuals within each province—in the vegetal world from the unicellular cryptogam to the highest phanerogam, in the animal world from the amorphous amoeba to Man—is at least suspected, the gradual rise of types being at all events a fact. But now, at last, we see the Kingdoms themselves evolving. And that supreme law which has guided the development from simple to complex in matter, in individual, in sub-Kingdom, and in Kingdom, until only two or three great Kingdoms remain, now begins at the beginning again, directing the evolution of these million-peopled worlds as if they were simple cells or organisms. Thus, what applies to the individual applies to the family, what applies to the family applies to the Kingdom, what applies to the Kingdom applies to the Kingdoms. And so, out of the infinite complexity there rises an infinite simplicity, the foreshadowing of a final unity, of that

> "One God, one law, one element,
> And one far-off divine event,
> To which the whole creation moves."

This is the final triumph of Continuity, the heart secret of Creation, the unspoken prophecy of Christianity. To Science, defining it as a working principle, this mighty process of amelioration is simply *Evolution*. To Christianity, discerning the end through the means, it is *Redemption*. These silent and patient processes, elaborating, eliminating, developing all from the first of time, conducting the evolution from millennium to millennium with unaltering purpose and unfaltering power, are the early stages in the redemptive work—the unseen approach of that Kingdom whose strange mark is that it "cometh without observation." And these Kingdoms rising tier above tier in ever increasing sublimity and beauty, their foundations visibly fixed in the past, their progress, and the direction of their progress, being facts in Nature still, are the signs which, since the Magi saw His star in the East, have never been wanting from the firmament of truth, and which in every age with growing clearness to the wise, and with ever-gathering mystery to the uninitiated, proclaim that "the Kingdom of God is at hand."

Stones Rolled Away and Other Addresses

Table of Contents

Introduction

Any one who had read "The Greatest Thing in the World" could not help but desire to see and hear its author; and, when Professor Drummond visited Boston in the spring of 1893, the capacity of lecture halls was taxed to the utmost. To accommodate thousands turned away, he repeated some of his lectures in the Lowell Institute Course, Boston. It was a crowded Boylston Hall or Appleton Chapel that invariably faced him when he addressed the students of Harvard University. He drew young men as few men can. He loved life and nature. He studied and knew men. He had read much. He had travelled in Europe, America, Africa, Australia and the New Hebrides, with eyes and ears wide open. With a charming personality and a rare grace of manner, he was a most attractive speaker and character, whether on the platform or in the quiet hour.

The student, the evangelist and pastor, the professor and lecturer, the traveller and writer, has passed away; but his words, his writing and his influence cannot. He willingly gave his life to help others. Many a soul was brought into a higher life. Many a life was led into the top flat. Many a one was shown his part in the Kingdom of God. Many a man who was down was set upon his feet. Many a stone of difficulty was rolled away.

The addresses here given to the public in permanent form for the first time, as they have already helped some, may yet help many more.

The first four were delivered to students of Harvard University, in April, 1893. The remaining three addresses were delivered at the World's Bible Students' Conference, Northfield, Mass., in July, 1893.

Luther Hess Waring
Scranton, PA.

Stones Rolled Away

Gentlemen, I am very much astonished at this spectacle. I told you last night it was against our principles in Scotland to have religious meetings on a week night. It seems to me that if you come to a meeting of this kind you mean business, and you may just as well own it. If a man comes to a shorthand class, it means that he wants to learn shorthand; and, if a man turns up at what I suppose I must call a religious meeting, it means that he is less or more interested in the subject.

Now I should say that I think a man has to give himself the benefit of that desire, and he should not be ashamed of it. The facts of religion are real; and, as mere students of life, you and I are bound to take cognizance of them. Of course, many very fair minded men are kept away from going into this subject as they would like by a number of exceedingly surface reasons. I cannot help calling them surface reasons. For instance, you meet a man who tells you that he doesn't like Christians, that they always put his back up.

Now, Christians often put my back up. There are many of them I find, with whom it takes all my time to get along. But that is not peculiar with Christians. It is only peculiar to peculiar Christians, and there are just as many of the other sort. A man might just as well say, I don't like sinners. A man might just as well keep out of the world because he doesn't like some people in the world, as to keep out of Christian circles because there are some objectionable creatures in it. We cannot be too fastidious. We cannot join any sect without having the weaker brethren in it. We cannot get on in this world entirely by ourselves. We must join this thing and that if we are going to be of any service at all, so that I think the difficulty of having to join ourselves with objectionable men applies pretty much all around.

Other men are kept away from Christianity by what I might call its phrases. A great many people, not so much in your country as in ours, talk in a dialect. The older people especially, our grandmothers, have a set of phrases in which all their religion is imbedded, and they can't talk to us about religion without using those phrases; and when we talk to them, if we do not use those phrases, we are put out of the synagogue. Now what we can do in this case is to translate their dialect into our own language, and then translate into their dialect when we speak back. It is a different dialect. We would put it upon a different basis; but after all we mean pretty much the same thing, and if we can once get into this habit of translating our more modern way of putting things into this antique language that those worthy people use to us we will find ourselves more at one with them than we think.

I meet another set of men who tell me that they don't like churches, that they find sermons stale, flat and unprofitable. Now, if any man here hates a dull sermon, I am with him. I have intense sympathy with any man who hates dullness. I think the world is far too dull, and that is one of the greatest reasons why the brightest men should throw themselves into Christianity to give it a broader phase to other people. One must confess that some church work, at all events, is not of a very cheerful or lively order. But of course that is not an argument why one should abstain from religious service. There are many reasons why we should even sacrifice ourselves and submit to a little dullness now and again if it is going to gain for us a greater good. After all, we live by institutions, and by fixed institutions. There are very few men who are able to get along without steady institutions of one kind and another. Some men are so tremendously free that they hate to be tied down to hours, to places and to seasons; but there are very few men big enough to stand that for a long time. If we look about for it, we will find some place that we can go and get some good. When a man goes to church really hungry and goes because he is hungry, he will pick up something, no matter where it is. Christ himself went to church, and even if we know something more than the minister knows, the fellowship, the sense of the solidarity of the Christian church throughout the whole world, the prayer and the inspiration of the hymn and the reading will at least do us some good. I do not say that a man cannot be very religious without that. There are tens of thousands of Christians who never go to church; and there are tens of thousands who go to church who are not Christians. But, as with substantial meals taken at intervals, man is no worse and may be much better for it.

The religious life needs keeping up just as the other parts of our life need keeping up. There is nothing more impossible than for a man to live a religious life on an hour's work or an hour's thought a week. A man could not learn French, German or Latin by giving an hour per week to it; and how can we expect a man to get in this great world of the spirit, this great moral world, this great ideal region, and learn anything about it by merely dabbling in it now and again? We must make it a regular business, and, if the religious part is a vital part of the whole nature, we may as well attend to it.

You may remember a passage in Mr. Darwin's life. He says: "In one respect my mind has changed during the last twenty or thirty years. Up to the age of thirty, or beyond it, the poetry of many kinds, such as the works of Milton, Gray, Byron, Coleridge and Shelley, gave me great pleasure; and even as a school boy I took intense delight in Shakespeare, and especially in the historical plays. I have always said that pictures gave me considerable, and music very great, delight. But now for many years I cannot endure to read a line of poetry. I have tried lately to read Shakespeare, but found it so intolerably dull that it nauseated me. I have also lost my taste for pictures and music. My mind seems to have become a kind of machine for grinding general laws out of large collections of facts. But why this should have caused the atrophy of that part of the brain, I cannot conceive. If I had my life to live over again" (this is the point) "I would have made the rule to read some poetry and listen to some music at least once every week." There is the greatest authority on degeneration confessing to his own personal degeneration, and in the same paragraph telling us how we may avoid it. He says by leaving these things out of his life for so many years, although he had a real liking for them, his nature at these points began to atrophy, and when he went back to them he found that they disgusted him; and then he says that, if he had his life to live again, he would have made it a rule to read some poetry and listen to some music at least once a week, and that would have kept the thing up. There is nothing magical about religion. If a man is to keep it up, he must use the means, just as he would use the means to keep up the violin, or his interest in art of any kind.

I find another set of men who have never got beyond this difficulty, that they find the Bible a somewhat arid and slow book. Now, in the first place, I want to say that I have, again, great sympathy with that objector because, as a matter of fact, there are whole tracts of the Bible which are distinctly dull, which are written in an archaic language, and about departments of history in the past which haven't any great living interest for us now. One must remember that the Bible is not a book, but a library consisting of a large number of books. By an accident, we have these books bound up in one as if they were one book; and to say that all the books of the Bible are dull is simply to pass a literary judgment which is incorrect. It is not true, as a matter of fact, that all these books of the Bible are dull. Of course a sailing directory is very flat on the shore; but when a man is at sea and wants to steer his way through difficult and dangerous wastes, where the currents are strong and the passages narrow, he wants the best chart he can get, and he wants to use it as carefully as he can; and when a man wakens up to the difficulty of life and the reality of its temptations, he wants some such chart as he gets in that book to help him through.

As a mere literary work, there are books there that are unsurpassed in the English tongue, and for their teaching, for their beauty and for their truth they have never been surpassed. Christ's words, of course, are beyond comparison; but even Paul had a far greater brain than almost any writer of history.

John's writing is far deeper and more beautiful than Emerson's, for instance. Let the man who is in love with Emerson, as I am happy to say I am, take up the book of John just as he would take up Emerson, and see if he doesn't get in it a great deal that Emerson has, and a great deal more. If a man doesn't like the Bible, it is because he has never struck the best parts of it, or because he has never felt any great need in his own life for its teaching. As a matter of fact, however, reading the Bible is a new thing. There were Christians for hundreds and hundreds of years before there was any people's Bible; so that it is not even essential, if you can't overcome this matter of taste, that you should read the Bible. There are hundreds of Christians at this moment who cannot read the Bible. There are Christians in heathen lands in whose language there is as yet no Bible; so that you see there is no absolute connection between these two things. Besides that, the Bible has now become diffused through literature to such an extent that you can often get the heart of the Bible in a very bright and living and practical form through other forms of literature. If you don't care to get it direct from the book itself, you can get it from our modern poetry, even from our modern novel; and Christianity has now been so long in the world and is diffused over so many things that it reflects itself in almost everything in life. Some one was once trying to convince a certain lady of that point as they were sitting at dinner; and he said to her that in the pudding which they had just eaten there was an egg, and that that morning at breakfast he had also eaten an egg. He saw the egg at breakfast, but he did not see the egg in the pudding; yet he had no doubt the egg in the pudding would nourish him just as much as the one he had for breakfast.

A man may get his nourishment straight out of the Bible. He may see it there, shell and all; but he may also get his nourishment mixed up with other ingredients, and it will do him just as much good.

There is another class of men, however, whom none of these minor difficulties touch—men who have come up to college, and who have got upset on almost all the main doctrines of Christianity. Now, I want to confess to you that, so far as I know my old friends, they have all passed through that stage. Every man who is worth a button passes through that stage. He loses all the forms of truth which he got in the Sunday School; and, if he is true to himself, gains them all back again in a richer and larger and more permanent form. But, between the loss and the gain, there is sometimes a very painful and dismal interlude, during which the man thinks that he is never going to believe again, when everything lies in ruin, and he doesn't see where any reconstruction is to come in. These are dark days and dark years in a man's life, and they are inevitable to every man who thinks. They are inevitable, because we are all born doubters. We came into the world asking questions. The world itself is a sphinx and tempts us to keep on asking questions. There are no great truths in the world which are not to some extent doubtable; and the instrument with which we look at truth is largely impaired, and has to be corrected by long years of experience for its early aberration. So that when we look at truth we only see part of it, and we see that part of it distorted. The result is a certain amount of twilight where we expected full day. One consolation to give that man is to tell him that we have all been through that. We take it like the measles. It lasts a certain number of months or years, and then we come out with our constitutions better than ever. There is a real rationale for that. Everything in the world passes through these stages, provided it be growing. You remember how the philosophers describe it. They describe the three great stages as position, opposition and composition. Position: Somebody lays down a truth, you look at it and say, "Yes, that is truth." I heard a clergyman say that when I was a boy, and I believed it. Then, one day, you read a book or hear some one else talk, and he put a query on it; and then there came the revolt against it, and for a long time your mind was seething with opposition to this original thing which was positive. And then you went on and put all these contradictory things together and composed them into a unity again. You reached the third stage—that of composition.

It is the same with everything. You begin to learn the piano, and after you have played about a year you think you know all about it; and you tackle the most difficult pieces, dash away at them, and think you can do it as well as anybody. Then you go into Boston and hear some great pianist, and come home a sad man. You see you know nothing about it. For the next six months you do not touch a single piece. You play scales day after day and practice finger exercises. Then, after six months, you say: "What is the use of playing scales? Music does not exist for scales;" and you turn to your old pieces and play them over again in an entirely different way. You have got it all back again. There are men here going through the scale period with regard to religious questions. What is the use of all this opposition? Is it not time to go back again, you ask, and put all this experience into something, and get at some truth at the other side? You see the same truth in a novel. Volume I., they will. Volume II., they won't. Volume III., they do.

We see the same thing in art. A man paints a picture. He thinks he has painted a grand one. After a few months, some one comes along and says: "Look here! Look at that boat! You don't call that a boat? And look at that leaf! That is not a leaf." And you discover that you have never looked at a boat and never seen a leaf. You are disheartened and do nothing the next six months but draw boats and leaves; and, after you have drawn boats and leaves until you are sick, you say: "What is the use of drawing boats and leaves?" and try again and produce your first landscape. But it is altogether a different thing from the picture you painted before. Now, when a man is working over the details of the Christian religion and struggling to get one thing adjusted and another, he will very soon find out that that does not amount to much. It is a useful thing, and he has to go through it, but he has to come out the other side also and put these things together.

The best advice, I think, that can be given to a man who is in this difficulty is, in the first place, to read the best authorities on the subject; not to put himself off with cheap tracts and popular sermons, but to go to the scientific authorities. There are as great scientific authorities in Germany, in England and in America on all the subject matter of theology as there are on the subject matter of chemistry or geology. Go to the authorities. You may not agree with them when you have read them. But if a man reads all the books on the opposition side he will very naturally get a distorted view of it. So, for every book he reads on the one side, he should, in justice, read a book on the other side.

Next, let a man remember that the great thing is not to think about religion, but to do it. We do not live in a "think" world. It is a real world. You do not believe that botany lies in the pages of Sachs. Botany lies out there in the flowers and in the trees, and it is living. And religion does not live in the pages of the doctrinal books, but in human life—in conflict with our own temptations, and in the conduct and character of our fellow beings. When we abandon this "think-world" of ours and get out into the real world, we will find that, after all, these doubts are not of such immense importance, and that we can do a great deal of good in the world.

For my part, I have as many doubts on all the great subjects connected with theology as probably any one here; but they do not interfere in the very slightest with my trying, in what humble way I can, to follow out the religion of Christ. They do not even touch that region; and I don't want to lose these doubts. I don't want any man to rob me of my problem. I have no liking and little respect for the cock-sure Christian—a man who can demonstrate some of the most tremendous verities of the faith, as he can the Fifth Book of Euclid. I want a religion and theology with some of the infinite about it, and some of the shadow as well as some of the light; and if, by reading up one of the great doctrines for five or six years, I get some little light upon it, it is only to find there are a hundred upon which I could spend another hundred lives. And if I should try to meet some specific point upon which you are at sea to-night, it would not do you much good. To-morrow a new difficulty would start in your mind, and you would be simply where you were. I would be stopping up only one of your wells. You would open another out of the first book you read. Try to separate theological doctrine from practical religion. Believe me that you can follow Christ in this University without having solved any of these problems. Why, there was a skeptic among the first twelve disciples, and one of the best of them, and one of the most loyal of them. That man sat down at the first Lord's table, and Christ never said any hard words against him. He tried to teach him. That is the only attitude, it seems to me, we can take to Christ still. We can enter His school as scholars, and sit at His feet and learn what we can; and by doing His will in the practical things of life, we shall know of this and that doctrine, whether it be of God. The only use of truth is that it can do somebody some good. The only use of truth is in its sanctifying power;

and that is the peculiarity of the truth of Christianity, that it has this sanctifying power and makes men better.

Now you say: "What am I to do? If I am to block up this avenue and am not to expect very much along the line of mere belief, in what direction am I to shape my Christian life?" Well, I cannot in the least answer that. Every man must shape his Christian life for himself, according as his own talents may lead him; but the great thing to do is simply to become a follower of Christ. That is to become a Christian. There is nothing difficult or mysterious about it. A Darwinian is a man who follows Darwin, studies his books, accepts his views and says, "I am a Darwinian." You look into Christ's life, into His influence; you look at the needs of the world; you see how the one meets the other; you look into your own life and see how Christ's life meets your life; and you say, "I shall follow this teacher and leader until I get a better." From the time you do that, you are a Christian. You may be a very poor one. A man who enlists is a very poor soldier for the first few years, but he is a soldier from the moment he enlists; and the moment a man takes Christ to be the center of his life that man becomes a Christian. Of course that makes a great change in his life. His friends will know it to-morrow. On the steam engine you have seen the apparatus at the side called the eccentric. It has a different center from all the other wheels. Now, the Christian man is to some extent an eccentric. His life revolves around a different center from many people round about him. Of course, it is the other people who are eccentric because the true center of life is the most perfect life, the most perfect man, the most perfect ideal; and the man who is circulating around that is living the most perfect. At the same time, that man's life will to some extent be different from the lives round about him, and to some extent he will be a marked man.

But what difference will it make to a man himself? For one thing, it will keep you straight. I fancy most of the men here are living straight lives as it is; but it is impossible that every man here is. Well, I will tell you how to keep your life straight from this time—how your hunger after righteousness can be met. If you become a Christian, you will lead a straight life. That is not all. If you become a Christian, you will help other men to lead straight lives. Seek first the kingdom of God and His righteousness. The only chance that this world has of becoming a righteous world is by the contagion of the Christian men in it. I do not know any country with the splendid pretensions and achievements of America where there is so much unrighteousness in politics and to some extent in commerce, and where shady things are not only winked at, but admired. That is acknowledged and deplored by every right thinking man in the country. I get it, not from observation, but from yourselves. There is not a day passes that I do not find men deploring political corruption and the want of commercial integrity, in some districts of this country, at all events. Now nothing can change that state of affairs unless such men as yourselves throw your influence on to the side of righteousness and determine that you will live to make this country a little straighter than you found it.

There is a career in Christianity as well as an individual life. How do you test the greatness of a career? You test it by its influence. Well, can you point me to any influence in the world in the past which has had anything like the influence of the name to which I have asked you to give your life's adherence? That life started without a chance of succeeding in anything, according to the received theories of a successful life. Christ was born in a manger. If you and I had been born in a manger, the shame of it would have accompanied us through our whole lives; and yet there is not one of us born to-day who is not baptized in the name of Christ and who has not a Christian name. Christ went to no university, and had no education; and there is not a university in Europe or in America which is not founded in the name of Christ. This university was founded in the name of Christ. Aye, and the very money which has gone to build the universities of the world has come from the followers of Christ. The education of the world, gentlemen, has been done by the followers of Jesus Christ. Christ had no political influence, and sought none; yet there is not a President placed in the White House, there is not a sovereign in Europe placed upon a throne, but acknowledges, in the doing of it and in public, that the power to do it has come from Christ, and that the object in doing it is to secure the coming of Christ's kingdom. Take it in any direction, and you will find that this influence, judged from mere worldly standards of success, has been supreme.

Napoleon said, "I do not understand that man. He must have been more than human. I used to be able," he said on St. Helena, "to get people to die for me. I got hundreds of thousands of them, but I had to be there. Now that I am here on this island, I can't get a man. But He," said he, "gets hundreds of thousands of the best men in the world to lay down their whole lives for Him every day." Judged as mere influence from the standpoint of an ambitious man like Napoleon, you see that that Life was supreme.

You remember the dinner that Charles Lamb gave to some literary men, and how they were discussing after dinner what their attitude would be if certain great figures of the past were to come into their dining room. After they had all spoken, Lamb said:

"Well, it looks to me like this, that if Shakespeare entered the room I should rise up to greet him; but if Christ entered the room, I should kneel down and keep silent."

And so I ask you if you have feelings of that kind about any figure in history compared to the feelings that spring into your mind when you try to contemplate that Life. Some of you have never read Christ's life. You have picked up a parable here and a miracle there, and a scrap of history between; but you have never read that biography as you have read the biography of Washington, Webster, or the life of Columbus. Read it. Go home and read one of the four little books which tell you about His life. Take Matthew, for instance; and if you don't run aground in the 5th chapter and find yourself compelled to spend a week over it, you haven't much moral nature left. I have known men who have tried that experiment, who have begun to read the gospel of Matthew, and by the time they had finished reading the 5th chapter, they had thrown in their lot with the Person who forms the subject of that book. There is no other way of getting to know about Christ unless you read His life, at least as a beginning. If you want to become a Christian you must read up, and that is the thing to read. If you like, after that you can read the other lives of Christ. How do men get to know one another? They simply take to one another. Two men meet here to-night. They go downstairs and exchange greetings. To-morrow night they meet in each other's rooms. By the end of a month they have got to know each other a little, and after another year of college life they have become sworn friends.

A man becomes a little attracted to Christ. That grows and grows, into a brighter friendship, and that grows into a great passion, and the man gives his life to Christ's interest. He counts it the highest ambition he can have to become a man such as Christ was. You see there is nothing profound about a religion of that kind. It is a religion that lies in the line of the ideals a young man forms, and that all the reading that he meets with from day to day fashions. In fact, it is a man's ideal turning up, and the man who turns his back upon that is simply turning his back upon his one chance of happiness in life and of making anything off life. Every life that is not lived in that time is out of the true current of history, to say nothing else. It is out of the stream —the main stream that is running through the ages, and that is going to sweep everything before it. A man who does not live that life may not be a bad man. The Bible does not say that everybody who is not a Christian is a notorious sinner; but it says that the man who lives outside that is wasting his life. He may not be doing wrong, but his life is lost. "He that loveth his life," Christ said, "shall lose it; and he that hateth his life in this world shall keep it unto life eternal." I am not ashamed to quote that to you; and I ask you to regard it with the same validity, and more, that you will give to any other quotation.

You will not accuse me of cant because I have used sacred words in this talk. There are technical terms in religion just as in science and philosophy. Just as in science I should speak of protoplasm, of oxygen or carbonic acid gas, so in talking of religion I must talk about faith and Jesus Christ. Just as I should quote authorities in speaking of chemistry or political economy, so I must use authorities in speaking about Christ. You will not take the words that I have said tonight as a mere expression of phraseology of a cant description, because it is not that; and I would ask those of you who are very much frightened to use such words to consider whether it is not a rational thing and a necessary thing, if you speak at all on this subject, to use these words. We must not be too fastidious, or thin-skinned, or particular on a point like that. While we are not in any degree to advertise our Christianity by our language, there are occasions, and this is one, when these things are necessary.

I want to say, in closing, that I hear almost extraordinary accounts of you Harvard men. Robert Browning once came to the Edinburgh students to talk to them; and he said, after he had gone away, that he had never in his life seen such a body of young men. Now I have no acquaintance with you whatever; but I have been asking up and down this district what sort of men the Harvard men are, and I want to let you know that you have a fairly good character. So far as I can learn, you have a character such as none of our Scotch universities have. Now live up to it. Let this university in the years to come be famous over America not only for its education, but for its sense of honor and manliness, and purity and Christianity. Seek first the kingdom of God. You know the whole truth. Live it. Want of interest in religion does not acquit you of taking your share in it. Why should I be here to talk to you? A Scotchman hates talking. I believe an American is dying to talk all the time. Well, I say want of religion does not absolve you from taking your share of it. The fact that you do not care about Christ does not alter the fact that Christ cares about you, that He wants you men, and that His kingdom cannot go on unless He gets such men as you. Are we to leave the greatest scheme that has ever been propounded to be carried out by duffers? It is easier, somebody says, to criticise the greatest scheme superbly than to do the smallest thing possible. The man who is looking on from the outside sees things in the game that the players do not see. He sees this bit of bad play and that. Well, stop criticising the game. Take off your coat, and come and help us. Our side is strong, and it is getting stronger; but we want the best men. Christianity ought to have the superlative men here in every department—in classics, in poetry, in literature, in humor, in everything that goes to the making of a man. The best gifts should be given to

Christ. We are apt to despise Christianity and keep away from it because there are many weak-minded people in it. That is one reason why we ought to take off our coats and throw ourselves into it, heart and soul. And I leave you with that appeal. I appeal to the strong men here to consider their position and see if they can do anything better with their life than to help on this great cause.

An Address to the Man Who Is down

To-night I want to talk to the man who is down, to the man who has his back to the wall, and who is being embattled by his own temptations. It is, perhaps, not an academic subject, but it is the greatest of all subjects on which one can speak to young men. There are men here who are lost in the abyss; but there are more men who are on the brink of the precipice. Temptation is a universal experience—the one thing that makes every man his brother, and creates within any one who thinks about it a grave sense of tenderness as he thinks of those around him, when he remembers that every man he meets has the same black spot in his nature that he has, and the same terrible fight going on from day to day. But, gentlemen, temptation is more than a universal experience. It is an individual thing. Just as you have your own handwriting, your own face, or your own walk, you have your own temptation— different in every case, but generally some one temptation which means everything to you, which sums up the whole battle of life, and which, if you could conquer, you would conquer the world. That temptation follows you wherever you go like your shadow. I have gone into the heart of Africa. When I opened the curtains of my tent in the morning, the first face I saw was the hideous face of my own temptation. Go where you like, you cannot avoid that. It will follow you wherever you go, and lie with you in the grave. Temptation is not only a universal experience and a personal experience, but you have doubtless noticed this about it, that it is very lonely. It cuts a man off in a moment from all his fellowmen; and in the silence of his own heart he finds himself fighting out that battle on which the issues of life hang. Christ trod the wine press alone, and so do you and I. That is one of the things that makes it harder, because there is no one to blame us when we go wrong, and there is no one to applaud us when we do right.

More than that, temptation is a pitiless thing. It goes into the church and picks off the man in the pulpit. It goes into the university and picks off the flower of the class. It goes into the Senate and picks off the great man. Let him that thinketh he standeth, however high up, however sheltered, take heed lest he fall. Why is it that we have to run the gauntlet of temptation all our lives, and what does it mean? Can we analyze it? We have seen its strength. Can we find out whence it comes and how to meet it? There are many theories as to how it came into our nature. Some think there is a virus in human nature somewhere, a bias towards wrong; but I don't think we need to look very far for the origin at least of a great many of our temptations. We have in our bodies the residua of the animal creation. We have bones and muscles and organs which are now mere curiosities, but which once played a great part in the life of our progenitor; and I suppose it is now accepted as a scientific fact, at all events so far as the body is concerned, that it has come down the long ladder from the invertebrate world. That is to say, we have in our nature a part of the animal; and if we have an animal's body in us, we have to a certain extent the residua of an animal's mind, of an animal's proclivities and passions. Whether that is the origin of them or not, it is certain every man among us has a certain residuum of the animal in him. After passing through the animal stage, it is believed that man passed through a long, long discipline in the savage state; so that, in addition to the animal, relics of the savage are still left in our nature.

There are two great classes of sins—sins of the body and sins of the disposition. The prodigal son is a typical instance of sins of the body; and the elder brother a typical illustration of sins of the disposition. He was just as bad as the prodigal, probably worse. The one set of temptations comes from the animal and the other from the savage. What are the characteristics of the savage? Laziness for one thing, and selfishness for another. The savage does nothing but lie in the sun all day and allow the fruits to drop into his mouth. He has no struggle for life. Nature has been so kind as to supply all his wants; and he is, above all, characteristic of selfishness. He has no one to think about or care for, nor has he any capacity. A great preacher said not long ago to his congregation that he would tell them the mark of the beast, and that he also knew its number. He said the mark of the beast was selfishness, and its number was No. 1. Now the mark of the beast, selfishness, is in every man's breast, less or more. We are built in three stories—the bottom, the animal; a little higher up, the savage; and on the top, the man. That is the old Pauline trichotomy—body, soul, spirit. Paul spoke of this body of death. Science speaks of it in almost precisely the same language. Whatever the origin, that is the construction of a man. He is built in those three layers. With this analysis, it is perhaps easier to see how temptation may be met.

Many a man goes through life hanging his head with shame and living without his self-respect because he has never discovered the distinction between temptation and sin. It is only when a man sees temptation coming and goes out to meet it, welcomes it, plays with it and invites it to be his guest that it passes from temptation into sin; but, until he has opened the door of his own accord and let it in, he has done no wrong. He has been a tempted man—not a sinful man. The proof, of course, that temptation is no sin is that Christ was tempted in all points like as we are, yet without sin. Many a man is thrown back in his attempts to live a new life by the clinging to him of this residua of his past; and he does not discover until perhaps too late that there is nothing wrong in these things until they have passed a certain point. If he sees them coming and turns his back upon them, he has not sinned. Indeed, temptation is not only not sin, but it is the most valuable ingredient in human nature. Who was it that said, "The greatest of all temptations is to be without any"? The man who has no temptation has no chance of becoming a man at all. The only way to get character is to have temptation. If a man never exercises his muscle, he will get no muscle. If a man never exercises his moral nature in opposing temptation, he will get no muscle in his character. Temptation is an opportunity of virtue. What makes a good picture? Practice. What makes a good oarsman? Practice. What makes a good cricketer? Practice. Temptation is the practice of the soul; and the man who has most temptations has most practice. I fancy we all imagine we have more temptations than anybody else. That is a universal delusion. But, instead of praying to be delivered from our temptations, we ought to try to understand their essential place in the moral world. Taken from us, these would leave us without a chance of becoming strong men. We should be insipid characters, flaxen and useless. That is why the New Testament says the almost astonishing thing: "Count it all joy when ye fall into divers temptations." We are apt to call it hard lines because we are tempted. James says, count it joy; congratulate yourself because of your own temptation. It is the struggle for life almost solely which has helped on the evolution of the animal kingdom, passing on into the moral region and giving you practice in growth.

Now, then, granting that this discipline is to be ours, that every day of our lives we have to face temptation, how are we to set about it? We have seen that temptation lies in the projection on the human area of our life of the animal and of the savage. I think the first thing we have to do is to deal decisively with those two parts of our nature. The animal body was finished thousands and thousands of years ago. Nature took a long time to work it out, then stopped and went on to develop the mind. Let us recognize the development of the body as a fact in the past, and have no more to do with it. The body is finished. The hand of creation is done working at it. That is what Paul meant very largely when he gave it as his advice to men to get over temptation, "Reckon ye yourselves dead." Reckon that all beneath. It is not only wrong to allow the body to prevail in a man's life, but it is a denial of his development. It is unnatural and irrational. It is contrary to the teachings of science, borrowed altogether from the teachings of religion. Therefore, the first thing a man must do is to make up his mind that the body which is prompting him is a dead thing and is to be taken as a dead thing. If we can give our animal nature its true place, we will soon learn to rise above it. What did Cato do when he was buffeted? Ask Seneca. He did not strike back, fly into a passion: he did not resent it, but denied that it had been done. That is to say, the body being nothing, nothing had happened.

But that is not enough. We cannot live negatively. It is not enough to forsake the old life, the old habit; but we must take another piece of advice which I think the New Testament also sums up for us in language of exceeding simplicity and yet of absolute scientific accuracy. Paul says: "Walk in the spirit." Live in the top flat. You find yourself living in the animal part of your being. Escape and get into the upper story, where the roof is open to God, and whre you can move amongst beautiful things, and amongst holy memories and amongst high ideals. Walk in the spirit and ye shall not fulfill the lusts of the flesh. A man can't do it. That is to say, he has to evolve the past, the animal and the savage, and develop the new nature. The new nature is renewed from day to day, little by little. Just as the body is built up, microscopic cell by microscopic cell, so the new nature is built up by a long series of crucifixions of the old nature, by taking in food from the higher world and getting those things built into our nature which work for righteousness and truth and beauty and purity.

Now, the man who encourages the higher part of his nature continuously will get an absolute victory over the lower parts of his being. He will come to live in those higher parts of his being. It will become as habitual to live there as it was to live in the lower; and, while this building up is going on within, there will be the degeneration of the old nature. How has man evolved past the animal and the savage, and how has so much that is in them passed away from him? By mere disuse. And so, by the mere disuse of the propensities of the body and the discouragement of selfish and petty interests, by merely giving up the animal ways and the animal passions, and the savage tempers and the savage laziness, the impulse, the function which makes these things, will wither—atrophy. As the one goes on, the other inevitably follows. As the old man passes away, the new man is renewed in righteousness. That can be explained not only in the language of development but in the language of psychology as a perfectly rational principle. A man cannot have two things in consciousness at the same moment. Suppose a man has been lost out in the West and wandered away from the railway depot where he had put up at a hotel. Perhaps he has been four or five days on the prairie. One day he staggers back, almost dropping with hunger and calls out for food; but finds lying upon his table, while waiting for food, a telegram reporting the sudden death of his wife. The hunger is gone, completely gone. The man who was perishing a few moments ago is now absolutely above it; and if I could keep up the emotion of sorrow, I could keep down forever the appetite of hunger. If you want to get over an appetite on philosophical principles, not to speak of religion, the thing to do is to pass into another region, and let your mind be preoccupied with something higher. Unless you take in the higher, it is tremendously difficult to crush out the lower. The new man can only be put on as the old man is put off.

You remember Augustine's history of temptation in four words—cogitatio, imaginatio, delectatio and assensio: a thought, a picture, a fascination, and a fall. You can cut off the series between the first and second. Between the second and third, it is almost impossible. Between the third and fourth, it is absolutely impossible. When the image is thrown upon the screen and you are delighting in it and it is just beginning to enthrall you, you can still do one thing. You can suddenly throw another image on the screen and look at that. If you look for two seconds at the first image you are lost; but if you look one second you are not yet lost, and there is still a chance to be saved. You can throw another image over it and let the first dissolve away; and, by the mere possession of consciousness, you have got over that temptation.

You see, then, how, upon merely natural principles, it is possible to fight temptation. If we simply walk in the spirit, we shall not fulfill the lusts of the flesh. We must evolve past them, in plain words. By cultivating ideals of all kinds and by strengthening our moral nature by all the opportunities we can get in society, in literature and in the church, we will gradually accumulate a body, a higher body, of life and mind and truth, in which we can live; and the old tenements in which we lived will not only be uninhabited but uninhabitable. Hence the value of everything that is beautiful and pure and lovely and wholesome in the world; and not only their use as auxiliaries to the religious life, but as indispensable to it; because all these are things in the higher nature, and the man who cultivates them is building up a region in which he can live. A man must live. He must live in the body, in the savage or in the man. At every moment he must live, and so at every moment he must make his choice. He cannot suppress it. If you take this subject in terms of energy, you will find that the energy which leads to sin must not be suppressed, but must be transformed into an energy which leads to virtue; so that when the desire to do something wrong comes in, instead of trying to suppress that desire, we have simply to turn the helm in the right direction; and in the new channel it will not only save us from a fall which we would have had, if we had allowed it to go the other way, but it will carry us higher towards the new life.

Now I have tried to explain the way in which any man here can rise above himself and be a man. I care not how far he has dropped. It is an historical fact that a man can be saved to the uttermost. You say to me, is there no religion in all this? It is all religion. You say, do I not need to put more religion into it? The more the better. I have spoken of walking in the spirit. I have spoken of ideals. I know no ideal that will act so promptly as the ideal of the perfect Man. I know no picture that you can throw upon the screen which will fascinate more immediately than the picture of the character of Christ. You may throw people upon the screen, a line of poetry, an epigram from a moralist, a memory of your mother, a warning of some one you love, and all these are reflections in some form of Christ; and they will all be effective up to a point. But most of all effective is the power of Christ Himself; and, unless a man has a moral environment which is full of these things, he cannot live. There is no hope for his new life, unless he has that. No man can live without these things morally. Take that gas which gives us light. The light is not in the gas. It is half in the air and half in the gas. Take away the half from the air, and the gas goes out. "Without me, ye can do nothing." Your life will go out. Without Me, whether as the Light of the world itself, or as diffused through books, and through men and through churches, without that your life will come to nothing; but, if you take that and all the reflections of it, and let these constitute a spiritual atmosphere about you, your redemption from this hour is a certainty. There is no haphazard about Christianity. It is based upon the laws of nature and the laws of the human mind.

The man who lives in Christ cannot go wrong. He will be kept. In the nature of things, he must be kept. He cannot sin. You remember John said: "Whosoever sinneth hath not seen Him, neither known Him." John's Friend was such, so inspiring and so influential, that it was inconceivable to John that anybody could ever have met Him without forevermore trying to live like Him. Sin is abashed in the presence of the purity of Jesus Christ. There are many heroes in life. They will all help a man; but we will get on better and quicker by giving ourselves to Christ.

I have just two things to add. The first is: if any man here to-night takes this seriously and means business; if he means for the future not to keep up the sham fight that he has been pretending to wage, and means to get to the bottom of things, let me ask him for a few days from this time to treat himself as a man who has been very ill and dare not do anything. Let him consider himself as a convalescent for a few weeks and take care where he goes, what he reads, what he looks at, and the people he speaks to. He is not strong enough for the outer air. When he first begins the new life, he is young and tender. Therefore, let him beware of the first few days. Mortality is greatest amongst children for the first few hours: then it is greater for the first few days; then it is great for the next few months, and lessens as the children grow older. If you are careful not to catch cold for the first few weeks after you begin to lead a new life, you will succeed; but, if you do to-morrow what you did to-day, you will go wrong, because you are not strong enough to resist. You will have to build up this new body cell by cell, day by day, just as the old body of temptation has been built up. If any man here knows any other man who is in that convalescent condition, let him take care, and neither by jest, or word, or temptation, throw that man back. Stand by him, if you know such a man. If you are such a man, do not be ashamed to get somebody else to back you and go along with you. Very few men can live a solitary Christian life. You will find it a great source of strength to get another man's life wound about you. You can help each other.

The other thing I want to say is this: Do not imagine that you can get deliverance from sin alone—I mean without getting other things, and without doing other things. Deliverance from sin is only a part of the Christian life—by no means the whole. It is only one wing of the new nature; but no man can get on with one wing. Deliverance from temptation is only one function of the new nature. Therefore, you must consecrate your whole life to Christianity, and go into it wholly and with a whole heart, if you expect to get deliverance in this one direction; and the best way you can do that is to make up your mind that you will give much of your life to Christianity, to purify the air of the world, so that other men will feel less temptation than you do. Sin is a kind of bacillus, and it cannot take root in the world unless there is a soil, and it is our business to make the world's soil pure and sanitarily sweet, so that the disease of sin cannot exist.

One Way to Help Boys

I am very much pleased to find the Boys' Brigade receiving University recognition. I am not aware that it has had this honor before in its history.

The idea of the Brigade is this. It is a new movement for turning out boys, instead of savages. The average boy, as you know, is a pure animal. He is not evolved; and, unless he is taken in hand by somebody who cares for him and who understands him, he will be very apt to make a mess of his life—not to speak of the lives of other people. We endeavor to get hold of this animal. You do not have the article here, and do not quite understand the boy I mean. The large cities of the old world are infested by hundreds and thousands of these ragamuffins, as we call them—young roughs who have nobody to look after them. The Sunday-school cannot handle these boys. The old method was for somebody to form them into a class and try to get even attention from them. Half the time was spent in securing order.

The new method is simply this: You get a dozen boys together, and, instead of forming them into a class, you get them into some little hall and put upon every boy's head a little military cap that costs in our country something like twenty cents, and you put around his waist a belt that costs about the same sum, and you call him a soldier. You tell him, "Now, Private Hopkins, stand up. Hold up your head. Put your feet together." And you can order that boy about till he is black in the face, just because he has a cap on his head and a belt around his waist. The week before you could do nothing with him. If he likes it, you are coming next Thursday night. He is not doing any favor by coming. You are doing him a favor; and if he does not turn up at eight o'clock, to the second, the door will be locked. If his hair is not brushed and his face washed, he cannot enter. Military discipline is established from the first moment. You give the boys three-fourths of an hour's drill again, and in a short time you have introduced quite a number of virtues into that boy's character. You have taught him instant obedience. If he is not obedient, you put him into the guard house, or tell him he will be drummed out of the regiment; and he will never again disobey. If he is punctual and does his drill thoroughly, tell him that at the end of the year he will get a stripe. He will get a cent's worth of braid. You have his obedience, punctuality, intelligence and attention for a year for one cent. Then you have taught him courtesy. He salutes you and feels a head taller. Everything is done as if you were a real captain and he a real private. He calls you "Captain." Each boy has a rifle that costs a dollar; but there is no firing. There is a bayonet drill without a bayonet. The first year they have military drill, and the second year bayonet exercises—an absolute copy of the army drill. The Brigade inculcates a martial, but not a warlike, spirit. The only inducement to bring the boys together at first is the drill. You might think it is a very poor one; but it is about the strongest inducement you could offer.

That is the outward machinery; but it is a mere take-in. The boy doesn't know it. The real object of the Brigade is to win that boy for Christianity—to put it quite plainly. It does not make the slightest secret of its aims.

On all its literature is: "The object of the Brigade shall be the advancement of Christ's Kingdom among boys, and the promotion of habits of reverence, discipline, self-respect, and all that tends toward a true Christian manhood."

After you have your boy and are sure of him, every drill is opened with a couple of minutes of prayer. The boys stand in line at "attention," with caps off, while a sort of blessing is asked. Then drill for three-fourths of an hour. After that the Captain gives them a little talk about anything—business prosperity, courtesy, courage, temptation, or anything. After that, all repeat the Lord's Prayer and dismiss. Then on Sunday almost all the companies have Bible class, with the same punctuality, interest and attention as during the week day. The boy treats his Captain as before. They sit like statues during the Bible lesson; and, if they are not there to the minute, they are shut out. Having influence over them, the Captain maintains it, and how much more apt the boys will be to pick up what he says. The thorough-going Captain will of course do a great deal more than in the Bible class; and very few stop at that. Some men get up football clubs and get fields, give up their own Saturday afternoons —which are a great holiday with us—to act as umpire for the boys' matches. Our captains are just one remove from the boys whom they teach, so that the boys are not at all afraid of them. The presence of the captain on the athletic field means, in the first place, that there will be no foul language and no foul play. And he, of course, thus increases his influence over them tenfold. Then in many cases they start a boys' club where they have a room open every night, where they have debates, newspapers and books. Then the captain gets to know the boys personally. He has them up to tea now and then, and gets to know their people.

In addition to that general work, there are one or two additions which are thrown in by special companies according to their own inclination. A great many have started military bands. Ambulance classes are becoming exceedingly popular. After drilling two or three winters the work gets flat; so they invent new things. Boys cannot join this Brigade until they are twelve years of age, and cannot clear out until they are seventeen. The boys hate to clear out; and the fact that they will have to leave induces them to make better use of their time. Of course they are not turned adrift. The captain sees that they get into good hands. Then every year, in a city of the size of Boston, for instance, all the boys belonging to the Brigade would be gathered together for a church service. If too many for one church, two would be secured, and the boys would assemble and march to the service and get a boys' sermon. At Christmas, every boy in the Brigade gets from his officer a little two-cent book. And there are a number of other little things that link the captain and the boys together and the different companies together.

This organization was started within a mile of where I live in Glasgow in 1883, by a Mr. Smith, who was a soldier, and who was not making much of a Sunday-school class he taught, and who conceived the idea of giving them military discipline. In our country we have grown to such an extent that already there are, I think, 22,000 boys belonging to the Brigade, and I think between 1,100 and 1,200 officers—captains and lieutenants. This Brigade has been worth starting for the sake of the officers alone.

Perhaps one thousand of these officers would have belonged to the unemployed rich and educated, if they had not struck this particular line of work. There are multitudes of young men who do not go to prayer meeting or see their way to teach in Sunday-school. Many are extremely fastidious as to what particular work they will do, and many are not cut out for these recognized fields. But here is a work that does not make any particular strain on any part of his nature. He simply gives himself and his muscular Christianity. So we think this has been worth pushing for the sake of the officers alone. We know a great many men have been made for life simply by a year or two of contact with these boys. If they develop the boys, the boys develop them.

Now, you have this movement started in America. I find the most crass ignorance on this subject here; but in some respects you are ahead of us. One of the first things you do with the boys is to start a newspaper. The conflagration has broken out in a somewhat remarkable way in California, and they must have a great many companies. As usual, when you take up anything in this country from anywhere else, you improve upon it or carry it to development in other directions.

Now, you do some things here we do not do, and of which I am not perfectly sure we would wholly approve. They strike us as being slightly against some of the fundamental principles for which we work. For instance, I notice that the boys here have a uniform, and that the officers have a uniform. We can make a boy for about fifty cents, not including the brass in his face; but here in America the uniform costs as follows:

(See Boys' Brigade Manual, U. S. of A.)
Fatigue blouses (I suppose they have paid duty on these blouses) $3.35
Pants 3.35
Fatigue caps, first quality 0.75
Belts 0.75
Plain bugles 0.25
Signal service 1.20
U. S. Army bunting flags 9.50
Silk cord for same 3.50
Bugler's stripes for pants 1.50
Extra fine officers' fatigue blouses 6.75
Pants with stripes 6.50
U. S. Army officers' overcoats with hoods $27 to 32.00

Well, you see that means business at any rate. But what we dislike about it is that it emphasizes the military side too much. We have refused to admit any company into the Brigade that wears a uniform. There are one or two in the country, but we don't have them. We don't want the boys to feel soldiers beyond the point that we need them to feel soldiers. We don't want them to thirst for blood and come over here and fight you or anybody else. We simply want to get them disciplined. I suppose there must be in this country quite a number of companies equipped at very considerable expense. These boys cannot afford to buy these uniforms for themselves, and they are very frequently bought by subscription.

This organization in America is almost always organized within the church. In the old country every organization must be associated, not necessarily with the church, but with some stable body that will be back of it and be a sponsor for it. It is usually the church—sometimes the Y. M. C. A. In this country the initiatory is frequently taken by the minister. I find the ministers here preserve the dew of their youth and the freshness of their manhood, and they are not at all the starchy kind of people one meets in some other countries. It is not because they are not fit for this, but the ministers must not have all the plums. They have enough to do. Here and there we have some keen ministers at this work, but, as a rule, we try to keep it among the laity.

In this country you make the boys promise that as long as they are members of the Boys' Brigade they will not use liquor and tobacco, will obey the rules and set an example of good conduct. The question is whether pledges are right fair to a boy at all. I very much question whether it is wise to put a strong pledge like that upon anybody. We exact no pledge whatever. It seems to me to be the difference between compulsory chapel attendance and optional, as it is here, to make a boy not smoke by compulsion. If he can be made moral by the influences that are brought to bear upon him, it is more apt to last.

Now I suppose I was asked to present this subject to you in behalf of enlisting one or two of you in the service. I do not know myself of any bit of work to which I would rather give what spare time I have than this. The boy is open to receive impressions in a way that is marked. It is possible to get hold of him. There are thousands of these boys who have been turned outside in. I have watched them. I remember the annual inspection of one of the first companies. When the prizes were given, it was my duty to pin the medals on the two leading boys' breasts. When the first boy came up, there was scarcely a place on his coat strong enough to bear the pin. His coat was one mass of patches that could scarcely hold together. He was clean. The next year I noticed he had on a much better coat, and I am sure he is now on his way to turn out to be a good man. I do not know anything that would pay any of you better than this. It lies near a young man's nature to take up such work. I do not think there is anything easier than to win a boy. You get him wound about you, and he lives through your spectacles and tries to please you. Adapt it any way you please; but I should like very much if after to-night some of you would write for some of this literature and take the trouble to spread it.

We gave the boys books each Christmas. Two years ago I wrote a book and offered fifty-three prizes. The boys competing were to write a letter addressed to "My Dear Baxter," and answer the question, "What are a Boy's Temptations, and How is He to Meet Them?" Well, I got about 450 dissections of the boys in answer to that offer. One of the thirty prizes went to California. I never saw such a revelation of the interior of a boy as I saw after reading those letters. Every boy, almost, out of the lot, pleaded guilty to four sins. Every boy, apparently, is a liar and a thief. These were the first two things that they all confessed. The third confession was that they all swore; and the fourth great temptation or sin to a boy was smoking—which is not a sin at all. It showed me that the boys were very badly taught, and that they have no definite conception of sin.

Every one of these Brigades, almost without an exception, is connected with the church. The Bible class is held in the church; and the drill is usually there, too. It is thoroughly under the wing of the church. The movement is so religious that there is never any religious opposition to it, and it is entirely undenominational.

An Appeal to the Outsider; or the Claims of Christianity

I am asked to talk specially to what we call in Scotland "the outsider"—the man who has not seen his way to throw in his lot with Christian men. We have made a specialty of the outsider in our university work in the old country. We have laid all our plans to interest him. He is generally the best man in the university; and for some years we have arranged all our Christian work and worship with a view to that type of man. We have laid down one or two principles. The first one is that none of us in any shape or form shall encourage cant. By that I mean sanctimoniousness, anything that is falsetto, any unreal expression of emotion or exaggeration of feeling. A second principle we have had to lay down is that no religious man shall interfere in any shape or form with the university amusements. Time after time I have seen at our religious meetings twelve out of the fifteen university football team; and we have always had amongst our foremost men the best athletes in the university. We have also laid it down as a principle that we shall not interfere with any university work. We have tried to get hold of the busiest men and interest them in whatever is going on, believing that a man may do his university work thoroughly and yet do something in the way of helping on the Christian life of his fellow students. In the Medical Faculty, where we have from 1,800 to 2,000 students, and which is our largest faculty in Edinburgh University, at the end of the four years' course we have the "Blue Ribbon Medical Course" scholarship. It is given to the man who has stood first all along the line for four years. Now the man who for the last four years has taken this scholarship has been not only one of the most active workers in the Christian community, but actually the secretary of the movement. I do not mean that one man has done that for four years; but the last four men have been not only the leading men in the scientific and professional studies, but the leading men in the Christian life of the place. With such a record as that you can understand that Christianity is, at all events, respected.

We never have any religious meetings on week days. We do not want the professors to say we are taking up the time the men ought to give other things. We believe a man's business at a college, and his religion, too, is to do his work. The meetings we have had, therefore, were on Sundays.

Another rule that we have had to make is never to interfere with a man's views. We want a man's life. We do not want his opinion. We do not start a man with a creed. We believe that the man arrives at a creed; and we take into our ranks any man who has any desire to seek the Kingdom of God. That, of course, had widened the door to a very large number of men who would have kept out, if we had been exclusive. But while we do not underrate a creed, while we believe that theological doctrines are just as scientific doctrines; yet religion is an art, and we can get men to practice the art who will arrive, we hope, in their future life, at something of the scientific principles which underlie it; but we make it a barrier to no man at the start that he knows little. In fact, a man enters the school of Christ as he enters a university. That is to say, he enters, not as a professor, but as a student. He comes to learn; and we believe the best way to learn is to let the man matriculate and begin.

If you ask me what obstacles we find specially in the way, I think the chief obstacle we meet is the revolt in thinking men's minds against popular and spurious and weak forms of Christianity. Men come to the institution who have been very strictly brought up, and they are not able, after a few months' college discipline, to believe the things they used to believe. A gentleman in Boston said to me a few days ago that he had a son at Harvard and that the young man had the audacity to come to him not long ago and tell him that he didn't believe so and so. I said to him: "Sir, what a splendid fellow your son must be." He preferred truth to comfort. A man is to be encouraged to think about religious matters. If Christianity cannot bear thinking about, it is not worth going in for.

One other thing that one finds is the idea many men have that it is a dull thing to go in for Christianity. Now, of course, that is simply not true. It is not true in fact, and it is not true in theory. It has, doubtless, more concern for a man's temperament and body than his creed; but if there is anything that can put sunniness or brightness into a man's life, it is Christianity. Christianity professes to cure dullness. Some of the greatest words in the Bible are "joy," "rest," "comfort." Christianity cures depression and gloom by removing the causes of it. What makes men depressed? Self-concentration, as a rule. When a man is wrapped up in himself, seeking only his own, he finds he is seeking a very shallow object, and very soon gets to the end of it; hence all the springs of life have nothing to act upon, and depression follows. Now, Christianity cures that by trying to take a man out of himself, and by showing him that his true life is in living out of himself.

Another source of dullness is the thwarting of the ambitions that we have. We get down in spirits because we do not get the recognition we think we deserve, because we are snubbed and slighted, because we are not at the top. Christianity cures that by a single sentence. It says: "The meek shall inherit the earth." There is no connection between Christianity and a dull life. It is the want of Christianity that makes any life dull. Christianity offers a young man, or an old man, or any man, a more abundant life than the life he is living—more life as life goes, more happiness in life, more intensity in life, more worthiness in life.

That, however, is perhaps not so great an obstacle, comparatively a trifling one, as the thought many men have that it is an unscientific thing in these days to endorse Christianity. Now it may be unscientific to endorse some forms in which Christianity is presented, but Christianity itself is a thoroughly scientific thing. There is nothing the least narrow about anything that Christ ever said. On the contrary, Christ said the broadest things that have ever been said; and he never rebuked breadth, but constantly rebuked narrowness. In His day there were three great philosophical, theological schools. There were the Pharisees, who were so narrow that they could not see spirit for form. There were the Sadducees, who were so narrow that they could not see spirit for matter. And there were the Essenes, who could not see matter for spirit. Christ was always rebuking these sects simply on account of their narrowness. His own view of life was as broad as the heavens. He took in every man and every part of every man. His religion was not kept back by any geographical or ethnographical limits. It was the religion of humanity.

You say, "But it is well known that many scientific men are opposed to Christianity." I ask you to give me their names. If you run over the names of the large figures in science at this moment, you will find that the majority are not only in favor of Christianity, but have expressed themselves in favor of it.

Mr. Huxley has never said anything against Christianity. He has defined the position of science. He says, "Science is not Christianity, nor is it anti-Christianity. It is extra-Christianity." He has thrown an arrow, with a little poison on it, perhaps, at some of the outworks of Christianity; but he has never said one word against Christ or the words or spirit of Christ. And it matters little what a man does to the outworks so long as he respects and is compelled to respect Christ; and Christianity is always respected, however humbly it is lived, by the wisest men.

The other day I came upon a statement by a Fellow of the Royal Society with regard to this subject, a sentence of which I should like to read to you. The Royal Society of London, as you know, is probably one of the first scientific bodies in the world. This man says: "I have known the British Association for the Advancement of Science under forty-one different presidents—all leading men of science. On looking over these forty-one names, I count twenty, who, judged by their public utterances or private communications, are men of Christian belief and character; while, judged by the same test, only four disbelieve in direct divine revelation."

You point to Mr. Darwin. Mr. Darwin never had, and never gave himself, a chance. He was brought up on Paley's Natural Theology—a great book in its day, but a book which Darwin himself made it impossible to read to-day; and he was bombarded with that book, and with religion along that line; and we have no evidence that he ever studied Christianity in any other form. But wherever he saw it, he respected it. When he was on the Island of Terra del Fuego, he saw the lowest subjects in the world. He told the missionaries they might go home. It was an impossibility, from the point of view of science, that these men could ever be elevated. A very few years after, Mr. Darwin wrote a letter to the secretary of that missionary society saying that he had found out what a great change had come over these islands—a certain amount of civilization had been introduced, and morality had been established; and he would like to withdraw what he had said. He enclosed a check for twenty five dollars for the work of the society; and he continued sending in his annual contribution to the end of his life.

Perhaps the greatest name known to you in the old country is that of Sir William Thompson, now Lord Kelvin, Professor of Physics in Glasgow University. If you go into his class room any day you like, you will hear him open his lecture with prayer.

It is not true that the scientific men have given up Christianity. Many of them have given up imitations of Christianity, spurious forms of it; but the thing itself stands untouched.

You ask me, "What, then, do you retain? Do you dilute Christianity until it means little or nothing—so little that anybody can call himself a Christian?" On the contrary, we make it the most severe thing, the most definite thing, that a man could choose for his object in life. We make it a necessity that a man shall be turning, that he shall seek first the Kingdom of God. He may choose his own way of doing it; but he must put that before him as an ambition and as his career to seek first the Kingdom of God. We say nothing to those men about saving their souls. We say to them: "Gentlemen, save your lives. Do something with your life. Let that energy, that talent, go out to some purpose. The world needs the knowledge you have, the impulses you can give; aye, and the criticisms that you can offer upon the religious forms round about. It needs all these things. Save your lives. Do something with them." The Kingdom of God, according to Christ's own definition, is leaven; it is salt; it is light. Can you tell me what is going to raise this country, for instance, if it is not to be Christianity? If you take the Christianity out of Boston, weak as some of it may be, and inconsistent as some of it may be, in fifty years it will be uninhabitable by a respectable man or woman. Was it Mr. Lowell who said: "Show me ten square miles in any part of the world, outside of Christianity, where the life of man and the purity of woman are safe, and I will give up Christianity"? There are no such ten square miles in any part of the world. Many things can lift society a little; but, as a matter of fact and history, the thing that has lifted the nations of the world to their present level has been, in some form or other, direct or diffused, the Christianity of Christ. Christian men are to be not only the leaven of the world, but they are to be the salt of the earth. The world is not only sunken, needing to be raised, but it is rotten, and needing to be purified. Salt is that which saves from corruption. Christianity is the salt of the earth. It is the great antiseptic of society. Christian men are the light of the world. The light of Christ was the light of men; and other men are to catch that light and radiate it upon the world.

You point me to other teachers, many of them very great, many of them with great messages for the world—Socrates, Plato—a long list of names; but, allowing all their goodness, can one of them be put beside Christ as a mere teacher? Socrates went about the world asking questions. Christ went about the world answering questions. That was the difference. Socrates was looking for truth. Christ said truth is in living. I am the truth; and the man who lives like Me will live true, and all the wrong in the mind will be corrected. You cannot help seeing truth.

Now, gentlemen, what do you think of that for a life, for a career? You do not know what to do with yourself. What do you think of being a crystal of salt in a community such as this city, or a little cell of leaven which cannot help, by the mere contagion of its presence, passing on influence and life to things round about it, or being a light to the dark people, perhaps the dark Christians, if you like, round about, too?

Do the workingmen of this country not need light? What is to alter the critical condition of the working classes in this country, if it is not to be the teaching of Christianity in some form? What is to guide these labor movements and to work upon the minds in all directions, to make this country continuously prosperous? Men who have looked deepest into these problems have either given them up or seen only one solution, and that is in the teaching of Christ and the application of His principles to common life. These principles are not in the air. They are justified by every fact and law of nature.

I believe in Christianity, first of all, not because I believe in this book. I believe in this book because I believe in Christianity. Religion does not come out of the Bible. The Bible comes out of religion. I believe in Christianity because I believe in evolution. Christianity is to me further evolution. I know no better definition of it than that. The forces of nature carry a man up to a certain point and there they stop. Then the psychic forces carry him up another point to the evolution of mind.

Then the moral forces come in and carry him up a little further. Then the vis a tergo, the struggle for life that pushes him on, is reinforced by a vis a fronto; and he sees ideals before him, and is drawn up higher and higher, from strength to strength, until he reaches the fullness of the stature of the perfect man. That is pure evolution, the evolution of the man toward the ideal, toward the perfect man Jesus Christ. This principle of which I have been speaking, of a man giving his life to other people, to help on his country, is in the very, heart of nature. There are two great principles in nature by which all things work and by which all things are moved. The one is the struggle for life. Every plant and animal starts out to nourish itself. That struggle goes on along the line of the function of nutrition. There is the struggle for the life of others—the function of reproduction. These two functions make up life. Now, most of us live along the line of the first. All our lives, nearly, are centered in that; but that is only one half of the life appointed by nature. There is the struggle for the life of others, the function of reproduction, and in its higher forms everything that is high lies. All the happiness in life, in reality, has come along the second of these two lines, and not along the first. All the life of the world, in reality, lies on the side of reproduction. A plant takes a little bit of itself and gives it away. It lives by death. It dies; the life goes on. This chapel is built upon death. That book is death. Those pillars are the death of men. Those clothes are the death of animals. Every part of life and everything in life is kept alive by death. The animal gives off a part of itself and dies. Its life goes on—has passed on; and I say all the comfort and happiness and beauty and luxury of life come along that line. Three-fourths of the world at this moment live upon rice. What is rice? It is a seed —a fruit, therefore, of reproduction. The world lives upon this altruistic principle. All the fruits of the world are the gifts of reproduction. All the drinks of the world are the fruits of reproduction —the milk of the cow, the sprouting grain, the malted liquor, the withered hop, the fruit of the vine, wine itself. All the beauty of the world comes along the line of reproduction—the feathers of the bird, the fire of the glow-worm, the face of a woman. All the music of the world is love music—the chorus of the insect, the song of the nightingale, the serenade of the lover. We live by what the function of reproduction has done for us; and the man who gives his life for what is going on in that line is living for the highest end in nature.

The struggle for life is waning every century, and by and by it will give place entirely to this other. Therefore, when Christ said, "Seek first the Kingdom of God," he propounded a perfectly scientific doctrine. He was offering man a life which would include all other lives, to which all other things would be heir.

Let me give you an illustration of what I mean. You are here at the university. You can't yet begin to do anything for your country, as you might. What you can do now is to leaven this university. What you can do is to get hold of some one man, whose life is of no account, and which is apparently not going to be of any account, and save that man, not for his own sake only, but because that is a piece of energy which has gone off but can be brought in and reclaimed and utilized for the good of man.

There was a medical student in Edinburgh University in his second year (our course is four years), who saw that he had been living there eighteen months entirely for himself. He had never done a hand's turn to be of any good or use to any one, and it hurt him. One day he determined that he would do something to help another man, and he remembered another undergraduate, who had come from the same country town as himself, and who had gone to pieces. He hunted him up. He found him half drunk in a very poor and shabby lodging. He told him that he would like him to come and live in his rooms; that he had nice rooms, and it was snugger than where he was. The other man stated he was in debt and could not leave. No. 1 went out of the room, paid the man's bill, sent for a carriage, bundled up his friend's things—and a newspaper held them all—and took him off to his own lodgings. The next morning he said: "Now, you and I are going to live together. Let us make a contract and both sign it."

There were four articles in it.

"First, neither one of us is to go out alone, unless absolutely necessary.

"Second, twenty minutes to be allowed to go from room to college for recitations. Overtime to be accounted for.

"Third, one hour to be given every night to recreation.

"Fourth, bygones to be bygones."

They both signed it. Everything went on well. They had lived together for six weeks when one night No. 2 sprang up, shut his book with a bang and said: "I can't stand this slow life. I must have a bust." "Very well," said No. 1, "you shall bust here. What do you want?" "I want some drink." "Well, you shall have it," said No. 1, and he got him something to drink and brought it to the room. No. 2 took it. Do you say it was a risk? His thirst was allayed and the wild beast was calmed. He settled down to his books for six weeks again, when the wild beast once more asserted itself. No. 1 gave it a meal to satisfy it, as before. No. 2 worked faithfully this time for three months before another outbreak. And so the thing went on. A year afterward No. 2 said to No. 1: "You never tell me what you are reading at the recreation hour. I think I see you read the Bible sometimes. You never talked to me on that subject." Talked to him about it! What was the use of talking to a man about Christianity when he was living it every hour of his life? He had done his work without ever having said a word. No. 2 was dying to learn his secret. I need not detail the rest. These two men passed out of the University at the end of their course. No. 1 passed a fairly good examination. No. 2, the man who was lost, graduated with honors and took the medal for his thesis. The last time I heard of No. 1 he was filling an important appointment in London, and No. 2 is known as "the Christian Doctor" of a village in Wales. Now that seems to me to be a thing worth living for; something to look back upon after one's college life is over.

No one knew anything about this. No. 1 was never known as a specially religious man, and yet, in his quiet way, he was living Christ in every direction; and he left more fragrance behind him when he was gone than a dozen of the noisier men.

I ask you, gentlemen, to save your lives, to save your college days, and I appeal to the generous side of you and ask you to remember your fellow men. Remember the man who is going to pieces; remember the man who is down, the man who is tempted. Perhaps if you would stand by him you could help him through. You need not make any great profession of religion. But, if you do that, you will make a great practice of it. It will amount to little, after the college course is over, that you have merely done your work and passed. What is the use of your passing, what is the use of your getting any degree, unless it is going to be of some use to somebody else? There is no particular reason why nine-tenths of us should be alive at all; but the man who begins to live for the Kingdom of God, who sees a chance to do a good turn here and a little one there, and shed a little light here and a little sunniness there, has something to live for. That man's life will never be lost. He lives a more abundant life. There is no other joy or light in the world except that.

And if you gentlemen are going to seek the Kingdom of God, I want to ask you to seek it first. Do not touch it unless you promise to seek it first. I promise you a miserable life and influence and a poor, broken, lost career, if you seek it second. Seek it first, or let it alone. Do not be an amphibian; no man can serve two masters, and, if you only knew it, it is a thousand times easier to seek first the Kingdom of God than to seek it second. I have not the slightest doubt there are many men who are seeking second the Kingdom of God, and their religion is a nuisance to them. It is hard to keep up, and they would get rid of it if they could. The cure is to seek it first, to make it the helm of life. Then only can a man's life go straight, and then only can he fulfill the destiny for which God has put him into the world.

Life on the Top Floor

You have had a great time on the mountains, but remember the mountain is not a place to live on. The Mount of Transfiguration is an episode, coming to a man from time to time; but it is not in the ordinary course of nature that a man should always live on the top of the mountain. The mountain is of use to send streams into the valley of our ordinary life, to fertilize and nourish what is there. Perhaps it is not possible that we shall all be living at the same pitch at which you have lived during the days of this week. Before the sacramental wine was dry on the lips of Peter he was untrue to his Saviour. A breakdown to the moral life is just as natural, and just as much a matter of law as the breakdown of an engine. It is important to get to the bottom of these causes. One of the most important things for us to study is the anatomy of the soul, the anatomy of temptation, and the physiology of sin.

You will not agree with me, perhaps, but I have a strong suspicion that the evolutionists are on the right track when they tell us that man's body has come up through the animal creation. Bone for bone, muscle for muscle and nerve for nerve, you and I are exactly the same as the higher vertebrae of the animal kingdom; and after we passed through the animal kingdom, it is supposed by the theorists, we underwent a long probation in which we were somewhat in the condition of the red Indian; and, just as we had the bodies of animals, we had to some extent the minds of animals and the dispositions of savages. If the animal has left me as its legacy a vertebral column and certain nerves, why should it not leave me a legacy of its modes and passions? And if I have once had as my ancestors a long race of savages, why should not the modes and predilections of the savage nature be still in my blood? If I have the blood of the tiger, shall I not have to some extent the spirit of a tiger? If I have the blood of a shark, shall I not be inclined sometimes to play the shark? If I have the blood of a fox, shall I not be inclined sometimes to be foxy? Well, it doesn't matter in the least whether that is true or not, but I appeal to you if it is not a fact that you find in yourselves the residuum of many animals and the disposition of many savages. If there is a man who has nothing of the animal in him, I should like you to introduce me to him. It doesn't matter where it came from. It is there, as a matter of fact. That is to say, man is built in three stories. He is a three-storied structure. On the ground floor there dwells the animal. Above that, on the second story, there is the savage. And on the third floor there is the man. Now, my brother, when you go wrong, it is not you who goes wrong, it is the man who lives in the bottom story. And when you collapse, when you imagine that it is impossible for you to recover again, remember that the true man in you is still there; and that although temptations may come to you from these lower parts of your nature, it is not essential that you should live in idle acquiescence to them. By taking to pieces the moral nature, one sees very clearly what temptation really is. It is the appeal of the animal to the man; and it is no sin for man to hear that appeal. It is no sin for a man to be tempted. In virtue of his nature, man must be tempted. It is when a man leaves the top story and deliberately walks down and spends an hour in the cellar that temptation passes from temptation into sin.

In the same way, one sees very clearly from that little piece of anatomy, how it is possible to overcome temptation. The remedy, of course, is simply to decline ever to move in the lower regions of one's being at all, to regard that as a thing evolved past, and to live constantly in the higher regions. When a man does that, it is impossible for him to break down. Put it in this way. An image is thrown upon the screen of your mind and you look at it. How can you dismiss it? You can only dismiss it by throwing another image on the screen which will be more beautiful, more pure and more attractive, and which, above all, will pre-occupy your mind so that the other image will fade away. It is impossible, I think, in most cases, for the man to deliberately fight the temptation when it comes in certain forms. The only thing he can do is to replace that form by another form. You can do something with temptation at its first stage. You can do everything with it. You can do a little with it at the second stage, but you can do nothing with it after it passes to the third stage. If you let it pass that, you are over Niagara. You must fight it, not by direct fight, but by flight to the higher regions. Paul summed it up in a single sentence, where he said: "Walk in the spirit, and ye shall not fulfill the lusts of the flesh." In plain English, walk in the fourth flat, and you will not do the things that people do in the cellar. You cannot be in two places at once. If you make up your mind to live continuously in the spirit, ye shall not fulfill the lusts of the flesh. Spirit is there contrasted with flesh. It does not mean primarily the Holy Spirit, although it includes that. It is here contrasted primarily with the flesh. Either live a cellar or a top-story life, a dog life or a man life. Walk among spiritual things, among high people—not necessarily religious things, but spiritual things. Look not on the things which are seen, but the things which are unseen. Be in the company of good books, beautiful pictures, and charming, delightful and inspiring music; and let all that one hears, sees, reads and thinks lift and inspire the higher. The man who does that is kept above the lower nature. Many and many a thing which is not directly religious, therefore, comes in to make up a part of the nourishment of the spiritual life.

We can always live a high life. We can always have before us beautiful, divine ideals, and the sudden attempt to get from the lower to the higher is the transition between the life of the flesh and the life of the spirit, and the passing from the one region into the other is done by a sudden act, by a sudden mental movement, by a transference of one's interests from one region to another. That mental movement, I think, may be dignified with the name of prayer. That sudden appeal to the purer image which is to displace the other and let it fade away is the spasmodic act of prayer, which instantly places one in the spiritual region; and that is one of the highest uses of prayer, not to get something directly from heaven, but to switch everything up, and not down. If you could keep a Christian and a God-like spirit, it would be impossible for you to have the lower appetites again.

If you want to get a man on his feet again, the thing to do is not to preach or read the Bible to him, but to get him out of the cellar in which he lives. Take him by the hand, and he will be led away from his former life. Those are psychological principles founded upon the fact that the attention cannot be directed to two things at the same moment. You see that, upon merely psychological principles, the man who understands his nature and applies that remedy for his case when he finds himself becoming a lower man than he ought to, is bound to get the victory. It is not by magic that men are able to succeed in living a high and Christian life. It is by living according to nature and according to the revelation of our higher nature. It is by living along the line of the laws under which this system of our human nature is founded. That is put in other words by Christ, where he says, "Abide in me"—the same thing on a still higher plane. The man who lives with Christ cannot sin. "If any man sin," John says, "he hath not known Christ." Sin is abashed in the presence of Christ. The man who lives in Christ as his ideal finds in Him a continuous living Saviour, drawing him away from himself and making it impossible for him to live for himself.

Let no man here to-night think or say that he can get victory over sin alone. He cannot get that out of religion unless he gets a great many other things as well, and is compelled to accept them. Deliverance from sin is only one of the functions of the new nature; and a man is not a new man if he has got only one arm. The one arm is to fight sin. He must be a full, perfect man; and the man who has simply got the muscle in his spiritual nature which is to deal with sin is not a Christian man at all necessarily. The man who attempts to live in one function alone will find it impossible. Religion is not a blue ribbon to wear against a single set of things. It is not an inoculation against a single disease. A man must accept Christ all around, not only as his Deliverer from sin, but as his friend and guide, his ideal and Saviour. He must walk his whole life, and every day of his life, in the spirit, not merely rushing into the top story when temptations are at his heels, but dwelling there, in that place where the air is always sweet, where the company is always pure, and where there is nothing to hinder the soul from communing with God and with the stars. If a man can continuously live in that region, he is bound to grow better and better. That is the picture of temptation chasing a man who walks in the Spirit. He hears its bark and feels its bite, like a dog's; but if he is off its ground it cannot touch him. Just in proportion as we live in the higher regions are we able to evade temptations.

In dealing with others, it is not enough to preach to them, to give them tracts, texts or prayers: but we must give them a new environment, in which the new nature can bud and flower and grow into perfection. Gentlemen, it is not such an easy business to save a man as some people think. It is not to be done by a few earnest words. That is why so many college men have been passed over untouched by our college Y. M. C. A.'s. It is not because we do not have meetings enough, not because we do not know the Bible well enough, not because we are not earnest enough; but it is because we do not proceed rationally enough. It is because we do not sow seeds for individuals and live so that they may be compelled to live this higher life with us. We do not do our work half thoroughly enough. Unless we lay down our lives to save men, we are not following the Master as we ought. It is good business to devote our lives to individuals. It may not be so picturesque, but individual work, where every man singles out his individual to help and save, and stands by him, if multiplied through the universities, would soon win our universities for Christ.

Make a continuous effort by will power and prayer power and the power of the Spirit of God to walk in the spiritual region; for nature abhors a vacuum. If we allow any pause to occur in our high living, if we leave this place, the enemy will come upon us, and we will be worse off after this Conference than we were before it.

The Kingdom of God and Your Part in it

"The futility of saving men by speech" is not a whole truth, but it is the large part of a truth. Imagine a life-saving crew trying to save wrecked mariners simply by calling to them, and not throwing out a life line or putting off in a boat after them! It is a case of life for life—a man laying down his own life for others, as Christ did.

In talking to a man you want to win, talk to him in his own language. If you want to get hold of an agnostic, try to translate what you have to say into simple words—words that will not be in every case the words in which you got it. It is not cant. Religion has its technical terms just as science, but it can be overdone; and, besides, it is an exceedingly valuable discipline for one's self. Take a text and say, "What does that mean in 19th century English ;" and in doing that you will learn the lesson that it is the spirit of truth that does one good, and not the form of words. The form does not matter, if it does you good and draws you nearer to God. Do not be suspicious of it, if it is God's truth, in whatever form it may be.

One has to do a great deal more than display his Christianity. He must not only talk it, but live it. What is the secret of Christianity? It is not picking out a man here and a man there and making them fit to go to heaven. Christ came to this world, as He Himself said, to found a society. Have you ever thought of that conception of Christianity? For hundreds of years it has been utterly lost sight of. It is only lately that men are getting to see the great Christian doctrine of the Kingdom of God. This great phrase was never off Christ's lips. "The Kingdom of God" is by far the commonest phrase in His speech. Have you ever given a month of your life to find out what Christ meant by "the Kingdom of God?" Every day as we pray, "Thy Kingdom come," has our Christian consciousness taken in the tremendous sweep of that prayer, and seen how it covers the length and breadth of this great world and every human being? Christ was continually telling what it was. The Kingdom of heaven is like unto this. The kingdom of heaven is like unto that. If there is one thing more prominent than another in Christ's language it is in explaining what the kingdom of heaven is, and in what the subjects of that kingdom are to busy themselves. The kingdom of God is a society for the best men working for the best end, with the highest motive according to the best principle. The Kingdom of God was to come without observation. Christ likened it to leaven, and one cannot get a better understanding of the meaning of His phrase than by taking His own metaphors. The world is sunken, Christ said, and it must be raised. Leaven comes from the same word as lever. It is that which lifts, elevates, or raises. Christ founded a society of men for the purpose of raising men. This leaven was not to disturb the form of or overturn any institution. When you put leaven into a vessel with anything that is to be leavened, it does not affect the outward form of it; but it changes its spirit.

The Kingdom of God is like leaven. It is to act, raising men by contagion, by the contact of one life with another. Did you ever put a little leaven under a microscope? If you did, you found it was a minute plant, perhaps one six-thousandth of an inch in diameter, with such an amazing power of propagation that, simply in contact with the dough, it has the effect of lifting it by means of the life that is in it. And so the virtue of the Christian's life, not by tempting it in the way of forcing it, but by its spontaneous, natural and beautiful goodness, reacts upon others. When men observe the fragrance of Christ and are reminded of Him, a longing comes over them to live like Him and breathe that air and have that calm, that beauty of character, and all that unconscious influence going out as a contagion to others. By these men the world is raised.

But that is not all. The world is not only sunken, it is sinful. Those of you who know life even an inch below the surface, know that even in this Christian country, in our great cities, the world is rotten. Have you ever thought of the sin of the world? Think of the sin in your own being. Think that the man in the next house has the same amount of sin in him, and all the people in your street are like that. Multiply that by the number of all the streets in your city, and that by the number of cities in your country, and that by the number of countries in the world, and you have a ghastly spectre under which your imagination staggers.

That, however, is only a single glimpse of this sinful world, for the sin can be taken away: "Behold the Lamb of God, which taketh away the sin of the world." How does He do it? By forgiving the sin of the world, and by taking it away, through you and me and other subjects of His kingdom.

Christians, the followers of Christ, He said, are the salt of the earth, and it is that salt that takes away the rottenness of the world. He takes away the guilt and the power of it, and you help Him to remove it by being salt in the society in which you live. Salt is that which keeps society from becoming rotten. You put salt upon fish or meat to prevent it from becoming rotten; and it is the Christian men and women in this country who prevent it from becoming absolutely rotten. Christianity is the great antiseptic of society. If you were to take Christianity out of New York, Chicago, Berlin, or Paris, those cities, in a few generations, would go to pieces, even physically, and be swept off the earth. Now, we are to be the salt of Chicago, New York and the great cities of the world. It is our business to make cities and to keep those cities sweet—not only to scavenge away the rottenness after it has grown there, but to prevent the new generation that is growing up from becoming rotten. The work of salt is to prevent this, as well as to cure it. Keep those children pure to the end of their lives. We do not emphasize half enough the prevention side of Christian society. We do not emphasize half enough the making of Christian environment in which a Christ-like life shall be possible—new houses, pure air and water, good schools, bringing the influences of sweetest life and purity to keep those young lives from succumbing to the influences which surround them. The world which you and I have to lift is not only the world of the poor; but we have to lift up our country.

One thing, gentlemen, strikes the stranger in coming to this country. He goes to a city like Boston, and finds the merchants of that city with their heads buried in their ledgers, wholly occupied with their private business, while a few Irishmen, holding the city offices, are carrying on their municipal government. Some one has defined dirt as matter in the wrong place; and it is matter in the wrong place for a company of Irishmen to regulate the affairs of the city of Boston. Therefore, gentlemen, if you are the subjects of the Kingdom of God, you must give to the world and to your country a reformed Boston, a reformed Chicago, above all a reformed New York. You have been taught in your schools of your duties as citizens; but you are taught in this Book just as plainly your duties as Christian citizens. These cities are making the people that are living in them. People will not be righteous. In this country there is not only little honesty and honorableness in municipal life; but, what is a thousand times worse, there is little in its possibility. In my country I have never known or heard of a member of the government, either municipal or state, proving false to his trust. It is your duty to restore righteousness in the high places of this government. Let the people see examples which will help them in their Christian life. I cannot speak too strongly about that, because I know that the thing in process of time can be done. We have had rotten municipal government, and the Christian men of the place have taken the thing up and said, we have determined this shall not be. In the old cities, they have put man after man into the municipal chair simply because they were Christian men, because they would deal with the people righteously, and carry out the programme of Christianity for the city. Let me tell you of the work of some university men in the city of London. They went to a district in the East End—a God-forsaken and sunken place, occupied for miles entirely by working people. They rented a house and became known as settlers in that poor district. They gave themselves no airs of superiority. They did not tell the people they had come to do them good. They went in there and made friends with the people. The leaven went in among the dough. The salt went in beside that which was corrupt. We keep the grains of salt all together, and the other things all together; but the very place where the salt ought not to be is beside the salt. It ought to be scattered over the meat. Well, these men were not in a great hurry. They waited some months and got to know a number of the workmen, and got to understand one another. They had studied the city, and the workingmen were astonished at how much the young fellows knew about city government, city life and education, and sanitation, cleansing and purity in all directions. One day there came a great war of labor. The working men put their heads together and said, "These young fellows have heads. Let us go and talk the matter over with them." In a few months those young men were the arbiters of a strike, and at a single word from them three or four thousand families were saved from being thrown out of work on a great strike. Is that not a Christian thing to do? If you understand the conception of the Kingdom of God as a society of the best men working for the best ends for the amelioration of human life, you will agree with me. One of these young men at the next election was elected a member of one of the municipal boards, and in a few months he was the head of the Board. Another got into the School Board, and in a short time was the head of it. These men did not claim to be superior. They were elected kings by the people because the people felt their kingship. By and by the time came when a member of Parliament was to be returned. The workingmen came again to their university friends and said, ``Whom shall we put in?'' Those men told them, and they put him in. And so those men have taken possession of that city in the name of Jesus Christ, and have been gradually working, leavening and salting. First, the blade; then, the ear; and then, the full corn in the ear.

It is coming without observation. It is not the work of a day. Christians are the only agents God has for carrying out His purposes. Think of that. He could Himself, with a single breath, cleanse the whole of London or New York, but he does not do it. It is by the members of His body that he carries on His work. We all have different parts of that work to do. Some of us are thumbs, some of us are fingers, and some of us are only a little bit of the little finger. Some, again, are limbs.

Now, that conception of Christianity as a kingdom is beginning to grow throughout Christendom at this hour. Every age has had its peculiar side of Christianity emphasized; and the side that is being emphasized now is the social side, that large conception of what Christ came to do, how He came to save men in the bulk, as it were —by the city and by the country; and many of the movements that are going on just now in society, in education, in sanitation, in university extension and philanthropy, are all working together for good in that direction. Let not us, who believe in the salvation of the individual soul as the supreme thing, shut our eyes to the Christianity of Christ, to His great conception of the Kingdom of God.

All the activities of Christianity may be classed under one or the other of these two heads—entering the kingdom of God ourselves, and spreading it to the lives of others. The individual life has been at this Conference. How is it to help on this movement for the bringing of the world to Christ? I know many of you are puzzled to know in what direction you can start off to help Christ. Let me simply say this to you. Once in my own life I came to crossroads. I did not know in which direction God wanted me to help His kingdom, and I started to read this Book to find out what the ideal life was. I knew I had only one life, and didn't want to miss it; and I found out that the only thing worth doing in the world was to do the will of God. Whether that was done in the pulpit or in the slums, whether done in the college class room or in the street, didn't matter at all. "My meat and my drink," Christ said, "is to do the will of Him that sent me;" and if you make up your mind to do the will of God, it matters little in what direction. There are more posts waiting for men than there are men waiting for posts. Christ needs men in every community and in every land. It makes little difference whether we go to foreign lands or stay at home, so it is where Gods puts us. I am not jealous of the great missionary movement which has swept this country. In my own college, at least one third of the men are going to the foreign mission field. I am not jealous of that movement. I rejoice in it. But I should like also to bid for men, both for my country and for yours, men who will give their lives to the Kingdom of God at home.

You will say, "How am I to know whether to go abroad or stay at home, be a lawyer or a Christian doctor?" The first thing is, course. The second thing is, think. Think over all the different lines of work—over all your own pray, of qualifications. If you are called to the missionary field, think of all the different kinds of missionary fields. There are some that do not need you at all; and there are others for which you are the very man. It is a great mistake to suppose that missionary fields are all alike, and that they are the same in Africa as in India or China. They are not the same at all. Study the field. The third thing is, regard his decision as final. Nobody can plan your life for you. Do take the advice of a wise friend, but do not not imagine that the most disagreeable of two or three alternative things before you is necessarily the will of God.

God's will does not always lie in the line of the disagreeable. God likes to see His children happy just as earthly fathers like to see their children happy, and there may be plums waiting for you as well as stones. Do not sacrifice to a thing that is disagreeable unless you are quite sure it is God's will.

The next thing is, when the time of decision comes, what light you have. We do not manufacture a act, go ahead with decision out of all these elements. We arrive at a decision. Some day, in a turn of the road, we find we are led. We do not know how. The subject just took shape in our minds somehow, and we arrived at a decision.

Having once decided, the next thing is, never reconsider your decision. The day after a man makes a great life's decision, if he reconsiders it, he reverses it. Never reconsider such a decision. You will never know for months or years whether you have done the right thing; but then, you will see that God has led every step of your way. One good general rule is to go in the direction of least resistance, if you find objections in every line and there is no one line positively drawing you out.

I want to return to the immediate purpose of those of you who are not yet out in the mission field, but who have a year or two at college before you. I ask you to study what Christianity is, and to spread the knowledge of that through your university. There are many men in the universities who do not know in the least what Christianity is. When I was in the university I thought Christianity was a thing you might put on the point of a needle, and that Jesus Christ was a being so small that you had to search closely for Him before you found Him; and now I know the whole earth is full of His glory. Study the Kingdom of God. See what Christ said was life, and how the members of that kingdom are to pass it on to others, to the lawyer and the doctor, until we have the professions Christianized, and the whole country will follow. It begins with you. Give your life for a life.

I will close with a specific case of one of your own countrymen. One night I got a letter from one of the students in the University of Edinburgh, with page after page of agnosticism and atheism. I went to see him, and spent a whole afternoon with him, but did not make the slightest impression. At Edinburgh University we have a students' evangelistic meeting Sunday nights, with an attendance of 800 or 1,000 men. A few nights after my conversation with this young man I saw him at one of these meetings. Beside him sat a man I had seen occasionally at the meetings, but whose name I did not know. After the meeting I spoke to the latter student and asked him if he knew the man sitting next to him. He said: "I am a graduate. After I finished my regular course of study, I wanted to take a post-graduate course; and last year I came to Edinburgh, where, in the dissecting room, I happened to be placed near this man. I took a singular liking to him. I found out he was not a religious man. A year passed without any change in him. I went to pack my trunks to go home at the end of my one year's post-graduate work; but I was uncertain whether I should go and take up my profession in America, or stay in Edinburgh and try to win that one man for Christ. I decided I would stay." "Well," I said, "my young fellow, it will pay you. You will get your man." Two or three months passed. It came to the night for our students' farewell meeting—a service some of you might well imitate. We have men in Edinburgh University from every part of the world. Every year five or six hundred of them go out never to meet again. In our religious work we get very close to one another; and on the last night of the university year we sit down together in our common hall to the Lord's Supper. This is entirely a students' meeting; but that night the members of the Theological Faculty participate, so that things may be done decently and in order. There you see hundreds of men—the cream and the youth of the world—sitting down to the Lord's table, many of them not members of the church, there for the first time pledging themselves to become members of the Kingdom of God. I saw one, sitting down, passing the communion cup to his American friend. The American had won the agnostic for Christ. A week after, he was back to his own country. I do not know his name, but he was a subject of Christ's Kingdom doing his Master's work. A few weeks passed, and the friend he rescued from agnosticism came to see me and said: "I want to tell you that I am going to be a medical missionary."

Before you leave here, make up your mind that, with God's help, you will try to land your man. Let us ask God to use us in His work.

The Three Elements of a Complete Life

Students are very often recommended to invest in certain books. I am going to take the liberty of suggesting to some of you to buy a certain picture which you can get for a very few cents. Most of you have already seen it. It is "The Angelus." It is an illuminated text. God speaks through you. He also speaks through art. I want to hang up this picture as an illuminated text. There are three things in the picture—a potato field, a country lad and a country girl standing on the ground, and on the far horizon the spire of the village church. That is the whole thing. There is no great scenery, no picturesque scenery; just a country lad and a country girl. In those Roman Catholic countries, at the hour of evening, the church bell rings out to summon the people to pray. Some go into the church to pray; and those that are caught in the fields when the Angelus rings bow their heads to engage for a few moments in silent prayer.

Now, that picture is a perfect picture of Christian life; and what is interesting about it is that it picks out the three great pedestals of life. Moody said it was not enough to have the root of the matter, we must have the whole thing.

I

The first element in life is work Three-fourths of our life is probably spent in work. Is that religious, or is it not? What is the meaning of it? It means, of course, that our work is just as religious as our worship; and unless we can make our work religious, three-fourths of our life remains unsanctified. The proof that work is religious is that the most of Christ's life was spent in work. It was not the Bible that was in His hands during these first thirty years of His life. It was the hammer and the plane. He was making chairs and tables and plows and yokes. That is to say, the highest conceivable life is in doing work. Christ's public ministry occupied only two and a half years. The great bulk of His time, He was simply at work; and from that moment work has had a new meaning given to it. When Christ came into the world He came to men at their work. He appealed to the shepherds, the working classes of those days. He also appealed to the wise men, the students of those days. Three deputations of the world went out to welcome him—first, the shepherds; second, the wise men; third, two old people, Simeon and Anna, in the temple. That is to say, Christ comes to men at their work, as the shepherds. He comes to men at their books—the wise men. He comes to men at their worship—Simeon and Anna. We find Christ, therefore, at our work, our books and our worship. But you will notice that it was the old people who found Christ at their worship, and, as we get older, we will cease to find Christ so much at our work and our books. We will then spend more of our time in worship than we are able to now, and as we get old we will repair to the prayer meeting and the House of God and meet Christ and worship Him as Simeon and Anna. We must try, until the time comes when much of our time shall be given to direct business, to find Christ in our books and at our common work.

Why should God have arranged that so many hours of every day should be occupied with work? It is because work makes men. A university is not a place for making scholars. It is a place for making Christians. A farm is not a place for growing grain. It is a place for growing character, and a man has no character except what is built up through the medium of the things he does from day to day. God's Spirit aids it through the actions which he performs during his life-work. The student turns up every word in his Latin, instead of consulting the translation. The result is that honesty is translated into the student's being. If he gets up his mathematics thoroughly he not only becomes a mathematician and a learned man, but he becomes a thorough man. If he attends to the instructions that are given to him in class intelligently and conscientiously he becomes a conscientious man, and it is just by such means that thoroughness, conscientiousness and honorableness are imbedded in our being. We do not get perfect character in our sleep. It comes to us as muscle comes, through doing things. It is the muscle of the soul, and it comes by exercising it upon actual things. Hence the meaning of our work is that it is the making of us, and it is only by and through our work that the great Christian graces are communicated to our souls. That is the means God requires for the growing of the Christian principles. We cannot have Christian character unless we use these means. Hence, gentlemen, the necessity of a student being true, first of all, to his work, and letting his Christianity show itself to his fellow students and his professors by the integrity and the thoroughness of his academic work. Unless he is faithful in that which is least, it is impossible for him to be faithful in that which is much. The world judges a student by the conscientiousness and faithfulness with which he does his college work. I know men who were led to pass their examinations simply because they had become Christians—men who struggled for years to pass their examinations, but who, when they became Christians, got to work and succeeded where they had previously failed. Christianity comes out in a man as much in his work as in his worship. Our work is not only to be done thoroughly, but it is to be done honestly. In dealing with that august thing called truth a man must be square with himself, fair to his own mind and to the principles and spirit of truth. We are students, and it is our business to get to the bottom of difficulties. Perhaps some truths which are revealed to us have deeper bottoms than we now know. We will get down to nuggets if we go below the surface, as our chairman said this morning. Christianity is the most important thing in the world, and the student ought to sound it in every direction and see if there is deep water and a safe place through which to steer his life. If there are shoals, he ought to know them. Therefore, when we come to difficulties, let us not be guilty of intellectual sin, jumping lightly over them. Let us be honest seekers after truth. We do not ask the public to sift doctrines, but it is the business of the student to exercise the intellect which God has given him. Faith is never opposed to reason in the New Testament. It is often supposed to be so, but it is not. Faith is opposed to sight, but never to reason. It is only by reason that we can sift and examine and criticise, and be sure of the forms of truth which are given us as Christians. Hence a great field of work has opened to the student even apart from his academic work. Let him be sure that in seeking after truth he is drawing very near Christ. "I am the way, the truth and the life." We talk a great deal about Christ as the way and about Christ as the life; but there is a side of Christ especially for the student, "I am the truth." Every student ought to be a truth-learner and a truth-seeker for Christ's sake.

II

The second element in life after work—and it ought to be put first in importance—is God. The Angelus is perhaps the most religious picture painted in this century. You cannot look at it and see that young man standing in the field with his hat off, and the girl opposite him with her hands clasped and her head bowed on her breast, without feeling a sense of God. Gentlemen, do we carry about with us wherever we go a sense of God? If not, we have missed the greatest part of life. Do we have that feeling and conviction of God's abiding presence wherever we are? Does He beset us behind and before? There is nothing more needed in this generation than a larger and more scriptural idea of God. A great American writer has told us that the conception of God that he got, in books and from sermons, when he was a boy, was that of a wise and very strict lawyer sitting in his office. I remember very well the awful conception I got when I was a boy. I was given a book of Watts' hymns, which was illustrated, and, amongst other hymns, there was one about God, and it represented a great black, scowling thunder cloud, and in the midst of that cloud there was a piercing eye. That was placed before my young imagination as God, and I got the idea that God was a great detective, playing the spy upon my actions, and, as the hymn says, writing now the story of what little children do. That was a bad lesson. It has taken years to obliterate it. We think of God as "up there." You know there is no such thing as "up there." What would be "up there" tonight will be "down there" twelve hours from this time. Do not think of God as "up there," because there is no such place. Science has been "up there," and it has not seen God. You say God made the world six thousand years ago and then He retired. That is the last that was seen of Him. He made the world and then went away into space somewhere to look on and keep things going. Geology has been away back there, and God has gone further and further back. These six thousand years have extended back into ages and ages of long, long years. Where is God, if He is not back there in time or up there in space? Where is He? God is in you. The Kingdom of God is within you and God Himself is within men. He is not "up there." When are we to exchange the terrible God of our childhood, the far-away God of our childhood, for the everywhere-present God of the Bible?

The God of theology has been largely taken from the old classical Christian-Roman writers, such as Augustine, who, great as they were, had nothing better to fling their conception of God upon than that of the greatest man. The greatest man was the Roman emperor, and therefore God became a kind of emperor. The Greeks had a far grander conception—the conception of Clement of Alexandria, which is coming again into modern theology. The Greek God is the God of this Book; the Spirit which moved upon the water; the God in whom we live and move and have our being; the God of whom Jesus spake to the woman at the well; the God who is a spirit. God is a spirit. Let us gather the conception of the immanent God. That is the theological word for it, and it is a splendid word. Immanuel, God with us, the inside God, the immanent God. You have had singular experiences since you have been here. What is it? It is God working in you. Have we really realized that God is in us and is working in us? God must be working in us. Long, long ago God made matter. Then He made flowers, trees and animals. Then he made man. Did He stop? Is God dead? If He lives, if He acts, what is He doing? He is making better men. He is carrying on the development of man. "It is God which worketh in you." The buds of our nature are not all out yet. The sap to make them come out comes from God, from the indwelling immanent Christ. Our bodies, therefore, are the temples of the Holy Ghost. We must bear Christ with us wherever we go, because the sense of God is not kept up by logic but by experience.

Most of you have heard of Hellen Kellar, the Boston girl who is deaf and dumb and blind. Until she was seven years of age her mind was an absolute blank. Nothing could get into that blank, because all the avenues to the other world were closed. Then, by that great process which Boston has discovered, by which the blind see, the deaf hear and the mute speak, that girl's soul was opened. Bit by bit they began to build up a mind —to give her a certain amount of information and to educate her. But no one liked to tell her about religion. They reserved that for Phillips Brooks. After some years had passed they took her to him and he began to talk to her, through the young lady who had been the means of opening her senses, and was able to communicate with her by the delicate process of touch. Phillips Brooks began to tell her about God, who God was, what He had done, how He loved men and what He was to us. The child listened very intently. Then she looked up and said: "Mr. Brooks, I knew all that before, but I didn't know His name." There was some mysterious pressure, some impelling power, some guide, some elevating impulse, within her soul. "It is *God*," said Phillips Brooks, "which worketh in you. God is with us and in us."

I wonder if you have heard the story of the two Americans who were once crossing the Atlantic and met in the cabin on Sunday night to sing hymns. As they sang the last hymn, "Jesus, Lover of my Soul," one of them heard an exceedingly rich and beautiful voice behind him. He looked around, and, although he did not know the face, he thought that he knew the voice. So, when the music ceased, he turned and asked the man if he had been in the Civil War.

The man replied that he had been a Confederate soldier.

"Were you at such a place at such a night?" asked the first.

"Yes," he replied, "and a curious thing happened that night which this hymn has recalled to my mind. I was posted on sentry duty near the edge of a wood. It was a dark night and very cold, and I was a little frightened because the enemy were supposed to be very near. About midnight, when everything was very still and I was feeling homesick and miserable and weary, I thought that I would comfort myself by praying and singing a hymn. I remember singing this hymn:

" 'All my trust on Thee is stayed,
All my help from Thee I bring;
Cover my defenseless head
With the shadow of Thy wing.'

"After singing that a strange peace came down upon me, and through the long night I felt no more fear."

"Now," said the other, "listen to my story. I was a Union soldier and was in the wood that night with a party of scouts. I saw you standing, although I did not see your face. My men had their rifles focused upon you, waiting the word to fire, but when you sang out:

" 'Cover my defenseless head
With the shadow of Thy wing'

I said: 'Boys, lower your rifles; we will go home.' It was God working in each of them. Just by such means, by this everywhere-acting, mysterious spirit, God keeps His Spirit moving. Hence that second great element in life, *God*, without Whom life is a living death.

III

A moment or two about the third element in life. The first is "work," the second is "God," the third is "love." You have noticed in that picture the sense of companionship, brought out by the young man and the young woman. It matters not whether they are brother and sister or lover and lover. There you have the idea of friendship, the final ingredient in our lives. If the man had been standing in that field alone, the scene would be almost weary. If the woman had been standing alone it would have been sentimental. You can carry much away from this Conference; but we can all carry away with us some enrichment of our human friendship, and that will complete our life, because no life is complete unless it has that additional element in it. That, after all, is the divine element in life, because God is love and because he that loveth is born of God. Therefore, gentlemen, after we leave one another, let us keep our friendships in repair, as some one says. They are worth while spending time on and keeping them up, because they constitute a large part of our life. I need not say that we must cultivate this spirit of friendship and let it grow into a great love not only for our friends, but for all humanity. Some of you are going into the mission field. Your mission field will be a failure unless you cultivate this element. Two years ago I was wandering about the coral islands of the Pacific, and I came to one island far remote from human gaze, inhabited solely by cannibals. At one end of the island was a missionary and his wife. At the other end of the island was another missionary and his wife. They never heard from other parts of the world for six months. You would suppose they would see each other every day, but they were not on loving terms. They were not on speaking terms. They were on war terms. One had actually assaulted the other. What was the trouble about? It was a quarrel over the word in the native language they should use for "God" in their translation of the New Testament. They needed and lacked charity, tenderness, tolerance, patience.

So these three things—work, God, love—form a complete life. If your life is not comfortable, if you are ill at ease, ask yourself if you are not lacking in one or other of these three things, and pray for them and work for them.

The Ascent of Man

Table of Contents

Preface

"The more I think of it," says Mr. Ruskin, "I find this conclusion more impressed upon me—that the greatest thing a human soul ever does in this world is to see something, and tell what it saw in a plain way." In these pages an attempt is made to tell "in a plain way" a few of the things which Science is now seeing with regard to the Ascent of Man. Whether these seeings are there at all is another matter. But, even if visions, every thinking mind, through whatever medium, should look at them. What Science has to say about himself is of transcendent interest to Man, and the practical bearings of this theme are coming to be more vital than any on the field of knowledge. The thread which binds the facts is, it is true, but a hypothesis As the theory, nevertheless. with which at present all scientific work is being done, it is assumed in every page that follows.

Though its stand-point is Evolution and its subject Man, this book is far from being designed to prove that Man has relations, compromising or otherwise, with lower animals. Its theme is Ascent, not Descent. It is a History, not an Argument. And Evolution, in the narrow sense in which it is often used when applied to Man, plays little part in the drama outlined here. So far as the general scheme of Evolution is introduced—and in the Introduction and elsewhere this is done at length —the object is the important one of pointing out how its nature has been misconceived, indeed how its greatest factor has been overlooked in almost all contemporary scientific thinking. Evolution was given to the modern world out of focus, was first seen by it out of focus, and has remained out of focus to the present hour. Its general basis has never been re-examined since the time of Mr. Darwin; and not only such speculative sciences as Teleology, but working sciences like Sociology have been led astray by a fundamental omission. An Evolution Theory drawn to scale, and with the lights and shadows properly adjusted—adjusted to the whole truth and reality of Nature and of Man—is needed at present as a standard for modern thought; and though a reconstruction of such magnitude is not here presumed, a primary object of these pages is to supply at least the accents for such a scheme.

Beyond an attempted readjustment of the accents there is nothing here for the specialist—except, it may be, the reflection of his own work. Nor, apart from Teleology, is there anything for the theologian. The limitations of a lecture-audience made the treatment of such themes as might appeal to him impossible; while owing to the brevity of the course, the Ascent had to be stopped at a point where all the higher interest begins. All that the present volume covers is the Ascent of Man, the Individual, during the earlier stages of his evolution. It is a study in embryos, in rudiments, in installations; the scene is the primeval forest; the date, the world's dawn. Tracing his rise as far as Family Life, this history does not even follow him into the Tribe; and as it is only then that social and moral life begin in earnest, no formal discussion of these high themes occurs. All the higher forces and phenomena with which the sciences of Psychology, Ethics, and Theology usually deal come on the world's stage at a later date, and no one need be surprised if the semi-savage with whom we leave off is found wanting in so many of the higher potentialities of a human being.

The Ascent of Mankind, as distinguished from the Ascent of the Individual, was originally summarized in one or two closing lectures, but this stupendous subject would require a volume for itself, and these fragments have been omitted for the present. Doubtless it may disappoint some that at the close of all the bewildering vicissitudes recorded here, Man should appear, after all, so poor a creature. But the great lines of his youth are the lines of his maturity, and it is only by studying these, in themselves and in what they connote, that the nature of Evolution and the quality of Human progress can be perceived.

Henry Drummond.

Introduction

I: Evolution in General

The last romance of Science, the most daring it has ever tried to pen, is the Story of the Ascent of Man. Withheld from all the wistful eyes that have gone before, whose reverent ignorance forbade their wisest minds to ask to see it, this final volume of Natural History has begun to open with our century's close. In the monographs of His and Minot, the Embryology of Man has already received a just expression; Darwin and Haeckel have traced the origin of the Animal-Body; the researches of Romanes mark a beginning with the Evolution of Mind; Herbert Spencer has elaborated theories of the development of Morals; Edward Caird of the Evolution of Religion. Supplementing the contributions of these authorities, verifying, criticizing, combating, rebutting, there works a multitude of others who have devoted their lives to the same rich problems, and already every chapter of the bewildering story has found its editors.

Yet, singular though the omission may seem, no connected outline of this great drama has yet been given us. These researches, preliminary reconnaissances though they be, are surely worthy of being looked upon as a whole. No one can say that this multitude of observers is not in earnest, nor their work honest, nor their methods competent to the last powers of science. Whatever the uncertainty of the field, it is due to these pioneer minds to treat their labour with respect. What they see in the unexplored land in which they travel belongs to the world. By just such methods, and by just such men, the map of the world of thought is filled in—here from the tracing up of some great river, there from a bearing taken roughly in a darkened sky, yonder from a sudden glint of the sun on a far-off mountain-peak, or by a swift induction of an adventurous mind from a momentary glimpse of a natural law. So knowledge grows; and in a century which has added to the sum of human learning more than all the centuries that are past, it is not to be conceived that some further revelation should not await us on the highest themes of all.

The day is for ever past when science need apologize for treating Man as an object of natural research. Hamlet's "being of large discourse, looking before and after" is withal a part of Nature, and can be made neither larger nor smaller, anticipate less nor prophesy less, because we investigate, and perhaps discover, the secret of his past. And should that past be proved to be related in undreamed-of ways to that of all other things in Nature, "all other things" have that to gain by the alliance which philosophy and theology for centuries have striven to win for them. Every step in the proof of the oneness in a universal evolutionary process of this divine humanity of ours is a step in the proof of the divinity of all lower things. And what is of infinitely greater moment, each footprint discovered in the Ascent of Man is a guide to the step to be taken next.

To discover the rationale of social progress is the ambition of this age. There is an extraordinary human interest abroad about this present world itself, a yearning desire, not from curious but for practical reasons, to find some light upon the course; and as the goal comes nearer the eagerness passes into suspense to know the shortest and the quickest road to reach it. Hence the Ascent of Man is not only the noblest problem which science can ever study, but the practical bearings of this theme are great beyond any other on the roll of knowledge.

Now that the first rash rush of the evolutionary invasion is past, and the sins of its youth atoned for by sober concession, Evolution is seen to be neither more nor less than the story of creation as told by those who know it best. "Evolution," says Mr. Huxley, "or development is at present employed in biology as a general name for the history of the steps by which any living being has acquired the morphological and the physiological characters which distinguish it. Though applied specifically to plants and animals this definition expresses the chief sense in which Evolution is to be used scientifically at present. We shall use the word, no doubt, in others of its many senses; but after all the blood spilt, Evolution is simply "history," a "history of steps," a "general name" for the history of the steps by which the world has come to be what it is. According to this general definition, the story of Evolution is narrative. It may be wrongly told; it may be coloured, exaggerated, over- or under-stated like the record of any other set of facts; it may be told with a theological bias or with an anti-theological bias; theories of the process may be added by this thinker or by that; but these are not of the substance of the story. Whether history is told by a Gibbon or a Green the facts remain, and whether Evolution be told by a Haeckel or a Wallace we accept the narrative so far as it is a rendering of Nature, and no more. It is true, before this story can be fully told, centuries still must pass. At present there is not a chapter of the record that is wholly finished. The manuscript is already worn with erasures, the writing is often blurred, the very language is uncouth and strange. Yet even now the outline of a continuous story is beginning to appear—a story whose chief credential lies in the fact that no imagination of man could have designed a spectacle so wonderful, or worked out a plot at once so intricate and so transcendently simple.

This story will be outlined here partly for the story and partly for a purpose. A historian dare not have a prejudice, but he cannot escape a purpose—the purpose, conscious or unconscious, of unfolding the purpose which lies behind the facts which he narrates. The interest of a drama—the authorship of the play apart—is in the players, their character, their motives, and the tendency of their action. It is impossible to treat these players as automata. Even if automata, those in the audience are not. Hence, where interpretation seems lawful, or comment warranted by the facts, neither will he withheld.

To give an account of Evolution, it need scarcely be remarked, is not to account for it. No living thinker has yet found it possible to account for Evolution. Mr. Herbert Spencer's famous definition of Evolution as "a change from an indefinite incoherent homogeneity to a definite coherent heterogeneity through continuous differentiations and integrations" —the formula of which the Contemporary Reviewer remarked that "the universe may well have heaved a sigh of relief when, through the cerebration of an eminent thinker, it had been delivered of this account of itself"—is simply a summary of results, and throws no light, though it is often supposed to do so, upon ultimate causes. While it is true, as Mr. Wallace affirms in his latest work, that "Descent with modification is now universally accepted as the order of nature in the organic world," there is everywhere at this moment the most disturbing uncertainty as to how the Ascent even of species has been brought about. The attacks on the Darwinian theory from the outside were never so keen as are the controversies now raging in scientific circles, over the fundamental principles of Darwinism itself. On at least two main points—sexual selection and the origin of the higher mental characteristics of man—Mr Alfred Russel Wallace, co-discoverer with Darwin of the principle of Natural Selection though he be, directly opposes his colleague. The powerful attack of Weismann on the Darwinian assumption of the inheritability of acquired characters has opened one of the liveliest controversies of recent years, and the whole field of science is hot with controversies and discussions. In his 'GermPlasm,' the German naturalist believes himself to have finally disposed of both Darwin's "gemmules" and Herbert Spencer's "primordial units," while Eimer breaks a lance with Weismann in defence of Darwin, and Herbert Spencer replies for himself, assuring us that "either there has been inheritance of acquired characters or there has been no evolution."

It is the greatest compliment to Darwinism that it should have survived to deserve this era of criticism. Meantime all prudent men can but hold their judgment in suspense both as to that specific theory of one department of Evolution which is called Darwinism, and as to the factors and causes of Evolution itself. No one asks more of Evolution at present than permission to use it as a working theory. Undoubtedly there are cases now before Science where it is more than theory—the demonstration from Yale, for instance, of the Evolution of the Horse; and from Steinheim of the transmutation of Planorbis. In these cases the missing links have come in one after another, and in series so perfect, that the evidence for their evolution is irresistible. "On the evidence of Palaeontology," says Mr. Huxley in the Encyclopaedia Britannica, "the evolution of many existing forms of animal life from their predecessors is no longer an hypothesis but an historical fact." And even as to Man, most naturalists agree with Mr. Wallace who "fully accepts Mr. Darwin's conclusion as to the essential identity of Man's bodily structure with that of the higher mammalia and his descent from some ancestral form common to man and the anthropoid apes," for "the evidence of such descent appears overwhelming and conclusive. But as to the development of the whole Man it is sufficient for the present to rank it as a theory, no matter how impressive the conviction be that it is more. Without some hypothesis no work can ever be done, and, as everyone knows, many of the greatest contributions to human knowledge have been made by the use of theories either seriously imperfect or demonstrably false. This is the age of the evolution of Evolution. All thoughts that the Evolutionist works with, all theories and generalizations, have been themselves evolved and are now being evolved. Even were his theory perfected, its first lesson would be that it was itself but a phase of the Evolution of further opinion, no more fixed than a species, no more final than the theory which it displaced. Of all men the Evolutionist, by the very nature of his calling, the mere tools of his craft, his understanding of his hourly shifting place in this always moving and ever more mysterious world, must be humble, tolerant, and undogmatic.

These, nevertheless, are cold words with which to speak of a Vision—for Evolution is after all a Vision—-which is revolutionizing the world of Nature and of thought, and, within living memory, has opened up avenues into the past and vistas into the future such as science has never witnessed before. While many of the details of the theory of Evolution are in the crucible of criticism, and while the field of modern science changes with such rapidity that in almost every department the textbooks of ten years ago are obsolete to-day, it is fair to add that no one of these changes, nor all of them together, have touched the general theory itself except to establish its strength, its value, and its universality. Even more remarkable than the rapidity of its conquest is the authority with which the doctrine of development has seemed to speak to the most authoritative minds of our time. Of those who are in the front rank, of those who by their knowledge have, by common consent, the right to speak, there are scarcely any who do not in some form employ it in working and in thinking. Authority may mean little; the world has often been mistaken; but when minds so different as those of Charles Darwin and of T. H. Green, of Herbert Spencer and of Robert Browning, build half the labours of their life on this one law, it is impossible, and especially in the absence of any other even competing principle at the present hour, to treat it as a baseless dream. Only the peculiar nature of this great generalization can account for the extraordinary enthusiasm of this acceptance. Evolution has done for Time what Astronomy has done for Space. As sublime to the reason as the Science of the Stars, as overpowering to the imagination, it has thrown the universe into a fresh perspective, and given the human mind a new dimension. Evolution involves not so much a change of opinion as a change in man's whole view of the world and of life. It is not the statement of a mathematical proposition which men are called upon to declare true or false. It is a method of looking upon Nature. Science for centuries devoted itself to the cataloguing of facts and the discovery of laws. Each worker toiled in his own little place—the geologist in his quarry, the botanist in his garden, the biologist in his laboratory, the astronomer in his observatory, the historian in his library, the archaeologist in his museum. Suddenly these workers looked up; they spoke to one another; they had each discovered a law; they whispered its name. It was Evolution. Henceforth their work was one, science was one, the world was one, and mind, which discovered the oneness, was one.

Such being the scope of the theory, it is essential that for its interpretation this universal character be recognized, and no phenomenon in nature or in human nature be left out of the final reckoning. It is equally clear that in making that interpretation we must begin with the final product, Man. If Evolution can be proved to include Man, the whole course of Evolution and the whole scheme of Nature from that moment assume a new significance The beginning must then be interpreted from the end, not the end from the beginning. An engineering workshop is unintelligible until we reach the room where the completed engine stands. Everything culminates in that final product, is contained in it, is explained by it. The Evolution of Man is also the complement and corrective of all other forms of Evolution. From this height only is there a full view, a true perspective, a consistent world. The whole mistake of naturalism has been to interpret Nature from the standpoint of the atom —to study the machinery which drives this great moving world simply as machinery, forgetting that the ship has any passengers, or the passengers any captain, or the captain any course. It is as great a mistake, on the other hand, for the theologian to separate off the ship from the passengers as for the naturalist to separate off the passengers from the ship. It is he who cannot include Man among the links of Evolution who has greatly to fear the theory of development. In his jealousy for that religion which seems to him higher than science, he removes at once the rational basis from religion and the legitimate crown from science, forgetting that in so doing he offers to the world an unnatural religion and an inhuman science. The cure for all the small mental disorders which spring up around restricted applications of Evolution is to extend it fearlessly in all directions as far as the mind can carry it and the facts allow, till each man, working at his subordinate part, is compelled to own, and adjust himself to, the whole.

If the theological mind be called upon to make this expansion, the scientific man must be asked to enlarge his view in another direction. If he insists upon including Man in his scheme of Evolution, he must see to it that he include the whole Man. For him at least no form of Evolution is scientific or is to be considered, which does not include the whole Man, and all that is in Man, and all the work and thought and life and aspiration of Man. The great moral facts, the moral forces so far as they are proved to exist, the moral consciousness so far as it is real, must come within its scope. Human History must be as much a part of it as Natural History. The social and religious forces must no more be left outside than the forces of gravitation or of life. The reason why the naturalist does not usually include these among the factors in Evolution is not oversight, but undersight. Sometimes, no doubt, he may take at their word those who assure him that Evolution has nothing to do with those higher things, but the main reason is simply that his work does not lie on the levels where those forces come into play. The specialist is not to be blamed for this; limitation is his strength. But when the specialist proceeds to reconstruct the universe from his little corner of it, and especially from his level of it, he not only injures science and philosophy, but may fatally mislead his neighbours. The man who is busy with the stars will never come across Natural Selection, yet surely must he allow for Natural Selection in his construction of the world as a whole. He who works among star-fish will encounter little of Mental Evolution, yet will he not deny that it exists. The stars have voices, but there are other voices; the star-fishes have activities, but there are other activities. Man, body, soul, spirit, are not only to be considered, but are first to be considered in any theory of the world. You cannot describe the life of kings, or arrange their kingdoms, from the cellar beneath the palace. "Art," as Browning reminds us,

"Must fumble for the whole, once fixing on a part,
However poor, surpass the fragment, and aspire
To reconstruct thereby the ultimate entire."

II: the Missing Factor in Current Theories

But it is not so much in ignoring Man that evolutionary philosophy has gone astray; for ,of that error it has seriously begun to repent. What we have now to charge against it, what is a main object of these pages to point out, is that it has misread Nature herself. In "fixing on a part" whereby to "reconstruct the ultimate," it has fixed upon a part which is not the most vital part, and the reconstructions, therefore, have come to be wholly out of focus. Fix upon the wrong "part," and the instability of the fabric built upon it is a foregone conclusion. Now, although reconstructions of the cosmos in the light of Evolution are the chief feature of the science of our time, in almost no case does even a hint of the true scientific standpoint appear to be perceived. And although it anticipates much that we should prefer to leave untouched until it appears in its natural setting, the gravity of the issues makes it essential to summarize the whole situation now.

The root of the error lies, indirectly rather than directly, with Mr. Darwin. In 1859, through the publication of the Origin of Species, he offered to the world what purported to be the final clue to the course of living Nature. That clue was the principle of the Struggle for Life. After the years of storm and stress which follow the intrusion into the world of all great thoughts, this principle was universally accepted as the key to all the sciences which deal with life. So ceaseless was Mr. Darwin's emphasis upon this factor, and so masterful his influence, that, after the first sharp conflict, even the controversy died down. With scarce a challenge the Struggle for Life became accepted by the scientific world as the governing factor in development, and the drama of Evolution was made to hinge entirely upon its action. It became the "part" from which science henceforth went on "to reconstruct the whole," and biology, sociology, and teleology, were built anew on this foundation.

That the Struggle for Life has been a prominent actor in the drama is certain. Further research has only deepened the impression of the magnitude and universality of this great and far-reaching law. But that it is the sole or even the main agent in the process of Evolution must be denied. Creation is a drama, and no drama was ever put upon the stage with only one actor. The Struggle for Life is the "Villain" of the piece, no more; and, like the "Villain" in the play, its chief function is to re-act upon the other players for higher ends. There is, in point of fact, a second factor which one might venture to call the Struggle for the Life of Others, which plays an equally prominent part. Even in the early stages of development, its contribution is as real, while in the world's later progress—under the name of Altruism— it assumes a sovereignty before which the earlier Struggle sinks into insignificance. That this second form of Struggle should all but have escaped the notice of Evolutionists is the more unaccountable since it arises, like the first, out of those fundamental functions of living organisms which it is the main business of biological science to investigate. The functions discharged by all living things, plant and animal, are two in number. The first is Nutrition, the second is Reproduction. The first is the basis of the Struggle for Life; the second, of the Struggle for the Life of Others. These two functions run their parallel course—or spiral course, for they continuously intertwine—from the very dawn of life. They are involved in the fundamental nature of protoplasm itself. They affect the entire round of life; they determine the whole morphology of living things; in a sense they are life. Yet, in constructing the fabric of Evolution, one of these has been taken, the other left.

Partly because of the limitations of its purely physical name, and partly because it has never been worked out as an evolutionary force, the function of Reproduction will require to be introduced to the reader in some detail. But to realize its importance or even to understand it, it will be necessary to recall to our minds the supreme place which function generally holds in the economy of life.

Life to an animal or to a Man is not a random series of efforts. Its course is set as rigidly as the courses of the stars. All its movements and changes, its apparent deflections and perturbations are guided by unalterable purposes; its energies and caprices definitely controlled. What controls it are its functions. These and these only determine life; living out these is life. Trace back any one, or all, of the countless activities of an animal's life, and it will be found that they are at bottom connected with one or other of the two great functions which manifest themselves in protoplasm. Take any organ of the body— hand or foot, eye or ear, heart or lung—or any tissue of the body—muscle or nerve, bone or cartilage—and it will be found to be connected either with Nutrition or with Reproduction. Just as everything about an engine, every bolt, bar, valve, crank, lever, wheel, has something to do with the work of that engine, everything about an animal's body has something to do with the work prescribed by those two functions. An animal, or a Man, is a consistent whole, a rational production. Now the rationale of living stands revealed to us in protoplasm. Protoplasm sets life its task. Living can only be done along its lines. There start the channels in which all life must run, and though the channels bifurcate endlessly as time goes on, and though more life and fuller is ever coursing through them, it can never overflow the banks appointed from the beginning.

But this is not all. The activities even of the higher life, though not qualitatively limited by the lower, are determined by these same lines. Were these facts only relevant in the domain of physiology, they would be of small account in a study of the Ascent of Man. But the more profoundly the Evolution of Man is investigated the more clearly is it seen that the whole course of his development has been conducted on this fundamental basis. Life, all life, higher or lower, is an organic unity. Nature may vary her effects, may introduce qualitative changes so stupendous as to make their affinities with lower things unthinkable, but she has never re-laid the foundations of the world. Evolution began with protoplasm and ended with Man, and all the way between, the development has been a symmetry whose secret lies in the two or three great crystallizing forces revealed to us through this first basis.

Having realized the significance of the physiological functions, let us now address ourselves to their meaning and connotations. The first, the function of Nutrition, on which the Struggle for Life depends, requires no explanation. Mr. Darwin was careful to give to his favourite phrase, the Struggle for Life, a wider meaning than that which associates it merely with Nutrition; but this qualification seems largely to have been lost sight of— to some extent even by himself—and the principle as it stands to-day in scientific and philosophical discussion is practically synonymous with the Struggle for Food. As time goes on this Struggle —at first a conflict with Nature and the elements, sustained by hunger, and intensified by competition —assumes many disguises, and is ultimately known in the modern world under the names of War and Industry. In these later phases the early function of protoplasm is obscured, but on the last analysis, War and Industry—pursuits in which half the world is now engaged—are seen to be simply its natural developments.

The implications of the second function, Reproduction, lie further from the surface. To say that Reproduction is synonymous with the Struggle for the Life of Others conveys at first little meaning, for the physiological aspects of the function persist in the mind, and make even a glimpse of its true character difficult. In two or three chapters in the text, the implications of this function will be explained at length, and the reader who is sufficiently interested in the immediate problem, or who sees that there is here something to be investigated, may do well to turn to these at once. Suffice it for the moment to say that the physiological aspects of the Struggle for the Life of Others are so overshadowed even towards the close of the Animal Kingdom by the psychical and ethical that it is scarcely necessary to emphasize the former at all. One's first and natural association with the Struggle for the Life of Others is with something done for posterity—in the plant the Struggle to produce seeds, in the animal to beget young. But this is a preliminary which, compared with what directly and indirectly rises out of it, may be almost passed over. The significant note is ethical, the development of Other-ism, as Altruism—its immediate and inevitable outcome. Watch any higher animal at that most critical of all hours—for itself, and for its species—the hour when it gives birth to another creature like itself. Pass over the purely physiological processes of birth; observe the behaviour of the animal-mother in presence of the new and helpless life which palpitates before her. There it lies, trembling in the balance between life and death. Hunger tortures it; cold threatens it; danger besets it; its blind existence hangs by a thread. There is the opportunity of Evolution. There is an opening appointed in the physical order for the introduction of a moral order. If there is more in Nature than the selfish Struggle for Life the secret can now be told. Hitherto, the world belonged to the Food-seeker, the Self-seeker, the Struggler for Life, the Father. Now is the hour of the Mother. And, animal though she be, she rises to her task. And that hour, as she ministers to her young, becomes to the world the hour of its holiest birth.

Sympathy, tenderness, unselfishness, and the long list of virtues which make up Altruism, are the direct outcome and essential accompaniment of the reproductive process. Without some rudimentary maternal solicitude for the egg in the humblest forms of life, or for the young among higher forms, the living world would not only suffer, but would cease. For a time in the life history of every higher animal the direct, personal, gratuitous, unrewarded help of another creature is a condition of existence. Even in the lowliest world of plants the labours of Maternity begin, and the animal kingdom closes with the creation of a class in which this function is perfected to its last conceivable expression. The vicarious principle is shot through and through the whole vast web of Nature; and if one actor has played a mightier part than another in the drama of the past, it has been self-sacrifice. What more has come into humanity along the line of the Struggle for the Life of Others will be shown later. But it is quite certain that, of all the things that minister to the welfare and good of Man, of all that make the world varied and fruitful, of all that make society solid and interesting, of all that make life beautiful and glad and worthy, by far the larger part has reached us through the activities of the Struggle for the Life of Others.

How grave the omission of this supreme factor from our reckoning, how serious the effect upon our whole view of nature, must now appear. Time was when the science of Geology was interpreted exclusively in terms of the action of a single force —fire. Then followed the theories of an opposing school who saw all the earth's formations to be the result of water. Any Biology, any Sociology any Evolution, which is based on a single factor, is as untrue as the old Geology. It is only when both the Struggle for Life and the Struggle for the Life of Others are kept in view, that any scientific theory of Evolution is possible. Combine them, contrast them, assign each its place, allow for their inter-actions, and the scheme of Nature may be worked out in terms of them to the last detail. All along the line, through the whole course of the development, these two functions act and react upon one another; and continually as they co-operate to produce a single result, their specific differences are never lost.

The first, the Struggle for Life, is, throughout, the Self-regarding function; the second, the Other-regarding function. The first, in lower Nature, obeying the law of self-preservation, devotes its energies to feed itself; the other, obeying the law of species-preservation, to feed its young. While the first develops the active virtues of strength and courage, the other lays the basis for the passive virtues, sympathy, and love. In the later world one seeks its end in personal aggrandizement, the other in ministration. One begets competition, self-assertion, war; the other unselfishness, self-effacement, peace. One is Individualism, the other, Altruism.

To say that no ethical content can be put into the discharge of either function in the earlier reaches of Nature goes without saying. But the moment we reach a certain height in the development, ethical implications begin to arise. These, in the case of the first, have been read into Nature, lower as well as higher, with an exaggerated and merciless malevolence. The other side has received almost no expression. The final result is a picture of Nature wholly painted in shadow—a picture so dark as to be a challenge to its Maker, an unanswered problem to philosophy, an abiding offence to the moral nature of Man. The world has been held up to us as one great battlefield heaped with the slain, an Inferno of infinite suffering, a slaughter-house resounding with the cries of a ceaseless agony.

Before this version of the tragedy, authenticated by the highest names on the roll of science, humanity was dumb, morality mystified, natural theology stultified. A truer reading may not wholly relieve the first, enlighten the second, or re-instate the third. But it at least re-opens the inquiry; and when all its bearings come to be perceived, the light thrown upon the field of Nature by the second factor may be more impressive to reason than the apparent shadow of the first to sense.

To relieve the strain of the position forced upon ethics by the one-sided treatment of the process of Evolution, heroic attempts have been made. Some have attempted to mitigate the amount of suffering it involves, and assure us that, after all, the Struggle, except as a metaphor, scarcely exists. "There is," protests Mr. Alfred Russel Wallace, "good reason to believe ... that the supposed `torments ` and `miseries ` of animals have little real existence, but are the reflection of the imagined sensations of cultivated men and women in similar circumstances; and that the amount of actual suffering caused by the Struggle for Existence among animals is altogether insignificant. Mr. Huxley, on the other hand, will make no compromise. The Struggle for Life to him is a portentous fact, unmitigated and unexplained. No metaphors are strong enough to describe the implacability of its sway. "The moral indifference of nature" and "the unfathomable injustice of the nature of things" everywhere stare him in the face. "For his successful progress, as far as the savage state, Man has been largely indebted to those qualities which he shares with the ape and the tiger. That stage reached, "for thousands and thousands of years, before the origin of the oldest known civilizations, men were savages of a very low type. They strove with their enemies and their competitors; they preyed upon things weaker or less cunning than themselves; they were born, multiplied without stint, and died, for thousands of generations, alongside the mammoth, the urus, the lion, and the hyaena, whose lives were spent in the same way; and they were no more to be praised or blamed, on moral grounds, than their less erect and more hairy compatriots.... Life was a continual free fight, and beyond the limited and temporary relations of the family, the Hobbesian war of each against all was the normal state of existence. The human species, like others, plashed and floundered amid the general stream of evolution, keeping its head above water as it best might, and thinking neither of whence nor whither.

How then does Mr. Huxley act—for it is instructive to follow out the consequences of an error—in the face of this tremendous problem? He gives it up. There is no solution. Nature is without excuse. After framing an indictment against it in the severest language at his command, he turns his back upon Nature—sub-human Nature, that is —and leaves teleology to settle the score as best it can. "The history of civilization," he tells us, "is the record of the attempts of the human race to escape from this position." But whither does he betake himself? Is he not part of Nature, and therefore a sharer in its guilt? By no means. For by an astonishing tour de force—the last, as his former associates in the evolutionary ranks have not failed to remind him, which might have been expected of him—he ejects himself from the world-order, and washes his hands of it in the name of Ethical Man. After sharing the fortunes of Evolution all his life, bearing its burdens and solving its doubts, he abandons it without a pang, and sets up an imperium in imperio, where, as a moral being, the ʻcosmic' Struggle troubles him no more. "Cosmic Nature," he says, in a parting shot at his former citadel, "is no school of virtue, but the head-quarters of the enemy of ethical nature. So far from the Ascent of Man running along the ancient line, "Social progress means a checking of the cosmic process at every step and the substitution for it of another, which may be called the ethical process; the end of which is not the survival of those who may happen to be the fittest, in respect of the whole of the conditions which exist, but of those who are ethically the best.

The expedient, to him, was a necessity. Viewing Nature as Mr. Huxley viewed it there was no other refuge. The "cosmic process" meant to him the Struggle for Life, and to escape from the Struggle for Life he was compelled to turn away from the world-order, which had its being because of it. As it happens, Mr. Huxley has hit upon the right solution, only the method by which he reaches it is wholly wrong. And the mischievous result of it is obvious —it leaves all lower Nature in the lurch. With a curious disregard of the principle of Continuity, to which all his previous work had done such homage, he splits up the world-order into two separate halves. The earlier dominated by the ʻcosmic ' principle— the Struggle for Life; the other by the ʻethical ' principle—virtually, the Struggle for the Life of Others. The Struggle for Life is thus made to stop at the ʻethical ' process; the Struggle for the Life of Others to begin. Neither is justified by fact. The Struggle for the Life of Others, as we have seen, starts its upward course from the same protoplasm as the Struggle for Life; and the Struggle for Life runs on into the ʻethical' sphere as much as the Struggle for the Life of Others. One has only to see where Mr. Huxley gets his ʻethical ' world to perceive the extent of the anomaly. For where does he get it, and what manner of world is it? "The history of civilization details the steps by which men have succeeded in building up an artificial world within the cosmos. An artificial world within the cosmos?

This suggested breach between the earlier and the later process, if indeed we are to take it seriously, is scientifically indefensible, and the more unfortunate since the same result, or a better, can be obtained without it. The real breach is not between the earlier and the later process, but between two rival, or two co-operating processes, which have existed from the first, which have worked together all along the line, and which took on ʻethical ' characters at the same moment in time. The Struggle for the Life of Others is sunk as deep in the "cosmic process" as the Struggle for Life; the Struggle for Life has a share in the "ethical process" as much as the Struggle for the Life of Others. Both are cosmic processes; both are ethical processes; both are both cosmical and ethical processes. Nothing but confusion can arise from a cross-classification which does justice to neither half of Nature.

The consternation caused by Mr. Huxley's change of front, or supposed change of front, is matter of recent history. Mr. Leslie Stephen and Mr. Herbert Spencer hastened to protest; the older school of moralists hailed it almost as a conversion.

But the one fact everywhere apparent throughout the discussion is that neither side apprehended either the ultimate nature or the true solution of the problem. The seat of the disorder is the same in both attackers and attacked—the one-sided view of Nature. Universally Nature, as far as the plant, animal, and savage levels, is taken to be synonymous with the Struggle for Life. Darwinism held the monopoly of that lower region, and Darwinism revenged itself in a manner which has at least shown the inadequacy of the most widely accepted premise of recent science.

That Mr. Huxley has misgivings on the matter himself is apparent from his Notes. "Of course," he remarks, in reference to the technical point, "strictly speaking, social life and the ethical process, in virtue of which it advances towards perfection, are part and parcel of the general process of Evolution. And he gets a momentary glimpse of the "ethical process" in the cosmos, which, if he had followed it out, must have modified his whole position. "Even in these rudimentary forms of society, love and fear come into play, and enforce a greater or less renunciation of self-will. To this extent the general cosmic process begins to be checked by a rudimentary ethical process, which is, strictly speaking, part of the former, just as the `governor' in a steam-engine is part of the mechanism of the engine.

Here the whole position is virtually conceded; and only the pre-conceptions of Darwinism and the lack of a complete investigation into the nature and extent of the "rudimentary ethical process" can have prevailed in the face of such an admission. Follow out the metaphor of the `governor,' and, with one important modification, the true situation almost stands disclosed. For what appears to be the `governor' in the rudimentary ethical process becomes the `steam-engine' in the later process. The mere fact that it exists in the "general cosmic process" alters the quality of that process; and the fact that, as we hope to show, it becomes the prime mover in the later process, entirely changes our subsequent conception of it. The beginning of a process is to be read from the end and not from the beginning. And if even a rudiment of a moral order be found in the beginnings of this process it relates itself and that process to a final end and a final unity.

Philosophy reads end into the earlier process by a necessity of reason. But how much stronger its position if it could add to that a basis in the facts of Nature? "I ask the evolutionist," pertinently inquires Mr. Huxley's critic, "who has no other basis than the Struggle for existence, how he accounts for the intrusion of these moral ideas and standards which presume to interfere with the cosmic process and sit in judgment upon its results. May we ask the philosopher how he accounts for them? As little can he account for them as he who has "no other basis than the Struggle for existence." Truly, the writer continues, the question "cannot be answered so long as we regard morality merely as an incidental result, a by-product, as it were, of the cosmical system." But what if morality be the main product of the cosmical system—of even the cosmical system? What if it can be shown that it is the essential and not the incidental result of it, and that so far from being a by-product, it is immorality that is the by-product?

These interrogations may be too strongly put. `Accompaniments' of the cosmical system might be better than `products'; `revelations through that process' may be nearer the truth than `results' of it. But what it is intended to show is that the moral order is a continuous line from the beginning, that it has had throughout, so to speak, a basis in the cosmos, that upon this, as a trellis-work, it has climbed upwards to the top. The one—the trelliswork—is to be conceived of as an incarnation; the other—the manifestation—as a revelation; the one is an Evolution from below, the other an Involution from above. Philosophy has long since assured us of the last, but because it was never able to show us the completeness of the first, science refused to believe it. The defaulter nevertheless was not philosophy but science. Its business was with the trellis-work. And it gave us a broken trellis-work, a ladder with only one side, and every step on the other side resting on air. When science tried to climb the ladder it failed; the steps refused to bear any weight. What did men of science do? They condemned the ladder and, balancing themselves on the side that was secure, proclaimed their Agnosticism to philosophy. And what did philosophy do? It stood on the other half of the ladder, the half that was not there, and rated them. That the other half was not there was of little moment. It was in themselves. It ought to be there; therefore it must be there. And it is quite true; it is there. Philosophy, like Poetry, is prophetic: "The sense of the whole," it says, "comes first.

But science could not accept the alternative. It had looked, and it was not there; from its standpoint the only refuge was Agnosticism— there were no facts. Till the facts arrived, therefore, philosophy was powerless to relieve her ally. Science looked to Nature to put in her own ends, and not to philosophy to put them in for her. Philosophy might interpret them after they were there, but it must have something to start from; and all that science had supplied her with mean time was the fact of the Struggle for Life. Working from the standpoint of the larger Nature, Human Nature itself, philosophy could put in other ends; but there appeared no solid backing for these in facts, and science refused to be satisfied. The position was a fair one. The danger of philosophy putting in the ends is that she cannot convince everyone that they are the right ones.

And what is the valid answer? Of course, that Nature has put in her own ends if we would take the trouble to look for them. She does not require them to be secretly manufactured upstairs and credited to her account. By that process mistakes might arise in the reckoning. The philosophers upstairs might differ about the figures, or at least in equating them. The philosopher requires fact, phenomenon, natural law, at every turn to keep him right; and without at least some glimpse of these, he may travel far afield. So long as Schopenhauer sees one thing in the course of Nature and Rousseau another, it will always be well to have Nature herself to act as referee. The end as read in Nature, and the end as re-read in, and interpreted by, the higher Nature of Man may be very different things; but nothing can be done till the End-in-the-phenomenon clears the way for the End-in-itself—till science overtakes philosophy with facts. When that is done, everything can be done. With the finding of the other half of the ladder, even Agnosticism may retire. Science cannot permanently pronounce itself "not knowing," till it has exhausted the possibilities of knowing. And in this case the Agnosticism is premature, for science has only to look again, and it will discover that the missing facts are there.

Seldom has there been an instance on so large a scale of a biological error corrupting a whole philosophy. Bacon's aphorism was never more true: "This I dare affirm in knowledge of Nature, that a little natural philosophy, and the first entrance into it, doth dispose the opinion to atheism, but on the other side, much natural philosophy, and wading deep into it, will bring about men's minds to religion. Hitherto, the Evolutionist has had practically no other basis than the Struggle for Life. Suppose even we leave that untouched, the addition of an Other-regarding basis makes an infinite difference. For when it is then asked on which of them the process turns, and the answer is given 'On both,' we perceive that it is neither by the one alone, nor by the other alone, that the process is to be interpreted, but by a higher unity which resolves and embraces all. And as both are equally necessary to the antinomy, even that of the two which seems irreconcilable with higher ends is seen to be necessary. Viewed simpliciter, the Struggle for Life appears irreconcilable with ethical ends, a prodigious anomaly in a moral world; but viewed in continuous reaction with the Struggle for the Life of Others, it discloses itself as an instrument of perfection the most subtle and far-reaching that reason could devise.

The presence of the second factor therefore, while it leaves the first untouched, cannot leave its implications untouched. It completely alters these implications. It has never been denied that the Struggle for Life is an efficient instrument of progress; the sole difficulty has always been to justify the nature of the instrument. But if even it be shown that this is only half the instrument, teleology gains something. If the fuller view takes nothing away from the process of Evolution, it imports something into it which changes the whole aspect of the case. For even from the first that factor is there. The Struggle for the Life of Others, as we have seen, is no interpolation at the end of the process, but radical, engrained in the world-order as profoundly as the Struggle for Life. By what right, then, has Nature been interpreted only by the Struggle for Life? With far greater justice might science interpret it in the light of the Struggle for the Life of Others. For, in the first place, unless there had been this second factor, the world could not have existed. Without the Struggle for the Life of Others, obviously there would have been no Others. In the second place, unless there had been a Struggle for the Life of Others, the Struggle for Life could not have been kept up. As will be shown later the Struggle for Life almost wholly supports itself on the products of the Struggle for the Life of Others. In the third place, without the Struggle for the Life of Others, the Struggle for Life as regards its energies would have died down, and failed of its whole achievement. It is the ceaseless pressure produced by the exuberant fertility of Reproduction that creates any valuable Struggle for Life at all. The moment "Others" multiply, the individual struggle becomes keen up to the disciplinary point. It was this, indeed— through the reading of Malthus on Over-population—that suggested to Mr. Darwin the value of the Struggle for Life. The law of Over-population from that time forward became the foundation-stone of his theory; and recent biological research has made the basis more solid than ever. The Struggle for the Life of Others on the plant and animal plane, in the mere work of multiplying lives, is a final condition of progress. Without competition there can be no fight, and without fight there can be no victory. In other words, without the Struggle for the Life of Others there can be no Struggle for Life, and therefore no Evolution. Finally, and all the reasons already given are frivolous beside it, had there been no Altruism—Altruism in the definite sense of unselfishness, sympathy, and self-sacrifice for Others, the whole higher world of life had perished as soon as it was created. For hours, or days, or weeks in the early infancy of all higher animals, maternal care and sympathy are a condition of existence. Altruism had to enter the world, and any species which neglected it was extinguished in a generation.

No doubt a case could be made out likewise for the imperative value of the Struggle for Life. The position has just been granted. So far from disputing it, we assume it to be equally essential to Nature and to a judgment upon the process of Evolution. But what is disputed is that the Struggle for Life is either the key to

Nature, or that it is more important in itself than the Struggle for the Life of Others. It is pitiful work pitting the right hand against the left, the heart against the head; but if it be insisted that there is neither right hand nor heart, the proclamation is necessary not only that they exist, but that absolutely they are as important and relatively to ethical Man of infinitely greater moment than anything that functions either in the animal or social organism.

But why, if all this be true of the Struggle for the Life of Others, has a claim so imperious not been recognized by science? That a phenomenon of this distinction should have attracted so little attention suggests a suspicion. Does it really exist? Is the biological basis sound? Have we not at least exaggerated its significance? The biologist will judge. Though no doubt the function of Reproduction is intimately connected in Physiology with the function of Nutrition, the facts as stated here are facts of Nature; and some glimpse of the influence of this second factor will be given in the sequel from which even the non-biological reader may draw his own conclusions. Difficult as it seems to account for the ignoring of an elemental fact in framing the doctrine of Evolution, there are circumstances which make the omission less unintelligible. Foremost, of course, there stands the overpowering influence of Mr. Darwin. In spite of the fact that he warned his followers against it, this largely prejudged the issue. Next is to be considered the narrowing, one had almost said the blighting, effect of specialism. Necessary to the progress of science, the first era of a reign of specialism is disastrous to philosophy. The men who in field and laboratory are working out the facts, do not speculate at all. Content with slowly building up the sum of actual knowledge in some neglected and restricted province, they are too absorbed to notice even what the workers in the other provinces are about. Thus it happens that while there are many scientific men, there are few scientific thinkers. The complaint is often made that science speculates too much. It is quite the other way. One has only to read the average book of science in almost any department to wonder at the wealth of knowledge, the brilliancy of observation, and the barrenness of idea. On the other hand, though scientific experts will not think themselves, there is always a multitude of onlookers waiting to do it for them. Among these what strikes one is the ignorance of fact and the audacity of the idea. The moment any great half-truth in Nature is unearthed, these unqualified practitioners leap to a generalization; and the observers meantime, on the track of the other half, are too busy or too oblivious to refute their heresies. Hence, long after its foundations are undermined, a brilliant generalization will retain its hold upon the popular mind; and before the complementary, the qualifying, or the neutralizing facts can be supplied, the mischief is done.

But while this is true of many who play with the double-edged tools of science, it is not true of a third class. When we turn to the pages of the few whose science is adequate and whose sweep is over the whole vast horizon, we find, as we should expect, some recognition of the altruistic factor. Though Mr. Herbert Spencer, to whom the appeal in this connection is obvious, makes a different use of the fact, it has not escaped him. Not only does the Other-regarding function receive recognition, but he allots it a high place in his system. Of its ethical bearings he is equally clear. "What," he asks, "is the ethical aspect of these [altruistic] principles? In the first place, animal life of all but the lowest kinds has been maintained by virtue of them. Excluding the Protozoa, among which their operation is scarcely discernible, we see that without gratis benefits to offspring, and earned benefits to adults, life could not have continued. In the second place, by virtue of them life has gradually evolved into higher forms. By care of offspring, which has become greater with advancing organization, and by survival of the fittest in the competition among adults, which has become more habitual with advancing organization, superiority has been perpetually fostered and further advances caused. Fiske, Littre, Romanes, Le Conte, L. Buchner, Miss Buckley, and Prince Kropotkin have expressed themselves partly in the same direction; and Geddes and Thomson, in so many words, recognize "the co-existence of twin-streams of egoism and altruism, which often merge for a space without losing their distinctness, and are traceable to a common origin in the simplest forms of life. The last named—doubtless because their studies have taken them both into the fields of pure biology and of bionomics—more clearly than any other modern writers, have grasped the bearings of this theme in all directions, and they fearlessly take their standpoint from the physiology of protoplasm. Thus, "in the hunger and reproductive attractions of the lowest organisms, the self-regarding and other-regarding activities of the higher find their starting-point. Though some vague consciousness is perhaps co-existent with life itself, we can only speak with confidence of psychical egoism and altruism after a central nervous system has been definitely established. At the same time, the activities of even the lowest organisms are often distinctly referable to either category.... Hardly distinguishable at the outset, the primitive hunger and love become the starting-points of divergent lines of egoistic and altruistic emotion and activity.

That at a much earlier stage than is usually supposed, Evolution visibly enters upon the "rudimentary ethical" plane, is certain, and we shall hope to outline the proof. But even if the thesis fails, it remains to challenge the general view that the Struggle for Life is everything, and the Struggle for the Life of Others nothing. Seeing not only that the second is the more important, but also this far more significant fact—which has not yet been alluded to—that as Evolution proceeds the one Struggle waxes, and the other wanes, would it not be wiser to study the drama nearer its denouement before deciding whether it was a moral, a non-moral, or an immoral play?

Lest the alleged waning of the Struggle for Life convey a wrong impression, let it be added that of course the word is to be taken qualitatively. The Struggle in itself can never cease. What ceases is its so-called anti-ethical character. For nothing is in finer evidence as we rise in the scale of life than the gradual tempering of the Struggle for Life. Its slow amelioration is the work of ages, may be the work of ages still, but its animal qualities in the social life of Man are being surely left behind; and though the mark of the savage and the brute still mar its handiwork, these harsher qualities must pass away. In that new social order which the gathering might of the altruistic spirit is creating now around us, in that reign of Love which must one day, if the course of Evolution holds on its way, be realized, the baser elements will find that solvent prepared for them from the beginning in anticipation of a higher rule on earth. Interpreting the course of Evolution scientifically, whether from its starting-point in the first protoplasm, or from the rallying-point of its two great forces in the social organism of to-day, it becomes more and more certain that only from the commingled achievement of both can the nature of the process be truly judged. Yet, as one sees the one sun set, and the other rise with a splendour the more astonishing and bewildering as the centuries roll on, it is impossible to withhold a verdict as to which may be most reasonably looked upon as the ultimate reality of the world. The path of progress and the path of Altruism are one. Evolution is nothing but the Involution of Love, the revelation of Infinite Spirit, the Eternal Life returning to Itself. Even the great shadow of Egoism which darkens the past is revealed as shadow only because we are compelled to read it by the higher light which has come. In the very act of judging it to be shadow, we assume and vindicate the light. And in every vision of the light, contrariwise, we resolve the shadow, and perceive the end for which both light and dark are given.

> "I can believe, this dread machinery
> Of sin and sorrow, would confound me else,
> Devised—all pain, at most expenditure
> Of pain by Who devised pain—to evolve,
> By new machinery in counterpart,
> The moral qualities of Man—how else?—
> To make him love in turn, and be beloved,
> Creative and self-sacrificing too,
> And thus eventually Godlike.

III: Why Was Evolution the Method Chosen?

One seldom-raised yet not merely curious question of Evolution is, why the process should be an evolution at all? If Evolution is simply a method of Creation, why was this very extraordinary method chosen? Creation tout d'un coup might have produced the same result; an instantaneous act or an age-long process would both have given us the world as it is? The answer of modern natural theology has been that the evolutionary method is the infinitely nobler scheme. A spectacular act, it is said, savours of the magician. As a mere exhibition of power it appeals to the lower nature; but a process of growth suggests to the reason the work of an intelligent Mind. No doubt this intellectual gain is real. While a catastrophe puts the universe to confusion at the start, a gradual rise makes the beginning of Nature harmonious with its end. How the surpassing grandeur of the new conception has filled the imagination and kindled to enthusiasm the soberest scientific minds, from Darwin downwards, is known to everyone. As the memorable words which close the Origin of Species recall: "There is a grandeur in this view of life, with its several powers, having been originally breathed by the Creator into a few forms or into one; and that whilst this planet has gone cycling on, according to the fixed law of gravity, from so simple a beginning endless forms most beautiful and most wonderful have been, and are being evolved.

But can an intellectual answer satisfy us any more than the mechanical answer which it replaced? As there was clearly a moral purpose in the end to be achieved by Evolution, should we not expect to find some similar purpose in the means? Can we perceive no high design in selecting this particular design, no worthy ethical result which should justify the conception as well as the execution of Evolution?

We go too far, perhaps, in expecting answers to questions so transcendent. But one at least suggests itself, whose practical value is apology enough for venturing to advance it. Whenever the scheme was planned, it must have been foreseen that the time would come when the directing of part of the course of Evolution would pass into the hands of Man. A spectator of the drama for ages, too ignorant to see that it was a drama, and too impotent to do more than play his little part, the discovery must sooner or later break upon him that Nature meant him to become a partner in her task, and share the responsibility of the closing acts. It is not given to him as yet to bind the sweet influences of Pleiades, or to unloose the bands of Orion. In part only can he make the winds and waves obey him, or control the falling rain. But in larger part he holds the dominion of the world of lower life. He exterminates what he pleases; he creates and he destroys; he changes; he evolves; his selection replaces natural selection; he replenishes the earth with plants and animals according to his will. But in a far grander sphere, and in an infinitely profounder sense, has the sovereignty passed to him, For, by the same decree, he finds himself the guardian and the arbiter of his personal destiny, and that of his fellow-men. The moulding of his life and of his children's children in measure lie with him. Through institutions of his creation, through Parliaments, Churches, Societies, Schools, he shapes the path of progress for his country and his time. The evils of the world are combated by his remedies; its passions are stayed, its wrongs redressed, its energies for good or evil directed by his hand. For unnumbered millions he opens or shuts the gates of happiness, and paves the way for misery or social health. Never before was it known and felt with the same solemn certainty that Man, within bounds which none can pass, must be his own maker and the maker of the world. For the first time in history not individuals only but multitudes of the wisest and the noblest in every land take home to themselves, and unceasingly concern themselves with, the problem of the Evolution of Mankind. Multitudes more, philanthropists, statesmen, missionaries, humble men and patient women, devote themselves daily to its practical solution, and everywhere some, in a God-like culmination of Altruism, give their very lives for their fellow-men. Who is to help these Practical Evolutionists—for those who read the book of Nature can call them by no other name, and those who know its spirit can call them by no higher—who is to help them in their tremendous task? There is the will—where is the wisdom?

Where but in Nature herself. Nature may have entrusted the further building to Mankind, but the plan has never left her hands. The lines of the future are to be learned from her past, and her fellow-helpers can most easily, most loyally, and most perfectly do their part by studying closely the architecture of the earlier world, and continuing the half-finished structure symmetrically to the top. The information necessary to complete the work with architectural consistency lies in Nature. We might expect that it should be there. When a business is transferred, or a partner assumed, the books are shown, the methods of the business explained, its future developments pointed out. All this is now done for the Evolution of Mankind. In Evolution Creation has shown her hand. To have kept the secret from Man would have imperilled the further evolution. To have revealed it sooner had been premature. Love must come before knowledge, for knowledge is the instrument of Love, and useless till it arrives. But now that there is Altruism enough in the world to begin the new era, there must be wisdom enough to direct it. To make Nature spell out her own career, to embody the key to the development in the very development itself, so that the key might be handed over along with the work, was to make the transference of responsibility possible and rational. In the seventeenth century, Descartes, who with Leibnitz already foresaw the adumbration of the evolutionary process, almost pointed this out; for speaking, in another connection, of the intellectual value of a slow development of things he observes, "their nature is much more easy to conceive when they are seen originating by degrees in this way, than when they are considered as entirely made.

The past of Nature is a working-model of how worlds can be made. The probabilities are there is no better way of making them. If Man does as well it will be enough. In any case he can only begin where Nature left off, and work with such tools as are put into his hands. If the new partner had been intended merely to experiment with world-making, no such legacy of useful law had been ever given him. And if he had been meant to begin de novo on a totally different plan, it is unlikely either that that should not have been hinted at, or that in his touching and beautiful endeavour he should be embarrassed and thrown off the track by the old plan. As a child set to complete some fine embroidery is shown the stitches, the colours, and the outline traced upon the canvas, so the great Mother in setting their difficult task to her later children provides them with one superb part finished to show the pattern.

IV: Evolution and Sociology

The moment it is grasped that we may have in Nature a key to the future progress of Mankind, the study of Evolution rises to an imposing rank in human interest. There lies the programme of the world from the first of time, the instrument, the charter, and still more the prophecy of progress. Evolution is the natural directory of the sociologist, the guide through that which has worked in the past to what—subject to modifying influences which Nature can always be trusted to give full notice of—may be expected to work in the future. Here, for the individual, is a new and impressive summons to public action, a vocation chosen of Nature which it will profit him to consider, for thereby he may not only save the whole world, but find his own soul. "The study of the historical development of man," says Prof. Edward Caird, "especially in respect of his higher life, is not only a matter of external or merely speculative curiosity; it is closely connected with the development of that life in ourselves. For we learn to know ourselves, first of all, in the mirror of the world: or, in other words, our knowledge of our own nature and of its possibilities grows and deepens with our understanding of what is without us, and most of all with our understanding of the general history of man. It has often been noticed that there is a certain analogy between the life of the individual and that of the race, and even that the life of the individual is a sort of epitome of the history of humanity. But, as Plato already discovered, it is by reading the large letters that we learn to interpret the small.... It is only through a deepened consciousness of the world that the human spirit can solve its own problem. Especially is this true in the region of anthropology. For the inner life of the individual is deep and full, just in proportion to the width of his relations to other men and things; and his consciousness of what he is in himself as a spiritual being is dependent on a comprehension of the position of his individual life in the great secular process by which the intellectual and moral life of humanity has grown and is growing. Hence the highest practical as well as speculative interests of men are connected with the new extension of science which has given fresh interest and meaning to the whole history of the race.

If, as Herbert Spencer reminds us, "it is one of those open secrets which seem the more secret because they are so open, that all phenomena displayed by a nation are phenomena of Life, and are dependent on the laws of Life," we cannot devote ourselves to study those laws too earnestly or too soon. From the failure to get at the heart of the first principles of Evolution the old call to "follow Nature" has all but become a heresy. Nature, as a moral teacher, thanks to the Darwinian interpretation, was never more discredited than at this hour; and friend and foe alike agree in warning us against her. But a further reading of Nature may decide not that we must discharge the teacher but beg her mutinous pupils to try another term at school. With Nature studied in the light of a true biology, or even in the sense in which the Stoics themselves employed their favourite phrase, it must become once more the watchword of personal and social progress. With Mr. Huxley's definition of what the Stoics meant by Nature as "that which holds up the ideal of the supreme good and demands absolute submission of the will to its behests . . . which commands all men to love one another, to return good for evil, to regard one another as citizens of one great state, the phrase, "Live according to Nature," so far from having no application to the modern world or no sanction in modern thought, is the first commandment of Natural Religion.

The sociologist has grievously complained of late that he could get but little help from science. The suggestions of Bagehot, the Synthetic Philosophy of Herbert Spencer, the proposals of multitudes of the followers of the last who announced the redemption of the world the moment they discovered the "Social Organism," raised great expectations. But somehow they were not fulfilled. Mr. Spencer's work has been mainly to give this century, and in part all time, its first great map of the field. He has brought all the pieces on the board, described them one by one, defined and explained the game. But what he has failed to do with sufficient precision, is to pick out the King and Queen. And because he has not done so, some men have mistaken his pawns for kings; others have mistaken the real kings for pawns; every ism has found endorsement in his pages, and men have gathered courage for projects as hostile to his whole philosophy as to social order. Theories of progress have arisen without any knowledge of its laws, and the ordered course of things has been done violence to by experiments which, unless the infinite conservatism of Nature had neutralized their evils, had been a worse disaster than they are. This inadequacy, indeed, of modern sociology to meet the practical problems of our time, has become a by-word. Mr. Leslie Stephen pronounces the existing science "a heap of vague empirical observation, too flimsy to be useful"; and Mr. Huxley, exasperated with the condition in which it leaves the human family, protests that "if there is no hope of a large improvement" he should "hail the advent of some kindly comet which would sweep the whole affair away."

The first step in the reconstruction of Sociology will be to escape from the shadow of Darwinism— or rather to complement the Darwinian formula of the Struggle for Life by a second factor which will turn its darkness into light. A new morphology can only come from a new physiology, and vice versa, and for both we must return to Nature. The one-sided induction has led Sociology into a wilderness of empiricism, and only a complete induction can reinstate it among the sciences. The vacant place is there awaiting it; and every earnest mind is prepared to welcome it, not only as the coming science, but as the crowning Science of all the sciences, the Science, indeed, for which it will one day be seen every other science exists. What it waits for meantime is what every science has had to wait for, exhaustive observation of the facts and ways of Nature. Geology stood still for centuries waiting for those who would simply look at the facts. Men speculated in fantastic ways as to how the world could have been made, and the last thing that occurred to them was to go and see it making. Then came the observers, men who, waiving all theories of the process, addressed themselves to the natural world direct, and in watching its daily programme of falling rain and running stream laid bare the secret for all time. Sociology has had its Werners; it awaits its Huttons. The method of Sociology must be the method of all the natural sciences. It also must go and see the world making, not where the conditions are already abnormal beyond recall, or where Man, by irregular action, has already obscured everything but the conditions of failure; but in lower Nature which makes no mistakes, and in those fairer reaches of a higher world where the quality and the stability of the progress are guarantees that the eternal order of Nature has had her uncorrupted way.

It cannot be that the full programme for the perfect world lies in the imperfect part. Nor can it ever be that science can find the end in the beginning, get moral out of non-moral states, evolve human societies from ant-heaps, or philanthropies from protoplasm. But in every beginning we get a beginning of an end; in every process a key to the single step to be taken next. The full corn is not in the ear, but the first cell of it is, and though 'it doth not yet appear' what the million-celled ear shall be, there is rational ground for judging what the second cell shall be. The next few cells of the Social Organism are all that are given to Sociology to affect. And, in dealing with them, its business is with the forces; the phenomena will take care of themselves. Neither the great forces of Nature, nor the great lines of Nature, change in a day, and however apparently unrelated seem the phenomena as we ascend—here animal, there human; at one time non-moral, at another moral—the lines of progress are the same. Nature, in horizontal section, is broken up into strata which present to the eye of ethical Man the profoundest distinctions in the universe; but Nature in the vertical section offers no break, or pause, or flaw. To study the first is to study a hundred unrelated sciences, sciences of atoms, sciences of cells, sciences of Souls, sciences of Societies; to study the second is to deal with one science—Evolution. Here, on the horizontal section, may be what Geology calls an unconformability; there is overlap; changes of climate may be registered from time to time, each with its appropriate reaction on the things contained; upheavals, depressions, denudations, glaciations, faults, vary the scene; higher forms of fossils appear as we ascend; but the laws of life are continuous throughout, the eternal elements in an ever temporal world. The Struggle for Life, and the Struggle for the Life of Others, in essential nature, have never changed. They find new expression in each further sphere, become coloured to our eye with different hues, are there the rivalries or the affections of the brute, and here the industrial or the moral conflicts of the race; but the factors themselves remain the same, and all life moves in widening spirals round them. Fix in the mind this distinction between the horizontal and the vertical view of Nature, between the phenomena and the law, between all the sciences that ever were and the one science which resolves them all, and the confusions and contradictions of Evolution are reconciled. The man who deals with Nature statically, who catalogues the phenomena of life and mind, puts on each its museum label, and arranges them in their separate cases, may well defy you to co-relate such diverse wholes. To him Evolution is alike impossible and unthinkable. But these items that he labels are not wholes. And the world he dissects is not a museum, but a living, moving, and ascending thing. The sociologist's business is with the vertical section, and he who has to do with this living, moving, and ascending thing must treat it from the dynamic point of view.

The significant thing for him is the study of Evolution on its working side. And he will find that nearly all the phenomena of social and national life are phenomena of these two principles—the Struggle for Life, and the Struggle for the

Life of Others. Hence he must betake himself in earnest to see what these mean in Nature, what gathers round them as they ascend, how each acts separately, how they work together, and whither they seem to lead. More than ever the method of Sociology must be biological. More urgently than ever "the time has come for a better understanding and for a more radical method; for the social sciences to strengthen themselves by sending their roots deep into the soil underneath from which they spring; and for the biologist to advance over the frontier and carry the methods of his science boldly into human society, where he has but to deal with the phenomena of life, where he encounters life at last under its highest and most complex aspect.

Would that the brilliant writer whose words these are, and whose striking work appears while these sheets are almost in the press, had "sent his roots deep enough into biological soil" to discover the true foundation for that future Science of Society which he sees to be so imperative. No modern thinker has seen the problem so clearly as Mr. Kidd, but his solution, profoundly true in itself, is vitiated in the eyes of science and philosophy by a basis wholly unsound. With an emphasis which Darwin himself has not excelled, he proclaims the enduring value of the Struggle for Life. He sees its immense significance even in the highest ranges of the social sphere. There it stands with its imperious call to individual assertion, inciting to a rivalry which Nature herself has justified, and encouraging every man by the highest sanctions ceaselessly to seek his own. But he sees nothing else in Nature; and he encounters therefore the difficulty inevitable from this standpoint. For to obey this voice means ruin to Society, wrong and anarchy against the higher Man. He listens for another voice; but there is no response. As a social being he cannot, in spite of Nature, act on his first initiative. He must subordinate himself to the larger interest, present and future, of those around him. But why, he asks, must he, since Nature says "Mind thyself"? Till Nature adds the further precept, "Look not every man on his own things, but also on the things of Others," there is no rational sanction for morality. And he finds no such precept. There is none in Nature. There is none in Reason. Nature can only point him to a strenuous rivalry as the one condition of continued progress; Reason can only endorse the verdict. Hence he breaks at once with reason and with Nature, and seeks an "ultra-rational sanction" for the future course of social progress.

Here, in his own words, is the situation. "The teaching of reason to the individual must always be that the present time and his own interests therein are all-important to him. Yet the forces which are working out our development are primarily concerned not with those interests of the individual, but with those widely different interests of a social organism subject to quite other conditions and possessed of an indefinitely longer life. . . . The central fact with which we are confronted in our progressive societies is, therefore, that the interests of the social organism and those of the individuals comprising it at any time are actually antagonistic; they can never be reconciled; they are inherently and essentially irreconcilable. Observe the extraordinary dilemma. Reason not only has no help for the further progress of Society, but Society can only go on upon a principle which is an affront to it. As Man can only attain his highest development in Society, his individual interests must more and more subordinate themselves to the welfare of a wider whole. "How is the possession of reason ever to be rendered compatible with the will to submit to conditions of existence so onerous, requiring the effective and continual subordination of the individual's welfare to the progress of a development in which he can have no personal interest whatever?

Mr. Kidd's answer is the bold one that it is not compatible. There is no rational sanction whatever for progress. Progress, in fact, can only go on by enlisting Man's reason against itself. "All those systems of moral philosophy, which have sought to find in the nature of things a rational sanction for human conduct in society, must sweep round and round in futile circles. They attempt an inherently impossible task. The first great social lesson of those evolutionary doctrines which have transformed the science of the nineteenth century is, that there cannot be such a sanction. . . . The extraordinary character of the problem presented by human society begins thus slowly to come into view. We find man making continual progress upwards, progress which it is almost beyond the power of the imagination to grasp. From being a competitor of the brutes he has reached a point of development at which he cannot himself set any limits to the possibilities of further progress, and at which he is evidently marching onwards to a high destiny. He has made this advance under the sternest conditions, involving rivalry and competition for all, and the failure and suffering of great numbers. His reason has been, and necessarily continues to be, a leading factor in this development; yet, granting, as we apparently must grant, the possibility of the reversal of the conditions from which his progress results, those conditions have not any sanction from his reason. They have had no such sanction at any stage of his history, and they continue to be as much without such sanction in the highest civilizations of the present day as at any past period.

These conclusions will not have been quoted in vain if they show the impossible positions to which a writer, whose contribution otherwise is of profound and permanent value, is committed by a false reading of Nature. Is it conceivable, a priori, that the human reason should be put to confusion by a breach of the Law of Continuity at the very point where its sustained action is of vital moment? The whole complaint, which runs like a dirge through every chapter of this book, is founded on a misapprehension of the fundamental laws which govern the processes of Evolution. The factors of Darwin and Weismann are assumed to contain an ultimate interpretation of the course of things. For all time the conditions of existence are taken as established by these authorities. With the Struggle for Life in sole possession of the field no one, therefore, we are warned, need ever repeat the gratuitous experiment of the past, of Socrates, Plato, Kant, Hegel, Comte, and Herbert Spencer, to find a sanction for morality in Nature. "All methods and systems alike, which have endeavoured to find in the nature of things any universal rational sanction for individual conduct in a progressive society, must be ultimately fruitless. They are all alike inherently unscientific in that they attempt to do what the fundamental conditions of existence render impossible." And Mr. Kidd puts a climax on his devotion to the doctrine of his masters by mourning over "the incalculable loss to English Science and English Philosophy" because Herbert Spencer's work "was practically complete before his intellect had any opportunity of realizing the full transforming effect in the higher regions of thought, and, more particularly, in the department of sociology, of that development of biological science which began with Darwin, which is still in full progress, and to which Professor Weismann has recently made the most notable contributions. Whether Mr. Spencer's ignorance or his science has been at the bottom of the escape, it is at least a lucky one. For if Mr. Kidd had realized "the full transforming effect" of the following paragraph, much of his book could not have been written. "The most general conclusion is that in order of obligation, the preservation of the species takes precedence of the preservation of the individual.

It is true that the species has no existence save as an aggregate of individuals; and it is true that, therefore, the welfare of the species is an end to be subserved only as subserving the welfare of individuals. But since disappearance of the species, implying absolute disappearance of all individuals, involves absolute failure in achieving the end, whereas disappearance of individuals, though carried to a great extent, may leave outstanding such numbers as can, by continuance of the species, make subsequent fulfilment of the end possible; the preservation of the individual must, in a variable degree according to circumstances, be subordinated to the preservation of the species, where the two conflict.

What Mr. Kidd has succeeded, and splendidly succeeded, in doing is to show that Nature as interpreted in terms of the Struggle for Life contains no sanction either for morality or for social progress. But instead of giving up Nature and Reason at this point, he should have given up Darwin. The Struggle for Life is not "the supreme fact up to which biology has slowly advanced." It is the fact to which Darwin advanced; but if biology had been thoroughly consulted it could not have given so maimed an account of itself. With the final conclusion reached by Mr. Kidd we have no quarrel. Eliminate the errors due to an unrevised acceptance of Mr. Darwin's interpretation of Nature, and his work remains the most important contribution to Social Evolution which the last decade has seen. But what startles us is his method. To put the future of Social Science on an ultra-rational basis is practically to give it up. Unless thinking men have some sense of the consistency of a method they cannot work with it, and if there is no guarantee of the stability of the results it would not be worth while.

But all that Mr. Kidd desires is really to be found in Nature. There is no single element even of his highest sanction which is not provided for in a thorough-going doctrine of Evolution—a doctrine, that is, which includes all the facts and all the factors, and especially which takes into accounts that evolution of Environment which goes on pari passu with the evolution of the organism and where the highest sanctions ultimately lie. With an Environment which widens and enriches until it includes—or consciously includes, for it has never been absent—the Divine; and with Man so evolving as to become more and more conscious that that Divine is there, and above all that it is in himself, all the materials and all the sanctions for a moral progress are for ever secure. None of the sanctions of religion are withdrawn by adding to them the sanctions of Nature. Even those sanctions which are supposed to lie over and above Nature may be none the less rational sanctions. Though a positive religion, in the Comtian sense, is no religion, a religion that is not in some degree positive is an impossibility. And although religion must always rest upon faith, there is a reason for faith, and a reason not only in Reason, but in Nature herself. When Evolution comes to be worked out along its great natural lines, it may be found to provide for all that religion assumes, all that philosophy requires, and all that science proves.

Theological minds, with premature approval, have hailed Mr. Kidd's solution as a vindication of their supreme position. Practically, as a vindication of the dynamic power of the religious factor in the Evolution of Mankind, nothing could be more convincing. But as an apologetic, it only accentuates a weakness which scientific theology never felt more keenly than at the present hour. This weakness can never be removed by an appeal to the ultra-rational. Does Mr. Kidd not perceive that anyone possessed of reason enough to encounter his dilemma, either in the sphere of thought or of conduct, will also have reason enough to reject any "ultra-rational" solution? This dilemma is not one which would occur to more than one in a thousand; it has tasked all Mr. Kidd's powers to convince his reader that it exists; but if exceptional intellect is required to see it, surely exceptional intellect must perceive that this is not the way out of it. One cannot, in fact, think oneself out of a difficulty of this kind; it can only be lived out. And that precisely is what Nature is making all of us, in greater or less degree, do, and every day making us do more. By the time, indeed, that the world as a whole is sufficiently educated to see the problem, it will already have been solved. There is little comfort, then, for apologetics in this direction. Only by bringing theology into harmony with Nature and into line with the rest of our knowledge can the noble interests given it to conserve retain their vitality in a scientific age. The first essential of a working religion is that it shall be congruous with Man; the second that it shall be congruous with Nature. Whatever its sanctions, its forces must not be abnormal, but reinforcements and higher potentialities of those forces which, from eternity, have shaped the progress of the world. No other dynamic can enter into the working schemes of those who seek to guide the destinies of nations or carry on the Evolution of Society on scientific principles. A divorce here would be the catastrophe of reason, and the end of faith. We believe with Mr. Kidd that "the process of social development which has been taking place, and which is still in progress, in our Western civilization, is not the product of the intellect, but the motive force behind it has had its seat and origin in the fund of altruistic feeling with which our civilization has become equipped." But we shall endeavour to show that this fund of altruistic feeling has been slowly funded in the race by Nature, or through Nature, and as the direct and inevitable result of that Struggle for the Life of Others, which has been from all time a condition of existence. What religion has done to build up this fund, it may not be within the scope of this introductory volume to inquire; it has done so much that students of religion may almost be pardoned the oversight of the stupendous natural basis which made it possible. But nothing is gained by protesting that "this altruistic development, and the deepening and softening of character which has accompanied it, are the direct and peculiar product of the religious system." For nothing can ever be gained by setting one half of Nature against the other, or the rational against the ultra-rational. To affirm that Altruism is a peculiar product of religion is to excommunicate Nature from the moral order, and religion from the rational order. If science is to begin to recognize religion, religion must at least end by recognizing science. And so far from religion sacrificing vital distinctions by allying itself with Nature, so far from impoverishing its immortal quality by accepting some contribution from the lower sphere, it thereby extends itself over the whole rich field, and claims all—matter, life, mind, space, time—for itself. The present danger is not in applying Evolution as a method, but only in not carrying it far enough. No man, no man of science even, observing the simple facts, can ever rob religion of its due. Religion has done more for the development of Altruism in a few centuries than all the millenniums of geological time. But we dare not rob Nature of its due. We dare not say that Nature played the prodigal for ages, and reformed at the eleventh hour. If Nature is the Garment of God, it is woven without seam throughout; if a revelation of God, it is the same yesterday, to-day, and for ever; if the expression of His Will, there is in it no variableness nor shadow of turning. Those who see great gulfs fixed—and we have all begun by seeing them—end by seeing them filled up. Were these gulfs essential to any theory of the universe or of Man, even the establishment of the unity of Nature were a dear price to pay for obliterating them. But the apparent loss is only gain, and the seeming gain were infinite loss. For to break up Nature is to break up Reason, and with it God and Man.

The Ascent of the Body

The earliest home of Primitive Man was a cave in the rocks—the simplest and most unevolved form of human habitation. One day, perhaps driven by the want within his hunting-grounds of the natural cave, he made himself a hut—an artificial cave. This simple dwelling-place was a one-roomed hut or tent of skin and boughs, and so completely does it satisfy the rude man's needs that down to the present hour no ordinary savage improves upon the idea. But as the hut surrounds itself with other huts and grows into a village, a new departure must take place. The village must have its chief, and the chief, in virtue of his larger life, requires a more spacious home. Each village, therefore, adds to its one-roomed huts, a hut with two rooms. From the two-roomed hut we pass, among certain tribes, to three- and four-roomed huts, and finally to the many-chambered lodge of the Head-Chief or King.

This passage from the simple cave to the many-chambered lodge is an Evolution, and a similar development may be traced in the domestic architecture of all civilized societies. The labourer's cottage of modern England and the shieling of the Highland crofter are the survivals of the one-roomed hut of Primitive Man, scarcely changed in any essential with the lapse of years. In the squire's mansion also, and the nobleman's castle, we have the representatives, but now in an immensely developed form, of the many-roomed home of the chief. The steps by which the cottage became the castle are the same as those by which the cave in the rocks became the lodge of the chief. Both processes wear the hall-mark of all true development—they arise in response to growing necessities, and they are carried out by the most simple and natural steps.

In this evolution of a human habitation we have an almost perfect type of the evolution of that more august habitation, the complex tenement of clay in which Man's mysterious being has its home. The Body of Man is a structure of a million, or a million million cells. And the history of the unborn babe is, in the first instance, a history of additions, of room being added to room, of organ to organ, of faculty to faculty. The general process, also, by which this takes place is almost as clear to modern science as in the case of material buildings. A special class of observers has carefully watched these secret and amazing metamorphoses, and so wonderful has been their success with mind and microscope that they can almost claim to have seen Man's Body made. The Science of Embryology undertakes to trace the development of Man from a stage in which he lived in a one-roomed house—a physiological cell. Whatever the multitude of rooms, the millions and millions of cells, in which to-day each adult carries on the varied work of life, it is certain that when he first began to be he was the simple tenant of a single cell. Observe, it is not some animal-ancestor or some human progenitor of Man that lived in this single cell—that may or may not have been—but the individual Man, the present occupant himself. We are dealing now not with phylogeny—the history of the race—but with ontogeny—the problem of Man's Ascent from his own earlier self. And the point at the moment is not that the race ascends; it is that each individual man has once, in his own life-time, occupied a single cell, and starting from that humble cradle, has passed through stage after stage of differentiation, increase, and development, until the myriad-roomed adult-form was attained. Whence that first cradle came is at present no matter. Whether its remote progenitor rocked among the waves of primeval seas or swung from the boughs of forests long since metamorphosed into coal does not affect the question of the individual ascent of Man. The answers to these questions are hypotheses. The fact that now arrests our wonder is that when the earliest trace of an infant's organization meets the eye of science it is nothing but a one-celled animal. And so closely does its development from that distant point follow the lines of the evolution just described in the case of the primitive savage hut, that we have but to make a few changes in phraseology to make the one process describe the other. Instead of rooms and chambers we shall now read cells and tissues; instead of the builder's device of adding room to room, we shall use the physiologist's term segmentation; the employments carried on in the various rooms will become the functions discharged by the organs of the human frame, and line for line the history of the evolution will be found to be the same.

The embryo of the future man begins life. Like the primitive savage, in a one-roomed hut, a single simple cell. This cell is round and almost microscopic in size. When fully formed it measures only one-tenth of a line in diameter, and with the naked eye can be barely discerned as a very fine point. An outer covering, transparent as glass, surrounds this little sphere, and in the interior, embedded in protoplasm, lies a bright globular spot. In form, in size, in composition there is no apparent difference between this human cell and that of any other mammal. The dog, the elephant, the lion, the ape, and a thousand others begin their widely different lives in a house the same as Man's. At an earlier stage indeed, before it has taken on its pellucid covering, this cell has affinities still more astonishing. For at that remoter period the earlier forms of all living things, both plant and animal, are one. It is one of the most astounding facts of modern science that the first embryonic abodes of moss and fern and pine, of shark and crab and coral polyp, of lizard, leopard, monkey, and Man are so exactly similar that the highest powers of mind and microscope fail to trace the smallest distinction between them.

But let us watch the development of this one-celled human embryo. Increase of rooms in architecture can be effected in either of two ways by building entirely new rooms, or by partitioning old ones. Both of these methods are employed in Nature. The first, gemmation, or budding, is common among the lower forms of life. The second, differentiation by partition, or segmentation, is the approved method among higher animals, and is that adopted in the case of Man. It proceeds, after the fertilized ovum has completed the complex preliminaries of karyokinesis, by the division of the interior-contents into two equal parts, so that the original cell is now occupied by two nucleated cells with the old cell-wall surrounding them outside. The two-roomed house is, in the next development, and by a similar process of segmentation, developed into a structure of four rooms, and this into one of eight, and so on. In a short time the number of chambers is so great that count is lost, and the activity becomes so vigorous in every direction that one ceases to notice individual cells at all. The tenement in fact consists now of innumerable groups of cells congregated together, suites of apartments as it were, which have quickly arranged themselves in symmetrical, definite, and withal different forms. Were these forms not different as well as definite we should hardly call it an evolution, nor should we characterize the resulting aggregation as a higher organism. A hundred cottages placed in a row would never form a castle. What makes the castle superior to the hundred cottages is not the number of its rooms, for they are possibly fewer; nor their difference in shape, for that is immaterial. It lies in the number and nature and variety of useful purposes to which the rooms are put, the perfection with which each is adapted to its end, and the harmonious co-operation among them with reference to some common work. This also is the distinction between a higher animal and a humble organism such as the centipede or the worm. These creatures are a monotony of similar rings, like a string of beads. Each bead is the counterpart of the other; and with such an organization any high or varied life becomes an impossibility. The fact that any growing embryo is passing through a real development is decided by the new complexity of structure, by the more perfect division of labour, and of better kinds of labour, and by the increase in range and efficiency of the correlated functions discharged by the whole. In the development of the human embryo the differentiating and integrating forces are steadily acting and co-operating from the first, so that the result is not a mere aggregation of similar cells, but an organism with different parts and many varied functions. When all is complete we find that one suite of cells has been specially set apart to provide the commissariat, others have devoted themselves exclusively to assimilation. The ventilation of the house—respiration—has been attended to by others, and a central force-pump has been set up, and pipes and ducts for many purposes installed throughout the system. Telegraph wires have next been stretched in every direction to keep up connection between the endless parts; and other cells developed into bony pillars for support. Finally, the whole delicate structure has been shielded by a variety of protective coverings, and after months and years of further elaboration and adjustment the elaborate fabric is complete. Now all these complicated contrivances —bones, muscles, nerves, heart, brain, lungs—are made out of cells; they are themselves, and in their furthest development, simply masses or suites of cells modified in various ways for the special department of household work they are meant to serve. No new thing, except building material, has entered into the embryo since its first appearing. It seized whatever matter lay to hand, incorporated it with its own quickening substance, and built it in to its appropriate place. So the structure rose in size and symmetry, till the whole had climbed, a miracle of unfolding, to the stature of a Man.

But the beauty of this development is not the significant thing to the student of Evolution; nor is it the occultness of the process nor the perfection of the result that fill him with awe as he surveys the finished work. It is the immense distance Man has come. Between the early cell and the infant's formed body, the ordinary observer sees the uneventful passage of a few brief months. But the evolutionist sees concentrated into these few months the labour and the progress of incalculable ages. Here before him is the whole stretch of time since life first dawned upon the earth; and as he watches the nascent organism climbing to its maturity he witnesses a spectacle which for strangeness and majesty stands alone in the field of biological research. What he sees is not the mere shaping or sculpturing of a Man. The human form does not begin as a human form. It begins as an animal; and at first, and for a long time to come, there is nothing wearing the remotest semblance of humanity. What meets the eye is a vast procession of lower forms of life, a succession of strange inhuman creatures emerging from a crowd of still stranger and still more inhuman creatures; and it is only after a prolonged and unrecognizable series of metamorphoses that they culminate in some faint likeness to the image of him who is one of the newest yet the oldest of created things. Hitherto we have been taught to look among the fossiliferous formations of Geology for the buried lives of the earth's past. But Embryology has startled the world by declaring that the ancient life of the earth is not dead. It is risen. It exists to-day in the embryos of still-living things, and some of the most archaic types find again a resurrection and a life in the frame of man himself.

It is an amazing and almost incredible story. The proposition is not only that Man begins his earthly existence in the guise of a lower animal embryo, but that in the successive transformations of the human embryo there is reproduced before our eyes a visible, actual, physical representation of part of the life-history of the world. Human Embryology is a condensed account, a recapitulation or epitome of some of the main chapters in the Natural History of the world. The same processes of development which once took thousands of years for their consummation are here condensed, foreshortened, concentrated into the space of weeks. Each platform reached by the human embryo in its upward course represents the embryo of some lower animal which in some mysterious way has played a part in the pedigree of the human race, which may itself have disappeared long since from the earth, but is now and for ever built into the inmost being of Man. These lower animals, each at its successive stage, have stopped short in their development; Man has gone on. At each fresh advance his embryo is found again abreast of some other animal-embryo a little higher in organization than that just passed. Continuing his ascent that also is overtaken, the now very complex embryo making up to one animal-embryo after another until it has distanced all in its series, and stands alone. As the modern stem-winding watch contains the old clepsydra and all the most useful features in all the timekeepers that were ever made; as the Walter printing-press contains the rude hand-machine of Gutenberg, and all the best in all the machines that followed it; as the modern locomotive of to-day contains the engine of Watt, the locomotive of Hedley, and most of the improvements of succeeding years, so Man contains the embryonic bodies of earlier and humbler and clumsier forms of life. Yet in making the Walter press in a modern workshop, the artificer does not begin by building again the press of Gutenberg, nor in constructing the locomotive does the engineer first make a Watt's machine and then incorporate the Hedley, and then the Stephenson, and so on through all the improving types of engines that have led up to this. But the astonishing thing is that, in making a Man, Nature does introduce the framework of these earlier types, displaying each crude pattern by itself before incorporating it in the finished work. The human embryo, to change the figure, is a subtle phantasmagoria, a living theatre in which a weird transformation scene is being enacted, and in which countless strange and uncouth characters take part. Some of these characters are well known to science, some are strangers. As the embryo unfolds, one by one these animal actors come upon the stage, file past in phantom-like procession, throw off their drapery, and dissolve away into something else. Yet, as they vanish, each leaves behind a vital portion of itself, some original and characteristic memorial, something itself has made or won, that perhaps it alone could make or win—a bone, a muscle, a ganglion, or a tooth— to be the inheritance of the race. And it is only after nearly all have played their part and dedicated their gift, that a human form, mysteriously compounded of all that has gone before, begins to be discerned in their midst.

The duration of this process, the profound antiquity of the last survivor, the tremendous height he has scaled, are inconceivable by the faculties of Man. But measure the very lowest of the successive platforms passed in the ascent, and see how very great a thing it is even to rise at all. The single cell, the first definite stage which the human embryo attains, is still the adult form of countless millions both of animals and plants. Just as in modern England the millionaire's mansion—the evolved form—is surrounded by labourers' cottages—the simple form—so in Nature, living side by side with the many-celled higher animals, is an immense democracy of unicellular artizans. These simple cells are perfect living things. The earth, the water, and the air teem with them everywhere. They move, they eat, they reproduce their like. But one thing they do not do—they do not rise. These organisms have, as it were, stopped short in the ascent of life. And long as Evolution has worked upon the earth, the vast numerical majority of plants and animals are still at this low stage of being. So minute are some of these forms that if their one-roomed huts were arranged in a row it would take twelve thousand to form a street a single inch in length. In their watery cities—for most of them are Lake-Dwellers—a population of eight hundred thousand million could be accommodated within a cubic inch. Yet, as there was a period in human history when none but cave-dwellers lived in Europe, so was there a time when the highest forms of life upon the globe were these microscopic things. See, therefore, the meaning of Evolution from the want of it. In a single hour or second the human embryo attains the platform which represents the whole life-achievement of myriads of generations of created things, and the next day or hour is immeasurable centuries beyond them.

Through all what zoological regions the embryo passes in its great ascent from the one-celled forms, one can never completely tell. The changes succeed one another with such rapidity that it is impossible at each separate stage to catch the actual likeness to other embryos. Sometimes a familiar feature suddenly recalls a form well-known to science, but the likeness fades, and the developing embryo seems to wander among the ghosts of departed types. Long ago these crude ancestral forms were again the highest animals upon the earth. For a few thousand years they reigned supreme, furthered the universal evolution by a hair-breadth, and passed away. The material dust of their bodies is laid long since in the Palaeozoic rocks, but their life and labour are not forgotten. For their gains were handed on to a succeeding race. Transmitted thence through an endless series of descendants, sifted, enriched, accentuated, still dimly recognizable, they re-appeared at last in the physical frame of Man. After the early stages of human development are passed, the transformations become so definite that the features of the contributary animals are almost recognizable. Here, for example, is a stage at which the embryo in its anatomical characteristics resembles that of the Vermes or Worms. As yet there is no head, nor neck, nor backbone, nor waist, nor limbs. A roughly cylindrical headless trunk—that is all that stands for the future man. One by one the higher Invertebrates are left behind, and then occurs the most remarkable change in the whole life-history. This is the laying down of the line to be occupied by the spinal chord, the presence of which henceforth will determine the place of Man in the Vertebrate sub-kingdom. At this crisis, the eye which sweeps the field of lower Nature for an analogue will readily find it. It is a circumstance of extraordinary interest that there should be living upon the globe at this moment an animal representing the actual transition from Invertebrate to Vertebrate life. The acquisition of a vertebral column is one of the great marks of height which Nature has bestowed upon her creatures; and in the shallow waters of the Mediterranean she has preserved for us a creature which, whether degenerate or not, can only be likened to one of her first rude experiments in this direction. This animal is the Lancelet, or Amphioxus, and so rudimentary is the backbone that it does not contain any bone at all, but only a shadow or prophecy of it in cartilage. The cartilaginous notochord of the Amphioxus nevertheless is the progenitor of all vertebral columns, and in the first instance this structure appears in the human embryo exactly as it now exists in the Lancelet. But this is only a single example. In living Nature there are a hundred other animal characteristics which at one stage or another the biologist may discern in the ever-changing kaleidoscope of the human embryo.

Even with this addition, nevertheless, the human infant is but a first rough draft, an almost formless lump of clay. As yet there is no distinct head, no brain, no jaws, no limbs; the heart is imperfect, the higher visceral organs are feebly developed, everything is elementary. But gradually new organs loom in sight, old ones increase in complexity. By a magic which has never yet been fathomed the hidden Potter shapes and re-shapes the clay. The whole grows in size and symmetry. Resemblances, this time, to the embryos of the lower vertebrate series, flash out as each new step is attained—first the semblance of the Fish, then of the Amphibian, then of the Reptile, last of the Mammal. Of these great groups the leading embryonic characters appear as in a moving panorama, some of them pronounced and unmistakable, others mere sketches, suggestions, likenesses of infinite subtlety. At last the true Mammalian form emerges from the crowd. Far ahead of all at this stage stand out three species—the Tailed Catarrhine Ape, the Tailless Catarrhine, and last, differing physically from these mainly by an enlargement of the brain and a development of the larynx, Man.

Whatever views be held of the doctrine of Evolution, whatever theories of its cause, these facts of Embryology are proved. They have taken their place in science wholly apart from the discussion of theories of Evolution, and as the result of laboratory investigation, made for quite other ends. What is true for Man, moreover, is true of all other animals. Every creature that lives climbs up its own genealogical tree before it reaches its mature condition. "All animals living, or that ever have lived, are united together by blood relationship of varying nearness or remoteness, and every animal now in existence has a pedigree stretching back, not merely for ten or a hundred generations, but through all geologic time since life first commenced on the earth. The study of development has revealed to us that each animal bears the mark of its ancestry, and is compelled to discover its parentage in its own development; the phases through which an animal passes in its progress from the egg to the adult are no accidental freaks, no mere matters of developmental convenience, but represent more or less closely, in more or less modified manner, the successive ancestral stages through which the present condition has been acquired. Almost foreseen by Agassiz, suggested by Von Baer, and finally applied by Fritz Muller, this singular law is the key-note of modern Embryology. In no case, it is true, is the recapitulation of the past complete. Ancestral stages are constantly omitted, others are over-accentuated, condensed, distorted, or confused; while new and undecipherable characters occasionally appear. But it is a general scientific fact, that over the graves of a myriad aspirants the bodies of Man and of all higher Animals have risen. No one knows why this should be so. Science, at present, has no rationale of the process adequate to explain it. It was formerly held that the entire animal creation had contributed something to the anatomy of Man; or that as Serres expressed it, "Human Organogenesis is a transitory Comparative Anatomy." But though Man has not such a monopoly of the past as is here inferred—other types having here and there diverged and developed along lines of their own—it is certain that the materials for his body have been brought together from an unknown multitude of lowlier forms of life.

Those who know the Cathedral of St. Mark's will remember how this noblest of the Stones of Venice owes its greatness to the patient hands of centuries and centuries of workers, how every quarter of the globe has been spoiled of its treasures to dignify this single shrine. But he who ponders over the more ancient temple of the Human Body will find imagination fail him as he tries to think from what remote and mingled sources, from what lands, seas, climates, atmospheres, its various parts have been called together, and by what innumerable contributory creatures, swimming, creeping, flying, climbing, each of its several members was wrought and perfected. What ancient chisel first sculptured the rounded columns of the limbs? What dead hands built the cupola of the brain, and from what older ruins were the scattered pieces of its mosaic-work brought? Who fixed the windows in its upper walls? What winds and weathers wrought strength into its buttresses? What ocean-beds and forest glades worked up its colourings? What Love and Terror and Night called forth the Music? And what Life and Death and Pain and Struggle put all together in the noiseless workshop of the past, and removed each worker silently when its task was done? How these things came to be, Biology is one long record. The architects and builders of this mighty temple are not anonymous. Their names, and the work they did, are graven forever on the walls and arches of the Human Embryo. For this is a volume of that Book in which Man's members were written, which in continuance were fashioned, when as yet there was none of them.

The Descent of Man from the Animal Kingdom is sometimes spoken of as a degradation. It is an unspeakable exaltation. Recall the vast antiquity of that primal cell from which the human embryo first sets forth. Compass the nature of the potentialities stored up in its plastic substance. Watch all the busy processes, the multiplying energies, the mystifying transitions, the inexplicable chemistry of this living laboratory. Observe the variety and intricacy of its metamorphoses, the exquisite gradation of its ascent, the unerring aim with which the one type unfolds—never pausing, never uncertain of its direction, refusing arrest at intermediate forms, passing on to its flawless maturity without waste or effort or fatigue. See the sense of motion at every turn, of purpose and of aspiration. Discover how, with identity of process and loyalty to the type, a hair-breadth of deviation is yet secured to each so that no two forms come out the same, but each arises an original creation, with features, characteristics, and individualities of its own. Remember, finally, that even to make the first cell possible, stellar space required to be swept of matter, suns must needs be broken up, and planets cool, the agents of geology labour millennium after millennium at the unfinished earth to prepare a material resting-place for the coming guest. Consider all this, and judge if Creation could have a sublimer meaning, or the Human Race possess a more splendid genesis.

From the lips of the Prophet another version, an old and beautiful story, was told to the childhood of the earth, of how God made Man; how with His own hands He gathered the Bactrian dust, modelled it, breathed upon it, and it became a living soul. Later, the insight of the Hebrew Poet taught Man a deeper lesson. He saw that there was more in Creation than mechanical production. He saw that the Creator had different kinds of Hands and different ways of modelling. How it was done he knew not, but it was not the surface thing his forefathers taught him. The higher divinity and mystery of the process broke upon him. Man was a fearful and wonderful thing. He was modelled in secret. He was curiously wrought in the lowest parts of the earth. When Science came, it was not to contradict the older versions. It but gave them content and a still richer meaning. What the Prophet said, and the Poet saw, and Science proved, all and equally will abide forever. For all alike are voices of the Unseen, commissioned to different peoples and for different ends to declare the mystery of the Ascent of Man.

When the multicellular globe, made up of countless offshoots or divisions of the original pair, has reached a certain size, its centre becomes filled with a tiny lakelet of watery fluid. This fluid gradually increases in quantity, and, pushing the cells outward, packs them into a single layer, circumscribing it on every side as with an elastic wall. At one part a dimple soon appears, which slowly deepens, until a complete hollow is formed. So far does this invagination of the sphere go on that the cells at the bottom of the hollow touch those at the opposite side. The ovum has now become an open bag or cup, such as one might make by doubling in an india-rubber ball, and thus is formed the gastrula of biology. The evolutional interest of this process lies in the fact that probably all animals above the Protozoa pass through this gastrula stage. That some of the lower Metazoa, indeed, never develop much beyond it, a glance at the structure of the humbler Coelenterates will show—the simplest of all illustrations of the fact that embryonic forms of higher animals are often permanently represented by the adult forms of lower. The chief thing however to mark here is the doubling-in of the ovum to gain a double instead of a single wall of cells. For these two different layers, the ectoderm and the endoderm, or the animal layer and the vegetal layer, play a unique part in the after-history. All the organs of movement and sensation spring from the one, all the organs of nutrition and reproduction develop from the other.

The Scaffolding Left in the Body

The spectacle which we have just witnessed is invisible, and therefore more or less unimpressive, except to the man of science. Embryology works in the dark. Requiring not only the microscope, but the comparative knowledge of intricate and inaccessible forms of life, its all but final contribution to the theory of Evolution carries no adequate conviction to the general mind. We must therefore follow the fortunes of the Body further into the open day. If the Embryo in every changing feature of its growth contains some reminiscence of an animal ancestry, the succeeding stages of its development may be trusted to carry on the proof. And though here the evidence is neither so beautiful nor so exact, we shall find that there is in the adult frame, and even in the very life and movement of the newborn babe, a continuous witness to the ancient animal strain.

We are met, unfortunately, at the outset by one of those curious obstacles to inquiry which have so often barred the way of truth and turned discovery into ridicule. It happens that the class of animals in which Science, in the very nature of the case, is compelled to look for the closest affinities to human beings is that of the Apes. This simple circumstance has told almost fatally against the wide acceptance of the theory of Descent. There is just as much truth in the sarcasm that man is a "reformed monkey" as to prejudge the question to the unscientific mind. But the statement is no nearer the truth itself than if one were to say that a gun is an adult form of the pistol. The connection, if any, between Man and Ape is simply that the most Man-like thing in creation is the Ape, and that, in his Ascent, Man probably passed through a stage when he more nearly resembled the Ape than any other known animal. Apart from that accident, Evolution owes no more to the Ape than to any other creature. Man and Ape are alike in being two of the latest terms of an infinite series, each member of which has had a share in making up the genealogical tree. To single out the Ape, therefore, and use the hypothetical relationship for rhetorical purposes is, to say the least, unscientific. It is certainly the fact that Man is not descended from any existing ape. The anthropoid apes branched off laterally at a vastly remote period from the nearest human progenitors. The challenge even to produce links between Man and the living man-like apes is difficult to take seriously. Should anyone so violate the first principles of Evolution as to make it, it is only to be said that it cannot be met. For an anthropoid ape could as little develop into a Man as could a Man pass backwards into an anthropoid ape. References to a Simian stem play no necessary part in the story of the Ascent of Man. In those pages the compromising name will scarcely occur. If historical sequence compels us to make an apparent exception here at the very outset, it will be seen that the allusion is harmless. For the analogy we are about to make might with equal relevancy have been drawn from a squirrel or a sloth.

On the theory that human beings were once allied in habit as well as in body with some of the apes, that they probably lived in trees, and that baby-men clung to their climbing mothers as baby-monkeys do to-day, Dr. Louis Robinson prophesied that a baby's power of grip might be found to be comparable in strength to that of a young monkey at the same period of development. Having special facilities for such an investigation, he tested a large number of just-born infants with reference to this particular. Now although most people have some time or other been seized in the awful grasp of a baby, few have any idea of the abnormal power locked up in the tentacles of this human octopus. Dr. Robinson's method was to extend to infants, generally of one hour old, his finger, or a walking stick, to imitate the branch of a tree, and see how long they would hang there without, what the newspapers call, "any other visible means of support." The results are startling. Dr. Robinson has records of upwards of sixty cases in which the children were under a month old, and in at least half of these the experiment was tried within an hour of birth: "In every instance, with only two exceptions, the child was able to hang on to the finger or a small stick, three-quarters of an inch in diameter, by its hands, like an acrobat from a horizontal bar, and sustain the whole weight of its body for at least ten seconds. In twelve cases, in infants under an hour old, half a minute passed before the grasp relaxed, and in three or four nearly a minute. When about four days old, I found that the strength had increased, and that nearly all, when tried at this age, could sustain their weight for half a minute. About a fortnight or three weeks after birth the faculty appeared to have attained its maximum, for several at this period succeeded in hanging for over a minute and a half, two for just over two minutes, and one infant of three weeks old for two minutes thirty-five seconds. . . . In one instance, in which the performer had less than one hour's experience of life, he hung by both hands to my forefinger for ten seconds, and then deliberately let go with his right hand (as if to seek a better hold), and maintained his position for five seconds more by the left hand only. Invariably the thighs are bent nearly at right angles to the body, and in no case did the lower limbs hang down and take the attitude of the erect position. This attitude, and the disproportionately large development of the arms compared with the legs, give the photographs a striking resemblance to a well-known picture of the celebrated Chimpanzee Sally at the Zoological Garden. I think it will be acknowledged that the remarkable strength shown in the flexor muscle of the fore-arm in these young infants, especially when compared with the flaccid and feeble state of the muscular system generally, is a sufficiently striking phenomenon to provoke inquiry as to its cause and origin. The fact that a three-week-old baby can perform a feat of muscular strength that would tax the powers of many a healthy adult is enough to set one wondering. A curious point is that in many cases no sign of distress is evident, and no cry uttered until the grasp begins to give way.

Place side by side with this the following account, which Mr. Wallace gives us in his Malay Archipelago of a baby Orang-outang, whose mother he happened to shoot:

"This little creature was only about a foot long, and had evidently been hanging to its mother when she first fell. Luckily it did not appear to have been wounded, and after we had cleaned the mud out of its mouth it began to cry out, and seemed quite strong and active. While carrying it home it got its hands in my beard, and grasped so tightly that I had great difficulty in getting free, for the fingers are habitually bent inward at the last joint so as to form complete hooks. For the first few days it clung desperately with all four hands to whatever it could lay hold of, and I had to be careful to keep my beard out of its way, as its fingers clutched hold of hair more tenaciously than anything else, and it was impossible to free myself without assistance. When restless, it would struggle about with its hands up in the air trying to find something to take hold of, and when it had got a bit of stick or rag in two or three of its hands, seemed quite happy. For want of something else, it would often seize its own feet, and after a time it would constantly cross its arms and grasp with each hand the long hair that grew just below the opposite shoulder. The great tenacity of its grasp soon diminished, and I was obliged to invent some means to give it exercise and strengthen its limbs. For this purpose I made a short ladder of three or four rounds, on which I put it to hang for a quarter of an hour at a time. At first it seemed much pleased, but it could not get all four hands in a comfortable position, and, after changing about several times, would leave hold of one hand after the other and drop on to the floor. Sometimes when hanging only by two hands, it would loose one, and cross it to the opposite shoulder, grasping its own hair; and, as this seemed much more agreeable than the stick, it would then loose the other and tumble down, when it would cross both and lie on its back quite contentedly, never seeming to be hurt by its numerous tumbles. Finding it so fond of hair, I endeavoured to make an artificial mother, by wrapping up a piece of buffalo-skin into a bundle, and suspending it about a foot from the floor. At first this seemed to suit it admirably, as it could sprawl its legs about and always find some hair, which it grasped with the greatest tenacity.

Whatever the value of these facts as evidence, they form an interesting if slight introduction to the part of the subject that lies before us. For we have now to explore the Body itself for actual betrayals—not mere external movements which might have come as well from early Man as from later animal; but veritable physical survivals, the material scaffolding itself—of the animal past. And the facts here are as numerous and as easily grasped as they are authentic. As the traveller, wandering in foreign lands, brings back all manner of curios to remind him where he has been—clubs and spears, clothes and pottery, which represent the ways of life of those whom he has met—so the body of Man, emerging from its age-long journey through the animal kingdom, appears laden with the spoils of its distant pilgrimage. These relics are not mere curiosities; they are as real as the clubs and spears, the clothes and pottery. Like them, they were once a part of life's vicissitude; they represent organs which have been outgrown; old forms of apparatus long since exchanged for better, yet somehow not yet destroyed by the hand of time. The physical body of Man, so great is the number of these relics, is an old curiosity shop, a museum of obsolete anatomies, discarded tools, outgrown and aborted organs. All other animals also contain among their useful organs a proportion which are long past their work; and so significant are these rudiments of a former state of things, that anatomists have often expressed their willingness to stake the theory of Evolution upon their presence alone.

Prominent among these vestigial structures, as they are called, are those which smack of the sea. If Embryology is any guide to the past, nothing is more certain than that the ancient progenitors of Man once lived an aquatic life. At one time there was nothing else in the world but water-life; all the land animals are late inventions. One reason why animals began in the water is that it is easier to live in the water—anatomically and physiologically cheaper—than to live on the land. The denser element supports the body better, demanding a less supply of muscle and bone; and the perpetual motion of the sea brings the food to the animal, making it unnecessary for the animal to move to the food. This and other correlated circumstances call for far less mechanism in the body, and, as a matter of fact, all the simplest forms of life at the present day are inhabitants of the water.

A successful attempt at coming ashore may be seen in the common worm. The worm is still so unacclimatized to land life that instead of living on the earth like other creatures, it lives in it, as if it were a thicker water, and always where there is enough moisture to keep up the traditions of its past. Probably it took to the shore originally by exchanging first the water for the ooze at the bottom, then by wriggling among muddy flats when the tide was out, and finally, as the struggle for life grew keen, it pushed further and further inland, continuing its migration so long as dampness was to be found.

More striking examples are found among the molluscs, the sea-faring animals par excellence of the past. A snail wandering over the earth with a sea-shell on its back is one of the most anomalous sights in nature—as preposterous as the spectacle of a Red Indian perambulating Paris with a birch canoe on his head. The snail not only carries this relic of the sea everywhere with it, but when it cannot get moisture to remind it of its ancient habitat, it actually manufactures it. That the creature itself has discovered the anomaly of its shell is obvious, for in almost every class its state of dilapidation betrays that its up-keep is no longer an object of much importance. In nearly every species the stony houses have already lost their doors, and most have their shells so reduced in size that not half of the body can get in. The degeneration in their cousins, the slugs, is even more pathetic. All that remains of the ancestral home in the highest ranks is a limpet-like cap on the tip of the tail; the lowest are sans everything; and in the intermediate forms the former glory is ironically suggested by a few grains of sand or a tiny shield so buried beneath the skin that only the naturalist's eye can see it.

When Man left the water, however—or what was to develop into Man—he took very much more ashore with him than a shell. Instead of crawling ashore at the worm stage, he remained in the water until he evolved into something like a fish; so that when, after an amphibian interlude, he finally left it, many "ancient and fish-like" characters remained in his body to tell the tale. The chief characteristic of a fish is its apparatus for breathing the air dissolved in the water. This consists of gills—delicate curtains hung on strong arches and dyed scarlet with the blood which continually courses through them. In many fishes these arches are five or seven in number, and communicating with them—in order to allow the aerated water, which has been taken in at the mouth, to pass out again after bathing the gills— an equal number of slits or openings is provided in the neck. Sometimes the slits are bare and open so that they are easily seen on the fish's neck—anyone who looks at a shark will see them—but in modern forms they are generally covered by the operculum or lid. Without these holes in their neck all fishes would instantly perish, and we may be sure Nature took exceptional care in perfecting this particular piece of the mechanism.

Now it is one of the most extraordinary facts in natural history that these slits in the fish's neck are still represented in the neck of Man. Almost the most prominent feature, indeed, after the head, in every mammalian embryo, are the four clefts or furrows of the old gill-slits. They are still known in Embryology by the old name—gill-slits—and so persistent are these characters that children are known to have been born with them not only externally visible which is a common occurrence but open through and through, so that fluids taken in at the mouth could pass through and trickle out at the neck. This last fact was so astounding as to be for a long time denied. It was thought that, when this happened, the orifice must have been accidentally made by the probe of the surgeon. But Dr. Sutton has recently met with actual cases where this has occurred. "I have seen milk," he says, "issue from such fistulae in individuals who have never been submitted to sounding." In the common case of children born with these vestiges, the old gill-slits are represented by small openings in the skin on the sides of the neck, and capable of admitting a thin probe. Sometimes even the place where they have been in childhood is marked throughout life by small round patches of white skin.

Almost more astonishing than the fact of their persistence is the use to which Nature afterwards put them. When the fish came ashore, its water-breathing apparatus was no longer of any use to it. At first it had to keep it on, for it took a long time to perfect the air-breathing apparatus destined to replace it. But when this was ready the problem arose, What was to be done with the earlier organ? Nature is exceedingly economical, and could not throw all this mechanism away. In fact, Nature almost never parts with any structure she has once made. What she does is to change it into something else. Conversely, Nature seldom makes anything new; her method of creation is to adapt something old. Now, when Nature had done with the old breathing-apparatus, she proceeded to adapt it for a new and important purpose. She saw that if water could pass through a hole in the neck, air could pass through likewise. But it was no longer necessary that air should pass through for purposes of breathing, for that was already provided for by the mouth. Was there any other purpose for which it was desirable that air should enter the body? There was, and a very subtle one. For hearing. Sound is the result of a wave-motion conducted by many things, but in a special way by air. To leave holes in the head was to let sound into the head. The mouth might have done for this, but the mouth had enough to do as it was, and, moreover, it must often be shut. In the old days, certainly, sound was conveyed to fishes in a dull way without any definite opening. But animals which live in water do not seem to use hearing much, and the sound-waves in fishes are simply conveyed through the walls of the head to the internal ear without any definite mechanism. But as soon as land-life began, owing to the changed medium through which sound-waves must now be propagated, and the new uses for sound itself, a more delicate instrument was required. And hence one of the first things attended to as the evolution went on was the construction and improvement of the ear. And this seems to have been mainly effected by a series of remarkable developments of one of the now superfluous gill-slits.

It has long been a growing certainty to Comparative Anatomy that the external and middle ear in Man are simply a development, an improved edition, of the first gill-cleft and its surrounding parts. The tympano-Eustachian passage is the homologue or counterpart of the spiracle associated in the shark with the first gill-opening. Prof. His of Leipsic has worked out the whole development in minute detail, and conclusively demonstrated the mode of origin of the external ear from the coalescence of six rounded tubercles surrounding the first branchial cleft at an early period of embryonic life.

Now, bearing in mind this theory of the origin of ears, an extraordinary corroboration confronts us. Ears are actually sometimes found bursting out in human beings half-way down the neck, in the exact position—namely, along the line of the anterior border of the sterno-mastoid muscle—which the gill-slits would occupy if they still persisted. In some human families, where the tendency to retain these special structures is strong, one member sometimes illustrates the abnormality by possessing the clefts alone, another has a cervical-ear, while a third has both a cleft and a neck-ear—all these, of course, in addition to the ordinary ears. This cervical auricle has all the characters of the ordinary ear, "it contains yellow elastic cartilage, is skin-covered, and has muscle-fibre attached to it. Dr Sutton calls attention to the fact that on ancient statues of fauns and satyrs cervical auricles are sometimes found, and he figures the head of a satyr from the British Museum, carved long before the days of anatomy, where a sessile ear on the neck is quite distinct. A still better illustration may be seen in the Art Museum at Boston on a full-sized cast of a faun, belonging to the later Greek period; and there are other examples in the same building. One interest of these neck-ears in statues is that they are not, as a rule, modelled after the human ear, but taken from the cervical-ear of the goat, from which the general idea of the faun was derived. This shows that neck-ears were common on the goats of that period—as they are on goats to this day. The occurrence of neck-ears in goats is no more than one would expect. Indeed, one would look for them not only in goats and in Man, but in all the Mammalia, for so far as their bodies are concerned all the higher animals are near relations. Observations on vestigial structures in animals are sadly wanting; but these cervical-ears are also certainly found in the horse, pig, sheep, and others.

That the human ear was not always the squat and degenerate instrument it is at present may be seen by a critical glance at its structure. Mr. Darwin records how a celebrated sculptor called his attention to a little peculiarity in the external ear, which he had often noticed both in men and women. "The peculiarity consists in a little blunt point, projecting from the inwardly folded margin or helix. When present, it is developed at birth, and, according to Professor Ludwig Meyer, more frequently in man than in woman. The helix obviously consists of the extreme margin of the ear folded inwards; and the folding appears to be in some manner connected with the whole external ear being permanently pressed backwards. In many monkeys who do not stand high in the order, as baboons and some species of macacus, the upper portion of the ear is slightly pointed, and the margin is not at all folded inwards; but if the margin were to be thus folded, a slight point would necessarily project towards the centre. Here then, in this discovery of the lost tip of the ancestral ear, is further and visible advertisement of Man's Descent, a surviving symbol of the stirring times and dangerous days of his animal youth. It is difficult to imagine any other theory than that of Descent which could account for all these facts. That Evolution should leave such clues lying about is at least an instance of its candour.

But this does not exhaust the betrayals of this most confiding organ. If we turn from the outward ear to the muscular apparatus for working it, fresh traces of its animal career are brought to light. The erection of the ear, in order to catch sound better, is a power possessed by almost all mammals, and the attached muscles are large and greatly developed in all but domesticated forms. This same apparatus, though he makes no use of it whatever, is still attached to the ears of Man. It is so long since he relied on the warnings of hearing, that by a well-known law, the muscles have fallen into disuse and atrophied. In many cases, however, the power of twitching the ear is not wholly lost, and every school-boy can point to some one in his class who retains the capacity, and is apt to revive it in irrelevant circumstances.

One might run over all the other organs of the human body and show their affinities with animal structures and an animal past. The twitching of the ear, for instance, suggests another obsolete, or obsolescent power—the power, or rather the set of powers, for twitching the skin, especially the skin of the scalp and forehead by which we raise the eyebrows. Subcutaneous muscles for shaking off flies from the skin, or for erecting the hair of the scalp, are common among quadrupeds, and these are represented in the human subject by the still functioning muscles of the forehead, and occasionally of the head itself. Everyone has met persons who possess the power of moving the whole scalp to and fro, and the muscular apparatus for effecting it is identical with what is normally found in some of the Quadrumana.

Another typical vestigial structure is the plica semi-lunaris, the remnant of the nictitating membrane characteristic of nearly the whole vertebrate sub-kingdom. This membrane is a semi-transparent curtain which can be drawn rapidly across the external surface of the eye for the purpose of sweeping it clean. In birds it is extremely common, but it also exists in fish, mammals, and all the other vertebrates. Where it is not found of any functional value it is almost always represented by vestiges of some kind. In Man all that is left of it is a little piece of the curtain draped at the side of the eye.

Passing from the head to the other extremity of the body one comes upon a somewhat unexpected but very pronounced characteristic—the relic of the tail, and not only of the tail, but of muscles for wagging it. Everyone who first sees a human skeleton is amazed at this discovery. At the end of the vertebral column, curling faintly outward in suggestive fashion, are three, four, and occasionally five vertebrae forming the coccyx, a true rudimentary tail. In the adult this is always concealed beneath the skin, but in the embryo, both in Man and ape, at an early stage it is much longer than the limbs. What is decisive as to its true nature, however, is that even in the embryo of Man the muscles for wagging it are still found. In the grown-up human being these muscles are represented by bands of fibrous tissue, but cases are known where the actual muscles persist through life. That a distinct external tail should not still be found in Man may seem disappointing to the evolutionist. But the want of a tail argues more for the theory of Evolution than its presence would have done. For all the anthropoids most allied to Man have long since also parted with theirs.

With regard to the presence of Hair on the body, and its disposition and direction, some curious facts may be noticed. No one, until Evolution supplied the impulse to a fresh study of the commonplace, thought it worth while to study such trifles as the presence of hair on the fingers and hands, and the slope of the hair on the arms. But now that attention is called to it, every detail is seen to be full of meaning. In all men the rudimentary hair on the arm, from the wrist to the elbow, points one way, from the elbow to the shoulder it points the opposite way. In the first case it points upwards from the wrist towards the elbow, in the other downwards from the shoulder to the elbow. This occurs nowhere else in the animal kingdom, except among the anthropoid apes and a few American monkeys, and has to do with the arboreal habit. As Mr. Romanes, who has pointed this out, explains it, "When sitting on trees, the Orang, as observed by Wallace, places its hands above its head with its elbows pointing downwards; the disposition of hair on the arms and fore-arms then has the effect of thatch in turning the rain. Again, I find that in all species of apes, monkeys, and baboons which I have examined (and they have been numerous), the hair on the back of the hands and feet is continued as far as the first row of phalanges; but becomes scanty, or disappears altogether, on the second row. I also find that the same peculiarity occurs in man. We have all rudimentary hair on the first row of phalanges, both of hands and feet, when present at all, it is more scanty on the second row: and in no case have I been able to find any on the terminal row. In all cases those peculiarities are congenital, and the total absence or partial presence of hair on the second phalanges is constant in different species of Quadrumana. . . . The downward direction of the hair on the backs of the hands is exactly the same in man as it is in all the anthropoid apes. Again, with regard to hair, Darwin notices that occasionally there appear in man a few hairs in the eyebrows much longer than the others; and that they seem to be a representation of similarly long and scattered hairs which occur in the chimpanzee, macacus, and baboon. Lastly, about the sixth month the human foetus is often thickly covered with somewhat long dark hair over the entire body, except the soles of the feet and palms of the hands, which are likewise bare in all quadrumanous animals. This covering, which is called the lanugo, and sometimes extends even to the whole forehead, ears, and face, is shed before birth. So that it appears to be useless for any purpose other than that of emphatically declaring man a child of the monkey. The uselessness of these relics, apart from the remarkable and detailed nature of the homologies just brought out, is a circumstance very hard to get over on any other hypothesis than that of Descent.

Caution, of course, is required in deciding as to the inutility of any character, since its seeming uselessness may only mean that we do not know its use. But there are undoubtedly cases where we know that certain vestigial structures are not only useless to Man but worse than useless. Coming under this category is perhaps the most striking of all the vestigial organs, that of the Vermiform Appendix of the Caecum. Here is a structure which is not only of no use to man now, but is a veritable death-trap. In herbivorous animals this "blind-tube" is very large—longer in some cases than the body itself—and of great use in digestion, but in Man it is shrunken into the merest rudiment, while in the Orang-outang: it is only a little larger. In the human subject, owing to its diminutive size, it can be of no use whatever, while it forms an easy receptacle for the lodgment of foreign bodies, such as fruit-stones, which set up inflammation, and in various ways cause death. In man this tube is the same in structure as the rest of the intestine; it is "covered with peritoneum, possesses a muscular coat, and is lined with mucous membrane. In the early embryo it is equal in calibre to the rest of the bowel, but at a certain date it ceases to grow pari passu with it, and at the time of birth appears as a thin tubular appendix to the caecum. In the newly-born child it is often absolutely as long as in the full-grown man. This precocity is always an indication that the part was of great importance to the ancestors of the human species.

So important is the key of Evolution to the modern pathologist that in cases of malformation his first resort is always to seek an explanation in earlier forms of life. It is found that conditions which are pathological in one animal are natural in others of a lower species. When any eccentricity appears in a human body the anatomist no longer sets it down as a freak of Nature. He proceeds to match it lower down. Mr. Darwin mentions a case of a man who, in his foot alone, had no less than seven abnormal muscles. Each of these was found among the muscles of lower animals. Take, again, a common case of malformation—club-foot. All children before birth display the most ordinary form of this deformity—that, namely, where the sole is turned inwards and upwards and the foot is raised—and it is only gradually that the foot attains the normal adult position. The abnormal position, abnormal that is in adult Man, is the normal condition of things in the case of the gorilla. Club-foot, hence, is simply gorilla-foot—a case of the arrested development of a character which apparently came along the line of the direct Simian stock. So simple is this method of interpreting the present by the past, and so fruitful, that the anatomist has been able in many instances to assume the role of prophet. Adult man possesses no more than twelve pair of ribs; the prediction was hazarded by an older Comparative Anatomy that in the embryonic state he would be found with thirteen or fourteen. This prophecy has since been verified. It was also predicted that at this early stage he would be found to possess the insignificant remnant of a very small bone in the wrist, the so-called os centrale, which must have existed in the adult condition of his extremely remote ancestors. This prediction has also been fulfilled, as Weismann aptly remarks, "just as the planet Neptune was discovered after its existence had been predicted from the disturbances induced in the orbit of Uranus.

But the enumeration becomes tedious. Though we are only at the beginning of the list, sufficient has been said to mark the interest of this part of the subject, and the redundancy of the proof. In the human body alone, there are at least seventy of these vestigial structures. Take away the theory that Man has evolved from a lower animal condition, and there is no explanation whatever of any one of these phenomena. With such facts before us, it is mocking human intelligence to assure us that Man has not some connection with the rest of the animal creation, or that the processes of his development stand unrelated to the other ways of Nature. To say that Providence, in making a new being, should deliberately have inserted these eccentricities, without their having any real connection with the things they so well imitate, or any working relation to the rest of his body, is, with our present knowledge, simple irreverence.

Were it the present object to complete a proof of the descent of Man, one might go on to select from other departments of science evidence not less striking than that from vestigial structures. From the side of palaeontology it might be shown that Man appears in the earth's crust like any other fossil, and in the exact place where science would expect to find him. When born, he is ushered into life like any other animal; he is subject to the same diseases; he yields to the same treatment. When fully grown there is almost nothing in his anatomy to distinguish him from his nearest allies among other animals—almost bone for bone, nerve for nerve, muscle for muscle he is the same. There is in fact a body of evidence now before science for the animal origin of Man's physical frame which it is impossible for a thinking mind to resist. Up to this point two only out of the many conspiring lines of testimony have been drawn upon for their contribution; but enough has been said to encourage us, with this as at least a working theory, to continue the journey. It is the Ascent of Man that concerns us and not the Descent. And these amazing facts about the past are cited for a larger purpose than to produce conviction on a point which, after all, is of importance only in its higher implications.

Haeckel has given an earlier account of the process in the following words:—"All the essential parts of the middle ear—the tympanic membrane, tympanic cavity, and Eustachian tube—develop from the first gill-opening with its surrounding parts, which in the Primitive Fishes (Selachii) remains throughout life as an open blow-hole, situated between the first and second gill-arches. In the embryos of higher Vertebrates it closes in the centre, the point of concrescence forming the tympanic membrane. The remaining outer part of the first gill-opening is the rudiment of the outer ear-canal. From the inner part originates the tympanic cavity, and further inward, the Eustachian tube. In connection with these, the three bonelets of the ear develop from the first two gill-arches; the hammer and anvil from the first, and the stirrup from the upper end of the second gill-arch. Finally, as regards the external ear, the ear-shell (concha auris), and the outer ear canal, leading from the shell to the tympanic membrane— these parts develop in the simplest way from the skin-covering which borders the outer orifice of the first gill-opening. At this point the ear-shell rises in the form of a circular fold of skin, in which cartilage and muscles afterwards form." —Haeckel, Evolution of Man, Vol. II., p. 269.

The Arrest of the Body

"On the Earth there will never be a higher Creature than Man. It is a daring prophecy, but every probability of Science attests the likelihood of its fulfilment. The goal looked forward to from the beginning of time has been attained. Nature has succeeded in making a Man; she can go no further; Organic Evolution has done its work.

This is not a conceit of Science, nor a reminiscence of the pre-Copernican idea that the centre of the universe is the world, and the centre of the world Man. It is the sober scientific probability that with the body of Man the final fruit of the tree of Organic Evolution has appeared; that the highest possibilities open to flesh and bone and nerve and muscle have now been realized; that in whatever direction, and with whatever materials, Evolution still may work, it will never produce any material thing more perfect in design or workmanship; that in Man, in short, about this time in history, we are confronted with a stupendous crisis in Nature, —the Arrest of the Animal. The Man, the Animal Man, the Man of Organic Evolution, it is at least certain, will not go on. It is another Man who will go on, a Man within this Man; and that he may go on the first Man must stop. Let us try for a moment to learn what it is to stop. Nothing could teach Man better what is meant by his going on.

One of the most perfect pieces of mechanism in the human body is the Hand. How long it has taken to develop may be dimly seen by a glance at the long array of less accurate instruments of prehension which shade away with ever decreasing delicacy and perfectness as we descend the scale of animal life. At the bottom of that scale is the Amoeba. It is a speck of protoplasmic jelly, headless, footless, and armless. When it wishes to seize the microscopic particle of food on which it lives a portion of its body lengthens out, and, moving towards the object, flows over it, engulfs it, and melts back again into the body. This is its Hand. At any place, and at any moment, it creates a Hand. Each Hand is extemporized as it is needed; when not needed it is not. Pass a little higher up the scale and observe the Sea-Anemone. The Hand is no longer extemporized as occasion requires, but lengthened portions of the body are set apart and kept permanently in shape for the purpose of seizing food. Here, in the capital of twining tentacles which crowns the quivering pillar of the body, we get the rude approximation to the most useful portion of the human Hand—the separated fingers. It is a vast improvement on the earlier Hand, but the jointless digits are still imperfect; it is simply the Amoeba Hand cut into permanent strips.

Passing over a multitude of intermediate forms, watch, in the next place, the Hand of an African Monkey. Note the great increase in usefulness due to the muscular arm upon which the Hand is now extended, and the extraordinary capacity for varied motion afforded by the three-fold system of jointing at shoulder, elbow, and wrist. The Hand itself is almost the human Hand; there are palm and nail and articulated fingers. But observe how one circumstance hinders the possessor from taking full advantage of these great improvements,—this Hand has no thumb, or if it has, it is but a rudiment. To estimate the importance of this apparently insignificant organ, try for a moment without using the thumb to hold a book, or write a letter, or do any single piece of manual work. A thumb is not merely an additional finger, but a finger so arranged as to be opposable to the other fingers, and thus possesses a practical efficacy greater than all the fingers put together. It is this which gives the organ the power to seize, to hold, to manipulate, to do higher work; this simple mechanical device in short endows the Hand of intelligence with all its capacity and skill. Now there are animals, like the Colobi, which have no thumb at all; there are others, like the Marmoset, which possess the thumb, but in which it is not opposable; and there are others, the Chimpanzee for instance, in which the Hand is in all essentials identical with Man's. In the human form the thumb is a little longer, and the whole member more delicate and shapely, but even for the use of her highest product, Nature has not been able to make anything much more perfect than the hand of this anthropoid ape.

Is the Hand then finished? Can Nature take out no new patent in this direction? Is the fact that no novelty is introduced in the case of Man a proof that the ultimate Hand has appeared? By no means. And yet it is probable for other reasons that the ultimate Hand has appeared; that there will never be a more perfectly handed animal than Man. And why? Because the causes which up to this point have furthered the evolution of the Hand have begun to cease to act. In the perfecting of the bodily organs, as of all other mechanical devices, necessity is the mother of invention. As the Hand was given more and more to do, it became more and more adapted to its work. Up to a point, it responded directly to each new duty that was laid upon it. But only up to a point. There came a time when the necessities became too numerous and too varied for adaptation to keep pace with them. And the fatal day came, the fatal day for the Hand, when he who bore it made a new discovery. It was the discovery of Tools. Henceforth what the Hand used to do, and was slowly becoming adapted to do better, was to be done by external appliances. So that if anything new arose to be done, or to be better done, it was not a better Hand that was now made but a better tool. Tools are external Hands. Levers are the extensions of the bones of the arm. Hammers are callous substitutes for the fist. Knives do the work of nails. The vice and the pincers replace the fingers. The day that Cave-man first split the marrow bone of a bear by thrusting a stick into it, and striking it home with a stone—that day the doom of the Hand was sealed.

But has not Man to make his tools, and will not that induce the development of the Hand to an as yet unknown perfection? No. Because tools are not made with the Hand. They are made with the Brain. For a time, certainly, Man had to make his tools, and for a time this work recompensed him physically, and the arm became elastic and the fingers dexterous and strong. But soon he made tools to make these tools. In place of shaping things with the Hand, he invented the turning-lathe; to save his fingers he requisitioned the loom; instead of working his muscles he gave out the contract to electricity and steam. Man, therefore, from this time forward will cease to develop materially these organs of his body. If he develops them outside his body, filling the world everywhere with artificial Hands, supplying the workshops with fingers more intricate and deft than Organic Evolution could make in a millennium, and loosing energies upon them infinitely more gigantic than his muscles could generate in a life-time, it is enough. Evolution after all is a slow process. Its great labour is to work up to a point where

Invention shall be possible, and where, by the powers of the human mind, and by the mechanical utilization of the energies of the universe, the results of ages of development may be anticipated. Further changes, therefore, within the body itself are made unnecessary. Evolution has taken a new departure. For the Arrest of the Hand is not the cessation of Evolution but its immense acceleration, and the re-direction of its energies into higher channels.

Take up the functions of the animal body one by one, and it will be seen how the same arresting finger is laid upon them all. To select an additional illustration, consider the power of Sight. Without pausing to trace the steps by which the Eye has reached its marvellous perfection, or to estimate the ages spent in polishing its lenses and adjusting the diaphragms and screws, ask the simple question whether, under the conditions of modern civilization, anything now is being added to its quickening efficiency, or range. Is it not rather the testimony of experience that if anything its power has begun to wane? Europe even now affords the spectacle of at least one nation so short-sighted that it might almost be called a myopic race. The same causes, in fact, that led to the Arrest of the Hand are steadily working to stop the development of the Eye. Man, when he sees with difficulty, does not now improve his Eye; he puts on a pince-nez. Spectacles—external eyes—have superseded the work of Evolution. When his sight is perfect up to a point, and he desires to examine objects so minute as to lie beyond the limit of that point, he will not wait for Evolution to catch up upon his demand and supply him, or his children's children, with a more perfect instrument. He will invest in a microscope. Or when he wishes to extend his gaze to the moon and stars, he does not hope to reach to-morrow the distances which to-day transcend him. He invents the telescope. Organic Evolution has not even a chance. In every direction the external eye has replaced the internal, and it is even difficult to suggest where any further development of this part of the animal can now come in. There are still, and in spite of all instruments, regions in which the unaided organs of Man may continue to find a field for the fullest exercise, but the area is slowly narrowing, and in every direction the appliances of Science tempt the body to accept those supplements of the Arts, which, being accepted, involve the discontinuance of development for all the parts concerned. Even where a mechanical appliance, while adding range to a bodily sense, has seemed to open a door for further improvement, some correlated discovery in a distant field of science, as by some remorseless fate, has suddenly taken away the opportunity and offered to the body only an additional inducement for neglect. Thus it might be thought that the continuous use of the telescope, in the attempt to discover more and more indistinct and distant heavenly bodies, might tend to increase the efficiency of the Eye. But that expectation has vanished already before a further fruit of Man's inventive power. By an automatic photographic apparatus fixed to the telescope, an Eye is now created vastly more delicate and in many respects more efficient than the keenest eye of Man. In at least five important particulars the Photographic Eye is the superior of the Eye of Organic Evolution. It can see where the human Eye, even with the best aids of optical instruments, sees nothing at all; it can distinguish certain objects with far greater clearness and definition; owing to the rapidity of its action it can instantly detect changes which are too sudden for the human eye to follow; it can look steadily for hours without growing tired; and it can record what it sees with infallible accuracy upon a plate which time will not efface. How long would it take Organic Evolution to arrive at an Eye of such amazing quality and power? And with such a piece of mechanism available, who, rather than employ it even to the neglect of his organs of vision, would be content to await the possible attainment of an equal perfection by his descendants some million years hence? Is there not here a conspicuous testimony to the improbability of a further Evolution of the sense of Sight in civilized communities—in other words, another proof of the Arrest of the Animal? What defiance of Evolution, indeed, what affront to Nature, is this? Man prepares a complicated telescope to supplement the Eye created by Evolution, and no sooner is it perfected than it occurs to him to create another instrument to aid the Eye in what little work is left for it to do. That is to say, he first makes a mechanical supplement to his Eye, then constructs a mechanical Eye, which is better than his own, to see through it, and ends by discarding, for many purposes, the Eye of Organic Evolution altogether.

As regards the other functions of civilized Man, the animal in almost every direction has reached its maximum. Civilization—and the civilized state, be it remembered, is the ultimate goal of every race and nation—is always attended by deterioration of some of the senses. Every man pays a definite price or forfeit for his taming. The sense of smell, compared with its development among the lower animals, is in civilized Man already all but gone. Compared even with a savage, it is an ascertained fact that the civilized Man in this respect is vastly inferior. So far as hearing is concerned, the main stimulus—fear of surprise by enemies—has ceased to operate, and the muscles for the erection of the ears have fallen into disuse. The ear itself in contrast with that of the savage is slow and dull, while compared with the quick sense of the lower animals, the organ is almost deaf. The skin, from the continuous use of clothes, has forfeited its protective power. Owing to the use of viands cooked, the muscles of the jaw are rapidly losing strength. The teeth, partly for a similar reason, are undergoing marked degeneration. The third molar, for instance, among some nations is already showing symptoms of suppression, and that this threatens ultimate extinction may be reasoned from the fact that the anthropoid apes have fewer teeth than the lower monkeys, and these fewer than the preceding generation of insectivorous mammals.

In an age of vehicles and locomotives the lower limbs find their occupation almost gone. For mere muscle, that on which his whole life once depended, Man has almost now no use. Agility, nimbleness, strength, once a stern necessity, are either a luxury or a pastime. Their outlet is the cricket-field or the tennis-court. To keep them up at all, artificial means—dumb-bells, parallel-bars, clubs—have actually to be devised. Vigour of limb is not to be found in common life, we look for it in the Gymnasium; agility is relegated to the Hippodrome. Once all men were athletes; now you have to pay to see them. More or less with all the animal powers it is the same. To some extent at least some phonograph may yet speak for us, some telephone hear for us, the typewriter write for us, chemistry digest for us, and incubation nurture us. So everywhere the Man as Animal is in danger of losing ground. He has expanded until the world is his body. The former body, the hundred and fifty pounds or so of organized tissue he carries about with him, is little more than a mark of identity. It is not he who is there, he cannot be there, or anywhere, for he is everywhere. The material part of him is reduced to a symbol; it is but a link with the wider framework of the Arts, a belt between machinery and machinery. His body no longer generates, but only utilizes energy; alone he is but a tool, a medium, a turncock of the physical forces.

Now with what feelings do we regard all this? Is not the crowning proof of the thesis under review that we watch this evidence accumulating against the body with no emotion and hear the doom of our clay pronounced without a regret? It is nothing to aspiring Man to watch the lower animals still perfecting their mechanism and putting all his physical powers and senses to the shame. It is nothing to him to be distanced in nimbleness by the deer: has he not his bullet? Or in strength by the horse: has he not bit and bridle? Or in vision by the eagle: his field-glass out-sees it. How easily we talk of the body as a thing without us, as an impersonal it And how naturally when all is over, do we advertise its irrelevancy to ourselves by consigning its borrowed atoms to the anonymous dust. The fact is, in one aspect, the body, to Intelligence, is all but an absurdity. One is almost ashamed to have one. The idea of having to feed it, and exercise it, and humour it, and put it away in the dark to sleep, to carry it about with one everywhere, and not only it but its wardrobe—other material things to make this material thing warm or keep it cool—the whole situation is a comedy. But judge what it would be if this exacting organism went on evolving, multiplied its members, added to its intricacy, waxed instead of waned? So complicated is it already that one shrinks from contemplating a future race having to keep in repair an apparatus more involved and delicate. The practical advantage is enormous of having all improvements henceforth external, of having insensate organs made of iron and steel rather than of wasting muscle and palpitating nerve. For these can be kept at no physiological cost, they cannot impede the other machinery, and when that finally comes to the last break-down there will be the fewer wheels to stop.

So great indeed is the advantage of increasing mechanical supplements to the physical frame rather than exercising the physical frame itself, that this will become nothing short of a temptation; and not the least anxious task of future civilization will be to prevent degeneration beyond a legitimate point, and keep up the body to its highest working level. For the first thing to be learned from these facts is not that the Body is nothing and must now decay, but that it is most of all and more than ever worthy to be preserved. The moment our care of it slackens, the Body asserts itself. It comes out from under arrest—which is the one thing to be avoided. Its true place by the ordained appointment of Nature is where it can be ignored; if through disease, neglect, or injury it returns to consciousness the effect of Evolution is undone. Sickness is degeneration; pain the signal to resume the evolution. On the one hand, one must "reckon the Body dead"; on the other, one must think of it in order not to think of it.

This arrest of physical development at a specific point is not confined to Man. Everywhere in the organic world science is confronted with arrested types. While endless groups of plant and animal forms have advanced during the geological ages, other whole groups have apparently stood still— stood still, that is to say, not in time but in organization. If Nature is full of moving things, it is also full of fixtures. Thirty-one years ago Mr. Huxley devoted the anniversary Address of the Geological Society to a consideration of what he called "Persistent Types of Life," and threw down to Evolutionists a puzzle which has never yet been fully solved. While some forms attained their climacteric tens of thousands of years ago and perished, others persevered, and, without advancing in any material respect, are alive to this day. Among the most ancient Carboniferous plants, for instance, are found certain forms generically identical with those now living. The cone of the existing Araucaria is scarcely to be distinguished from that of an Oolite form. The Tabulate Corals of the Silurian period are similar to those which exist to-day. The Lamp-shells of our present seas so abounded at the same ancient date as to give their name to one of the great groups of Silurian rocks—the Lingula Flags.

Star-fishes and urchins, almost the same as those which tenant the coast-lines of our present seas, crawled along what are now among the most ancient fossiliferous rocks. Both of the forms just named, the Brachiopods and the Echinoderms, have come down to us almost unchanged through the nameless gap of time which separates the Silurian and Old Red Sandstone periods from the present era.

This constancy of structure reveals a conservatism in Nature, as unexpected as it is widespread. Does it mean that the architecture of living things has a limit beyond which development cannot go? Does it mean that the morphological possibilities along certain lines of bodily structure have exhausted themselves, that the course of conceivable development in these instances has actually run out? In Gothic Architecture, or in Norman, there are terminal points which, once reached, can be but little improved upon. Without limiting working efficiency, they can go no further. These styles in the very nature of things seem to have limits. Mr. Ruskin has indeed assured us that there are only three possible forms of good architecture in the world; Greek, the architecture of the Lintel; Romanesque, the architecture of the Rounded Arch; Gothic, the architecture of the Gable. "All the architects in the world will never discover any other way of bridging a space than these three, the Lintel, the Round Arch, the Gable; they may vary the curve of the arch, or curve the sides of the gable, or break them down; but in doing this they are merely modifying or sub-dividing, not adding to the generic form."

In some such way, there may be terminal generic forms in the architecture of animals; and the persistent types just named may represent in their several directions the natural limits of possible modification. No further modification of a radical kind, that is to say, could in these instances be introduced without detriment to practical efficiency. These terminal forms thus mark a normal maturity, a goal; they represent the ends of the twigs of the tree of life.

Now consider the significance of that fact. Nature is not an interminable succession. It is not always a becoming. Sometimes things arrive. The Lamp-shells have arrived, they are part of the permanent furniture of the world; along that particular line, there will probably never be anything higher. The Star-fishes also have arrived, and the Sea-urchins, and the Nautilus, and the Bony Fishes, the Tapirs, and possibly the Horse—all these are highly divergent forms which have run out the length of their tether and can go no further. When the plan of the world was made, to speak teleologically, these types of life were assigned their place and limit, and there they have remained. If it were wanted to convey the impression that Nature had some large end in view, that she was not drifting aimlessly towards a general higher level, it could not have been done more impressively than by everywhere placing on the field of Science these fixed points, these innumerable consummations, these clean-cut mountain peaks, which for millenniums have never grown. Even as there is a plan in the parts, there is a plan in the whole.

But the most certain of all these "terminal points" in the evolution of Creation is the body of Man. Anatomy places Man at the head of all other animals that were ever made; but what is infinitely more instructive, with him, as we have just seen, the series comes to an end. Man is not only the highest branch, but the highest possible branch Take as a last witness the testimony of anatomy itself with regard to the human brain. Here the fact is not only re-affirmed but the rationale of it suggested in terms of scientific law. "The development of the brain is in connection with a whole system of development of the head and face which cannot be carried further than in Man. For the mode in which the cranial cavity is gradually increased in size is a regular one, which may be explained thus: we may look on the skull as an irregular cylinder, and at the same time that it is expanded by increase of height and width it also undergoes a curvature or bending on itself, so that the base is crumpled together while the roof is elongated. This curving has gone on in Man till the fore end of the cylinder, the part on which the brain rests above the nose, is nearly parallel to the aperture of communication of the skull with the spinal canal, i.e. the cranium has a curve of 180deg. or a few degrees more or less. This curving of the base of the skull involves change in position of the face bones also, and could not go on to a further extent without cutting off the nasal cavity from the throat. . . . Thus there is anatomical evidence that the development of the vertebrate form has reached its limit by completion in Man.

This author's conception of the whole field of living nature is so suggestive that we may continue the quotation: "To me the animal kingdom appears not in indefinite growth like a tree, but a temple with many minarets, none of them capable of being prolonged—while the central dome is completed by the structure of man. The development of the animal kingdom is the development of intelligence chained to matter; the animals in which the nervous system has reached the greatest perfection are the vertebrates, and in Man that part of the nervous system which is the organ of intelligence reaches, as I have sought to show, the highest development possible to a vertebrate animal, while intelligence has grown to reflection and volition. On these grounds, I believe, not that Man is the highest possible intelligence, but that the human body is the highest form of human life possible, subject to the conditions of matter on the surface of the globe, and that the structure completes the design of the animal kingdom.

Never was the body of Man greater than with this sentence of suspension passed on it, and never was Evolution more wonderful or more beneficent than when the signal was given to stop working at Man's animal frame. This was an era in the world's history. For it betokened nothing less than that the cycle of matter was now complete, and the one prefatory task of the ages finished. Henceforth the Weltanschauung is for ever changed. From this pinnacle of matter is seen at last what matter is for, and all the lower lives that ever lived appear as but the scaffolding for this final work. The whole sub-human universe finds its reason for existence in its last creation, its final justification in the new immaterial order which opened with its close. Cut off Man from Nature, and, metaphysical necessity apart, there remains in Nature no divinity. To include Man in Evolution is not to lower Man to the level of Nature, but to raise Nature to his high estate. There he was made, these atoms are his confederates, these plant cells raised him from the dust, these travailing animals furthered his Ascent: shall he excommunicate them now that their work is done? Plant and animal have each their end, but Man is the end of all the ends. The latest science reinstates him, where poet and philosopher had already placed him, as at once the crown, the master, and the rationale of creation. "Not merely," says Kant, "is he like all organized beings an end in nature, but also here on earth the last end of nature, in reference to whom all other natural things constitute a system of ends." Yet it is not because he is the end of ends, but the beginning of beginnings, that the completion of the Body marks a crisis in the past. At last Evolution had culminated in a creation so complex and exalted as to form the foundation for an inconceivably loftier super-organic order. The moment an organism was reached through which Thought was possible, nothing more was required of matter. The Body was high enough. Organic Evolution might now even resign its sovereignty of the world; it had made a thing which was now its master. Henceforth Man should take charge of Evolution even as up till now he had been the one charge of it. Henceforth his selection should replace Natural Selection; his judgment guide the struggle for life; his will determine for every plant upon the earth whether it should bloom or fade, for every animal whether it should increase, or change, or die. So Man entered into his Kingdom.

Science is charged, be it once more recalled, with numbering Man among the beasts, and levelling his body with the dust. But he who reads for himself the history of creation as it is written by the hand of Evolution will be overwhelmed by the glory and honour heaped upon this creature. To be a Man, and to have no conceivable successor; to be the fruit and crown of the long past eternity, and the highest possible fruit and crown; to be the last victor among the decimated phalanxes of earlier existences, and to be nevermore defeated; to be the best that Nature in her strength and opulence can produce; to be the first of that new order of beings who by their dominion over the lower world and their equipment for a higher, reveal that they are made in the Image of God—to be this is to be elevated to a rank in Nature more exalted than any philosophy or any poetry or any theology have ever given to Man. Man was always told that his place was high; the reason for it he never knew till now; he never knew that his title deeds were the very laws of Nature, that he alone was the Alpha and Omega of Creation, the beginning and the end of Matter, the final goal of Life.

Nature is full of new departures; but never since time began was there anything approaching in importance that period when the slumbering animal, Brain, broke into intelligence, and the Creature first felt that it had a Mind. From that dateless moment a higher and swifter progress of the world began. Henceforth, Intelligence triumphed over structural adaptation. The wise were naturally selected before the strong. The Mind discovered better methods, safer measures, shorter cuts. So the body learned to refer to it, then to defer to it. As the Mind was given more to do, it enlarged and did its work more perfectly. Gradually the favours of Evolution— exercise, alteration, differentiation, addition—which were formerly distributed promiscuously among the bodily organs—were now lavished mainly upon the Brain. The gains accumulated with accelerating velocity; and by sheer superiority and fitness for its work, the Intellect rose to commanding power, and entered into final possession of a monopoly which can never be disturbed.

Now this means not only that an order of higher animals has appeared upon the earth, but that an altogether new page in the history of the universe has begun to be written. It means nothing less than that the working of Evolution has changed its course. Once it was a physical universe, now it is a psychical universe. And to say that the working of Evolution has changed its course, and set its compass in psychical directions, is to call attention to the most remarkable fact in Nature. Nothing so original or so revolutionary has ever been given to science to discover, to ponder, or to proclaim. The power of this event to strike and rouse the mind will depend upon one's sense of what the working of Evolution has been to the world; but those who realize this even dimly will see that no emphasis of language can exaggerate its significance. Let imagination do its best to summon up the past of Nature. Beginning with the panorama of the Nebular Hypothesis, run the eye over the field of Palaeontology, Geology, Botany, and Zoology. Watch the majestic drama of Creation unfolding, scene by scene and act by act. Realize that one power, and only one, has marshalled the figures for this mighty spectacle; that one hand, and only one, has carried out these transformations; that one principle, and only one, has controlled each subsidiary plot and circumstance; that the same great patient unobtrusive law has guided and shaped the whole from its beginnings in bewilderment and chaos to its end in order, harmony, and beauty. Then watch the curtain drop. And as it moves to rise again, behold the new actor upon the stage. Silently, as all great changes come, Mental Evolution has succeeded Organic. All the things that have been now lie in the far background as forgotten properties. And Man stands alone in the foreground, and a new thing, Spirit, strives within him.

The Dawn of Mind

The most beautiful witness to the Evolution of Man is the Mind of a little child. The stealing in of that inexplicable light—yet not more light than sound or touch—called consciousness, the first flicker of memory, the gradual governance of will, the silent ascendancy of reason—these are studies in Evolution the oldest, the sweetest, and the most full of meaning for mankind. Evolution, after all, is a study for the nursery. It was ages before Darwin or Lamarck or Lucretius that Maternity, bending over the hollowed cradle in the forest for a first smile of recognition from her babe, expressed the earliest trust in the doctrine of development. Every mother since then is an unconscious Evolutionist, and every little child a living witness to Ascent.

Is the Mind a new or an old thing in the world? Is it an Evolution from beneath or an original gift from heaven? Did the Mind, in short, come down the ages like the Body, and does the mother's faith in the intellectual unfolding of her babe include a remoter origin for all human faculty? Let the mother look at her child and answer. "It is the very breath of God," she says; "this Child-Life is Divine." And she is right. But let her look again. That forehead, whose is it? It is hers. And the frown which darkened it just now? Is hers also. And that which caused the frown to darken, that something or nothing, behind the forehead, that flash of pride, or scorn, or hate? Alas, it is her very own. And as the years roll on, and the budding life unfolds, there is scarcely a mood or gesture or emotion that she does not know is borrowed. But whence in turn did she receive them? From an earlier mother. And she? From a still earlier mother. And she? From the savage-mother in the woods. And the savage-mother?

Shall we hesitate here? We well may. So Godlike a gift is intellect, so wondrous a thing is consciousness, that to link them with the animal world seems to trifle with the profoundest distinctions in the Universe. Yet to associate these supersensuous things with the animal kingdom is not to identify them with the animal-body. Electricity is linked with metal rods, it is not therefore metallic. Life is associated with protoplasm, it is not therefore albuminous. Instinct is linked with matter, but it is not therefore material; Intellect with animal matter, but is not therefore animal. As we rise in the scale of Nature we encounter new orders of phenomena, Matter, Life, Mind, each higher than that before it, each totally and forever different, yet each using that beneath it as the pedestal for its further progress. Associated with animal-matter— how associated no psychology, no physiology, no materialism, no spiritualism, has even yet begun to hint—may there not have been from an early dawn the elements of a future Mind? Do the wide analogies of Nature not make the suggestion worthy at least of inquiry? The fact, to which there is no exception, that all lesser things evolve, the suggestion, which is daily growing into a further certainty, that there is a mental evolution among animals from the Coelenterate to the Ape; the fact that the unfolding of the Child-Mind is itself a palpable evolution; the infinitely more significant circumstance that the Mind in a child seems to unfold in the order in which it would unfold if its mental faculties were received from the Animal world, and in the order in which they have already asserted themselves in the history of the race. These seem formidable facts on the side of those consistent evolutionists who, in the face of countless difficulties and countless prejudices, still press the lawful inquiry into the development of human faculty.

The first feeling in most minds when the idea of mental evolution is presented, is usually one of amusement. This not seldom changes, when the question is seen to be taken seriously, into wonder at the daring of the suggestion or pity for its folly. All great problems have been treated in this way. All have passed through the inevitable phases of laughter, contempt, opposition. It ought to be so. And if this problem is "perhaps the most interesting that has ever been submitted to the contemplation of our race, its basis cannot be criticized with too great care. But none have a right to question either the sanity or the sanctity of such investigations, still less to dismiss them idly on a priori grounds, till they have approached the practical problem for themselves, and heard at least the first few relevant words from Nature. For one has only to move for a little among the facts to see what a world of interest lies here, and to be forced to hold the judgment in suspense till the sciences at work upon the problem have further shaped their verdict. Thinkers who are entitled to respect have even gone further. They include mental evolution not only among the hypotheses of Science but among its facts and its necessary facts. "Is it conceivable," asks Mr. Romanes, "that the human mind can have arisen by way of a natural genesis from the minds of the higher quadrumana? I maintain that the material now before us is sufficient to show, not only that this is conceivable, but inevitable.

It is no part of the present purpose to discuss the ultimate origin or nature of Mind. Our subject is its development. At the present moment the ultimate origin of Mind is as inscrutable a mystery as the origin of Life. It is sometimes charged against Evolution that it tries to explain everything and to rob the world of all its problems. There does not appear the shadow of a hope that it is about to rob it of this. On the contrary the foremost scientific exponents of the theory of mental evolution are ceaselessly calling attention to the inscrutable character of the element whose history they attempt to trace. "On the side of its philosophy," says Mr. Romanes, "no one can have a deeper respect for the problem of self-consciousness than I have; for no one can be more profoundly convinced than I am that the problem on this side does not admit of solution. In other words, so far as this aspect of the matter is concerned, I am in complete agreement with the most advanced idealist I am as far as any one can be from throwing light upon the intrinsic nature of the probable origin of that which I am endeavouring to trace. Mr. Darwin himself recoiled from a problem so transcendent: "I have nothing to do with the origin of the mental powers, any more than I have with that of life itself. "In what manner," he elsewhere writes, "the mental powers were first developed in the lowest organisms, is as hopeless an inquiry as how life itself first originated."

Notwithstanding his appreciation of the difficulty of the ultimate problem, Mr. Darwin addressed his whole strength to the question of the Evolution of Mind—the Evolution as distinguished from its origin and nature; and in this he has recently had many followers, as well as many opponents. Among the latter stand the co-discoverer with him of Natural Selection, Mr. Alfred Russel Wallace, and Mr. St. George Mivart. Mr. Wallace's opposition, from a scientific point of view, is not so hostile, however, as is generally supposed. While holding his own view as to the origin of Mind, what he attacks in Mr. Darwin's theory of mental evolution is, not the development itself, but only the supposition that it could have been due to Natural Selection. Mr. Wallace's authority is frequently quoted to show that the mathematical, the musical and the artistic faculties could not have been evolved, whereas all he has really emphasized is that "they could not have been developed under the law of Natural Selection. In short the conclusion of Mr. Darwin which his colleague found "not to be supported by adequate evidence, and to be directly opposed to many well ascertained facts," was not a general theorem, but a specific one. And many will agree with Mr. Wallace in doubting "that man's entire nature and all his faculties, whether moral, intellectual, or spiritual, have been derived from their rudiments in the lower animals, in the same manner and by the action of the same general laws as his physical structure has been derived.

The more this problem has been investigated, the difficulties of the whole field increase, and the off-hand acceptance of any specific evolution theory finds less and less encouragement. No serious thinker, on whichever side of the controversy, has succeeded in lessening to his own mind the infinite distance between the Mind of Man and everything else in Nature, and even the most consistent evolutionists are as unanimous as those who oppose them, in their assertion of the uniqueness of the higher intellectual powers. The concensus of scientific opinion here is extraordinary. "I know nothing," says Huxley, in the name of biology, "and never hope to know anything, of the steps by which the passage from molecular movement to states of consciousness is effected. "The two things," emphasizes the physicist, "are on two utterly different platforms, the physical facts go along by themselves, and the mental facts go along by themselves. "It is all through and for ever inconceivable," protests the German physiologist, "that a number of atoms of Carbon, Hydrogen, Nitrogen, Oxygen, and so on, shall be other than indifferent as to how they are disposed and how they move, how they were disposed and how they moved, how they will be disposed and how they will be moved. It is utterly inconceivable how consciousness shall arise from their joint action.So impressed is even Mr. Lloyd Morgan, mental evolutionist though he be, with the gap between the Minds of Man and brute that his language is almost as strong: "I for one do not for a moment question that the mental processes of man and animals are alike products of evolution. The power of cognizing relations, reflection and introspection, appear to me to mark a new departure in evolution, and "I am not prepared to say that there is a difference in kind between the mind of man and the mind of a dog. This would imply a difference in origin or a difference in the essential nature of its being. There is a great and marked difference in kind between the material processes which we call physiological and the mental processes we call psychical. They belong to wholly different orders of being. I see no reason for believing that mental processes in man differ thus in kind from mental processes in animals. But I do think that we have, in the introduction of the analytic faculty, so definite and marked a new departure that we should emphasize it by saying that the faculty of perception, in its various specific grades, differs generically from the faculty of conception. And believing, as I do, that conception is beyond the power of my favourite and clever dog, I am forced to believe that his mind differs generically from my own.

Should anyone feel it necessary either to his view of Man or of the Universe to hold that a great gulf lies here, it is open to him to cling to his belief. The present thesis is simply that Man has ascended. After all, little depends on whether the slope is abrupt or gentle, whether Man reaches the top by a uniform flight or has here and there by invisible hands to be carried across a bridgeless space. In any event it is Nature's staircase. To say that self-consciousness has arisen from sensation, and sensation from the function of nutrition, let us say, in the Mimosa pudica or Sensitive Plant, may be right or wrong; but the error can only be serious when it is held that that accounts either for self-consciousness or for the transition. Mimosa can be defined in terms of Man; but Man cannot be defined in terms of Mimosa. The first is possible because there is the least fraction in that which is least in Man of that which is greatest in Mimosa; the last is impossible because there is nothing in Mimosa of that which is greatest in Man. What the two possess in common, or seem to possess, may be a basis for comparison, for what it is worth; but to include in the comparison the ninety-nine and nine-tenths per cent of what is over and above that common fraction is by no sort of reasoning lawful. Man, in the last resort, has self-consciousness, Mimosa sensation; and the difference is qualitative as well as quantitative.

If, however, it is a fallacy to ignore the qualitative differences arising in the course of the transition, it may be a mistake, on the other hand, to make nothing of the transition. If in the name of Science the advocate of the Law of Continuity demands that it be rectified, he may well make the attempt. The partial truth for the present perhaps amounts to this, that earlier phases of life exhibit imperfect manifestations of principles which in the higher structure and widened environment of later forms are more fully manifested and expressed, yet are neither contained in the earlier phases nor explained by them. At the same time, everything that enters into Man, every sensation, emotion, volition, enters with a difference, a difference due to the fact that he is a rational and self-conscious being, a difference therefore which no emphasis of language can exaggerate. The music varies with the ear; varies with the soul behind the ear; relates itself with all the music that ear has ever heard before; with the mere fact that what that ear hears, it hears as music; that it hears at all; that it knows that it hears. Man differs from every other product of the evolutionary process in being able to see that it is a process, in sharing and rejoicing in its unity, and in voluntarily working through the process himself. If he is part of it he is also more than part of it, since he is at once its spectator, its director, and its critic. "Even on the hypothesis of a psychic life in all matter we come to an alteration indeed, but not an abolition, of the contrast between body and soul. Of course on that hypothesis they are distinguished by no qualitative difference in their natures, but still less do they blend into one; the one individual ruling soul always remains facing, in an attitude of complete isolation, the homogeneous but ministrant monads, the joint multitude of which forms the living body.

With these preliminary cautions, let us turn for a little to the facts. The field here is so full of interest in itself that apart from its forming a possible chapter in the history of Man it is worth a casual survey.

The difficulty of establishing even the general question of Ascent is of course obvious. After Mind emerged from the animal state, for a long time, and in the very nature of the case, no record of its progress could come down to us. The material Body has left its graduated impress upon the rocks in a million fossil forms; the Spirit of Man, at the other extreme of time, has traced its ascending curve on the tablets of civilization, in the drama of history, and in the monuments of social life; but the Mind must have risen into its first prominence during a long, silent and dateless interval which preceded the era of monumental records. Mind - cannot be exhumed by Palaeontology or fully embalmed in unwritten history, and apart from the analogies of Embryology we have nothing but inference to guide us until the time came when it was advanced enough to leave some tangible register behind.

But so far as knowledge is possible there are mainly five sources of information with regard to the past of Mind. The first is the Mind of a little child; the second the Mind of lower animals; the third, those material witnesses—flints, weapons, pottery—to primitive states of Mind which are preserved in anthropological museums; the fourth is the Mind of a Savage; and the fifth is Language.

The first source—the Mind of a little child—has just been referred to Mind, in Man, does not start into being fully ripe. It dawns; it grows; it mellows; it decays. This growing moreover is a gradual growing, an infinitely gentle, never abrupt unfolding—the kind of growing which in every other department of Nature we are taught by Nature to associate with an Evolution. If the Mind of the infant had been evolved, and that not from primeval Man, but from some more ancient animal, it could not to more perfection have simulated the appearance of having so come.

But this is not all. The Mind of a child not only grows, but grows in a certain order. And the astonishing fact about that order is that it is the probable order of evolution of mental faculty as a whole. Where Science gets that probable order will be referred to by and by. Meantime, simply note the fact that not only in the manner but in the order of its development, the human Mind simulates a product of Evolution. The Mind of a child, in short, is to be treated as an unfolding embryo; and just as the embryo of the body recapitulates the long life-history of all the bodies that led up to it, so this subtler embryo in running its course through the swift years of early infancy runs up the psychic scale through which, as evidence from another field will show, Mind probably evolved. We have seen also that in the case of the body, each step of progress in the embryo has its equivalent either in the bodies, or in the embryos of lower forms of life. Now each phase of mental development in the child is also permanently represented by some species among the lower animals, by idiots, or by the Mind of some existing savage.

Let us turn, however, to the second source of information—Mind in the lower Animals.

That animals have "Minds" is a fact which probably no one now disputes. Stories of "Animal Intelligence" and "Animal Sagacity" in dogs and bees and ants and elephants and a hundred other creatures have been told us from childhood with redundant reiteration. The old protest that animals have no Mind but only instinct has lost its point. In addition to instincts, animals betray intelligence, and often a high degree of intelligence; they share our feelings and emotions; they have memories; they form percepts; they invent new ways of satisfying their desires, they learn by experience. It is true their Minds want much, and all that is highest; but the point is that they actually have Minds, whatever their quantity and whatever their quality. If abstraction, as Locke says, "is an excellency which the faculties of brutes do by no means attain to," we cannot on that account deny them Mind, but only that height of Mind which men have, and which Evolution would never look for in any living thing but Man. An Evolutionist would no more expect to find the higher rational characteristics in a wolf or a bear than to unearth the modern turbine from a Roman aqueduct.

Though the possession even of a few rudiments of Mind by animals is a sufficient starting point for Mental Evolution, to say that they have only a few rudiments is to understate the facts. But we know so little what Mind is that speculation in this region can only be done in the rough. On one hand lies the danger of minimizing tremendous distinctions, on the other, of pretending to know all about these distinctions, because we have learned to call them by certain names. Mind, when we come to see what it is, may be one; perhaps must be one. The habit of unconsciously regarding the powers and faculties of Mind as separate entities, like the organs of the body, has its risks as well as its uses; and we cannot too often remind ourselves that this is a mere device to facilitate thought and speech.

It is mainly to Mr. Romanes that we owe the working out of the evidence in this connection; and even though his researches be little more than a preliminary exploration their general results are striking. Realizing that the most scientific way to discover whether there are any affinities between Mind in Animals and Mind in Man is to compare the one with the other, he began a laborious study of the Animal world. His conclusions are contained in Animal Intelligence and Mental Evolution in Animals—volumes which no one can read without being convinced at least of the thoroughness and fairness of the investigation. That abundant traces were found of Mind in the lower animals goes without saying. But the range of mental phenomena discovered there may certainly excite surprise. Thus, to consider only one set of phenomena—that of the emotions—all the following products of emotional development are represented at one stage or another of animal life:

Fear, emulation, benevolence, surprise, pride, revenge, affection, resentment, rage, pugnacity, emotion of the beautiful, shame, curiosity, regret, jealousy, grief, deceitfulness, anger, hate, emotion of the ludicrous, play, cruelty, sympathy

But this list is something more than a bare catalogue of what human emotions exist in the animal world. It is an arranged catalogue, a more or less definite psychological scale. These emotions did not only appear in animals, but they appeared in this order. Now to find out order in Evolution is of first importance. For order of events is history, and Evolution is history. In creatures very far down the scale of life—the Annelids—Mr. Romanes distinguished what appeared to him to be one of the earliest emotions—Fear. Somewhat higher up, among the Insects, he met with the Social Feelings, as well as Industry, Pugnacity, and Curiosity. Jealousy seems to have been born into the world with Fishes; Sympathy with Birds. The Carnivora are responsible for Cruelty, Hate, and Grief; the Anthropoid Apes for Remorse, Shame, the Sense of the Ludicrous, and Deceit.

Now, when we compare this table with a similar table compiled from a careful study of the emotional states in a little child, two striking facts appear. In the first place, there are almost no emotions in the child which are not here—this list, in short, practically exhausts the list of human emotions. With the exception of the religious feelings, the moral sense, and the perception of the sublime, there is nothing found even in adult Man which is not represented with more or less vividness in the Animal Kingdom. But this is not all. These emotions, as already hinted, appear in the Mind of the growing child in the same order as they appear on the animal scale. At three weeks, for instance, Fear is perceptibly manifest in a little child. When it is seven weeks old the Social Affections dawn. At twelve weeks emerges Jealousy, with its companion Anger. Sympathy appears after five months; Pride, Resentment, Love of Ornament, after eight; Shame, Remorse, and Sense of the Ludicrous after fifteen. These dates, of course, do not indicate in any mechanical way the birthdays of emotions; they represent rather stages in an infinitely gentle mental ascent, stages nevertheless so marked that we are able to give them names, and use them as landmarks in psychogenesis. Yet taken even as representing a rough order it is a circumstance to which some significance must be attached that the tree of Mind as we know it in lower Nature, and the tree of Mind as we know it in a little child, should be the same tree, starting its roots at the same place, and though by no means ending its branches at the same level, at least growing them so far in a parallel direction.

Do we read these emotions into the lower animals or are they really there? That they are not there in the sense in which we think them there is probably certain. But that they are there in some sense, a sense sufficient to permit us cautiously to reason from, seems an admissible hypothesis. No doubt it takes much for granted,—partly, indeed, the very thing to be proved. But discounting even the enormous limitations of the inquiry, there is surely a residuum of general result to make it at least worth making.

If we turn from emotional to intellectual development, the parallelism though much mole faint is at least shadowed. Again we find a list of intellectual products common to both Animal and Man, and again an approximate order common to both. It is true, Man's development beyond the highest point attained by any animal in the region of the intellect, is all but infinite. Of rational judgment he has the whole monopoly. Wherever the roots of Mind be, there is no uncertainty as to where, and where exclusively, the higher branches are. Grant that the mental faculties of Man and Animal part company at a point, there remains to consider the vast distance—in the case of the emotions almost the whole distance—where they run parallel with one another. Comparative psychology is not so advanced a science as comparative embryology; yet no one who has felt the force of the recapitulation argument for the evolution of bodily function, even making all allowances for the differences of the things compared, will deny the weight of the corresponding argument for the evolution of Mind. Why should the Mind thus recapitulate in its development the psychic life of animals unless some vital link connected them?

A singular complement to this argument has been suggested recently—though as yet only in the form of the vaguest hint—from the side of Mental Pathology. When the Mind is affected by certain diseases, its progress downward can often be followed step by step. It does not tumble down in a moment into chaos like a house of cards, but in a definite order, stone by stone, or storey by storey. Now the striking thing about that order is, that it is the probable order in which the building has gone up. The order of descent, in short, is the inverse of the order of ascent. The first faculty to go, in many cases of insanity, is the last faculty which arrived; the next faculty is affected next; the whole spring uncoiling as it were in the order and direction in which, presumably, it had been wound up. Sometimes even in the phenomenon of old age the cycle may be clearly traced. "Just as consciousness is slowly evolved out of vegetative life, so is it, through the infirmities of old age, the gradual approach of death, and in advanced mental disease, again resolved into it. The highest, most differentiated phenomena of consciousness are the first to give way; impulse, instinct, and reflex movements become again predominant. The phrase 'to grow childish' expresses the resemblance between the first stage and the stage of dissolution.

That the highest part of man should totter first is what, on the theory of mental evolution, one would already have expected. The highest part is the latest added part, and the latest added part is the least secured part. As the last arrival, it is not yet at home; it has not had time to get lastingly embedded in the brain; the competition of older faculties is against it; the hold of the will upon it is slight and fitful; its tenure as a tenant is precarious and often threatened. Among the older and more permanent residents, therefore, it has little chance. Hence if anything goes wrong, as the last added, the most complex, the least automatic of all the functions, it is the first to suffer.

We are but too familiar with cases where men of lofty intellect and women of most pure mind, seized in the awful grasp of madness, are transformed in a few brief months into beings worse than brutes. How are we to account, on any other principle than this, for that most shocking of all catastrophes the sudden and total break-up, the devolution, of a saint? That the wise man should become a chattering idiot is inexplicable enough, but that the saintly soul should riot in blasphemy and immorality so foul that not among the lowest races is there anything to liken to it— these are phenomena so staggering that if Evolution hold any key to them at all, its suggestion must come as at least a partial relief to the human mind. These are possibly cases of actual reversion, cases where all the beautiful later buildings of humanity had been swept away and only the elemental brute foundations left. Devolution is thus assumed to be a co-relative of Evolution. And as the morbid states of the Mind are more and more studied in this relation, it may yet be possible from the phenomena of insanity to lay bare to some extent the outline of intellectual ascent. In the present state both of psychology, and especially of our knowledge of the brain, nothing probably could be more precarious than this as an argument. The very statement involves modes of expression which exact science would rule out of court. The best that can be said is that it is a suggestion awaiting further light before it can even rank as a theory. Complex as the source of knowledge is, the Mind itself must ever be the final authority on its own biography. Analogy from lower nature may do much to confirm the reading; the mental history of the human race, from the rudiments of intellect in the savage to its development in civilized life, may contribute some closing chapters; but unless the Mind tell its own story it will never be fully told. Yet should it ever thus be told, the mystery of Mind itself would remain the same. For the most this could do would be to replace one mystery by a greater. For what greater mystery could there be than that within the mystery of the Mind itself there should lie concealed the very key to unlock its mystery?

To pass from this fascinating region to the material contributions of Anthropology is a somewhat abrupt transition. But this third line of approach to a knowledge of the earlier phases of Mind need not detain us long.

So patient has been the search over almost the whole world for relics of pre-historic Man, that vast collections are now everywhere available where the arts, industries, weapons, and, by inference, the mental development, of the earlier inhabitants of this planet can be practically studied. On the two main points at issue in the discussion of mental evolution these collections are unanimous. They reveal in the first instance, traces of Mind of a very low order existing from an unknown antiquity; and in the second place, they show a gradual improving of this Mind as we approach the present day. It may be that in some cases the evidence suggests a degenerating rather than an ascending civilization; but perturbations of this sort do not affect the main question, nor neutralize the other facts. Evolution is constantly confronted with statements as to the former glory of now decadent nations, as if that were an argument against the theory. Granting that nations have degenerated, it still remains to account for that from which they degenerated. That Egypt has fallen from a great height is certain; but the real problem is how it got to that height. When a boy's kite descends in our garden, we do not assume that it came from the clouds. That it went up before it came down is obvious, from all that we know of kite-making. And that nations went up before they came down is obvious from all that we know of nation-making. The gravitation, moreover, which brings down nations is just as real as the gravitation which brings down kites; and instead of a falling nation being a stumbling block to Evolution, it is a necessity of the theory. The degeneration and extinction of the unfit are as infallibly brought about by natural laws as the survival of the fit. Evolution is by no means synonymous with uninterrupted progress, but at every turn means relapse, extinction, and decay.

It is pretty clear that, applying the old Argument from Design to the case of the most ancient human relics, Man began the Ascent of Civilization at zero. There has been a time in the history of every nation when the only supplements to the organs of the body for the uses of Man were the stones of the field and the sticks of the forest. To use these natural, abundant, and portable objects, was an obvious resource with early tribes. If Mind dawned in the past at all, it is with such objects that we should expect its first associations, and as a matter of fact it seems everywhere to have been so. Relics of a Stick Age would of course be obliterated by time, but traces of a Stone Age have been found, not in connection with the first beginnings of a few tribes only, but with the first beginnings—from the point that any representation is possible—of probably every nation in the world. The wide geographical use of stone implements is one of the most striking facts in Anthropology. Instead of being confined to a few peoples, and to outlying districts, as is sometimes asserted, their distribution is universal. They are found throughout the length and breadth of Europe, and on all its islands; they occur everywhere in Western Asia, and north of the Himalayas. In the Malay Peninsula they strew the ground in endless numbers; and again, in Australia, New Zealand, New Caledonia, the New Hebrides, and the Coral Islands of the Pacific. Known in China, they are scattered broadcast throughout Japan, and the same is true of America, Mexico, and Peru. If a child playing with a toy spade is a proof that it is a child, a nation working with stone axes is proved to be a child-nation. Erroneous conclusions may easily be drawn, and indeed have been, from the fact of a nation using stone, but the general law stands. Partly, perhaps, by mutual intercourse, this use of stone became universal; but it arose, more likely, from the similarity in primitive needs, and the available means of gratifying them. Living under widely different conditions, and in every variety of climate, all early peoples shared the instincts of humanity which first called in the use of tools and weapons. All felt the same hunger; all had the instinct of self-preservation; and the universality of these instincts and the commonness of stone led the groping Mind to fasten upon it, and make it one of the first steps to the Arts. A Stone Age, thus, was the natural beginning. In the nature of things there could have been no earlier. If Mind really grew by infinitely gradual ascents, the exact situation the theory requires is here provided in actual fact.

The next step from the Stone Age, so far as further appeal to ancient implements can guide us is also exactly what one would expect. It is to a better Stone Age. Two distinct grades of stone implements are found, the rough and the smooth, or the unground and the ground. For a long period the idea never seems to have dawned that a smooth stone made a better axe than a rough one. Mind was as yet unequal to this small discovery, and there are vast remains representing long intervals of time where all the stone implements and tools are of the unground type. Even when the hour did come, when savage vied with savage in putting the finest polish on his flints, his inspiration probably came from Nature. The first lapidary was the sea; the smoothed pebble on the beach, or the rounded stone of a mountain stream, supplied the pattern. There is no question that the rough stone came earlier than the ground stone. Thus the implements of the Drift Period, those of the Danish Mounds, the Bone Caves, and the gravels of St. Acheul are mostly unground, while those of the later Lake-Dwellers are almost wholly of the smooth type.

To follow the Stone Age upward into the Bronze Period, and from that to the Age of Iron, is not necessary for the present purpose. For at this point the order of succession passes from shell-mound and crannog, into living hands. There are nations with us still who have climbed so short a distance up the psychic scale as to be still in the Age of Stone—peoples whose mental culture and habits are often actual witnesses to the mental states of early Man. These children of Nature take up the thread of mental progress where the Troglodyte and Drift Man left it; and the modern traveller, starting from the civilization of Europe can follow Mind downwards step by step, in ever descending order, tracing its shadings backwards to a first simplicity, till he finds himself with the still living Lake-dweller of Nyasaland or the Bushman of the African forest. Time was when these humble tribes, with their strange and artless ways, were mere food for the curious. Now the study of the lower native races has risen to the first rank in comparative psychology; and the student of beginnings, whether they be the beginnings of Art or of Ethics, of Language or of Letters, of Law or of Religion, goes to seek the roots of his science in the ways, traditions, faiths, and institutions of savage life.

This leads us, however, to the fourth of the sources from which we were to gather a hint or two with regard to the past of Mind—the savage. No one should pronounce upon the Evolution of Mind till he has seen a savage. By this is not meant the show savage of an Australian town, or the quay Kaffir of a South African port, or the Reservation Indian of a Western State; but the savage as he is in reality, and as he may be seen to-day by any who care to look upon so weird a spectacle. No study from the life can compare with this in interest or in pathos, nor stir so many strange emotions in the mind of a thoughtful man. To sit with this incalculable creature in the heart of the great forest; to live with him in his natural home as the guest of Nature; to watch his ways and moods and try to resolve the ceaseless mystery of his thoughts—this, whether the existing savage represents the primitive savage or not, is to open one of the workshops of Creation and behold the half-finished product from which humanity has been evolved.

The world is getting old, but the traveller who cares to follow the daybreak of Mind for himself can almost do so still. Selecting a region where the wand of western civilization has scarcely reached, let him begin with a cruise in the Malay Archipelago or in the Coral Seas of the Southern Pacific. He may find himself there even yet on spots on which no white foot has ever trod, on islands where unknown races have worked out their destiny for untold centuries, whose teeming peoples have no name, and whose habits and mode of life are only known to the outer world through a ship's telescope. As he coasts along, he will see the dusky figures steal like shades among the trees, or hurry past in their bark canoes, or crouch in fear upon the coral sand. He can watch them gather the bread-fruit from the tree and pull the cocoa-nut from the palm and root out the taro for a meal which, all the year round and all the centuries through, has never changed. In an hour or two he can compass almost the whole round of their simple life, and realize the gulf between himself and them in at least one way—in the utter impossibility of framing to himself an image of the mental world of men and women whose only world is this.

Let him pass on to the coast of Northern Queensland, and, landing where fear of the white man makes landing possible, penetrate the Australian bush. Though the settlements of the European have been there for a generation, he will find the child of Nature still untouched, and neither by intercourse nor imitation removed by one degree from the lowest savage state. These aboriginal peoples know neither house nor home. They neither sow nor reap. Their weapons are those of Nature, a pointed stick and a knotted club. They live like wild things on roots and berries and birds and wallabies, and in the monotony of their life and the uncouthness of their Mind represent almost the lowest level of humanity.

From these rudiments of mankind let him make his way to the New Hebrides, to Tanna, and Santo, and Ambrym, and Aurora. These islands, besides Man, contain only three things, coral, lava, and trees. Until but yesterday their peoples had never seen anything but coral, lava, and trees. They did not know that there was anything else in the world. One hundred years ago Captain Cook discovered these islanders and gave them a few nails. They planted them in the ground that they might grow into bigger nails. It is true that in other lands a very rich life and a very wide world could be made out of no more varied materials than coral, lava, and trees; but on these Tropical Islands Nature is disastrously kind. All that her children need is provided for them ready-made. Her sun shines on them so that they are never either cold or hot; she provides crops for them in unexampled luxuriance, and arranges the year to be one long harvest; she allows no wild animals to prowl among the forests; and surrounding them with the alienating sea she preserves them from the attacks of human enemies. Outside the struggle for life, they are out of life itself. Treated as children, they remain children. To look at them now is to recall the long holiday of the childhood of the world. It is to behold one's natural face in a glass.

Pass on through the other Cannibal Islands and, apart from the improvement of weapons and the construction of a hut, throughout vast regions there is still no sign of mental progress. But before one has completed the circuit of the Pacific the change begins to come. Gradually there appear the beginnings of industry and even of art. In the Solomon Group and in New Guinea, carving and painting may be seen in an early infancy. The canoes are large and good, fish-hooks are manufactured, and weaving of a rude kind has been established. There can be no question at this stage that the Mind of Man has begun its upward path. And what now begins to impress one is not the poverty of the early Mind, but the enormous potentialities that lie within it, and the exceeding swiftness of its Ascent towards higher things. When the Sandwich Islands are reached, the contrast appears in its full significance. Here, a century ago, Captain Cook, through whom the first knowledge of their existence reached the outer world, was killed and eaten. To-day the children of his murderers have taken their place among the civilized nations of the world, and their Kings and Queens demand acknowledgment at modern Courts.

Books have been given to the world on the Mind of animals. It is strange that so little should have been written specifically on the Mind of the savage. But though this living mine has not yet been drawn upon for its last contribution to science, facts to suggest and sustain a theory of mental evolution are everywhere abundant. Waiving individual cases where nations have fallen from a higher intellectual level the proof indicates a rising potentiality and widening of range as we pass from primitive to civilized states. It is open to debate whether during the historic period mere intellectual advance has been considerable, whether more penetrating or commanding intellects have ever appeared than those of Job, Isaiah, Plato, Shakespeare. But that is matter of yesterday. What concerns us now to note is that the Mind of Man as a whole has had a slow and gradual dawn: that it has existed, and exists to-day, among certain tribes at almost the lowest point of development with which the word human can be associated; and that from that point an Ascent of Mind can be traced from tribe to nation in an ever increasing complexity and through infinitely delicate shades of improvement, till the highest civilized states are reached. In the very nature of things we should have expected such a result. For this is not only a question of faculty. In a far more intimate sense than we are apt to imagine, it is a question of a gradually evolving environment. Every infinitesimal enrichment of the soil for Mind to grow in meant an infinitesimal enrichment of the Mind itself. "It needs but to ask what would happen to ourselves were the whole mass of existing knowledge obliterated, and were children with nothing beyond their nursery-language left to grow up without guidance or instruction from adults, to perceive that even now the higher intellectual faculties would be almost inoperative, from lack of the materials and aids accumulated by past civilization. And seeing this, we cannot fail to see that development of the higher intellectual faculties has gone on pari passu with social advance alike as cause and consequence; that the primitive man could not evolve these higher intellectual faculties in the absence of a fit environment; and that in this, as in other respects, his progress was retarded by the absence of capacities which only progress could bring.

The last testimony is that of Language. It has already been pleaded in excuse for the absence of actual proof for mental evolution that Mind leaves no material footprints by which the palaeontologist can trace its upward path. Yet this is not wholly true. The flints and arrow-heads, the celts and hammers, of early Man are fossil intelligence; the remains of primitive arts and industries are petrified Mind. But there is one mould into which Mind has run more large and beautiful than any of these. When its contents are examined they carry us back not only to what men worked at with their hands, but to what they said to one another as they worked and what they thought as they spoke. That mould is Language. Language, says Jean Paul, is "ein Worterbuch erblasster Metaphern"— a dictionary of faded metaphors. But it is much more. A word is a counter of the brain, a tangible expression of a mental state, an heirloom of the wealth of culture of a race. And an old word, like an ancient coin, speaks to us of a former currency of thought, and by its image and superscription reveals the mental life and aspiration of those who minted it. "Language is the amber in which a thousand precious and subtle thoughts have been safely embalmed and preserved. It is the embodiment, the incarnation, of the feelings and thoughts and experiences of a nation, yea often of many nations, and of all which through long centuries they have attained to and won. It stands like the Pillars of Hercules, to mark how far the moral and intellectual conquests of mankind have advanced, only not like those pillars, fixed and immovable, but even itself advancing with the progress of these. The mighty moral instincts which have been working in the popular mind have found therein their unconscious voice; and the single kinglier spirits that have looked deeper into the heart of things have oftentimes gathered up all they have seen into some one word, which they have launched upon the world, and with which they have enriched it for ever—making in the new word a new region of thought to be henceforward in some sort the common heritage of all.

What then, when we open this marvellous structure, is the revelation yielded us of the mental states of those who lived at the dawn of speech? An impression of poverty, great and pathetic. All fossils teach the same lesson—the lesson of life, beauty, structure, waning into a poverty-stricken past. Whether they be the shells which living creatures once inhabited, or the bones of departed vertebrate types, or the forms of words where wisdom lay entombed, the structures became simpler and simpler, cruder and cruder, less full of the richness and abundance of life as we near the birth of time. They tell of days when the world was very young, when plants were flowerless and animals backboneless, of later years when primeval Man prowled the forest and chipped his flints and chattered in uncouth syllables of battle and the chase. No words entered at that time into human speech except those relating to the activities, few and monotonous, of an almost animal lot. These were the days of the protoplasm of speech. There was no differentiation between verbs or adverbs, nouns or adjectives. The sentence as yet was not; each word was a sentence. There was no grammatical inflection but the inflection of the voice; the moods of the verb were uttered by intonation or grimace. The pronouns "him" and "you" were made by pointing at him and you. Man had even no word for himself, for he had not yet discovered himself. This fact, when duly considered, raises the witness of Language to the Ascent of Mind to an almost unique importance. Nothing more significant could be said as to Man's mental past than that there was a time when he was scarcely conscious of himself, as a self. He knew himself, not as subject, but like a little child, as one of the objects of the external world. The words might have been written historically of mankind, "When I was a child, I spake as a child."

This evidence will meet us again in other forms when we pass to consider the Evolution of Language itself. Meantime let us close this chapter by pointing out a relation of a much more significant order between Language and the whole subject of Mental Evolution. For the point is not only of special interest, but it touches upon, and helps to solve, one of the vital problems of the Ascent of Man.

The enormous distance travelled by the Mind of Man beyond the utmost limit of intelligence reached by any animal is a puzzling circumstance, a circumstance only equalled in strangeness by another— the suddenness with which that rise took place. Both facts are without a parallel in nature. Why, of the countless thousands of species of animals, each with some shadowy rudiment of a Mind, all should have remained comparatively at the same dead level, while Man alone shot past and developed powers of a quality and with a speed unknown in the world's history, is a question which it is impossible not to raise. That by far the greatest step in the world's history should not only have been taken at the eleventh hour, but that it took only an hour to do it—for compared with the time when animals began their first activities, the birth of Man is a thing of yesterday—seems almost the denial of Evolution. What was it in Man's case that gave his mental powers their unprecedented start or facilitated a growth so rapid and so vast?

The factors in all Evolution, and above all in this, are too subtle to encourage one to speculate with final assurance on so fine a problem. Nevertheless, when it is asked, What brought about this sudden rise of intelligence in the case of Man? there is a wonderful unanimity among men of science as to the answer. It came about, it is supposed, in connection with the acquisition by Man of the power to express his mind, that is to speak. Evolution, up to this time, had only one way of banking the gains it won—heredity. To hand on any improvement physically was a slow and precarious work. But with the discovery of language there arose a new method of passing on a step in progress. Instead of sowing the gain on the wind of heredity, it was fastened on the wings of words. The way to make money is not only to accumulate small gains steadily, but to put them out at a good rate of interest. Animals did the first with their mental acquisitions: Man did the second. At a comparatively early date, he found out a first-rate and permanent investment for his money, so that he could not only keep his savings and put them out at the highest rate of interest, but have a share in all the gain that was made by other men. That discovery was Language. Many animals had hit upon an imperfect form of this discovery; but Man alone succeeded in improving it up to a really paying point. The condition of all growth is exercise, and till he could find a further field and a larger opportunity to work what little brains he had, he had little chance of getting more. Speech gave him this opportunity. He rapidly ran up a fortune in brain-matter, because he had found out new uses for it, new exercises of it, and especially a permanent investment for husbanding in the race each gain as it was made in the individual. When he did anything he could now say it; when he learned anything he could pass it on; when he became wise wisdom did not die with him, it was banked in the Mind of humanity. So one man lent his mind to another. The loans became larger and larger, the interest greater and greater; Man's fortune was secured. In the mere Struggle for Life, his wits were sharpened up to a point; but unless he had learned to talk, he could never have passed very far beyond the animal.

Apart from the saving of time and the facility for increased knowledge, the acquisition of speech meant a saving of brain. A word is a counter for a thought. To use language is to make thinking easy. Hence the release of brain energy for further developments in new directions. In these and other ways speech became the main factor in the intellectual development of mankind. Language formed the trellis on which Mind climbed upward, which continuously sustained the ripening fruits of knowledge for later minds to pluck. Before the savage's son was ten years old he knew all that his father knew. The ways of the game, the habits of birds and fish, the construction of traps and snares—all these would be taught him. The physical world, the changes of season, the location of hostile tribes, the strategies of war, all the details and interests of savage life would be explained. And before the boy was in his teens he was equipped for the Struggle for Life as his forefathers had never been even in old age. The son, in short, started to evolve where his father left off. Try to realize what it would be for each of us to begin life afresh, to be able to learn nothing by the experiences of others, to live in a dumb and illiterate world, and see what chance the animal had of making pronounced progress until the acquisition of speech. It is not too much to say that speech, if mental evolution is to come to anything or is to be worth anything, is a necessary condition. By it alone, in any degree worth naming, can the fruits of observation and experience of one generation be husbanded to form a new starting point for a second, nor without it could there be any concerted action or social life. The greatness of the human Mind, after all, is due to the tongue, the material instrument of reason, and to Language, the outward expression of the inner life.

As to the exact point of the difference, Mr. Romanes draws the line at the exclusive possession by Man of the power of introspective reflection in the light of self-consciousness. "Wherein," he asks, "does the distinction truly consist? It consists in the power which the human being displays of objectifying ideas, or of setting one state of mind before another state, and contemplating the relation between them. The power to think is—or, as I should prefer to state it, the power to think at all is—the power which is given by introspective reflection in the light of self-consciousness. . . . We have no evidence to show that any animal is capable of thus objectifying its own ideas; and, therefore, we have no evidence that any animal is capable of judgment. Indeed, I will go further and affirm that we have the best evidence which is derivable from what are necessarily ejective sources, to prove that no animal can possibly attain to these excellencies of subjective life." Mr. Romanes proceeds to state the reason why. It is because of "the absence in brutes of the needful conditions to the occurrence of those excellencies as they obtain in themselves . . . the great distinction between the brute and the man really lies behind the faculties both of conception and prediction; it resides in the conditions to the occurrence of either."—Mental Evolution in Animals, p. 175.

The situation is dramatic, that from end to end of the region occupied by these tribes, there stretches the Telegraph connecting Australia with Europe. But what is at once dramatic and pathetic is that the natives know it only in its material relations —as so much wire, the first metal they have ever seen, to cut into lengths for spear-heads.

The Evolution of Language

If Evolution is the method of Creation, the faculty of Speech was no sudden gift. Man's mind is not to be thought of as the cylinder of a phonograph to which ready-made words were spoken and stored up for future use. Before Homo sapiens was evolved he must necessarily have been preceded for a longer or shorter period by Homo alalus, the not-speaking man; and this man had to make his words, and beginning with dumb signs and inarticulate cries to build up a body of Language word by word as the body was built up cell by cell.

The alternative theory of the origin of Language universally held until lately, and expressed in so many words even by the eighth edition of the Encyclopaedia Britannica, that "our first parents received it by immediate inspiration," has the same relation to exact science as the view that the world was made in six days by direct creative fiat. Both are poetically true. But to science, seeking for precise methods of operation, neither is an adequate statement of now ascertained facts. The same processes of research that made the poetic view of creation untenable in the physical realm are now slowly beginning to displace the older view of the origin of speech. That Language should be outside a law whose universality is being established with every step of progress is itself improbable; and now that the field is being exhaustively explored, the proofs that it is no exception multiply on every side. The living interest the mere suggestion gives to the study of Language is obvious. Evolution enters no region—dull, neglected, or remote—of the temple of knowledge without transforming it. Philology, since this wizard touched it, has become one of the most entrancing of the sciences. And Language, from a study which interested only a few specialists, is disclosed as one vast palimpsest, every word and phrase luminous with the inner mind and soul of the past. To penetrate far into this tempting region is beyond our province now. The immediate object is to give a simple sketch of the possible conditions which first led Man to speak; of the principles which apparently guided the formation of his early vocabulary; and of the gradual refining of the means of intercommunication between him and his fellow-men as time passed on. Instead of beginning with words, therefore, we shall begin with Man. For the first condition for understanding the Evolution of Speech is that we take it up as a study from the life, that we place ourselves in the primeval forest with early Man, in touch with the actual scenes in which he lived, and note the real experiences and necessities of such a lot. We may indeed discover in this research small trace of a miraculous inbreathing of formal words. But to make Speech and fit it into a man, after all is said, is less miraculous than to fit a man to make Speech.

One of the earliest devices hit upon in the course of Evolution was the principle of co-operation. Long before men had learned to form themselves into tribes and clans for mutual strength and service, gregariousness was an established institution. The deer had formed themselves into herds, and the monkeys into troops; the birds were in flocks, and the wolves in packs; the bees in hives, and the ants in colonies. And so abundant and dominant in every part of the world are these social types to-day that we may be sure the gregarious state has exceptional advantages in the upward struggle.

One of these advantages, obviously, is the mere physical strength of numbers. But there is another and a much more important one—the mental strength of a combination. Here is a herd of deer, scattered, as they love to be, in a string, quarter of a mile long. Every animal in the herd not only shares the physical strength of all the rest, but their powers of observation. Its foresight in presence of possible danger is the foresight of the herd. It has as many eyes as the herd, as many ears, as many organs of smell, its nervous system extends throughout the whole space covered by the line; its environment, in short, is not only what it hears, sees, smells, touches, tastes, but what every single member hears, sees, smells, touches, tastes. This means an enormous advantage in the Struggle for Life. What deer have to arm themselves most against is surprise. When it comes to an actual fight, comrades are of little use. At that crisis the others run away and leave the victims to their fate. But in helping one another to avert that crisis, the value of this mutual aid is so great that gregarious animals, for the most part timid and defenceless as individuals, have survived to occupy in untold multitudes the highest places in Nature.

The success of the co-operative principle, however, depends upon one condition: the members of the herd must be able to communicate with one another. It matters not how acute the senses of each animal may be, the strength of the column depends on the power to transmit from one to another what impressions each may receive at any moment from without. Without this power the sociality of the herd is stultified; the army, having no signalling department, is powerless as an army. But if any member of the herd is able by motion of head or foot or neck or ear, by any sign or by any sound, to pass on the news that there is danger near, each instantly enters into possession of the faculties of the whole. Each has a hundred eyes, noses, ears. Each has quarter of a mile of nerves. Thus numbers are strength only when strength is coupled with some power of inter-communication by signs. If one herd develops this signalling system and another does not, its chances of survival will be greater. The less equipped herds will be slowly decimated and driven to the wall; and those which survive to propagate their kind will be those whose signal-service is most efficient and complete. Hence the Evolution of the signal-system. Under the influence of Natural Selection its progress was inevitable. New circumstances and relations would in time arise, calling for additions, vocal, visible, audible, to the sign-vocabulary. And as time went on each set of animals would acquire a definite signal-service of its own, elementary to the last degree, yet covering the range of its ordinary experiences and adequate to the expression of its limited mental states.

Now what interests us with regard to these signs is that they are Language. The evolution we have been tracing is nothing less than the first stage in the evolution of Speech. Any means by which information is conveyed from one mind to another is Language. And Language existed on the earth from the day that animals began to live together. The mere fact that animals cling to one another, live together, move about together, proves that they communicate. Among the ants, perhaps the most social of the lower animals, this power is so perfect that they are not merely endowed with a few general signs but seem able to convey information upon matters of detail. Sweeping across country in great armies they keep up communication throughout the whole line, and succeed in conveying to one another information as to the easiest routes, the presence of enemies or obstacles, the proximity of food supplies, and even of the numbers required on emergencies to leave the main band for any special service. Everyone has observed ants stop when they meet one another and exchange a rapid greeting by means of their waving antennae, and it is possibly through these perplexing organs that definite intercourse between one creature and another first entered the world. The exact nature of the antenna-language is not yet fathomed, but the perfection to which it is carried proves that the idea of language generally has existed in nature from the earliest time. Among higher animals various outward expressions of emotions are made, and these become of service in time for the conveyance of information to others. The howl of the dog, the neigh of the horse, the bleat of the lamb, the stamp of the goat, and other signs are all readily understood by other animals. One monkey utters at least six different sounds to express its feelings; and Mr. Darwin has detected four or five modulations in the bark of the dog: "the bark of eagerness, as in the chase; that of anger as well as growling; the yelp or howl of despair when shut up; the baying at night; the bark of joy when starting on a walk with his master; and the very distinct one of demand or supplication, as when wishing for a door or window to be opened.

Now these signs are as much language as spoken words. You have only to evolve this to get all the language the dictionary-maker requires. Any method of communication, as already said, is Language, and to understand Language we must fix in our minds- the idea that it has no necessary connection with actual words. In the simple instances just given there are illustrations of at least three kinds of Language. When a deer throws up its head suddenly, all the other deer throw up their heads. That is a sign. It means "listen." If the first deer sees the object, which has called its attention, to be suspicious, it utters a low note. That is a word. It means "caution." If next it sees the object to be not only suspicious but dangerous it makes a further use of Language—intonation. Instead of the low note "listen," it utters a sharp loud cry that means "Run for your life." Hence these three kinds of Language—a sign or gesture, a note or word, an intonation.

Down to this present hour these are still the three great kinds of Language. The movement of foot or ear have been evolved into the modern gesture or grimace; the note or cry into a word, and the intonation into an emphasis or inflexion of the voice. These are still, indeed, not only the main elements in Language but the only elements. The eloquence which enthrals the legislators of St Stephen's, or the appeal which melts the worshippers at St. Paul's, originated in the voices of the forest and the activities of the ant-hill. To those who have not realized the exceeding smallness of the beginnings of all new developments, the suggestion of science as to the origin of Language, like many of its other suggestions about early stages, will seem almost ludicrous. But a knowledge of two things warns one not to look for surprises at the beginning of Evolution but at the end. In the first place, it is all but a cardinal principle that developments are brought about by minute, slow and insensible degrees. The second fact is even more important. The theatre of change is the actual world, and the exciting cause something really happening in every-day life. Few departures are not made in the air. They arise in connection with some commonplace event; and usually take the shape of some slightly new response. In other connections, of course, the converse is also true, but when a change occurs for the first time in the life of an organism the exciting cause, whatever the internal adaptation, or want of it, is some change in the environment. Among the events then, actually happening in the day's round, we are to seek for the exciting cause of the earliest forms of speech.

The simplest Language open to Man was that which we have already seen to mark the beginning of all Language, the Language of gesture or sign. To the word gesture, however, it is necessary to attach a larger meaning than the term ordinarily expresses to us. It is not to be limited, for example, to visible movements of the limbs or facial muscles. The ejaculations of the savage, the drumming of the gorilla, the screech of the parrot, the crying, growling, purring, hissing, and spitting of other animals are all forms of gesture. Nor is it possible to separate the Language of gesture from the Language of intonation. These have grown up side by side and can neither be distinguished psychologically nor as to priority in the order of Evolution. Intonation, though it has grown to be infinitely the more delicate instrument of the two and is still so important a part of some Languages —the Chinese, for example—as to be an integral part of them, has its roots in the same soil and must be looked upon as, along with it, the earliest form of Language.

That this Gesture-Language marked, if not the dawn, at least a very early stage of Language in the case of Man, there is abundant evidence. Apart from analogy, there are at least three witnesses who may be cited in proof not only of the fact, but of the high perfection to which a Gesture-Language may be carried. The first of these witnesses is the homo alalus, the not-speaking man, of to-day, the deaf-mute. As an actual case of a human being reduced as regards the power of speech to the level of early Man his evidence, even with all allowances for the high development of his mental faculties, is of scientific value. The mere fact that a deaf man is also a dumb man is almost a final answer to the affirmation that the power of speech is an original and intuitive faculty of Man. If it were so, there is no reason why a deaf man should not speak. The vocal apparatus in his case is complete; all that is required to make him utter a definite sound is to hear one. When he hears one, but not till then, he can imitate it. Language, so far as the testimony of the deaf-mute goes, is clearly a matter of imitation. Unable to attain the second stage of Language—words—he has to content himself with the first—signs. And this Language he has evolved to its last perfection. It shows how little the mere utterance of words has to do with Language, that the deaf-mute is able to converse on every-day subjects almost as perfectly as those who can speak. The permutations and combinations that can be produced with ten pliable fingers, or with the varying expressions of the muscles of the face, are endless, and everything that he cares to know can be uttered or translated to him by motion, gesture, and grimace. To give an idea how far gestures can be made to do the work of spoken words, the signs may be described in which a deaf-and-dumb man once told a child's story in presence of Mr. Tylor. "He began by moving his hand, palm down, about a yard from the ground, as we do to show the height of a child— this meant that it was a child he was thinking of. Then he tied an imaginary pair of bonnet-strings under his chin (his usual sign for female), to make it understood that the child was a little girl. The child's mother was then brought on the scene in a similar way. She beckons to the child and gives her twopence, these being indicated by pretending to drop two coins from one hand into the other; if there had been any doubt as to whether they were copper or silver coins, this would have been settled by pointing to something brown or even by one's contemptuous way of handling coppers which at once distinguishes them from silver. The mother also gives the child a jar, shown by sketching its shape with the forefingers in the air, and going through the act of handing it over. Then by imitating the unmistakable kind of twist with which one turns a treacle-spoon, it is made known that it is treacle the child has to buy. Next, a wave of the hand shows the child being sent off on her errand, the usual sign of walking being added, which is made by two fingers walking on the table. The turning of an imaginary door-handle now takes us into the shop, when the counter is shown by passing the flat hands as it were over it. Behind this counter a figure is pointed out; he is shown to be a man by the usual sign of putting one's hand to one's chin and drawing it down where the beard is or would be; then the sign of tying an apron around one's waist adds the information that the man is the shopman. To him the child gives her jar, dropping the money into his hand, and moving her forefinger as if taking up treacle to show what she wants. Then we see the jar put into an imaginary pair of scales which go up and down; the great treacle-jar is brought from the shelf and the little one filled, with the proper twist to take up the last trickling thread; the grocer puts the two coins in the till, and the little girl sets off with the jar. The deaf-and-dumb story-teller went on to show in pantomime how the child, looking down at the jar, saw a drop of treacle on the rim, wiped it off with her finger, and put the finger in her mouth, how she was tempted to take more, how her mother found her out by the spot of treacle on her pinafore, and so forth.

A second witness is savage Man. Some of the more primitive races, far as they have evolved past the alalus stage, still cling to the gesture-language which bulked so largely in the intercourse of their ancestors. No one who has witnessed a conversation—one says "witnessed," for it is more seeing than hearing—between two different tribes of Indians can have any doubt of the working efficiency of this method of speech. After ten minutes of almost pure pantomime each will have told the other everything that it is needful to say. Indians of different tribes, indeed, are able to communicate most perfectly on all ordinary subjects with no more use of the voice than that required for the emission of a few different kinds of grunts. The fact that stranger tribes make so large a use of gesture in expressing themselves to one another does not, of course, imply that each has not a word-language of its own. But few of the Languages of primitive peoples are complete without the additions which gesture offers. There are gaps in the vocabulary of almost all savage tribes due to the fact that in actual speech the lacunae are bridged by signs, and many of their words belong more to the category of signs than to that of words.

The final witness is the first attempt at Language of a little child. Universally an infant opens communication with the mental world around it in the primitive language of gesture and tone. Long before it has learned to speak, without the use of a single word it conveys information as to fundamental wants, and expresses all its varying moods and wishes with a vehemence and point which are almost the envy of riper years. The interesting thing about this is that it is spontaneous. In later childhood it has to be taught to speak—because speech is a fine art—but to utter the hereditary and primitive Language of mankind requires no prompting. Words are conventional, movements and sounds are natural. The Language of the nursery is the native Language of the forest, the inarticulate cry of the animal, the intonation of the savage. To quote from Mallery:—"The wishes and emotions of very young children are conveyed in a small number of sounds, but in a great variety of gestures and facial expressions. A child's gestures are intelligent long in advance of speech; although very early and persistent attempts are made to give it instruction in the latter but none in the former, from the time when it begins risu cognoscere matrem. It learns words only as they are taught, and learns them through the medium of signs which are not expressly taught. Long after familiarity with speech it consults the gestures and facial expressions of its parents and nurses, as if seeking them to translate or explain their words. These facts are important in reference to the biologic law that the order of development of the individual is the same as that of the species. . . . The insane understand and obey gestures when they have no knowledge whatever of words. It is also found that semi-idiotic children who cannot be taught more than the merest rudiment of speech can receive a considerable amount of information through signs, and can express themselves by them. Sufferers from aphasia continue to use appropriate gestures. A stammerer, too, works his arms and features as if determined to get his thoughts out, in a manner not only suggestive of the physical struggle, but of the use of gesture as a hereditary expedient.

The survival both of gesture and intonation in modern adult speech, and especially the unconsciousness of their use, illustrate how indelibly these primitive forms of Language are embedded in the human race. There are doubtless exceptions, but it is probably the rule that gestures are mainly called in to supplement expression when the subject-matter of discourse does not belong to the highest ranges of thought, or the speaker to the loftiest type of oratory. The higher levels of thought were reached when the purer forms of spoken Language had become the vehicle of expression; and, as has often been noticed, when a speaker soars into a very lofty region, or allows his mind to grapple intensely and absorbingly with an exalted theme, he becomes more and more motionless, and only resumes the gesture-language when he descends to commoner levels. It is not only that a fine speaker has a greater command of words and is able to dispense with auxiliaries —as a master of style can dispense with the use of italics—but that, at all events, in the case of abstract thought, it is untranslatable into gesture-speech. Gestures are suggestions and reminders of things seen and heard. They are nearly all attached to objects or to moods, and rival words only when used of every-day things. "No sign talker," Mr. Romanes reminds us, "with any amount of time at his disposal, could translate into the language of gesture a page of Kant.

The next stage in the Evolution of Language must have been reached as naturally as the Language of gesture and tone. From the gesture-language to mixtures of signs and sounds, and finally to the specialization of sound into words, is a necessary transition. Apart from the fact that gestures and tones have limits, circumstances must often have arisen in the life of early Man when gesture was impossible. A sign Language is of no use when one savage is at one end of a wood and his wife at the other. He must now roar; and to make his roar explicit, he must have a vocabulary of roars, and of all shades of roars. In the darkness of night also, his signs are useless, and he must now whisper and have a vocabulary of whispers. Nor is it difficult to conceive where he got his first brief list of words. Instead of drawing things in the air with his finger, he would now try to imitate their sounds. Everything around him that conveyed any impression of sound would have associated with it some self-expressive word, which all familiar with the original sound could instantly recognize. Imagine, for instance, a herd of buffalo browsing in a glade of the African forest. The vanguard, some little distance from its neighbours, hears the low growl of a lion. That growl, of course, is Language, and the buffalo understands it as well as we do when the word "lion" is pronounced. Between the word "lion" spoken, and the object lion growled, there is no difference in the effect. Suppose, next, the buffalo wished to convey to its comrades the knowledge that a lion was near, a lion and not some other animal, it might imitate this growl. It is not likely that it would do so; some other sign expressing alarm in general would probably be used, for the discrimination of the different sources of danger is probably an achievement beyond this animal's power. But if Primitive Man was placed under the same circumstances, granting that he had begun in a feeble way to exercise mind, he would almost certainly come in time to denote a lion by an imitated growl, a wolf by an imitated whine, and so on. The sighing of the wind, the flowing of the stream, the beat of the surf, the note of the bird, the chirp of the grasshopper, the hiss of the snake, would each be used to express these things. And gradually a Language would be built up which included all the things in the environment with which sound was either directly, indirectly, or accidentally associated.

That this method of word-making is natural is seen in the facility with which it is still used by children; and from the early age at which they begin to employ it, the sound Language is clearly one of the very first forms of speech. All a child's words are of course gathered through the sense of hearing, but if it can itself pick up a word direct from the object, it will use it long before it elects to repeat the conventional name taught it by its nurse. The child who says moo for cow, or bow-wow for dog, or tick-tick for watch, or puff-puff for train, is an authority on the origin of human speech. Its father, when he talks of the hum of machinery or the boom of the cannon, when he calls champagne fizz or a less aristocratic beverage pop, is following in the wake of the inventors of Language. Among savage peoples, and especially those encountering the first rush of new things and thoughts brought them by the advancing wave of civilization, word-making is still going on; and wherever possible the favourite principle seems to be that of sound.

How full all Languages are of these sound-words is known to the philologist, though multitudes of words in every Language have had their pedigree effaced or obscured by time. "An Englishman would hardly guess from the present pronunciation and meaning of the word pipe what its origin was; yet when he compares it with the Low Latin pipa, French pipe, pronounced more like our word peep, to chirp, and meaning such a reed-pipe as shepherds played on, he then sees how cleverly the very sound of the musical pipe has been made into a word for all kinds of tubes, such as tobacco-pipes and water-pipes. Words like this travel like Indians on the war-path, wiping out their footmarks as they go. For all we know multitudes of our ordinary words may have thus been made from real sounds, but have now lost beyond recovery the traces of their first expressiveness. In the Chinuk language of the West Coast of America, to cite a few more of Tylor's instances, a tavern is called a "heehee-house," that is a laughter house, or an amusement house, the word for amusement being taken by an obvious association from the laughter which it excites. How indirect a derivation may be is illustrated by the word which the Basutos of South Africa use for courtier. The buzz of a certain fly resembles the sound ntsi-ntsi, and they apply this word to those who buzz round the chief as a fly buzzes round a piece of meat. As everyone knows "papa" for father, is evolved into papa the pope, and "abba" the Hebrew for father into abbot. For plurals, a doubling of the word is often used, but no doubt at first quantity was expressed by gestures or by numbering on the fingers. "Orang" is the Malay for Man, "Orang-orang" for men, while "Orangutan" is wild man. Verbs are formed on the same principle as nouns. In the Tecuna language of Brazil the verb

to sneeze is haitschu, while the Welsh for a sneeze is tis. Other verbs which came
to have large and comprehensive meanings arose out of the simple activities and
occupations of primitive life. Thus the first verb in the Bible, the Hebrew "bara"
now meaning create, was originally used for cutting or hewing, the first step in
making things. In the Borneo language of Africa, the verb "to make" comes from
the word tando, to weave. In English, "to suffer" meant to bear as a burden, and
to "apprehend an idea" was originally to "catch hold" of some "sight." Even Max
Muller, who opposes the onomatopoetic theory with regard to the origin of most
words, agrees that the sounds of the occupation of men, and especially of men
working together, and making special sounds at their task—such as builders,
soldiers, and sailors—are widely represented in modern speech.

Though mimicry, sometimes exact, but probably more often a mere echo or
suggestion of the sound to be recalled, is responsible for some of the material of
Language, multitudes of words appear to have no such origin. There are infinitely
more words than sounds in the world; and even things which have very distinct
sounds have been named without any regard to them. The inventors of the word
watch, for instance, did not call it tick-tick but watch, the idea being taken from
the watchman who walked about at night and kept the time; and when the
steam-engine appeared, instead of taking the obvious sound-name puff-puff, it
was called engine (Lat. ingenium), to signify that it was a work of genius. These
modern words, however, are the coinages of an intellectual age, and it was to be
expected that the inventors should look deeper below the surface. How those
words which have no apparent association with sound were formed in early times
remains a mystery. With some the original sound-association has probably been
lost; in the case of others, the association may have been so indirect as to be now
untraceable. The sounds available in savage life for word-making could never
have been so numerous as the things requiring names, and as civilization
advanced the old words would be used in new connections, while wholly new
terms must have been coined from time to time. Both these methods—the habit
of generalizing unconsciously from single terms, and the trick of coining new
words in a wholly conventional way—are still continually employed by savages as
well as by children. Thus, to take an example of the first, Mr. John Moir, one of the
earliest white men to settle in East Central Africa, was at once named by the
natives Mandala, which means "a reflection in still water," because he wore on his
eyes what looked to them a still water (spectacles). Afterwards they came to call
not only Mr. Moir by that name, but spectacles, and finally—when it entered the
country—glass itself. Examples of generalization among children abound in every
nursery. A child is taken to the window by his nurse to see the moon. The easy
monosyllable is caught up at once, and for some time the child applies it
indiscriminately to anything bright or shining—the gas, the candle, the firelight
are each "the moon." Mr. Romanes records a case where a child made a similar
use of the word star—the gas, the candle, the firelight were each "a star." If the
makers of Language proceeded on this principle, no wonder the philologist has
riddles to read. How often must the savage children of the world have started off
naming things from two such different points? Mr. Romanes mentions a still more
elaborate example which was furnished him by Mr. Darwin: "The child, who was
just beginning to speak, called a duck `quack,' and, by special association, it also
called water `quack.' By an appreciation of the resemblance of qualities, it next
extended the term `quack' to denote all birds and insects on the one hand, and all
fluid substances on the other. Lastly, by a still more delicate appreciation of

resemblance, the child eventually called all coins `quack,' because on the back of a French sou it had once seen the representation of an eagle. Hence, to the child, the sign `quack,' from having originally had a very specialized meaning, became more and more extended in its significance, until it now seems to designate such apparently-different objects as `fly,' `wine,' and `coin.'

The instructiveness of this, in showing the reason why philology is often so helplessly at a loss in tracking far-strayed words to their original sense, is plain. In the nature of the case, the onomatopoetic theory can never be proved in more than a fraction of cases. So cunning is the mind in associating ideas, so swift in making new departures, that the clue to multitudes of words must be obliterated by time, even if the first forms and spellings of the words themselves remain in their original integrity —which rarely happens—to offer a feasible point to start the search from.

But it is far from necessary to assume that all words should have had a rational ancestry. On the contrary many words are probably deliberate artificial inventions. When not only every human being, but every savage and every child has the ability as well as the right to call anything it likes by any name it chooses, it is vain in every case to seek for any general principle underlying the often arbitrary conjunctions of letters and sounds which we call words. Words cannot all at least be treated with the same scientific regard as we would treat organic forms. When dissected, in the nature of the case, they cannot be expected to reveal specific structure such as one finds in a fern or a cray-fish. A fern or a cray-fish is the expression of an infinitely subtle and intricate adaptation, while a word may be a mere caprice. Perhaps, indeed, the greatest marvel about philology is that there should be a philology at all—that Languages should be so rich in association, so pregnant with the history and poetry of the past. Into the problem, therefore, of how the infinite variety of words in a Language was acquired it is unnecessary to enter at length. Once the idea had dawned of expressing meaning by sounds, the formation of words and even of Languages is a mere detail. We have probably all invented words. Almost every family of children invents words of its own, and cases are known where quite considerable Languages have been manufactured in the nursery. When boys play at brigands and pirates they invent pass-words and names, and from mere love of secrets and mysteries concoct vocabularies which no one can understand but themselves.

This simple fact indeed has been used with great plausibility to account for differences in dialect among different tribes, and even for the partial origin of new Languages. Thus the structure of the Indian languages has long puzzled philologists. Whitney informs us that as regards the material of expression, there is "irreconcilable diversity" among them. "There are a very considerable number of groups between whose significant signs exist no more apparent correspondences than between those of English, Hungarian, and Malay; none namely which may not be merely fortuitous." To account for these dialects a suggestion, as interesting as it is ingenious, has been advanced by Dr. Hale. Imagine the case of a family of Red Indians, father, mother, and half a dozen children, in the vicissitudes of war, cut off from their tribe. Suppose the father to be scalped and the mother soon to die. The little ones left to themselves in some lonely valley, living upon roots and herbs, would converse for a time by using the few score words they had heard from their parents. But as they grew up they would require new words and would therefore coin them. As they became a tribe they would require more words, and so in time a Language might arise, all the words expressive of the simpler relations—father, mother, tent, fire—being common to other Indian Languages, but all the later words purely arbitrary and necessarily a standing puzzle to philology. The curious thing is that this theory is borne out by some most interesting geographical facts. "If, under such circumstances, disease, or the casualties of a hunter's life should carry off the parents, the survival of the children would, it is evident, depend mainly upon the nature of the climate and the ease with which food could be procured at all seasons of the year. In ancient Europe, after the present climatal conditions were established, it is doubtful if a family of children under ten years of age could have lived through a single winter. We are not, therefore, surprised to find that no more than four or five linguistic stocks are represented in Europe. Of North America, east of the Rocky Mountains and north of the tropics, the same may be said. The climate and the scarcity of food in winter forbid us to suppose that a brood of orphan children could have survived, except possibly, by a fortunate chance, in some favoured spot on the shore of the Mexican Gulf, where shell-fish, berries, and edible roots are abundant and easy of access. But there is one region where Nature seems to offer herself as the willing nurse and bountiful stepmother of the feeble and unprotected. Of all countries on the globe, there is probably not one in which a little flock of very young children would find the means of sustaining existence more readily than in California. Its wonderful climate, mild and equable beyond example, is well known. Half the months are rainless. Snow and ice are almost strangers. There are fully two hundred cloudless days in every year. Roses bloom in the open air through all seasons. Berries of many sorts are indigenous and abundant. Large fruits and edible nuts on low and pendant boughs may be said in Milton's phrase to `hang amiable.' Need we wonder that in such a mild and fruitful region, a great number of separate tribes were found speaking languages which careful investigation has classed in nineteen distinct linguistic stocks?" Even more striking is the case of Oregon on the Californian border, which is also a favoured and luxuriant land. "The number of linguistic stocks in this narrow district is more than twice as large as in the whole of Europe.

In such ways as these we may conceive of early Man building up the fabric of speech. In time his vocabulary would enlarge and become, so far as objects in the immediate environment were concerned, fairly complete. As Man gained more knowledge of the things around him, as he came into larger relations with his fellows, as life became more rich and complex, this accumulation of words would go on, each art as it was introduced creating new terms, each science pouring in contributions to the fund, until the materials of human speech became more and more complete. This process was never finished. The evolution of Language is still going on. No corroboration of the theory of the evolution of Language could be more perfect than the simple fact that it has gone on steadily down to the present hour and is going on now. Tens of thousands of words—no longer now onomatopoetic—have been evolved since Johnson compiled his dictionary, and every year sees additions not only to technical terms but to the Language of the people. The English Language is now being grown on two or three different kinds of soil, and the different fruits and flavours that result are intercharged and mixed, to enrich, or adulterate, the common English tongue. The mere fact that Language-making is a living art at the present hour, if not an argument against the theory that Language is a special gift, at least shows that Man has a special gift of making Language. If Man could manufacture words in any quantity, there was little reason why he should have been presented with them ready-made. The power to manufacture them is gift enough, and none the less a gift that we know some of the steps by which it was given, or at least through which it was exercised. But if the very words were given him as they stand, it is more than singular that so many of them should bear traces of another origin. Even Trench at this point succumbs to the theory of development, and his testimony is the more valuable that it is evidently so very much against the grain to admit it. He begins by stating apparently the opposite:—"The truer answer to the inquiry how language arose is this: God gave man language just as He gave him reason, and just because He gave him reason; for what is man's word but his reason coming forth that it may behold itself? They are indeed so essentially one and the same that the Greek language has one word for them both. He gave it to him, because he could not be man, that is, a social being, without it." Yet he is too profound a student of words to fail to qualify this, and had he failed to do so every page in his well-known book had judged him. "Yet," he continues, "this must not be taken to affirm that man started at the first furnished with a full-formed vocabulary of words, and as it were with his first dictionary and first grammar ready-made to his hands. He did not thus begin the world with names, but with the power of naming: for man is not a mere speaking machine; God did not teach him words, as one of us teaches a parrot, from without; but gave him a capacity, and then evoked the capacity which He gave.

If the theory just given as to the formation of Language, or at least as to the possible formation of Language, be more than a fairy tale, there is another quarter in which corroboration of an important kind should lie. Hitherto we have examined, as witnesses, the makers of words; it may be worth while for a moment to place in the witness-box the words themselves. A chemist has two methods of determining the composition of any body, analysis and synthesis. Having seen how words may be built up, it remains for us to see whether on analysis they bear trace of having been built up in the way, and from the elements, suggested. Comparative Philology has now made an actual investigation into the words and structure of all known Languages, and the information sought by the evolutionist lies ready-made to his hand. So far as controversy might be expected to arise here on the theory of development itself, there is none. For the first fact to interest us in this new region is that every student of Language seems to have been compelled to give in his adherence to the general theory of Evolution. All agree with Renan that "Sans doute les langues, comme tout ce qui est organise, sont sujettes a la loi du development graduel." And even Max Muller, the least thorough-going from an evolutionary point of view of all philologists, asserts that "no student of the science of Language can be anything but an evolutionist, for, wherever he looks, he sees nothing but evolution going on all around him."

The outstanding discovery of the dissector of words is that, vast and complex as Languages appear, they are really composed of few and simple elements. Take the word "evolutionary." The termination "ary" is a late addition added to this and to thousands of other words for a special purpose; the same applies to the syllable "tion." The first letter e distinguishes evolution from convolution, revolution, involution, and is also a later growth. None of these extra syllables is of first importance; by themselves they have almost no meaning. The part which will not disappear or melt away into mere grammar, on which the stress of the sense hangs, is the syllable "vol" or "volv," and, so far as the English language is concerned, it is to be looked upon as the root. By running it to earth in older languages its source is found in a still more radical word, and therefore it must next be blotted out of the list of primitive words. By patient comparison of all other words with all other words, of Languages with Languages, and apparent roots with apparent roots, the supposed primitive roots of Language have been found. Just as all the multifarious objects in the material world—water, air, earth, flesh, bone, wood, iron, paper, cloth—are resolvable by the chemist into some sixty-eight elements, so all the words in each of the three or four great groups of Language yield on the last analysis only a few hundred original roots. That still further analysis may break down some or many of these is not impossible. But the facts as they stand are all significant. The further we go back into the past the Languages become thinner and thinner, the words fewer and fewer, the grammar poorer and poorer. Of the thousand known Languages it has been found possible to reduce all to three or four—probably three —great families; and each of these in turn is capable of almost unlimited philological pruning. In analyzing the Sanskrit language, Professor Max Muller reduces its whole vocabulary to 121 roots—the 121 "original concepts." "These 121 concepts constitute the stock-in-trade with which I maintain that every thought that has ever passed through the mind of India, so far as known to us in its literature, has been expressed. It would have been easy to reduce that number still further, for there are several among them which could be ranged together under more general concepts. But I leave this further reduction to others, being satisfied as a first attempt with having shown how small a number of seeds may produce, and has produced, the enormous intellectual vegetation that has covered the soil of India from the most distant antiquity to the present day.

That a "first attempt" should have succeeded in reducing this vast family of Languages to 121 words is significant. The exhumation by philology of this early cluster reminds one of the discovery of the segmented ovum in embryology. Such clusters appear at an early stage in the history of all developments. The processes which precede this stage are of the utmost subtlety, but in embryology they have yielded to the later analysis of the microscope. So it may be one day with the natural history of Language. We may never, for obvious reasons, get back to the actual beginning, but we may get nearer. When the embryologist reached his cluster of cells in the segmented ovum, he did not believe he had found the dawn of life. What further the philologist may find remains a mystery. Where these 121 words came from may never be known. But the development from that point sufficiently shows that words, like everything else, have followed the universal law, and that Languages, starting from small beginnings, have grown in volume, intricacy, and richness, as time rolled on. "All philologists," says Romanes, "will now agree with Geiger—'Language diminishes the further we look back, in such a way that we cannot forbear concluding it must once have had no existence at all.'"

The history of progress for a long time henceforth is the history of the progress of language and the increase in intelligence which necessarily went along with it. From being able to say what he knew, Man went on to write what he knew. The Evolution of writing went through the same general stages as the Evolution of Speech. First there was the onomatopoetic writing—as it were, the growl-writing—the ideograph, the imitation of an actual object. This is the form we find fossil in the Egyptian hieroglyphic. For a man a man was drawn, for a camel a camel, for a hut a hut. Then intonation was added—accents, that is, for extra meaning or extra emphasis. Then to save time the objects were drawn in shorthand—a couple of dashes for the limbs and one across, as in the Chinese for man; a square in the same language for a field; two strokes at an obtuse angle, suggesting the roof, for a house. To express further qualities, these abbreviated pictures were next compounded in ingenious ways. A man and a field together conveyed the idea of wealth, and because a man with a field was rich, he was supposed to be happy, and the same combination stood, and stands to this day, for contentment. When a roof is drawn and a woman beneath it—or the strokes which represent a roof and a woman—we have the idea of a woman at home, a woman at peace, and hence the symbol comes to stand for quietness and rest. Chinese writing is picture-writing with the pictures degenerated into dashes—a lingual form of the modern impressionism.

When writing was fully evolved, this height was only the starting-point for some new development. Every summit in Evolution is the base of some grander peak. Speech, whether by writing or by spoken word, is too crude and slow to keep pace with the needs of the now swiftly ascending mind. Man's larger life demands a further specialization of this power. He learned to speak at first because he could not convey his thoughts to his wife at the other side of the wood. It was Space that made him speak. He now learns to speak better because he cannot convey his thoughts to the other end of the world. This new distance-language began again at the beginning, just as all Language does, by employing signs. Man invented the telegraph—a little needle which makes signs to some one at the other side of the world. The telegraph is a gesture-language, and is therefore only a primitive stage. Man found this out and from signs went on to sounds—he invented the telephone. By all the traditions of Evolution this marvellous instrument ought to be, and is even now on the verge of being, the vehicle of the distance-language of the future.

Is this the end? It is by no means likely. The mind is feeling about already for more perfect forms of human intercourse than telegraphed or telephoned words. As there was a stage in the ascent of Man at which the body was laid aside as a finished product, and made to give way to Mind, there may be a stage in the Evolution of Mind when its material achievements—its body—shall be laid aside and give place to a higher form of Mind. Telepathy has already become a word, not a word for thought-reading or muscle-reading, but a scientific word. It means "the ability of one mind to impress, or to be impressed by another mind otherwise than through the recognized channels of sense. By men of science, adepts in mental analysis, aware of all sources of error, armed against fraud, this subject is now being made the theme of exhaustive observation. It is too soon to pronounce. Practically we are in the dark. But there are those in this fascinating and mysterious region who tell us that the possibilities of a more intimate fellowship of man with man, and soul with soul, are not to be looked upon as settled by our present views of matter or of mind. However little we know of it, however remote we are from it, whether it ever be realized or not, telepathy is theoretically the next stage in the Evolution of Language. As we have seen, the introduction of speech into the world was delayed, not because the possibilities of it were not in Nature, but because the instrument was not quite ready. Then the instrument came, and Man spoke. The development of the organ and the development of the function went on together, arrived together, were perfected together. What delayed the gesture-language of the telegraph was not that electricity was not in Nature, but the want of the instrument. When that came, the gesture-language came, and both were perfected together. What delayed the telephone was not that its principle was not in Nature, but that the instrument was not ready. What now delays its absolute victory of space is not that space cannot be bridged, but that it is not ready. May it not be that that which delays the power to transport and drive one's thought as thought to whatever spot one wills, is not the fact that the possibility is withheld by Nature, but that the hour is not quite come—that the instrument is not yet fully ripe? Are there no signs, is the feeling after it no sign, are there not even now some facts, to warrant us in treating it, after all that Evolution has given us, as a still possible gift to the human race? What strikes one most in running the eye up this graduated ascent is that the movement is in the direction of what one can only call spirituality. From the growl of a lion we have passed to the whisper of a soul; from the motive fear, to the motive sympathy; from the icy physical barriers of space, to a nearness closer than breathing; from the torturing slowness of time to time's obliteration. If Evolution reveals anything, if science itself proves anything, it is that Man is a spiritual being and that the direction of his long career is towards an ever larger, richer, and more exalted life. On the final problem of Man's being the voice of science is supposed to be dumb. But this gradual perfecting of instruments, and, as each arrives, the further revelation of what lies behind in Nature, this gradual refining of the mind, this increasing triumph over matter, this deeper knowledge, this efflorescence of the soul, are facts which even Science must reckon with. Perhaps, after all, Victor Hugo is right: "I am the tadpole of an archangel."

Before closing this outline two of the many omitted points may be briefly referred to. In thinking of Language as a "discovery," it is not necessary to assume that that discovery involved the pre-existence of very high mental powers. These were probably developed pari passu with Speech, but did not necessarily ante-date it to such a degree as to make the preceding argument a petitio principii. Obviously the discovery of Language could not in the first instance have been responsible for the Evolution of Mind since Man must already have had Mind enough to discover it. But this does not necessarily imply any very high grade of intellect—very high, that is to say, as compared with other contemporary animals—for it is possible that a comparatively slight rise in intelligence might have led to the initial step from which all the others might follow in rapid succession. An illustration, suggested by a remark of Cope's, may help to make plain how a very slight cause may initiate changes of an almost radical order and on the most gigantic scale.

In part of the Arctic regions at this moment there is no such thing as liquid. Matter is only known there in the solid form. The temperature may be thirty-one degrees below zero, or thirty-one degrees above zero without making the slightest difference; there can be nothing there but ice, glacier, and those crystals of ice which we call snow. But suppose the temperature rose two degrees, the difference would be indescribable. While no change for sixty degrees below that point made the least difference, the almost inappreciable addition of two degrees changes the country into a world of water. The glaciers, under the new conditions, retreat into the mountains, the vesture of ice drops into the sea, a garment of greenness clothes the land. So, in the animal world, a very small rise beyond the animal maximum may open the door for a revolution. With a brain of so many cubic inches, and so many pounds of brain matter, we have animal intelligence. Everything below that limit is animal, and the number of inches or pounds below it makes no difference. But pass to a brain not a few but many pounds heavier, many cubic inches larger, and very much more convoluted, and it is conceivable that in passing from the lower to the higher figures some such change might occur as that which differentiates solid from liquid in the case of water. What the chemist calls a "critical point" might thus be passed, and from a condition associated with certain properties—though in the brain we must speak of accompaniments rather than properties—a condition associated with certain other properties might be the result. Thus, as Cope says, "some Rubicon has been crossed, some flood-gate has been opened, which marks one of Nature's great transitions, such as have been called `expression-points' of progress." A slight rise in intelligence might lead to the first acquisition of Speech, and from this point the rise might be at once exceedingly swift and in directions wholly new. The illustration is not to be taken for more than it seeks to illustrate—which is not the method of transition as to qualitative detail, but simply the fact that an apparently slight change may have startling and indefinite results.

The last difficulty is this. If the connection between Mind and Language is so vital, why do not Birds, many of which apparently speak, emulate Man in mental power? If his speech is largely responsible for his intelligence, why have not Birds —the parrot, for instance—attained the same intelligence? Several answers might be suggested to the question, and several kinds of answers— biological, physiological, philological, and psychological. But the real answer is the general one, that to make animals human required a conspiracy of circumstances which neither Birds nor any other animal fell heir to. It was one chance in a million that the multitude of co-operating conditions which pushed Man onward were fulfilled; and though it may never be known what these conditions were, it was doubtless from the failure on the one hand to meet one or more of them, and on the other from the success with which openings in other directions were pursued by competing species, that Man was left alone during the later aeons of his ascent.

The progenitors of Birds and the progenitors of Man at a very remote period were probably one. But at a certain point they parted company and diverged hopelessly and for ever. The Birds took one road, the Mammals another; the Mammals for the most part kept to the ground, the Birds took to the air. One consequence of this expedient in the case of the Birds was disastrous. For observe the cost to them of the aerial mode of life. The wing was made at the expense of the hand. With this consummate organ buried in feathers, the use which the higher Vertebrates made of it was denied them. Birds have the bones for a hand, could have had a hand, but they waived their right to it. When it is considered how much Man owes to the hand it may be conceived how much they have lost by the want of it. Had Man not been a "tool-using animal," he had probably never become a Man; the Bird, partly because it placed itself out of the running here, has never been anything but a Bird. To one organism only was it given to keep on the path of progress from the beginning to the end, and so fulfil without deviation or relapse the final purpose of Evolution.

Among the Coral Islands of the Pacific the savages everywhere speak of the white residents in New Caledonia as the Wee-wee men, or Wee-wees. Cannibals on a dozen different islands, speaking as many languages, have all this name in common. New Caledonia is a French Penal Settlement, containing thousands of French convicts, and one's first crude thought is that the Wee-wees are so named from their size. A moment's reflection, however, shows that it is taken from their sounds—that in fact we have here a very pretty example of modern onomatopoeia. These convicts, freed or escaped, find their way over the Pacific group; and the natives, seizing at once upon their characteristic sound, know them as

Oui-oui's—a name which has now become general for all Frenchmen in the Southern Pacific.

The construction of the mouth and lips has of course had something to do with differences in Languages, and even with the possibility of language in the case of Man. You must have your trumpet before you can get the sound of a trumpet. One reason why many animals have no speech is simply that they have not the mechanism which by any possibility could produce it. They might have a Language, but nothing at all like human Language. It is one of the significant notes in Evolution that Man, almost alone among vertebrates, has a material body so far developed as to make it an available instrument for speech. There was almost certainly a time when this was to him a physical impossibility.

"The acquisition of articulate speech," says Prof. Macalister, "became possible to man only when the alveolar arch and palatine area became shortened and widened, and when his tongue, by its accommodation to the modified mouth, became shorter and more horizontally flattened, and the higher refinements of pronunciation depend for their production upon the more extensive modifications in the same direction." Even for differences in dialect, as the same writer points out, there is a physical basis. "With the macrodont alveolar arch and the corresponding modified tongue, sibilation is a difficult feat to accomplish, and hence the sibilant sounds are practically unknown in all the Australian dialects."—British Association: Anthropological Section. Edinb., 1891.

The Struggle for Life

Matthew Arnold, in a well -remembered line, describes a bird in Kensington Gardens "deep in its unknown day's employ." But, peace to the poet, its employ is all too certain. Its day is spent in struggling to get a living; and a very hard day it is. It awoke at daybreak and set out to catch its morning meal; but another bird was awake before it, and it lost its chance. With fifty other breakfastless birds, it had to bide its time, to scour the country; to prospect the trees, the grass, the ground; to lie in ambush; to attack and be defeated; to hope and be forestalled. At every meal the same programme is gone through, and every day. As the seasons change the pressure becomes more keen. Its supplies are exhausted, and it has to take wing for hundreds and thousands of miles to find new hunting-ground. This is how birds live, and this is how birds are made. They are the children of Struggle. Beak and limb, claw and wing, shape, strength, all down to the last detail, are the expressions of their mode of life.

This is how the early savage lived, and this is how he was made. The first practical problem in the Ascent of Man was to get him started on his upward path. It was not enough for Nature to equip him with a body, and plant his foot on the lowest rung of the ladder. She must introduce into her economy some great principle which should secure, not for him alone but for every living thing, that they should work upward toward the top. The inertia of things is such that without compulsion they will never move. And so admirably has this compulsion been applied that its forces are hidden in the very nature of life itself—the very act of living contains within it the principles of progress. An animal cannot be without becoming.

The first great principle into the hands of which this mighty charge was given is the Struggle for Life. It is one of the chief keys for unlocking the mystery of Man's Ascent, and so important in all development that Mr. Darwin assigns it the supreme rank among the factors in Evolution. "Unless," he says "it be thoroughly engrained in the mind, the whole economy of Nature, with every fact on distribution, rarity, abundance, extinction, and variation, will be dimly seen or quite misunderstood." How, under the pressures of this great necessity to work for a living, the Ascent of Man has gone on, we have now to inquire. Though not to the extent that is usually supposed, yet in part under this stimulus, he has slowly emerged from the brute-existence, and, entering a path where the possibilities of development are infinite, has been pushed on from stage to stage, without premeditation, or design, or thought on his part, until he arrived at that further height where, to the unconscious compulsions of a lower environment, there were added those high incitements of conscious ideals which completed the work of creating him a Man.

Start with a comparatively unevolved savage, and see what the Struggle for Life will do for him. When we meet him first he is sitting, we shall suppose, in the sun. Let us also suppose—and it requires no imagination to suppose it—that he has no wish to do anything else than sit in the sun, and that he is perfectly contented, and perfectly happy. Nature around him, visible and invisible, is as still as he is, as inert apparently, as unconcerned. Neither molests the other; they have no connection with each other. Yet it is not so. That savage is the victim of a conspiracy. Nature has designs upon him, wants to do something to him. That something is to move him. Why does it wish to move him? Because movement is work, and work is exercise, and exercise may mean a further evolution of the part of him that is exercised. How does it set about moving him? By moving itself. Everything else being in motion, it is impossible for him to resist. The sun moves away to the west and he must move or freeze with cold. As the sun continues to move, twilight falls and wild animals move from their lairs and he must move or be eaten. The food he ate in the morning has dissolved and moved away to nourish the cells of his body, and more food must soon be moved to take its place or he must starve. So he starts up, he works, he seeks food, shelter, safety; and those movements make marks in his body, brace muscles, stimulate nerves, quicken intelligence, create habits, and he becomes more able and more willing to repeat these movements and so becomes a stronger and a higher man. Multiply these movements and you multiply him. Make him do things he has never done before, and he will become what he never was before. Let the earth move round in its orbit till the sun is far away and the winter snows begin to fall. He must either move away, and move away very fast, to find the sun again; or he must chase, and also very fast, some thick-furred animal, and kill it, and clothe himself with its skin. Thus from a man he has become a hunter, a different kind of a man, a further man. He did not wish to become a hunter; he had to become a hunter. All that he wished was to sit in the sun and be let alone, and but for a Nature around him which would not rest, or let him alone, he would have sat on there till he died. The universe has to be so ordered that that which Man would not have done alone he should be compelled to do. In other words it was necessary to introduce into Nature, and into Human Nature, some such principle as the Struggle for Life. For the first law of Evolution is simply the first law of motion. "Every body continues in a state of rest, or of uniform motion in a straight line, unless it is compelled by impressed forces to change that state." Nature supplied that savage with the impressed forces, with something which he was compelled to respond to. Without that, he would have continued for ever as he was.

Apart from the initial appetite, Hunger, the stimulus of Environment—that which necessitates Man to struggle for life—is two-fold. The first is inorganic nature, including heat and cold, climate and weather, earth, air, water—the material world. The second is the world of life, comprehending all plants and animals, and especially those animals against whom primitive Man has always to struggle most—other primitive Men. All that Man is, all the arts of life, all the gifts of civilization, all the happiness and joy and progress of the world, owe much of their existence to that double war.

Follow it a little further. Go back to a time when Man was just emerging from the purely animal state, when he was in the condition described by Mr. Darwin, "a tailed quadruped probably arboreal in its habits," and when in his glimmering consciousness mind was feeling about for its first uses in snatching some novel success in the Struggle for Life. This hypothetical creature, so far as bodily structure was concerned, was presumably not very vigorous. Had he been more vigorous he might never have evolved at all; as it was, he fled for refuge not to his body but to a stratagem of the Mind. When threatened by a comrade, or pressed by an alien-species, he called in a simple foreign aid to help him in the

Struggle—the branch of a tree. Whether the discovery was an accident; whether the idea was caught from the falling of a bough, or a blow from a branch waving in the wind, is of no consequence. This broken branch became the first weapon. It was the father of all clubs. The day this discovery was made, the Struggle for Life took a new departure. Hitherto animals fought with some specialized part of their own bodies—tooth, limb, claw. Now they took possession of the armoury of material Nature.

This invention of the club was soon followed by another change. To use a club effectively, or to keep a good look-out for enemies or for food, a man must stand erect. This alters the centre of gravity of the body, and as the act becomes a habit, subsidiary changes slowly take place in other parts. In time the erect position becomes confirmed. Man owes what Burns calls his "heaven-erected face" to the Struggle for Life. How recent this change is, how new the attitude still is to him, is seen from the simple fact that even yet he has not attained the power of retaining the erect position long. Most men sit down when they can, and so unnatural is the standing position, so unstable the equilibrium, that when slightly sick or faint, Man cannot stand at all.

Possibly both the erect position and the Club had another origin, but the detail is immaterial. This "hairy-tailed quadruped, arboreal in its habits," must sometimes have wandered or been driven into places where trees were few and far between. It is conceivable that an animal, accustomed to get along mainly by grasping something, should have picked up a branch and held it in its hand, partly to use as a crutch, partly as a weapon, and partly to raise itself from the ground in order to keep a better look-out in crossing treeless spaces. An Orang-outang may now be seen in the Zoological gardens in Java which promenades about its bower continually with the help of a stick, and seems to prefer the erect position so long as the stick or any support is at hand.

The next stage after the invention of anything is to improve upon it, or to make a further use of it. Both these things now happened. One day the stick, wrenched rapidly from the tree, happened to be left with a jagged end. The properties of the point were discovered. Now there were two classes of weapons in the world—the blunt stick and the pointed stick—that is to say, the Club and the Spear.

In using these weapons at first, neither probably was allowed to leave the hand. But already their owners had learned to hurl down branches from the tree-tops and bombard their enemies with nuts and fruits. Hence they came to throw their clubs and spears, and so missiles were introduced. Under this new use the primitive weapons themselves received a further specialization. From the heavy bludgeon would arise on the one hand the shaped war-club, and on the other the short throwing club, or waddy. The spear would pass into the throwing assegai, or the ponderous weapon such as the South Sea Islanders use to-day. From the natural point of a torn branch to the sharpening of a point deliberately is the next improvement. From rubbing the point against the sharp edge of a large stone, to picking up a sharp-edged small stone and using it as a knife, is but a step. So, by the mere necessities of the Struggle for Life, development went on. Man became a tool-using animal, and the foundations of the Arts were laid. Next, the man who threw his missile furthest, had the best chance in the Struggle for Life. To throw to still greater distances, and with greater precision, he sought out mechanical aids—the bow, the boomerang, the throwing-stick, and the sling. Then instead of using his own strength he borrowed strength from nature, mixed different kinds of dust together and invented gunpowder. All our modern weapons of precision, from the rifle to the long range gun, are evolutions from the missiles of the savage. These suggestions are not mere fancies; in savage tribes existing in the world to-day these different stages in Evolution may still be seen.

After weapons of offence came weapons of defence. At first the fighting savage sheltered himself at the back of a tree. Then when he wished to pass to another tree he tore off part of the bark, took it with him, and made the first shield. Where the trees were without suitable bark, he would plait his shield from canes, grasses, and the midribs of the leaves, or construct them from frameworks of wood and skins. In times of peace these hollow shields, lying idly about the huts, would find new uses—baskets, cradles, and, in an evolved form, coracles or boats. In leisure hours also, new virtues discovered themselves in the earlier implements of war and of the chase. The twang of his bow suggested memories that were pleasant to his ear; he kept on twanging it, and so made music. Because two bows twanged better than one, he twanged two bows; then he made himself a two-stringed bow from the first, and ended with a "ten-stringed instrument." By and by came the harp; later, the violin. The whistling of the wind in a hollow reed prepared the way for the flute; a conch-shell, broken at the helix, gave him the trumpet. Two flints struck together yielded fire.

Trifling, almost puerile, as these beginnings look to us now, remember they were once the serious realities of life. The club and spear of the savage are toys to us to-day; but we forget that the rude shafts of wood which adorn our halls were all the world to early Man, and represented the highest expression and daily instrument of his evolution. These primitive weapons are the pathetic expression of the world's first Struggle. As the earliest contribution of mankind to solve its still fundamental difficulty —the problem of Nutrition—they are of enduring interest to the human race. So far from being, as one might suppose, mere implements of destruction, they are implements of self-preservation; they entered the world not from hate of Man but for love of life. Why was the spear invented, and the sling, and the bow? In the first instance because Man needed the bird and the deer for food. Why from implements of the chase did they change into implements of war? Because other men wanted the bird and the deer, and the first possessor, as populations multiplied, must protect his food-supply. The parent of all industries is Hunger: the creator of civilization in its earlier forms is the Struggle for Life.

By hollowing a pit in the ground, planting his spear, or a pointed stake, upright in the centre, and covering the mouth with boughs, Man could trap even the largest game. When the climate became cold, he stripped off the skin and became the possessor of clothes. With a stone for a hammer, he broke open molluscs on the shore, or speared or trapped the fish in the shoals. Digging for roots with his pointed stick in time suggested agriculture. From imitating the way wild fruits and grains were sown by Nature he became a gardener and grew crops. To possess a crop means to possess an estate, and to possess an estate is to give up wandering and begin that more settled life in which all the arts of industry must increase. Catching the young of wild animals and keeping them, first as playthings, then for supplies of meat or milk, or in the case of the dog for helping in the chase, he perceived the value of domestic animals. So Man slowly passed from the animal to the savage, so his mind was tamed, and strengthened, and brightened, and heightened; so the sense of power grew strong, and so virtus, which is to say virtue, was born.

In struggling with Nature, early Man not only found material satisfactions: he found himself. It was this that made him, body, mind, character, and disposition; and it was this largely that gave to the world different kinds of men, different kinds of bodies, minds, characters, and dispositions. The first moral and intellectual diversifiers of men are to be sought for in geography and geology—in the factors which determine the circumstances in which men severally conduct their Struggle for Life. If the land had been all the same the Struggle for Life had been all the same, and if the Struggle for Life had been all the same, life itself had been all the same. But to no two sets of men is the world ever quite the same. The theatre of struggle varies with every degree of latitude, with every change of altitude, with every variation of soil. In most countries three separate regions are found—a maritime region, an agricultural region, a pastoral region. In the first, the belt along the shore, the people are fishermen; in the second, the lowlands and alluvial plains, the people are farmers; in the third, the highlands and plateaux, they are shepherds. As men are nothing but expressions of their environments, as the kind of life depends on how men get their living, each set of men becomes changed in different ways. The fisherman's life is a precarious life; he becomes hardy, resolute, self-reliant. The farmer's life is a settled life; he becomes tame, he loves home, he feeds on grains and fruits which take the heat out of his blood and make him domestic and quiet. The shepherd is a wanderer; he is much alone; the monotonies of grass make him dull and moody; the mountains awe him: the protector of his flock, he is a man of war. So arise types of men, types of industries; and by and bye, by exogamous marriage, blends of these types, and further blends of infinite variety. "It is so ordered by Nature, that by so striving to live they develop their physical structure; they obtain faint glimmerings of reason; they think and deliberate; they become Man. In the same way, the primeval men have no other object than to keep the clan alive. It is so ordered by Nature that in striving to preserve the existence of the clan, they not only acquire the arts of agriculture, domestication, and navigation; they not only discover fire, and its uses in cooking, in war, and in metallurgy; they not only detect the hidden properties of plants, and apply them to save their own lives from disease, and to destroy their enemies in battle; they not only learn to manipulate Nature and to distribute water by machinery; but they also, by means of the life-long battle, are developed into moral beings. Nature being "everything that is," and Man being in every direction immersed in it and dependent on it, can never escape its continuous discipline. Some environment there must always be; and some change of environment, no matter how minute, there must always be; and some change, no matter how imperceptible, must be always wrought in him.

We now see, perhaps, more clearly why Evolution at the dawn of life entered into league with so strange an ally as Want. The Evolution of Mankind was too great a thing to entrust to any uncertain hand. The advantage of attaching human progress to the Struggle for Life is that you can always depend upon it. Hunger never fails. All other human appetites have their periods of activity and stagnation; passions wax and wane; emotions are casual and capricious. But the continuous discharge of the function of Nutrition is interrupted only by the final interruption—Death. Death means, in fact, little more than an interference with the function of Nutrition; it means that the Struggle for Life having broken down, there can be no more life, no further evolution. Hence, it has been ordained that Life and Struggle, Health and Struggle, Growth and Struggle, Progress and Struggle, shall be linked together; that whatever the chances of misdirection, the apparent losses, the mysterious accompaniments of strife and pain, the Ascent of Man should be bound up with living. When it is remembered that, at a later day, Morality and Struggle, and even Religion and Struggle, are bound so closely that it is impossible to conceive of them apart, the tremendous value of this principle and the necessity for providing it with indestructible foundations, will be perceived.

This association of the Struggle for Life with the physiological function of Nutrition must be continually borne in mind. For the essential nature of the principle has been greatly obscured by the very name which Mr. Darwin gave to it. Probably no other was possible; but the effect has been that men have emphasized the almost ethical substantive 'Struggle' and ignored the biological term 'Life.' A secondary implication of the process has thus been elevated into the prime one; and this, exaggerated by the imagination, has led to Nature being conceived of as a vast murderous machine for the annihilation of the majority and the survival of the few. But the Struggle for Life, in the first instance, is simply living itself; at the best, it is living under a healthily normal maximum of pressure; at the worst, under an abnormal maximum. As we have seen, initially, it is but another name for the discharge of the supreme physiological function of Nutrition. If life is to go on at all, this function must be discharged and continuously discharged. The primary characteristic of protoplasm, the physical basis of all life, is Hunger, and this has dictated the first law of being—"Thou shalt eat." What distinguishes scientifically the organic from the inorganic, the animal from the stone? That the animal eats, the stone does not. Almost all achievement in the early history of the living world has been due to Hunger. For millenniums nearly the whole task of Evolution was to perfect the means of satisfying it, and in so doing to perfect life itself. The lowest forms of life are little more than animated stomachs, and in higher groups the nutritive system is the first to be developed, the first to function, and the last to cease its work. Almost wholly, indeed, in the earlier vicissitude of the race, and largely in the more ordered course of later times, Hunger rules the life and work and destiny of men; and so profoundly does this mysterious deity still dominate the round of even the highest life that the noblest occupations which engage the human mind must be interrupted two or three times a day to do it homage.

Whatever Man came ultimately to wish and to achieve for himself, it was essential at first that such arrangements should be made for him. The machinery for his development had not only to be put into Nature, but he had to be placed in the machine and held there, and brought back there as often as he tried to evade it. To say that man evolved himself, nevertheless, is as absurd as to say that a newspaper prints itself. To say even that the machinery evolved him is as preposterous as to say of a poem that the printing-press made it. The ultimate problem is, Who made the machine? and Who thought the poem that was to be printed?

If you say that you do not unreservedly approve of the machine, that it lacerates as well as binds, the difficulty is more real. But it is a principle in the study of history to suspend judgment both of the meaning and of the value of a policy until the chain of sequences it sets in motion should be worked out to its last fulfilment. When the full tale of the Struggle for Life is told, when the record of its victories is closed, when the balance of its gains and losses has been struck, and especially when it is proved that there actually have been losses, it will be time to pass judgment on its moral value. Of course this principle cuts both ways; it warns

off a favourable as well as an unfavourable verdict on the beneficence of the
system of things. But Evolution is a study in history, and its results are largely
known. And it would be affectation to deny that on the whole these results are
good, and appear the worthier the more we penetrate into their inner meaning.
Men forget when they denounce the Struggle for Life, that it is to be judged not
only on the ground of sentiment but of reason, that not its local or surface effects
only, but its permanent influence on the order of the world, must be taken into
account.

Even on the lower ranges of Nature the unfavourable implications of the
Struggle for Life have probably been exaggerated. While it is essential to an
understanding of the course of evolution to retain in the imagination a vivid sense
of the Struggle itself, we must beware of over-colouring the representation, or
flooding it with accompaniments of emotion borrowed from our own sensations.
The word Struggle at all in this connection is little more than a metaphor. When
it is said that an animal struggles, all that is really meant is that it lives. An
animal, that is to say, does not, in addition to all its other activities, have to employ
a vast number of special activities, to the exercise of which the term Struggle is to
be applied. It is Life itself which is the Struggle: and the whole Life, and the whole
of the activities and powers which make up Life are involved in it. To speak of
Struggle in the sense of some special and separate struggle, to conceive of battle,
or even a series of battles, is misleading, where all is struggle and where all is
battle. Especially must we beware of reading into it our personal ideas with regard
to accompaniments of pain. The probabilities are that the Struggle for Life in the
lower creation is, to say the least, less painful than it looks. Whether we regard the
dulness of the states of consciousness among lower animals, or the fact that the
condition of danger must become habitual, or that death when it comes is sudden,
and unaccompanied by that anticipation which gives it its chief dread to Man, we
must assume that whatever the Struggle for Life subjectively means to the lower
animals, it can never approach in terror what it means to us. And as to putting
any moral content into it, until a late stage in the world's development, that is not
to be thought of. Judged of even by later standards there is much to relieve one's
first unfavourable impression. With exceptions, the fight is a fair fight. As a rule
there is no hate in it, but only Hunger. It is seldom prolonged, and seldom wanton.
As to the manner of death, it is generally sudden. As to the fact of death, all
animals must die. As to the meaning of an existence prematurely closed, it is
better to be to be eaten than not to be at all. And, as to the last result, it is better
to be eaten out of the world and, dying, help another to live, than pollute the world
by lingering decay. The most, after all, that can be done with life is to give it to
others. Till Nature taught her creatures of their own free will to offer the sacrifice,
is it strange that she took it by force?

There are those indeed who frown upon Science for predicating a Struggle for
Life in Nature at all, lest the facts should impugn the beneficence of the universe.
But Science did not invent the Struggle for Life. It is there. What Science has
really done is to show not only its meaning but its great moral purpose. There are
others, again, like Mill, who, seeing the facts, but not seeing that moral purpose,
impugn natural theology for still believing in the beneficence of that purpose.
Neither attitude, probably, is quite worthy of the names with which these
conclusions are associated. Much more reasonable are the verdicts of the two men
who are first responsible for bringing the facts before the world, Mr. Alfred Russel
Wallace and Mr. Darwin. "When we reflect," says Mr. Darwin, "on this struggle,

we may console ourselves with the full belief that the war of nature is not incessant, that no fear is felt, that death is generally prompt, and that the vigorous, the healthy, and the happy survive and multiply." And in much stronger language Mr. Wallace: "On the whole, the popular idea of the struggle for existence entailing misery and pain on the animal world is the very reverse of the truth. What it really brings about is the maximum of life and of the enjoyment of life, with the minimum of suffering and pain. Given the necessity of death and reproduction, and without these there could have been no progressive development of the organic world—and it is difficult even to imagine a system by which a greater balance of happiness could have been secured.

We may safely leave Nature here to look after her own ethic. That a price, a price in pain, and assuredly sometimes a very terrible price, has been paid for the evolution of the world, after all is said, is certain. There may be difference of opinion as to the amount of this price, but on one point there can be no dispute—that even at the highest estimate the thing which was bought with it was none too dear. For that thing was nothing less than the present progress of the world. The Struggle for Life has been a victorious struggle; it has succeeded in its stupendous task; and there is nothing of order or beauty or perfection in living Nature that does not owe something to its having been carried on. The first duty of those who demur to the cost of progress is to make sure that they comprehend in all its richness the infinity of the gift this sacrifice has purchased for humanity. The end of the Struggle for Life is not battle; it is not even victory, it is evolution. The result is not wounds, it is health. Nature is a vast and complicated system of devices to keep things changing, adjusting, and, as it seems, progressing. The Struggle for Life is a species of necessitated aspiration, the vis a tergo which keeps living things in motion. It does not follow, of course, that that motion should be upward; that is dependent on other considerations. But the point to mark is, that without the struggle for food and the pressure of want, without the conflict with foes and the challenge of climate, the world would be left to stagnation. Change, adventure, temptation, vicissitude even to the verge of calamity, these are the life of the world.

There is another side to this principle from which its higher significance becomes still more apparent. It follows from the Struggle for Life that those animals which struggle most successfully will prosper, while the less successful will disappear—hence the well-known principle of Natural Selection or the Survival of the Fittest. Waiving the discussion of this law in general, and the. varying meanings which "fitness" assumes as we rise in the scale of being, observe the role it plays in Nature. The object of the Survival of the Fittest is to produce fitness. And it does so both negatively and positively. In the first place it produces fitness by killing off the unfit. Without the rigorous weeding out of the imperfect the progress of the world had not been possible. If fit and unfit indiscriminately had been allowed to live and reproduce their kind, every improvement which any individual might acquire would be degraded to the common level in the course of a few generations. Progress can only start by one or two individuals shooting ahead of their species; and their life-gain can only be conserved by their being shut off from their species—or by their species being shut off from them. Unless shut off from their species their acquisition will either be neutralized in the course of time by the swamping effect of inter-breeding with the common herd, or so diluted as to involve no real advance. The only chance for Evolution, then, is either to carry off these improved editions into "physiological isolation," or to remove the unimproved editions by wholesale death.. The first of these alternatives is only occasionally possible; the second always. Hence the death of the unevolved, or of the unadapted in reference to some new and higher relation with environment, is essential to the perpetuation of a useful variation. Although Natural Selection by no means invariably works in the direction of progress,—in parasites it has consummated almost utter degeneration,—no progress can take place without it. It is only when one considers the working of the Struggle for Life on the large scale, and realizes its necessity to the Evolution of the world as a whole, that one can even begin to discuss its ethical or teleological meanings. To make a fit world, the unfit at every stage must be made to disappear; and if any self-acting law can bring this about, though its bearing upon this or that individual case may seem unjust, its necessity for the world as a whole is vindicated. If more of any given species are born into the world than can possibly find food, and if a given number must die, that number must be singled out upon some principle; and we cannot quarrel with the principle in Physical Nature which condemns to death the worst. By placing the death-penalty upon the slightest shortcoming, Natural Selection so discourages imperfection as practically to eliminate it from the world. The fact that any given animal is alive at all is almost a token of its perfectness. Nothing living can be wholly a failure. For the moment that it fails, it ceases to live. Something more fit, were it even by a hairbreadth, secures its place; so that all existing lives must, with reference to their environment, be the best possible lives. Natural Selection is the means employed in Nature to bring about perfect health, perfect wholeness, perfect adaptation, and in the long run the Ascent of all living things.

This being so, the Law of the Struggle for Life is elevated to a unique place in Nature as a first necessity of progress. It involves that every living thing in Nature shall live its best, that every resource shall be called out to its utmost, that every individual faculty shall be kept in the most perfect order and work up to its fullest strength. So far from being a drag on life, it is the one thing which not only makes life go on at all, but which in the very act perfects it. The result may sometimes involve the dethroning of a species, or its entire extinction: it may lead in the case of others to degeneration; but in the end it must result in the gradual perfecting of organisms upon the whole, and the steady advance of the final type. In fixing the eye on the murderous side of this Struggle, it is therefore well to remember to what it leads. There could be no higher end in the universe than to make a perfect world, and no more perfect law than that which at the same moment eliminates the unfit and establishes the fit. Too frequently the moralist's attention is diverted to the negative side, to what seems the quite immoral spectacle of the massacre of the innocent, the rout and murder of the unfit. But in earlier Nature there is no such word as innocent; and no ethical meaning at that stage can attach itself to the term 'unfit.' Fitness in the stormy days of the world's animal youth was necessarily fighting-fitness; no higher end was present anywhere than simply to gain for life a footing in the world, and perfect it up to the highest physical form. The creature which did that fulfilled its destiny, and no higher destiny was possible or conceivable. The Survival of the Fittest, of course, does not mean the survival of the strongest. It means the Survival of the Adapted—the survival of the most fitted to the circumstances which surround it. A fish survives in water when a leaking ironclad goes to the bottom, not because it is stronger but because it is better adapted to the element in which it lives. A Texas bull is stronger than a mosquito, but in an autumn drought the bull dies, the mosquito lives. Fitness to survive is simply fittedness, and has nothing to do with strength or courage, or intelligence or cunning as such, but only with adjustments as fit or unfit to the world around. A prize-fighter is stronger than a cripple; but in the environment of modern life the cripple is cared for by the people, is judged fit to live by a moral world, while the pugilist, handicapped by his very health, has to conduct his own struggle for existence. Physical fitness here is actually a disqualification; what was once unfitness is now fitness to survive. As we rise in the scale, the physical fitness of the early world changes to fitness of a different quality, and this law becomes the guardian of a moral order. In one era the race is to the swift, in another the meek inherit the earth. In a material world social survival depends on wealth, health, power; in a moral world the fittest are the weak, the pitiable, the poor. Thus there comes a time when this very law, in securing survival for those who would otherwise sink and fall, is the minister of moral ends.

When we pass from the animal and the savage states to watch the working of the Struggle for Life in later times, the impression deepens that, after all, the "gladiatorial theory" of existence has much to say for itself. To trace its progress further is denied us for the present, but observe before we close what it connotes in modern life. Its lineal descendants are two in number, and they have but to be named to show the enormous place this factor has been given to play in the world's destiny. The first is War, the second is Industry. These in all their forms and ramifications are simply the primitive Struggle continued on the social and political plane. War is not a casual thing like a thunderstorm, nor a specific thing like a battle. It is that ancient Struggle for Life carried over from the animal kingdom, which, in the later as in the earlier world, has been so perfect an instrument of evolution. Along with Industry, and for a time before it, War was the foster-mother of civilization. The patron of the heroic virtues, the purifier of societies, the solidifier of states, the military form of this Struggle—despite the awful balance on the other side—stands out on every page of history as the maker and educator of the human race. Industry is but the same Struggle in another disguise. The industrial conflict of to-day is the old attempt of primitive Man to get the most out of Nature—to grow foods, to find clothes, to raise fuel, to gain wealth. Owing to the ever-increasing number of the Strugglers the supplies fall short of the demands, with the result of perpetuating on the industrial plane, and often in hard and degrading forms, the primitive Struggle for Life. When society wonders at its labour troubles it forgets that Industry is a stage but one or two removes from the purely animal Struggle. And when morality impugns the Struggle for Life, it forgets that nearly the whole later fabric of civilization is its creation.

But one has only to look at these further phases of the Struggle to observe the most important fact of all—the change that passes over the principle as time goes on. Examine it on the higher levels as carefully as we have examined it on the lower, and though the crueler elements persist with fatal and appalling vigour, there are whole regions, and daily enlarging regions, where every animal feature is discredited, discouraged, or driven away. Already, with the social tragedy still at its height around us, the amelioration in many directions makes constant progress; and partly through the rise of opposing forces, and partly through the very civilization which it has helped to create, the maligner power must disappear. The Struggle for Life, as life's dynamic, can never wholly cease. In the keenness of its energies, the splendour of its stimulus, its bracing effect on character, its wholesome tensions throughout the whole range of action, it must remain with us to the end. But in the virulence of its animal qualities it must surely pass away. There are those who, without reflecting on this qualitative change, would govern Society by the merely animal Struggle; those who claim for this the sanction of Nature, and lay down the principle of selfishness as the eternally working law. The eternal law, as we shall presently see, is unselfishness. But even the selfishness of early Nature loses its sting with time; the self that is in it becomes a higher self; and the world in which it acts is so much a better world that if self gave full rein to the animal it would be instantly extinguished.

The amelioration of the Struggle for Life is the most certain prophecy of Science. If this universe is a moral universe, it was a necessity that sooner or later this conflict should abate, that in the course of Evolution this particular change should come, that there should be put into the very machinery of Nature that which should bring it about. And what do we find? We find the Animal side of the Struggle for Life attacked in such directions, and with such weapons, that its defeat is sure. These weapons are in the armoury of Nature; they have been there from the beginning; and they are now engaged upon the enemy so hotly and so openly that we can discover what some of them are. The first is one which has begun to mine the Struggle for Life at its roots. Essentially, as we have seen, the Struggle for Life is the attempt to solve the fundamental problem of all life—Nutrition. If that could be solved apart from the Struggle for Life, its occupation would be gone. Now, it is more than probable that that problem will be otherwise solved. It will be solved by science. At the present moment Chemistry is devoting itself to the experiment of manufacturing nutrition, and with an enthusiasm which only immediate hope begets. It is not the visionaries who have dared to prophesy here. In a hundred laboratories the problem is being practically worked out, and, as one of the highest authorities assures us, "The time is not far distant when the artificial preparation of articles of food will be accomplished. Already, through the labours of other sciences, the Struggle for Food has been made infinitely easier than it was; but when the immediate quest succeeds, and the food of Man is made direct from the elements, the Struggle in all its coarser forms will practically be abolished. Civilization cannot ease the whole burden at once; the Struggle for Life will go on, but it will be the Struggle with its fangs drawn.

But there is a higher hope than Science. Attacked from below by Man's intellect, the final blow will be struck from a deeper source. It is impossible to conceive that the Ascent of Man should always depend upon his appetites, that in God's world there should be nothing better to attract him than food and raiment, that he should take no single step towards a higher life except when driven to it. As there comes a time in a child's life when coercion gives place to free and conscious choice, the day comes to the world when the aspirations of the spirit begin to compete with, to neutralize, and to supplant the compulsions of the body. Against that day, in the heart of humanity, Nature had made full provision. For there, prepared by a profounder chemistry than that which was to relieve the strain on the physical side, had gathered through the ages a force in whose presence the energies of the Animal Struggle are as naught. Beside the Struggle for the Life of Others the Struggle for Life is but a passing phase. As old, as deeply sunk in Nature, this further force was destined from the first to replace the Struggle for Life, and to build a nobler superstructure on the foundations which it laid. To establish these foundations was all that the Animal Struggle was ever designed to do. It has laid them well; yet it is only when the Struggle for Life stands projected against the larger influence with which all through history—and in an infinitely profound sense through moral history —it has been allied, that at once its worth and its ignominy are seen.

The Struggle for the Life of Others

We now open a wholly new, and by far the most important, chapter in the Evolution of Man. Up to this time we have found for him a Body, and the rudiments of Mind. But Man is not a Body, nor a Mind. The temple still awaits its final tenant—the higher human Soul.

With a Body alone, Man is an animal: the highest animal, yet a pure animal; struggling for its own narrow life, living for its small and sordid ends. Add a Mind to that and the advance is infinite. The Struggle for Life assumes the august form of a struggle for light: he who was once a savage, pursuing the arts of the chase, realizes Aristotle's ideal man, "a hunter after Truth." Yet this is not the end. Experience tells us that Man's true life is neither lived in the material tracts of the body, nor in the higher altitudes of the intellect, but in the warm world of the affections. Till he is equipped with these, Man is not human. He reaches his full height only when Love becomes to him the breath of life, the energy of will, the summit of desire. There at last lies all happiness, and goodness, and truth, and divinity:

"For the loving worm within its clod
Were diviner than a loveless God."

That Love did not come down to us through the Struggle for Life, the only great factor in Evolution which up to this time has been dwelt upon, is self-evident. It has a lineage all its own. Yet inexplicable though the circumstance be, the history of this force, the most stupendous the world has ever known, has scarcely even begun to be investigated. Every other principle in Nature has had a thousand prophets; but this supreme dynamic has run its course through the ages unobserved; its rise, so far as science is concerned, is unknown; its story has never been told. But if any phenomenon or principle in Nature is capable of treatment under the category of Evolution, this is. Love is not a late arrival, an after-thought, with Creation. It is not a novelty of a romantic civilization. It is not a pious word of religion. Its roots began to grow with the first cell of life which budded on this earth. How great it is the history of humanity bears witness; but how old it is and how solid, how bound up with the very constitution of the world, how from the first of time an eternal part of it, we are only now beginning to perceive. For the Evolution of Love is a piece of pure Science. Love did not descend out of the clouds like rain or snow. It was distilled on earth. And few of the romances which in after years were to cluster round this immortal word are more wonderful than the story of its birth and growth. Partly a product of crushed lives and exterminated species, and partly of the choicest blossoms and sweetest essences that ever came from the tree of life, it reached its spiritual perfection after a history the most strange and chequered that the pages of Nature have to record. What Love was at first, how crude and sour and embryonic a thing, it is impossible to conceive. But from age to age, with immeasurable faith and patience, by cultivations continuously repeated, by transplantings endlessly varied, the unrecognizable germ of this new fruit was husbanded to its maturity, and became the tree on which humanity, society, and civilization were ultimately borne.

As the story of Evolution is usually told, Love— the evolved form, as we shall see, of the Struggle for the Life of Others—has not even a place. Almost the whole emphasis of science has fallen upon the opposite—the animal Struggle for Life. Hunger was early seen by the naturalists to be the first and most imperious appetite of all living things, and the course of Nature came to be erroneously interpreted in terms of a never-ending strife. Since there are vastly more creatures born than can ever survive, since for every morsel of food provided a hundred claimants appear, life to an animal was described to us as one long tragedy; and Poetry, borrowing the imperfect creed, pictured Nature only as a blood-red fang. Before we can go on to trace the higher progress of Love itself, it is necessary to correct this misconception. And no words can be thrown away if they serve, in whatever imperfect measure, to restore to honour what is in reality the supreme factor in the Evolution of the world. To interpret the whole course of Nature by the Struggle for Life is as absurd as if one were to define the character of St. Francis by the tempers of his childhood. Worlds grow up as well as infants; their tempers change, the better nature opens out, new objects of desire appear, higher activities are added to the lower. The first chapter or two of the story of Evolution may be headed the Struggle for Life; but take the book as a whole and it is not a tale of battle. It is a Love-story.

The circumstances, as has been already pointed out in the Introduction, under which the world at large received its main impression of Evolution, obscured these later and happier features. The modern revival of the Evolution theory occurred almost solely in connection with investigations in the lower planes of Nature, and was due to the stimulus of the pure naturalists, notably of Mr. Darwin. But what Mr. Darwin primarily undertook to explain was simply the Origin of Species. His work was a study in infancies, in rudiments; he emphasized the earliest forces and the humblest phases of the world's development. The Struggle for Life was there the most conspicuous fact—at least, on the surface; it formed the key-note of his teaching; and the tragic side of Nature fixed itself in the popular mind. The mistake the world made was two-fold: it mistook Darwinism for Evolution—a specific theory of Evolution applicable to a single department for a universal scheme; and it misunderstood Mr. Darwin himself. That the foundations of Darwinism—or what was taken for Darwinism—were the foundations of all Nature was assumed. Dazzled with the apparent solidity of this foundation, men made haste to run up a structure which included the whole vast range of life—vegetal, animal, social—based on a law which explained but half the facts, and was only relevant, in the crude form in which it was universally stated, for the childhood of the world. It was impossible for such an edifice to stand. Natural history cannot in any case cover the whole facts of human history, and, so interpreted, can only fatally distort them. The mistake had been largely qualified had Mr. Darwin's followers even accepted his foundation in its first integrity; but, perhaps because the author of the theory himself but dimly apprehended the complement of his thesis, few seem to have perceived that anything was amiss. Mr. Darwin's sagacity led him distinctly to foresee that narrow interpretations of his great phrase "Struggle for Existence" were certain to be made; and in the opening chapters of the Origin of Species, he warns us that the term must be applied in its "large and metaphorical sense, including dependence of one being on another, and including (which is more important) not only the life of the individual, but success in leaving progeny. In spite of this warning, his overmastering emphasis on the individual Struggle for Existence seems to have obscured, if not to his own mind, certainly to almost all his followers, the truth that any other great factor in Evolution existed.

The truth is there are two Struggles for Life in every living thing—the Struggle for Life, and the Struggle for the Life of Others. The web of life is woven upon a double set of threads, the second thread distinct in colour from the first, and giving a totally different pattern to the finished fabric. As the whole aspect of the after-world depends on this distinction of strands in the warp, it is necessary to grasp the distinction with the utmost clearness. Already, in the introductory chapter, the nature of the distinction has been briefly explained. But it is necessary to be explicit here, even to redundancy. We have arrived at a point from which the Ascent of Man takes a fresh departure, a point from which the course of Evolution begins to wear an entirely altered aspect. No such consummation ever before occurred in the progress of the world as the rise to potency in human life of the Struggle for the Life of Others. The Struggle for the Life of Others is the physiological name for the greatest word of ethics—Other-ism, Altruism, Love. From Self-ism to Other-ism is the supreme transition of history. It is therefore impossible to lodge in the mind with too much solidity the simple biological fact on which the Altruistic Struggle rests. Were this a late phase of Evolution, or a factor applicable to single genera, it would still be of supreme importance; but it is radical, universal, involved in the very nature of life itself. As matter is to be interpreted by Science in terms of its properties, life is to be interpreted in terms of its functions. And when we dissect down to that form of matter with which all life is associated, we find it already discharging, in the humblest organisms visible by the microscope, the function on which the stupendous superstructure of Altruism indirectly comes to rest. Take the tiniest protoplasmic cell, immerse it in a suitable medium, and presently it will perform two great acts—the two which sum up life, which constitute the eternal distinction between the living and the dead—Nutrition and Reproduction. At one moment, in pursuance of the Struggle for Life, it will call in matter from without, and assimilate it to itself; at another moment, in pursuance of the Struggle for the Life of Others, it will set a portion of that matter apart, add to it, and finally give it away to form another life. Even at its dawn life is receiver and giver; even in protoplasm is Self-ism and Other-ism. These two tendencies are not fortuitous. They have been lived into existence. They are not grafts on the tree of life, they are its nature, its essential life. They are not painted on the canvas, but woven through it.

The two main activities, then, of all living things are Nutrition and Reproduction. The discharge of these functions in plants, and largely in animals, sums up the work of life. The object of Nutrition is to secure the life of the individual; the object of Reproduction is to secure the life of the Species. These two objects are thus wholly different. The first has a purely personal end; its attention is turned inwards; it exists only for the present. The second in a greater or less degree is impersonal; its attention is turned outwards; it lives for the future. One of these objects, in other words, is Self-regarding; the other is Other-regarding. Both, of course, at the outset are wholly selfish; both are parts of the Struggle for Life. Yet see already in this non-ethical region a parting of the ways. Selfishness and unselfishness are two supreme words in the moral life. The first, even in physical Nature, is accompanied by the second. In the very fact that one of the two mainsprings of life is Other-regarding there lies a prophecy, a suggestion, of the day of Altruism. In organizing the physiological mechanism of Reproduction in plants and animals Nature was already laying wires on which, one far-off day, the currents of all higher things might travel.

In itself, this second Struggle, this effort to maintain the life of the species, is not less real than the first; the provisions for effecting it are not less wonderful; the whole is not less a part of the system of things. And, taken prophetically, the function of Reproduction is as much greater than the function of Nutrition as the Man is greater than the Animal, as the Soul is higher than the Body, as Co-operation is stronger than Competition, as Love is stronger than Hate. If it were ever to be charged against Nature that she was wholly selfish, here is the refutation at the very start. One of the two fundamental activities of all life, whether plant or animal, is Other-regarding. It is not said that the function of Reproduction, say in a fern or in an oak, is an unselfish act, yet in a sense, even though begotten of self, it is an other-regarding act. In the physical world, to speak of the Struggle for Food as selfish, or to call the Struggle for Species unselfish, are alike incongruous. But if the morality of Nature is impugned on the ground of the universal Struggle for Life, it is at least as relevant to refute the charge - by putting moral content into the universal Struggle for Species. No true moral content can be put into either, yet the one marks the beginning of Egoism, the other of Altruism. Almost the whole self-seeking side of things has come down the line of the individual Struggle for Life; almost the whole unselfish side of things is rooted in the Struggle to preserve the life of others.

That an Other-regarding principle should sooner or later appear on the world's stage was a necessity if the world was ever to become a moral world. And as everything in the moral world has what may be called a physical basis to begin with, it is not surprising to find in the mere physiological process of Reproduction a physical forecast of the higher relations, or, more accurately, to find the higher relations manifesting themselves at first through physical relations. The Struggle for the Life of Others formed an indispensable stepping-stone to the development of the Other-regarding virtues. Nature always works with long roots. To conduct Other-ism upward into the higher sphere without miscarriage, and to establish it there for ever, Nature had to embed it in the most ancient past, so organizing and endowing protoplasm that life could not go on without it, and compelling its continuous activity by the sternest physiological necessity.

To say that there is a certain protest of the mind against associating the highest ethical ends with forces in their first stage almost physical, is to confess a truth which all must feel. Even Haeckel, in contrasting the tiny rootlet of sex-attraction between two microscopic cells with the mighty after-efflorescence of love in the history of mankind, is staggered at the audacity of the thought, and pauses in the heart of a profound scientific investigation to reflect upon it. After a panegyric in which he says, "We glorify love as the source of the most splendid creations of art; of the noblest productions of poetry, of plastic art and of music; we reverence in it the most powerful factor in human civilization, the basis of family life, and, consequently, of the development of the state"; ... he adds, "So wonderful is love, and so immeasurably important is its influence on mental life, that in this point, more than in any other, `supernatural' causation seems to mock every natural explanation." It is the mystery of Nature, that between the loftiest spiritual heights and the lowliest physical depths, there should seem to run a pathway which the intellect of Man may climb. Haeckel has spoken, and rightly, from the standpoint of humanity; yet he continues, and with equal right, from the standpoint of the naturalist. "Notwithstanding all this, the comparative history of evolution leads us back very clearly and indubitably to the oldest and simplest source of love, to the elective affinity of two differing cells.

Self-Sacrifice in Nature

It is not, however, in Haeckel's "elective affinity of differing cells" that we must seek the physical basis of Altruism. That may be the physical basis of a passion which is frequently miscalled Love; but Love itself, in its true sense as Self-sacrifice, Love with all its beautiful elements of sympathy, tenderness, pity, and compassion, has come down a wholly different line. It is well to be clear about this at once, for the function of Reproduction suggests to the biological mind a view of this factor which would limit its action to a sphere which in reality forms but the merest segment of the whole. The Struggle for the Life of Others has certainly connected with it sex relations, as we shall see; but we can only use it scientifically in its broad physiological sense, as literally a Struggling for Others, a giving up self for Others. And these others are not Other-sexes. They have nothing to do with sex. They are the fruits of Reproduction—the egg, the seed, the nestling, the little child. So far from its chief manifestation being within the sphere of sex it is in the care and nurture of the young, in the provision everywhere throughout Nature for the seed and egg, in the endless and infinite self-sacrifices of Maternity, that Altruism finds its main expression.

That this is the true reading of the work of this second factor appears even in the opening act of Reproduction in the lowest plant or animal. Pledged by the first law of its being—the law of self-preservation—to sustain itself, the organism is at the same moment pledged by the second law to give up itself. Watch one of the humblest unicellular organisms at the time of Reproduction. The cell, when it grows to be a certain size, divides itself into two, and each part sets up an independent life. Why it does so is now known. The protoplasm inside the cell—the body as it were—needs continually to draw in fresh food. This is secured by a process of imbibition or osmosis through the surrounding wall. But as the cell grows large, there is not wall enough to pass in all the food the far interior needs, for while the bulk increases as the cube of the diameter the surface increases only as the square. The bulk of the cell, in short, has outrun the absorbing surface; its hunger has outgrown its satisfactions; and unless the cell can devise some way of gaining more surface it must starve. Hence the splitting into two smaller cells. There is now more absorbing surface than the two had when combined. When the two smaller cells have grown as large as the original parent, income and expenditure will once more balance. As growth continues, the waste begins to exceed the power of repair and the life of the cell is again threatened. The alternatives are obvious. It must divide, or die. If it divides, what has saved its life? Self-sacrifice. By giving up its life as an individual it has brought forth two individuals, and these will one day repeat the surrender. Here, with differences appropriate to their distinctive spheres, is the first great act of the moral life. All life, in the beginning, is self-contained, self-centred, imprisoned in a single cell. The first step to a more abundant life is to get rid of this limitation. And the first act of the prisoner is simply to break the walls of its cell. The plant does this by a mechanical or physiological process; the moral being by a conscious act which means at once the breaking-up of Self-ism and the recovery of a larger self in Altruism. Biologically, Reproduction begins as rupture. It is the release of the cell, full-fed, yet unsatiated, from itself. "Except a corn of wheat fall into the ground and die, it abideth alone; but if it die, it bringeth forth much fruit."

These facts are not coloured to suit a purpose. There is no other language in which science itself can state them. "Reproduction begins as rupture. Large cells beginning to die, save their lives by sacrifice. Reproduction is literally a life-saving against the approach of death. Whether it be the almost random rupture of one of the more primitive forms such as Schizogenes, or the overflow and separation of multiple buds as in Arcella, or the dissolution of a few of the Infusorians, an organism, which is becoming exhausted, saves itself and multiplies in reproducing. There is no Reproduction in plant, animal, or Man which does not involve self-sacrifice. All that is moral, and social, and other-regarding has come along the line of this function. Sacrifice, moreover, as these physiological facts disclose, is not an accident, nor an accompaniment of Reproduction, but an inevitable part of it. It is the universal law and the universal condition of life. The act of fertilization is the anabolic restoration, renewal, and rejuvenescence of a katabolic cell: it is a resurrection of the dead brought about by a sacrifice of the living, a dying of part of life in order to further life.

Pass from the unicellular plant to one of the higher phanerogams, and the self-sacrificing function is seen at work with still greater definiteness, for there we have a clearer contrast with the other function. To the physiologist a tree is not simply a tree, but a complicated piece of apparatus for discharging, in the first place, the function of Nutrition. Root, trunk, branch, twig, leaf, are so many organs—mouths, lungs, circulatory-system, alimentary canal—for carrying on to the utmost perfection the Struggle for Life. But this is not all. There is another piece of apparatus within this apparatus of a wholly different order. It has nothing to do with Nutrition. It has nothing to do with the Struggle for Life. It is the flower. The more its parts are studied, in spite of all homologies, it becomes more clear that this is a construction of a unique and wonderful character. So important has this extra apparatus seemed to science, that it has named the great division of the vegetable kingdom to which this and all higher plants belong, the Phanerogams—the flowering plants; and it recognizes the complexity and physiological value of this reproductive specialty by giving them the place of honour at the top of the vegetable creation. Watch this flower at work for a little, and behold a miracle. Instead of struggling for life it lays down its life. After clothing itself with a beauty which is itself the minister of unselfishness, it droops, it wastes, it lays down its life. The tree still lives; the other leaves are fresh and green; but this life within a life is dead. And why? Because within this death is life. Search among the withered petals, and there, in a cradle of cunning workmanship, are a hidden progeny of clustering seeds—the gift to the future which this dying mother has brought into the world at the cost of leaving it. The food she might have lived upon is given to her children, stored round each tiny embryo with lavish care, so that when they waken into the world the first helplessness of their hunger is met. All the arrangements in plant-life which concern the flower, the fruit, and the seed are the creations of the Struggle for the Life of Others.

No one, though science is supposed to rob all the poetry from Nature, reverences a flower like the biologist. He sees in its bloom the blush of the young mother; in its fading, the eternal sacrifice of Maternity. A yellow primrose is not to him a yellow primrose. It is an exquisite and complex structure added on to the primrose plant for the purpose of producing other primrose plants. At the base of the flower, packed in a delicate casket, lie a number of small white objects no larger than butterflies' eggs. These are the eggs of the primrose. Into this casket, by a secret opening, filmy tubes from the pollen grains—now enticed from their hiding-place on the stamens and clustered on the stigma—enter and pour their fertilizing fovilla through a microscopic gateway which opens in the wall of the egg and leads to its inmost heart. Mysterious changes then proceed. The embryo of a future primrose is born. Covered with many protective coats, it becomes a seed. The original casket swells, hardens, is transformed into a rounded capsule opening by valves or a deftly constructed hinge. One day this capsule, crowded with seeds, breaks open and completes the cycle of Reproduction by dispersing them over the ground. There, by and by, they will burst their enveloping coats, protrude their tiny radicles, and repeat the cycle of their parents' sacrificial life.

With endless variations in detail, these are the closing acts in the Struggle for the Life of Others in the vegetable world. We have illustrated the point from plants, because this is the lowest region where biological processes can be seen in action, and it is essential to establish beyond dispute the fundamental nature of the reproductive function. From this level onwards it might be possible to trace its influence, and growing influence, throughout the whole range of the animal kingdom until it culminates in its most consummate expression— a human mother. Some of the links in this unbroken ascent will be filled in at a later stage— for the Evolution of Maternity is so wonderful and so intricate as to deserve a treatment of its own —but meantime we must pass on to notice a few of the other gifts which Reproduction has bestowed upon the world. In a rigid sense, it is impossible to separate the gains to humanity from the Reproductive function as distinguished from those of the Nutritive. They are co-operators, not competitors, and their apparently rival paths continuously intertwine. But mark a few of the things that have mainly grown up around this second function, and decide whether or not it be a worthy ally of the Struggle for Life in the Evolution of Man.

To begin at the most remote circumference, consider what the world owes to-day to the Struggle for the Life of Others in the world of plants. This is the humblest sphere in which it can offer any gifts at all, yet these are already of such a magnitude that without them the higher world would not only be inexpressibly the poorer, but could not continue to exist. As we have just seen, all the arrangements in plant life which concern the flower are the creations of the Struggle for the Life of Others. For Reproduction alone the flower is created; when the process is over it returns to the dust. This miracle of beauty is a miracle of Love. Its splendour of colour, its variegations, its form, its symmetry, its perfume, its honey, its very texture, are all notes of Love—Love-calls or Love-lures or Love-provisions for the insect world, whose aid is needed to carry the pollen from anther to stigma, and perfect the development of its young. Yet this is but a thing thrown in, in giving something else. The Flower, botanically, is the herald of the Fruit. The Fruit, botanically, is the cradle of the Seed. Consider how great these further achievements are, how large a place in the world's history is filled by these two humble things—the Fruits and Seeds of plants. Without them the Struggle for Life itself would almost cease. The animal Struggle for Life is a struggle for what? For Fruits and Seeds. All animals in the long run depend for food upon Fruits and Seeds, or upon lesser creatures which have utilized Fruits and Seeds. Three-fourths of the population of the world at the present moment subsist upon rice. What is rice? It is a seed; a product of Reproduction. Of the other fourth, three-fourths live upon grains—barley, wheat, oats, millet. What are these grains? Seeds—stores of starch or albumen which, in the perfect forethought of Reproduction, plants bequeath to their offspring. The foods of the world, especially the children's foods, are the foods of the children of plants, the foods which unselfish activities store round the cradles of the helpless, so that when the sun wakens them to their new world they may not want. Every plant in the world lives for Others. It sets aside something, something costly, cared for, the highest expression of its nature. The Seed is the tithe of Love, the tithe which Nature renders to Man. When Man lives upon Seeds he lives upon Love. Literally, scientifically, Love is Life. If the Struggle for Life has made Man, braced and disciplined him, it is the Struggle for Love that sustains him.

Pass from the foods of Man to drinks, and the, gifts of Reproduction once more all but exhaust the list. This may be mere coincidence, but a coincidence which involves both food and drink is at least worth noting The first and universal food of the world is milk, a product of Reproduction. All distilled spirits are products of Reproduction. All malted liquors are made from the embryos of plants. All wines are juices of the grape. Even on the plane of the animal appetites, in mere relation to Man's hunger and his thirst, the factor of Reproduction is thus seen to be fundamental. To interpret the course of Evolution without this would be to leave the richest side even of material Nature without an explanation. Retrace the ground even thus hastily travelled over, and see how full Creation is of meaning, of anticipation of good for Man, how far back begins the undertone of Love. Remember that nearly all the beauty of the world is Love-beauty—the corolla of the flower and the plume of the grass, the lamp of the firefly, the plumage of the bird, the horn of the stag, the face of a woman; that nearly all the music of the natural world is Love-music—the song of the nightingale, the call of the mammal, the chorus of the insect, the serenade of the lover; that nearly all the foods of the world are Love-foods—the date and the raisin, the banana and the bread-fruit, the locust and the honey, the eggs, the grains, the seeds, the cereals, and the legumes; that all the drinks of the world are Love-drinks—the juices of the sprouting grain and the withered hop, the milk from the udder of the cow, the wine from the Love-cup of the vine. Remember that the Family, the crown of all higher life, is the creation of Love; that Co-operation, which means power, which means wealth, which means leisure, which therefore means art and culture, recreation and education, is the gift of Love. Remember not only these things, but the diffusions of feeling which accompany them, the elevations, the ideals, the happiness, the goodness, and the faith in more goodness, and ask if it is not a world of Love in which we live.

Co-operation in Nature

Though Co-operation is not exclusively the gift of Reproduction, it is so closely related to it that we may next observe a few of the fruits of this most definitely altruistic principle. For here is a principle, not merely a series of interesting phenomena, profoundly rooted in Nature and having for its immediate purpose the establishment of Other-ism. In innumerable cases, doubtless, Co-operation has been induced rather by the action of the Struggle for Life—a striking circumstance in itself, as showing how the very selfish side of life has had to pay its debt to the larger law—but in multitudes more it is directly allied with the Struggle for the Life of Others.

For illustrations of the principle in general we may begin with the very dawn of life. Every life at first was a single cell. Co-operation was unknown. Each cell was self-contained and self-sufficient, and as new cells budded from the parent they moved away and set up life for themselves. This self-sufficiency leads to nothing in Evolution. Unicellular organisms may be multiplied to infinity, but the vegetable kingdom can never rise in height, or symmetry, or productiveness without some radical change. But soon we find the co-operative principle beginning its mysterious integrating work. Two, three, four, eight, ten cells club together and form a small mat, or cylinder, or ribbon—the humblest forms of corporate plant-life—in which each individual cell divides the responsibilities and the gains of living with the rest. The colony succeeds; grows larger; its co-operations become more close and varied. Division of labour in new directions arises for the common good; leaves are organized for nutrition, and special cells for reproduction. All the organs increase in specialization; and the time arrives when from cryptogams the plant world bursts into flowers. A flower is organized for Co-operation. It is not an individual entity, but a commune, a most complex social system. Sepal, petal, stamen, anther, each has its separate role in the economy, each necessary to the other and to the life of the species as a whole. Mutual aid having reached this stage can never be arrested short of the extinction of plant-life itself.

Even after this stage, so triumphant is the success of the Co-operative Principle, that having exhausted the possibilities of further development within the vegetable kingdom, it overflowed these boundaries and carried the activities of flowers into regions which the plant-world never invaded before. With a novelty and audacity unique in organic Nature, the higher flowering plants, stimulated by Co-operation, opened communication with two apparently forever unrelated worlds, and established alliances which secured from the subjects of these distant states a perpetual and vital service. The history of these relations forms the most entrancing chapter in botanical science. But so powerfully has this illustration of the principle appealed already to the popular imagination that it becomes a mere form to re-state it. What interests us anew in these novel enterprises, nevertheless, is that they are directly connected with the Reproductive Struggle. For it is not for food that the plant-world voyages into foreign spheres, but to perfect the supremer labour of its life.

The vegetable world is a world of still life. No higher plant has the power to move to help its neighbour, or even to help itself, at the most critical moment of its life. And it is through this very helplessness that these new Co-operations are called forth. The fertilizing pollen grows on one part of the flower, the stigma which is to receive it grows on another, or it may be on a different plant. But as these parts cannot move towards one another, the flower calls in the aid of moving things. Unconscious of their vicarious service, the butterfly and the bee, as they flit from flower to flower, or the wind as it blows across the fields, carry the fertilizing dust to the waiting stigma, and complete that act without which in a generation the species would become extinct. No flower in the world, at least no entomophalous flower, can continuously develop healthy offspring without the Co-operations of an insect; and multitudes of flowers without such aid could never seed at all. It is to these Co-operations that we owe all that is beautiful and fragrant in the flower-world. To attract the insect and recompense it for its trouble, a banquet of honey is spread in the heart of the flower; and to enable the visitor to find the nectar, the leaves of the flower are made showy or conspicuous beyond all other leaves. To meet the case of insects which love the dusk, many flowers are coloured white; for those which move about at night and cannot see at all, the night-flowers load the darkness with their sweet perfume. The loveliness, the variegations of shade and tint, the ornamentations, the scents, the shapes, the sizes of flowers, are all the gifts of Co-operation. The flower in every detail, in fact, is a monument to the Co-operative Principle.

Scarcely less singular are the Co-operations among flowers themselves, the better to attract the attention of the insect world. Many flowers are so small and inconspicuous that insects might not condescend to notice them. But Altruism is always inventive. Instead of dispersing their tiny florets over the plant, these club together at single points, so that by the multitude of numbers an imposing show is made. Each of the associating flowers in these cases preserves its individuality, and—as we see in the Elder or the Hemlock—continues to grow on its own flower-stalk. But in still more ingenious species the partners to a floral advertisement sacrifice their separate stems and cluster close together on a common head. The Thistle, for example, is not one flower, but a colony of flowers, each complete in all its parts, but all gaining the advantage of conspicuousness by densely packing themselves together. In the Sunflowers and many others the sacrifice is carried still further. Of the multitude of florets clustered together to form the mass of colour, a few cease the development of the reproductive organs altogether, and allow their whole strength to go towards adding visibility to the mass. The florets in the centre of the group, packed close together, are unable to do anything in this direction; but those on the margin expand the perianth into a blazing circle of flame, and leave the deep work of Reproduction to those within. What are the advantages gained by all this mutual aid? That it makes them the fittest to survive. These Co-operative Plants are among the most numerous, most vigorous, and most widely diffused in Nature. Self-sacrifice and Co-operation are thus recognized as sound in principle. The blessing of Nature falls upon them. The words themselves, in any more than a merely physical sense, are hopelessly out of court in any scientific interpretation of things. But the point to mark is, that on the mechanical equivalents of what afterwards come to have ethical relations Natural Selection places a premium. Non-co-operative or feebly co-operative organisms go to the wall. Those which give mutual aid survive and people the world with their kind.

Without pausing to note the intricate Co-operations of flowers which reward the eye of the specialist—the subtle alliance with Space in Dioecious flowers; with Time in Dichogamous species, and with Size in the Dimorphic and Trimorphic forms—consider for a moment the extension of the principle to the Seed and Fruit. Helpless, single-handed, as is a higher plant, with regard to the efficient fertilizing of its flowers, an almost more difficult problem awaits it when it comes to the dispersal of its seeds. If each seed fell where it grew, the spread of the species would shortly be at an end. But Nature, working on the principle of Co-operation, is once more redundant in its provisions. By a series of new alliances the offspring are given a start on distant and unoccupied ground; and so perfect are the arrangements in this department of the Struggle for the Life of Others that single plants, immovably rooted in the soil, are yet able to distribute their children over the world. By a hundred devices the fruits and seeds when ripe are entrusted to outside hands provided with wing or parachute and launched upon the wind, attached by cunning contrivances to bird and beast, or dropped into stream and wave and ocean-current, and so transported over the earth.

If we turn to the Animal Kingdom, the Principle of Co-operation everywhere once more confronts us. It is singular that, with few exceptions, science should still know so little of the daily life of even the common animals. A few favourite mammals, some birds, three or four of the more picturesque and clever of the insects—these almost exhaust the list of those whose ways are thoroughly known. But, looking broadly at Nature, one general fact is striking—the more social animals are in overwhelming preponderance over the unsocial. Mr. Darwin's dictum, that "those communities which included the greatest number of the most sympathetic members would flourish best" is wholly proved. Run over the names of the commoner or more dominant mammals, and it will be found that they are those which have at least a measure of sociability. The cat-tribe excepted, nearly all live together in herds or troops—the elephant, for instance, the buffalo, deer, antelope, wild-goat, sheep, wolf, jackal, reindeer, hippopotamus, zebra, hyena, and seal. These are mammals, observe—an association of sociability in its highest developments with reproductive specialization. Cases undoubtedly exist where the sociability may not be referable primarily to this function; but in most the chief Co-operations are centred in Love. So advantageous are all forms of mutual service that the question may be fairly asked, whether after all Co-operation and Sympathy—at first instinctive, afterwards reasoned—are not the greatest facts even in organic Nature? To quote the words of Prince Kropotkin: "As soon as we study animals—not in laboratories and museums only, but in the forest and the prairie, in the steppes and the mountains—we at once perceive that though there is an immense amount of warfare and extermination going on amidst various species, and especially amidst various classes of animals, there is, at the same time, as much, or perhaps more, of mutual support, mutual aid, and mutual defence, amidst animals belonging to the same species or, at least, to the same society. Sociability is as much a law of Nature as mutual struggle. . . . If we resort to an indirect test and ask Nature 'Who are the fittest: those who are continually at war with each other, or those who support one another?' we at once see that those animals which acquire habits of mutual aid are undoubtedly the fittest. They have more chances to survive, and they attain, in their respective classes, the highest development of intelligence and bodily organization. If the numberless facts which can be brought forward to support this view are taken into account, we may safely say that mutual aid is as much a law of animal life as mutual struggle; but that, as a factor of evolution, it most probably has a far greater importance, inasmuch as it favours the development of such habits and character as ensure the maintenance and further development of the species, together with the greatest amount of welfare and enjoyment of life for the individual, with the least waste of energy.

In the large economy of Nature, almost more than within these specific regions, the interdependence of part with part is unalterably established. The system of things, from top to bottom, is an uninterrupted series of reciprocities. Kingdom corresponds with kingdom, organic with inorganic. Thus, to carry on the larger agriculture of Nature, myriads of living creatures have to be retained in the earth itself—in the earth—and to prepare and renew the soils in which the otherwise exhausted ground may keep up her continuous gifts of vegetation. Ages before Man appeared with his tools of husbandry, these agriculturists of Nature—in humid countries the Worm, in sub-tropical regions the White Ant—ploughed and harrowed the earth, so that without the Co-operations of these most lowly forms of life, the higher beauty and fruitfulness of the world had been impossible. The very existence of animal life, to take another case of broad economy, is possible only through the mediation of the plant. No animal has the power to satisfy one single impulse of hunger without the Co-operation of the vegetable world. It is one of the mysteries of organic chemistry that the Chlorophyll contained in the green parts of plants alone among substances has the power to break up the mineral kingdom and utilize the products as food. Though detected recently in the tissues of two of the very lowest animals, Chlorophyll is the peculiar possession of the vegetable kingdom, and forms the solitary point of contact between Man and all higher animals and their supply of food. Every grain of matter therefore eaten by Man, every movement of the body, every stroke of work done by muscle or brain, depends upon the contribution of a plant, or of an animal which has eaten a plant. Remove the vegetable kingdom, or interrupt the flow of its unconscious benefactions, and the whole higher life of the world ends. Everything, indeed, came into being because of something else, and continues to be because of its relations to something else. The matter of the earth is built up of co-operating atoms; it owes its existence, its motion, and its stability to co-operating stars. Plants and animals are made of co-operating cells, nations of cooperating men. Nature makes no move, Society achieves no end, the Cosmos advances not one step that is not dependent on Co-operation; and while the discords of the world disappear with growing knowledge, Science only reveals with increasing clearness the universality of its reciprocities.

But to return to the more direct effects of Reproduction. After creating Others there lay before Evolution a not less necessary task—the task of uniting them together. To create units in indefinite quantities and scatter them over the world is not even to take one single step in progress. Before any higher evolution can take place these units must by some means be brought into relation so as not only to act together, but to react upon each other. According to well-known biological laws, it is only in combinations, whether of atoms, cells, animals, or human beings, that individual units can make any progress, and to create such combinations is in every case the first condition of development. Hence the first commandment of Evolution everywhere is "Thou shalt mass, segregate, combine, grow large." Organic Evolution, as Mr. Herbert Spencer tells us, "is primarily the formation of an aggregate." No doubt the necessities of the Struggle for Life tended in many ways to fulfil this condition, and the organization of primitive societies, both animal and human, are largely its creation. Under its influence these were called together for mutual protection and mutual help; and Co-operations induced in this way have played an important part in Evolution. But the Co-operations brought about by Reproduction are at once more radical, more universal, and more efficient. The Struggle for Life is in part a disruptive force. The Struggle for the Life of Others is wholly a social force. The social efforts of the first are secondary; those of the last are primary. And had it not been for the stronger and unbreakable bond which the Struggle for the Life of Others introduced into the world, the organization of Societies had never even been begun. How subtly Reproduction effects its purpose an illustration will make plain. And we shall select it again from the lowest world of life, so that the fundamental nature of this factor may be once more vindicated on the way.

More than two thousand years ago Herodotus observed a remarkable custom in Egypt. At a certain season of the year the Egyptians went into the desert, cut off branches from the wild palms, and, bringing them back to their gardens, waved them over the flowers of the date-palm. Why they performed this ceremony they did not know; but they knew that if they neglected it the date crop would be poor or wholly lost. Herodotus offers the quaint explanation that along with these branches there came from the desert certain flies possessed of a "vivific virtue," which somehow lent an exuberant fertility to the dates. But the true rationale of the incantation is now explained. Palm trees, like human beings, are male and female. The garden plants, the date bearers, were females; the desert plants were males; and the waving of the branches over the females meant the transference of the fertilizing pollen dust from the one to the other.

Now consider, in this far away province of the vegetable kingdom, the strangeness of this phenomenon. Here are two trees living wholly different lives, they are separated by miles of desert sand; they are unconscious of one another's existence; and yet they are so linked together that their separation into two is a mere illusion. Physiologically they are one tree; they cannot dwell apart. It is nothing to the point that they are neither dowered with locomotion nor the power of conscious choice. The point is that there is that in Nature which unites these seemingly disunited things, which effects combinations and co-operations where one would least believe them possible, which sustains by arrangements of the most elaborate kind inter-relations between tree and tree. By a device the most subtle of all that guard the higher Evolution of the world—the device of Sex—Nature accomplishes this task of throwing irresistible bonds around widely separate things, and establishing such sympathies between them that they must act together or forfeit the very life of their kind. Sex is a paradox; it is that which separates in order to unite. The same mysterious mesh which Nature threw over the two separate palms, she threw over the few and scattered units which were to form the nucleus of Mankind.

Picture the state of primitive Man; his fear of other primitive Men; his hatred of them; his unsociability; his isolation; and think how great a thing was done by Sex in merely starting the crystallization of humanity. At no period, indeed, was Man ever utterly alone. There is no such thing in nature as a man, or for the matter of that as an animal, except among the very humblest forms. Wherever there is a higher animal there is another animal; wherever there is a savage there is another savage—the other half of him, a female savage. This much, at least Sex has done for the world-it has abolished the numeral one. Observe, it has not simply discouraged the existence of one; it has abolished the existence of one. The solitary animal must die, and can leave no successor. Unsociableness, therefore, is banished out of the world: it has become the very condition of continued existence that there should always be a family group, or at least pair. The determination of Nature to lay the foundation stone of corporate national life at this point, and to embed Sociability for ever in the constitution of humanity, is only obvious when we reflect with what extraordinary thoroughness this Evolution of Sex was carried out. There is no instance in Nature of Division of Labour being brought to such extreme specialization. The two sexes were not only to perform different halves of the same function, but each so entirely lost the power of performing the whole function that even with so great a thing at stake as the continuance of the species, one could not discharge it. Association, combination, mutual help, fellowship, affection—things on which all material and moral progress would ultimately turn—were thus forced upon the world at the bayonet's point.

This hint, that the course of development is taking a social, rather than an individual direction, is of immense significance. If that can be brought about by the Struggle for the Life of Others—and in the next chapters we shall see that it has been—there can be no dispute about the rank of the factor which consummates it. Along the line of the physiological function of Reproduction, in association with its induced activities and relations, not only has Altruism entered the world, but along with it the necessary field for its expansion and full expression. If Nature is to be read solely in the light of the Struggle for Life, these ethical anticipations—and as yet we are but at the beginning of them—for a social world and a moral life, must remain the stultification both of science and of teleology.

The Ethical Significance of Sex

Next among the gifts of Reproduction fall to be examined some further contributions yielded by the new and extraordinary device which a moment ago leaped into prominence—Sex. The direct, and especially the collateral, issues here are of such significance that it will be essential to study them in detail. Realize the novelty and originality of this most highly specialized creation, and it will be seen at once that something of exceptional moment must lie behind it. Here is a phenomenon which stands absolutely alone on the field of Nature. There is not only nothing at all like it in the world, but while everything else has homologues or analogues somewhere in the cosmos, this is without any parallel. Familiarity has so accustomed us to it that we accept the sex separation as a matter of course; but no words can do justice to the wonder and novelty of this strange line of cleavage which cuts down to the very root of being in everything that lives.

No theme of equal importance has received less attention than this from evolutionary philosophy. The single problems which sex suggests have been investigated with a keenness and brilliance of treatment never before brought to bear in this mysterious region; and Mr. Darwin's theory of sexual selection, whether true or false, has called attention to a multitude of things in living Nature which seem to find a possible explanation here. But the broad and simple fact that this division into maleness and femaleness should run between almost every two of every plant and every animal in existence, must have implications of a quite exceptional kind.

How deep, from the very dawn of life, this rent between the two sexes yawns is only now beginning to be seen. Examine one of the humblest water weeds—the Spirogyra. It consists of waving threads or necklaces of cells, each plant to the eye the exact duplicate of the other. Yet externally alike as they seem, the one has the physiological value of the male, the other of the female. Though a primitive method of Reproduction, the process in this case foreshadows the law of all higher vegetable life. From this point upwards, though there are many cases where Reproduction is asexual, in nearly every family of plants a Reproduction by spores takes place, and where it does not take place its absence is abnormal, and to be accounted for by degeneration. When we reach the higher plants the differences of sex become as marked as among the higher animals. Male and female flowers grow upon separate trees, or live side by side on the same branch, yet so unlike one another in form and colour that the untrained eye would never know them to be relatives. Even when male and female are grown on the same flower-stalk and enclosed in a common perianth, the hermaphroditism is generally but apparent, owing to the physiological barriers of heteromorphism and dichogamy. Sex-separation, indeed, is not only distinct among flowering plants, but is kept up by a variety of complicated devices, and a return to hermaphroditism is prevented by the most elaborate precautions.

When we turn to the animal kingdom again, the same great contrast arrests us. Half a century ago, when Balbiani described the male and female elements in microscopic infusorians, his facts were all but rejected by science. But further research has placed it beyond all doubt that the beginnings of sex are synchronous almost with those shadowings in of life. From a state marked by a mere varying of the nuclear elements, a state which might almost be described as one antecedent to sex, the sex-distinction slowly gathers definition, and passing through an infinite variety of forms, and with countless shades of emphasis, reaches at last the climax of separateness which is observed among birds and mammals. Often, even in the Metazoa, this separateness is outwardly obscured, as in star-fishes and reptiles; often it is matter of common observation; while sometimes it is carried to such a pitch of specialization that only the naturalist identifies the two wholly unlike creatures as male and female. Through the whole wide field of Nature then this gulf is fixed. Each page of the million-leaved Book of Species must be as it were split in two, the one side for the male, the other for the female. Classification naturally takes little note of this distinction; but it is fundamental. Unlikenesses between like things are more significant than unlikenesses of unlike things. And the unlikenesses between male and female are never small, and almost always great. Though the fundamental difference is internal the external form varies; size, colour, and a multitude of more or less striking secondary sexual characteristics separate the one from the other. Besides this, and more important than all, the cycle of a year's life is never the same for the male as for the female; they are destined from the beginning to pursue different paths, to live for different ends.

Now what does all this mean? To say that the sex-distinction is necessary to sustain the existence of life in the world is no answer, since it is at least possible that life could have been kept up without it. From the facts of Parthenogenesis, illustrated in bees and termites, it is now certain that Reproduction can be effected without fertilization; and the circumstance that fertilization is nevertheless the rule, proves this method of Reproduction, though not a necessity, to be in some way beneficial to life. It is important to notice this absence of necessity for sex having been created—the absence of any known necessity— from the merely physiological standpoint. Is it inconceivable that Nature should sometimes do things with an ulterior object, an ethical one, for instance? To no one with any acquaintance with Nature's ways will it be possible to conceive of such a purpose as the sole purpose. In these early days when sex was instituted it was a physical universe. Undoubtedly sex then had physiological advantages; but when in a later day the ethical advantages become visible, and rise to such significance that the higher world nearly wholly rests upon them, we are entitled, as viewing the world from that higher level, to have our own suspicions as to a deeper motive underlying the physical.

Apart from bare necessity, it is further remarkable that no very clear advantage of the sex-distinction has yet been made out by Science. Hensen and Van Beneden are able to see in conjugation no more than a Verjungung or rejuvenescence of the species. The living machinery in its wearing activities runs down and has to be wound up again; to keep life going some - fresh impulse must be introduced from time to time; or the protoplasm, exhausting itself, seeks restoration in fertilization and starts afresh. To Hatschek it is a remedy against the action of injurious variations; while to Weismann it is simply the source of variations. "I do not know," says the latter, "what meaning can be attributed to sexual reproduction other than the creation of hereditary individual characters to form the material on which natural selection may work. Sexual reproduction is so universal in all classes of multicellular organisms, and nature deviates so rarely from it, that it must necessarily be of pre-eminent importance. If it be true that new species are produced by processes of selection, it follows that the development of the whole organic world depends on these processes, and the part that amphigony has to play in nature, by rendering selection possible among multicellular organisms, is not only important, but of the very highest imaginable importance.

These views may be each true; and probably, in a measure, are; but the fact remains that the later psychical implications of sex are of such transcendent character as to throw all physical considerations into the shade. When we turn to these, their significance is as obvious as in the other case it was obscure. This will appear if we take even the most distinctively biological of these theories—that of Weismann. Sex, to him, is the great source of variation in Nature, in plainer English, of the variety of organisms in the world. Now this variety, though not the main object of sex, is precisely what it was essential for Evolution by some means to bring about. The first work of Evolution always is, as we have seen, to create a mass of similar things—atoms, cells, men—and the second is to break up that mass into as many different kinds of things as possible. Aggregation masses the raw material, collects the clay for the potter; differentiation destroys the featureless monotonies as fast as they are formed, and gives them back in new and varied forms. Now if Evolution designed, among other things, to undertake the differentiation of Mankind, it could not have done it more effectively than through the device of sex. To the blending, or to the mosaics, of the different characteristics of father and mother, and of many previous fathers and mothers, under the subtle wand of heredity, all the varied interest of the human world is due. When one considers the passing on, not so much of minute details of character and disposition, but of the dominant temperament and type; the new proportion in which already inextricably mingled tendencies are re-arranged, and the changed environment in which, with each new generation, they must unfold; it is seen how perfect an instrument for variegating humanity lies here. Had sex done nothing more than make an interesting world, the debt of Evolution to Reproduction had been incalculable.

The Ethical Significance of Maternity

But let us not be diverted from the main stream by these secondary results of the sex-distinction. A far more important implication lies before us. The problem that remains for us to settle is as to how the merely physical forms of Other-ism began to be accompanied or overlaid by ethical characters. And the solution of this problem requires nothing more than a consideration of the broad and fundamental fact of sex itself. In what it is, and in what it necessarily implies, we shall find the clue to the beginnings of the social and moral order of the world. For, rising on the one hand out of maleness and on the other hand out of femaleness, developments take place of such a kind as to constitute this the turning-point of the world's moral history. Let it be said at once that these developments are not to be sought for in the direction in which, from the nature of the factors, one might hastily suppose that they lay. What seems to be imminent at this stage, and as the natural end to which all has led up, is the institution of affection in definite forms between male and female. But we are on a very different track. Affection between male and female is a later, less fundamental, and, in its beginnings, less essential growth; and long prior to its existence, and largely the condition of it, is the even more beautiful development whose progress we have now to trace. The basis of this new development is indeed far removed from the mutual relations of sex with sex. For it lies in maleness and femaleness themselves, in their inmost quality and essential nature, in what they lead to and what they become. The superstructure, certainly, owes much to the psychical relations of father and mother, husband and wife, but the Evolution of Love began ages before these were established.

What exactly maleness is, and what femaleness, has been one of the problems of the world. At least five hundred theories of their origin are already in the field, but the solution seems to have baffled every approach. Sex has remained almost to the present hour an ultimate mystery of creation, and men seem to know as little what it is as whence it came. But among the last words of modern science there are one or two which spell out a partial clue to both of these mysterious problems. The method by which this has been reached is almost for the first time a purely biological one, and if its inferences are still uncertain, it has at least established some important facts.

Starting with the function of nutrition as the nearest ally of Reproduction, the newer experimenters have discovered cases in which sex apparently has been determined by the quantity and quality of the food-supply. And in actual practice it has been found possible, in the case of certain organisms, to produce either maleness or femaleness by simply varying their nutrition—femaleness being an accompaniment of abundant food, maleness of the reverse. When Yung, to take an authentic experiment, began his observations on tadpoles, he ascertained that in the ordinary natural condition the number of males and females produced was not far from equal—the percentage being about 57 female to 43 male, thus giving the females a preponderance of seven. But when a brood of tadpoles was sumptuously fed the percentage of females rose to 78, and when a second brood was treated even more liberally, the number amounted to 81. In a third experiment with a still more highly nutritious diet, the result of the high feeding was more remarkable, for in this case 92 females were produced and only 8 males. In the case of butterflies and moths, it has been found that if caterpillars are starved before entering the chrysalis state the offspring are males, while others of the same brood, when highly nourished, develop into females. A still more instructive case is that of the aphides, the familiar plant-lice of our gardens. During the warmth of summer, when food is abundant, these insects produce parthenogenetically nothing but females, while in the famines of later autumn they give birth to males. In striking confirmation of this fact it has been proved that in a conservatory where the aphides enjoy perpetual summer, the parthenogenetic succession of females continued to go on for four years and stopped only when the temperature was lowered and food diminished. Then males were at once produced. It will no longer be said that science is making no progress with this unique problem when it is apparently able to determine sex by turning off or on the steam in a green house. With regard to bees the relation between nutrition and sex seems equally established. "The three kinds of inmates in a bee-hive are known to everyone as queens, workers, and drones; or, as fertile females, imperfect females, and males. What are the factors determining the differences between these three forms? In the first place, it is believed that the eggs which give rise to drones are not fertilized, while those that develop into queens and workers have the normal history. But what fate rules the destiny of the two latter, determining whether a given ovum will turn out the possible mother of a new generation, or remain at the lower level of a non-fertile working female? It seems certain that the fate mainly lies in the quantity and quality of the food. Royal diet, and plenty of it, develops the future queens . . Up to a certain point the nurse bees can determine the future destiny of their charge by changing the diet, and this in some cases is certainly done. If a larva on the way to become a worker receive by chance some crumbs from the royal superfluity, the reproductive function may develop, and what are called 'fertile workers,' to a certain degree above the average abortiveness, result; or, by direct intention, a worker grub may be reared into a queen bee.

It is unnecessary to prolong the illustration, for the point it is wished to emphasize is all but in sight. As we have just witnessed, the tendency of abundant nutrition is to produce females, while defective nutritive conditions produce males. This means that in so far as nutrition reacts on the bodies of animals—and nothing does so more—there will be a growing difference, as time begins to accumulate the effects, between the organization and life-habit of male and female respectively. In the male, destructive processes, a preponderance of waste over repair, will prevail; the result will be a katabolic habit of body; in the female the constructive processes will be in the ascendant, occasioning an opposite or anabolic habit. Translated into less technical language, this means that the predominating note in the male will be energy, motion, activity; while passivity, gentleness, repose, will characterize the female. These words, let it be noticed, psychical though they seem, are yet here the coinages of physiology. No other terms indeed would describe the difference. Thus Geddes and Thomson: "The female cochineal insect, laden with reserve-products in the form of the well-known pigment, spends much of its life like a mere quiescent gall on the cactus plant. The male, on the other hand, in his adult state, is agile, restless, and short-lived. Now this is no mere curiosity of the entomologist, but in reality a vivid emblem of what is an average truth throughout the world of animals—the preponderating passivity of the females, the freedomness and activity of the males." Rolph's words, because he writes neither of men nor of animals, but goes back to the furthest recess of Nature and characterizes the cell itself, are still more significant: "The less nutritive and therefore smaller, hungrier, and more mobile organism is the male; the more nutritive and usually more quiescent is the female."

Now what do these facts indicate? They indicate that maleness is one thing and femaleness another, and that each has been specialized from the beginning to play a separate role in the drama of life. Among primitive peoples, as largely in modern times, "The tasks which demand a powerful development of muscle and bone, and the resulting capacity for intermittent spurts of energy, involving corresponding periods of rest, fall to the man; the care of the children and all the various industries which radiate from the hearth, and which call for an expenditure of energy more continuous, but at a lower tension, fall to the woman. Whether this or any theory of the origin of Sex be proved or unproved, the fact remains, and is everywhere emphasized in Nature, that a certain constitutional difference exists between male and female, a difference inclining the one to a robuster life, and implanting in the other a certain mysterious bias in the direction of what one can only call the womanly disposition.

On one side of the great line of cleavage have grown up men—those whose lives for generations and generations have been busied with one particular set of occupations; on the other side have lived and developed women—those who for generations have been busied with another and a widely different set of occupations. And as occupations have inevitable reactions upon mind, character, and disposition, these two have slowly become different in mind and character and disposition. That cleavage therefore, which began in the merely physical region, is now seen to extend into the psychical realm, and ends by supplying the world with two great and forever separate types. No efforts, or explanations, or expostulations can ever break down that distinction between maleness and femaleness, or make it possible to believe that they were not destined from the first of time to play a different part in human history. Male and female never have been and never will be the same. They are different in origin; they have travelled to their destinations by different routes; they have had different ends in view. The result is that they are different, and the contribution therefore of each to the evolution of the human race is special and unique. By and by it will be our duty to mark what Man, in virtue of his peculiar gift, has done for the world; part indeed of his contribution has been already recorded here. To him has been mainly assigned the fulfilment of the first great function—the Struggle for Life. Woman, whose higher contribution has not yet been named. is the chosen instrument for carrying on the Struggle for the Life of Others. Man's life, on the whole, is determined chiefly by the function of Nutrition; Woman's by the function of Reproduction. Man satisfies the one by going out into the world, and in the rivalries of war and the ardours of the chase, in conflict with Nature, and amid the stress of industrial pursuits, fulfilling the law of Self-preservation; Woman completes her destiny by occupying herself with the industries and sanctities of the home, and paying the debt of Motherhood to her race.

Now out of this initial difference—so slight at first as to amount to no more than a scarcely perceptible bias—have sprung the most momentous issues. For by every detail of their separate careers the two original tendencies—to outward activity in the man; to inward activity, miscalled passivity, in the woman—became accentuated as time went on. The one life tended towards selfishness, the other towards unselfishness. While one kept Individualism alive, the other kept Altruism alive. Blended in the children, these two master-principles from this their starting-point acted and reacted all through history, seeking that mean in which true life lies. Thus by a Division of Labour appointed by the will of Nature, the conditions for the Ascent of Man were laid.

But by far the most vital point remains. For we have next to observe how this bears directly on the theme we set out to explore—the Evolution of Love. The passage from mere Other-ism, in the physiological sense, to Altruism, in the moral sense, occurs in connection with the due performance of her natural task by her to whom the Struggle for the Life of Others is assigned. That task, translated into one great word, is Maternity—which is nothing but the Struggle for the Life of Others transfigured, transferred to the moral sphere. Focused in a single human being, this function, as we rise in history, slowly begins to be accompanied by those heaven-born psychical states which transform the femaleness of the older order into the Motherhood of the new. When one follows Maternity out of the depths of lower Nature, and beholds it ripening in quality as it reaches the human sphere, its character, and the character of the processes by which it is evolved, appear in their full divinity. For of what is Maternity the mother? Of children? No; for these are the mere vehicle of its spiritual manifestation. Of affection between female and male? No; for that, contrary to accepted beliefs, has little to do in the first instance with sex-relations. Of what then? Of Love itself, of Love as Love, of Love as Life, of Love as Humanity, of Love as the pure and undefiled fountain of all that is eternal in the world. In the long stillness which follows the crisis of Maternity, witnessed only by the new and helpless life which is at once the last expression of the older function and the unconscious vehicle of the new, Humanity is born. By an alchemy which remains, and must ever remain, the secret of Nature, the physiological forces give place to those higher principles of sympathy, solicitude, and affection which from this time onwards are to change the course of Evolution and determine a diviner destiny for a Human Race:

> "Earth's insufficiency
> Here grows to event;
> The indescribable
> Here it is done;
> The woman-soul leadeth us
> Upward and on.

So stupendous is this transition that the mere possibility staggers us. Separated by the whole diameter of conscious intelligence and will, what possible affinities can exist between the Reproductive and the Altruistic process? What analogy can ever exist between the earlier physiological Struggle for the Life of Others and the later Struggle of Love? Yet, different though their accompaniments may be, when closely examined they are seen, at every essential point, running parallel with each other. The object in either case is to continue the life of the Species; the essence of both is self-sacrifice; the first manifestation of the sacrifice is to make provision for Others by helping them to draw the first few breaths of life. But what has Love to do with Species? Can Altruism have reference to mere life? The answer is, that in its first beginnings it has almost nothing to do with anything else. For, consider the situation. Reproduction, let us suppose, has done its most perfect work on the physiological plane: the result is that a human child is born into the world. But the work of Reproduction being to Struggle for the Life of the Species, its task is only complete when it secures that the child, representing the Species, shall live. If the child dies, Reproduction has failed; the Species, so far as this effort is concerned, comes to an end. Now, can Reproduction as a merely physiological function complete this process? It can not. What can? Only the Mother's Care and Love. Without these, in a few hours or days, the new life must perish; the earlier achievement of Reproduction is in vain. Hence there comes a moment when these two functions meet, when they act as complements to each other; when Physiology hands over its unfinished task to Ethics; when Evolution—if for once one may use a false distinction—depends upon the 'moral' process to complete the work the 'cosmic' process has begun.

At what precise stage of the Ascent, in association with what class of animals, Other-ism began to shade into Altruism in the ethical sense, is immaterial. Whether the Altruism in the early stages is real or apparent, profound or superficial, voluntary or automatic, does not concern us. What concerns us is that the Altruism is there; that the day came when, even though a rudiment, it was a reality; above all that the arrangements for introducing and perfecting it were realities. The prototype, for ages, may have extended only to form, to the outward relation; for further ages no more Altruism may have existed than was absolutely necessary to the preservation of the species. But to fix the eye upon it at that remote stage and assert that, because it was apparently then automatic, it must therefore have been automatic ever after, is to forget the progressive character of Evolution as well as to ignore facts. While many of the apparent Other-regarding acts among animals are purely selfish and purely automatic, undoubtedly there are instances where more is involved. Apart from their own offspring—in relation to which there may always be the suspicion of automatism; and apart from domestic animals—which are open to the further suspicion of having been trained to it— animals act spontaneously towards other animals; they have their playmates; they make friendships, and very attached friendships. Much more, indeed, has been claimed for them; but it is not necessary to claim even this much. No evolutionist would expect among animals—domestic animals always excepted—any considerable development of Altruism, because the physiological and psychical conditions which directly led to its development in Man's case were fulfilled in no other creature.

Simple as seems the method by which the first few sparks of Love were nursed into flame in the bosom of Maternity, the details of the evolution are so intricate as to require a chapter to themselves. But the emphasis which Nature puts on this process may be judged of by the fact that one half the human race had to be set apart to sustain and perfect it. To the evolutionist who discerns the true proportions of the forces which made for the Ascent of Man, one of the two or three great events in the natural history of the world was the institution of sex. It is here that the master-forces which were to dominate the latest and highest stages of the process start; here, specialized into Egoism and Altruism, they part; and here, each having run its different course, they meet to distribute their gains to a succeeding race. With the initial impulses of their sex strengthened by the different life-routine to which each led, these two forces ran their course through history, determining by their ceaseless reactions the order and progress of the world, or when wrongly balanced, its disorder and decay. According to evolutional philosophy there are three great marks or necessities of all true development—Aggregation, or the massing of things; Differentiation, or the varying of things ; and Integration, or the re-uniting of things into higher wholes. All these processes are brought about by sex more perfectly than by any other factor known. From a careful study of this one phenomenon, science could almost decide that Progress was the object of Nature, and that Altruism was the object of Progress.

This vital relation between Altruism in its early stages and physiological ends, neither implies that it is to be limited by these ends nor defined in terms of them. Everything must begin somewhere. And there is no aphorism which the labours of Evolution, at each fresh beginning, have tended more consistently to endorse than "first that which is natural, then that which is spiritual." How this great saying also disposes of the difficulty, which appears and reappears with every forward step in Evolution, as to the qualitative terms in which higher developments are to be judged, is plain. Because the spiritual to our vision emerges from the natural, or, to speak more accurately, is convoyed upwards by the natural for the first stretches of its ascent, it is not necessarily contained in that natural, nor is it to be defined in terms of it. What comes "first" is not the criterion of what comes last. Few things are more forgotten in criticism of Evolution than that the nature of a thing is not dependent on its origin, that one's whole view of a long, growing, and culminating process is not to be governed by the first sight the microscope can catch of it. The processes of Evolution evolve as well as the products; evolve with the products. In the Environments they help to create, or to make available, they find a field for new creations as well as further reinforcements for themselves. With the creation of human children Altruism found an area for its own expansion such as had never before existed in the world. In this new soil it grew from more to more, and reached a potentiality which enabled it to burst the trammels of physical conditions, and overflow the world as a moral force. The mere fact that the first uses of Love were physical shows how perfectly this process bears the stamp of Evolution. The later function is seen to relieve the earlier at the moment when it would break down without it, and continue the ascent without a pause.

If it be hinted that Nature has succeeded in continuing the Ascent of Life in Animals without any reinforcement from psychical principles, the first answer is that owing to physiological conditions this would not have been possible in the case of Man. But even among animals it is not true that Reproduction completes its work apart from higher principles, for even there, there are accompaniments, continually increasing in definiteness, which at least represent the instincts and emotions of Man. It is no doubt true that in animals the affections are less voluntarily directed than in the case of a human mother. But in either case they must have been involuntary at first. It can only have been at a late stage in Evolution that Nature could trust even her highest product to carry on the process by herself. Before Altruism was strong enough to take its own initiative, necessity had to be laid upon all mothers, animal and human, to act in the way required. In part physiological, this necessity was brought about under the ordinary action of that principle which had to take charge of everything in Nature until the will of Man appeared—Natural Selection. A mother who did not care for her children would have feeble and sickly children. Their children's children would be feeble and sickly children. And the day of reckoning would come when they would be driven off the field by a hardier, that is a better-mothered, race. Hence the premium of Nature upon better mothers. Hence the elimination of all the reproductive failures, of all the mothers who fell short of completing the process to the last detail. And hence, by the law of the Survival of the Fittest, Altruism, which at this stage means good-motherism, is forced upon the world.

This consummation reached, the foundations of the human world are finished. Nothing foreign remains to be added. All that need happen henceforth is that the Struggle for the Life of Others should work out its destiny. To follow out the gains of Reproduction from this point would be to write the story of the nations, the history of civilization, the progress of Social Evolution. The key to all these processes is here. There is no intelligible account of the world which is not founded on the realization of the place of this factor in development. Sociology, practically, can only beat the air, can make no step forward as a science, until it recognizes this basis in biology. It is the failure, not so much to recognize the supremacy of this second factor, but to see that there is any second factor at all, that has vitiated almost every attempt to construct a symmetrical social philosophy. It has long, indeed, been perceived that society is an organism, and an organism which has grown by natural growth like a tree. But the tree to which it is usually likened is such a tree as never grew on this earth. For it is a tree without flowers; a tree with nothing but stem and leaves; a tree that performed the function of Nutrition, and forgot all about Reproduction. The great unrecognized truth of social science is that the Social Organism has grown and flowered and fruited in virtue of the continuous activities and inter-relations of the two co-related functions of Nutrition and Reproduction, that these two dominants being at work it could not but grow, and grow in the way it has grown. When the dual nature of the evolving forces is perceived; when their reactions upon one another are understood; when the changed material with which they have to work from time to time, the further obstacles confronting them at every stage, the new Environments which modify their action as the centuries add their growths and disencumber them of their withered leaves,— when all this is observed, the whole social order falls into line. From the dawn of life these two forces have acted together, one continually separating, the other continually uniting; one continually looking to its own things, the other to the things of Others. Both are great in Nature—but "the greatest of these is Love."

The answer to the argument in favour of automatism is thus summarized by C. M. Williams: "(1) That functions which are preserved and inherited must evidently be, not only in animals and plants, but also and equally in man, such as favour the preservation of the species; those which do not so favour it must perish with the individuals or species to which they belong; (2) that it cannot, indeed, be assumed that a result which has never come within the experience of the species can be willed as an end, although, with the species, function securing results which, from a human point of view, might be regarded as such, may be preserved; but (3) that, as far as we assume the existence of consciousness at all in any species or individual, we must assume pleasure and pain, pleasure in customary function, pain in its hindrance; and (4) that, as far as we can assume memory, we may also feel authorized to assume that a remembered action may be associated with remembered results that come within the experience of the animal, some phases of which may thus become, as combined with pleasure or pain, ends to seek or consequences to avoid."—Evolutional Ethics, p. 386.

The Evolution of a Mother

The Evolution of a Mother, in spite of its half-humorous, half-sacrilegious sound, is a serious study in Biology. Even on its physical side this was the most stupendous task Evolution ever undertook. It began when the first bud burst from the first plant-cell, and was only completed when the last and most elaborately wrought pinnacle of the temple of Nature crowned the animal creation.

What was that pinnacle? There is no more instructive question in science. For the answer brings into relief one of the expression-points of Nature—one of these great teleological notes of which the natural order is so full, and of which this is by far the most impressive. Run the eye for a moment up the scale of animal life. At the bottom are the first animals, the Protozoa. The Coelenterates follow, then in mixed array, the Echinoderms, Worms, and Molluscs. Above these come the Pisces, then the Amphibia, then the Reptilia, then the Aves, then—What? The Mammalia, *the Mothers*. There the series stops. Nature has never made anything since.

Is it too much to say that the one motive of organic Nature was to make Mothers? It is at least certain that this was the chief thing she did. Ask the Zoologist what, judging from science alone, Nature aspired to from the first, he could but answer Mammalia—Mothers. In as real a sense as a factory is meant to turn out locomotives or clocks, the machinery of Nature is designed in the last resort to turn out Mothers. You will find Mothers in lower Nature at every stage of imperfection; you will see attempts being made to get at better types; you find old ideas abandoned and higher models coming to the front. And when you get to the top you find the last great act was but to present to the world a physiologically perfect type. It is a fact which no human Mother can regard without awe, which no man can realize without a new reverence for woman and a new belief in the higher meaning of Nature, that the goal of the whole plant and animal kingdoms seems to have been the creation of a family, which the very naturalist has had to call Mammalia.

That care for others, from which the Mammalia take their name, though reaching its highest expression there, is introduced into Nature in cruder forms almost from the dawn of life. In the vegetable kingdom, from the motherlessness of the early Cryptogams, we rise to find a first maternity foreshadowed in the flowering tree. It elaborates a seed or nut or fruit with infinite precaution, surrounding the embryo with coat after coat of protective substance, and storing around it the richest foods for its future use. And rudimentary though the manifestation be, when we remember that this is not an incident in the tree's life but its whole blossom and crown, it is impossible but to think of this solicitude and Motherhood together. So exalted in the tree's life is this provision for others that the Botanist, like the Zoologist, places the mothering plants at the top of his department of Nature. His highest division is the Phanerogams—named, literally, in terms of their reproductive specialization.

Crossing into the animal kingdom we observe the same motherless beginning, the same cared-for end. All elementary animals are orphans; they know neither home nor care; the earth is their only mother or the inhospitable sea; they waken to isolation, to apathy, to the attentions only of those who seek their doom. But as we draw nearer the apex of the animal kingdom, the spectacle of a protective Maternity looms into view. At what precise point it begins it is difficult to say. But that it does not begin at once, that there is a long and gradual Evolution of Maternity, is clear. From casual observation, and from popular books, it might be inferred that care of offspring—we cannot yet speak of affection—is characteristic of the whole field of Nature. On the contrary, it is doubtful whether in the Invertebrate half of Nature it exists at all. If it does it is very rare; and in the Vertebrates it is met with only exceptionally till we reach the two highest classes. What does exist, and sometimes in marvellous perfection, is care for eggs; but that is a wholly different thing, both in its physical and psychical aspect, from love of offspring. The truth is, Nature so made animals in the early days that they did not need Mothers. The moment they were born they looked after themselves, and were perfectly able to look after themselves. Mothers in these days would have been a superfluity. All that Nature worked at at that dawning date was Maternity in a physical sense— Motherhood came as a later and a rarer growth. The children of those days were not really children at all; they were only offspring, springers off, deserters from home. At one bound they were out into life on their own account, and she who begat them knew them no more. That early world, therefore, for millions and millions of years was a bleak and loveless world. It was a world without children and a world without Mothers. It is good to realize how heartless Nature was till these arrived.

In the lower reaches of Nature, things remain still unchanged. The rule is not that the Mother ignores, but that she never sees her child. The land-crabs of the West Indies descend from their homes in the mountains once a year, march in procession to the sea, commit their eggs to the waves, and come away. The burying-beetles deposit their fragile capsules in the dead carcase of a mouse or bird, plant all together in the earth, and leave them to their fate. Myriads of other creatures are born into the world, and ordained so to be born, whose Mothers are dead before they begin to live. The moment of birth with the Ephemeridae is also the moment of death. These are not cases nevertheless where there has been no care. On the contrary, there is a solicitude for the egg of the most extreme kind—for its being placed exactly in the right spot, at the right time, protected from the weather, shielded from enemies, and provided with a first supply of food. The butterfly places the eggs of its young on the very leaf which the coming caterpillar likes the most, and on the under side of the leaf, where they will be least exposed—a case which illustrates in a palpable way the essential difference between Motherhood and Maternity. Maternity here, in the restricted sense of merely adequate physical care, is carried to its utmost perfection. Everything that can be done for the egg is done. Motherhood, on the other hand, is non-existent, is even an anatomical impossibility. If a butterfly could live till its egg was hatched—which does not happen—it would see no butterfly come out of the egg, no airy likeness of itself, but an earth-bound caterpillar. If it recognized this creature as its child, it could never play the Mother to it. The anatomical form is so different that were it starving it could not feed it, were it threatened it could not save it, nor is it possible to see any direction in which it could be of the slightest use to it. It is obvious that Nature never intended to make a Mother here; that all that she desired as yet was to perfect the first maternal instinct. And the tragedy of the situation is that on that day when its training to be a true Mother should begin, the butterfly passes out of the world.

But there is another reason, in addition to the precocity of the offspring, why parental care is a drug in the market in lower Nature. There are such multitudes of these creatures that it is scarcely worth caring for them. The humbler denizens of the world produce offspring, not by units or tens, but by thousands and millions; and with populations so vast, maternal protection is not required to sustain the existence of the species. It was probably on the whole a better arrangement to produce a million and let them take their chance, than to produce one and take special trouble with it. It was easier, moreover, a thousand times easier, for Nature to make a million young than one Mother. But the ethical effect, if one may use such a term here, of this early arrangement was nil. All this saving of Motherly trouble meant for a long space in Nature complete absence of maternal training. With children of this sort Motherhood had no chance. There was no time to love, no opportunity to love, and no object to love. It was a period of physical installations; and of psychical installations only as establishing the first stages of the maternal instinct—the prenatal care of the egg. This is a necessary beginning, but it is imperfect; it arrests itself at the critical point—where care can react upon the Mother.

Now, before Maternal Love can be evolved out of this first care, before Love can be made a necessity, and carried past the unhatched egg to the living thing which is to come out of it, Nature must alter all her ways. Four great changes at least must be introduced into her programme. In the first place, she must cause fewer young to be produced at a birth. In the second place, she must have these young produced in such outward form that their Mothers will recognize them. In the third place, instead of producing them in such physical perfection that they are able to go out into life the moment they are born, she must make them helpless, so that for a time they must dwell with her if they are to live at all. And fourthly, it is required that she shall be made to dwell with them; that in some way they also should be made necessary—physically necessary— to her to compel her to attend to them. All these beautiful arrangements we find carried out to the last detail. A mother is made, as it were, in four processes. She requires, like the making of a coloured picture, four separate printings, each adding some new thing to the effect. Let us note the way in which woman—savage woman—became caretaker, and watcher, and nurse, and passed from femaleness to the higher heights of Motherhood.

The first great change that had to be introduced into Nature was the diminishing of the number of young produced at a birth. As we have seen, nearly all the lower animals produce scores, or hundreds, or thousands, or millions, at one time. Now, no mother can love a million. Clearly, if Nature wishes to make care-takers, she must moderate her demands. And so she sets to work to bring down the numbers, reducing them steadily until so few remain that Motherhood becomes a possibility. How great this change is can only be understood when one realizes the almost incalculable fecundity of the first created forms of life. When we examine the progeny of the lowest plants we find ourselves among figures so high that no microscope can count them. The Protococcus Nivalis shows its exuberant reproductive power by reddening the Arctic landscape with its offspring in a single night. When we break or shake the Puff-ball of the well-known fungus, the cloud of progeny darkens the air with a smoke made up of uncountable millions of spores. Hydatina Senta, one of the Rotifera, propagates four times in thirty-four hours, and in twelve days is the parent of sixteen million young. Among fish the number is still very great. The herring and the cod give birth to a million ova, the frog spawns eggs by the thousand, and most of the creatures at and below that level in a like degree. Then comes a gradual change. When we pass on to the Reptiles, the figures fall into hundreds. On reaching the birds the young are to be counted by tens or units. In the highest of Mammals the rule is one. This bringing down of the numbers is a remarkable circumstance. It means the calling in of a diffused care, to focus it upon one, and concentrate it into Love.

The next thing was to make it possible for the parent to recognize its young. If it was difficult to love a million it was impossible to love an embryo. In the lower reaches the young are never in the smallest degree like their parents, and, granting the highest power of recognition to the Mother, it is impossible that she should recognize her own offspring. For generations even Science was imposed upon here, for many forms of life were described and classified as distinct species which have turned out to be simply the young of other species. It may be useless to contrast so striking a case as the ciliated Planula with the adult Aurelia—vagaries of form which for generations deceived the naturalist— for it is doubtful whether creatures of the Medusoid type have eyes; but in the higher groups where power of recognition is more certain, the unlikeness of progeny to parent is often as decided. The larval forms of the Star-fish or the Sea Urchin, or their kinsman the Holothurian, are disguised past all recognition; and among the Insects the relation between Butterflies and Moths and their respective caterpillars is beyond any possible clue. No doubt there are other modes of recognition in Nature than those which depend on the sense of sight. But looked at on every side, the fact remains that the power to identify their young is all but absent until the higher animals appear.

The next work of Nature, therefore, was to make the young resemble the parent, to make, in short, the children presentable at birth. And the means taken to effect this are worth noting. Nature always makes her changes with a marvellous economy, and generally, as in this case, with a quite startling simplicity. To start making a new kind of embryo, a plan obvious to us, was not thought of. That would have been to have lost all the time spent on them already. If Nature begins a thing and wishes to make a change, she never goes back to the beginning and starts de novo. Her respect for her own work is profound. To begin at the beginning again would not only be lost work, but waste of future time; and Evolution, slow as it may seem, never fails to take the quickest path. She did not then start making new embryos. She did not even touch up the old embryos. All that she did was to keep them hidden till they grew more presentable. She left them exactly as they were, only she drew a veil over them. Instead of saying "Let us re-create these little things," she passed the word "Let us delay them till they are fair to see." And from the day that word was passed, the embryos were hindered in the eggs, and the eggs were hindered in the nest, and the young were hindered in the body, retained in the dark for weeks and months, so that when first they caught the Mother's eye they were "strong and of a good liking."

Though in no case in higher Nature is the young an exact reproduction of its parent, it will be admitted that the likeness is very much greater than among any of the lower animals. The young of many birds are at least a colourable imitation of their parents; Nature's young geese are at least like enough geese not to be mistaken for swans; no dog could be misled into mistaking—even apart from the sense of smell—a kitten for a puppy, nor would a hare ever be taken in by the young of a rabbit. Among domestic animals like the sheep and cow there is a culmination of adaptation in this direction, the lamb and the calf when born being almost facsimiles of their Mothers. But this point need not be dwelt on. It is of insignificant importance, and belongs to the surface. The idea of Nature going out of her way to make better family likenesses will not stand scrutiny as a final end in physiology. These illustrations are simply adduced to confirm the impression that Nature is working not aimlessly, not even mysteriously, but in a specific direction; that somehow the idea of Mothers is in her mind, and that she is trying to draw closer and closer the bonds which are to unite the children of men. It will be enough if we have gathered from this parenthesis that some time in the remote past, parent and child came to be introduced to one another; that the young when born into the world gradually approached the parental form, that they no longer "shocked them by their larval ugliness"; so that "the first human mother on record, seeing her first-born son, exclaimed: `I have gotten a Man from the Lord.'

If this second process in the Evolution of Motherhood is of minor importance, the necessity for the third will not be doubted. What use is there for perfecting the power of recognition between parent and child if the latter act like the run of offspring in lower nature—spring off into independent life the moment they are born? If the Mother is to be taught to know her progeny, surely the progeny also must be taught not to abandon their Mother. And hence Nature had to set about a somewhat novel task—to teach the youth of the world the Fifth Commandment. Glance once more over the Animal series and see how thoroughly she taught them the lesson. It is sometimes said that Nature has no imperatives. In reality it is all imperative. This Commandment was thrust upon the early world under penalties for disobedience the most exacting that could be devised—the threat of death. Pick out a few children and inspect them. Take one from the bottom of Nature, one from the middle, and one from the top, and see if any progress in filial duty is visible as we ascend. The first,—the young of Aurelia will do, or a ciliated Infusorian,—representing countless millions like itself, is the Precocious Child. The moment this embryo is born it leaves the domestic hearth; the chances are it has never seen its parents. If it has, it disowns them on the spot. A better swimmer in many cases—for many of the parents have forgotten how to swim—it cannot be overtaken. It ignores its Mother and despises her. The second is the Good Intentioned Child. This child—a bird, let us say—begins well, stays much at home in the early days, but plays the prodigal towards the close. For some weeks it remains quietly in the egg; for more weeks it remains—not quite so quietly—in the nest; and for more weeks still—but with an obvious itching to be off—in the neighbourhood of the nest. This, nevertheless, is a good subject. It is really a kind of child, and its Mother is truly a Mother. The third is the Model Child—the Mammal. In this child, which is only found in the high places of Nature, infancy reaches its last perfection. Housed, protected, sumptuously fed, the luxurious children keep to their Mother's side for months and years, and only quit the parental roof when their filial education is complete.

On a casual view of the Examiner's Report on these various children of Nature, the physiologist, as distinguished from the educationalist, might object that so far from being the subject of congratulation it is a clear case for censure. If early Nature could turn out ready-made animals in a single hour, is it not a retrograde move to have to take so long about it later on? When one contrasts the free swimming embryo of a Medusa, dashing out into its heroic life the moment it is born, with the helpless kitten or the sightless pup, is it unfair to ask if Nature has not lost the trick of making lusty lives? Is she not trying the new experiment at the risk of blundering the old one, and why cannot she continue the earlier and more brilliant device of making her children knight-errants from the first? Because brilliance is not her object. Her object is ethical as well as physiological; and though when we look below the surface a purely physiological explanation of the riddle will appear, the ethical gain is not less clear. By curbing them she is educating them, taming them, rescuing them from a wild and lawless life. These roving embryos are mere bandits; their nature and habits must be changed; not a sterner race but a gentler race must be born. New words must come into the world—Home, Love, Mother. And these imperceptibly slow drawings together of parent and child are the inevitable preliminaries of the domestication of the Human Race. Regarded from the ethical point of view there are few things more significant than this reining-in of the world's rampant youth, this tightening the bonds of family life, this most gentle introduction of gentleness into a world cold with motherless children and heartless with childless mothers.

The personal tie once formed between parent and offspring could never be undone, and from this moment onwards must grow from more to more. For observe what has happened. A generation has grown up to whom this tie is the necessity of existence. Every Mammalian child born into the world must come to be fed, must, for a given number of hours each day, be in the maternal school, and whether it like it or not, learn its lessons. No young of any Mammal can nourish itself. There is that in it therefore at this stage which compels it to seek its Mother; and there is that in the Mother which compels it even physically—and this is the fourth process, on which it is needless to dwell—to seek her child. On the physiological side, the name of this impelling power is lactation; on the ethical side, it is Love. And there is no escape henceforth from communion between Mother and child, or only one—death. Break this new bond and the Mammalia become extinct. Nature is in earnest here, if anywhere. The training of Humanity is seen to be under a compulsory education act. It is in the severity and dread of her penalties, coupled with the impossibility of evading the least of them, that the will of Nature and the seriousness of her purposes are most declared. For the physiological gains which underlie these ethical relations are all-important. It is largely owing to them that the Mammalia have taken their place in the van of the procession of life. Under the earlier system life had a bad start; each animal had to push its way upward single-handed from the egg. It was planted, so to speak, on the first rung of the ladder, and as the risks of life are immeasurably great in infancy, it had all these risks to take. Under the new system it is launched into the battle already nourished and strong, and passed scatheless through the first vicissitudes of youth. In the higher Mammalia, in virtue of the possession by this group of a placenta in addition to the ordinary Mammalian characteristics, the young have a double chance of a successful start. The development, in fact, of higher forms of life on the earth has depended on the physical perfecting of Mothers, and of the physiological ties which bind them to their young. With the immense structural advance of the Mammalia, an order of being was introduced into Nature whose continuity as an all but immortal series could never be broken. Thus whatever moral relations underlie the extraordinary physical characteristic of this highest class of animals, there is the added guarantee that they can never be destroyed.

With the physical programme carried out to the last detail, the ethical drama opened. An early result, partly of her sex, and partly of her passive strain, is the founding through the instrumentality of the first savage Mother of a new and a beautiful social state—Domesticity. While Man, restless, eager, hungry, is a wanderer on the earth, Woman makes a Home. And though this Home be but a platform of sticks and leaves, such as the gorilla builds on a tree, it becomes the first great schoolroom of the human race. For one day there appears in this roofless room that which is to teach the teachers of the world—a Little Child.

No greater day ever dawned for Evolution than this on which the first human child was born. For there entered then into the world the one thing wanting to complete the Ascent of Man—a tutor for the affections. It may be that a Mother teaches a Child, but in a far deeper sense it is the Child who teaches the Mother. Millions of millions of Mothers had lived in the world before this, but the higher affections were unborn. Tenderness, gentleness, unselfishness, love, care, self-sacrifice—these as yet were not, or were only in the bud. Maternity existed in humble forms, but not yet Motherhood. To create Motherhood and all that enshrines itself in that holy word required a human child. The creation of the Mammalia established two schools in the world—the two oldest and surest and best equipped schools of Ethics that have ever been in it—the one for the Child, who must now at least know its Mother, the other for the Mother, who must as certainly attend to her Child. The only thing that remains now is to secure that they shall both be kept in that school as long as it is possible to detain them. The next effort of Evolution, therefore—the fifth process as one might call it—is to lengthen out these school days, and give affection time to grow.

No animal except Man was permitted to have his education thus prolonged. Many creatures were allowed to stay at school for a few days or weeks, but to one only was given a curriculum complete enough to accomplish its exalted end. Watch two of the highest organisms during their earliest youth, and observe the striking contrast in the time they are made to remain at their Mother's side. The first is a human infant; the second, born, let us suppose, on the same day is a baby monkey. In a few days or weeks the baby monkey is almost able to leave its Mother. Already it can climb, and eat, and chatter like its parents; and in a few weeks more the creature is as independent of them as the winged-seed is of the parent tree. Meantime, and for many months to come, its little twin is unable to feed itself, or clothe itself, or protect itself; it is a mere semi-unconscious chattel, a sprawling ball of helplessness, the world's one type of impotence. The body is there in all its parts, bone for bone and muscle for muscle, like the other. But somehow this body will not do its work. Something as yet hangs fire. The body has eyes but they see not, ears but they hear not, limbs but they walk not. This body is a failure. Why does the human infant lie like a log on the forest-bed while its nimble prototype mocks it from the bough above? Why did that which is not human step out into life so long before that which is?

The question has been answered for us by Mr. John Fiske, and the world here owes to him one of the most beautiful contributions ever made to the Evolution of Man. We know what this delay means ethically—it was necessary for moral training that the human child should have the longest possible time by its Mother's side—but what determines it on the physical side? The thing that constitutes the difference between the baby monkey and the baby man is an extra piece of machinery which the last possesses and the first does not. It is this which is keeping back the baby man. What is that piece of machinery? A brain, a human brain. The child, nevertheless, is not using it. Why? Because it is not quite fitted up. Nature is working hard at it; but owing to its intricacy and delicacy the process requires much time, and till all is ready the babe must remain a thing. And why does the monkey-brain get ready first? Because it is an easier machine to make. And why should it be easier to make? Because it is only required to do the life-work of an Animal; the other has to do the life-work of a Man. Mental Evolution, in fact, here steps in, and makes an unexpected contribution to the ethical development of the world.

An apparatus for controlling one of the lower animals can be turned out from the workshop of Nature sometimes in a day. The wheels are few, the works are simple, the connections require little time for adjustment or correction. Everything that a humble organism will do has been done a million times by its parents, and already the faculties have been carefully instructed by heredity and will automatically repeat the whole life and movement of their race. But when a Man is made, it is not an automaton that is made. This being will do new things, think new thoughts, originate new ways of life. His immediate ancestors have done the same, but done some of them so seldom, and others of them for so short a time, that heredity has failed to notice them. For half the life therefore that lies before the human offspring no storage of habit has been handed down from the past. Each descendant must carve a way through the world for itself, and learn to comport itself through all the varying incidents of life as best it can. Now the equipment for this is very complex. Into the infant's frame must be fitted not only the apparatus for automatic repetition of what its parents have done, but the apparatus for intelligent initiation; not only the machinery for carrying on the involuntary and reflex actions—involuntary and reflex because they have been done so often by its ancestors as to have become automatic—but for the voluntary and self-conscious life which will do new things, choose fresh alternatives, seek higher and more varied ends. The instrument which will attend to breathing even when we forget it; the apparatus which will make the heart beat even though we try to stop it; the self-acting spring which makes the eyelid close the moment it is threatened—these and a hundred others are old and well-tried inventions which, from ceaseless practice generation after generation, work perfectly in each new individual from the start. Nature therefore need waste no time at this late day on their improvement. But the higher brain is comparatively a new thing in the world. It has to undertake a vaster range of duties, often totally new orders of duties; it has to do things which its forerunners had not quite learned to do, or had not quite learned to do unthinkingly, and the inconceivably complex machinery requires time to settle to its work. The older brain-processes have been greatly accelerated even now, and appear in full activity at an early stage in the infant's life, but the newer and the higher are in perfect order only after a considerable interval of adjustment and elaboration.

Now Infancy, physiologically considered, means the fitting up of this extra machinery within the brain; and according to its elaborateness will be the time required to perfect it. A sailing vessel may put to sea the moment the rigging is in; a steamer must wait for the engines. And the compensation to the steamer for the longer time in dock is discovered by and by in its vastly greater usefulness, its power of varying its course at will, and in its superior safety in time of war or storm. For its greater after-usefulness also, its more varied career, its safer life, humanity has to pay tribute to Evolution by a delayed and helpless Infancy, a prolonged and critical constructive process. Childhood in its early stage is a series of installations and trials of the new machinery, a slow experimenting with powers and faculties so fresh that heredity in handing them down has been unable to accompany them with full directions as to their use.

The Brain of Man, to change the figure—if indeed any figure of that marvellous molecular structure can be attempted without seriously misleading—is an elevated table-land of stratified nervous matter, furrowed by deep and sinuous canons, and traversed by a vast net-work of highways along which Thoughts pass to and fro. The old and often-repeated Thoughts, or mental processes, pass along beaten tracks; the newer Thoughts have less marked footpaths; the newer still are compelled to construct fresh Thought-routes for themselves. Gradually these become established thoroughfares; but in the increasing traffic and complexity of life, new paths in endless multitudes have to be added, and bye lanes and loops between the older highways must be thrown into the system. The stations upon these roads from which the travellers set out are cells; the roads are transit fibres; the travellers themselves are in physiological language nervous discharges, in psychological language mental processes. Each new mental process involves a new redistribution of nervous matter among the cells, a new travelling of nervous discharge along one or many of the transit fibres. Now in every new connection of ideas multitudes of cells and even multitudes of groups of cells may be concerned, so that should it happen that a combination of these precise centres had never been made before, it is obvious that no routes could possibly exist between them, and these must then and there be prospected. Each new Thought is therefore a pioneer, a road-maker, or road-chooser, through the brain; and the exhaustless possibilities of continuous development may be judged from the endlessness of the possible combinations. In the oldest and most-used brain there must always remain vast territories still to be explored, and, as it were, civilized; and in all men multitudes of possible connections continue to the last unrealized. When it is remembered, indeed, that the brain itself is very large, the largest mass of nerve-matter in the organic world; when it is further realized that each of the cells of which it is built up measures only one ten-thousandth of an inch in diameter, that the transit fibres which connect them are of altogether unimaginable fineness, the limitlessness of the powers of Thought and the inconceivable complexity of these processes will begin to be understood.

Now it is owing to the necessity for having a certain number of the more useful routes established before the babe can be trusted from its Mother's side, that the delay of Infancy is required. And even after the child has begun to practise the art of living for itself, time has still to be granted for many purposes—for new route-making, for becoming familiar with established thoroughfares, for practising upon obstacles and gradients, for learning to perform the journeys quickly and without fatigue, for allowing acts repeated to accelerate and embody themselves as habits. In the savage state, where the after-life is simple, the adjustments are made with comparative ease and speed; but as we rise in the scale of civilization the necessary period of Infancy lengthens step by step until in the case of the most highly educated man, where adjustments must be made to a wide intellectual environment, the age of tutelage extends for almost a quarter of a century.

The use of all this to morals, the reactions especially upon the Mother, are too obvious to dwell on. Till the brain arrived, everything was too brief, too rapid for ethical achievements; animals were in a hurry to be born, children thirsted to be free. There was no helplessness to pity, no pain to relieve, no quiet hours, no watching; to the Mother no moment of suspense—the most educative moment of all—when the spark of life in her little one burned low. Parents could be no use to their offspring physically, and the offspring could be no use to their parents psychically. The young required no Infancy; the old acquired no Sympathy. Even among the other Mammalia or the Birds the Mother's chance was small. There Infancy extends to a few days or weeks, yet is but an incident in a life preoccupied with sterner tasks. A lioness will bleed for her cub to-day, and in tomorrow's struggle for life contend with it to the death. A sheep knows its lamb only while it is a lamb. The affection in these cases, fierce enough while it lasts, is soon forgotten, and the traces it left in the brain are obliterated before they have furrowed into habit. Among the Carnivora it is instructive to observe that while the brief span of infancy admits of the Mother learning a little Love, the father, for want of even so brief a lesson, remains untouched, so wholly untouched indeed that the Mother has often to hide her offspring from him lest they be devoured. Love then had no chance till the Human Mother came. To her alone was given a curriculum prolonged enough to let her graduate in the school of the affections. Not for days or weeks, but for months, as the cry of her infant's helplessness went forth, she must stand between the flickering flame and death; and for years to come, until the budding intellect could take its own command, this Love dare not grow cold, or pause an hour in its unselfish ministry

Begin at the beginning again and recall the fact of woman's passive strain. A tendency to passivity means, among other things, a capacity to sit still. Be it but for a minute or an hour does not matter; the point is that the faintest possible capacity is there. For this is the embryo of Patience, and if much and long nursed a fully fledged Patience will come out of it. Supply next to this new virtue some definite object on which to practise, let us say a child. When this child is in trouble the Mother will observe the signs of pain. Its cry will awaken associations, and in some dull sense the Mother will feel with it. But "feeling with another" is the literal translation of the name of a second virtue—Sympathy. From feeling with it, the parent will sooner or later be led to do something to help it; then it will do more things to help it; finally it will be always helping it. Now, to care for things is to become Careful; to tend things is to become Tender. Here are four virtues—Patience, Sympathy, Carefulness, Tenderness—already dawning upon mankind.

On occasion Sympathy will be called out in unusual ways. Crises will occur—dangers, famines, sicknesses. At first the Mother will be unable to meet these extreme demands—her fund of Sympathy is too poor. She cannot take any exceptional trouble, or forget herself, or do anything very heroic. The child, unable to breast the danger alone, dies. It is well that this should be so. It is the severity and righteous justice of Nature—the tragedy of Ivan Ivanovitch anticipated by Evolution. A Mother who has failed in helpfulness must leave no successor to perpetuate her unworthiness in posterity. Somewhere else, however, developing along similar lines, there is another fractionally better Mother. When the emergency occurs, she rises to the occasion. For one hour she transcends herself. That day a cubit is added to the moral stature of mankind; the first act of Self-Sacrifice is registered in favour of the human race. It may or may not be that the child will acquire its Mother's virtue. But unselfishness has scored; its child has proved itself fitter to survive than the child of Selfishness. It does not follow that in all circumstances the nobler will be always victorious: but it has a great chance. A few score more of centuries, a few more millions of Mothers, and the germs of Patience, Carefulness, Tenderness, Sympathy, and Self-Sacrifice will have rooted themselves in Humanity.

See then what the Savage Mother and her Babe have brought into the world. When the first Mother awoke to her first tenderness and warmed her loneliness at her infant's love, when for a moment she forgot herself and thought upon its weakness or its pain, when by the most imperceptible act or sign or look of sympathy she expressed the unutterable impulse of her Motherhood, the touch of a new creative hand was felt upon the world. However short the earliest infancies, however feeble the sparks they fanned, however long heredity took to gather fuel enough for a steady flame, it is certain that once this fire began to warm the cold hearth of Nature and give humanity a heart, the most stupendous task of the past was accomplished. A softened pressure of an uncouth hand, a human gleam in an almost animal eye, an endearment in an inarticulate voice—feeble things enough. Yet in these faint awakenings lay the hope of the human race. "From of old we have heard the monition, `Except ye be as babes ye cannot enter the kingdom of Heaven`; the latest science now shows us—though in a very different sense of the words—that unless we had been as babes, the ethical phenomena which give all its significance to the phrase `Kingdom of Heaven` would have been non-existent for us. Without the circumstances of Infancy we might have become formidable among animals through sheer force of sharp-wittedness. But except for these circumstances we should never have comprehended the meaning of such phrases as `self-sacrifice` or `devotion.' The phenomena of social life would have been omitted from the history of the world, and with them the phenomena of ethics and religion.

The Evolution of a Father

In last chapter we watched the beautiful experiment of Nature making Mothers. We saw how the young produced at one birth were gradually reduced in numbers until it was possible for affection to concentrate upon a single object; how that object was delayed in birth till it was a likeable and presentable thing; how it was tied to its mother's side by physical bonds, and hindered there for years to give time for the Mother's care to ripen into love. We saw, what was still more instructive, that Nature, when she had laid the train for perfecting these arrangements, gave up making any more animals; and that there were physiological reasons why this well-mothered class should survive beyond all others, and, by sheer physiological fitness, henceforth dominate the world.

But there was still a crowning task to accomplish. The world was now beginning to fill with Mothers, but there were no Fathers. During all this long process the Father has not even been named. Nothing that has been done has touched or concerned him almost in the least degree. He has gone his own way, lived outside all these changes; and while Nature has succeeded in moulding a human Mother and a human child, he still wanders in the forest a savage and unblessed soul.

This time for him, nevertheless, is not lost. In his own way he is also at school, and learning lessons which will one day be equally needed by humanity. The acquisitions of the manly life are as necessary to human character as the virtues which gather their sweetness by the cradle; and these robuster elements—strength, courage, manliness, endurance, self-reliance—could only have been secured away from domestic cares. Apart from that, it was not necessary to put the Father through the same mill as the Mother. Whatever the Mother gained would be handed on to her boys as well as to her girls, and with the law of heredity to square accounts, it was unnecessary for each of the two great sides of humanity to make the same investments. By one acquiring one set of virtues and the other another, the blend in the end would be the richer; and, without obliterating the eternal individualities of each, the measure of completeness would be gained more quickly for the race. Before heredity, however, could do its work upon the Father a certain basis had to be laid. With his original habits he would squander the hereditary gains as fast as he received them, and unless some change was brought about in his mode of life the old wild blood in his veins would counteract the gentler influence, and leave all the Mother's work in vain. Hence Nature had to set about another long and difficult process—to make the savage Father a reformed character.

The Evolution of a Father is not so beautiful a process as the Evolution of a Mother, but it was almost as formidable a problem to attack. As much depended on it, as we shall see, as the training of the mother; and though it began later, it required the bringing about of one or two changes in Nature as novel as any that preceded it. When the work was begun, the Father was in a much worse plight, so far as training for family life was concerned, than the Mother. If Maternity was at a feeble level in the lower reaches of Nature, Paternity was non-existent. Among a few Invertebrates the male parent took a passing share in the care of the egg, but it is not until we are all but at the top that fatherly interest finds any real expression. Among the Birds, the parents unite together in most cases to build the nest, the Father doing the rough work of bringing in moss and twigs, while the more trusty Mother does the actual work. When the eggs are laid, the male parent also takes his turn at incubation; supplies food and protection; and lingers round the place of birth to defend the fledglings to the last. When we leave the Birds, however, and pass on to the Mammals, the Fathers are nearly all backsliders. Many are not only indifferent to their young, but hostile: and among the Carnivora the Mothers have frequently to hide their little ones in case the father eats them.

We have another and a more serious count against early Fatherhood. If the Love of Father for child was in this backward state, infinitely more grave was the condition of things between him and the Mother. Probably we have all taken it for granted that husbands and wives have always loved one another. Evolution takes nothing for granted. The affection between husband and wife is, of all the immeasurable forms of Love, the most beautiful, the most lasting, and the most divine: yet up to this time we have not been able even to record its existence. The finished results of Evolution appear so natural to us, looking back from this late day, that we continually ignore the difficulties it had to meet, and forget how every single step in progress from the lowest to the highest had to be carried at the bayonet's point. The most informed naturalist probably has never given Nature credit for a thousandth part of the work she has done, or has succeeded in presenting to his mind more than a surface outline of the gigantic series of problems she had to solve. In lower Nature, as a simple fact, male and female do not love one another; and in the lower reaches of Human-Nature, husband and wife do not love one another. Among exceptional nations, for the last few hours of the world's history, husbands and wives have truly loved; but for the vast mass of Mankind, during the long ages which preceded historic times, conjugal love was probably all but unknown.

Now here is a very pretty problem for Evolution. She has at once to make good Husbands and good Fathers out of lawless savages. Unless this problem is solved the higher progress of the world is at an end. It is the mature opinion of every one who has thought upon the history of the world, that the thing of highest importance for all times and to all nations is Family Life. When the Family was instituted, and not till then, the higher Evolution of the world was secured. Hence the exceptional value of the Father's development. As the other half of the arch on which the whole higher world is built, his taming, his domestication, his moral discipline, are vital; and in the nature of things this was the next great operation undertaken by Evolution.

The first step in the transition was to relate him, definitely and permanently, to the Mother. And here a formidable initial obstacle had to be encountered. The apathy and estrangement between husband and wife in the animal world is radical and universal. There is almost no such thing there as married life. Marriage, in anthropology, is not a word for an occasion, but for a state; it is not, that is to say, a wedding, but a dwelling together throughout life of husband and wife. Now when Man emerged from the animal creation this institution of conjugal life had not been arrived at. Marriage like everything else has been slowly evolved, and until it was evolved, until they learned to dwell continually together, there was no chance for mutual love to spring up between male and female. In Nature the pairing season is usually but an incident. It lasts only a very short time, and during the rest of the year, with some exceptions, the sexes remain apart. From the investigations of Westermarck, who has lately contributed to sociology the most masterly account of the Evolution of Marriage we possess—it appears more than probable that the earliest progenitors of Man had also a pairing season, and that the young were born at a particular time of the year, and never at any other time. All the animals nearest to Man in Nature have such a season, and there are only a few known—the elephant for instance, and some of the whales—which have none. Now the brevity of this period in the father's case must have told against his developing any real affection. If he is to run away a few days after the young are born he will miss all the discipline of the home, and as this discipline is essential, as this is the only way in which love can be acquired, or inherited love developed, some method must be adopted in his case to extend the period of home life during which it can act.

Now let us see how this was done. The problem being to give Love time, the solution was in some way to alter the circumstances which confined the pairing season to a specific date—to abolish, in fact, the pairing season in the case of Man, and lengthen out the time in which husband and wife should stay together. And as this was actually the method adopted, we have first to ask what these special circumstances were. Why should animals have specific dates at all? . The clue will be found if we examine carefully what these dates are and the reasons Nature has had for choosing them. Some wise principle must underlie this, or it would not be the universal rule it is. The pairing time with Birds, as everyone knows, occurs in the Spring. With Reptiles this is also the case; but among Mammals each species has a season peculiar to itself, every separate month being selected by one or other, and invariably adhered to. "The bat pairs in January and February; the wild camel in the desert to the east of Lake Lob-nor, from the middle of January nearly to the end of February; the Canis Azarae and the Indian bison in winter; the weasel in March; the kulan from May to July; the musk-ox at the end of August; the elk, in the Baltic Provinces, at the end of August, and, in Asiatic Russia, in September or October; the wild Yak in Tibet in September; the reindeer in Norway at the end of September; the badger in October; the Capra pyrenaica in November; the chamois, the musk-deer, and the orongo-antelope in November and December; the wolf, from the end of December to the middle of February. It might seem that no law governed these various dates, but their very variety is the proof of an underlying principle. For these dates show that each animal in each particular country chooses that time of the year to give birth to her young when they will have the best chance of surviving—that is to say, when the climate is mildest, food most abundant, and the prospects of life on the whole most favourable. The dormouse thus brings forth its young in August, when the nuts begin to ripen; and the young deer sees the light just before the first grass shoots into greenness. Because those born at this season survived and those born out of it perished, by the prolonged action of Natural Selection these dates in time probably became engrained in the species, and would only alter with climate itself.

But when Man's Evolution made a certain progress, and when the Mother's care reached mature perfection, it was no longer imperative for children to be born only when the sun was shining, and the fruits grew ripe. The parents could now make provision for any weather and for any dearth. They could give their little ones clothes when nights grew cold; they could build barns and granaries against times of famine. In any climate, and at any time, their young were safe; and the old marriage dates, with their subsequent desertions, were struck from the human calendar. So arose, or at least was inaugurated, Family Life, the first and the last nursery of the higher sympathies, and the home of all that was afterwards holy in the world. One could not find a simpler instance of the growing sovereignty of Mind over the powers of Nature. So remote a cause as the inclination of the earth's axis, and the consequent changes of the seasons, determines the time of Marriage for almost the whole animal creation, while Man, and a few other forms of life whose environment is exceptional, are able to refuse all such dictations. It was when Man's mind became capable of making its own provisions against the weather and the crops that the possibility of Fatherhood, Motherhood, and the Family were realized.

The supporters of the hypothesis of promiscuity have tried to show, what would almost follow from their theory, that the children in primitive times belonged rather to the tribe. But it is not likely that this was the case. The hypothesis of promiscuity itself, notwithstanding its support from M'Lennan, Morgan, Lubbock, Bastian, Post, and other authorities, has probably received its death-blow; and the ancientness of the family as well as of the institution of Marriage are both vindicated by later facts. "Everywhere," writes Westermarck, "we find the tribes or clans composed of several families, the members of each family being more closely connected with one another than with the rest of the tribe. The Family, consisting of parents, children, and often also their next descendants, is a universal institution among existing people. And it seems extremely probable that among our early human ancestors, the Family proved, if not the Society itself, at least the nucleus of it. I do not, of course, deny that the tie which bound the children to the Mother was much more intimate and more lasting than that which bound them to the Father; but it seems to me that the only result to which a critical investigation of facts can lead us is, that in all probability there has been no stage of human development where marriage has not existed, and that the father has always been, as a rule, the protector of his Family.

But the process is not yet quite completed. With the longer time together husband and wife may get to know and lean upon one another a little, but the time is still too short for deep affection, and there remain one or two serious obstacles to remove. Indeed, unless some further steps are taken, this first achievement must end in failure. As a matter of fact, it has often ended in failure, and there have been and still are tribes and nations where love between husband and wife is non-existent. Among the Hovas, we are assured by authorities, the idea of love between husband and wife is "hardly thought of"; that at Winnebah "not even the appearance of affection" exists between them; that among the Beni-Amer it is "considered even disgraceful for a wife to show any affection for her husband"; that the Chittagong Hill tribes have "no idea of tenderness nor of chivalrous devotion"; and that the Eskimo treat their wives "with great coldness and neglect." The savage cruelty with which wives are treated by the Australian aborigines is indicated even in their weapons. The very names "Servant, Slave," by which the Brahman address their wives, and the wife's reply, "Master, Lord," symbolize the gulf between the two. There are exceptions, it is true, and often touching exceptions. Travellers cite instances of constancy among savage peoples which reach the region of romance. Probably there never was a time, indeed, nor a race, when some measure of sympathy did not stir between husband and wife. But when we consider all the facts, it is impossible to doubt that in the region of all the higher affections the savage wife and the savage husband were all but strangers to each other.

What then was wanting for the perfecting of the domestic tie, and how did Evolution secure it? In the animal creation, we have already witnessed the methods which Nature took to get more care out of little care, to make a short-lived sympathy grow into a great sympathy. Her method was first, concentration; and second, extension of time. By giving a Mother one or two young to care for instead of a hundred, she made care practicable, and by lengthening the period of infancy from hours to years she made it inevitable. And these are again her methods in perfecting love between man and wife. By abolishing the pairing season she lengthened the time for love to grow in; the next step is to perfect the object on which it shall focus. For there was again the same sort of barrier to a full-blown love which we saw before in the animal kingdom. An animal mother could not truly love in the early days because she had a hundred or a thousand young. Man could not love in the early days because he had a dozen wives. This love was too diluted to come to anything. What Evolution next worked at was to get a quintessence. Polygamy, in other words, the scattered love of many, must, from this time forward, be changed into monogamy—the absorbing love of one. And this transposition was gradually introduced. A few polygamous people, a very few at first, become monogamous. The new system worked better, it spread, and was finally adopted by those higher nations which it also helped to create. It is an instance, nevertheless, of the slowness with which radical changes succeed in leavening great masses of mankind, that the older system, with the ban of Evolution upon it, still survives in Modern Europe. Yet there are signs, even among the uncivilized, that polygamy is passing away. Among some almost savage tribes it is unknown; among others prohibited. Even in a polygamous community it is usually only a minority who have more wives than one. And where the plural system is in full force, the tendency—the Evolutionist would say the transition —to monogamy is plainly marked, for among the many wives possessed by any individual, there is generally one who is first favourite and ranks as helpmeet or wife. The stress just laid upon the ethical gains of the monogamous state as contrasted with the polygamous, of course only emphasizes one side of the question, and by the pure naturalist might be ruled out of court. Were the physiologist to go over the same ground he could give a parallel account of the development, and show that on the merely Physiological plane the transition to monogamy and the rise of the Family was a likely if not an inevitable result. It is at least certain that during those later stages of social Evolution in which Monogamy has prevailed, the change has been in the best physical interests alike of the parents, the offspring, and of society.

This barrier removed, Evolution had still much to do to the other—the brevity of the time during which husband and wife remained together. What short work Nature had already made of this obstacle—by abolishing the pairing season—we have just seen. But that requires supplementing. It is not enough to give time for mutual knowledge and affection after marriage. Nature must deepen the result by extending it to the time before marriage. In primitive times there was no such thing as courtship. Men secured their wives in three ways, and in uncivilized nations so find them still. Among barbarous nations marriage is not a case of love, but of capture; among the semi-barbarous it is a case of barter; and among the imperfectly civilized— among whom we must often include ourselves—a matter of convention. The second of these, the purchase system—a slightly evolved form of marriage by capture—is probably one through which all human Marriage has passed; and relics of it still exist in the dos and other symbols among nations with whom the custom of buying a bride has long since passed away. By degrading the object of barter to the level of a chattel, this system is a barrier to high affection. But in most cases this is heightened by the impossibility of that preliminary courtship which leads to mutual knowledge and intelligent love. The bride and bridegroom, in the extremer cases, meet as total strangers; and though affection may bud in after years, the mingling of unknown temperaments, together with the destruction of reverence for woman by treating her as an article of barter, make the chances small of it blossoming into a flower.

Courtship, with its vivid perceptions and quickened emotions, is a great opportunity for Evolution; and to institute and lengthen reasonably a period so rich in impression is one of its latest and highest efforts. To give love time, indeed, has been all along, and through a great variety of arrangements, the chief means of establishing it on the earth. Unfortunately, the lesson of Nature here is being all too slowly learned, even among nations with its open book before them. In some of the greatest of civilized countries real mutual knowledge between the youth of the sexes is unattainable; marriages are made only by a higher kind of purchase, and the supreme step in life is taken in the dark. Whatever safeguards this method provides, it cannot be final, nor can those nations rise to any exalted social height or moral greatness till some change occurs. It has been given especially to one nation to lead the world in its assault upon this mistaken law, and to demonstrate to mankind that in the unconstrained and artless relations of youth lie higher safeguards than the polite conventions of society can afford. The people of America have proved that the blending of the sweet currents of different family-lives in social intercourse, in recreation, and—most original of all—in education, can take place freely and joyously without any sacrifice of man's reverence for woman, or woman's reverence for herself; and, springing out of these naturally mingled lives, there must more and more come those sacred and happy homes which are the surest guarantees for the moral progress of a nation. So long as the first concern of a country is for its homes, it matters little what it seeks second or third. Long before Evolution showed its scientific interest in this first social aggregate, and proclaimed it the strategic point in moral progress, poetry, philosophy, and history assigned the same great place to Family-life. The one point, indeed, where all students of the past agree, where all prophets of the future meet, where all the sciences from biology to ethics are enthusiastically at one, is in their faith in the imperishable potentialities of this yet most simple institution.

With all these barriers removed it might now be supposed that the process was at last complete. But one of the surprises of Evolution here awaits us. All the arrangements are finished to fan the flame of love, yet out of none of them was love itself begotten. The idea that the existence of sex accounts for the existence of love is untrue. Marriage among early races, as we have seen, has nothing to do with love. Among savage peoples the phenomenon everywhere confronts us of wedded life without a grain of love. Love then is no necessary ingredient of the sex relation; it is not an outgrowth of passion. Love is love, and has always been love, and has never been anything lower. Whence, then, came it? If neither the Husband nor the Wife bestowed this gift upon the world, Who did? It was A Little Child. Till this appeared, Man's affection was non-existent; Woman's was frozen. The Man did not love the Woman; the Woman did not love the Man. But one day from its Mother's very heart, from a shrine which her husband never visited nor knew was there, which she herself dared scarce acknowledge, a Child drew forth the first fresh bud of a Love which was not Passion, a Love which was not selfish, a Love which was an incense from its Maker, and whose fragrance from that hour went forth to sanctify the world. Later, long later, through the same tiny and unconscious intermediary, the father's soul was touched. And one day, in the love of a little child, Father and Mother met.

That this is the true lineage of love, that it has descended not from Husbands and Wives but through children, is proved by the simplest study of savage life. Love for children is always a prior and a stronger thing than love between Father and Mother. The indifference of the Husband to his Wife—though often greatly exaggerated by anthropology—is all too manifest, and throughout whole regions the Wife does not love but only fears her Husband. For the children on the other hand both parents have almost always a regard. The universality of a Mother's Love is one of the revelations of travel. Even among cannibals, where the shocking treatment of Wives by their Husbands is in daily evidence, a case of cruelty to children from the Mother's side—apart from infanticide, which has a rationale of its own—is rarely heard of. The status of children if not ideal forms a most striking contrast to the general moral and social level: and one cannot but decide that they have been unconsciously the true moral teachers of the world. Had the institution of the Family depended on Sex and not on affection it would probably never have endured for any time. Love is eternal; Sex, transient. Its unbridled expression in individual natures, and its recklessness when thwarted, have given rise to exaggerated ideas of its power. In all uncontrolled forms, however, it becomes so immediate a menace to social order that if it does not die out in self-destruction it is checked by the community and forced into lawful channels. The only thing that could bear the heavy burden of social order and adapt itself to every change and fresh demand was the indestructibly solid, yet elastic, strength of love. The care and culture of love therefore became thenceforth the first great charge of Evolution, and every obstruction to its path began to be swept away. Whatever facilities could further its career were gradually adopted, and changes which soon began to pass over the face of all human societies seemed but parts of one great conspiracy to hasten its final reign.

For a prolonged and protective Fatherhood, once introduced into the world, was immediately taken charge of by Natural Selection. The children who had fathers to fight for them grew up; those who had not were killed or starved. The lengthening of the period during which Father and Mother kept together meant double protection for the little ones; and the more they kept together for the first few days or weeks, and the more the Father helped to defend mother and child, the more chance for all three in the end. The picture which Koppenfells draws of the female Gorilla and her young ensconced in a nest upon the fork of a tree, while Gorilla pere sat all night at the foot with his back against the trunk to protect them from the leopards, is a fair object-lesson in the first or protective stage of the Father's Evolution. When Man passed, however, as he probably did, from the frugivorous to the carnivorous state, the Father had the additional responsibility of keeping his family in food. It would be impossible for a Mother to hunt for game and attend to her young; and for a long time the young themselves were useless in the chase, and must be entirely dependent on their parents' bounty. But this means promotion to the Father. He is not only protector but food-provider. It is impossible to. believe that in process of time the discharge of this office did not bring some faint satisfactions to himself, that the mere sight of his offspring fed instead of famished did not give him a certain pleasure. And though the pleasure at first may have been no more than the absence of the annoyance they caused by the clamorousness of their want, it became a stimulus to exertion, and led in the end to rudimentary forms of sympathy and self-denial.

Once established in the world as a winning force, love could only yield to a greater force than itself, and greater force there is none. In the hands of Natural Selection, therefore, it ran its course. Whatever physiological adjustments continued to go on beneath the surface, ethical factors now determined extinction or survival. Bad parents mean starved children, and starved children will be replaced in the Struggle for Life by full-fed children, and ere a few generations parents without love will exist no more. The child, on the other hand, which has drunk most deeply of its Father's or its Mother's love lives to hand on that which has spared it to a succeeding race. How much of affection is handed on, or how little, matters not, for Heredity works with the finest microscope, and sees, and seizes, the invisible. In a second child, reared by parents one degree more loving than the last, this ultimate particle of love will grow a little more, and each succeeding Family in this royal line will be richer in the elements which make for progress than the last.

When we reach the human Family, we find that this simple combination was already strong enough to become the nucleus of the social and national life of the world. For the moment the new forces of Sympathy, Brotherhood, Self-denial, or Love, began to work among the isolated units which made up primitive Man, the whole composition and character of the aggregate began to change. Sooner or later in the recurring necessities of savage existence there came an opportunity for the members of the first combination, the little group of Father, Mother, and Sons, to act together. However unworthily this primitive group merited the name of Family, there was here what at that time was of final importance— the elements of physical strength. He who formerly stood alone in the Struggle for Life now found himself backed on occasion by an inner circle. Those who outside this circle ventured to oppose or offend an individual within it had the Family to reckon with. Ends were gained by the new alliance which were unattainable single-handed by any individual member of the tribe, and whether enlisted to evade disaster or secure a prey, to resist an injustice or avenge a wrong, the odds henceforth and always were in favour of the combination. When it is remembered how, owing to the comparative equality of the competitors in the conflict of savage existence, even an infinitesimal advantage on one side or the other determines health or starvation, survival or extinction, the importance of the first feeble effort at federation must be recognized. Shoulder to shoulder has been the watchword all through history of national development. Almost from the very first, indeed, the Family and not the individual must have been the unit of Tribal life; and as Families grew more and more definite, they became the recognized piers of the social structure and gave a first stability to the race of men.

But great as are the physical advantages of the Family, the ethical uses, even in the early days of its existence, place this institution at the head of all the creations of Evolution. For the Family is not only its greatest creation, but its greatest instrument for further creation. The ethical changes begin almost the moment it is formed. One immediate effect, for instance, of the formation of Family groups was to take off from any single individual the perpetual strain of the Struggle for Life. The Family as a whole must sometimes fight, but the responsibility and the duty are now distributed, and those who were once solely preoccupied with the personal struggle will have respites, during which other things will occupy their minds. Attention thus called off from environing enemies, the members of the Family will, as it were, discover one another. New relations among them will spring up, new adjustments to one another's presence and to one another's needs, and hitherto unknown elements of character will be gradually called to the surface. That unselfishness, in some rude form, should now grow up is a necessity of living together. A man cannot be a member of a Family and remain an utter egoist. His interests are perforce divided, and though the Family group is a small surface for unselfishness to spread to and to practise on, no greater feat could as yet be attempted, and Evolution never runs risks of too rapid development or over-strain. With the incorporation of the Family into a Clan or Tribe the area will presently be extended, and the necessity of controlling self-interest more thoroughly, or merging it in a wider interest, become more obligatory. But to prepare the altruistic sentiment for so great an abnegation, the simpler discipline of the Family was required. How firmly Families in time became welded together in mutual interest and support, and how much crude Altruism this implies, is evident from the place of Family feuds and the power of great Families and Houses both in ancient and modern history. A striking instance is the Vendetta. To avenge a Family insult in countries where this prevails was a sacred duty to all the relatives, and even the last surviving member willingly gave up his life to vindicate its honour. So strong indeed sometimes has grown the power of individual Families that the more desirable spread of Altruism to the Nation was threatened, and wider interests so much forgotten that the Family became the enemy of the State. Nothing could more forcibly show the tremendous power of self-development contained within the Family circle, and the solidity and strength to which it can grow, than that, time after time in history, it has had to be crushed and broken up by all the forces of the State.

Among other elements in human nature fostered in the Family is one of exceptional interest. The attempt has been made to show that from the inevitable relations of early Family life, the sense of Duty first dawned upon the world. The theme is too great, too intricate, and too dangerous to open under the limitations of the present inquiry, for these deny us the appeal to Society, to Religion, and even to the Conscience of the higher Man. But it is due to the Father, whose Evolution we are tracing, that the share he is supposed by some authorities to take in it should be at least named.

That morality in general has something to do with the relations of people to one another is evident, as everyone knows, from the mere derivation of the word. Mores, morals are in the first instance customs, the customs or ways which people have when they are together. Now, the Family is the first occasion of importance where we get people together. And as there are not only a number of people in a Family, but different kinds of people, there will be a variety in the relations subsisting between them, in the customs which stereotype the most frequently repeated actions necessitated by these relations, and in the moods and attitudes of mind accompanying them. Leaving out of sight differences of kind among brothers and sisters, consider the probably more divergent and certainly more dominant influences of Father and Mother. What the relation of child to Mother has crystallized into we have sufficiently marked—it is a relation of direct dependence, and its product is Love. But the Father is a wholly different influence. What attitude does the Child take up in this austerer presence, and what ways of acting, what customs, mores, morals, are engrained in the child's mind through it? The acknowledged position of the Father in most early tribes is head of the Family. To the children, and generally even to the Mother, he represents Authority. He is the children's chief. Bachoven has familiarized us with the idea of a Matriarchate, or Maternal Family; but although exceptional tribes have given supremacy to the Mother, the rule is for the Father to be supreme. As head of the Family, therefore, it was his business to make the Family laws. No doubt the Mother also made laws; but the Father, as the more terrible person, exacted obedience with greater severity, and his laws acquired more force. To do what was pleasing in his eyes was a necessity with the children, and his favour or his frown became standards of what was "good" and what was "bad." Low as this standard was—the fear or favour of a savage Father—it was a beginning of right mores, good conduct, proper manners. Plant in the mind, or evoke from it, the idea of acting in a given way with reference to some half-dozen daily trifles when done in the presence of one authoritative individual, and Evolution has already found something to work on. The children have got six, if not ten commandments. Extend the half-dozen things done rightly to a whole dozen, and then to a score, and then to a hundred; and let it become habitual to do these things rightly. When the right doing of these things commends the doer to one person, he will next be apt to commend himself by similar conduct to other persons, if their standard happens to be the same. Whether good behaviour purchases favour or simply succeeds in evading penalties is at first immaterial. All that is required, under whatever sanctions, is that some standard of good or bad shall arise. No abstract sense of duty, of course, here exists; no perfect law; it is a purely personal and local code; but the word duty has at least received a first imperfect meaning; and the Father, in some rough way, forms an external conscience to those beneath him.

Such is the tentative theory of the advocates of Evolutional Ethics. It may or may not be a possible account of the rise of a sense of obligation, but it is certain that it does not account for the whole of it. Why, also, that particular thing should be elicited under the circumstances described is an unanswered question. In attempting to trace its rise, no rationale appears of its origin; all proofs, in short, of its evolution take for granted its previous existence. A latent thing has become active; an invisible thing has become apparent. In one sense a relation has been created, in another sense a quality in that relation has been revealed. A new experiment upon human nature has been tried; a new discovery of its properties has been the result.

That these moral elements, on the other hand, must have a beginning somewhere in space and time is certain enough. Not less necessary to the world than the Mother's gift of Love is the twin offering of the Father—Righteousness. And if, almost before the soul is born, the shadowy outline of a moral order should begin to loom out in history, the later phases and the later sanctions lose nothing of their quality, are all the more wonderful and all the more divine, because met by moral adumbrations in the distant past. If the later children had their ten commandments given them in one way, they cannot grudge that the world's earlier children should have been given their two or three commandments in another way—another way which, nevertheless, did we know all, might turn out to be but another phase of the same way. But it is impossible even to approach the Evolution of Morality until we have carried Man some stages further up his Ascent. It is only when he reaches the social stage, when he becomes aggregated into clans, tribes, and nations, that this problem opens. For the present we must content ourselves with having witnessed his arrival in the Human Family—the starting-point and threshold of the true moral life.

For a long time, it is true, the Family circle, as a circle, was incomplete. Machinery must itself evolve before its products evolve. Scarcely defined at all, broken as soon as formed, the earlier circles allowed their strongest forces to escape almost at the moment they generated. But the walls grew higher and higher with the advance of history. The leakage became less and less. With the Christian era the machinery was complete; the circle finally closed in, and became a secluded shrine where the culture of everything holy and beautiful was carried on. The path by which this ideal consummation was reached was not, as we have seen, a straight path; nor has the integrity of the institution been always preserved through the later centuries. The difficulty of realizing the ideal may be judged of by the fewness of the nations now living who have reached it, and by the multitude of peoples and tribes who have vanished from the earth without attaining. From the failure to fulfil some one or other of the required conditions people after people and nation after nation have come together only to disperse, and leave no legacy behind except the lesson—as yet in few cases understood—of why they failed.

Yet whether the road be straight or devious is of little moment. The one significant thing is that it rises. We have reached a stage in Evolution at which physiological gains are guarded and accentuated, if not in an ethical interest, at least by ethical factors becoming utilized by natural selection. Henceforth affection becomes a power in the world; and whatever physiological adjustments continue to perfect themselves, the most attached Families will have a better chance of surviving and of transmitting their moral characteristics to succeeding generations. The completion of the arch of Family Life forms one of the great, if not the greatest of the landmarks of history. If the crowning work of Organic Evolution is the Mammalia, the consummation of the Mammalia is the Family. Physically, psychically, ethically, the Family is the masterpiece of Evolution. The creation of Evolution, it was destined to become the most active instrument and ally which Evolution has ever had. For what is its evolutionary significance? It is the generator and the repository of the forces which alone can carry out the social and moral progress of the world. There they rally when they become enfeebled, there their excesses are counterbalanced, and thence they radiate out, refined and reinforced, to do their holy work.

Looking at the mere dynamics of the question, the Family contains all the machinery, and nearly all the power, for the moral education of mankind. Feebly, but adequately, in the early chapters of Man's history it fulfilled its function of nursing Love, the Mother of all morality, and Righteousness, the Father of all morality, so preparing a parentage for all the beautiful spiritual children which in later years should spring from them. If life henceforth is to go on at all, it must be a better life, a more loving life, a more abundant life; and this premium upon Love means—if it means anything—that Evolution is taking henceforth an ethical direction. It is no more possible to interpret Nature physically from this point than to interpret a "Holy Family" of Raphael's in terms of the material structure of canvas or the qualities of pigments. Canvas may be coarse or fine, pigments may be vegetable or mineral; but whether the colours be crushed out of madder or ground out of arsenic or lead is of no importance now. Once these things were important; by infinitely slow processes Nature formed them; by clever arts the colourman prepared them. But the "Holy Family" did not lie potentially in the madder-bud, nor in the earth with the lead and arsenic, nor in the laboratory with the colourman. He who claims Nature for Matter and Physical force makes the same assumption that these would do if they claimed the painting. In a far truer sense than Raphael produced his "Holy Family" Nature has produced a Holy Family. Not for centuries but for millenniums the Family has survived. Time has not tarnished it; no later art has improved upon it; nor genius discovered anything more lovely; nor religion anything more divine. From the bee's cell and the butterfly's wing men draw what they call the Argument from Design; but it is in the kingdoms which come without observation, in these great immaterial orderings which Science is but beginning to perceive, that the purposes of Creation are revealed.

Involution

Many years ago, in the clay which in every part of the world is found underlying beds of coal, a peculiar fossil was discovered and named by science Stigmaria. It occurred in great abundance and in many countries, and from the strange way in which it ramified through the clay it was supposed to be some extinct variety of a gigantic water-weed. In the coal itself another fossil was discovered, almost as abundant but far more beautiful, and from the exquisite carving which ornamented its fluted stem it received the name of Sigillaria. One day a Canadian geologist, studying Sigillaria in the field, made a new discovery. Finding the trunk of a Sigillaria standing erect in a bed of coal, he traced the column downwards to the clay beneath. To his surprise he found it ended in Stigmaria. This branching fossil in the clay was no longer a water-weed. It was the root of which Sigillaria was the stem, and the clay was the soil in which the great coal-plant grew.

Through many chapters, often in the dark, everywhere hampered by the clay, we have been working among roots. Of what are they the roots? To what order do they belong? By what process have they grown? What connection have they with the realm above, or the realm beneath? Is it a Stigmaria or a Sigillaria world?

Till yesterday Science did not recognize them even as roots. They were classified apart. They led to nothing. No organic connection was known between lower Nature and that wholly separate and all but antagonistic realm, the higher world of Man. Atoms, cells, plants, animals were the material products of a separate creation, the clay from which Man took his clay-body, and no more. The higher world, also, was a system by itself. It rose out of nothing; it rested upon nothing. Clay, where the roots lay, was the product of inorganic forces; Coal, which enshrined the tree, was a creation of the sunlight. What fellowship had light with darkness? What possible connection could exist between that beautiful organism which stood erect in the living, and that which lay prone in the dead? Yet, by a process doubly verified, the organic connection between these two has now been traced. Working upwards through the clay the biologist finds what he took to be an organism of the clay leaving his domain and passing into a world above —a world which he had scarcely noticed before, and into which, with such instruments as he employs, he cannot follow it. Working downward through the higher world, the psychologist, the moralist, the sociologist, behold the even more wonderful spectacle of the things they had counted a peculiar possession of the upper kingdom, burying themselves in ever attenuating forms in the clay beneath. What is to be made of this discovery? Once more, Is it a Stigmaria or a Sigillaria world? Is the biologist to give up his clay or the moralist his higher kingdom? Are Mind, Morals, Men, to be interpreted in terms of roots, or are atoms and cells to be judged by the flowers and fruits of the tree?

The first fruit of the discovery must be that each shall explore with new respect the other's world, and, instead of delighting to accentuate their contrasts, strive to magnify their infinite harmonies. Old as is the world's vision of a cosmos, and universal as has been its dream of the unity of Nature, neither has ever stood before the imagination complete. Poetry felt, but never knew, that the universe was one; Biology perceived the profound chemical balance between the inorganic and organic kingdoms, and no more; Physics, discovering the correlation of forces, constructed a cosmos of its own; Astronomy, through the law of gravitation, linked us, but mechanically, with the stars. But it was reserved for Evolution to make the final revelation of the unity of the world, to comprehend everything under one generalization, to explain everything by one great end. Its omnipresent eye saw every phenomenon and every law. It gathered all that is and has been into one last whole—a whole whose very perfection consists in the all but infinite distinctions of the things which it unites.

What is often dreaded in Evolution—the danger of obliterating distinctions that are vital—is a groundless fear. Stigmaria can never be anything more than root, and Sigillaria can never be anything less than stem. To show their connection is not to transpose their properties. The wider the distinctions seen among their properties the profounder is the Thought which unites them, the more rich and rational the Cosmos which comprehends them. For "the unity which we see in Nature is that kind of Unity which the Mind recognizes as the result of operations similar to its own—not a unity which consists in mere sameness of material, or in mere identity of composition, or in mere uniformity of structure; but a unity which consists in the subordination of all these to similar aims, not to similar principles of action—that is to say, in like methods of yoking a few elementary forces to the discharge of special functions, and to the production, by adjustment, of one harmonious whole.

Yet did Sigillaria grow out of Stigmaria? Did Mind, Morals, Men, evolve out of Matter? Surely if one is the tree and the other the root of that tree, and if Evolution means the passage of the one into the other, there is no escape from this conclusion—no escape therefore from the crassest materialism? If this is really the situation, the lower must then include the higher, and Evolution, after all, be a process of the clay? This is a frequent, a natural, and a wholly unreflecting inference from a very common way of stating the Evolution theory. It arises from a total misconception of what a root is. Because a thing is seen to have roots, it is assumed that it has grown out of these roots, and must therefore belong to the root-order. But neither of these things is true in Nature. Are the stem, branch, leaf, flower, fruit of a tree roots? Do they belong to the root-order? They do not. Their whole morphology is different; their whole physiology is different; their reactions upon the world around are different. But it must be allowed that they are at least contained in the root? No single one of them is contained in the root. If not in the root, then in the clay? Neither are they contained in the clay. But they grow out of clay, are they not made out of clay? They do not grow out of clay, and they are not made out of clay. It is astounding sometimes how little those who venture to criticize biological processes seem to know of its simplest facts. Fill a flower-pot with clay, and plant in it a seedling. At the end of four years it has become a small tree; it is six feet high; it weighs ten pounds. But the clay in the pot is still there? A moiety of it has gone, but it is not appreciably diminished; it has not, except the moiety, passed into the tree; the tree does not live on clay nor on any force contained in the clay. It cannot have grown out of the seedling, for the seedling contained but a grain for every pound contained in the tree. It cannot have grown from the root, because the root is there now, has lost nothing to the tree, has itself gained from the tree, and at first was no more there than the tree.

Sigillaria, then, as representing the ethical order, did not grow out of Stigmaria as representing the organic or the material order. Trees not only do not evolve out of their roots, but whole classes in the plant world—the sea-weeds for instance—have no roots at all. If any possible relation exists it is exactly the opposite one—it is the root which evolves from the tree. Trees send down roots in a far truer sense than roots send up trees. Yet neither is the whole truth. The true function of the root is to give stability to the tree, and to afford a medium for conveying into it inorganic matter from without. And this brings us face to face with the real relation. Tree and root—the seed apart—find their explanation not in one another nor in something in themselves, but mainly in something outside themselves. The secret of Evolution lies, in short, with the Environment. In the Environment, in that in which things live and move and have their being, is found the secret of their being, and especially of their becoming. And what is that in which things live and move and have their being? It is Nature, the world, the cosmos—and something more, some One more, an Infinite Intelligence and an Eternal Will. Everything that lives, lives in virtue of its correspondences with this Environment. Evolution is not to unfold from within; it is to infold from without. Growth is no mere extension from a root but a taking possession of, or a being possessed by, an ever widening Environment, a continuous process of assimilation of the seen or Unseen, a ceaseless redistribution of energies flowing into the evolving organism from the Universe around it. The supreme factor in all development is Environment. Half the confusions which reign round the process of Evolution, and half the objections to it, arise from considering the evolving object as a self-sufficient whole. Produce an organism, plant, animal, man, society, which will evolve in vacuo and the right is yours to say that the tree lies in the root, the flower in the bud, the man in the embryo, the social organism in the family of an anthropoid ape. If an organism is to be judged in terms of the immediate Environment of its roots, the tree is a clay tree; but if it is to be judged by stem, leaves, fruit, it is not a clay tree. If the moral or social organism is to be judged in terms of the Environment of its roots, the moral and social organism is a material organism; but if it is to be judged in terms of the higher influences which enter into the making of its stem, leaves, fruit, it is not a material organism. Everything that lives, and every part of everything that lives, enters into relation with different parts of the Environment and with different things in the Environment; and at every step of its Ascent it compasses new ranges of the Environment, and is acted upon, and acts, in different ways from those in which it was acted upon, or acted, at the previous stage.

For what is most of all essential to remember is that not only is Environment the prime factor in development, but that the Environment itself rises with every evolution of any form of life. To regard the Environment as a fixed quantity and a fixed quality is, next to ignoring the altruistic factor, the cardinal error of evolutional philosophy. With every step a climber rises up a mountain side his Environment must change. At a thousand feet the air is lighter and purer than at a hundred, and as the effect varies with the cause, all the reactions of the air upon his body are altered at the higher level. His pulse quickens ; his spirit grows more buoyant; the energies of the upper world flow in upon him. All the other phenomena change—the plants are Alpine, the animals are a hardier race, the temperature falls, the very world he left behind wears a different look. At three thousand feet the causes, the effects, and the phenomena change again. The horizon is wider, the light intenser, the air colder, the top nearer; the nether world recedes from view. At six thousand feet, if we may accentuate the illustration till it contains more of the emphasis of the reality, he enters the region of snow. Here is a change brought about by a small and perfectly natural rise which yet amounts to a revolution. Another thousand feet and there is another revolution—he is ushered into the domain of mist. Still another thousand, and the climax of change has come. He stands at the top, and, behold, the Sun. None of the things he has encountered in his progress toward the top are new things. They are the normal phenomena of altitude—the scenes, the energies, the correspondences, natural to the higher slopes. He did not create any of these things as he rose; they were not created as he rose; they did not lie potentially in the plains or in the mountain foot. What has happened is simply that in rising he has encountered them— some for the first time, which are therefore wholly new to him; others which, though known before, now flow into his being in such fuller measure, or enter into such fresh relations among themselves, or with the changed being which at every step he has become, as to be also practically new.

Man, in his long pilgrimage upwards from the clay, passes through regions of ever varying character. Each breath drawn and utilized to make one upward step brings him into relation with a fractionally higher air, a fractionally different world. The new energies he there receives are utilized, and in virtue of them he rises to a third, and from a third to a fourth. As in the animal kingdom the senses open one by one—the eye progressing from the mere discernment of light and darkness to the blurred image of things near, and then to clearer vision of the more remote; the ear passing from the tremulous sense of vibration to distinguish with ever increasing delicacy the sounds of far-off things —so in the higher world the moral and spiritual senses rise and quicken till they compass qualities unknown before and impossible to the limited faculties of the earlier life. So Man, not by any innate tendency to progress in himself, nor by the energies inherent in the protoplasmic cell from which he first set out, but by a continuous feeding and reinforcing of the process from without, attains the higher altitudes, and from the sense-world at the mountain foot ascends with ennobled and ennobling faculties until he greets the Sun.

What is the Environment of the Social tree? It is all the things, and all the persons, and all the influences, and all the forces with which, at each successive stage of progress, it enters into correspondence. And this Environment inevitably expands as the Social tree expands and extends its correspondences. At the savage stage Man compasses one set of relations, at the rude social stage another, at the civilized stage a third, and each has its own reactions. The social, the moral, and the religious forces beat upon all social beings in the order in which the capacities for them unfold, and according to the measure in which the capacities themselves are fitted to contain them. And from what ultimate source do they come? There is only one source of everything in the world. They come from the same source as the Carbonic Acid Gas, the Oxygen, the Nitrogen, and the Vapour of Water, which from the outer world enter into the growing plant. These also visit the plant in the order in which the capacities for them unfold, and according to the measure in which these capacities can contain them.

The fact that the higher principles come from the same Environment as those of the plant, nevertheless does not imply that they are the same as those which enter into the plant. In the plant they are physical, in Man spiritual. If anything is to be implied it is not that the spiritual energies are physical, but that the physical energies are spiritual. To call the things in the physical world "material" takes us no nearer the natural, no further away from the spiritual The roots of a tree may rise from what we call a physical world; the leaves may be bathed by physical atoms; even the energy of the tree may be solar energy, but the tree is itself; The tree is a Thought, a unity, a rational purposeful whole; the "matter" is but the medium of their expression. Call it all—matter, energy, tree —a physical production, and have we yet touched its ultimate reality? Are we even quite sure that what we call a physical world is, after all, a physical world? The preponderating view of science at present is that it is not. The very term "material world," we are told, is a misnomer; that the world is a spiritual world, merely employing "matter" for its manifestations.

But surely here is still a fallacy. Are not these so-called social forces the effect of Society and not its cause? Has not Society to generate them before they regenerate Society? True, but to generate is not to create. Society is machinery, a medium for the transmission of energy, but no more a medium for its creation than a steam engine is for the creation of its energy. Whence then the social energies? The answer is as before. Whence the physical energies? And Science has only one answer to that. "Consider the position into which Science has brought us. We are led by scientific logic to an unseen, and by scientific analogy to the spirituality of this unseen. In fine, our conclusion is, that the visible universe has been developed by an intelligence resident in the Unseen. There is only one theory of the method of Creation in the field, and that is Evolution; but there is only one theory of origins in the field, and that is Creation. Instead of abolishing a creative Hand, Evolution demands it. Instead of being opposed to Creation, all theories of Evolution begin by assuming it. If Science does not formally posit it, it never posits anything less. "The doctrine of Evolution," writes Mr. Huxley, "is neither theistic nor anti-theistic. It has no more to do with theism than the first book of Euclid has. It does not even come in contact with theism considered as a scientific doctrine." But when it touches the question of origins, it is either theistic or silent. "Behind the co-operating forces of Nature," says Weismann, "which aim at a purpose, we must admit a cause, . . . inconceivable in its nature. of which we can only say one thing with certainty, that it must be theological."

The fallacy of the merely quantitative theory of Evolution is apparent. To interpret any organism in terms of the organism solely is to omit reference to the main instrument of its Evolution, and therefore to leave the process, scientifically and philosophically, unexplained. It is as if one were to construct a theory of the career of a millionaire in terms of the pocket-money allowed him when a schoolboy. Disregard the fact that more pocket-money was allowed the schoolboy as he passed from the first form to the sixth; that his allowance was increased as he came of age; that now, being a man, not a boy, he was capable of more wisely spending it; that being wise he put his money to paying uses; and that interest and capital were invested and re-invested as years went on—disregard all this and you cannot account for the rise of the millionaire. As well construct the millionaire from the potential gold contained in his first sixpence—a sixpence which never left his pocket—as construct a theory of the Evolution of Man from the protoplasmic cell apart from its Environment. It is only when interpreted, not in terms of himself, but in terms of Environment, and of an Environment increasingly appropriated, quantitatively and qualitatively, with each fresh stage of the advance, that a consistent theory is possible, or that the true nature of Evolution can appear.

A child does not grow out of a child by spontaneous unfoldings. The process is fed from without. The body assimilates food, the mind assimilates books, the moral nature draws upon affection, the religious faculties nourish the higher being from Ideals. Time brings not only more things, but new things; the higher nature inaugurates possession of, or by, the higher order. "It lies in the very nature of the case that the earliest form of that which lives and develops is the least adequate to its nature, and therefore that from which we can get the least distinct clue to the inner principle of that nature. Hence to trace a living being back to its beginning, and to explain what follows by such beginning, would be simply to omit almost all that characterizes it, and then to suppose that in what remains we have the secret of its existence. That is not really to explain it, but to explain it away; for on this method, we necessarily reduce the features that distinguish it to a minimum and, when we have done so, the remainder may well seem to be itself reducible to something in which the principle in question does not manifest itself at all. If we carry the animal back to protoplasm, it may readily seem possible to explain it as a chemical compound. And, in like manner, by the same minimizing process, we may seem to succeed in reducing consciousness and self-consciousness in its simplest form to sensation, and sensation in its simplest form to something not essentially different from the nutritive life of plants. The fallacy of the sorites may thus be used to conceal all qualitative changes under the guise of quantitative addition or diminution, and to bridge over all difference by the idea of gradual transition. For, as the old school of etymologists showed, if we are at liberty to interpose as many connecting links as we please, it becomes easy to imagine that things the most heterogeneous should spring out of each other. While, however, the hypothesis of gradual change—change proceeding by infinitesimal stages which melt into each other so that the eye cannot detect where one begins and the other ends—makes such a transition easier for imagination, it does nothing to diminish the difficulty or the wonder of it for thought.

The value of philosophical criticism to science has seldom appeared to more advantage than in these words of the Master of Balliol. The following passage from Martineau may be fitly placed beside them:—"In not a few of the progressionists the weak illusion is unmistakable, that, with time enough, you may get everything out of next-to-nothing. Grant us, they seem to say, any tiniest granule of power, so close upon zero that it is not worth begrudging—allow it some trifling tendency to infinitesimal movement—and we will show you how this little stock became the kosmos, without ever taking a step worth thinking of, much less constituting a case for design. The argument is a mere appeal to an incompetency in the human imagination, in virtue of which magnitudes evading conception are treated as out of existence; and an aggregate of inappreciable increments is simultaneously equated,—in its cause to nothing, in its effect to the whole of things. You manifestly want the same causality, whether concentrated in a moment or distributed through incalculable ages; only in drawing upon it a logical theft is more easily committed piecemeal than wholesale. Surely it is a mean device for a philosopher thus to crib causation by hair-breadths, to put it out at compound interest through all time, and then disown the debt."

It is not said that the view here given of the process of Evolution has been the actual process. The illustrations have been developed rather to clear up difficulties than to state a theory. The time is not ripe for daring to present to our imaginations even a partial view of what that transcendent process may have been. At present we can only take our ideas of growth from the growing things around us, and in this analogy we have taken no account of the most essential fact—the seed. Nor is it asserted, far as these illustrations point in that direction, that the course of Evolution has been a continuous, uninterrupted, upward rise. On the whole it has certainly been a rise; but whether a rise without leap or break or pause, or—what is more likely—a progress in rhythms, pulses, and waves, or—what is unlikely— a cataclysmal ascent by steps abrupt and steep, may possibly never be proved.

There are reverent minds who ceaselessly scan the fields of Nature and the books of Science in search of gaps—gaps which they will fill up with God. As if God lived in gaps? What view of Nature or of Truth is theirs whose interest in Science is not in what it can explain but in what it cannot, whose quest is ignorance not knowledge, whose daily dread is that the cloud may lift, and who, as darkness melts from this field or from that, begin to tremble for the place of His abode? What needs altering in such finely-jealous souls is at once their view of Nature and of God. Nature is God's writing, and can only tell the truth; God is light, and in Him is no darkness at all.

If by the accumulation of irresistible evidence we are driven—may not one say permitted—to accept Evolution as God's method in creation, it is a mistaken policy to glory in what it cannot account for. The reason why men grudge to Evolution each of its fresh claims to show how things have been made is the groundless fear that if we discover how they are made we minimize their divinity. When things are known, that is to say, we conceive them as natural, on Man's level; when they are unknown, we call them divine—as if our ignorance of a thing were the stamp of its divinity. If God is only to be left to the gaps in our knowledge, where shall we be when these gaps are filled up? And if they are never to be filled up, is God only to be found in the dis-orders of the world? Those who yield to the temptation to reserve a point here and there for special divine interposition are apt to forget that this virtually excludes God from the rest of the process. If God appears periodically, He disappears periodically. If He comes upon the scene at special crises, He is absent from the scene in the intervals. Whether is all-God or occasional-God the nobler theory? Positively, the idea of an immanent God, which is the God of Evolution, is infinitely grander than the occasional wonder-worker, who is the God of an old theology. Negatively, the older view is not only the less worthy, but it is discredited by science. And as to facts, the daily miracle of a flower, the courses of the stars, the upholding and sustaining day by day of this great palpitating world, need a living Will as much as the creation of atoms at the first. We know growth as the method by which things are made in Nature, and we know no other method. We do not know that there are not other methods; but if there are, we do not know them. Those cases which we do not know to be growths, we do not know to be anything else, and we may at least suspect them to be growths. Nor are they any the less miraculous because they appear to us as growths. A miracle is not something quick. The doings of these things may seem to us no miracle, nevertheless it is a miracle that they have been done.

But, after all, the miracle of Evolution is not the process but the product. Beside the wonder of the result, the problem of the process is a mere curiosity of Science. For what is the product? It is not mountain and valley, sky and sea, flower and star, this glorious and beautiful world in which Man's body finds its home. It is not the god-like gift of Mind nor the ordered cosmos where it finds so noble an exercise for its illimitable powers. It is that which of all other things in the universe commends itself, with increasing sureness as time goes on, to the reason and to the heart of Humanity—Love. Love is the final result of Evolution. This is what stands out in Nature as the supreme creation. Evolution is not progress in matter. Matter cannot progress. It is a progress in spirit, in that which is limitless, in that which is at once most human, most rational, and most divine. Whatever controversy rages as to the factors of Evolution, whatever mystery enshrouds its steps, no doubt exists of its goal. The great landmarks we have passed, and we are not yet half-way up the Ascent, each separately and all together have declared the course of Nature to be a rational course, and its end a moral end. At the furthest limit of time, in protoplasm itself, we saw start forth the two great currents which by their action and reaction, as Selfishness and Unselfishness, were to supply in ever accentuating clearness the conditions of the moral life. Following their movements upward through the organic kingdom, we watched the results which each achieved —always high, and always waxing higher; and though what we call Evil dogged each step with sinister and sometimes staggering malevolence, the balance when struck was always good upon the whole. Then came the last great act of the organic process, the act which finally revealed to teleology its hitherto obscured end, the organization of the Mammalia, the Kingdom of the Mothers. So full of ethical possibility is this single creation that one might stake the character of Evolution upon the Mammalia alone. On the biological side, as we have seen, the Evolution of the Mammalia means the Evolution of Mothers; on the sociological side, the Evolution of the Family; and on the moral side, the Evolution of Love. How are we to characterize a process which ripened fruits like these? That the very animal kingdom had for its end and crown a class of animals who owe their name, their place, and their whole existence to Altruism; that through these Mothers society has been furnished with an institution for generating, concentrating, purifying, and redistributing Love in all its enduring forms; that the perfecting of Love is thus not an incident in Nature but everywhere the largest part of her task, begun with the first beginnings of life, and continuously developing quantitatively and qualitatively to the close—all this has been read into Nature by our own imaginings, or it is the revelation of a purpose of benevolence and a God whose name is Love. The sceptic, we are sometimes reminded, has presented crucial difficulties to the theist founded on the doctrine of Evolution. Here is a problem which the theist may leave with the sceptic. That that which has emerged has the qualities it has, that even the Mammalia should have emerged, that that class should stand related to the life of Man in the way it does, that Man has lived because he loved, and that he lives to love—these, on any theory but one, are insoluble problems.

Forbidden to follow the Evolution of Love into the higher fields of history and society, we take courage to make a momentary exploration in a still lower field—a field so far beneath the plant and animal level that hitherto we have not dared it conceivable that in inorganic Nature, among the very material bases of the world, there should be anything to remind us of the coming of this Tree of Life? To expect even foreshadowings of ethical characters there were an anachronism too great for expression. Yet there is something there, something which is at least worth recalling in the present connection.

The earliest condition in which Science allows us to picture this globe is that of a fiery mass of nebulous matter. At the second stage it consists of countless myriads of similar atoms, roughly outlined into a ragged cloud-ball, glowing with heat, and rotating in space with inconceivable velocity. By what means can this mass be broken up, or broken down, or made into a solid world? By two things—

mutual attraction and chemical affinity. The moment when within this cloud-ball the conditions of cooling temperature are such that two atoms could combine together the cause of the Evolution of the Earth is won. For this pair of atoms are chemically "stronger" than any of the atoms immediately surrounding them. Gradually, by attraction or affinity, the primitive pair of atoms—like the first pair of savages— absorb a third atom, and a fourth, and a fifth, until a "Family" of atoms is raised up which possesses properties and powers altogether new, and in virtue of which it holds within its grasp the conquest and servitude of all surrounding units. From this growing centre, attraction radiates on every side, until a larger aggregate, a family group—a Tribe—arises and starts a more powerful centre of its own. With every additional atom added, the power as well as the complexity of the combination increases. As the process goes on, after endless vicissitudes, repulsions, and readjustments, the changes become fewer and fewer, the conflict between mass and mass dies down, the elements passing through various stages of liquidity finally combine in the order of their affinities, arrange themselves in the order of their densities, and the solid earth is finished.

Now recall the names of the leading actors in this stupendous reformation. They are two in number, mutual attraction and chemical affinity. Notice these words—Attraction, Affinity. Notice that the great formative forces of physical Evolution have psychical names. It is idle to discuss whether there is or can be any identity between the thing represented in the one case and in the other. Obviously there cannot be. Yet this does not exhaust the interest of the analogy. In reality, neither here nor anywhere, have we any knowledge whatever of what is actually meant by Attraction; nor, in the one sphere or in the other, have we even the means of approximating to such knowledge. To Newton himself the very conception of one atom or one mass, attracting through empty space another atom or another mass, put his mental powers to confusion. And as to the term Affinity, the most recent Chemistry, finding it utterly unfathomable in itself, confines its research at present to the investigation of its modes of action. Science does not know indeed what forces are; it only classifies them. Here, as in every deep recess of physical Nature, we are in the presence of that which is metaphysical, that which bars the way imperiously at every turn to a materialistic interpretation of the world. Yet name and nature of force apart, what affinity even the grossest, what likeness even the most remote, could one have expected to trace between the gradual aggregation of units of matter in the condensation of a weltering star, and the slow segregation of men in the organization of societies and nations? However different the agents, is there no suggestion that they are different stages of a uniform process, different epochs of one great historical enterprise, different results of a single evolutionary law?

Read from the root, we define this age-long process by a word borrowed from the science of roots—a word from the clay—Evolution. But read from the top, Evolution is an impossible word to describe it. The word is Involution. It is not a Stigmaria world, but a Sigillaria world; a spiritual, not a material universe. Evolution is Advolution; better, it is Revelation—the phenomenal expression of the Divine, the progressive realization of the Ideal, the Ascent of Love. Evolution is a doctrine of unimaginable grandeur. That Man should discern the prelude to his destiny in the voices of the stars; that the heart of Nature should be a so human heart; that its eternal enterprise should be one with his ideals; that even in the Universe beyond, the Reason which presides should have so strange a kinship with that measure of it which he calls his own; that he, an atom in that

Universe, should dare to feel himself at home within it, should stand beside Immensity, Infinity, Eternity, unaffrighted and undismayed—these things bewilder Man the more that they bewilder him so little.

But one verdict is possible as to the practical import of this great doctrine, as to its bearing upon the individual life and the future of the race. Evolution has ushered a new hope into the world. The supreme message of science to this age is that all Nature is on the side of the man who tries to rise. Evolution, development, progress are not only on her programme, these are her programme. For all things are rising, all worlds, all planets, all stars and suns. An ascending energy is in the universe, and the whole moves on with one mighty idea and anticipation. The aspiration in the human mind and heart is but the evolutionary tendency of the universe becoming conscious. Darwin's great discovery, or the discovery which he brought into prominence, is the same as Galileo's—that the world moves. The Italian prophet said it moves from west to east; the English philosopher said it moves from low to high. And this is the last and most splendid contribution of science to the faith of the world.

The discovery of a second motion in the earth has come into the world of thought only in time to save it from despair. As in the days of Galileo, there are many even now who do not see that the world moves—men to whom the earth is but an endless plain, a prison fixed in a purposeless universe where untried prisoners await their unknown fate. It is not the monotony of life which destroys men, but its pointlessness; they can bear its weight, its meaninglessness crushes them. But the same great revolution that the discovery of the axial rotation of the earth effected in the realm of physics, the announcement of the doctrine of Evolution makes in the moral world. Already, even in these days of its dawn, a sudden and marvellous light has fallen upon earth and heaven. Evolution is less a doctrine than a light; it is a light revealing in the chaos of the past a perfect and growing order, giving meaning even to the confusions of the present, discovering through all the deviousness around us the paths of progress, and flashing its rays already upon a coming goal. Men begin to see an undeviating ethical purpose in this material world, a tide, that from eternity has never turned, making for perfectness. In that vast progression of Nature, that vision of all things from the first of time moving from low to high, from incompleteness to completeness, from imperfection to perfection, the moral nature recognizes in all its height and depth the eternal claim upon itself. Wholeness, perfection, love—these have always been required of Man. But never before on the natural plane have they been proclaimed by voices so commanding, or enforced by sanctions so great and rational.

Is Nature henceforth to become the ethical teacher of the world? Shall its aims become the guide, its spirit the inspiration of Man's life? Is there no ground here where all the faiths and all the creeds may meet—nay, no ground for a final faith and a final creed? For could but all men see the inner meaning and aspiration of the natural order should we not find at last the universal religion—a religion congruous with the whole past of Man, at one with Nature, and with a working creed which Science could accept?

The answer is a simple one: We have it already. There exists a religion which has anticipated all these requirements—a religion which has been before the world these eighteen hundred years, whose congruity with Nature and with Man stands the tests at every point. Up to this time no word has been spoken to reconcile Christianity with Evolution, or Evolution with Christianity. And why? Because the two are one. What is Evolution? A method of creation. What is its object? To make more perfect living beings. What is Christianity? A method of creation. What is its object? To make more perfect living beings. Through what does Evolution work? Through Love. Through what does Christianity work? Through Love. Evolution and Christianity have the same Author, the same end, the same spirit. There is no rivalry between these processes. Christianity struck into the Evolutionary process with no noise or shock; it upset nothing of all that had been done; it took all the natural foundations precisely as it found them; it adopted Man's body, mind, and soul at the exact level where Organic Evolution was at work upon them; it carried on the building by slow and gradual modifications; and, through processes governed by rational laws, it put the finishing touches to the Ascent of Man.

No man can run up the natural lines of Evolution without coming to Christianity at the top. One holds no brief to buttress Christianity in this way. But science has to deal with facts and with all facts, and the facts and processes which have received the name of Christian are the continuations of the scientific order, as much the successors of these facts and the continuations of these processes—due allowances being made for the differences in the planes, and for the new factors which appear with each new plane—as the facts and processes of biology are of those of the mineral world. We land here, not from choice, but from necessity. Christianity—it is not said any particular form of Christianity—but Christianity, is the Further Evolution.

"The glory of Christianity," urged Jowett, "is not to be as unlike other religions as possible, but to be their perfection and fulfilment." The divinity of Christianity, it might be added, is not to be as unlike Nature as possible, but to be its coronation; the fulfilment of its promise; the rallying point of its forces; the beginning not of a new end, but of an infinite acceleration of the processes by which the end, eternal from the beginning, was henceforth to be realized. A religion which is Love and a Nature which is Love can never but be one. The infinite exaltation in quality is what the progressive revelation from the beginning has taught us to expect. Christianity, truly, has its own phenomena: its special processes; its factors altogether unique. But these do not excommunicate it from God's order. They are in line with all that has gone before, the latest disclosure of Environment. Most strange to us and new, most miraculous and supernatural when looked at from beneath, they are the normal phenomena of altitude, the revelation natural to the highest height. While Evolution never deviates from its course, it assumes new developments at every stage of the Ascent; and here, as the last and highest, these specializations, accelerations, modifications, are most revolutionary of all. For the evolving products are now no longer the prey and tool of the Struggle for Life—the normal dynamic of the world's youth. For them its appeal is vain; its force is spent ; a quicker road to progress has been found. No longer driven from below by the Animal Struggle, they are drawn upward from above; no longer compelled by hate or hunger, by rivalry or fear, they feel impelled by Love; they realize the dignity reserved for Man alone in evolving through Ideals. This development through Ideals, the Perfect Ideal through which all others come, are the unique phenomena of the closing act—unique not because they are out of relation to what has gone before, but because the phenomena of the summit are different from the phenomena of the plain. Apart from these, and not absolutely apart from these—for nothing in the world can be absolutely apart from anything else, there is nothing in Christianity which is not in germ in Nature. It is not an excrescence on Nature but its efflorescence. It is not a side track where a few enthusiasts live impracticable lives on impossible ideals. It is the main stream of history and of science, and the only current set from eternity for the progress of the world and the perfecting of a human race.

We began these chapters with the understanding that Evolution is history, the scientific history of the world. Christianity is history, a history of some of the later steps in the Evolution of the world. The continuity between them is a continuity of spirit; their forms are different, their forces confluent. Christianity did not begin at the Christian era, it is as old as Nature; did not drop like a bolt from Eternity, came in the fulness of Time. The attempt to prove an alibi for Christianity; to show that it was in the skies till the Christian era opened, is as fatal to its acceptance by Science as it is useless for defence to Theology. What emerges from Nature as the final result of Creation is none other than that immortal principle which, reinforced, is the instrument and end of the new Creation.

The attempt of Science, on the other hand, to hold itself aloof from the later phases of developments which in their earlier stages it so devotes itself to trace, is either ignorance or sheer affectation. For that Altruism which we found struggling to express itself throughout the whole course of Nature, What is it? "Altruism is the new and very affected name for the old familiar things which we used to call Charity, Philanthropy, and Love. Only by shutting its eyes can Science evade the discovery of the roots of Christianity in every province that it enters; and when it does discover them, it is only by disguising words that it can succeed in disowning the relationship. There is nothing unscientific in accepting that relationship; there is much that is unscientific in dishonouring it. The Will behind Evolution is not dead; the heart beneath Nature is not stilled. Love not only was; it is; it moves; it spreads. To ignore the later and most striking phases is to fail to see what the earlier process really was, and to leave the ancient task of Evolution historically incomplete. That Christian development, social, moral, spiritual, which is going on around us, is as real an evolutionary movement as any that preceded it, and at least as capable of scientific expression. A system founded on Self-Sacrifice, whose fittest symbol is the Leaven, whose organic development has its natural analogy in the growth of a Mustard Tree, is not a foreign thing to the Evolutionist; and that prophet of the Kingdom of God was no less the spokesman of Nature who proclaimed that the end of Man is "that which we had from the beginning, that we love."

In the profoundest sense, this is scientific doctrine. The Ascent of Man and of Society is bound up henceforth with the conflict, the intensification, and the diffusion of the Struggle for the Life of Others. This is the Further Evolution, the page of history that lies before us, the closing act of the drama of Man. The Struggle may be short or long; but by all scientific analogy the result is sure. All the other Kingdoms of Nature were completed; Evolution always attains; always rounds off its work. It spent an eternity over the earth, but finished it. It struggled for millenniums to bring the Vegetable Kingdom up to the Flowering Plants, and attained. In the Animal Kingdom it never paused until the possibilities of organization were exhausted in the Mammalia. Kindled by this past, Man may surely say, "I shall arrive." The succession cannot break. The Further Evolution must go on, the Higher Kingdom come—first the blade, where we are to-day; then the ear, where we shall be to-morrow; then the full corn in the ear, which awaits our children's children, and which we live to hasten.

The Greatest Thing in the World and Other Addresses

Table of Contents

Introduction

I was staying with a party of friends in a country house during my visit to England in 1884. On Sunday evening as we sat around the fire, they asked me to read and expound some portion of Scripture. Being tired after the services of the day, I told them to ask Henry Drummond, who was one of the party. After some urging he drew a small Testament from his hip pocket, opened it at the 13th chapter of I Corinthians, and began to speak on the subject of Love.

It seemed to me that I had never heard anything so beautiful, and I determined not to rest until I brought Henry Drummond to Northfield to deliver that address. Since then I have requested the principals of schools to have it read before the students every year. The one great need in our Christian life is love, more love to God and to each other. Would that we could all move into that Love chapter, and live there.

This volume contains, in addition to the address on Love, some other addresses which I trust will bring help and blessing to many.

D. L. Moody.

Love: The Greatest Thing in the World

Every one has asked himself the great question of antiquity as of the modern world: What is the 'summum bonum'—the supreme good? You have life before you. Once only you can live it. What is the noblest object of desire, the supreme gift to covet?

We have been accustomed to be told that the greatest thing in the religious world is Faith. That great word has been the key-note for centuries of the popular religion; and we have easily learned to look upon it as the greatest thing in the world. Well, we are wrong. If we have been told that, we may miss the mark. In the 13th chapter of I Corinthians, Paul takes us to Christianity at its source; and there we see, "the greatest of these is love."

It is not an oversight. Paul was speaking of faith just a moment before. He says, "If I have all faith, so that I can remove mountains, and have not love, I am nothing." So far from forgetting, he deliberately contrasts them, "Now abideth Faith, Hope, Love," and without a moment's hesitation the decision falls, "The greatest of these is Love."

And it is not prejudice. A man is apt to recommend to others his own strong point. Love was not Paul's strong point. The observing student can detect a beautiful tenderness growing and ripening all through his character as Paul gets old; but the hand that wrote "The greatest of these is love," when we meet it first, is stained with blood.

Nor is this letter to the Corinthians peculiar in singling out love as the "summum bonum." The masterpieces of Christianity are agreed about it. Peter says, "Above all things have fervent love among yourselves." *Above all things.* And John goes farther, "God is love."

You remember the profound remark which Paul makes elsewhere, "Love is the fulfilling of the law." Did you ever think what he meant by that? In those days men were working the passage to Heaven by keeping the Ten Commandments, and the hundred and ten other commandments which they had manufactured out of them. Christ came and said, "I will show you a more simple way. If you do one thing, you will do these hundred and ten things, without ever thinking about them. If you *love*, you will unconsciously fulfill the whole law."

You can readily see for yourselves how that must be so. Take any of the commandments. "Thou shalt have no other gods before Me." If a man love God, you will not require to tell him that. Love is the fulfilling of that law. "Take not His name in vain." Would he ever dream of taking His name in vain if he loved him?

"Remember the Sabbath day to keep it holy." Would he not be too glad to have one day in seven to dedicate more exclusively to the object of his affection? Love would fulfill all these laws regarding God.

And so, if he loved man, you would never think of telling him to honor his father and mother. He could not do anything else. It would be preposterous to tell him not to kill. You could only insult him if you suggested that he should not steal—how could he steal from those he loved? It would be superfluous to beg him not to bear false witness against his neighbor. If he loved him it would be the last thing he would do. And you would never dream of urging him not to covet what his neighbors had. He would rather they possess it than himself. In this way "Love is the fulfilling of the law." It is the rule for fulfilling all rules, the new commandment for keeping all the old commandments, Christ's one.

Secret of the Christian life.

Now Paul has learned that; and in this noble eulogy he has given us the most wonderful and original account extant of the "summum bonum." We may divide it into three parts. In the beginning of the short chapter we have Love *contrasted*; in the heart of it, we have Love *analyzed*; toward the end, we have Love *defended* as the supreme gift.

I. The Contrast

Paul begins by contrasting Love with other things that men in those days thought much of. I shall not attempt to go over these things in detail. Their inferiority is already obvious.

He contrasts it with *eloquence*. And what a noble gift it is, the power of playing upon the souls and wills of men, and rousing them to lofty purpose and holy deeds! Paul says, If I speak with the tongues of men and of angels, and have not love, I am become sounding brass, or a tinkling cymbal." We all know why. We have all felt the brazenness of words without emotion, the hollowness, the unaccountable unpersuasiveness, of eloquence behind which lies no Love.

He contrasts it with *prophecy*. He contrasts it with *mysteries*. He contrasts it with *faith*. He contrasts it with *Charity*. Why is Love greater than faith? Because the end is greater than the means. And why is it greater than charity? Because the whole is greater than the part.

Love is greater than *faith*, because the end is greater than the means. What is the use of having faith? It is to connect the soul with God. And what is the object of connecting man with God? That he may become like God. But God is Love. Hence Faith, the means, is in order to Love, the end. Love, therefore, obviously is greater than faith. "If I have all faith, so as to remove mountains, but have not love, I am nothing."

It is greater than *charity*, again, because the whole is greater than a part. Charity is only a little bit of Love, one of the innumerable avenues of Love, and there may even be, and there is, a great deal of charity without Love. It is a very easy thing to toss a copper to a beggar on the street; it is generally an easier thing than not to do it. Yet Love is just as often in the withholding. We purchase relief from the sympathetic feelings roused by the spectacle of misery, at the copper's cost. It is too cheap—too cheap for us, and often too dear for the beggar. If we really loved him we would either do more for him, or less. Hence, "If I bestow all my goods to feed the poor, but have not love it profiteth me nothing."

Then Paul contrasts it with *sacrifice* and martyrdom: "If I give my body to be burned, but have not love, it profiteth me nothing." Missionaries can take nothing greater to the heathen world than the impress and reflection of the Love of God upon their own character. That is the universal language. It will take them years to speak in Chinese, or in the dialects of India. From the day they land, that language of Love, understood by all, will be pouring forth its unconscious eloquence.

It is the man who is the missionary, it is not his words. His character is his message. In the heart of Africa, among the great Lakes, I have come across black men and women who remembered the only white man they ever saw before—David Livingstone; and as you cross his footsteps in that dark continent, men's faces light up as they speak of the kind doctor who passed there years ago. They could not understand him; but they felt the love that beat in his heart. They knew that it was love, although he spoke no word.

Take into your sphere of labor, where you also mean to lay down your life, that simple charm, and your lifework must succeed. You can take nothing greater, you need take nothing less. You may take every accomplishment; you may be braced for every sacrifice; but if you give your body to be burned, and have not Love, it will profit you and the cause of Christ nothing.

II. The Analysis

After contrasting Love with these things, Paul, in three verses, very short, gives us an amazing analysis of what this supreme thing is.

I ask you to look at it. It is a compound thing, he tells us. It is like light. As you have seen a man of science take a beam of light and pass it through a crystal prism, as you have seen it come out on the other side of the prism broken up into its component colors—red, and blue, and yellow, and violet, and orange, and all the colors of the rainbow—so Paul passes this thing, Love, through the magnificent prism of his inspired intellect, and it comes out on the other side broken up into its elements.

In these few words we have what one might call The spectrum of Love, the analysis of love. Will you observe what its elements are? Will you notice that they have common names; that they are virtues which we hear about every day; that they are things which can be practiced by every man in every place in life; and how, by a multitude of small things and ordinary virtues, the supreme thing, the "summum bonum," is made up?

The Spectrum of Love has nine ingredients:

Patience . . . . "Love suffereth long."
Kindness . . . . "And is kind."
Generosity . . . . "Love envieth not."
Humility . . . . "Love vaunteth not itself, is not puffed up."
Courtesy . . . . "Doth not behave itself unseemly."
Unselfishness . . . . "Seeketh not its own."
Good temper . . . . "Is not provoked."

Guilelessness . . . . "Taketh not account of evil."
Sincerity . . . . "Rejoiceth not in unrighteousness, but rejoiceth with the truth."

Patience; kindness; generosity; humility; courtesy; unselfishness; good temper; guilelessness; sincerity—these make up the supreme gift, the stature of the perfect man.

You will observe that all are in relation to men, in relation to life, in relation to the known to-day and the near to-morrow, and not to the unknown eternity. We hear much of love to God; Christ spoke much of love to man. We make a great deal of peace with heaven; Christ made much of peace on earth. Religion is not a strange or added thing, but the inspiration of the secular life, the breathing of an eternal spirit through this temporal world. The supreme thing, in short, is not a thing at all, but the giving of a further finish to the multitudinous words and acts which make up the sum of every common day.

Patience. This is the normal attitude of love; Love passive, love waiting to begin; not in a hurry; calm; ready to do its work when the summons comes, but meantime wearing the ornament of a meek and quiet spirit. Love suffers long; beareth all things; believeth all things; hopeth all things. For Love understands, and therefore waits.

Kindness. Love active. Have you ever noticed how much of Christ's life was spent in doing kind things—in *merely* doing kind things? Run over it with that in view, and you will find that He spent a great proportion of His time simply in making people happy, in doing good turns to people. There is only one thing greater than happiness in the world, and that is holiness; and it is not in our keeping; but what God *has* put in our power is the happiness of those about us, and that is largely to be secured by our being kind to them.

"The greatest thing," says some one, "a man can do for his Heavenly Father is to be kind to some of His other children." I wonder why it is that we are not all kinder than we are? How much the world needs it! How easily it is done! How instantaneously it acts! How infallibly it is remembered! How superabundantly it pays itself back—for there is no debtor in the world so honorable, so superbly honorable, as Love. "Love never faileth." Love is success, Love is happiness, Love is life. "Love," I say with Browning, "is energy of life."

"For life, with all it yields of joy or woe And hope and fear, Is just our chance o' the prize of learning love,— How love might be, hath been indeed, and is."

Where Love is, God is. He that dwelleth in Love dwelleth in God. God is Love. Therefore *love*. Without distinction, without calculation, without procrastination, love. Lavish it upon the poor, where it is very easy; especially upon the rich, who often need it most; most of all upon our equals, where it is very difficult, and for whom perhaps we each do least of all. There is a difference between *trying to please* and *giving pleasure*. Give pleasure. Lose no chance of giving pleasure; for that is the ceaseless and anonymous triumph of a truly loving spirit. "I shall pass through this world but once. Any good thing, therefore, that I can do, or any kindness that I can show to any human being, let me do it now. Let me not defer it or neglect it, for I shall not pass this way again."

Generosity. "Love envieth not." This is love in competition with others. Whenever you attempt a good work you will find other men doing the same kind of work, and probably doing it better. Envy them not. Envy is a feeling of ill-will to those who are in the same line as ourselves, a spirit of covetousness and detraction. How little Christian work even is a protection against un-Christian feeling! That most despicable of all the unworthy moods which cloud a Christian's soul assuredly waits for us on the threshold of every work, unless we are fortified with this grace of magnanimity. Only one thing truly need the Christian envy—the large, rich, generous soul which "envieth not."

And then, after having learned all that, you have to learn this further thing, *humility*—to put a seal upon your lips and forget what you have done. After you have been kind, after Love has stolen forth into the world and done its beautiful work, go back into the shade again and say nothing about it. Love hides even from itself. Love waives even self-satisfaction. "Love vaunteth not itself, is not puffed up." Humility—love hiding.

The fifth ingredient is a somewhat strange one to find in this "summum bonum:" *courtesy*. This is Love in society, Love in relation to etiquette. "Love doe not behave itself unseemly."

Politeness has been defined as love in trifles. Courtesy is said to be love in little things. And the one secret of politeness is to love.

Love *cannot* behave itself unseemly. You can put the most untutored persons into the highest society, and if they have a reservoir of Love in their hearty they will not behave themselves unseemly. They simply cannot do it. Carlisle said of Robert Burns that there was no truer gentleman in Europe than the ploughman-poet. It was because he loved everything—the mouse, and the daisy, and all the things, great and small, that God had made. So with this simple passport he could mingle with any society, and enter courts and palaces from his little cottage on the banks of the Ayr.

You know the meaning of the word "gentleman." It means a gentle man—a man who does things gently, with love. That is the whole art and mystery of it. The gentle man cannot in the nature of things do an ungentle, an ungentlemanly thing. The ungentle soul, the inconsiderate, unsympathetic nature, cannot do anything else. "Love doth not behave itself unseemly."

Unselfishness. "Love seeketh not her own." Observe: Seeketh not even that which is her own. In Britain the Englishman is devoted, and rightly, to his rights. But there come times when a man may exercise even the higher right of giving up his rights.

Yet Paul does not summon us to give up our rights. Love strikes much deeper. It would have us not seek them at all, ignore them, eliminate the personal element altogether from our calculations.

It is not hard to give up our rights. They are often eternal. The difficult thing is to give up *ourselves*. The more difficult thing still is not to seek things for ourselves at all. After we have sought them, bought them, won them, deserved them, we have taken the cream off them for ourselves already. Little cross then to give them up. But not to seek them, to look every man not on his own things, but on the things of others—that is the difficulty. "Seekest thou great things for thyself?" said the prophet; "*seek them not.*" Why? Because there is no greatness in *things*. Things cannot be great. The only greatness is unselfish love. Even self-denial in itself is nothing, is almost a mistake. Only a great purpose or a mightier love can justify the waste.

It is more difficult, I have said, not to seek our own at all than, having sought it, to give it up. I must take that back. It is only true of a partly selfish heart. Nothing is a hardship to Love, and nothing is hard. I believe that Christ's "yoke" is easy. Christ's yoke is just His way of taking life. And I believe it is an easier way than any other. I believe it is a happier way than any other. The most obvious lesson in Christ's teaching is that there is no happiness in having and getting anything, but only in giving. I repeat, *there is no happiness in having or in getting, but only in giving.* Half the world is on the wrong scent in the pursuit of happiness. They think it consists in having and getting, and in being served by others. It consists in giving, and in serving others. "He that would be great among you," said Christ, "let him serve." He that would be happy, let him remember that there is but one way—"it is more blessed, it is more happy, to give than to receive."

The next ingredient is a very remarkable one: good temper. "Love is not provoked."

Nothing could be more striking than to find this here. We are inclined to look upon bad temper as a very harmless weakness. We speak of it as a mere infirmity of nature, a family failing, a matter of temperament, not a thing to take into very serious account in estimating a man's *character*. And yet here, right in the heart of this analysis of love, it finds a place; and the Bible again and again returns to condemn it as one of the most destructive elements in human nature.

The peculiarity of ill temper is that it is the vice of the virtuous. It is often the one blot on an otherwise noble character. You know men who are all but perfect, and women who would be entirely perfect, but for an easily ruffled, quick-tempered, or "touchy" disposition. This compatibility of ill temper with high moral character is one of the strangest and saddest problems of ethics. The truth is, there are two great classes of sins—sins of the *body* and sins of the *disposition*. The Prodigal Son may be taken as a type of the first, the Elder Brother of the second. Now, society has no doubt whatever as to which of these is the worse. Its brand falls, without a challenge, upon the Prodigal. But are we right? We have no balance to weigh one another's sins, and coarser and finer are but human words; but faults in the higher nature may be less venal than those in the lower, and to the eye of Him who is Love, a sin against Love may seem a hundred times more base. No form of vice, not worldliness, not greed of gold, not drunkenness itself, does more to un-Christianize society than evil temper. For embittering life, for breaking up communities, for destroying the most sacred relationships, for devastating homes, for withering up men and women, for taking the bloom of childhood, in short, for sheer gratuitous misery-producing power this influence stands alone.

Look at the Elder Brother—moral, hard-working, patient, dutiful—let him get all credit for his virtues—look at this man, this baby, sulking outside his own father's door. "He was angry," we read, "and would not go in." Look at the effect upon the father, upon the servants, upon the happiness of the guests. Judge of the effect upon the Prodigal—and how many prodigals are kept out of the Kingdom of God by the unlovely character of those who profess to be inside. Analyze, as a study in Temper, the thunder-cloud itself as it gathers upon the Elder Brother's brow. What is it made of? Jealousy, anger, pride, uncharity, cruelty, self-righteousness, touchiness, doggedness, sullenness—these are the ingredients of this dark and loveless soul. In varying proportions, also, these are the ingredients of all ill temper. Judge if such sins are of the disposition are not worse to live in, and for others to live with, than the sins of the body. Did Christ indeed not answer the question Himself when He said, "I say unto you that the publicans and the harlots go into the Kingdom of Heaven before you"? There is really no place in heaven for a disposition like this. A man with such a mood could only make heaven miserable for all the people in it. Except, therefore, such a man be born again, he cannot, simply *cannot*, enter the kingdom of heaven.

You will see then why Temper is significant. It is not in what it is alone, but in what it reveals. This is why I speak of it with such unusual plainness. It is a test for love, a symptom, a revelation of an unloving nature at bottom. It is the intermittent fever which bespeaks unintermittent disease within; the occasional bubble escaping to the surface which betrays some rottenness underneath; a sample of the most hidden products of the soul dropped involuntarily when off one's guard; in a word, the lightning form of a hundred hideous and un-Christian sins. A want of patience, a want of kindness, a want of generosity, a want of courtesy, a want of unselfishness, are all instantaneously symbolized in one flash of Temper.

Hence it is not enough to deal with the Temper. We must go to the source, and change the inmost nature, and the angry humors will die away of themselves. souls are made sweet not by taking the acid fluids out, but by putting something in—a great Love, a new Spirit, the Spirit of Christ. Christ, the Spirit of Christ, interpenetrating ours, sweetens, purifies, transforms all. This only can eradicate what is wrong, work a chemical change, renovate and regenerate, and rehabilitate the inner man. Will-power does not change men. Time does not change men. Christ does. Therefore, "Let that mind be in you which was also in Christ Jesus."

Some of us have not much time to lose. Remember, once more, that this is a matter of life or death. I cannot help speaking urgently, for myself, for yourselves. "Whoso shall offend one of these little ones, which believe in me, it were better for him that a millstone were hanged about his neck, and that he were drowned in the depth of the sea." That is to say, it is the deliberate verdict of the Lord Jesus that it is better not to live than not to love. *It is better not to live than not to love.*

Guilelessness and *sincerity* may be dismissed almost without a word. Guilelessness is the grace for suspicious people. The possession of it is the great secret of personal influence.

You will find, if you think for a moment, that the people who influence you are people who believe in you. In an atmosphere of suspicion men shrivel up; but in that atmosphere they expand, and find encouragement and educative fellowship.

It is a wonderful thing that here and there in this hard, uncharitable world there should still be left a few rare souls who think no evil. this is the great unworldliness. Love "thinketh no evil," imputes no motive, sees the bright side, puts the best construction on every action. What a delightful state of mind to live in! What a stimulus and benediction even to meet with it for a day! To be trusted is to be saved. And if we try to influence or elevate others, we shall soon see that success is in proportion to their belief of our belief in them. The respect of another is the first restoration of the self-respect a man has lost; our ideal of what he is becomes to him the hope and pattern of what he may become.

"Love rejoiceth not in unrighteousness, but rejoiceth with the truth." I have called this *sincerity* from the words rendered in the Authorized Version by "rejoiceth in the truth." And, certainly, were this the real translation, nothing could be more just; for he who loves will love Truth not less than men. He will rejoice in the Truth—rejoice not in what he has been taught to believe; not in this church's doctrine or in that; not in this ism or in that ism; but "in *the truth*." He will accept only what is real; he will strive to get at facts; he will search for *truth* with a humble and unbiased mind, and cherish whatever he finds at any sacrifice. But the more literal translation of the Revised Version calls for just such a sacrifice for truth's sake here. For what Paul really meant is, as we there read, "Rejoiceth not in unrighteousness, but rejoiceth with the truth," a quality which probably no one English word—and certainly not *sincerity*—adequately defines. It includes, perhaps more strictly, the self-restraint which refuses to make capital out of others' faults; the charity which delights not in exposing the weakness of others, but "covereth all things"; the sincerity of purpose which endeavors to see things as they are, and rejoices to find them better than suspicion feared or calumny denounced.

So much for the analysis of Love. Now the business of our lives is to have these things fitted into our characters. That is the supreme work to which we need to address ourselves in this world, to learn Love. Is life not full of opportunities for learning Love? Every man and woman every day has a thousand of them. The world is not a playground; it is a schoolroom. Life is not a holiday, but an education. And the one eternal lesson for us all is *how better we can love*.

What makes a man a good cricketer? Practice. What makes a man a good artist, a good sculptor, a good musician? Practice. What makes a man a good linguist, a good stenographer? Practice. What makes a man a good man? Practice. Nothing else. There is nothing capricious about religion. We do not get the soul in different ways, under different laws, from those in which we get the body and the mind. If a man does not exercise his arm he develops no biceps muscle; and if a man does not exercise his soul, he acquires no muscle in his soul, no strength of character, no vigor of moral fibre, no beauty of spiritual growth. Love is not a thing of enthusiastic emotion. It is a rich, strong, manly, vigorous expression of the whole round Christian character—the Christlike nature in its fullest development. And the constituents of this great character are only to be built up by ceaseless practice.

What was Christ doing in the carpenter's shop? Practicing. Though perfect, we read that he *learned* obedience, and grew in wisdom and in favor with God. Do not quarrel, therefore, with your lot in life. Do not complain of its never-ceasing cares, its petty environment, the vexations you have to stand, the small and sordid souls you have to live and work with. Above all, do not resent temptation; do not be perplexed because it seems to thicken round you more and more, and ceases neither for effort nor for agony nor prayer. That is your practice. That is the practice which god appoints you; and it is having its work in making you patient, and humble, and generous, and unselfish, and kind, and courteous. Do not grudge the hand that is mounding the still too shapeless image within you. It is growing more beautiful, though you see it not; and every touch of temptation may add to its perfection. Therefore keep in the midst of life. Do not isolate yourself. Be among men and among things, and among troubles, and difficulties, and obstacles. You remember Goethe's words: "Talent develops itself in solitude; character in the stream of life." Talent develops itself in solitude—the talent of prayer, of faith, of meditation, of seeing the unseen; character grows in the stream of the world's life. That chiefly is where men are to learn love.

How? Now, how? To make it easier, I have named a few of the elements of love. But these are only elements. Love itself can never be defined. Light is a something more than the sum of its ingredients—a glowing, dazzling, tremulous ether. And love is something more than all its elements—a palpitating, quivering, sensitive, living thing. By synthesis of all the colors, men can make whiteness, they cannot make light. By synthesis of all the virtues, men can make virtue, they cannot make love. How then are we to have this transcendent living whole conveyed into our souls? We brace our wills to secure it. We try to copy those who have it. We lay down rules about it. We watch. We pray. But these things alone will not bring love into our nature. Love is an *effect*. And only as we fulfill the right condition can we have the effect produced. Shall I tell you what the *cause* is?

If you turn to the Revised Version of the First Epistle of John you find these words: "We love because He first loved us." "We love," not "We love *him*." That is the way the old version has it, and it is quite wrong. "*We love*—because He first loved us." Look at that word "because." It is the *cause* of which I have spoken. "*Because* He first loved us," the effect follows that we love, we love Him, we love all men. We cannot help it. Because He loved us, we love, we love everybody. Our heart is slowly changed. contemplate the love of Christ, and you will love. Stand before that mirror, reflect Christ's character, and you will be changed into the same image from tenderness to tenderness. There is no other way. You cannot love to order. You can only look at the lovely object, and fall in love with it, and grow into likeness to it. And so look at this Perfect Character, this Perfect Life. Look at the great sacrifice as He laid down Himself, all through life, and upon the Cross of Calvary; and you must love Him. And loving Him, you must become like Him. Love begets love. It is a process of induction. Put a piece of Iron in the presence of an electrified body, and that piece of iron for a time becomes electrified. It is changed into a temporary magnet in the mere presence of a permanent magnet, and as long as you leave the two side by side, they are both magnets alike. Remain side by side with Him who loved us, and gave himself for us, and you, too, will become a permanent magnet, a permanently attractive force; and like Him you will draw all men unto you, like Him you will be drawn unto all men. that is the inevitable effect of Love. Any man who fulfills that cause must have that effect produced in him.

Try to give up the idea that religion comes to us by chance, or by mystery, or by caprice. It comes to us by natural law, or by supernatural law, for all law is Divine.

Edward Irving went to see a dying boy once, and when he entered the room he just put his hand on the sufferer's head, and said, "My boy, God loves you," and went away. The boy started from his bed, and called out to the people in the house, "God loves me! God loves me!"

One word! It changed that boy. The sense that God loved him overpowered him, melted him down, and began the creating of a new heart in him. And that is how the love of God melts down the unlovely heart in man, and begets in him the new creature, who is patient and humble and gentle and unselfish. And there is no other way to get it. There is no mystery about it. We love others, we love everybody, we love our enemies, *because he first loved us.*

III. The Defense.

Now I have a closing sentence or two to add about Paul's reason for singling out love as the supreme possession.

It is a very remarkable reason. In a single word it is this: *it lasts*. "Love," urges Paul, "never faileth." Then he begins again one of his marvelous lists of the great things of the day, and exposes them one by one. He runs over the things that men thought were going to last, and shows that they are all fleeting, temporary, passing away.

"Whether there be *prophecies*, they shall be done away." It was the mother's ambition for her boy in those days that he should become a prophet. For hundreds of years God had never spoken by means of any prophet, and at that time the prophet was greater than the king. Men waited wistfully for another messenger to come, and hung upon his lips when he appeared, as upon the very voice of God. Paul says, "Whether there be prophecies, they shall fail." The Bible is full of prophecies. One by one they have "failed"; that is, having been fulfilled, their work is finished; they have nothing more to do now in the world except to feed a devout man's faith.

Then Paul talks about *tongues*. That was another thing that was greatly coveted. "Whether there be tongues, they shall cease." As we all know, many, many centuries have passed since tongues have been known in this world. They have ceased. Take it in any sense you like. Take it, for illustration merely, as languages in general—a sense which was not in Paul's mind at all, and which though it cannot give us the specific lesson, will point the general truth. Consider the words in which these chapters were written—Greek. It has gone. Take the Latin—the other great tongue of those days. It ceased long ago. Look at the Indian language. It is ceasing. The language of Wales, of Ireland, of the Scottish Highlands is dying before our eyes. The most popular book in the English tongue at the present time, except the bible, is one of Dickens' works, his "Pickwick Papers." It is largely written in the language of London street-life; and experts assure us that in fifty years it will be unintelligible to the average English reader.

Then Paul goes farther, and with even greater boldness adds, "Whether there by *knowledge*, it shall be done away." The wisdom of the ancients, where is it? It is wholly gone. A schoolboy to-day knows more than Sir Isaac Newton knew; his knowledge has vanished away. You put yesterday's newspaper in the fire: its knowledge has vanished away. You buy the old editions of the great encyclopedias for a few cents: their knowledge has vanished away. Look how the coach has been superseded by the use of steam. Look how electricity has superseded that, and swept a hundred almost new inventions into oblivion. One of the greatest living authorities, Sir William Thompson, said in Scotland, at a meeting at which I was present, "The steam-engine is passing away." "Whether there be knowledge, it shall vanish away." At every workshop you will see, in the back yard, a heap of old iron, a few wheels, a few levers, a few cranks, broken and eaten with rust. Twenty years ago that was the pride of the city. Men flocked in from the country to see the great invention; not it is superseded, its day is done. And all the boasted science and philosophy of this day will soon be old.

In my time, in the university of Edinburgh, the greatest figure in the faculty was Sir James Simpson, the discoverer of chloroform. Recently his successor and nephew, Professor Simpson, was asked by the librarian of the University to go to the library and pick out the books on his subject (midwifery) that were no longer needed. His reply to the librarian was this: "Take every text-book that is more than ten years old and put it down in the cellar."

Sir James Simpson was a great authority only a few years ago: men came from all parts of the earth to consult him; and almost the whole teaching of that time is consigned by the science of to-day to oblivion. And in every branch of science it is the same. "Now we know in part. We see through a glass darkly." Knowledge does not last.

Can you tell me anything that is going to last? Many things Paul did not condescend to name. He did not mention money, fortune, fame; but he picked out the great things of his time, the things the best men thought had something in them, and brushed them peremptorily aside. Paul had no charge against these things in themselves. All he said about them was that they would not last. They were great things, but not supreme things. There were things beyond them. What we are stretches past what we do, beyond what we possess. Many things that men denounce as sins are not sins; but they are temporary. And that is a favorite argument of the New Testament. John says of the world, not that it is wrong, but simply that it "passeth away." There is a great deal in the world that is delightful and beautiful; there is a great deal in it that is great and engrossing; but it will not last.

All that is in the world, the lust of the eye, the lust of the flesh, and the pride of life, are but for a little while. Love not the world therefore. Nothing that it contains is worth the life and consecration of an immortal soul. The immortal soul must give itself to something that is immortal. And the only immortal things are these: "Now abideth faith, hope, love, but the greatest of these is love."

Some think the time may come when two of these three things will also pass away—faith into sight, hope into fruition. Paul does not say so. We know but little now about the conditions of the life that is to come. But what is certain is that Love must last. God, the Eternal God, is Love. Covet, therefore, that everlasting gift, that one thing which it is certain is going to stand, that one coinage which will be current in the Universe when all the other coinages of all the nations of the world shall be useless and unhonored. You will give yourself to many things, give yourself first to Love. Hold things in their proportion. *Hold things in their proportion.* Let at least the first great object of our lives be to achieve the character defended in these words, the character—and it is he character of Christ—which is built round Love.

I have said this thing is eternal. Did you ever notice how continually John associates love and faith with eternal life? I was not told when I was a boy that "God so loved the world that He gave His only-begotten Son, that whosoever believeth in Him should have everlasting life." What I was told, I remember, was, that God so loved the world that, if I trusted in Him, I was to have a thing called peace, or I was to have rest, or I was to have joy, or I was to have safety. But I had to find out for myself that whosoever trusteth in Him—that is, whosoever loveth Him, for trust is only the avenue to Love—hath everlasting life.

The Gospel offers a man a life. Never offer a man a thimbleful of Gospel. Do not offer them merely joy, or merely peace, or merely rest, or merely safety; tell them how Christ came to give men a more abundant life than they have, a life abundant in love, and therefore abundant in salvation for themselves, and large

Henry Drummond

in enterprise for the alleviation and redemption of the world. Then only can the Gospel take hold of the whole of a man, body, soul and spirit, and give to each part of his nature its exercise and reward. Many of the current Gospels are addressed only to a part of man's nature. They offer peace, not life; faith, not Love; justification, not regeneration. And men slip back again from such religion because it has never really held them. Their nature was not all in it. It offered no deeper and gladder life-current than the life that was lived before. Surely it stands to reason that only a fuller love can compete with the love of the world.

To love abundantly is to live abundantly, and to love forever is to live forever. Hence, eternal life is inextricably bound up with love. We want to live forever for the same reason that we want to live to-morrow. Why do we want to live to-morrow? Is it because there is some one who loves you, and whom you want to see to-morrow, and be with, and love back? There is no other reason why we should live on than that we love and are beloved. It is when a man has no one to love him that he commits suicide. So long as he has friends, those who love him and whom he loves, he will live, because to live is to love. Be it but the love of a dog, it will keep him in life; but let that go, he has no contact with life, no reason to live. He dies by his own hand.

Eternal life also is to know God, and God is love. This is Christ's own definition. Ponder it. "This is life eternal, that they might know Thee the only true God, and Jesus Christ whom Thou hast sent." Love must be eternal. It is what God is. On the last analysis, then, love is life. Love never faileth, and life never faileth, so long as there is love. That is the philosophy of what Paul is showing us; the reason why in the nature of things love should be the supreme thing—because it is going to last; because in the nature of things it is an Eternal Life. It is a thing that we are living now, not that we get when we die; that we shall have a poor chance of getting when we die unless we are living now.

No worse fate can befall a man in this world than to live and grow old alone, unloving and unloved. To be lost is to live in an unregenerate condition, loveless and unloved; and to be saved is to love; and he that dwelleth in love dwelleth already in God. For God is Love.

Now I have all but finished. How many of you will join me in reading this chapter once a week for the next three months? A man did that once and it changed his whole life. Will you do it? It is for the greatest thing in the world. You might begin by reading it every day, especially the verses which describe the perfect character. "Love suffereth long, and is kind; love envieth not; love vaunteth not itself." Get these ingredients into your life. Then everything that you do is eternal. It is worth doing. It is worth giving time to. No man can become a saint in his sleep; and to fulfill the condition required demands a certain amount of prayer and meditation and time, just as improvement in any direction, bodily or mental, requires preparation and care. Address yourselves to that one thing; at any cost have this transcendent character exchanged for yours.

You will find as you look back upon your life that the moments that stand out, the moments when you have really lived, are the moments when you have done things in a spirit of love. As memory scans the past, above and beyond all the transitory pleasures of life, there leap forward those supreme hours when you have been enabled to do unnoticed kindnesses to those round about you, things too trifling to speak about, but which you feel have entered into your eternal life.

I have seen almost all he beautiful things God has made; I have enjoyed almost every pleasure that He has planned for man; and yet as I look back I see standing out above all the life that has gone four or five short experiences, when the love of God reflected itself in some poor imitation, some small act of love of mine, and these seem to be the things which alone of all one's life abide. Everything else in all our lives is transitory. Every other good is visionary. But the acts of love which no man knows about, or can ever know about—they never fail.

In the book of Matthew, where the Judgement Day is depicted for us in the imagery of One seated upon a throne and dividing the sheep from the goats, the test of a man then is not, "How have I believed?" but "How have I loved?" The test of religion, the final test of religion, is not religiousness, but Love. I say the final test of religion at that great Day is not religiousness, but Love; not what I have done, not what I have believed, not what I have achieved, but how I have discharged the common charities of life. Sins of commission in that awful indictment are not even referred to. By what we have not done, *by sins of omission*, we are judged. It could not be otherwise. For the withholding of love is the negation of the spirit of Christ, the proof that we never knew Him, that for us He lived in vain. It means that He suggested nothing in all our thoughts, that He inspired nothing in all our lives, that we were not once near enough to Him to be seized with the spell of His compassion for the world. It means that—

"I lived for myself, I thought for myself, For myself, and none beside— Just as if Jesus had never lived, As if He had never died."

Thank God the Christianity of today is coming nearer the world's need. Live to help that on. Thank God men know better, by a hair's breadth, what religion is, what God is, who Christ is, where Christ is. Who is Christ? He who fed the hungry, clothed the naked, visited the sick. And where is Christ? Where?—"Whoso shall receive a little child in My name receiveth Me.' And who are Christ's? "Every one that loveth is born of God."

Lessons from the Angelus

God often speaks to men's souls through music; He also speaks to us through art. Millet's famous painting entitled "The Angelus" is an illuminated text, upon which I am going to say a few words to you to-night.

There are three things in this picture—a potato field, a country lad and a country girl standing in the middle of it, and on the far horizon the spire of a village church. That is all there is to it—no great scenery and no picturesque people. In Roman Catholic countries at the evening hour the church bell rings out to remind the people to pray. Some go into the church, while those that are in the fields bow their heads for a few moments in silent prayer.

That picture contains the three great elements which go to make up a perfectly rounded Christian life. It is not enough to have the "root of the matter" in us, but that we must be whole and entire, lacking nothing. The Angelus may bring to us suggestions as to what constitutes a complete life.

I. The first element in a symmetrical life is *work*.

Three-fourths of our time is probably spent in work. Of course the meaning of it is that our work should be just as religious as our worship, and unless we can work for the glory of God three-fourths of life remains unsanctified.

The proof that work is religious is that most of Christ's life was spent in work. During a large part of the first thirty years of His life He worked with the hammer and the plane, making ploughs and yokes and household furniture. Christ's public ministry occupied only about two and a half years of His earthly life; the great bulk of His time was simply spent in doing common everyday tasks, and ever since then work has had a new meaning.

When Christ came into the world He was revealed to three deputations who went to meet and worship Him. First came the shepherds, or working class; second, the wise men, or student class; and third, the two old people in the temple, Simeon and Anna; that is to say, Christ is revealed to men at their work, He is revealed to men at their books, and He is revealed to men at their worship. It was the old people who found Christ at their worship, and as we grow older we will spend more time exclusively in worship than we are able to do now. In the mean time we must combine our worship with our work, and we may expect to find Christ at our books and in our common task.

Why should God have provided that so many hours of every day should be occupied with work? It is because work makes men.

A university is not merely a place for making scholars, it is a place for making Christians. A farm is not a place for growing corn, it is a place for growing character, and a man has no character except that which is developed by his life and thought. God's Spirit does the building through the acts which a man performs from day to day. A student who cons out every word in his Latin and Greek instead of consulting a translation finds that honesty is translated into his character. If he works out his mathematical problems thoroughly, he not only becomes a mathematician, but becomes a thorough man. It is by constant and conscientious attention to daily duties that thoroughness and conscientiousness and honorableness are imbedded in our beings. Character is the music of the soul, and is developed by exercise. Active use of the power entrusted to us is one of the chief means which God employs for producing the Christian graces. Hence the religion of a student demands that he be true to his work, and that he let his Christianity be shown to his fellow students and to his professors by the integrity and the conscientiousness of his academic life. A man who is not faithful in that which is least will not be faithful in that which is great. I have known men who struggled unsuccessfully for years to pass their examinations who, when they became Christians, found a new motive for work and thus were able to succeed where previously they had failed. A man's Christianity comes out as much in his work as in his worship.

Our work is not only to be done thoroughly, but it is to be done honestly. A man is not only to be honorable in his academic relations, but he must be honest with himself and in his attitude toward the truth. Students are not entitled to dodge difficulties, they must go down to the foundation principles. Perhaps the truths which are dear to us go down deeper even than we think, and we will get more out of them if we dig down for the nuggets than we will if we only pick up those that are on the surface. Other theories may perhaps be found to have false bases; if so, we ought to know it. It is well to take our surroundings in every direction to see if there is deep water; if there are shoals we ought to find out where they are. Therefore, when we come to difficulties, let us not jump lightly over them, but let us be honest as seekers after truth.

It may not be necessary for people in general to sift the doctrines of Christianity for themselves, but a student is a man whose business it is to think, to exercise the intellect which God has given him in finding out the truth. Faith is never opposed to reason, thought it is sometimes supposed by Bible teachers that it is; but you will find it is not. Faith is opposed to sight, but not to reason, thought it is not limited to reason. In employing his intellect in the search for truth a student is drawing nearer to the Christ who said, "I am the way, the truth and the life." We talk a great deal about Christ as the way and Christ as the life, but there is a side of Christ especially for the student: "I am the truth," and every student ought to be a truth-lover and a truth-seeker for Christ's sake.

II. Another element in life, which of course is first in importance, is *God*.

The Angelus is perhaps the most religious picture painted this century. You cannot look at it and see that young man standing in the field with his hat off and the girl opposite him with her hands clasped and her head bowed on her breast, without feeling a sense of God.

Do we carry about with us the thought of God wherever we go? If not, we have missed the greatest part of life. Do we have a conviction of god's abiding presence wherever we are? There is nothing more needed in this generation than a larger and more Scriptural idea of God. A great American writer has told us that when he was a boy the conception of God which he got from books and sermons was that of a wise and very strict lawyer. I remember well the awful conception of God which I had when a boy. I was given an illustrated edition of Watts' hymns, in which God was represented as a great piercing eye in the midst of a great black thunder cloud. The idea which that picture gave to my young imagination was that of God as a great detective, playing the spy upon my actions, as the hymn says: "Writing now the story of what little children do."

That was a very mistaken and harmful idea which it has taken me years to obliterate. We think of God as "up there," or as one who made the world six thousand years ago and then retired. We must learn that He is not confined either to time or space. God is not to be thought of as merely back there in time, or up there in space. If not, where is He? "The word is nigh thee, even in thy mouth." The Kingdom of God is within you, and God Himself is among men. When are we to exchange the terrible, far-away, absentee God of our childhood for the everywhere present God of the Bible? Too many of the old Christian writers seem to have conceived of God as not much more than the greatest man—a kind of divine emperor. He is infinitely more; He is a spirit, as Jesus said to the woman at the well, and in Him we live and move and have our being. Let us think of God as Immanuel—God with us—an ever-present, omnipresent, eternal One. Long, long ago, God made matter, then He made the flowers and trees and animals, then He made man. Did He stop? Is God dead? If He lives and acts what is He doing? He is making men better.

He it is that "worketh in you." The buds of our nature are not all out yet; the sap to make them comes from the God who made us, from the indwelling Christ. Our bodies are the temples of the Holy Ghost, and we must bear this in mind, because the sense of God is kept up, not by logic, but by experience.

Until she was seven years of age the life of Helen Keller, the Boston girl who was deaf and dumb and blind, was an absolute blank; nothing could go into that mind because the ears and eyes were closed to the outer world. Then by that great process which has been discovered, by which the blind see, and the deaf hear, and the mute speak, that girl's soul became opened, and they began to put in little bits of knowledge, and bit by bit they began to educate her. They reserved her religious instruction for Phillips Brooks. After some years, when she was twelve years old, they took her to him and he began to talk to her through the young lady who could communicate with her by the exceedingly delicate process of touch. He began to tell her about God and what He had done, and how He loved men, and what He is to us. The child listened very intelligently, and finally said: "Mr. Brooks, I knew all that before, but I didn't know His name."

How often we have felt something within us impelling us to do something which we would not have conceived of by ourselves, or enabling us to do something which we could not have done alone. "It is God which worketh in you." This great simple fact explains many of the mysteries of life,

and takes away the fear which we would otherwise have in meeting the difficulties which lie before us.

Two Americans who were crossing the Atlantic met on Sunday night to sing hymns in the cabin. As they sang the hymn, "Jesus, Lover of my Soul," one of the Americans heard an exceedingly rich and beautiful voice behind him. He looked around, and although he did not know the face he thought that he recognized the voice. So when the music ceased he turned and asked the man if he had not been in the Civil war. The man replied that he had been a Confederate soldier. "Were you at such a place on such a night?" asked the first. "Yes," he said, "and a curious thing happened that night; this hymn recalled it to my mind. I was on sentry duty on the edge of the wood. It was a dark night and very cold, and I was a little frightened because the enemy was supposed to be very near at hand. I felt very homesick and miserable, and about midnight, when everything was very still, I was beginning to feel very weary and thought that I would comfort myself by praying and singing a hymn. I remember singing this hymn, 'All my trust on thee is stayed, all my help from thee I bring, cover my defenseless head with the shadow of thy wing.'

After I had sung those words a strange peace came down upon me, and through the long night I remember having felt no more fear."

"Now," said the other man, "listen to my story. I was a Union soldier, and was in the wood that night with a party of scouts. I saw you standing up, although I didn't see your face, and my men had their rifles focused upon you waiting the word to fire, but when you sang out,

'Cover my defenseless head with the shadow of Thy wing.'

I said, 'Boys, put down your rifles, we will go home.' I couldn't kill you after that."

God was working in each of them, in His own way carrying out His will. God keeps his people and guides them and without Him life is but a living death.

III. The third element in life about which I wish to speak is *love.*

In this picture we notice the delicate sense of companionship, brought out by the young man and the young woman. It matters not whether they are brother and sister, or lover and loved; there you have the idea of friendship, the final ingredient in our life, after the two I have named. If the man or the woman had been standing in that field alone it would have been incomplete.

Love is the divine element in life, because "God is love." "He that loveth is born of God," therefore, as some one has said, let us "keep our friendships in repair." Let us cultivate the spirit of friendship, and let the love of Christ develop it into a great love, not only for our friends, but for all humanity. Wherever you go and whatever you do, your work will be a failure unless you have this element in your life.

These three things go far toward forming a well-rounded life. Some of us may not have these ingredients in their right proportion, but if you are lacking in one or the other of them, then pray for it and work for it that your life may be rounded and complete as God intended it should be.

Pax Vobiscum

I once heard a sermon by a distinguished preacher upon "Rest." It was full of beautiful thoughts; but when I came to ask myself, "How does he say I can get Rest?" there was no answer. The sermon was sincerely meant to be practical, yet it contained no experience that seemed to me to be tangible, nor any advice that I could grasp—any advice, that is to say, which could help me to find the thing itself as I went about the world.

Yet this omission of what is, after all, the only important problem, was not the fault of the preacher. The whole popular religion is in the twilight here. And when pressed for really working specifics for the experiences with which it deals, it falters, and seems to lose itself in mist.

The want of connection between the great words of religion and every-day life has bewildered and discouraged all of us. Christianity possesses the noblest words in the language; its literature overflows with terms expressive of the greatest and happiest moods which can fill the soul of man. Rest, Joy, Peace, Faith, Love, Light—these words occur with such persistency in hymns and prayers that an observer might think they formed the staple of Christian experience. But on coming to close quarters with the actual life of most of us, how surely would he be disenchanted. I do not think we ourselves are aware of how much our religious life is made up of phrases; how much of what we call Christian Experience is only a dialect of the Churches, a mere religious phraseology with almost nothing behind it in what we really feel and know.

To some of us, indeed, the Christian experiences seem further away than when we took the first steps in the Christian life. That life has not opened out as we had hoped. We do not regret our religion, but we are disappointed with it. There are times, perhaps, when wandering notes form a diviner music stray into our spirits; but these experiences come at few and fitful moments. We have no sense of possession in them. When they visit us, it is as surprise. When they leave us, it is without explanation. When we wish their return, we do not know how to secure it.

All of which means a religion without solid base, and a poor and flickering life. It means a great bankruptcy in those experiences which give Christianity its personal solace and make it attractive to the world, and a great uncertainty as to any remedy. It is as if we knew everything about health—except the way to get it.

I am quite sure that the difficulty does not lie in the fact that men are not in earnest. This is simply not the fact. All around us Christians are wearing themselves out in trying to be better. The amount of spiritual longing in the world—in the hearts of unnumbered thousands of men and women in whom we should never suspect it; among the wise and thoughtful, among the young and gay, who seldom assuage and never betray their thirst—this is one of the most wonderful and touching facts of life. It is not more heart that is needed, but more light; not more force, but a wiser direction to be given to very real energies already there.

The usual advice when one asks for counsel on these questions is, "Pray." But this advice is far from adequate. I shall qualify the statement presently; but let me urge it here, with what you will perhaps call daring emphasis, that to pray for these things is not the way to get them. No one will get them without praying; but that men do not get them by praying is a simple fact. We have all prayed, and sincerely prayed, for such experiences as I have named; prayed, believing that that was the way to get them. And yet have we got them? The test is experience. I dare not limit prayer; still less the grace of God. If you have got them in this way, it is well. I am speaking to those, be they few or many, who have not got them; to ordinary men in ordinary circumstances. But if we have not got them, it by no means follows that prayer is useless. The correct conclusion is only that it is useless, or inadequate rather, for this particular purpose. To make prayer the sole resort, the universal panacea for every spiritual ill, is as radical a mistake as to prescribe only one medicine for every bodily trouble. The physician who does the last is a quack; the spiritual advisor who dies the first is grossly ignorant of his profession.

To do nothing but pray is a wrong done to prayer itself, and can only end in disaster. It is as if one tried to live only with the lungs, as if one assimilated only air and neglected solid food. The lungs are a first essential; the air is a first essential; but the body has many members, given for different purposes, secreting different things, and each has a method of nutrition as special to itself as its own activity. While prayer, then, is the characteristic sublimity of the Christian life, it is by no means the only one. And those who make it the sole alternative, and apply it to purposes for which it was never meant, are really doing the greatest harm to prayer itself. To couple the word "inadequate" with this might word is not to dethrone prayer, but to exalt it.

What dethrones prayer is unanswered prayer. When men pray for things which do not come that way—pray with sincere belief that prayer, unaided and alone, will compass what they ask—then, not getting what they ask, they often give up prayer.

This is the natural history of much atheism, not only an atheism of atheists, but a more terrible atheism of Christians, an unconscious atheism, whose roots have struck far into many souls whose last breath would be spent in denying it. So, I repeat, it is a mistaken Christianity which allow men to cherish a blind belief in the omnipotence of prayer. Prayer, certainly, when the appropriate conditions are fulfilled, is omnipotent, but not blind prayer. Blind prayer is superstition. Prayer, in its true sense, contains the sane recognition that while man prays in faith, *God acts by law*. What that means in the immediate connection we shall see presently.

What, then, is the remedy? It is impossible to doubt that there is a remedy, and it is equally impossible to believe that it is a secret. The idea that some few men, by happy chance or happier temperament, have been given the secret—as if there were some sort of knack or trick of it—is wholly incredible and wrong. Religion must be for all, and the way into its loftiest heights must be by a gateway through which the peoples of the world may pass.

I shall have to lead up to this gateway by a very familiar path. But as this path is strangely unfrequented where it passes into the religious sphere, I must ask your forbearance for dwelling for a moment upon the commonest of commonplaces.

I. Effects Require Causes

Nothing that happens in the world happens by chance. God is a God of order. Everything is arranged upon definite principles, and never at random. the world, even the religious world, is governed by law. Character is governed by law. Happiness is governed by law. The Christian experiences are governed by law. Men, forgetting this, expect Rest, Joy, Peace, Faith to drop into their souls from the air like snow or rain. But in point of fact they do not do so; and if they did, they would no less have their origin in previous activities and be controlled by natural laws. Rain and snow do drop from the air, but not without a long previous history. They are the mature effects of former causes. Equally so are Rest and Peace and Joy. They, too, have each a previous history. Storms and winds and calms are not accidents, but brought about by antecedent circumstances. Rest and Peace are but calms in man's inward nature, and arise through causes as definite and as inevitable.

Realize it thoroughly; it is a methodical, not an accidental world. If a housewife turns out a good cake, it is the result of a sound receipt, carefully applied. She cannot mix the assigned ingredients and fire them for the appropriate time without producing the result. It is not she who has made the cake; it is nature. She brings related things together; sets causes at work; these causes bring about the result. she is not a creator, but an intermediary. She does not expect random causes to produce specific effects—random ingredients would only produce random cakes. So it is in the making of Christian experiences. Certain lines are followed; certain effects are the result. These effects cannot but be the result. But the result can never take place without the previous cause. To expect results without antecedents is to expect cakes without ingredients. That impossibility is precisely the almost universal expectation.

Now what I mainly wish to do is to help you firmly to grasp this simple principle of Cause and Effect in the spiritual world. And instead of applying the principle generally to each of the Christian experiences in turn, I shall examine its application to one in some little detail. The one I shall select is Rest. And I think any one who follows the application in this single instance will be able to apply it for himself to the others.

Take such a sentence as this: African explorers are subject to fevers which cause restlessness and delirium.

Note the expression, "cause restlessness." *Restlessness has a cause.* Clearly, then, any one who wished to get rid of restlessness would proceed at once to deal with the cause. If that were not removed, a doctor might prescribe a hundred things, and all might be taken in turn, without producing the least effect. Things are so arranged in the original planning of the world that certain effects must follow certain causes, and certain causes must be abolished before certain effects can be removed. Certain parts of Africa are inseparably linked with the physical experience called fever; this fever is in turn infallibly linked with a mental experience called restlessness and delirium. To abolish the mental experience the radical method would be to abolish the physical experience, and the way of abolishing the physical experience would be to abolish Africa, or to cease to go there.

Now this hold good for all other forms of Restlessness. Every other form and kind of Restlessness in the world had a definite cause, and the particular kind of Restlessness can only be removed by removing the allotted cause.

All this is also true of Rest. Restlessness has a cause: must not *rest* have a cause? Necessarily. If it were a chance world we would not expect this; but, being a methodical world, it cannot be otherwise. Rest, physical rest, moral rest, spiritual rest, every kind of rest has a cause, as certainly as restlessness. Now causes are discriminating. There is one kind of cause for every particular effect and no other, and if one particular effect is desired, the corresponding cause must be set in motion. It is no use proposing finely devised schemes, or going through general pious exercises in the hope that somehow Rest will come. The Christian life is not casual, but causal. All nature is a standing protest against the absurdity of expecting to secure spiritual effects, or any effects, without the employment of appropriate causes. The Great Teacher dealt what ought to have been the final blow to this infinite irrelevancy by a single question, "Do men gather grapes of thorns or figs of thistles?"

Why, then, did the Great Teacher not educate His followers fully? Why did He not tell us, for example, how such a thing as Rest might be obtained? The answer is that *he did*. But plainly, explicitly, in so many words? Yes, plainly, explicitly, in so many words. He assigned Rest to its cause, in words with which each of us has been familiar from his earliest childhood.

He begins, you remember—for you at once know the passage I refer to—almost as if Rest could be had without any cause; "Come unto me," He says, "and I will *give* you Rest."

Rest, apparently, was a favor to be bestowed; men had but to come to Him; He would give it to every applicant. But the next sentence takes that all back. The qualification, indeed, is added instantaneously. For what the first sentence seemed to give was next thing to an impossibility. For how, in a literal sense, can Rest be *given*? One could no more give away Rest than he could give away Laughter. We speak of "causing" laughter, which we can do; but we can not give it away. When we speak of "giving" pain, we know perfectly well we can not give pain away. And when we aim at "giving" pleasure, all that we can do is to arrange a set of circumstances in such a way as that these shall cause pleasure. Of course there is a sense, and a very wonderful sense, in which a Great Personality breathes upon all who come within its influence an abiding peace and trust. Men can be to other men as the shadow of a great rock in a weary land; much more Christ; much more Christ as Perfect Man; much more still as Savior of the world. But it is not this of which I speak. When Christ said He would give men Rest, He meant simply that he would put them in the way of it. By no act of conveyance would or could He make over His own Rest to them. He could give them his receipt for it. That was all. But He would not make it for them. For one thing it was not in His plan to make it for them; for another thing, men were not so planned that it could be made for them; and for yet another thing, it was a thousand times better that they should make it for themselves.

That this is the meaning becomes obvious from the wording of the second sentence: "Learn of me, and ye shall *find* Rest." Rest, (that is to say), is not a thing that can be *given*, but a thing to be *Acquired*. It comes not by an act, but by a process. It is not to be found in a happy hour, as one finds a treasure; but slowly, as one finds knowledge. It could indeed be no more found in a moment than could knowledge. A soil has to be prepared for it. Like a fine fruit, it will grow in one climate, and not in another; at one altitude, and not at another. Like all growth it will have an orderly development and mature by slow degrees.

The nature of this slow process Christ clearly defines when He says we are to achieve Rest by *learning*. "Learn of me," He says, "and ye shall find rest to your souls."

Now consider the extraordinary originality of this utterance how novel the connection between these two words "Learn" and "Rest." How few of us have ever associated them—ever thought that Rest was a thing to be learned; ever laid ourselves out for it as we would to learn a language; ever practiced it as we would practice the violin? Does it not show how entirely new Christ's teaching still is to the world, that so old and threadbare an aphorism should still be so little known? The last thing most of us would have thought of would have been to associate *rest* with *work*.

What must one work at? What is that which if duly learned will find the soul of man in Rest? Christ answers without the least hesitation. He specifies two things—Meekness and Lowliness. "Learn of me," He says, "for I am *meek* and *lowly* in heart."

Now these two things are not chosen at random. To these accomplishments, in a special way, Rest is attached. Learn these, in short, and you have already found Rest. These as they stand direct causes of Rest; will produce it at once; cannot but produce it at once. And if you think for a single moment, you will see how this is necessarily so, for causes are never arbitrary, and the connection between antecedent and consequent her and everywhere lies deep in the nature of things.

What is the connection, then? I answer by a further question.

What are the chief causes of unrest?

If you know yourself, you will answer—Pride, Selfishness, Ambition. As you look back upon the past years of your life, is it not true that its unhappiness has chiefly come from the succession of personal mortifications and almost trivial disappointments which the intercourse of life has brought you? Great trials come at lengthened intervals, and we rise to breast them; but it is the petty friction of our every-day life with one another, the jar of business or of work, the discord of the domestic circle, the collapse of our ambition, the crossing of our will or the taking down of our conceit, which make inward peace impossible. Wounded vanity, then, disappointed hopes, unsatisfied selfishness—these are the old, vulgar, universal sources of man's unrest.

Now it is obvious why Christ pointed out as the two chief objects for attainment the exact opposites of these. To meekness and lowliness these things simply do not exist. They cure unrest by making it impossible. These remedies do not trifle with surface symptoms; they strike at once at removing causes. The ceaseless chagrin of a self-centered life can be removed at once by learning meekness and lowliness of heart. He who learns them is forever proof against it. He lives henceforth a charmed life. Christianity is a fine inoculation, a transfusion of healthy blood into an anaemic or poisoned soul. No fever can attack a perfectly sound body; no fever of unrest can disturb a soul which has breathed the air or learned the ways of Christ.

Men sigh for the wings of a dove that they may fly away and be at Rest. But flying away will not help us. "The Kingdom of God is *within you.*" We aspire to the top to look for Rest; it lies at the bottom. Water rests only when it gets to the lowest place. So do men. Hence, *be lowly.* The man who has no opinion of himself at all can never be hurt if others do not acknowledge him. Hence, *be meek.* He who is without expectation cannot fret if nothing comes to him. It is self-evident that these things are so. The lowly man and the meek man are really above all other men, above all other things. They dominate the world because they do not care for it. The miser does not possess gold, gold possesses him. But the meek possess it. "The meek," said Christ, "inherit the earth." They do not buy it; they do not conquer it; but they inherit it.

There are people who go about the world looking out for slights, and they are necessarily miserable, for they find them at every turn—especially the imaginary ones. One has the same pity for such men as for the very poor. They are the morally illiterate. They have had no real education, for they have never learned how to live.

Few men know how to live. We grow up at random carrying into mature life the merely animal methods and motives which we had as little children. And it does not occur to us that all this must be changed that much of it must be reversed; that life is the finest of the Fine Arts; that it has to be learned with life-long patience, and that the years of our pilgrimage are all too short to master it triumphantly.

Yet this is what Christianity is for—to teach men the art of life; and its whole curriculum lies in one word—"Learn of me." Unlike most education, this is almost purely personal; it is not to be had from books, or lectures or creeds or doctrines. It is a study from the life. Christ never said much in mere words about the Christian graces. He lived them, He was them. Yet we do not merely copy Him. We learn His art by living with Him, like the old apprentices with their masters.

Now we understand it all? Christ's invitation to the weary and heavy-laden is a call to begin life over again upon a new principle—upon His own principle. "Watch my way of doing things," He says; "Follow me. Take life as I take it. Be meek and lowly, and you will find Rest."

I do not say, remember, that the Christian life to every man, or to any man, can be a bed of roses. No educational process can be this. And perhaps if some men knew how much was involved in the simple "learn" of Christ, they would not enter His school with so irresponsible a heart. For there is not only much to learn, but much to unlearn.

Many men never go to this school at all till their disposition is already half ruined and character has taken on its fatal set. To learn arithmetic is difficult at fifty—much more to learn Christianity. To learn simply what it is to be meek and lowly, in the case of one who has had no lessons in that in childhood, may cost him half of what he values most on earth. Do we realize, for instance, that the way of teaching humility is generally by *humiliation*? There is probably no other school for it. When a man enters himself as a pupil in such a school it means a very great thing. There is much Rest there, but there is also much Work.

I should be wrong, even though my theme is the brighter side, to ignore the cross and minimize the cost. Only it gives to the cross a more definite meaning, and a rarer value, to connect it thus directly and casually with the growth of the inner life. Our platitudes on the "benefits of affliction" are usually about as vague as our theories of Christian Experience. "Somehow" we believe affliction does us good. But it is not a question of "Somehow." The result is definite, calculable, necessary. It is under the strictest law of cause and effect. The first effect of losing one's fortune, for instance, is humiliation; and the effect of humiliation, as we have just seen, is to make one humble; and the effect of being humble is to produce Rest. It is a roundabout way, apparently, of producing Rest; but Nature generally works by circular processes; and it is not certain that there is any other way of becoming humble, or of finding Rest. IF a man could make himself humble to order, it might simplify matters; but we do not find that this happens. Hence we must all go through the mill. Hence death, death to the lower self, is the nearest gate and the quickest road to life.

Yet this is only half the truth. Christ's life outwardly was one of the most troubled lives that was ever lived: tempest and tumult, tumult and tempest, the waves breaking over it all the time till the worn body was laid in the grave. But the inner life was a sea of glass. The great calm was always there. At any moment you might have gone to Him and found Rest. Even when the blood-hounds were dogging Him in the streets of Jerusalem, He turned to His disciples and offered them, as a last legacy, "My peace." Nothing ever for a moment broke the serenity of Christ's life on earth. Misfortune could not reach Him; He had no fortune. Food, raiment, money—fountain-heads of half the world's weariness—He simply did not care for; they played no part in His life; He "took no thought" for them. It was impossible to affect Him by lowering His reputation. He had already made Himself of no reputation. He was dumb before insult. When he was reviled, He reviled not again. In fact, there was nothing that the world could do to him that could ruffle the surface of His spirit.

Such living, as mere living, is altogether unique. It is only when we see what it was in Him that we can know what the word Rest means. It lies not in emotions, or in the absence of emotions. It is not a hallowed feeling that comes over us in church. It is not something that the preacher has in his voice. It is not in nature, or in poetry, or in music—though in all these there is soothing. It is the mind at leisure from itself. It is the perfect poise of the soul; the absolute adjustment of the inward man to the stress of all outward things; the preparedness against every emergency; the stability of assured convictions; the eternal calm of an invulnerable faith; the repose of a heart set deep in God. It is the mood of the man who says, with Browning, "God's in His Heaven, all's well with the world."

Two painters each painted a picture to illustrate his conception of rest. The first chose for his scene a still lone lake among the far-off mountains. The second threw on his canvas a thundering waterfall, with a fragile birch-tree bending over the foam; at the fork of a branch, almost wet with the cataract's spray, a robin sat on its nest. The first was only *stagnation*; the last was *rest*. For in Rest there are always two elements—tranquility and energy; silence and turbulence; creation and destruction; fearlessness and fearfulness. This it was in Christ.

It is quite plain from all this that whatever else He claimed to be or to do, He at least knew how to live.

All this is the perfection of living, of living in the mere sense of passing through the world in the best way. Hence His anxiety to communicate His idea of life to others. He came, He said, to give men life, true life, a more abundant life than they were living; "the life," as the fine phrase in the Revised Version has it, "that is life indeed." This is what He Himself possessed, and it was this which He offers to mankind. And hence His direct appeal for all to come to Him who had not made much of life, who were weary and heavy-laden. These He would teach His secret. They, also, should know "the life that is life indeed."

II. What yokes are for.

There is still one doubt to clear up. After the statement, "Learn of Me," Christ throws in the disconcerting qualification: "*Take my yoke* upon you, and learn of Me."

Why, if all this be true, does He call it a *yoke*? Why, while professing to give Rest, does He with the next breath whisper "*burden*"? Is the Christian life, after all, what its enemies take it for—an additional weight to the already great woe of life, some extra punctiliousness about duty, some painful devotion to observances, some heavy restriction and trammeling of all that is joyous and free in the world? Is life not hard and sorrowful enough without being fettered with yet another yoke?

It is astounding how so glaring a misunderstanding of this plain sentence should ever have passed into currency. Did you ever stop to ask what a yoke is really? Is it to be a burden to the animal which wears it? It is just the opposite. It is to make its burden light. Attached to the oxen in any other way than by a yoke, the plough would be intolerable. Worked by means of a yoke, it is light. A yoke is not an instrument of torture; it is an instrument of mercy.

It is not a malicious contrivance for making work hard; it is a gentle device to make hard labor light. It is not meant to give pain, but to save pain. And yet men speak of the yoke of Christ as if it were slavery, and look upon those who wear it as objects of compassion. For generations we have had homilies on "The Yoke of Christ"—some delighting in portraying its narrow exactions; some seeking in those exactions the marks of its divinity; others apologizing for it, and toning it down; still others assuring us that, although it be very bad, it is not to be compared with the positive blessings of Christianity. How many, especially among the young, has this one mistaken phrase driven forever away from the kingdom of God? Instead of making Christ attractive, it makes Him out a taskmaster, narrowing life by petty restrictions, calling for self-denial where none is necessary, making misery a virtue under the plea that it is the yoke of Christ, and happiness criminal because it now and then evades it. According to this conception, Christians are at best the victims of a depressing fate; their life is a penance; and their hope for the next world purchased by a slow martyrdom in this.

The mistake has arisen from taking the word "yoke" here in the same sense as in the expression "under the yoke," or "wear he yoke in his youth." But in Christ's illustration it is not the "jugum" of the Roman soldier, but the simple "harness" or "ox-collar" of the Eastern peasant. It is the literal wooden yoke which He, with His own hands in the carpenter shop, had probably often made. He knew the difference between a smooth yoke and a rough one, a bad fit and a good fit; the difference also it made to the patient animal which had to wear it. The rough yoke galled, and the burden was heavy; the smooth yoke caused no pain, and the load was lightly drawn. The badly fitted harness was a misery; the well-fitted collar was "easy."

And what was the "burden"? It was not some special burden laid upon the Christian, some unique infliction that they alone must bear. It was what all men bear. It was simply life, human life itself, the general burden of life which all must carry with them from the cradle to the grave. Christ saw that men took life painfully. To some it was a weariness, to others a failure, to many a tragedy, to all a struggle and a pain. How to carry this burden of life had been the whole world's problem. It is still the whole world's problem. And here is Christ's solution: "Carry it as I do. Take life as I take it. Look at it from My point of view. Interpret it upon My principles. Take My yoke and learn of me, and you will find it easy. For my yoke is easy, works easily, sits right upon the shoulders, and *therefore* My burden is light."

There is no suggestion here that religion will absolve any man from bearing burdens. That would be to absolve him from living, since it is life itself that is the burden. What Christianity does propose is to make it tolerable.

Christ's yoke is simply His secret for the alleviation of human life, His prescription for the best and happiest method of living. Men harness themselves to the work and stress of the world in clumsy and unnatural ways. The harness they put on is antiquated. A rough, ill-fitted collar at best, they make its strain and friction past enduring, by placing it where the neck is most sensitive; and by mere continuous irritation this sensitiveness increases until the whole nature is quick and sore.

This is the origin, among other things, of a disease called "touchiness"—a disease which, in spite of its innocent name, is one of the gravest sources of restlessness in the world. Touchiness, when it becomes chronic, is a morbid condition of the inward disposition. It is self-love inflamed to the acute point; conceit, *with a hair-trigger*. The cure is to shift the yoke to some other place; to let men and things touch us through some new and perhaps as yet unused part of our nature; to become meek and lowly in heart while the old sensitiveness is becoming numb from want of use.

It is the beautiful work of Christianity everywhere to adjust the burden of life to those who bear it, and them to it. It has a perfectly miraculous gift of healing. Without doing any violence to human nature it sets it right with life, harmonizing it with all surrounding things, and restoring those who are jaded with the fatigue and dust of the world to a new grace of living. In the mere matter of altering the perspective of life and changing the proportions of things, its function in lightening the care of man is altogether its own.

The weight of a load depends upon the attraction of the earth. Suppose the attraction of the earth were removed? A ton on some other planet, where the attraction of gravity is less, does not weigh half a ton. Now Christianity removes the attraction of the earth; and this is one way in which it diminishes man's burden. It makes them citizens of another world. What was a ton yesterday is not half a ton today. So without changing one's circumstances, merely by offering a wider horizon and a different standard, it alters the whole aspect of the world.

Christianity as Christ taught is the truest philosophy of life ever spoken. but let us be quite sure when we speak of Christianity that we mean Christ's Christianity. Other versions are either caricatures, or exaggerations, or misunderstandings, or shortsighted and surface readings. For the most part their attainment is hopeless and the results wretched. But I care not who the person is, or through what vale of tears he has passed, or is about to pass, there is a new life for him along this path.

III. How fruits grow

Were Rest my subject, there are other things I should wish to say about it, and other kinds of Rest of which I should like to speak. But that is not my subject. My theme is that the Christian experiences are not the work of magic, but come under the law of Cause and Effect. I have chosen Rest only as a single illustration of the working of that principle. If there were time I might next run over all the Christian experiences in turn, and show the same wide law applies to each; but I think it may serve the better purpose if I leave this further exercise to yourselves. I know no Bible study that you will find more full of fruit, of which will take you nearer to the ways of God, or make the Christian life itself more solid or more sure. I shall add only a single other illustration of what I mean, before I close.

Where does Joy come from? I knew a Sunday scholar whose conception of Joy was that it was a thing made in lumps and kept somewhere in Heaven, and that when people prayed for it, pieces were somehow let down and fitted into their souls. I am not sure that views as gross and material are not often held by people who ought to be wiser. In reality, Joy is as much a matter of Cause and Effect as pain. No one can get Joy by merely asking for it. It is one of the ripest fruits of the Christian life, and, like all fruits, must be grown. There is a very clever trick in India called the mango trick. A seed is put in the ground and covered up, and after diverse incantations a full-blown mango-bush appears within five minutes. I never met any one who knew how the thing was done, but I never met any one who believed it to be anything else than a conjuring trick. The world is pretty unanimous now in its belief in the orderliness of Nature. Men may not know how fruits grow, but they do know that they cannot grow in an hour. Some lives have not even a stalk on which fruits could hang, even if they did grow in an hour. Some have never planted one seed of Joy in all their lives; and others who may have planted a germ or two have lived so little in sunshine that they never could come to maturity.

Whence, then, is joy? Christ put His teaching upon this subject into one of the most exquisite of His parables. I should in any instance have appealed to His teaching here, as in the case of Rest, for I do not wish you to think I am speaking words of my own. But it so happens that He has dealt with it in words of unusual fullness.

I need not recall the whole illustration. It is the parable of the Vine. Did you ever think why Christ spoke that parable? He did not merely throw it into space as a find illustration of general truths. It was not simply a statement of the mystical union, and the doctrine of an indwelling Christ. It was that; but it was more. After He had said it, He did what was not an unusual thing when He was teaching His greatest lessons—He turned to the disciples and said He would tell them why He had spoken it. It was to tell them how to get joy.

"These things I have spoken unto you," He said, "that My Joy might remain in you, and that your Joy might be full." It was a purposed and deliberate communication of His Secret of Happiness.

Go back over these verses, then, and you will find the Causes of this Effect, the spring, and the only spring, out of which true Happiness comes. I am not going to analyze them in detail. I ask you to enter into the words for yourselves.

Remember, in the first place, that the Vine was the Eastern symbol of Joy. It was its fruit that made glad the heart of man. Yet, however innocent that gladness—for the expressed juice of the grape was the common drink at every peasant's board—the gladness was only a gross and passing thing. This was not true happiness, and the vine of the Palestine vineyards was not the true vine. "*Christ* was the *true* Vine." Here, then, is the ultimate source of Joy. Through whatever media it reaches us, all true Joy and Gladness find their source in Christ.

By this, of course, is not meant that the actual Joy experienced is transferred from Christ's nature, or is something passed on from Him to us. What is passed on is His method of getting it. There is, indeed, a sense in which we can share another's joy or another's sorrow. But that is another matter. Christ is the source of Joy to men in the sense in which He is the source of Rest. His people share His life, and therefore share its consequences, and one of these is Joy. His method of living is one that in the nature of things produces Joy. When He spoke of His Joy remaining with us He meant in part that the causes which produced it should continue to act. His followers, (that is to say), by *repeating* His life would experience its accompaniments. His Joy, His kind of Joy, would remain with them.

The medium through which this Joy comes is next explained: "He that abideth in Me, the same bringeth forth much fruit." Fruit first, Joy next; the one the cause or medium of the other. Fruit-bearing is the necessary antecedent; Joy both the necessary consequent and the necessary accompaniment. It lay partly in the bearing fruit, partly in the fellowship which made that possible. Partly, that is to say, Joy lay in mere constant living in Christ's presence, with all that that implied of peace, of shelter, and of love; partly in the influence of that Life upon mind and character and will; and partly in the inspiration to live and work for others, with all that that brought of self-riddance and joy in others' gain. All these, in different ways and at different times, are sources of pure happiness.

Even the simplest of them—to do good to other people—is an instant and infallible specific. There is no mystery about Happiness whatever. Put in the right ingredients and it must come out. He that abideth in Him will bring forth much fruit; and bringing forth much fruit is Happiness. The infallible receipt for Happiness, then, is to do good; and the infallible receipt for doing good is to abide in Christ. The surest proof that all this is a plain matter of Cause and Effect is that men may try every other conceivable way of finding happiness, and they will fail. Only the right cause in each case can produce the right effect.

Then the Christian experiences are our own making? In the same sense in which grapes are our own making and no more. All fruits *grow*—whether they grow in the soil or in the soul; whether they are the fruits of the wild grape or of the True Vine. No man can *make* things grow. He can *get them to grow* by arranging all the circumstances and fulfilling all the conditions. But the growing is done by God. Causes and effects are eternal arrangements, set in the constitution of the world; fixed beyond man's ordering. What man can do is to place himself in the midst of a chain of sequences. Thus he can get things to grow. But the power is the Spirit of God.

What more need I add but this—test the method by experiment. Do not imagine that you have got these things because you know how to get them. As well try to feed upon a cookery book. But I think I can promise that if you try in this simple and natural way, you will not fail. Spend the time you have spent in sighing for fruits in fulfilling the conditions of their growth. The fruits will come, must come. We have hitherto paid immense attention to *effects*, to the mere experiences themselves; we have described them, extolled them, advised them, prayed for them—done everything but find out what *caused* them. Henceforth let us deal with causes.

"To be," says Lotze, "is to be in relations." About every other method of living the Christian life there is an uncertainty. About every other method of acquiring the Christian experiences there is a "perhaps." But in so far as this method is the way of nature, it cannot fail. Its guarantee is the laws of the universe—and these are "the Hands of the Living God."

The true vine.

"I am the true vine, and my Father is the husbandman. Every branch in me that beareth not fruit he taketh away; and every branch that beareth fruit, he purgeth it, that it may bring forth more fruit. Now ye are clean through the word which I have spoken unto you. Abide in me, and I in you. As the branch cannot bear fruit of itself, except it abide in the vine; no more can ye, except ye abide in me. I am the vine, ye are the branches: He that abideth in me, and I in him, the same bringeth forth much fruit: for without me ye can do nothing. If a man abide not in me, he is cast forth as a branch, and is withered; and men gather them, and cast them into the fire, and they are burned. If ye abide in me, and my word abide in you, ye shall ask what ye will, and it shall be done unto you. Herein is my Father glorified, that ye bear much fruit; so ye shall be my disciples. As the Father hath loved me, so have I loved you: continue ye in my love. If ye keep my commandments, ye shall abide in my love; even as I have kept my Father's commandments, and abide in his love. These things have I spoken unto you, that my joy might remain in you, and that your joy might be full."

First! an Address to Boys.

I have three heads to give you. The first is "Geography," the second is "Arithmetic," and the third is "Grammar."

I: First. Geography tells us where to find places.

Where is the Kingdom of God? It is said that when a Prussian officer was killed in the Franco-Prussian war, a map of France was very often found in his pocket. When we wish to occupy a country, we ought to know its geography. Now, *where* is the Kingdom of God? A boy over there says, "It is in heaven." No; it is not in heaven. Another boy says, "It is in the Bible." No; it is not in the Bible. Another boy says, "It must be in the Church," No; it is not in the Church. Heaven is only the capital of the Kingdom of God; the Bible is the guide-book to it; the Church is the weekly parade of those who belong to it. If you turn to the seventeenth chapter of Luke you will find out where the Kingdom of God really is: "The Kingdom of God is within you"—within *you*. The Kingdom of God is *inside people*.

I remember once taking a walk by the river near where the Falls of Niagara are, and I noticed a remarkable figure walking along the river bank. I had been some time in America. I had seen black men, and red men, and yellow men, and white men; black men, the Negroes; red men, the Indians; yellow men, the Chinese; white men, the Americans. But this man looked quite different in his dress from anything I had ever seen. When he came a little closer, I saw he was wearing a kilt; when he came a little nearer still, I saw that he was dressed exactly like a Highland soldier. When he came quiet near, I said to him: "What are you doing here?"

"Why should I not be here?" he replied; "don't you know this is British soil? When you cross the river you come into Canada."

This soldier was thousands of miles from England, and yet he was in the Kingdom of England. Wherever there is an English heart beating loyal to the Queen of Britain, there is England. Wherever there is a boy whose heart is loyal to the Kingdom of God, the Kingdom of God is within him.

What is the Kingdom of God? Every Kingdom has its exports, it products. Go down the river here and you will find ships coming in with cotton; you know they come from America. You will find ships with tea; you know they are from China. Ships with wool; you know they come from Australia. Ships with sugar; you know they come from Java.

What comes from the Kingdom of God? Again, we must refer to our Guide-book. Turn to Romans, and we shall find what the Kingdom of God is. I will read it: "The Kingdom of God is righteousness, peace, joy"—three things. "The Kingdom of God is righteousness, peace, joy." Righteousness, of course is just doing what is right. Any boy who does what is *right* has the Kingdom of God within him. Any boy who, instead of being quarrelsome, lives at peace with the other boys, has the Kingdom of God within him. Any boy whose heart is filled with joy because he does what is right, has the Kingdom of God within him. The Kingdom of God is not going to religious meetings, and hearing strange religious experiences; the Kingdom of God is doing what is right—living at peace with all men, being filled with joy in the Holy Ghost.

Boys, if you are going to be Christians, be Christians as boys, and not as your grandmothers. A grandmother has to be a Christian as a grandmother, and that is the right and the beautiful thing for her; but if you cannot read your Bible by the hours as your grandmother can, or delight in meetings as she can, don't think you are necessarily a bad boy. When you are your grandmother's age you will have your grandmother's kind of religion. Meantime, be a Christian as a boy. Live a boy's life. Do the straight thing; seek the kingdom of righteousness and honor and truth. Keep the peace with the boys about you, and be filled with the joy of being a loyal, and simple, and natural, and boy-like servant of Christ.

You can very easily tell a house, or a workshop, or an office where the Kingdom of God is *not*. The first thing you see in that pace is that the "straight thing" is not always done. Customers do not get fair play. You are in danger of learning to cheat and to lie. Better a thousand times to starve than to stay in a place where you cannot do what is right.

Or, when you go into your workshop, you find everybody sulky, touchy, and ill-tempered, everybody at daggers-drawn with everybody else, some of the men not on speaking terms with some of the others, and the whole *feel* of the place miserable and unhappy. The Kingdom of God is not thee, for IT is peace. It is the Kingdom of the Devil that is anger, and wrath and malice.

If you want to get the Kingdom of God into your workshop, or into your home, let the quarreling be stopped. Live in peace and harmony and brotherliness with everyone. For the Kingdom of God is a kingdom of brothers. It is a great Society, founded by Jesus Christ, of all the people who try to live like Him, and to make the world better and sweeter and happier. Wherever boy is trying to do that, in the house or on the street, in the workshop or on the baseball field, there is the Kingdom of God. And every boy, however small or obscure or poor, who is seeking that, is a member of it. You see now, I hope, what the Kingdom is.

II: I pass, therefore, to the second head; What was it? Arithmetic.

Are there any arithmetic words in this text? "Added." What other arithmetic words? "First."

Now, don't you think you could not have anything better to seek "first" than the things I have named to do what is right, to live at peace, and be always making those about you happy? You see at once why Christ tells us to seek these things first—because they are the best worth seeking.

Do you know anything better than these three things, anything happier, purer, nobler? If you do, seek them first. But if you do not, seek first the Kingdom of God. I do not tell you to be religious. You know that. I do not tell you to seek the Kingdom of God. I tell you to seek the Kingdom of God *first*. *First*. Not many people do that. They put a little religion into their life—once a week, perhaps. They might just as well let it alone. It is not worth seeking the Kingdom of God unless we seek it *first*.

Suppose you take the helm out of a ship and hang it over the bow, and send that ship to sea, will it ever reach the other side? Certainly not. It will drift about anyhow. Keep religion in its place, and it will take you straight through life and straight to your Father in heaven when life is over. But if you do not put it in its place, you may just as well have nothing to do with it. Religion out of its place in a human life is the most miserable thing in the world. There is nothing that requires so much to be kept in its place as religion, and its place is what? second? third? "First." Boys, *first* the Kingdom of God; make it so that it will be natural to you to think about that the very first thing.

There was a boy in Glasgow apprenticed to a gentleman who made telegraphs. (The gentleman told me this himself.) One day this boy was up on the top of a four-story house with a number of men fixing up a telegraph wire. The work was all but done. It was getting late, and the men said they were going away home, and the boy was to nip off the ends of the wire himself. Before going down they told him to be sure to go back to the workshop, when he was finished, with his master's tools.

"Do not leave any of them lying about, whatever you do," said the foreman.

The boy climbed up the pole and began to nip off the ends of the wire. It was a very cold winter night, and the dusk was gathering. He lost his hold and fell upon the slates, slid down, and then over and over to the ground below. A clothes-rope stretched across the "green" on which he was just about to fall, caught him on the chest and broke his fall; but the shock was terrible, and he lay unconscious among some clothes upon the green.

An old woman came out; seeing her rope broken and the clothes all soiled, thought the boy was drunk, shook him, scolded him, and went for the policeman. The boy with the shaking came back to consciousness, rubbed his eyes, and got back on his feet. What do you think he did? He staggered, half-blind, up the stairs. He climbed the ladder. He got on to the roof of the house. He gathered up his tools, put them into his basket, took them down, and when he got to the ground again fainted dead away.

Just then the policeman came, saw there was something seriously wrong, and carried him away to the hospital, where he lay for some time. I am glad to say he got better.

What was his first thought at that terrible moment? His duty. He was not thinking of himself; he was thinking about his master. First, the Kingdom of God.

But there is another arithmetic word. What is it? "Added."

You know the difference between *addition* and *subtraction*. Now, that is a very important difference in religion, because—and it is a very strange thing—very few people know the difference when they begin to talk about religion. They often tell boys that if they seek the Kingdom of God, everything else is going to be *subtracted* from them. They tell them that they are going to become gloomy, miserable, and will lose everything that makes a boy's life worth living—that they will have to stop baseball and story-books, and become little old men, and spend all their time in going to meetings and in singing hymns.

Now, that is not true. Christ never said anything like that. Christ said we are to "Seek first the Kingdom of God," and everything else worth having is to be *added* unto us. If there is anything I would like you to remember, it is these two arithmetic words—"first" and "added."

I do not mean by "added" that if you become religious you are all going to become *rich*. Here is a boy, who, in sweeping out the shop tomorrow, finds a quarter lying among the orange boxes. Well, nobody has missed it. He puts it in his pocket, and it begins to burn a hole there. by breakfast time he wishes that money were in his master's pocket. And by-and-by he goes to his master. He says (to *himself*, and not to his master), "I was at the Boys' Brigade yesterday and I was told to seek *first* that which was right." Then he says to his master: "Please, sir, here is a quarter that I found upon the floor."

The master puts it in the till. What has the boy got in his pocket? Nothing; *But he has got the kingdom of God in his heart.* He has laid up treasure in heaven, which is of infinitely more worth than the quarter.

Now, that boy does not find a dollar on his way home. I have known that to happen, but that is not what is meant by "adding." It does not mean that God is going to pay him in his own coin, for He pays in better coin.

Yet I remember once hearing of a boy who was paid in both ways. He was very, very poor. He lived in a foreign country, and his mother said to him one day that he must go into the great city and start in business, and she took his coat and cut it open and sewed between the lining and the coat forty golden dinars, which she had saved up for many years to start him in life. She told him to take care of robbers as he went across the desert; and as he was going out of the door she said:

"My boy, I have only two words for you—'Fear God, and never tell a lie.'"

The boy started off, and towards evening he saw glittering in the distance the minarets of the great city. But between the city and himself he saw a cloud of dust. It came nearer. Presently he saw that it was a band of robbers.

One of the robbers left the rest and rode toward him, and said: "Boy, what have you got?"

The boy looked him in the face and said: "I have forty golden dinars sewed up in my coat."

The robber laughed and wheeled around his horse and went away back. He would not believe the boy.

Presently another robber came and he said: "Boy, what have you got?"

"Forty golden dinars sewed up in my coat."

The robber said: "The boy is a fool," and wheeled his horse and rode away back.

By and by the robber captain came and he said: "Boy, what have you got?"

"I have forty golden dinars sewed up in my coat."

The robber dismounted, and put his hand over the boy's breast, felt something round, counted one, two, three, four, five, till he counted out the forty golden coins. He looked the boy in the face and said: "Why did you tell me that?"

The boy said: "Because of God and my mother."

The robber leaned on his spear and thought and said: "Wait a moment."

He mounted his horse, rode back to the rest of the robbers, and came back in about five minutes with his dress changed. This time he looked not like a robber, but like a merchant. He took the boy up on his horse and said: "My boy, I have long wanted to do something for my God and for my mother, and I have this moment renounced my robber's life. I am also a merchant. I have a large business house in the city. I want you to come and live with me, to teach me about your God; and you will be rich, and your mother some day will come and live with us."

And it all happened. By seeing first the Kingdom of God, all these things were added unto him.

Boys, banish forever from your minds the idea that religion is *subtraction*. It does not tell us to give things up, but rather gives us something so much better that they give themselves up. When you see a boy on the street whipping a top, you know, perhaps, that you could not make that boy happier than by giving him a top, a whip, and half an hour to whip it. But next birthday, when he looks back he says, "What a goose I was last year to be delighted with a top. What I want now is a baseball bat."

Then when he becomes an old man, he does not care in the least for a baseball bat; he wants rest, and a snug fireside and a newspaper every day. He wonders how he could ever have taken up his thoughts with baseball bats and whipping-tops.

Now, when a boy becomes a Christian, he grows out of the evil things one by one—that is to say, if they are really evil—which he used to set his heart upon; (of course I do not mean baseball bats, for they are not evils); and so instead of telling people to give up things, we are safer to tell them to "seek first the Kingdom of God," and then they will get new things and better things, and

The old things will drop off of themselves. This is what is meant by the "new heart." It means that God puts into us new thoughts and new wishes, and we become quite different.

III: Lastly, and very shortly. What was the third head? "Grammar." Right.

Now, I require a clever boy to answer the next question. What is the verb? "Seek." Very good: "seek." What mood is it in? "Imperative mood." What does that mean? "A command." What is the soldier's first lesson? "Obedience." Have you obeyed this command? Remember the imperative mood of these words, "*seek* first the Kingdom of God."

This is the command of your King. It *must* be done. I have been trying to show you what a splendid thing it is; what a reasonable thing it is; what a happy thing it is; but beyond all these reasons, it is a thing that *must* be done, because we are *commanded* to do it by our Captain. Now, there is His command to seek *first* the Kingdom of God. Have you done it?

"Well," I know some boys will say, "we are going to have a good time, enjoy life, and then we are going to seek—*last*—the Kingdom of God."

Now, that is mean; it is nothing else than mean for a boy to take all the good gifts that God has given him, and then give him nothing back in return but his wasted life.

God wants boys' *lives*, not only their souls. It is for active, service that soldiers are drilled, and trained, and fed, and armed. That is why you and I are in the world at all—not to prepare to go out of it some day, but to serve God actively in it *now*. It is monstrous, and shameful, and cowardly to talk of seeking the Kingdom *last*. It is shirking duty, abandoning one's rightful post, playing into the enemy's hand by doing nothing to turn his flank. Every hour a Kingdom is coming in your heart, in your home, in the world near you, be it a Kingdom of Darkness or a Kingdom of Light. You are placed where you are, in a particular business, in a particular street, to help on there the Kingdom of God. You cannot do that when you are old and ready to die. By that time your companions will have fought their fight, and lost or won. If they lose, will you not be sorry that you did not help them? Will you not regret that only at the last you helped the Kingdom of God? Perhaps you will not be able to do it then. And then your life has been lost indeed.

Very few people have the opportunity to seek the Kingdom of God at the end. Christ, knowing all that, knowing that religion was a thing for our life, not merely for our death-bed, has laid this command upon us now: "Seek *first* the Kingdom of God."

I am going to leave you with this text itself. Every boy in the world should obey it.

Boys, before you go to work to-morrow, before you go to sleep to-night, resolve that, God helping you, you are going to seek *first* the Kingdom of God. Perhaps some boys here are deserters; they began once before to serve Christ, and they deserted. Come back again, come back again today! Others have never enlisted at all. Will you not do it now? You are old enough to decide. The grandest moment of a boy's life is that moment when he decides to *"seek first the kingdom of God."*

The Changed Life: The Greatest Need of the World

God is all for quality; man is for quantity. The immediate need of the world at this moment is not more of us, but, if I may use the expression, a better brand of us. To secure ten men of an improved type would be better than if we had ten thousand more of the average Christians distributed all over the world. There is such a thing in the evangelistic sense as winning the whole world and losing our own soul. And the first consideration of our own life—our own spiritual relations to God—our own likeness to Christ. And I am anxious, briefly, to look at the right and the wrong way of becoming like Christ—of becoming better men: the right and the wrong way of sanctification.

Let me begin by naming, and in part discarding some processes in vogue already for producing better lives. These processes are far from wrong; in their place they may even be essential. One ventures to disparage them only because they do not turn out the most perfect possible work.

1. The first imperfect method is to rely on resolution.

In will power, in mere spasms of earnestness, there is no salvation. Struggle, effort, even agony, have their place in Christianity, as we shall see; but this is not where they come in.

In mid-Atlantic the Etruria, in which I was sailing, suddenly stopped. Something had gone wrong with the engines. There were five hundred able-bodied men on board the ship. Do you think that if we had gathered together and pushed against the mast we could have pushed it on?

When one attempts to sanctify himself by effort, he is trying to make his boat go by pushing against the mast. He is like a drowning man trying to lift himself out of the water by pulling at the hair of his own head.

Christ held up this method almost to ridicule when He said, "Which of you by taking thought can add a cubit to his stature?" Put down that method forever as being futile.

The one redeeming feature of the self-sufficient method is this—that those who try it find out almost at once that it will not gain the goal.

2. Another experimenter says: "But that is not my method. I have seen the folly of a mere wild struggle in the dark. I work on a principle. My plan is not to waste power on random effort, but to concentrate on a single sin. By taking one at a time and crucifying it steadily, I hope in the end to extirpate all."

To this, unfortunately, there are four objections: For one thing, life is too short; the name of sin is legion. For another thing, to deal with individual sins is to leave the rest of the nature for the time untouched. In the third place, a single combat with a special sin does not affect the root and spring of the disease. If you dam up a stream at one place, it will simply overflow higher up. If only one of the channels of sin be obstructed, experience points to an almost certain overflow through some other part of the nature. Partial conversion is almost always accompanied by such moral leakage, for the pent-up energies accumulate to the bursting point, and the last state of that soul may be worse than the first. In the last place, religion does not consist in negatives, in stopping this sin and stopping that. The perfect character can never be produced with a pruning knife.

3. But a third protests: "So be it. I make no attempt to stop sins one by one. My method is just the opposite. I copy the virtues one by one."

The difficulty about the copying method is that it is apt to be mechanical. One can always tell an engraving from a picture, an artificial flower from a real flower. To copy virtues one by one has somewhat the same effect as eradicating the vices one by one; the temporary result is an overbalanced and incongruous character. Some one defines a *prig* as "a creature that is over-fed for its size." One sometimes finds Christians of this species—over-fed on one side of their nature, but dismally thin and starved looking on the other. The result, for instance, of copying Humility, and adding it on to an otherwise worldly life, is simply grotesque. A rabid temperance advocate, for the same reason, is often the poorest of creatures, flourishing on a single virtue, and quite oblivious that his Temperance is making a worse man of him and not a better. These are examples of fine virtues spoiled by association with mean companions. Character is a unity, and all the virtues must advance together to make the perfect man.

This method of sanctification, nevertheless, is in the true direction. It is only in the details of execution that it fails.

4. A fourth method I need scarcely mention, for it is a variation on those already named. It is the very young man's method; and the pure earnestness of it makes it almost desecration to touch it. It is to keep a private note-book with columns for the days of the week, and a list of virtues, with spaces against each for marks. this, with many stern rules for preface, is stored away in a secret place, and from time to time, at nightfall, the soul is arraigned before it as before a private judgment bar.

This living by code was Franklin's method; and I suppose thousands more could tell how they had hung up in their bedrooms, or hid in locked-fast drawers, the rules which one solemn day they drew up to shape their lives.

This method is not erroneous, only somehow its success is poor. You bear me witness that it fails. And it fails generally for very matter-of-fact reasons—most likely because one day we forget the rules.

All these methods that have been named—the self-sufficient method, the self-crucifixion method, the mimetic method, and the diary method—are perfectly human, perfectly natural, perfectly ignorant, and as they stand perfectly inadequate. It is not argued, I repeat, that they must be abandoned. Their harm is rather that they distract attention from the true working method, and secure a fair result at the expense of the perfect one. What that perfect method is we shall now go on to ask.

I. The formula of sanctification.

A formula, a receipt for Sanctification—can one seriously speak of this mighty change as if the process were as definite as for the production of so many volts of electricity?

It is impossible to doubt it. Shall a mechanical experiment succeed infallibly, and the one vital experiment of humanity remain a chance? Is corn to grow by method, and character by caprice? If we cannot calculate to a certainty that the forces of religion will do their work, then is religion vain. And if we cannot express the law of these forces in simple words, then is Christianity not the world's religion, but the world's conundrum.

Where, then, shall one look for such a formula? Where one would look for any formula—among the text-books. And if we turn to the text-books of Christianity we shall find a formula for this problem as clear and precise as any in the mechanical sciences. If this simple rule, moreover, be but followed fearlessly, it will yield the result of a perfect character as surely as any result that is guaranteed by the laws of nature.

The finest expression of this rule in Scripture, or indeed in any literature, is probably one drawn up and condensed into a single verse by Paul. You will find it in a letter—the second to the Corinthians—written by him to some Christian people who, in a city which was a byword for depravity and licentiousness, were seeking the higher life. To see the point of the words we must take them from the immensely improved rendering of the Revised translation, for the older Version in this case greatly obscures the sense. They are these: "We all, with unveiled face reflecting as a mirror the glory of the Lord, are transformed into the same image from glory to glory, even as from the Lord, the Spirit."

Now observe at the outset the entire contraction of all our previous efforts, in the simple passive: "*We are transformed.*"

We *are changed*, as the Old Version has it—we do not change ourselves. No man can change himself. Throughout the New Testament you will find that wherever these moral and spiritual transformations are described the verbs are in the passive. Presently it will be pointed out that there is a *rationale* in this; but meantime do not toss these words aside as if this passivity denied all human effort or ignored intelligible law. What is implied for the soul here is no more than is everywhere claimed for the body. In physiology the verbs describing the processes of growth are in the passive. Growth is not voluntary; it takes place, it happens, it is wrought upon matter. So here. "Ye must be born again"—we cannot be born ourselves. "Be not conformed to this world, but *be ye transformed*"—we are subjects to transforming influence, we do not transform ourselves. Not more certain is it that it is something outside the thermometer that produces a change in the thermometer, that it is something outside the soul of man that produces a moral change upon him. That he must be susceptible to that change, that he must be a party to it, goes without saying; but that neither his aptitude nor his will can produce it, is equally certain.

Obvious as it ought to seem, this may be to some an almost startling revelation. The change we have been striving after is not to be produced by any more striving. It is to be wrought upon us by the mounding of hands beyond our own. As the branch ascends, and the bud bursts, and the fruit reddens under the co-operation of influences from the outside air, so man rises to the higher stature under invisible pressures from without. the radical defect of all our former methods of sanctification was the attempt to generate from within that which can only be wrought upon us from without. The radical defect of all our former methods of sanctification was the attempt to generate from within that which can only be wrought upon us from without. According to the first Law of Motion, every body continues in its state of rest, or of uniform motion in a straight line, except in so far as it may be compelled *by impressed forces* to change that state. This is also a first law of Christianity. Every man's character remains as it is, or continues in the direction in which it is going, until it is compelled *by impressed forces* to change that state. Our failure has been the failure to put ourselves in the way of the impressed forces. There is a clay, and there is a Potter; we have tried to get the clay to mold the clay.

Whence, then, these pressures, and where this Potter? The answer of the formula is—"By reflecting as a mirror the glory of the Lord we are changed." But this is not very clear. What is the "glory" of the Lord, and how can mortal man reflect it, and how can that act as an "impressed force" in mounding him to a nobler form? The word "glory"—the word which has to bear the weight of holding these "impressed forces"—is a stranger in current speech, and our first duty is to seek out its equivalent in working English. It suggests at first a radiance of some kind, something dazzling or glittering, some halo such as the old masters loved to paint round the head of their Ecce Homos. But that is paint, mere matter, the visible symbol of some unseen thing. What is that unseen thing? It is that of all unseen things the most radiant, the most beautiful, the most Divine, and that is *character*. On earth, in Heaven, there is nothing so great, so glorious as this. The word has many meanings; in ethics it can have but one. Glory is character, and nothing less, and it can be nothing more. The earth is "full of the glory of the Lord," because it is full of His character. The "Beauty of the Lord" is character. "The Glory of the Only Begotten" is character, the character which is "fullness of grace and truth." And when God told His people HIS NAME, He simply gave them His character, His character which was Himself: "And the Lord proclaimed the name for the Lord...the Lord, the Lord God, merciful and gracious, long-suffering and abundant in goodness and truth." Glory then is not something intangible, or ghostly, or transcendental. If it were this, how could Paul ask men to reflect it? Stripped of its physical enswathement it is Beauty, moral and spiritual Beauty, Beauty infinitely real, infinitely exalted, yet infinitely near and infinitely communicable.

With this explanation read over the sentence once more in paraphrase: We all reflecting as a mirror the character of Christ are transformed into the same Image from character to character—from a poor character to a better one, from a better one to a little better still, from that to one still more complete, until by slow degrees the Perfect Image is attained. Here the solution of the problem of sanctification is compressed into a sentence: Reflect the character of Christ. You will be changed, in spite of yourself and unknown to yourself, into the same image from character to character.

(1.) All men are reflectors—that is the first law on which this formula is based. One of the aptest descriptions of a human being is that he is a mirror. As we sat at table to-night the world in which each of us lived and moved through this day was focused in the room. What we saw when we looked at one another was not one another, but one another's world. We were an arrangement of mirrors. The scenes we saw were all reproduced; the people we met walked to and fro; they spoke, they bowed, they passed us by, did everything over again as if it had been real. When we talked, we were but looking at our own mirror and describing what flitted across it; our listening was not hearing, but seeing—we but looked on our neighbor's mirror.

All human intercourse is a seeing of reflections. I meet a stranger in a railway carriage. The cadence of his first words tell me he is English and comes from Yorkshire. Without knowing it he has reflected his birthplace, his parents, and the long history of their race. Even physiologically he is a mirror. His second sentence records that he is a politician, and a faint reflection in the way he pronounces **the Times** reveals his party. In his next remarks I see reflected a whole world of experiences. The books he has read, the people he has met, the companions he keeps, the influences that have played upon him and made him the man he is—these are all registered there by a pen which lets nothing pass, and whose writing can never be blotted out.

What I am reading in him meantime he is also reading in me; and before the journey is over we could half write each other's lives. Whether we like it or not, we live in glass houses. The mind, the memory, the soul, is simply a vast chamber paneled with looking-glass. And upon this miraculous arrangement and endowment depends the capacity of mortal souls to "reflect the character of the Lord."

(2). But this is not all. If all these varied reflections from our so-called secret life are patent to the world, how close the writing, complete the record within the soul itself! For the influences we meet are not simply held for a moment on the polished surface and thrown off again into space. Each is retained where first it fell, and stored up in the soul forever.

This law of assimilation is the second, and by far the most impressive truth which underlies the formula of sanctification—the truth that men are not only mirrors, but that these mirrors, so far from being mere reflectors of the fleeting things they see, transfer into their own inmost substance, and hold in permanent preservation the things that they reflect.

No one knows how the soul can hold these things. No one knows how the miracle is done. No phenomenon in nature, no process in chemistry, no chapter in necromancy can ever help us to begin to understand this amazing operation. For, think of it, the past is not only *focused* there, in a man's soul, it IS there. How could it be reflected from there if it were not there? All things that he has ever seen, known, felt, believed of the surrounding world are now within him, have become part of him, in part are him—he has been changed into their image. He may deny it, he may resent it, but they are there. They do not adhere to him, they are transfused through him. He cannot alter or rub them out. They are not in his memory, they are in *him*. His soul is as they have filled it, made it, left it. These things, these books, these events, these influences are his makers. In their hands are life and death, beauty and deformity. When once the image or likeness of any of these is fairy presented to the soul, no power on earth can hinder two things happening—it must be absorbed into the soul and forever reflected back again from character.

Upon these astounding yet perfectly obvious psychological facts, Paul bases his doctrine of sanctification. He sees that character is a thing built up by slow degrees, that it is hourly changing for better or for worse according to the images which flit across it. One step further and the whole length and breadth of the application of these ideas to the central problem of religion will stand before us.

II. The alchemy of influence.

If events change men, much more persons. No man can meet another on the street without making some mark upon him. We say we exchange words when we meet; what we exchange is souls. And when intercourse is very close and very frequent, so complete is this exchange that recognizable bits of the one soul begin to show in the other's nature, and the second is conscious of a similar and growing debt to the first.

Now, we become like those whom we habitually reflect. I could prove from science that applies even to the physical framework of animals—that they are influenced and organically changed by the environment in which they life.

This mysterious approximating of two souls, who has not witnessed? Who has not watched some old couple come down life's pilgrimage hand in hand, with such gentle trust and joy in one another that their very faces wore the self-same look? These were not two souls; it was a composite soul. It did not matter to which of the two you spoke, you would have said the same words to either. It was quite indifferent which replied, each would have said the same. Half a century's *reflecting* had told upon them; they were changed into the same image. It is the Law of Influence that *We become like those whom we habitually reflect*: these had become like because they habitually reflected. Through all the range of literature, of history, and biography this law presides. Men are all mosaics of other men. There was a savor of David about Jonathan, and a savor of Jonathan about David. Metempsychosis is a fact. George Eliot's message to the world was that men and women make men and women. The Family, the cradle of mankind, has no meaning apart from this. Society itself is nothing but a rallying point for these omnipotent forces to do their work. On the doctrine of Influence, in short, the whole vast pyramid of humanity is built.

But it was reserved for Paul to make the supreme application of the Law of Influence. It was a tremendous inference to make, but he never hesitated. He himself was a changed man; he knew exactly what had done it; it was Christ.

On the Damascus road they met, and from that hour his life was absorbed in His. The effect could not but follow—on words, on deeds, on career, on creed. The "impressed forces" did their vital work. He became like Him Whom he habitually loved. "So we all," he writes, "reflecting as a mirror the glory of Christ, are changed into the same image."

Nothing could be more simple, more intelligible, more natural, more supernatural. It is an analogy from an every-day fact. Since we are what we are by the impacts of those who surround us, those who surround themselves with the highest will be those who change into the highest. There are some men and some women in whose company we are always at our best.

While with them we cannot think mean thoughts or speak ungenerous words. Their mere presence is elevation, purification, sanctity. All the best stops in our nature are drawn out by their intercourse, and we find a music in our souls that was never there before. Suppose even *that* influence prolonged through a month, a year, a lifetime, and what could not life become? There, even on the common plane of life, talking our language, walking our streets, working side by side, are sanctifiers of souls; here, breathing through common clay, is Heaven; here, energies charged even through a temporal medium with the virtue of regeneration. If to live with men, diluted to the millionth degree with the virtue of the Highest, can exalt and purify the nature, what bounds can be set to the influence of Christ? To live with Socrates—with unveiled face—must have made one wise; with Aristides, just. Francis Assisi must have made one gentle; Savonarola, strong. But to have lived with Christ must have made one like Christ: that is to say, *a Christian*.

As a matter of fact, to live with Christ did produce this effect. It produced it in the case of Paul. And during Christ's lifetime the experiment was tried in an even more startling form. A few raw, unspiritual, uninspiring men, were admitted to the inner circle of His friendship. The change began at once. Day by day we can almost see the first disciple grow. First there steals over them the faintest possible adumbration of His character, and occasionally, very occasionally, they do a thing or say a thing that they could not have done or said had they not been living there. Slowly the spell of His Life deepens. Reach after reach of their nature is overtaken, thawed, subjugated, sanctified. Their manner softens, their words become more gentle, their conduct more unselfish. As swallows who have found a summer, as frozen buds the spring, their starved humanity bursts into a fuller life. They do not know how it is, but they are different men.

One day they find themselves like their Master, going about and doing good. To themselves it is unaccountable, but they cannot do otherwise. they were not told to do it, it came to them to do it. But the people who watch them know well how to account for it—"They have been," they whisper, "with Jesus." Already even, the mark and seal of His character is upon them—"They have been with Jesus." Unparalleled phenomenon, that these poor fishermen should remind other men of Christ! Stupendous victory and mystery of regeneration that mortal men should suggest *God* to the world!

There is something almost melting in the way his contemporaries, and John especially, speak of the influence of Christ. John lived himself in daily wonder at Him; he was overpowered, over-awed, entranced, transfigured. To his mind it was impossible for any one to come under this influence and ever be the same again. "Whosoever abideth in Him sinneth not," he said. It was inconceivable that he should sin, as inconceivable as that ice should live in a burning sun, or darkness coexist with noon. If any one did sin, it was to John the simple proof that he could never have met Christ. "Whosoever sinneth," he exclaims, "hath not seen *Him*, neither known *Him*." Sin was abashed in this Presence. Its root withered. Its sway and victory were forever at an end.

But these were His contemporaries. It was easy for *them* to be influenced by Him, for they were every day and all the day together. But how can we mirror that which we have never seen? How can all this stupendous result be produced by a Memory, by the scantiest of all Biographies, by One who lived and left this earth eighteen hundred years ago? How can modern men to-day make Christ, the absent Christ, their most constant companion still?

The answer is that friendship is a spiritual thing. It is independent of Matter, or Space, or Time. That which I love in my friend is not that which I see. What influences me in my friend is not his body but his spirit. He influences me about as much in his absence as in his presence. It would have been an ineffable experience truly to have lived at that time—

"I think when I read the sweet story of old,
How when Jesus was here among men,
He took little children like lambs to his fold,
I should like to have been with Him then.
"I wish that His hand had been laid on my head,
That His arms had been thrown around me,
And that I had seen His kind look when he said,
'Let the little ones come unto me.'"

And yet, if Christ were to come into the world again, few of us probably would ever have a chance of seeing Him. Millions of her subjects in the little country of England have never seen their own Queen. And there would be millions of the subjects of Christ who could never get within speaking distance of Him if He were here. We remember He said: "It is expedient for you (not *for me*) that I go away"; because by going away He could really be nearer to us than He would have been if He had stayed here. It would be geographically and physically impossible for most of us to be influenced by His person had He remained. And so our communion with Him is a spiritual companionship; but not different from most companionships, which, when you press them down to the roots, you will find to be essentially spiritual.

All friendship, all love, human and Divine, is purely spiritual. It was after He was risen that He influenced even the disciples most. Hence, in reflecting the character of Christ, it is no real obstacle that we may never have been in visible contact with Himself.

There lived once a young girl whose perfect grace of character was the wonder of those who knew her. She wore on her neck a gold locket which no one was ever allowed to open. One day, in a moment of unusual confidence, one of her companions was allowed to touch its spring and learn its secret. She saw written these words— "Whom having not seen I love."

That was the secret of her beautiful life. She had been changed into the Same Image.

Now this is not imitation, but a much deeper thing. Mark this distinction, for the difference in the process as well as in the result, may be as great as that between a photograph secured by the infallible pencil of the sun, and the rude outline from a school-boy's chalk. Imitation is mechanical, reflection organic. The one is occasional, the other habitual. In the one case, man comes to God and imitates him; in the other, God comes to man and imprints Himself upon him. It is quite true that there is an imitation of Christ which amounts to reflection. But Paul's term includes all that the other holds, and is open to no mistake.

What, then, is the practical lesson? It is obvious. "Make Christ your most constant companion"—this is what it practically means for us. Be more under His influences than under any other influence. Ten minutes spent in His society every day, ay, two minutes if it be face to face, and heart to heart, will make the whole day different. Every character has an inward spring,—let Christ be it. Every action has a key-note,—let Christ set it.

Yesterday you got a certain letter. You sat down and wrote a reply which almost scorched the paper. You picked the cruelest adjectives you knew and sent it forth, without a pang to do its ruthless work. You did that because your life was set in the wrong key. You began the day with the mirror placed at the wrong angle.

Tomorrow at day-break, turn it towards Him, and even to your enemy the fashion of your countenance will be changed. Whatever you then do, one thing you will find you could not do—you could not write that letter. Your first impulse may be the same, your judgement may be unchanged, but if you try it the ink will dry on your pen, and you will rise from your desk an unavenged, but greater and more Christian man. Throughout the whole day your actions, down to the last detail, will do homage to that early vision.

Yesterday you thought mostly about yourself. Today the poor will meet you, and you will feed them. The helpless, the tempted, the sad, will throng about you, and each you will befriend. Where were all these people yesterday? Where they are today, but you did not see them. It is in reflected light that the poor are seen. But your soul today is not at the ordinary angle.

"Things which are not seen" are visible. For a few short hours you live the Eternal Life. The eternal life, the life of faith, is simply the life of a higher vision. Faith is an attitude—a mirror set at the right angle.

When tomorrow is over, and in the evening you review it, you will wonder how you did it. You will not be conscious that you strove for anything, or imitated anything, or crucified anything. You will be conscious of Christ; that He was with you, that without compulsion you were yet compelled; that without force, or noise, or proclamation, the revolution was accomplished. You do not congratulate yourself as one who has done a mighty deed, or achieved a personal success, or stored up a fund of "Christian experience" to ensure the same result again. What you are conscious of is "the glory of the Lord." And what the world is conscious of, if the result be a true one, is also "the glory of the Lord." In looking at a mirror one does not see the mirror, or think of it, but only of what it reflects. For a mirror never calls the attention to itself—except when there are flaws in it.

Let me say a word or two more about the effects which necessarily must follow from this contact, or fellowship, with Christ. I need not quote the texts upon the subject—the texts about abiding in Christ. "He that abideth in Him sinneth not." You cannot sin when you are standing in front of Christ. You simply cannot do it. Again: "If ye abide in Me, and My words abide in you, ye shall ask what ye will, and it shall be done unto you." Think of that! That is another inevitable consequence. And there is yet another: "He that abideth in Me, the same bringeth forth much fruit." Sinlessness—answered prayer—much fruit.

But in addition to these things, see how many of the highest Christian virtues and experiences necessarily flow from the assumption of that attitude towards Christ. For instance, the moment you assume that relation to Christ you begin to know what the *child-spirit* is. You stand before Christ, and He becomes your Teacher, and you instinctively become docile. Then you learn also to become *charitable* and *tolerant*; because you are learning of Him, and He is "meek and lowly in heart," and you catch that spirit. That is a bit of His character being reflected into yours. Instead of being critical and self-asserting, you become humble and have the mind of a little child.

I think, further, the only way of learning what *faith* is is to know Christ and be in His company. You hear sermons about the nine different kinds of faith—distinctions drawn between the right kind of faith and the wrong—and sermons telling you how to get faith. So far as I can see, there is

Only one way in which faith is got, and it is the same in the religious world as it is in the world of men and women. I learn to trust you, my brother, just as I get to trust me just as you get to know me. I do not trust you as a stranger, but as I come into contact with you, and watch you, and live with you, I find out that you are trustworthy, and I come to trust myself to you, and to lean upon you. But I do not do that to a stranger.

The way to trust Christ is to know Christ. You cannot help trusting Him them. You are changed. By knowing Him faith is begotten in you, as cause and effect. To trust Him without knowing Him as thousands do, is not faith, but credulity. I believe a great deal of prayer for faith is thrown away. What we should pray for is that we may be able to fulfill the condition, and when we have fulfilled the condition, the faith necessarily follows. The way, therefore, to increase our faith is to increase our intimacy with Christ. We trust Him more and more the better we know Him.

And then another immediate effect of this way of sanctifying the character is the tranquility that it brings over the Christian life. How disturbed and distressed and anxious Christian people are about their growth in grace! Now, the moment you give that over into Christ's care—the moment you see that you are *being* changed—that anxiety passes away. You see that it must follow by an inevitable process and by a natural law if you fulfill the simple condition; so that peace is the reward of that life and fellowship with Christ.

Many other things follow. A man's usefulness depends to a large extent upon his fellowship with Christ. That is obvious. Only Christ can influence the world; but all that the world sees of Christ is what it sees of you and me. Christ said: "The world seeth Me no more, but ye see Me." You see Him, and standing in front of Him reflect Him, and the world sees the reflection. It cannot see Him. So that a Christian's usefulness depends solely upon that relationship.

Now, I have only pointed out a few of the things that follow from the standing before Christ—from the abiding in Christ. You will find, if you run over the texts about abiding in Christ, many other things will suggest themselves in the same relations. Almost everything in Christian experience and character follows and follows necessarily, from standing before Christ and reflecting his character. But the supreme consummation is that we are changed into *the same image*, "even as by the Lord the Spirit." That is to say that in some way, unknown to us, but possibly not more mysterious than the doctrine of personal influence, we are changed into the image of Christ.

This method cannot fail. I am not setting before you an opinion or a theory, but this is a certainly successful means of sanctification. "We all, with unveiled face, reflecting in a mirror the glory of Christ (the character of Christ) assuredly—without any miscarriage—without any possibility of miscarriage—are changed into the same image." It is an immense thing to be anchored in some great principle like that. Emerson says: "The hero is the man who is immovably centered." Get immovably centered in that doctrine of sanctification. Do not be carried away by the hundred and one theories of sanctification that are floating about in religious literature of the country at the present time; but go to the bottom of the thing for yourself, and see the *rationale* of it for yourself, and you will come to see that it is a matter of cause and effect, and that if you will fulfill the condition laid down by Christ, the effect must follow by a natural law.

What a prospect! To be changed into the same image. Think of that! That is what we are here for. That is what we are elected for. Not to be saved, in the common acceptation, but "whom He did foreknow He also did predestinate to be conformed to the image of His Son." Not merely to be saved, but *to be conformed to the image of his son.* Conserve that principle. And as we must spend time in cultivating our earthly friendships if we are to have their blessings, so we must

Spend time in cultivating the fellowship and companionship of Christ. And there is nothing so much worth taking into our lives as a profounder sense of what is to be had by living in communion with Christ, and by getting nearer to Him. It will matter much if we take away with us some of the thoughts about theology, and some of the new light that has been shed upon the text of Scripture; it will matter infinitely more if our fellowship with the Lord Jesus become a little closer, and our theory of holy living a little more rational. And then as we go forth, men will take knowledge of us, that we have been with Jesus, and as we reflect Him upon them, they will begin to be changed into the same image.

It seems to me the preaching is of infinitely smaller account than the life which mirrors Christ. That is bound to tell; without speech or language—like the voices of the stars. It throws out its impressions on every side. The one simple thing we have to do is to be there—in the right relation; to go through life hand in hand with Him; to have Him in the room with us, and keeping us company wherever we go; to depend upon Him and lean upon Him, and so have His life reflected in the fullness of its beauty and perfection into ours.

III. The first experiment.

Then you reduce religion to a common Friendship? A common Friendship—who talks of a *common* Friendship? There is no such thing in the world.

On earth no word is more sublime. Friendship is the nearest thing we know to what religion is. God is love. And to make religion akin to Friendship is simply to give it the highest expression conceivable by man. But if by demurring to "a common friendship" is meant a protest against the greatest and the holiest in religion being spoken of in intelligible terms, then I am afraid the objection is all to real. Men always look for a mystery when one talks of sanctification, some mystery apart from that which must ever be mysterious wherever Spirit works. It is thought some peculiar secret lies behind it, some occult experience which only the initiated know. Thousands of persons go to church every Sunday hoping to solve this mystery. At meeting, at conferences, many a time they have reached what they thought was the very brink of it, but somehow no further revelation came. Poring over religious books, how often were they not within a paragraph of it; the next page, the next sentence, would discover all, and they would be borne on a flowing tide forever. But nothing happened. The next sentence and the next page were read, and still it eluded them; and though the promise of its coming kept faithfully up to the end, the last chapter found them still pursuing.

Why did nothing happen? Because there was nothing to happen—nothing of the kind they were looking for. Why did it elude them? Because there was no "it." When shall we learn that the pursuit of holiness is simply the pursuit of Christ?

When shall we substitute for the "it" of a fictitious aspiration, the approach to a Living Friend? Sanctity is in character and not in moods; Divinity in our own plain calm humanity, and in no mystic rapture of the soul.

And yet there are others who, for exactly a contrary reason, will find scant satisfaction here. Their complaint is not that a religion expressed in terms of Friendship is too homely, but that it is still too mystical. To "abide" in Christ, to "make Christ our most constant companion," is to them the purest mysticism. They want something absolutely tangible and absolutely direct. These are not the poetical souls who seek a sign, a mysticism in excess, but the prosaic natures whose want is mathematical definition in details. Yet it is perhaps not possible to reduce this problem to much more rigid elements. The beauty of Friendship is its infinity. One can never evacuate life of mysticism. Home is full of it, love is full of it, religion is full of it. Why stumble at that in the relation of man to Christ which is natural in the relation of man to man?

If any one cannot conceive or realize a mystical relation with Christ, perhaps all that can be done is to help him to step on to it by still plainer analogies from common life. How do I know Shakespear or Dante? By communing with their words and thoughts. Many men know Dante better than their own fathers. Many men know Dante better than their own fathers. He influences them more. As a spiritual presence he is more near to them, as a spiritual force more real. Is there any reason why a greater than Shakspere or Dante, who also walked this earth, who left great words behind Him, who has greater works everywhere in the world now, should not also instruct, inspire and mold the characters of men? I do not limit Christ's influence to this: it is this, and it is more. But Christ, so far from resenting or discouraging this relation of Friendship, Himself proposed it. "Abide in me" was almost His last word to the world. And He partly met the difficulty of those who feel its intangibleness by adding the practical clause, "If ye abide in *Me, and my words abide in you.*"

Begin with His words. Words can scarcely ever be long impersonal. Christ himself was a Word, a word made Flesh. Make His words flesh; do them, live them, and you must live Christ. *"He that keepeth my commandments, he it is that loveth Me."* Obey Him and you must love Him. Abide in Him, and you must obey Him. *Cultivate* His Friendship. Live after Christ, in His Spirit, as in His Presence, and it is difficult to think what more you can do. Take this at least as a first lesson, as introduction.

If you cannot at once and always feel the play of His life upon yours, watch for it also indirectly. "The whole earth is full of the character of the Lord." Christ is the Light of the world, and much of his Light is reflected from things in the world—even from clouds. Sunlight is stored in every leaf, from leaf through coal, and it comforts us thence when days are dark and we cannot see the sun. Christ shines through men, through books, through history, through nature, music, art. Look for Him there. "Every day one should either look at a beautiful picture, or hear beautiful music, or read a beautiful poem." The real danger of mysticism is not making it broad enough.

Do not think that nothing is happening because you do not see yourself grow, or hear the whir of the machinery. All great things grow noiselessly. You can see a mushroom grow, but never a child. Paul said for the comforting of all slowly perfecting souls that they grew "from character to character." "The inward man," he says elsewhere, "is renewed from day to day." All thorough work is slow; all true development by minute, slight and insensible metamorphoses. The higher the structure, moreover, the slower the progress. As the biologist runs his eye over the long Ascent of Life, he sees the lowest forms of animals develop in an hour; the next above these reach maturity in a day; those higher still take weeks or months to perfect; but the few at the top demand the long experiment of years. If a child and an ape are born on the same day, the last will be in full possession of its faculties and doing the active work of life before the child has left its cradle. Life is the cradle of eternity. As the man is to the animal in the slowness of his evolution, so is the spiritual man to the natural man. Foundations which have to bear the weight of an eternal life must be surely laid. Character is to wear forever; who will wonder or grudge that it cannot be developed in a day?

To await the growing of a soul, nevertheless, is an almost Divine act of faith. How pardonable, surely, the impatience of deformity with itself, of a consciously despicable character standing before Christ, wondering, yearning, hungering to be like that! Yet must one trust the process fearlessly and without misgiving. "The Lord the Spirit" will do His part. The tempting expedient is, in haste for abrupt or visible progress, to try some method less spiritual, or to defeat the end by watching for effects instead of keeping the eye on the Cause. A photograph prints from the negative only while exposed to the sun. While the artist is looking to see how it is getting on he simply stops the getting on. Whatever of wise supervision the soul may need, it is certain it can never be over-exposed, or that, being exposed, anything else in the world can improve the result or quicken it. The creation of a new heart, the renewing of a right spirit, is an omnipotent work of God. Leave it to the Creator. "He which hath begun a good work in you will perfect it unto that day."

No man, nevertheless, who feels the worth and solemnity of what is at stake will be careless as to his progress. To become like Christ is the only thing in the world worth caring for, the thing before which every ambition of man is folly, and all lower achievement vain.

Those only who make this quest the supreme desire and passion of their lives can ever begin to hope to reach it. If, therefore, it has seemed up to this point as if all depended on passivity, let me now assert, with conviction more intense, that all depends on activity. A religion of effortless adoration may be a religion for an angel, but never for a man. No in the contemplative, but in the active, lies true hope; not in rapture, but in reality, lies true life; not in the realm of ideals, but among tangible things, is man's sanctification wrought. Resolution, effort, pain, self-crucifixion, agony—all the things already dismissed as futile in themselves, must now be restored to office, and a tenfold responsibility laid upon them. For what is their office? Nothing less than to move the vast inertia of the soul, and place it, and keep it where the spiritual forces will act upon it. It is to rally the forces of the will, and keep the surface of the mirror bright and ever in position.

It is to uncover the face which is to look at Christ, and draw down the veil when unhallowed sights are near.

You have, perhaps, gone with an astronomer to watch him photograph the spectrum of a star. As you enter the dark vault of the observatory you saw him being by lighting a candle. To see the star with? No; but to adjust the instrument to see the star with. It was the star that was going to take the photograph; it was, also, the astronomer. For a long time he worked in the dimness, screwing tubes and polishing lenses and adjusting reflectors, and only after much labor the finely focused instrument was brought to bear. Then he blew out the light, and left the start to do its work upon the plate alone.

The day's task for the Christian is to bring his instrument to bear. Having done that he may blow out his candle. All the evidences of Christianity which have brought him there, all aids to Faith, all acts of worship, all the leverages of the Church, all Prayer and Meditation, all girding of the Will—these lesser processes, these candle-light activities for that supreme hour, may be set aside. But, remember, it is but for an hour. The wise man will be he who quickest lights his candle; the wisest he who never lets it out. Tomorrow, the next moment, he, a poor, darkened, blurred soul, may need it again to focus the Image better, to take a mote off the lens, to clear the mirror from a breath with which the world has dulled it.

No readjustment is ever required on behalf of the Star. That is one great fixed point in this shifting universe. But *the world moves*. And each day, each hour, demands a further motion and readjustment for the soul. A telescope in an observatory follows a star by clockwork, but the clockwork of the soul is called *the Will*. Hence, while the soul in passivity reflects the Image of the Lord, the Will in intense activity holds the mirror in position lest the drifting motion of the world bear it beyond the line of vision. To "follow Christ" is largely to keep the soul in such position as will allow for the motion of the earth. And this calculated counteracting of the movements of the world, this holding of the mirror exactly opposite to the Mirrored, this steadying of the faculties unerringly through cloud and earthquake, fire and sword, is the stupendous co-operating labor of the Will. It is all man's work. It is all Christ's work. In practice it is both; in theory it is both. But the wise man will say in practice, "It depends upon myself."

In the Gallerie des Beaux Arts in Paris there stands a famous statue. It was the last work of a great genius, who, like many a genius, was very poor and lived in a garret, which served as a studio and sleeping-room alike. When the statue was all but finished, one midnight a sudden frost fell upon Paris. The sculptor lay awake in the fireless room and thought of the still moist clay, thought how the water would freeze in the pores and destroy in an hour the dream of his life. So the old man rose from his couch and heaped the bed-clothes reverently round his work. In the morning when the neighbors entered the room the sculptor was dead, but the statue was saved!

The Image of Christ that is forming within us—that is life's one charge. Let every project stand aside for that. The spirit of God who brooded upon the waters thousands of years ago, is busy now creating men, within these commonplace lives of ours, in the image of God. "Till Christ be formed," no man's work is finished, no religion crowned, no life has fulfilled its end. Is the infinite task begun? When, how, are we to be different? Time cannot change men. Death cannot change men. Christ can. Wherefore *put on Christ.*

Dealing With Doubt

There is a subject which I think workers amongst young men cannot afford to keep out of sight—I mean the subject of "Doubt." We are forced to face that subject. We have no choice. I would rather let it alone; but every day of my life I meet men who doubt, and I am quite sure that most Christian workers among men have innumerable interviews every year with men who raise skeptical difficulties about religion.

Now it becomes a matter of great practical importance that we should know how to deal wisely with these. Upon the whole, I think these are the best men in the country. I speak of my own country. I speak of the universities with which I am familiar, and I say that they men who are perplexed,—the men who come to you with serious and honest difficulties,—are the best men. They are men of intellectual honesty, and cannot allow themselves to be put to rest by words, or phrases, or traditions, or theologies, but who must get to the bottom of things for themselves. And if I am not mistaken,

Christ was very fond of these men. The outsiders always interested Him, and touched Him. The orthodox people—the Pharisees—He was much less interested in. He went with publicans and sinners—with people who were in revolt against the respectability, intellectual and religious, of the day. And following Him, we are entitled to give sympathetic consideration to those whom He loved and took trouble with.

First, let me speak for a moment or two about The origin of doubt.

In the first place, *we are born questioners.* Look at the wonderment of a little child in its eyes before it can speak. The child's great word when it begins to speak is, "Why?" Every child is full of every kind of question, about every kind of thing, that moves, and shines and changes, in the little world in which it lives.

That is the incipient doubt in the nature of man. Respect doubt for its origin. It is an inevitable thing. It is not a thing to be crushed. It is a part of man as God made him. Heresy is truth in the making, and doubt is the prelude of knowledge.

Secondly: *the world is a sphinx.* It is a vast riddle—an unfathomable mystery; and on every side there is temptation to questioning. In every leaf, in every cell of every leaf, there are a hundred problems. There are ten good years of a man's life in investigating what is in a leaf. God has planned the world to incite men to intellectual activity.

Thirdly: *The instrument with which we attempt to investigate truth is impaired.* Some say it fell, and the glass is broken. Some say prejudice, heredity, or sin, have spoiled its sight, and have blinded our eyes and deadened our ears. In any case the instruments with which we work upon truth, even in the strongest men, are feeble and inadequate to their tremendous task.

And in the fourth place, *all religious truths are doubtable*. There is no absolute truth for any one of them. Even that fundamental truth—the existence of a God—no man can prove by reason. The ordinary proof for the existence of a God involves either an assumption, argument in a circle, or a contradiction. The impression of God is kept up by experience, not by logic. And hence, when the experimental religion of a man, of a community, or of a nation wanes, religion wanes—their idea of God grows indistinct, and that man, community or nation becomes infidel.

Bear in mind, then, that all religious truths are doubtable—even those which we hold most strongly.

What does this brief account of the origin of doubt teach us? It teaches us great intellectual humility.

It teaches us sympathy and toleration with all men who venture upon the ocean of truth to find out a path through it for themselves. Do you sometimes feel yourself thinking unkind things about your fellow-students who have intellectual difficulty? I know how hard it is always to feel sympathy and toleration for them; but we must address ourselves to that most carefully and most religiously. If my brother is short-sighted I must not abuse him or speak against him; I must pity him, and if possible try to improve his sight, or to make things that he is to look at so bright that he cannot help seeing. But never let us think evil of men who do not see as we do. From the bottom of our hearts let us pity them, and let us take them by the hand and spend time and thought over them, and try to lead them to the true light.

What has been the church's treatment of doubt in the past? It has been very simple. "There is a heretic. Burn him!" That is all. "There is a man who has gone off the road. Bring him back and torture him!"

We have got past that physically; have we got past it morally? What does the modern Church say to a man who is skeptical? Not "Burn him!" but "Brand him!" "Brand him!"—call him a bad name. And in many countries at the present time, a man who is branded as a heretic is despised, tabooed and put out of religious society, much more than if he had gone wrong in morals. I think I am speaking within the facts when I say that a man who is unsound is looked upon in many communities with more suspicion and with more pious horror than a man who now and then gets drunk. "Burn him!" "Brand him!" "Excommunicate him!" That has been the Church's treatment of doubt, and that is perhaps to some extent the treatment which we ourselves are inclined to give to the men who cannot see the truths of Christianity as we see them.

Contrast Christ's treatment of doubt. I have spoken already of His strange partiality for the outsiders—for the scattered heretics up and down the country; of the care with which He loved to deal with them, and of the respect in which He held their intellectual difficulties. Christ never failed to distinguish between doubt and unbelief. Doubt is *"can't believe"*; unbelief is *"won't believe."* Doubt is honesty; unbelief is obstinacy. Doubt is looking for light; unbelief is content with darkness. Loving darkness rather than light—that is what Christ attacked, and attacked unsparingly. But for the intellectual questioning of Thomas, and Philip, and

Nicodemus, and the many others who came to Him to have their great problems solved, He was respectful and generous and tolerant.

And how did He meet their doubts? The Church, as I have said, says, "Brand him!" Christ said, "Teach him." He destroyed by fulfilling. When Thomas came to Him and denied His very resurrection, and stood before Him waiting for the scathing words and lashing for his unbelief, they never came. They never came! Christ gave him facts—facts! No men can go around facts. Christ said, "Behold My hands and My feet." The great god of science at the present time is a fact. It words with facts. Its cry is, "Give me facts. Found anything you like upon facts and we will believe it." The spirit of Christ was the scientific spirit. He founded His religion upon facts; and He asked all men to found their religion upon facts.

Now, get up the facts of Christianity, and take men to the facts. Theologies—and I am not speaking disrespectfully of theology; theology is as scientific a thing as any other science of facts—but theologies are

Human versions

of Divine truths, and hence the varieties of the versions and the inconsistencies of them. I would allow a man to select whichever version of this truth he liked *afterwards*; but I would ask him to begin with no version, but go back to the facts and base his Christian life upon these.

That is the great lesson of the New Testament way of looking at doubt—of Christ's treatment of doubt. It is not "Brand him!"—but lovingly, wisely and tenderly to teach him. Faith is never opposed to reason in the New Testament; it is opposed to sight. You will find that a principle worth thinking over. *Faith is never opposed to reason in the new testament, but to sight.*

With these principles in mind as to the origin of doubt, as to Christ's treatment of it, how are we ourselves to deal with those who are in intellectual difficulty?

In the first place, I think *we must make all the concessions to them that we conscientiously can.*

When a doubter first encounters you, he pours out a deluge of abuse of churches, and ministers, and creeds, and Christians. Nine-tenths of what he says is probably true. Make concessions. Agree with him. It does him good to unburden himself of these things. He has been cherishing them for years—laying them up against Christians, against the Church, and against Christianity; and now he is startled to find the first Christian with whom he has talked over the thing almost entirely agrees with him. We are, of course, not responsible for everything that is said in the name of Christianity; and now he is startled to find the first Christian with whom he has talked over the thing almost entirely agrees with him. We are, of course, not responsible for everything that is said in the name of Christianity; but a man does not give up medicine because there are quack doctors, and no man has a right to give up his Christianity because there are spurious or inconsistent Christians. Then, as I already said, creeds are human versions of Divine truths; and we do not ask a man to accept all the creeds, any more than we ask him to accept all the Christians. We ask him to accept Christ, and the facts about Christ and the words of Christ. You will find the battle is half won when you have endorsed the man's objections, and possibly added a great many more to the charges which he has against ourselves. These men are in revolt against the kind of religion which we exhibit to the world—against the cant that is taught in the name of Christianity. And if the men that have never seen the real thing—if you could show them that, they would receive it as eagerly as you do. They are merely in revolt against the imperfections and inconsistencies of those who represent Christ to the world.

Second: *beg them to set aside, by an act of will, all unsolved problems*: such as the problem of the origin of evil, the problem of the Trinity, the problem of the relation of human will and predestination, and so on—problems which have been investigated for thousands of years without result—ask them to set those problems aside as insoluble. In the meantime, just as a man who is studying mathematics may be asked to set aside the problem of squaring the circle, let him go on with what can be done, and what has been done, and leave out of sight the impossible.

You will find that will relieve the skeptic's mind of a great deal of unnecessary cargo that has been in his way.

Thirdly: *talking about difficulties, as a rule, only aggravates them.*

Entire satisfaction to the intellect is unattainable about any of the greater problems, and if you try to get to the bottom of them by argument, there is no bottom there; and therefore you make the matter worse. But I would say what is known, and what can be honestly and philosophically and scientifically said about one or two of the difficulties that the doubter raises, just to show him that you can do it—to show him that you are not a fool—that you are not merely groping in the dark yourself, but you have found whatever basis is possible. But I would not go around all the doctrines. I would simply do that with one or two; because the moment you cut off one, a hundred other heads will grow in its place. It would be a pity if all these problems could be solved. The joy of the intellectual life would be largely gone. I would not rob a man of his problems, nor would I have another man rob me of my problems. They are the delight of life, and the whole intellectual world would be stale and unprofitable if we knew everything.

Fourthly—and this is the great point: *turn away from the reason and go into the man's moral life.*

I don't mean, go into his moral life and see if the man is living in conscious sin, which is the great blinder of the eyes—I am speaking now of honest doubt; but open a new door into the practical side of man's nature.

Entreat him not to postpone life and his life's usefulness until he has settled the problems of the universe. Tell him those problems will never all be settled; that his life will be done before he has begun to settle them; and ask him what he is doing with his life meantime. Charge him with wasting his life and his usefulness; and invite him to deal with the moral and practical difficulties of the world, and leave the intellectual difficulties as he goes along. To spend time upon these is proving the less important before the more important; and, as the French say, "The good is the enemy of the best." It is a good thing to think; it is a better thing to work—it is a better thing to do good. And you have him there, you see. He can't get beyond that. You have to tell him, in fact that there are two organs of knowledge: the one reason, the other obedience. And now tell him there is but One, and lead him to the great historical figure who calls all men to Him: the one perfect life—the one Savior of mankind—the one Light of the world. Ask him to begin to obey Christ; and, doing His will, he shall now of the doctrine whether it be of God.

That, I think, is about the only thing you can do with a man: to get him into practical contact with the needs of the world, and to let him lose his intellectual difficulties meantime. Don't ask him to give them up altogether. Tell him to solve them afterward one by one if he can, but meantime to give his life to Christ and his time to the kingdom of God. You fetch him completely around when you do that. You have taken him away from the false side of his nature, and to the practical and moral side of his nature; and for the first time in his life, perhaps, he puts things in their true place. He puts his nature in the relations in which it ought to be, and he then only begins to live. And by obedience he will soon become a learner and pupil for himself, and Christ will teach him things, and he will find whatever problems are solvable gradually solved as he goes along the path of practical duty.

Now, let me, in closing, give an instance of how to deal with specific points. The question of miracles is thrown at my head every second day: "What do you say to a man when he says to you, 'Why do you believe in miracles?'" I say, "Because I have seen then." He asks, "When?" I say, "Yesterday." "Where?" "Down such-and-such a street I saw a man who was a drunkard redeemed by the power of an unseen Christ and saved from sin. That is a miracle."

The best apologetic for Christianity is a Christian. That is a fact which the man cannot get over. There are fifty other arguments for miracles, but none so good as that you have seen them. Perhaps, you are one yourself. But take a man and show him a miracle with his own eyes. Then he will believe.

A Life for A Life and Other Addresses

Table of Contents

A Tribute

It sometimes happens that a man, in giving to the world the truths that have most influenced his life, unconsciously writes the truest kind of a character sketch. This was so in the case of Henry Drummond, and no words of mine can better describe his life or character than those in which he has presented to us, "The Greatest Thing in the World." Some men take an occasional journey into the thirteenth of 1 Corinthians, but Henry Drummond was a man who lived there constantly, appropriating its blessings and exemplifying its teachings. As you read what he terms the analysis of love, you find that all its ingredients were interwoven into his daily life, making him one of the most lovable men I have ever known. Was it courtesy you looked for, he was a perfect gentleman. Was it kindness, he was always preferring another. Was it humility, he was simple and not courting favor. It could be said of him truthfully, as it was said of the early apostles, "that men took knowledge of him, that he had been with Jesus."

Nor was this love and kindness only shown to those who were close friends. His face was an index to his inner life. It was genial and kind, and made him, like his Master, a favorite with children. He could be the profound philosopher or the learned theologian, but I know that he preferred to be the simple friend of children and youth. Never have I known a man who, in my opinion, lived nearer the Master or sought to do His will more fully.

I well remember our first meeting in Edinburgh twenty-four years ago. He was still a divinity student in the university, but he generously gave himself to aiding me in every possible way. There was nothing that he would not undertake to do to help spread the evangelistic work among his friends in the university, and, later on, he began special meetings for young men in various towns in Great Britain. The friendship then begun has been strengthened ever since, not only by his lovable nature, but by the great blessing God has used him to be in my own life.

Never have I heard Henry Drummond utter one unkind or harsh word of criticism against any one. He was a man who was filled with love to his fellow men, because he knew by experience something of the love of Christ. He was one of the easiest men with whom to work, for he thought more of the common object than of aught else.

The news of his death has brought a sense of the deepest loss to all his friends in every part of the world. He was a man greatly beloved, and my own feelings are akin to those of David on the death of Jonathan. But although the life on earth is ended, God has called His servant higher to a sphere of greater usefulness. And when at last we meet again before our Lord and Master Jesus Christ, whom we both loved and served together in years gone, we shall no longer "see through a glass darkly; but then face to face;" and things which we could not see alike here below we shall fully know in the light of His countenances who brought our lives together and blessed them with a mutual love.

D. L. Moody

The following addresses were delivered at the Students' Conference in Northfield, 1893. They are now issued in permanent form for the first time.

A Life for a Life

The report to the Italian government describing a great shipwreck said, "A large ship was seen coming close to shore last night; we endeavored to give every assistance through the speaking trumpet, nevertheless four hundred and one bodies were washed ashore this morning." That shows the futility of attempting to save men by speech. It isn't the whole truth, but it is a part of the truth. In saving men it is very often a life for a life; you have to give your life to the men whom you are trying to better. About the least Christian act a man can do for his brother-man is to talk about Christianity; the case is of a man laying down his life as Christ laid down His life. Don't misunderstand me. I have an idea that some of you don't understand me: it is my fault, and I will tell you why. Because for the last three or four years of my life I have had very little to do with the ninety and nine: I have been after the one sheep that was lost, and I have got into the way of talking to that one and trying to make things plain to him. In most cases he has been a man who wouldn't accept the Bible to start with, and I have had to translate the Bible into words which he would accept, and therefore some of you don't recognize the old truth in the language of the street. If you want to get hold of an agnostic, or a man who doesn't start off by standing on the common ground with you of believing the Bible, let me ask you to try to translate what you have to say into the simplest words, into words which will not be in every case the words in which you ordinarily clothe your thought. Now while it is no more cant to talk about religion in the language of the Bible than it is cant to talk about Science in the words of Science—for religion has technical terms just as much as science has—yet it will be useful to the man who calls all that cant, and it will prove an exceedingly valuable discipline for oneself to take an old text that has been lingering in one's mind from childhood and say, "What does this really mean in nineteenth century speech?" You will find that an effort to go to the bottom of that text will give you a new grasp of it, and, that in so doing you have learned an exceedingly valuable lesson, that it doesn't matter into what phrase or words truth is put, so long as it is true.

I had an egg for breakfast this morning, and I saw that it was an egg; there it was, shell and all. God made that egg. I had an egg for dinner to-day, but it was in the pudding, and it didn't look in the least like an egg, but it did me just as much good as the egg which I had for breakfast and which I saw with my eyes. You get a ray of truth through a book, or a man, or a picture, or a tree, or the sky; it doesn't matter the form of it if it does you good, if it inspires you and draws you near to God. Don't be suspicious of it if it is God's truth, even if its form changes. In talking to a man,—if you are to win him in that way,—talk in the man's own language if you can. But I was going to say more particularly that one has to do a great deal more to display and live out his Christianity than merely to talk to people about religion. Have you ever tried to get at the real secret of what Christianity is? It isn't picking out a man here, and a man there and having them made fit to go to Heaven; Christ came into this world, as He himself said, to found a society. Have you ever thought of that conception of Christianity? For hundreds of years that conception of Christianity has been utterly lost sight of; it is only lately that men are getting back to see the great Christian doctrine of the kingdom of God. The great phrase that was never off Christ's lips was the "kingdom of God." It is by far the commonest phrase in his teaching. Have you ever given a month of your life to finding out what Christ meant by the kingdom of God? Every day as we have prayed, "Thy kingdom come," has our Christian consciousness taken in the tremendous sweep of that prayer and seen how it covers the length and breadth of this great world and every interest of human life? Christ was continually asking people to join his kingdom, and in order to get them to join it and to make no mistake about its meaning, he was continually telling them what it was: the kingdom of Heaven is like unto this, the kingdom of Heaven is like unto that; if there is one thing more common in Christ's teaching than another, it is His explanation of what the kingdom of God is, and what the subjects of that kingdom are to busy themselves in doing. Now the kingdom of God is a society of the best men, working for the best ends, with the highest motives, according to the best principles. The kingdom of God was to give them observation. Christ likened the kingdom of God to leaven, and one cannot get a better understanding of the meaning of this phrase than by taking His own metaphor. Christ saw that the world was sunken and that it had to be raised. Leaven comes from the same word as lever does, that which lifts or raises, and Christ founded a Society of men for the purpose of raising the world. The kingdom of God is like leaven. When you put leaven into a vessel with the thing which is to be leavened, it does not affect the outward form; and when leaven comes into a society, or into a church, or into a movement, or into a country, its first purpose is not to affect the outward form, but to lift the external form by changing the inward spirit of it. The kingdom of Heaven is like leaven: it is to raise men by the contact of one life with another. Did you ever put a little leaven under a microscope? If you did you found that it was a plant, perhaps six one-thousandths of an inch in diameter, with an amazing power of propagation; and that leaven simply by being in contact with the dough has the effect of lifting by means of the life that is in it; and the Christian man, simply by virtue of the life that is in him,—not by attempting much in the way of forcing it upon others,—but by his own spontaneous nature can so work upon men that they cannot but feel that he has been with Jesus. When they look through him and perceive the fragrance of his spirit and the Christlikeness of his life, they remember Christ,—they are reminded of Christ by him; and a longing comes over them to live like that, and breathe that air and have that calm, that meekness and that beauty of character; and by that unconscious influence going out as a contagious power, men are won to Christ, and by these men the world is raised. But that is not all.

The world is not only sunken; the world is rotten. Those of you who know life even an inch below the surface know that even in this Christian country, in our great cities the world is rotten. I lave you ever thought of the sin of the world? Think of the sin in your own being; think that the man in the next house to you has the same amount of sin in him, and that all the people in your street are like that. Multiply that by all the streets in your city, that city by all the cities in your country, go around the world and add to that all the sin that is in all the streets in all the cities in the world, and you conjure up a ghastly spectre before which your imagination quails, and that is only a single glimpse of the sin of the world. But it can be taken away, it can be taken away: "Behold the Lamb of God who taketh away the sin of the world." How does he do it? On the cross by forgiving the sin of t he world; that is one part of it, and through you and through me and through the subjects of his kingdom. Christ said that the followers of Him are the salt of the earth and it is that salt that helps to take away the rottenness of the world. God takes away the guilt of it, and you help him to remove it by being the salt in the society in which you live. Salt is that which keeps things from becoming rotten. You put salt upon meat and salt upon fish to prevent them from becoming rotten, and it is the Christian men and women in the city and in the country who prevent them from becoming absolutely rotten. Christianity is the great antiseptic of society, and if you take the Christianity out of New York, out of Chicago, out of Berlin, or out of Paris, those cities must go to pieces. In a few generations they would go to pieces even physically by the mere accumulation of their rottenness. Now we are to be the salt of New York and of Chicago and of all the great cities of America, and it is our business to make and to keep these cities sweet, not only to sweep away the rottenness, but to prevent the new generation that is growing up from becoming rotten. The work of salt is preventative as well as curative. We do not half enough emphasize the preventative side of Christian activity; we do not half enough emphasize the making of Christian environment, in which the Christ life shall be possible even in the slums of our great cities. That man is doing the work of Christ who is cleansing these places by building new houses, by giving pure air and pure water, by giving good schools, and by in any way bringing sweetness and light and purity to keep young lives from succumbing to the influences which surround them.

That is not all. The world which you and I have to help to lift up is not only the world of the poor, but we have to lift up our whole country. One thing that strikes a stranger very much in coming to this country is this: He comes to a city like Boston, and he finds the merchants of that city with their heads buried in their ledgers, while a few Irishmen carry on the city government. I do not object to an Irishman, but it is matter in the wrong place when a company of Irishmen regulate the affairs of the city of Boston. Therefore, if you are subjects of the kingdom of God, you must work to reform the world and reform your country and reform Boston and Chicago, and above all reform New York. You have been taught in school of your duties as citizens, but you are taught in this book very plainly your duties as Christian citizens. It is your duty to make these cities, and it is possible for you to do it. These cities are making the people that live in them, and unless they set examples of righteousness and honor, the people will not be righteous and honorable. In this country there is not only little honesty and honor in municipal life, but there is little belief in its possibility. In England I have never known of a member of a government or of a municipality, or of a city accepting a bribe. When I have told that to some in America, they have received it with incredulity, because the very conception of a pure government, and of honorable city and municipal authorities has been almost lost by the nation. It is your business to restore the integrity and the righteousness in the high places of this land, and let the people see examples which will be helpful to them in their Christian life. I cannot speak too strongly about that, because I know that it can be done. We have had rotten municipal government, and the Christian men of the place have taken it up, and have said, "we are determined that this shall not be," and in the old city they have put man after man into the municipal chairs simply because they were Christian men, and because they would deal with the people righteously and carry out a program of Christianity for the city, and that can be done here.

Let me tell you what happened to the work of some University men in the city of London. They went to a district in the East End, a God-forsaken, sunken place, entirely occupied for miles by working people. They took a little house and became settlers in that poor district. They gave themselves no airs of superiority; they didn't tell the people they had come to do them good; they went in there and made friends with the people. The leaven went in among the dough, and the salt went in beside that which was corrupting. The very place where the salt should not be is beside the salt; it ought to be scattered over the meat and rubbed well into it. Well, these men went to live there, and they were in no great hurry. They waited several months and came to know quite a number of the working people; they came to understand one another. These men had studied cities, and they knew about city government, and about city life, and about education, and about cleansing, and about purity. One day there came a great labor war, and the working men put their heads together and said, "Those young men up there have good heads, let's go and talk it over with them." So they did, and in a few moments those young men were the arbiters of the strike. By a single word of theirs, three or four thousand men could be kept at work, that is three or four thousand people could be kept out of want. One of these young men after a time was elected to a Board, and in a few months was the head of that Board, and could sway that district. The other edged his way to the School-board, and soon was head of the School-board. These men did not claim to be superior; they were elected kings of the common people, because the people felt their kingship. By and by there came a time when a member of Parliament was to be chosen, and these people put in one of these young men. And so they have taken possession of that city in the name of Jesus Christ, and they are gradually working and lifting and salting It is not to be done in a day,—"first the blade, then the ear, then the full corn in the ear." It is giving them observation, but the kingdom is coming in that way, and the sin of that place is being taken away by the work of these men.

Christians are the only agents God has for carrying out His purposes. Think of that! He could himself with a single breath cleanse the whole of New York or the whole of London, but he does not do it. We are members of His body, and it is by the members of His body that He carries on His work, and we all have a different piece of that work to do. Some of us are limbs and must use our fingers, and some of us are only a little bit of a little finger, and others are brains. God is in everyone, and all are essential to the coming of His kingdom.

Now that conception of Christianity as a kingdom is beginning to go throughout Christendom at this hour. Every age has emphasized its peculiar side of Christianity, and the side that is just now being emphasized above all others is that social side, that large conception of what Christ came to do, how He came to save men, as it were, in the bulk,—by the city and by the country—and the movements that are going on just now in society, in education, in sanitation, in University Extension, in philanthropy, are all working together for good in that direction; and let us who believe in the salvation of the individual soul as the supreme thing not startle away the supreme thing. Let us not shut our eyes to the Christianity of Christ, to His great conception of the kingdom of God.

There are two functions discharged by every living being, and by every plant: one is the struggle for its own life,—the function of nutrition; the other is the struggle for the life of others,—the function of reproduction. All the activities of life may be classed under one or the other of these two heads, and all the activities of the Christian may be classed under one or the other of these two heads, the function of nutrition and the function of reproduction. You go from a Conference fairly well fed; the individual life has been attended to, now what is to become of this unless it is to go out in different ways for the helping of this universal movement for the bringing of the world to Christ. I know that many of you are puzzled to know in what direction you can start to help Christ, to help this world. Let me simply say this to you in that connection: Once I came to crossroads in the old life, and did not know in which direction God wanted me to help to hasten His kingdom. I started to read the Book to find out what the ideal life was, and I found that the only thing worth doing in the world was to do the will of God; whether that was done in the pulpit or in the slums, whether it was done in the college or class-room or on the street did not matter at all. "My meat and my drink," Christ said, "is to do the will of him that sent me," and if you make up your mind that you are going to do the will of God above everything else, it matters little in what direction you work. There are more posts waiting for men than there are men waiting for posts. Christ needs men in every community and in every land; it matters little whether we go to foreign lands or stay at home, as long as we are sure that we are where God puts us. I am not jealous of the great missionary movement which has swept this country and which has also swept ours. In my own college at least one third of the men are going to the foreign mission field. I am not jealous of that movement, I rejoice in it, but I should like also to plead for my country and for your country. Men say, "How am I to know whether I am to go there or to stay at home?" Let me give you one or two points on the subject.

The first thing of course is, Pray. I need not enlarge upon that. The only reason that a man should speak at all is because he says things that are not being said. The second thing is, Think. Think over all the different lines of work and think over all your own qualifications. If you want to go to the missionary field, think over the different kinds of missionary fields. There are some kinds of missionary fields which do not need you at all, and there may be others for which you are just the right man. It is a mistake to imagine that missionary work is all the same. The man who is going to the missionary field had better not go to his field unequipped with a knowledge of the people and the country. A third thing is, Take the advice of wise friends, but do not regard their decision as final; no other man can plan your life for you. Let me say also in that connection, do not imagine that the most disagreeable of two or three alternatives that may be before you is necessarily the will of God. God's will does not always lie in the line of the disagreeable; God likes to see His children happy just as fathers like to see their children happy, and there may be plums waiting for you as well as stones. Do not sacrifice yourself to a thing that is disagreeable unless you are quite sure that it is the will of God. The fourth is, When the time comes for decision, act, go ahead with what light you have, you will find a turn of the road somewhere. The fifth thing is, Having once decided, don't reconsider your decision. The day after a man makes a great life decision, he does not always allow himself to think he has done the right thing. If you make a decision once, let that be final. And the last thing is, That you will probably not know for months or years that you have done the right thing, but then you will see that God has led you every step of the way. One good general rule is, go in the direction of least resistance. If you have nothing positive to urge you on, and find objections to every scheme, go in the direction where there is least resistance.

I want to return again just for a moment or two to the immediate purposes of those of you who have a year or two of college life before you, and I ask you to study what Christianity is, and to spread the knowledge of that through your University. There are many in the University who do not know in the least what Christianity is. When I was in the University I thought Christianity was something you could put upon the point of a needle, and I thought that Christ was a being so small that you had to search hard for Him before you found Him, but now I know that the whole earth is full of His glory, and I know that there is no scheme that has ever been conceived by the mind of man so great as the vision of Christ when he prayed, "Thy kingdom come," and saw the nations of the earth becoming subjects of His rule. Study the kingdom of God, see what Christ said it was like, and how it was coming to be great, and how the members of that kingdom were to act, and pass it on to the other men, pass it on to the lawyers, pass it on to the doctors, until we have the professions Christianized, and the country will follow.

Begin with individuals; give your life for a life. Let me illustrate by recalling to you the case of a man whom I shall never forget to my dying day. One night I got a letter from one of the students of the University of Edinburgh, page after page of agnosticism and atheism. I went over to see him and spent a whole afternoon with him and did not make the slightest impression. At Edinburgh University, we have a Students' Evangelistic meeting Sunday nights at which there are eight hundred or one thousand men present. A few nights after this, I saw that man in the meeting, and next to him sat another man whom I had seen occasionally at the meetings, I did not know his name, but I wanted to find out more about my skeptic, so when the meeting was over, I went up to him and said, "Do you happen to know Boyce?" "Yes," he replied, "it is he that has brought me to Edinburgh." "Are you an old friend?" I asked. "I am an American, a graduate of an American University," he said. "After I had finished there I wanted to take a post-graduate course, and finally decided to come to Edinburgh. In the dissecting room I happened to be placed next to Boyce, and I took a singular liking for him. I found out that he was a man of very remarkable ability, though not a religious man, and I thought I might be able to do something for him. A year passed and he was just where I found him." He certainly was blind enough, because it was only two or three weeks before that that he wrote me that letter. "I think you said," I resumed, "that you only came here to take a year of the postgraduate course." "Well," he said, "I packed my trunks to go home, and I thought of this friend, and I wondered whether a year of my life would be better spent to go and start in my profession in America, or to stay in Edinburgh and try to win that one man for Christ, and I stayed." Well," I said, "my dear fellow, it will pay you; you will get that man." Two or three months passed, and it came to the last night of our meetings. We have men in Edinburgh from every part of the world. Every year, five or six hundred of them go out never to meet again, and in our religious work, we get very close to one another, and on the last night of the year we sit down together in our common hall to the Lord's Supper. This is entirely a students' meeting. On that night we get in the members of the theological faculty, so that things may be done decently and in order. Hundreds of men are there, the cream of the youth of the world, sitting down at the Lord's Table. Many of them are not members of the church, but are there for the first time pledging themselves to become members of the kingdom of God. I saw Boyce sitting down and handing the communion cup to his American friend. He had got his man. A week after, he was back in his own country. I do not know his name; he made no impression in our country, nobody knew him. He was a subject of Christ's kingdom, doing His work in silence and in humility. A few weeks passed and Boyce came to see me I said, "What do you come here for?" He said, "I want to tell you I am going to be a Medical Missionary." It was worth a year, was it not?

Before you leave, gentlemen, before you leave Northfield, make up your mind that with God's help you will try and win your man. Let us try and lead souls to Christ, if He can use us in that way.

Lessons from the Angelus

Students are recommended to invest in certain books; I am going to take the liberty to suggest to you the buying of a certain picture which you can get for a very few cents; it is Millais' Angelus.

God speaks to men's souls through music, and He also speaks through art. This famous picture is an illuminated text, and upon it I want to hang what I have to say to-night.

There are three things in this picture—a potato field, a country lad and a country girl standing in the middle of it, and upon the far horizon the spire of a village church. That is all—no great scenery, and no picturesque people.

In Roman Catholic countries at the evening hour the church bell rings out to remind the people to pray. Some go into the church to pray, while those that are in the fields, when the Angelus rings, bow their heads for a few moments in silent prayer.

That picture is a perfect portraiture of the Christian life; and what is interesting about it apart from the fact that it singles out the three great pedestals upon which a symmetrical life is lived, is the completeness of the truth that it contains. I recall how often Mr. Moody has told us that it is not enough to have the roots of religion in us, but that we must be whole and entire, lacking nothing.

The Angelus, as we look upon it, will reveal to us the elements which constitute the complete life.

The first of these is work. Three-fourths of our life is probably spent in work. Is that religious or is it not? What is the meaning of it? Of course the meaning of it is that our work should be just as religious as our worship, and that unless we can make our work religious, three-fourths of life remains unsanctified.

The proof that work is religious is that the most of Christ's life was spent in work. During those first thirty years of his life, the Scriptures were not in His hands so much as the hammer and the plane; He was making chairs and tables and ploughs and yokes; which is to say that the highest conceivable life was mainly spent in doing common work. Christ's public ministry occupied only about two and a half years; the great bulk of His time He was simply at work, and ever since then work has had a new meaning.

When Christ came into the world, He came to men at their work. He appeared to the shepherds, the working classes of those days; He appeared also to the wise men, the students of those days. Three deputations went out to meet Him. First came the shepherds, second the wise men, and third the two old people, Simeon and Anna—that is to say, Christ comes to men at their work, He comes to men at their books, and He comes to men at their worship. But you will notice that it was the old people who found Christ at their worship, and as we grow older we will spend more time in worship, and will repair to the prayer meeting and the house of God to meet Christ and to worship Him as Simeon and Anna did. But until the age comes when much of our time will be given to direct vision, we must try to find Christ at our books and in our common work.

Now why should God have arranged it that so many hours of every day should be occupied with work? It is because work makes men. A University is not merely a place for making scholars, it is a place for making Christians. A farm is not a place for growing corn, it is a place for growing character, and a man has no character except what is built up through the medium of the things that he does from day to day. God's Spirit does the building through the acts which a man performs during his life work. If a student cons out every word in his latin instead of consulting a translation, the result is that honesty is translated into his character; if he works out his mathematical problems thoroughly, he not only becomes a mathematician, but a thorough man; if he attends to the instructions that are given him in the class-room intelligently and conscientiously, he becomes a conscientious man. It is just by such means that thoroughness and conscientiousness and honorableness are imbedded in our being. We cannot dream perfect character; we do not get it in our sleep; it comes to us as muscle comes, through doing things. Character is the muscle of the soul, and it is developed by the practice of the muscles, and by exercising it upon actual things; hence our work is the making of us, and it is by and through our work that the great Christian graces are communicated to our soul. That is the means which God employs for the growing of the Christian graces, and apart from that we cannot have a Christian character. Hence the religion of a student consists first of all in his being true to his work, and in letting his Christianity be shown to his fellow students and to his professors by the integrity and the thoroughness of his academic work. If he is not faithful in that which is least, it will be impossible for him to be faithful in that which is great. I have known men who struggled unsuccessfully for years to pass their examinations, who when they became Christians, found a new motive for work, and thus were able to succeed where previously they had failed.

There are men here who have much intellectual energy; if they can but see that a man's Christianity comes out as much in his work as in his worship, they will find a new motive and stimulus to do their work thoroughly. Our work is not only to be done thoroughly, it is to be done honestly. By this I mean not so much that a man must be honorable in his academic relations, as that he must be fair to his own mind, and to the principles of the truth. We are not entitled to dodge difficulties, when they arise it is our duty to go to the bottom of them. Perhaps the truths which are dear to us are deeper even than we think, and we can get more out of them if we dig down for the nuggets. Others may perhaps be found to have false bases; if so, we ought to know it.

Christianity is the most important thing in the world, and the student ought to sound it in every direction to see if there is deep water and a safe place in which to launch his life; if there are shoals he ought to know it. Therefore, when we come to difficulties, let us not be guilty of jumping lightly over them, but let us be honest as seekers after truth,—which is the definition of a student. It may not be necessary for people in general to sift the doctrines of Christianity for themselves, but it is required of a student, whose business it is to think, to exercise the intellect which God has given him in living out the truth. Faith is never opposed to reason, though it is often supposed that the Bible teaches that it is, but you will find that it is not. Faith is opposed to sight but not to reason. It is only by reason that we can sift and examine and criticise and be sure of the forms of truth which are given us as Christians. Hence the great field of work that is open to a student is in seeking for truth, and let him be sure that in seeking for truth he is drawing very near to Christ who said: "I am the way, and the truth, and the life." We talk a great deal about Christ as the Way and Christ as the Life, but there is a side of Christ especially for the student, "I am the Truth;" and every student ought to be a truth lover and a truth seeker for Christ's sake.

Another element in life which of course is first in importance, is God. The Angelus is perhaps the most religious picture painted during this century. You cannot look at it and see that young man standing in the field with his hat off and the girl opposite him with her hands clasped and her head bowed upon her breast without feeling a sense of God. Do we carry about with us a sense of God? Do we carry the thought of Him with us wherever we go? If not, we have missed the greatest part of life. Do we have that feeling and a conviction of God's abiding presence wherever we are? There is nothing more needed in this generation than a larger and more scriptural idea of God. A great American writer has told us that when he was a boy the conception of God which he got from books and sermons was that of a wise and very strict lawyer. I remember well the awful conception of God which I got when I was a boy. I was given an illustrated edition of Watts' hymns, and amongst others there was one hymn which represented God as a great piercing eye in the midst of a great black thunder cloud. The idea of God which that picture gave to my young imagination was of a great detective playing the spy upon my actions; as the hymn says:
"Writing now the story of what little children do."

Such lines as this gave me a bad idea which it has taken me years to obliterate. We think of God as "up there"; there is no such place as "up there." Do not think that God is "up there." You say, God made the world six thousand years ago, and then retired; that is the last that was seen of Him; He made the world and then went to look on, and keep things going. Geology has been away back there, and God has gone farther and farther back; this six thousand years has extended out into ages and ages, and long, long periods. Where is God if He is not "up there" or "back there?," "up there" in space, or "back there" in time—where is He? "The word is nigh thee, even in thy mouth." "The Kingdom of God is within you," and God Himself is among men. When are we to exchange the terrible far away, absentee God of our childhood for the everywhere present God of the Bible? The God of theology has been largely taken from the old Roman Christian writers, who, great as they were, had nothing better to form their conception of God upon than the greatest man. The greatest man to them was the Roman emperor, and therefore God to them became a kind of divine emperor. The Greeks had a far grander conception which is again finding expression in modern theology. The Greek God is the God of this Book; the Spirit which moved upon the waters; the God in whom we live, and move, and have our being; the God of whom Jesus spoke to the women at the well, the God who is a spirit. Let us gather the conception of an imminent God; that is the theological word for it, and it is a splendid word, Immanuel—God with us—an inside God, an imminent God.

Long, long ago, God made matter, then He made the flowers and trees and animals, then He made man. Did He stop? Is God dead? If He lives and acts what is He doing? He is making men better. He is carrying on the development of men. It is God which "worketh in you." The buds of our nature are not all out yet; the sap to make them bloom comes from the God who made us, from the indwelling Christ. Our bodies are the temples of the Holy Ghost, and we must bear this in mind because the sense of God is kept up not by logic, but by experience,—we must try to keep alive this sense of God.

You have heard of Helen Keller, the Boston girl, who was born deaf, and dumb, and blind; until she was seven years of age her life was an absolute blank; nothing could go into that mind because the ears and eyes were closed to the outer world. Then by that great process which has been discovered, by which the blind see, the deaf hear, and the mute speak, the girl's soul became opened, and they began to put in little bits of knowledge, and bit by bit to educate her. But they reserved the religious instruction for Phillips Brooks. When she was twelve years old they took her to him and he talked to her through the medium of the young lady who had been the means of opening her senses, and who could communicate with her by the exceedingly delicate process of touch. He began to tell her about God, and what He had done, and how He loves men and what He is to us. The child listened very intelligently, and finally said, "Mr. Brooks, I knew all of that before, but I did not know His name." Have you not often felt something within you that was not you, some mysterious pressure, some impulse, some guidance, something lifting you and impelling you to do that which you would not yourself ever have conceived of? Perhaps you did not know His name—"It is God that worketh in you." If we can really found our life upon that great simple fact, the first principle of religion, which we are so apt to forget, that God is with us and in us, we will have no difficulty or fear about our future life.

Two Americans who were crossing the Atlantic, met in the cabin on Sunday night to sing hymns. As they sang the last hymn, "Jesus lover of my soul," one of them heard an exceedingly rich and beautiful voice behind him. He looked around and although he did not know the face, he thought that he knew the voice, so when the music ceased, he turned around and asked the man if he had not been in the civil war. The man replied that he had been a confederate soldier. "Were you at such a place on such a night?" asked the first. "Yes," he replied, "and a curious thing happened that night which this hymn has recalled to my mind. I was posted on sentry duty in the edge of a wood. It was a dark night and very cold and I was a little frightened because the enemy were supposed to be very near. About midnight when everything was very still and I was feeling homesick and miserable and weary, I thought that I would comfort myself by praying and singing a hymn. I remember singing this hymn,

"'All my trust on Thee is stayed,
All my help from Thee I bring
Cover my defenceless head
With the shadow of Thy wing."

After singing that a strange peace came down upon me, and through the long night I remember having felt no more fear."

"Now," said the other, "Listen to my story. I was a Union soldier and was in the wood that night with a party of scouts. I saw you standing, although I did not see your face. My men had their rifles focused upon you, waiting the word to fire, but when you sang out,

"'Cover my defenceless head
With the shadow of Thy wing,'

I said, 'Boys, lower your rifles, we will go home.'"

God was working in each of them. By just such means, by His every where acting mysterious Spirit, God keeps His people and guides them, and hence that second great element in life, God; without Him life is but a living death.

The third element in life about which I wish to speak is Love. The first is Work, the second is God, and the third is Love. In this picture you notice the delicate sense of companionship brought out by the young man and the young woman. It matters not whether they are brother and sister, or lover and loved, there you have the idea of friendship, the final ingredient in our life, after the two I have named. If the man or the woman had been standing in that field alone it would have been incomplete. Love is the divine element in life, because "God is love," and because "he that loveth is born of God"; therefore, as one has said, let us "keep our friendships in repair." They are worth while spending time over, because they constitute so large a part of our life. Let us cultivate this spirit of friendship that it may grow into a great love, not only for our friends but for all humanity. Those of you who are going to the mission field must remember that your mission will be a failure unless you cultivate this element.

So these three things complete life. Some of us may not have these ingredients in their right proportion, but if our life is not comfortable, if we are incomplete, let us ascertain if we are not lacking in one or the other of these three things, and then let us pray for it and work for it.

The Ideal Man

You are to have many speakers tonight, and my words are necessarily exceedingly few, and I desire to devote them however informal they may be, to state principles; because when one gets hold of principles, one can arrange many facts and many ideas and many aspirations around them. And I want to be quite informal—this is an informal night, it is the last night we shall be together, and we talk to one another with more intimacy perhaps than we would be apt to do on a platform night.

I started out some years ago, when I was a student, to find out the meaning of life, to discover what was the ideal-life, and I went for my information to this Book, where I found a sketch of an ideal man, which I want to give you in a very few words, in the language of this book.

The definition of the ideal man I found to be this; "A man after my own heart who shall fulfil all my will."

The first thing a man needs is a reason for being born at all. What are we here for? What is the object of life? I found this answer to that question: "I come to do thy will, O God." And that is the principle which a Christian life ought to be built upon. Our Christian experience is very apt to be made of scraps, bits of sermons, stray texts, and isolated sentences instead of being of a piece and of increasing forces directed constantly from the beginning of life until the curtain drops. If we realized that we come into the world to do the will of God and set the helm steady from the beginning, our lives would work out to a great purpose. The real object of life is simply to do the will of God. When Mr. Moody was in London some years ago, they put up for his meetings, a building which held ten thousand people. After the meetings were over, this building which was put up at a great cost was to be taken down. A number of the committee said, "Well, it is rather a shame to take down this great house after only a few months' use; could we not get some of the great preachers to preach to the people? "They wrote to Mr. Spurgeon, and asked him to come there for a week. They said, "Here is a chance to reach ten thousand people every night," and they magnified the part Mr. Spurgeon would have to these vast crowds. Mr. Spurgeon wrote a letter back to Mr. Moody which I happened to see, and it began with these words, "I have no ambition to preach to ten thousand people, but to do the will of God;" and he declined. The responsibility lay with him to satisfy his own conscience as to why he declined, but what struck me about that letter was that it exposed the vertebral column of that great Christian life. "I have no ambition to do this or to do that, but to do the will of God."

The first thing a baby needs who comes into the world and begins to live is food. I searched my Bible for food for the ideal man, and I found it: "My meat is to do the will of Him who sent me."

After a child has food, the next thing needed is companionship. The hunger of the affections begins to speak, and the child begins to feel around after objects of affection. Hence, the next thing the ideal man needs is friends; and I started out to see what company he would have, and I found this: "Whosoever doeth the will of my Father which is in heaven, the same is my mother, and sister and brother." All the people in the world, black and white, rich and poor, educated and illiterate, who are doing the will of God, are my mother, my brother, and my sister. They may not believe as I believe; they may not hold the same form of church government as I hold; that doesn't disinherit them, or dismember them from the family. "Whosoever doeth the will of God, the same is my mother and sister and brother."

The next thing an ideal man wants, after he has his friends, is language. Although I cannot find any kind of language he is to talk to his earthly friends, yet I can learn a great deal what it ought to be from the ideal man's prayers, the language which he uses in talking to his Father: "Thy will be done." And let us notice that this prayer does not mean resignation; it is not passive, but active.

To pray this prayer is not in effect to say, "God evidently is going to have his way and we may just as well succumb; it is of no use to kick against the pricks; let us just resign at once; Thy will be done." It is an active prayer, and means, "Let that will work through the earth; let it be done in the world; let it be as energetic in the world, as it is triumphant in heaven, until it carries and sweeps everything in the earth along with it!" "Thy will be done!"

All men may be saved; hence the prayer Thy will be done is followed by the expression, "Thy kingdom come."

It is the will of God that Christ's program for the world should be carried out, and the ideal man will turn away from all the other objects and ambitions one by one until he has centred himself and gives the last drop of his blood to the coming of Christ's kingdom. The kingdom of God is coming in Northfield about as plain as in any other part of the world, perhaps a great deal plainer. Those who know Northfield to-day, and those who knew it twenty years ago, know that even in that short time the kingdom of Christ has been coming here. Things are possible here now that were impossible then; lives are lived here now that were not then; the whole atmosphere of the place has felt the influence of Christ. If you could pass that on to every town in America and to every city, we should see, even in our own lifetime, the kingdom of God coming; and it should be our business, if we try to lead the ideal life, to have God's will done in our town and in our state and city as it is clone in heaven. Let us localize that prayer; let us localize it and particularize it and get it into the bit of the world that we are responsible for and not lose it in space—"Thy will be done."

I will dwell for a few moments on the other parts of the ideal life. Education is the next thing an ideal man wants: "Teach me to do thy will, O God." One might go on to speak of the enjoyments of the ideal life: "I delight to do thy will, O God; thy statutes have been my song in the house of my pilgrimage." The pleasure of life consists in living along the lines of God's will.

The close of life, the final step of life, the end of it all, is an eternal life; all the other lives may be very fine, beautiful and interesting, and in their way useful, but this is an eternal life,—"He that doeth the will of God abideth forever." Not an hour of a life lived along that line can be lost, because it is a mere conductor to the eternal, a mere physical means of communicating the spiritual law to this natural world. George Eliot says, "I know no failure save failure in cleaving to the purposes which I know to be the best." I fancy we all know pretty well that this is the best purpose to which we can put our life,—to do the will of God, and our lives cannot fail so long as we do that. That principle equalizes all life, it makes a life lived in the kitchen and a life lived in the pulpit equally heroic, equally Christian and equally divine, because a servant girl in the kitchen can do the will of God just as much as Mr. Spurgeon from his platform. When life is all over, nothing greater can be said of any man than that he did the will of God, whatever that was.

I close by giving you a text indirectly connected with this: "Seek first the kingdom of God." Seek it first! It is not worth while being a Christian unless a man makes it his meat and drink to do the will of God, and help on Christ's kingdom; and I dare say many of you have found out a further secret, not only that it is not worth while, but that it is a hundred times easier to seek the kingdom of God first than it is to seek it second. A man is very apt to think that if he gets more religious and more earnest, life will be come more complicated, and everything will be very much more difficult. That is not true. Life becomes vastly more simple and vastly more easy the more that a man determines that he will seek first the kingdom of God. Just in proportion as we link our wills with the will of God, there will be a lasting outcome from our lives. Some years ago the Atlantic cable was broken, and the operator on the coast of Ireland used to stay at night and watch the needle, as it waved back and forth trying to utter itself in inarticulate words. For months and months this incoherent muttering went on without any meaning, but one night as he watched the needle, he thought he noticed a change, and he tried to follow what it was saying. He saw it spell out a coherent syllable, and that was followed by a second syllable and a third, and a fourth, until he read whole sentences. In mid ocean the cable had been joined. You know an incoherent, inarticulate muttering comes from a man's voice, or lips, or life, who is not linked with the will of God. The moment those two wills touch and are joined together, and keep together, life begins to spell out its great words, and the messages from the other side become real and intelligent. It is only as we can keep up this connection and live habitually in this great stream of existence in the will of God, which is the winning force in life, that our lives can count for Him.

The Changed Life

Table of Contents

We All
With unveiled face
Reflecting
As a Mirror
The Glory of the Lord
Are transformed
Into the same image
From Glory to Glory
Even as from the Lord
The Spirit

The Changed Life

"I protest that if some great power would agree to make me always think what is true and do what is right, on condition of being turned into a sort of clock and wound up every morning, I should instantly close with the offer."

These are the words of Mr. Huxley. The infinite desirability, the infinite difficulty of being good—the theme is as old as humanity. The man does not live from whose deeper being the same confession has not risen, or who would not give his all tomorrow, if he could "close with the offer" of becoming a better man.

I propose to make that offer now. In all seriousness, without being "turned into a sort of clock," the end can be attained. Under the right conditions it is as natural for character to become beautiful as for a flower; and if on God's earth, there is not some machinery for effecting it, the supreme gift to the world has been forgotten. This is simply what man was made for. With Browning: "I say that Man was made to grow, not stop." Or in the deeper words of an older Book: "Whom He did foreknow, He also did predestinate . . . to be conformed to the Image of his Son."

Let me begin by naming, and in part discarding, some processes in vogue already, for producing better lives. These processes are far from wrong; in their place they may even be essential. One ventures to disparage them only because they do not turn out the most perfect possible work.

The first imperfect method is to rely on Resolution. In will-power, in mere spasms of earnestness there is no salvation. Struggle, effort, even agony, have their place in Christianity as we shall see; but this is not where they come in. In mid-Atlantic the other day, the Etruria in which I was sailing, suddenly stopped. Something had gone wrong with the engines. There were five hundred able-bodied men on board the ship. Do you think if we had gathered together and pushed against the masts we could have pushed it on? When one attempts to sanctify himself by effort, he is trying to make his boat go by pushing against the mast. He is like a drowning man trying to lift himself out of the water by pulling at the hair of his own head. Christ held up this method almost to ridicule when He said, "Which of you by taking thought can add a cubit to his stature?" The one redeeming feature of the self-sufficient method is this—that those who try it find out almost at once that it will not gain the goal.

Another experimenter says:—"But that is not my method. I have seen the folly of a mere wild struggle in the dark. I work on a principle. My plan is not to waste power on random effort, but to concentrate on a single sin. By taking one at a time and crucifying it steadily, I hope in the end to extirpate all." To this, unfortunately, there are four objections. For one thing life is too short; the name of sin is Legion. For another thing, to deal with individual sins is to leave the rest of the nature for the time untouched. In the third place, a single combat with a special sin does not affect the root and spring of the disease. If one only of the channels of sin be obstructed, experience points to an almost certain overflow through some other part of the nature. Partial conversion is almost always accompanied by such moral leakage, for the pent-up energies accumulate to the bursting point, and the last state of that soul may be worse than the first. In the last place, religion does not consist in negatives, in stopping this sin and stopping that. The perfect character can never be produced with a pruning knife.

But a Third protests:— "So be it I make no attempt to stop sins one by one. My method is just the opposite. I copy the virtues one by one." The difficulty about the copying method is that it is apt to be mechanical. One can always tell an engraving from a picture, an artificial flower from a real flower. To copy virtues one by one has somewhat the same effect as eradicating the vices one by one; the temporary result is an overbalanced and incongruous character. Someone defines a prig as "a creature that is over-fed for its size." One sometimes finds Christians of this species— over-fed on one side of their nature, but dismally thin and starved-looking on the other. The result, for instance, of copying Humility, and adding it on to an otherwise worldly life, is simply grotesque. A rabid Temperance advocate, for the same reason, is often the poorest of creatures, flourishing on a single virtue, and quite oblivious that his Temperance is making a worse man of him and not a better. These are examples of fine virtues spoiled by association with mean companions. Character is a unity, and all the virtues must advance together to make the perfect man. This method of sanctification, nevertheless, is in the true direction. It is only in the details of execution that it fails.

A fourth method I need scarcely mention, for it is a variation on those already named. It is the very young man's method; and the pure earnestness of it makes it almost desecration to touch it. It is to keep a private note-book with columns for the days of the week, and a list of virtues with spaces against each for marks. This, with many stern rules for preface, is stored away in a secret place, and from time to time, at nightfall, the soul is arraigned before it as before a private judgment bar. This living by code was Franklin's method; and I suppose thousands more could tell how they had hung up in their bed-rooms, or hid in lock-fast drawers, the rules which one solemn day they drew up to shape their lives. This method is not erroneous, only somehow its success is poor. You bear me witness that it fails? And it fails generally for very matter-of-fact reasons—most likely because one day we forget the rules.

All these methods that have been named —the self-sufficient method, the self-crucifixion method, the mimetic method, and the diary method—are perfectly human, perfectly natural, perfectly ignorant, and, as they stand, perfectly inadequate. It is not argued, I repeat, that they must be abandoned. Their harm is rather that they distract attention from the true working method, and secure a fair result at the expense of the perfect one. What that perfect method is we shall now go on to ask.

The Formula of Sanctification

A Formula, a receipt, for Sanctification— can one seriously speak of this mighty change as if the process were as definite as for the production of so many volts of electricity? It is impossible to doubt it. Shall a mechanical experiment succeed infallibly, and the one vital experiment of humanity remain a chance? Is corn to grow by method, and character by caprice? If we cannot calculate to a certainty that the forces of religion will do their work, then is religion vain. And if we cannot express the law of these forces in simple words, then is Christianity not the world's religion but the world's conundrum.

Where, then, shall one look for such a formula? Where one would look for any formula—among the text books. And if we turn to the text books of Christianity we shall find a formula for this problem as clear and precise as any in the mechanical sciences. If this simple rule, moreover, be but followed fearlessly, it will yield the result of a perfect character as surely as any result that is guaranteed by the laws of nature. The finest expression of this rule in Scripture, or indeed in any literature, is probably one drawn up and condensed into a single verse by Paul. You will find it in a letter—the second to the Corinthians—written by him to some Christian people who, in a city which was a byword for depravity and licentiousness, were seeking the higher life. To see the point of the words we must take them from the immensely improved rendering of the Revised translation, for the older Version in this case greatly obscures the sense. They are these: "We all, with unveiled face reflecting as a mirror the glory of the Lord, are transformed into the same image from glory to glory, even as from the Lord the Spirit."

Now observe at the outset the entire contradiction of all our previous efforts, in the simple passive "we are transformed." We are changed, as the Old Version has it—we do not change ourselves. No man can change himself. Throughout the New Testament you will find that wherever these moral and spiritual transformations are described the verbs are in the passive. Presently it will be pointed out that there is a rationale in this; but meantime do not toss these words aside as if this passivity denied all human effort or ignored intelligible law. What is implied for the soul here is no more than is everywhere claimed for the body. In physiology the verbs describing the processes of growth are in the passive. Growth is not voluntary; it takes place, it happens, it is wrought upon matter. So here. "Ye must be born again" —we cannot born ourselves. "Be not conformed to this world but be ye transformed"—we are subjects to a transforming influence, we do not transform ourselves. Not more certain is it that it is something outside the thermometer that produces a change in the thermometer, than it is something outside the soul of man that produces a moral change upon him. That he must be susceptible to that change, that he must be a party to it, goes without saying; but that neither his aptitude nor his will can produce it, is equally certain.

Obvious as it ought to seem, this may be to some an almost startling revelation. The change we have been striving after is not to be produced by any more striving after. It is to be wrought upon us by the moulding of hands beyond our own. As the branch ascends, and the bud bursts, and the fruit reddens under the co-operation of influences from the outside air, so man rises to the higher stature under invisible pressures from without. The radical defect of all our former methods of sanctification was the attempt to generate from within that which can only be wrought upon us from without. According to the first Law of Motion: Every body continues in its state of rest, or of uniform motion in a straight line, except in so far as it may be compelled by impressed forces to change that state. This is also a first law of Christianity. Every man's character remains as it is, or continues in the direction in which it is going, until it is compelled by impressed forces to change that state. Our failure has been the failure to put ourselves in the way of the impressed forces. There is a clay, and there is a Potter; we have tried to get the clay to mould the clay.

Whence, then, these pressures, and where this Potter? The answer of the formula is "By reflecting as a mirror the glory of the Lord we are changed." But this is not very clear. What is the "glory" of the Lord, and how can mortal man reflect it, and how can that act as an "impressed force" in moulding him to a nobler form? The word "glory" —the word which has to bear the weight of holding those "impressed forces" —is a stranger in current speech, and our first duty is to seek out its equivalent in working English. It suggests at first a radiance of some kind, something dazzling or glittering, some halo such as the old masters loved to paint round the heads of their Ecce Homos. But that is paint, mere matter, the visible symbol of some unseen thing. What is that unseen thing? It is that of all unseen things, the most radiant, the most beautiful, the most Divine, and that is Character. On earth, in Heaven, there is nothing so great, so glorious as this. The word has many meanings; in ethics it can have but one. Glory is character and nothing less, and it can be nothing more. The earth is "full of the Glory of the Lord," because it is full of His character. The "Beauty of the Lord" is character. "The effulgence of His Glory" is character. "The Glory of the Only Begotten" is character, the character which is "fulness of grace and truth." And when God told His people His name He simply gave them His character, His character which was Himself. "And the Lord proclaimed the Name of the Lord . . . the Lord, the Lord God, merciful and gracious, long-suffering and abundant in goodness and truth." Glory then is not something intangible, or ghostly, or transcendental. If it were this, how could Paul ask men to reflect it? Stripped of its physical enswathement it is Beauty, moral and spiritual Beauty, Beauty infinitely real, infinitely exalted, yet infinitely near and infinitely communicable.

With this explanation read over the sentence once more in paraphrase: We all reflecting as a mirror the character of Christ are transformed into the same Image from character to character—from a poor character to a better one, from a better one to ane a little better still, from that to one still more complete, until by slow degrees the Perfect Image is attained. Here the solution of the problem of sanctification is compressed into a sentence: Reflect the character of Christ and you will become like Christ.

All men are mirrors—that is the first law on which this formula is based. One of the aptest descriptions of a human being is that he is a mirror. As we sat at table to-night, the world in which each of us lived and moved throughout this day was focussed in the room. What we saw as we looked at one another was not one another, but one mother's world. We were an arrangement of mirrors. The scenes we saw were all reproduced; the people we met walked to and fro; they spoke, they bowed, they passed us by, did everything over again as if it had been real. When we talked, we were but looking at our own mirror and describing what flitted across it; our listening was not hearing, but seeing—we but looked on our neighbour's mirror. All human intercourse is a seeing of reflections. I meet a stranger in a railway carriage. The cadence of his first word tells me he is English, and comes from Yorkshire. Without knowing it he has reflected his birthplace, his parents, and the long history of their race. Even physiologically he is a mirror. His second sentence records that he is a politician, and a faint inflexion in the way he pronounces The Times reveals his party. In his next remarks I see reflected a whole world of experiences. The books he has read, the people he has met, the influences that have played upon him and made him the man he is— these are all registered there by a pen which lets nothing pass, and whose writing can never be blotted out. What I am reading in him meantime he also is reading in me; and before the journey is over we could half write each other's lives. Whether we like it or not, we live in glass houses. The mind, the memory, the soul, is simply a vast chamber panelled with looking-glass. And upon this miraculous arrangement and endowment depends the capacity of mortal souls to "reflect the character of the Lord."

But this is not all. If all these varied reflections from our so-called secret life are patent to the world, how close the writing, how complete the record, within the soul itself? For the influences we meet are not simply held for a moment on the polished surface and thrown off again into space. Each is retained where first it fell, and stored up in the soul for ever.

This law of Assimilation is the second, and by far the most impressive truth which underlies the formula of sanctification—the truth that men are not only mirrors, but that these mirrors so far from being mere reflectors of the fleeting things they see, transfer into their own inmost substance, and hold in permanent preservation the things that they reflect. No one knows how the soul can hold these things. No one knows how the miracle is done. No phenomenon in nature, no process in chemistry, no chapter in necromancy can even help us to begin to understand this amazing operation. For, think of it, the past is not only focussed there, in a man's soul, it is there. How could it be reflected from there if it were not there? All things that he has ever seen, known, felt, believed of the surrounding world are now within him, have become part of him, in part are him—he has been changed into their image. He may deny it, he may resent it, but they are there. They do not adhere to him, they are transfused through him. He cannot alter or rub them out. They are not in his memory, they are in him. His soul is as they have filled it, made it, left it. These things, these books, these events, these influences are his makers. In their hands are life and death, beauty and deformity. When once the image or likeness of any of these is fairly presented to the soul, no power on earth can hinder two things happening—it must be absorbed into the soul, and for ever reflected back again from character.

Upon these astounding yet perfectly obvious psychological facts, Paul bases his doctrine of sanctification. He sees that character is a thing built up by slow degrees, that it is hourly changing for better or for worse according to the images which flit across it. One step further and the whole length and breadth of the application of these ideas to the central problem of religion will stand before us.

The Alchemy of Influence

If events change men, much more persons. No man can meet another on the street without making some mark upon him. We say we exchange words when we meet; what we exchange is souls. And when intercourse is very close and very frequent, so complete is this exchange that recognisable bits of the one soul begin to show in the other's nature, and the second is conscious of a similar and growing debt to the first. This mysterious approximating of two souls who has not witnessed? Who has not watched some old couple come down life's pilgrimage hand in hand with such gentle trust and joy in one another that their very faces wore the self-same look? These were not two souls; it was a composite soul. It did not matter to which of the two you spoke, you would have said the same words to either. It was quite indifferent which replied, each would have said the same. Half a century's reflecting had told upon them: they were changed into the same image. It is the Law of Influence that we become like those whom we habitually admire: these had become like because they habitually admired. Through all the range of literature, of history, and biography this law presides. Men are all mosaics of other men. There was a savour of David about Jonathan and a savour of Jonathan about David. Jean Valjean, in the masterpiece of Victor Hugo, is Bishop Bienvenu risen from the dead. Metempsychosis is a fact. George Eliot's message to the world was that men and women make men and women. The Family, the cradle of mankind, has no meaning apart from this. Society itself is nothing but a rallying point for these omnipotent forces to do their work. On the doctrine of Influence, in short, the whole vast pyramid of humanity is built.

But it was reserved for Paul to make the supreme application of the Law of Influence. It was a tremendous inference to make, but he never hesitated. He himself was a changed man: he knew exactly what had done it; it was Christ On the Damascus road they met, and from that hour his life was absorbed in His. The effect could not but follow—on words, on deeds, on career, on creed. The "impressed forces" did their vital work. He became like Him whom he habitually loved. "So we all," he writes, "reflecting as a mirror the glory of Christ are changed into the same image."

Nothing could be more simple, more intelligible, more natural, more supernatural. It is an analogy from an everyday fact Since we are what we are by the impacts of those who surround us, those who surround themselves with the highest will be those who change into the highest. There are some men and some women in whose company we are always at our best. While with them we cannot think mean thoughts or speak ungenerous words. Their mere presence is elevation, purification, sanctity. All the best stops in our nature are drawn out by their intercourse, and we find a music in our souls that was never there before. Suppose even that influence prolonged through a month, a year, a lifetime, and what could not life become? Here, even on the common plane of life, talking our language, walking our streets, working side by side, are sanctifiers of souls; here, breathing through common play, is Heaven; here, energies charged even through a temporal medium with a virtue of regeneration. If to live with men, diluted to the millionth degree with the virtue of the Highest, can exalt and purify the nature, what bounds can be set to the influence of Christ? To live with Socrates—with unveiled face—must have made one wise; with Aristides, just. Francis of Assisi must have made one gentle; Savonarola, strong. But to have lived with Christ? To have lived with Christ must have made one like Christ; that is to say, A Christian.

As a matter of fact, to live with Christ did produce this effect. It produced it in the case of Paul. And during Christ's lifetime the experiment was tried in an even more startling form. A few raw, unspiritual, uninspiring men, were admitted to the inner circle of His friendship. The change began at once. Day by day we can almost see the first disciples grow. First there steals over them the faintest possible adumbration of His character, and occasionally, very occasionally, they do a thing, or say a thing that they could not have done or said had they not been living there. Slowly the spell of His Life deepens. Reach after reach of their nature is overtaken, thawed, subjugated, sanctified. Their manners soften, their words become more gentle, their conduct more unselfish As swallows who have found a summer, as frozen buds the spring, their starved humanity bursts into a fuller life. They do not know how it is, but they are different men. One day they find themselves like their Master, going about and doing good. To themselves it is unaccountable, but they cannot do otherwise. They were not told to do it, it came to them to do it. But the people who watch them know well how to account for it—"They have been," they whisper, "with Jesus." Already even, the mark and seal of His character is upon them— "They have been with Jesus." Unparalleled phenomenon, that these poor fishermen should remind other men of Christ! Stupendous victory and mystery of regeneration that mortal men should suggest to the world, God!

There is something almost melting in the way His contemporaries, and John especially, speak of the Influence of Christ. John lived himself in daily wonder at Him; he was overpowered, overawed, entranced, transfigured. To his mind it was impossible for any one to come under this influence and ever be the same again. "Whosoever abideth in Him sinneth not," he said. It was inconceivable that he should sin, as inconceivable as that ice should live in a burning sun, or darkness co-exist with noon. If any one did sin, it was to John the simple proof that he could never have met Christ. "Whosoever sinneth," he exclaims, "hath not seen Him, neither known Him." Sin was abashed in this Presence. Its roots withered. Its sway and victory were for ever at an end.

But these were His contemporaries. It was easy for them to be influenced by Him, for they were every day and all the day together. But how can we mirror that which we have never seen? How can all this stupendous result be produced by a Memory, by the scantiest of all Biographies, by One who lived and left this earth eighteen hundred years ago? How can modern men to-day make Christ, the absent Christ, their most constant companion still? The answer is that Friendship is a spiritual thing. It is independent of Matter, or Space, or Time. That which I love in my friend is not that which I see. What influences me in my friend is not his body but his spirit. It would have been an ineffable experience truly to have lived at that time—

"I think when I read the sweet story of old,
How when Jesus was here among men,

He took little children like lambs to His fold,
I should like to have been with him then.

"I wish that His hand had been laid on my head,
That His arms had been thrown around me,
And that I had seen His kind look when He said,
Let the little ones come unto Me."

And yet, if Christ were to come into the world again few of us probably would ever have a chance of seeing Him. Millions of her subjects, in this little country, have never seen their own Queen. And there would be millions of the subjects of Christ who could never get within speaking distance of Him if He were here. Our companionship with Him, like all true companionship, is a spiritual communion. All friendship, all love, human and Divine, is purely spiritual. It was after He was risen that He influenced even the disciples most. Hence in reflecting the character of Christ it is no real obstacle that we may never have been in visible contact with Himself.

There lived once a young girl whose perfect grace of character was the wonder of those who knew her. She wore on her neck a gold locket which no one was ever allowed to open. One day, in a moment of unusual confidence, one of her companions was allowed to touch its spring and learn its secret. She saw written these words— "Whom having not seen, I love." That was the secret of her beautiful life. She had been changed into the Same Image.

Now this is not imitation, but a much deeper thing. Mark this distinction. For the difference in the process, as well as in the result, may be as great as that between a photograph secured by the infallible pencil of the sun, and the rude outline from a schoolboy's chalk. Imitation is mechanical, reflection organic. The one is occasional, the other habitual. In the one case, man comes to God and imitates Him; in the other, God comes to man and imprints Himself upon him. It is quite true that there is an imitation of Christ which amounts to reflection. But Paul's term includes all that the other holds, and is open to no mistake.

"Make Christ your most constant companion"—this is what it practically means for us. Be more under His influence than under any other influence. Ten minutes spent in His society every day, ay, two minutes if it be face to face, and heart to heart, will make the whole day different. Every character has an inward spring, let Christ be it. Every action has a key-note, let Christ set it. Yesterday you got a certain letter. You sat down and wrote a reply which almost scorched the paper. You picked the cruellest adjectives you knew and sent it forth, without a pang, to do its ruthless work. You did that because your life was set in the wrong key. You began the day with the mirror placed at the wrong angle. To-morrow, at daybreak, turn it towards Him, and even to your enemy the fashion of your countenance will be changed. Whatever you then do, one thing you will find you could not do—you could not write that letter. Your first impulse may be the same, your judgment may be unchanged, but if you try it the ink will dry on your pen, and you will rise from your desk an unavenged but a greater and more Christian man. Throughout the whole day your actions, down to the last detail, will do homage to that early vision. Yesterday you thought mostly about yourself. To-day the poor will meet you, and you will feed them. The helpless, the tempted, the sad, will throng about you, and each you will befriend. Where were all these people yesterday? Where they are to-day, but you did not see them. It is in reflected light that the poor are seen. But your soul to-day is not at the ordinary angle. "Things which are not seen" are visible. For a few short hours you live the Eternal Life. The eternal life, the life of faith, is simply the life of the higher vision. Faith is an attitude— a mirror set at the right angle.

When to-morrow is over, and in the evening you review it, you will wonder how you did it. You will not be conscious that you strove for anything, or imitated anything, or crucified anything. You will be conscious of Christ; that He was with you, that without compulsion you were yet compelled, that without force, or noise, or proclamation, the revolution was accomplished. You do not congratulate yourself as one who has done a mighty deed, or achieved a personal success, or stored up a fund of "Christian experience" to ensure the same result again. What you are conscious of is "the glory of the Lord." And what the world is conscious of, if the result be a true one, is also "the glory of the Lord." In looking at a mirror one does not see the mirror, or think of it, but only of what it reflects. For a mirror never calls attention to itself except when there are flaws in it.

That this is a real experience and not a vision, that this life is possible to men, is being lived by men to-day, is simple biographical fact. From a thousand witnesses I cannot forbear to summon one. The following are the words of one of the highest intellects this age has known, a man who shared the burdens of his country as few have done, and who, not in the shadows of old age, but in the high noon of his success, gave this confession—I quote it with only a few abridgments—to the world:—

'I want to speak to-night only a little, but that little I desire to speak of the sacred name of Christ, who is my life, my inspiration, my hope, and my surety. I cannot help stopping and looking back upon the past. And I wish, as if I had never done it before, to bear witness, not only that it is by the grace of God, but that it is by the grace of God as manifested in Christ Jesus, that I am what I am. I recognize the sublimity and grandeur of the revelation of God in His eternal fatherhood as one that made the heavens, that founded the earth, and that regards all the tribes of the earth, comprehending them in one universal mercy; but it is the God that is manifested in Jesus Christ, revealed by His life, made known by the inflections of His feelings, by His discourse, and by His deeds—it is that God that I desire to confess to-night, and of whom I desire to say, "By the love of God in Christ Jesus I am what I am."

'If you ask me precisely what I mean by that, I say, frankly, that more than any recognized influence of my father or my mother upon me; more than the social influence of all the members of my father's household; more, so far as I can trace it, or so far as I am made aware of it, than all the social influences of every kind, Christ has had the formation of my mind and my disposition. My hidden ideals of what is beautiful I have drawn from Christ. My thoughts of what is manly, and noble, and pure, have almost all of them arisen from the Lord Jesus Christ. Many men have educated themselves by reading Plutarch's Lives of the Ancient Worthies, and setting before themselves one and another of these that in different ages have achieved celebrity; and they have recognized the great power of these men on themselves. Now I do not perceive that poet, or philosopher, or reformer, or general, or any other great man, ever has dwelt in my imagination and in my thought as the simple Jesus has. For more than twenty-five years I instinctively have gone to Christ to draw a measure and a rule for everything. Whenever there has been a necessity for it, I have sought—and at last almost spontaneously—to throw myself into the companionship of Christ; and early, by my imagination, I could see Him standing and looking quietly and lovingly upon me. There seemed almost to drop from His face an influence upon me that suggested what was the right thing in the controlling of passion, in the subduing of pride, in the overcoming of selfishness; and it is from Christ, manifested to my inward eye, that I have consciously derived more ideals, more models, more influences, than from any human character whatever.

'That is not all. I feel conscious that I have derived from the Lord Jesus Christ every thought that makes heaven a reality to me, and every thought that paves the road that lies between me and heaven. All my conceptions of the progress of grace in the soul; all the steps by which divine life is evolved; all the ideals that overhang the blessed sphere which awaits us beyond this world —these are derived from the Saviour. The life that I now live in the flesh I live by the faith of the Son of God.

'That is not all. Much as my future includes all these elements which go to make the blessed fabric of earthly life, yet, after all, what the summer is compared with all its earthly products —flowers, and leaves, and grass—that is Christ compared with all the products of Christ in my mind and in my soul. All the flowers and leaves of sympathy; all the twining joys that come from my heart as a Christian—these I take and hold in the future, but they are to me what the flowers and leaves of summer are compared with the sun that makes the summer. Christ is the Alpha and Omega, the beginning and the end of my better life.

'When I read the Bible, I gather a great deal from the Old Testament, and from the Pauline portions of the New Testament; but after all, I am conscious that the fruit of the Bible is Christ. That is what I read it for, and that is what I find that is worth reading. I have had a hunger to be loved of Christ. You all know, in some relations, what it is to be hungry for love. Your heart seems unsatisfied till you can draw something more toward you from those that are dearest to you. There have been times when I have had an unspeakable heart-hunger for Christ's love. My sense of sin is never strong when I think of the law; my sense of sin is strong when I think of love—if there is any difference between law and love. It is when drawing near the Lord Jesus Christ, and longing to be loved, that I have the most vivid sense of unsymmetry, of imperfection, of absolute unworthiness, and of my sinfulness. Character and conduct are never so vividly set before me as when in silence I bend in the presence of Christ, revealed not in wrath, but in love to me. I never so much long to be lovely, that I may be loved, as when I have this revelation of Christ before my mind.

'In looking back upon my experience, that part of my life which stands out, and which I remember most vividly, is just that part that has had some conscious association with Christ. All the rest is pale, and thin, and lies like clouds on the horizon. Doctrines, systems, measures, methods— what may be called the necessary mechanical and external part of worship; the part which the senses would recognize—this seems to have withered and fallen off like leaves of last summer; but that part which has taken hold of Christ abides'

Can anyone hear this life-music, with its throbbing refrain of Christ, and remain unmoved by envy or desire? Yet till we have lived like this we have never lived at all.

The First Experiment

Then you reduce religion to a common Friendship? A common Friendship—Who talks of a common Friendship? There is no such thing in the world. On earth no word is more sublime. Friendship is the nearest thing we know to what religion is. God is love. And to make religion akin to Friendship is simply to give it the highest expression conceivable by man. But if by demurring to "a common friendship" is meant a protest against the greatest and the holiest in religion being spoken of in intelligible terms, then I am afraid the objection is all too real. Men always look for a mystery when one talks of sanctification; some mystery apart from that which must ever be mysterious wherever Spirit works. It is thought some peculiar secret lies behind it, some occult experience which only the initiated know. Thousands of persons go to church every Sunday hoping to solve this mystery. At meetings, at conferences, many a time they have reached what they thought was the very brink of it, but somehow no further revelation came. Poring over religious books, how often were they not within a paragraph of it; the next page, the next sentence, would discover all, and they would be borne on a flowing tide for ever. But nothing happened. The next sentence and the next page were read, and still it eluded them; and though the promise of its coming kept faithfully up to the end, the last chapter found them still pursuing. Why did nothing happen? Because there was nothing to happen—nothing of the kind they were looking for. Why did it elude them? Because there was no "it" When shall we learn that the pursuit of holiness is simply the pursuit of Christ? When shall we substitute for the "it" of a fictitious aspiration, the approach to a Living Friend? Sanctity is in character and not in moods; Divinity in our own plain calm humanity, and in no mystic rapture of the soul.

And yet there are others who, for exactly a contrary reason, will find scant satisfaction here. Their complaint is not that a religion expressed in terms of Friendship is too homely, but that it is still too mystical. To "abide" in Christ, to "make Christ our most constant companion" is to them the purest mysticism. They want something absolutely tangible and absolutely direct. These are not the poetical souls who seek a sign, a mysticism in excess; but the prosaic natures whose want is mathematical definition in details. Yet it is perhaps not possible to reduce this problem to much more rigid elements. The beauty of Friendship is its infinity, One can never evacuate life of mysticism. Home is full of it, love is full of it, religion is full of it. Why stumble at that in the relation of man to Christ which is natural in the relation of man to man?

If any one cannot conceive or realize a mystical relation with Christ, perhaps all that can be done is to help him to step on to it by still plainer analogies from common life. How do I know Shakespeare or Dante? By communing with their words and thoughts. Many men know Dante better than their own fathers. He influences them more. As a spiritual presence he is more near to them, as a spiritual force more real. Is there any reason why a greater than Shakespeare or Dante, who also walked this earth, who left great words behind Him, who has great works everywhere in the world now, should not also instruct, inspire, and mould the characters of men? I do not limit Christ's influence to this. It is this, and it is more. But Christ, so far from resenting or discouraging this relation of Friendship, Himself proposed it. "Abide in Me" was almost His last word to the world. And He partly met the difficulty of those who feel its intangibleness by adding the practical clause, "If ye abide in Me and My words abide in you."

Begin with His words. Words can scarcely ever be long impersonal. Christ Himself was a Word, a word made Flesh. Make His words flesh; do them, live them, and you must live Christ. "He that keepeth My commandments, he it is that loveth Me." Obey Him and you must love Him. Abide in Him and you must obey Him. Cultivate His Friendship. Live after Christ, in His Spirit, as in His Presence, and it is difficult to think what more you can do. Take this at least as a first lesson, as introduction. If you cannot at once and always feel the play of His life upon yours, watch for it also indirectly. "The whole earth is full of the character of the Lord." Christ is the Light of the world, and much of His Light is reflected from things in the world—even from clouds. Sunlight is stored in every leaf, from leaf through coal, and it comforts us thence when days are dark and we cannot see the sun. Christ shines through men, through books, through history, through nature, music, art. Look for Him there. "Every day one should either look at a beautiful picture, or hear beautiful music, or read a beautiful poem." The real danger of mysticism is not making it broad enough.

Do not think that nothing is happening because you do not see yourself grow, or hear the whirr of the machinery. All great things grow noiselessly. You can see a mushroom grow, but never a child. Mr. Darwin tells us that Evolution proceeds by "numerous, successive, and slight modifications." Paul knew that, and put it, only in more beautiful words, into the heart of his formula. He said for the comforting of all slowly perfecting souls that they grew "from character to character." "The inward man" he says elsewhere, "is renewed from day to day." All thorough work is slow; all true development by minute slight and insensible metamorphoses. The higher the structure, moreover, the slower the progress. As the biologist runs his eye over the long Ascent of Life he sees the lowest forms of animals develop in an hour; the next above these reach maturity in a day; those higher still take weeks or months to perfect; but the few at the top demand the long experiment of years. If a child and an ape are born on the same day the last will be in full possession of its faculties and doing the active work of life before the child has left its cradle. Life is the cradle of eternity. As the man is to the animal in the slowness of his evolution, so is the spiritual man to the natural man. Foundations which have to bear the weight of an eternal life must be surely laid. Character is to wear for ever; who will wonder or grudge that it cannot be developed in a day?

To await the growing of a soul, nevertheless, is an almost Divine act of faith. How pardonable, surely, the impatience of deformity with itself, of a consciously despicable character standing before Christ, wondering, yearning, hungering to be like that? Yet must one trust the process fearlessly, and without misgiving. "The Lord the Spirit" will do His part. The tempting expedient is, in haste for abrupt or visible progress, to try some method less spiritual, or to defeat the end by watching for effects instead of keeping the eye on the Cause. A photograph prints from the negative only while exposed to the sun. While the artist is looking to see how it is getting on he simply stops the getting on. Whatever of wise supervision the soul may need, it is certain it can never be over-exposed, or, that, being exposed, anything else in the world can improve the result or quicken it. The creation of a new heart, the renewing of a right spirit is an omnipotent work of God. Leave it to the Creator. "He which hath begun a good work in you will perfect it unto that day."

No man, nevertheless, who feels the worth and solemnity of what is at stake will be careless as to his progress. To become like Christ is the only thing in the world worth caring for, the thing before which every ambition of man is folly, and all lower achievement vain. Those only who make this quest the supreme desire and passion of their lives can even begin to hope to reach it. If, therefore, it has seemed up to this point as if all depended on passivity, let me now assert, with conviction more intense, that all depends on activity. A religion of effortless adoration may be a religion for an angel but never for a man. Not in the contemplative, but in the active lies true hope; not in rapture, but in reality lies true life; not in the realm of ideals but among tangible things is man's sanctification wrought. Resolution, effort, pain, self-crucifixion, agony—all the things already dismissed as futile in themselves must now be restored to office, and a tenfold responsibility laid upon them. For what is their office? Nothing less than to move the vast inertia of the soul, and place it, and keep it where the spiritual forces will act upon it. It is to rally the forces of the will, and keep the surface of the mirror bright, and ever in position. It is to uncover the face which is to look at Christ, and draw down the veil when unhallowed sights are near. You have, perhaps, gone with an astronomer to watch him photograph the spectrum of a star. As you entered the dark vault of the Observatory you saw him begin by lighting a candle. To see the star with? No; but to see to adjust the instrument to see the star with. It was the star that was going to take the photograph; it was, also, the astronomer. For a long time he worked in the dimness, screwing tubes and polishing lenses and adjusting reflectors, and only after much labour the finely focussed instrument was brought to bear. Then he blew out the light, and left the star to do its work upon the plate alone. The day's task for the Christian is to bring his instrument to bear. Having done that he may blow out his candle. All the evidences of Christianity which have brought him there, all aids to Faith, all acts of Worship, all the leverages of the Church, all Prayer and Meditation, all girding of the Will—these lesser processes, these candle-light activities for that supreme hour may be set aside. But, remember, it is but for an hour. The wise man will be he who quickest lights his candle; the wisest he who never let it out. To-morrow, the next moment, he, a poor, darkened, slurred soul, may need it again to focus the Image better, to take a mote off the lens, to clear the mirror from a breath with which the world has dulled it.

No re-adjustment is ever required on behalf of the Star. That is one great fixed point in this shifting universe. But the world moves. And each day, each hour, demands a further motion and re-adjustment for the soul. A telescope in an observatory follows a star by clockwork, but the clockwork of the soul is called the Will. Hence, while the soul in passivity reflects the Image of the Lord, the Will in intense activity holds the mirror in position lest the drifting motion of the world bear it beyond the line of vision. To "follow Christ" is largely to keep the soul in such position as will allow for the motion of the earth. And this calculated counteracting of the movements of a world, this holding of the mirror exactly opposite to the Mirrored, this steadying of the faculties unerringly, through cloud and earthquake, fire and sword, is the stupendous co-operating labour of the Will.

It is all man's work. It is all Christ's work. In practice, it is both; in theory it is both. But the wise man will say in practice, "It depends upon myself."

In the Galerie des Beaux Arts in Paris there stands a famous statue. It was the last work of a great genius, who, like many a genius, was very poor and lived in a garret which served as studio and sleeping-room alike. When the statue was all but finished, one midnight a sudden frost fell upon Paris. The sculptor lay awake in the fireless room and thought of the still moist clay, thought how the water would freeze in the pores and destroy in an hour the dream of his life. So the old man rose from his couch and heaped the bed-clothes reverently round his work. In the morning when the neighbours entered the room the sculptor was dead. But the statue lived.

The Image of Christ that is forming within us—that is life's one charge. Let every project stand aside for that "Till Christ be formed" no man's work is finished, no religion crowned, no life has fulfilled its end. Is the infinite task begun? When, how, are we to be different? Time cannot change men. Death cannot change men. Christ can. Wherefore, put on Christ.

The City Without a Church

Table of Contents

*I, John, Saw the Holy City, New Jerusalem, Coming down from God
out of Heaven.
And I saw no Temple therein.
And His servants shall serve Him;
And they shall see His Face;
And His Name shall be written on their foreheads.*

I Saw the City

Two very startling things arrest us in John's vision of the future. The first is that the likest thing to Heaven he could think of was a City; the second, that there was no Church in that City.

Almost nothing more revolutionary could be said, even to the modern world, in the name of religion. No Church—that is the defiance of religion; a City—that is the antipodes of Heaven. Yet John combines these contradictions in one daring image, and holds up to the world the picture of a City without a Church as his ideal of the heavenly life.

By far the most original thing here is the simple conception of Heaven as a City. The idea of religion without a Church— "I saw no Temple therein"—is anomalous enough; but the association of the blessed life with a City—the one place in the world from which Heaven seems most far away— is something wholly new in religious thought. No other religion which has a Heaven ever had a Heaven like this. The Greek, if he looked forward at all, awaited the Elysian Fields; the Eastern sought Nirvana. All other Heavens have been Gardens, Dreamlands—passivities more or less aimless. Even to the majority among ourselves Heaven is a siesta and not a City. It remained for John to go straight to the other extreme and select the citadel of the world's fever, the ganglion of its unrest, the heart and focus of its most strenuous toil, as the framework for his ideal of the blessed life.

The Heaven of Christianity is different from all other Heavens, because the religion of Christianity is different from all other religions. Christianity is the religion of Cities. It moves among real things. Its sphere is the street, the market-place, the working-life of the world.

And what interests one for the present in John's vision is not so much what it reveals of a Heaven beyond, but what it suggests of the nature of the heavenly life in this present world. Find out what a man's Heaven is— no matter whether it be a dream or a reality, no matter whether it refer to an actual Heaven or to a Kingdom of God to be realized on earth—and you pass by an easy discovery to what his religion is; And herein lies one value at least of this allegory. It is a touchstone for Christianity, a test for the solidity or the insipidity of one's religion, for the wholesomeness or the fatuousness of one's faith, for the usefulness or the futility of one's life. For this vision of the City marks off in lines which no eye can mistake the true area which the religion of Christ is meant to inhabit, and announces for all time the real nature of the saintly life.

City life is human life at its intensest, man in his most real relations. And the nearer one draws to reality, the nearer one draws to the working sphere of religion. Wherever real life is, there Christ goes. And He goes there, not only because the great need lies there, but because there is found, so to speak, the raw material with which Christianity works—the life of man. To do something with this, to infuse something into this, to save and inspire and sanctify this, the actual working life of the world, is what He came for. Without human life to act upon, without the relations of men with one another, of master with servant, husband with wife, buyer with seller, creditor with debtor, there is no such thing as Christianity. With actual things, with Humanity in its everyday dress, with the traffic of the streets, with gates and houses, with work and wages, with sin and poverty, with these things, and all the things and all the relations and all the people of the City, Christianity has to do and has more to do than with anything else. To conceive of the Christian religion as itself a thing—a something which can exist apart from life; to think of it as something added on to being, something kept in a separate compartment called the soul, as an extra accomplishment like music, or a special talent like art, is totally to misapprehend its nature. It is that which fills all compartments. It is that which makes the whole life music and every separate action a work of art. Take away action and it is not. Take away people, houses, streets, character, and it ceases to be. Without these there may be sentiment, or rapture, or adoration, or superstition; there may even be religion, but there can never be the religion of the Son of Man.

If Heaven were a siesta, religion might be conceived of as a reverie. If the future life were to be mainly spent in a Temple, the present life might be mainly spent in Church. But if Heaven be a City, the life of those who are going there must be a real life. The man who would enter John's Heaven, no matter what piety or what faith he may profess, must be a real man. Christ's gift to men was life, a rich and abundant life. And life is meant for living. An abundant life does not show itself in abundant dreaming, but in abundant living—in abundant living among real and tangible objects and to actual and practical purposes. "His servants," John tells us, "shall serve." In this vision of the City he confronts us with a new definition of a Christian man— the perfect saint is the perfect citizen.

To make Cities—that is what we are here for. To make good Cities—that is for the present hour the main work of Christianity. For the City is strategic. It makes the towns: the towns make the villages; the villages make the country. He who makes the City makes the world. After all, though men make Cities, it is Cities which make men. Whether our national life is great or mean, whether our social virtues are mature or stunted, whether our sons are moral or vicious, whether religion is possible or impossible, depends upon the City. When Christianity shall take upon itself in full responsibility the burden and care of Cities the Kingdom of God will openly come on earth. What Christianity waits for also, as its final apologetic and justification to the world, is the founding of a City which shall be in visible reality a City of God. People do not dispute that religion is in the Church. What is now wanted is to let them see it in the City. One Christian City, one City in any part of the earth, whose citizens from the greatest to the humblest lived in the spirit of Christ, where religion had overflowed the Churches and passed into the streets, inundating every house and workshop, and permeating the whole social and commercial life—one such Christian City would seal the redemption of the world.

Some such City, surely, was what John saw in his dream. Whatever reference we may find there to a world to come, is it not equally lawful to seek the scene upon this present world? John saw his City descending out of Heaven. It was, moreover, no strange apparition, but a City which he knew. It was Jerusalem, a new Jerusalem. The significance of that name has been altered for most of us by religious poetry; we spell it with a capital and speak of the New Jerusalem as a synonym for Heaven. Yet why not take it simply as it stands, as a new Jerusalem? Try to restore the natural force of the expression—suppose John to have lived to-day and to have said London? "I saw a new London?" Jerusalem was John's London. All the grave and sad suggestion that the word London brings up to-day to the modern reformer, the word Jerusalem recalled to him. What in his deepest hours he longed and prayed for was a new Jerusalem, a reformed Jerusalem. And just as it is given to the man in modern England who is a prophet, to the man who believes in God and in the moral order of the world, to discern a new London shaping itself through all the sin and chaos of the City, so was it given to John to see a new Jerusalem rise from the ruins of the old.

We have no concern—it were contrary to critical method—to press the allegory in detail. What we take from it, looked at in this light, is the broad conception of a transformed City, the great Christian thought that the very Cities where we live, with all their suffering and sin, shall one day, by the gradual action of the forces of Christianity, be turned into Heavens on earth. This is a spectacle which profoundly concerns the world. To the reformer, the philanthropist, the economist, the politician, this Vision of the City is the great classic of social literature. What John saw, we may fairly take it, was the future of all Cities. It was the dawn of a new social order, a regenerate humanity, a purified society, an actual transformation of the Cities of the world into Cities of God.

This City, then, which John saw is none other than your City, the place where you live—as it might be, and as you are to help to make it. It is London, Berlin, New York, Paris, Melbourne, Calcutta—these as they might be, and in some infinitesimal degree as they have already begun to be. In each of these, and in every City throughout the world to-day, there is a City descending out of Heaven from God. Each one of us is daily building up this City or helping to keep it back. Its walls rise slowly, but, as we believe in God, the building can never cease. For the might of those who build, be they few or many, is so surely greater than the might of those who retard, that no day's sun sets over any City in the land that does not see some stone of the invisible City laid. To believe this is faith. To live for this is Christianity.

The project is delirious? Yes—to atheism. To John it was the most obvious thing in the world. Nay, knowing all he knew, its realization was inevitable. We forget, when the thing strikes us as strange, that John knew Christ. Christ was the Light of the World—the Light of the World. This is all that he meant by his Vision, that Christ is the Light of the World. This Light, John saw, would fall everywhere—especially upon Cities. It was irresistible and inextinguishable. No darkness could stand before it. One by one the Cities of the world would give up their night. Room by room, house by house, street by street, they would be changed. Whatsoever worketh abomination or maketh a lie would disappear. Sin, pain, sorrow, would silently pass away. One day the walls of the City would be jasper; the very streets would be paved with gold. Then the kings of the earth would bring their glory and honour into it. In the midst of the streets there should be a tree of Life. And its leaves would go forth for the healing of the nations.

Survey the Cities of the world today, survey your own City—town, village, home —and prophesy. God's kingdom is surely to come in this world. God's will is surely to be done on earth as it is done in Heaven. Is not this one practicable way of realizing it? When a prophet speaks of something that is to be, that coming event is usually brought about by no unrelated cause or sudden shock, but in the ordered course of the world's drama. With Christianity as the supreme actor in the world's drama, the future of its Cities is even now quite clear. Project the lines of Christian and social progress to their still far off goal, and see even now that Heaven must come to earth.

His Servants Shall Serve

If any one wishes to know what he can do to help on the work of God in the world let him make a City, or a street, or a house of a City. Men complain of the indefiniteness of religion. There are thousands ready in their humble measure to offer some personal service for the good of men, but they do not know where to begin. Let me tell you where to begin—where Christ told His disciples to begin, at the nearest City. I promise you that before one week's work is over you will never again be haunted by the problem of the indefiniteness of Christianity. You will see so much to do, so many actual things to be set right, so many merely material conditions to alter, so much striving with employers of labour, and City councils, and trade agitators, and Boards, and Vestries, and Committees; so much pure unrelieved uninspiring hard work, that you will begin to wonder whether in all this naked realism you are on holy ground at all. Do not be afraid of missing Heaven in seeking a better earth. The distinction between secular and sacred is a confusion and not a contrast; and it is only because the secular is so intensely sacred that so many eyes are blind before it. The really secular thing in life is the spirit which despises under that name what is but part of the everywhere present work and will of God. Be sure that, down to the last and pettiest detail, all that concerns a better world is the direct concern of Christ.

I make this, then, in all seriousness as a definite practical proposal. You wish, you say, to be a religious man. Well, be one. There is your City; begin. But what are you to believe? Believe in your City. What else? In Jesus Christ. What about Him? That He wants to make your City better; that that is what He would be doing if He lived there. What else? Believe in yourself—that you, even you, can do some of the work which He would like done, and that unless you do it, it will remain undone. How are you to begin? As Christ did. First He looked at the City; then He wept over it; then He died for it.

Where are you to begin? Begin where you are. Make that one corner, room, house, office as like Heaven as you can. Begin? Begin with the paper on the walls, make that beautiful; with the air, keep it fresh; with the very drains, make them sweet; with the furniture, see that it be honest. Abolish whatsoever worketh abomination—in food, in drink, in luxury, in books, in art; whatsoever maketh a lie—in conversation, in social intercourse, in correspondence, in domestic life. This done, you have arranged for a Heaven, but you have not got it. Heaven lies within, in kindness, in humbleness, in unselfishness, in faith, in love, in service. To get these in, get Christ in. Teach all in the house about Christ—what He did, and what He said, and how He lived, and how He died, and how He dwells in them, and how He makes all one. Teach it not as a doctrine, but as a discovery, as your own discovery. Live your own discovery.

Then pass out into the City. Do all to it that you have done at home. Beautify it, ventilate it, drain it. Let nothing enter it that can defile the streets, the stage, the newspaper offices, the booksellers' counters; nothing that maketh a lie in its warehouses, its manufactures, its shops, its art galleries, its advertisements.

Educate it, amuse it, church it. Christianize capital; dignify labour. Join Councils and Committees. Provide for the poor, the sick, and the widow. So will you serve the City.

If you ask me which of all these things is the most important, I reply that among them there is only one thing of superlative importance and that is yourself. By far the greatest thing a man can do for his City is to be a good man. Simply to live there as a good man, as a Christian man of action and practical citizen, is the first and highest contribution any one can make to its salvation. Let a City be a Sodom or a Gomorrah, and if there be but ten righteous men in it, it will be saved.

It is here that the older, the more individual, conception of Christianity, did such mighty work for the world—it produced good men. It is goodness that tells, goodness first and goodness last. Good men even with small views are immeasurably more important to the world than small men with great views. But given good men, such men as were produced even by the self-centred theology of an older generation, and add that wider outlook and social ideal which are coming to be the characteristics of the religion of this age, and Christianity has an equipment for the reconstruction of the world, before which nothing can stand. Such good men will not merely content themselves with being good men. They will be forces—according to their measure, public forces. They will take the city in hand, some a house, some a street, and some the whole. Of set purpose they will serve. Not ostentatiously, but silently, in ways varied as human nature, and many as life's opportunities, they will minister to its good.

To help the people, also, to be good people good fathers, and mothers, and sons, and citizens—is worth all else rolled into one. Arrange the government of the City as you may, perfect all its philanthropic machinery, make righteous its relations great and small, equip it with galleries and parks, and libraries and music, and carry out the whole programme of social reform, and the one thing needful is still without the gates. The gospel of material blessedness is part of a gospel—a great and Christian part— but when held up as the whole gospel for the people it is as hollow as the void of life whose circumference even it fails to touch.

There are countries in the world—new countries—where the people, rising to the rights of government, have already secured almost all that reformers cry for. The lot of the working man there is all but perfect. His wages are high, his leisure great, his home worthy. Yet in tens of thousands of cases the secret of life is unknown.

It is idle to talk of Christ as a social reformer if by that is meant that His first concern was to improve the organization of society, or provide the world with better laws. These were among His objects, but His first was to provide the world with better men. The one need of every cause and every community still is for better men. If every workshop held a Workman like Him who worked in the carpenter's shop at Nazareth, the labour problem and all other workman's problems would soon be solved. If every street had a home or two like Mary's home in Bethany, the domestic life of the city would be transformed in three generations.

External reforms— education, civilization, public schemes, and public charities—have each their part to play. Any experiment that can benefit by one hairbreadth any single human life is a thousand times worth trying. There is no effort in any single one of these directions but must, as Christianity advances, be pressed by Christian men to ever further and fuller issues. But those whose hands have tried the ways, and the slow work of leavening men one by one with the spirit of Jesus Christ.

The thought that the future, that any day, may see some new and mighty enterprise of redemption, some new departure in religion, which shall change everything with a breath and make all that is crooked straight, is not at all likely to be realized. There is nothing wrong with the lines on which redemption runs at present except the want of faith to believe in them, and the want of men to use them. The Kingdom of God is like leaven, and the leaven is with us now. The quantity at work in the world may increase but that is all. For nothing can ever be higher than the Spirit of Christ or more potent as a regenerating power on the lives of men.

Do not charge me with throwing away my brief because I return to this old, old plea for the individual soul. I do not forget that my plea is for the City. But I plead for good men, because good men are good leaven. If their goodness stop short of that, if the leaven does not mix with that which is unleavened, if it does not do the work of leaven—that is, to raise something— it is not the leaven of Christ. The question or good men to ask themselves is: Is my goodness helping others? Is it a private luxury, or is it telling upon the City? Is it bringing any single human soul nearer happiness or righteousness?

If you ask what particular scheme you shall take up, I cannot answer. Christianity has no set schemes. It makes no choice between conflicting philanthropies, decides nothing between competing churches, favours no particular public policy, organizes no one line of private charity. It is not essential even for all of us to take any public or formal line. Christianity is not all carried on by Committees, and the Kingdom of God has other ways of coming than through municipal reforms. Most of the stones for the building of the City of God, and all the best of them, are made by mothers. But whether or no you shall work through public channels, or only serve Christ along the quieter paths of home, no man can determine but yourself.

There is an almost awful freedom about Christ's religion. "I do not call you servants." He said, "for the servant knoweth not what his lord doeth. I have called you friends." As Christ's friends, His followers are supposed to know what He wants done, and for the same reason they will try to do it—this is the whole working basis of Christianity. Surely next to its love for the chief of sinners the most touching thing about the religion of Christ is its amazing trust in the least of saints. Here is the mightiest enterprise ever launched upon this earth, mightier even than its creation, for it is its re-creation, and the carrying of it out is left, so to speak, to haphazard—to individual loyalty, to free enthusiasms, to uncoerced activities, to an uncompelled response to the pressures of God's Spirit. Christ sets His followers no tasks. He appoints no hours. He allots no sphere. He Himself simply went about and did good. He did not stop life to do some special thing which should be called religious. His life was His religion. Each day as it came brought round in the ordinary course its natural ministry. Each village along the highway had someone waiting to be helped. His pulpit was the hillside, His congregation a woman at a well. The poor, wherever He met them, were His clients; the sick, as often as He found them, His opportunity. His work was everywhere; His workshop was the world. One's associations of Christ are all of the wayside. We never think of Him in connection with a Church We cannot picture Him in the garb of a priest or belonging to any of the classes who specialize religion. His service was of a universal human order. He was the Son of Man, the Citizen.

This, remember, was the highest life ever lived, this informal citizen-life. So simple a thing it was, so natural, so human, that those who saw it first did not know it was religion, and Christ did not pass among them as a very religious man. Nay, it is certain, and it is an infinitely significant thought, that the religious people of His time not only refused to accept this type of religion as any kind of religion at all, but repudiated and denounced Him as its bitter enemy.

Inability to discern what true religion is, is not confined to the Pharisees. Multitudes still who profess to belong to the religion of Christ, scarcely know it when they see it. The truth is, men will hold to almost anything in the name of Christianity, believe anything, do anything—except its common and obvious tasks. Great is the mystery of what has passed in this world for religion.

I Saw No Temple There

"I saw no Church there," said John. Nor is there any note of surprise as he marks the omission of what one half of Christendom would have considered the first essential. For beside the type of religion he had learned from Christ, the Church type —the merely Church type—is an elaborate evasion. What have the pomp and circumstance, the fashion and the form, the vestures and the postures, to do with Jesus of Nazareth? At a stage in personal development. and for a certain type of mind, such things may have a place. But when mistaken for Christianity, no matter how they aid it, or in what measure they conserve it, they defraud the souls of men, and rob humanity of its dues. It is because to large masses of people Christianity has become synonymous with a Temple service that other large masses of people decline to touch it. It is a mistake to suppose that the working classes of this country are opposed to Christianity. No man can ever be opposed to Christianity who knows what it really is. The working men would still follow Christ if He came among them. As a matter of fact they do follow anyone, preacher or layman, in pulpit or on platform, who is the least like Him. But what they cannot follow, and must evermore live outside of, is a worship which ends with the worshipper, a religion expressed only in ceremony, and a faith unrelated to life.

Perhaps the most dismal fact of history is the failure of the great organized bodies of ecclesiasticism to understand the simple genius of Christ's religion. Whatever the best in the Churches of all time may have thought of the life and religion of Christ, taken as a whole they have succeeded in leaving upon the mind of a large portion of the world an impression of Christianity which is the direct opposite of the reality. Down to the present hour almost whole nations in Europe live, worship, and die under the belief that Christ is an ecclesiastical Christ, religion the sum of all the Churches' observances, and faith an adhesion to the Churches' creeds. I do not apportion blame; I simply record the fact. Everything that the spiritual and temporal authority of man could do has been done— done in ignorance of the true nature of Christianity—to dislodge the religion of Christ from its natural home in the heart of Humanity. In many lands the Churches have literally stolen Christ from the people; they have made the Son of Man the Priest of an Order; they have taken Christianity from the City and imprisoned it behind altar rails; they have withdrawn it from the national life and doled it out to the few who pay to keep the unconscious deception up.

Do not do the Church, the true Church at least, the injustice to think that she does not know all this. Nowhere, not even in the fiercest secular press, is there more exposure of this danger, more indignation at its continuance, than in many of the Churches of to-day. The protest against the confusion of Christianity with the Church is the most threadbare of pulpit themes. Before the University of Oxford, from the pulpit of St. Mary's, these words were lately spoken: "If it is strange that the Church of the darker ages should have needed so bitter a lesson (the actual demolition of their churches), is it not ten times stranger still that the Church of the days of greater enlightenment should be found again making the chief part of its business the organizing of the modes of worship; that the largest efforts which are owned as the efforts of the Church are made for the establishment and maintenance of worship; that our chief controversies relate to the teaching and the ministry of a system designed primarily, if not exclusively, for worship; that even the fancies and the refinements of such a system divide us; that the breach between things secular and things religious grows wider instead of their being made to blend into one; and that the vast and fruitful spaces of the actual life of mankind lie still so largely without the gates? The old Jerusalem was all temple. The mediaeval Church was all temple. But the ideal of the new Jerusalem was—no temple, but a God-inhabited society. Are we not reversing this ideal in an age when the church still means in so many mouths the clergy, instead of meaning the Christian society, and when nine men are striving to get men to go to church for one who is striving to make men realize that they themselves are the Church?"

Yet even with words so strong as these echoing daily from Protestant pulpits the superstition reigns in all but unbroken power. And everywhere still men are found confounding the spectacular services of a Church, the vicarious religion of a priest, and the traditional belief in a creed, with the living religion of the Son of Man.

"I saw no Temple there"—the future City will be a City without a Church. Ponder that fact, realize the temporariness of the Church, then—go and build one. Do not imagine, because all this has been said, that I mean to depreciate the Church. On the contrary, if it were mine to build a City, a City where all life should be religious, and all men destined to become members of the Body of Christ, the first stone I should lay there would be the foundation-stone of a Church Why? Because, among other reasons, the product which the Church on the whole best helps to develop, and in the largest quantity, is that which is most needed by the City.

For the present, and for a long time to come, the manufactory of good men, the nursery of the forces which are to redeem the City, will in the main be found to be some more or less formal, more or less imperfect, Christian Church. Here and there an unchurched soul may stir the multitudes to lofty deeds; isolated men; strong enough to preserve their souls apart from the Church, but shortsighted enough perhaps to fail to see that others cannot, may set high examples and stimulate to national reforms. But for the rank and file of us, made of such stuff as we are made of, the steady pressures of fixed institutions, the regular diets of a common worship, and the education of public Christian teaching are too obvious safeguards of spiritual culture to be set aside. Even Renan declares his conviction that "Beyond the family and outside the State, man has need of the Church ... Civil society, whether it calls itself a commune, a canton, or a province, a state, or fatherland, has many duties towards the improvement of the individual; but what it does is necessarily limited. The family ought to do much more, but often it is insufficient; sometimes it is wanting altogether. The association created in the name of moral principle can alone give to every man coming into this world a bond which unites him with the past, duties as to the future, examples to follow, a heritage to receive and to transmit, and a tradition of devotion to continue." Apart altogether from the quality of its contribution to society, in the mere quantity of the work it turns out it stands alone. Even for social purposes the Church is by far the greatest Employment Bureau in the world. And the man who, seeing where it falls short, withholds on that account his witness to its usefulness, is a traitor to history and to fact.

"The Church," as the preacher whom I have already quoted, most truly adds, "is a society which tends to embrace the whole life of mankind, to bind all their relations together by a Divine sanction. As such, it blends naturally with the institutions of common life—those institutions which, because they are natural and necessary, are therefore Divine. What it aims at is not the recognition by the nation of a worshipping body, governed by the ministers of public worship, which calls itself the Church, but that the nation and all classes in it should act upon Christian principle, that laws should be made in Christ's spirit of justice, that the relations of the powers of the state should be maintained on a basis of Christian equity, that all public acts should be done in Christ's spirit, and with mutual forbearance, that the spirit of Christian charity should be spread through all ranks and orders of the people. The Church will maintain public worship as one of the greatest supports of a Christian public life; but it will always remember that the true service is a life of devotion to God and man far more than the common utterance of prayer." I have said that were it mine to build a City, the first stone I should lay there would be the foundation-stone of a Church. But if it were mine to preach the first sermon in that Church, I should choose as the text, "I saw no Church therein." I should tell the people that the great use of the Church is to help men to do without it As the old ecclesiastical term has it, Church services are "diets" of worship. They are meals. All who are hungry will take them, and, if they are wise, regularly. But no workman is paid for his meals. He is paid for the work he does in the strength of them. No Christian is paid for going to Church. He goes there for a meal, for strength from God and from his fellow-worshippers to do the work of life —which is the work of Christ. The Church is a Divine institution because it is so very human an institution. As a channel of nourishment, as a stimulus to holy deeds, as a link with all holy lives, let all men use it, and to the utmost of their opportunity. But by all that they know of Christ or care for man, let them beware of mistaking its services for Christianity. What Church services really express is the want of Christianity. And when that which is perfect in Christianity is come, all this, as the mere passing stay and scaffolding of struggling souls, must vanish away.

If the masses who never go to Church only knew that the Churches were the mute expression of a Christian's wants and not the self-advertisement of his sanctity, they would have more respectful words for Churches. But they have never learned this. And the result in their case of confounding religion with the Church is even more serious than in the case of the professing Christian. When they break with the Church it means to them a break with all religion. As things are it could scarce be otherwise. With the Church in ceaseless evidence before their eyes as the acknowledged custodian of Christianity; with actual stone and lime in every street representing the place where religion dwells; with a professional class moving out and in among them, holding in their hands the souls of men, and almost the keys of Heaven—how is it possible that those who turn their backs on all this should not feel outcast from the Church's God? It is not possible. Without a murmur, yet with results to themselves most disastrous and pathetic, multitudes accept this false dividing-line and number themselves as excommunicate from all good. The masses will never return to the Church till its true relation to the City is more defined. And they can never have that most real life of theirs made religious so long as they rule themselves out of court on the ground that they have broken with ecclesiastical forms. The life of the masses is the most real of all lives. It is full of religious possibilities. Every movement of it and every moment of it might become of supreme religious value, might hold a continuous spiritual discipline, might perpetuate, and that in most natural ways, a moral influence which should pervade all Cities and all States. But they must first be taught what Christianity really is, and learn to distinguish between religion and the Church. After that, if they be taught their lesson well, they will return to honour both.

Our fathers made much of "meetness" for Heaven. By prayer and fasting, by self-examination and meditation they sought to fit themselves "for the inheritance of the saints in light." Important beyond measure in their fitting place are these exercises of the soul. But whether alone they fit men for the inheritance of the saints depends on what a saint is. If a saint is a devotee and not a citizen, if Heaven is a cathedral and not a City, then these things do fit for Heaven. But if life means action, and Heaven service; if spiritual graces are acquired for use and not for ornament, then devotional forms have a deeper function. The Puritan preachers were wont to tell their people to "practise dying." Yes; but what is dying? It is going to a City. And what is required of those who would go to a City? The practice of Citizenship—the due employment of the unselfish talents, the development of public spirit, the payment of the full tax to the great brotherhood, the subordination of personal aims to the common good. And where are these to be learned? Here; in Cities here. There is no other way to learn them. There is no Heaven to those who have not learned them.

No Church however holy, no priest however earnest, no book however sacred, can transfer to any human character the capacities of Citizenship—those capacities which in the very nature of things are necessities to those who would live in the kingdom of God. The only preparation which multitudes seem to make for Heaven is for its Judgment Bar. What will they do in its streets? What have they learned of Citizenship? What have they practised of love? How like are they to its Lord? To "practise dying" is to practise living. Earth is the rehearsal for Heaven. The eternal beyond is the eternal here. The street-life, the home-life, the business-life, the City-life in all the varied range of its activity, are an apprenticeship for the City of God. There is no other apprenticeship for it. To know how to serve Christ in these is to "practise dying."

To move among the people on the common street; to meet them in the market-place on equal terms; to live among them not as saint or monk, but as brother-man with brother-man; to serve God not with form or ritual, but in the free impulse of a soul; to bear the burdens of society and relieve its needs; to carry on the multitudinous activities of the City—social, commercial, political, philanthropic—in Christ's spirit and for His ends: this is the religion of the Son of Man, and the only meetness for Heaven which has much reality in it.

No Church however holy, no priest however earnest, no book however sacred, can transfer to any human character the capacities of Citizenship—those capacities which in the very nature of things are necessities to those who would live in the kingdom of God. The only preparation which multitudes seem to make for Heaven is for its Judgment Bar. What will they do in its streets? What have they learned of Citizenship? What have they practised of love? How like are they to its Lord? To "practise dying" is to practise living. Earth is the rehearsal for Heaven. The eternal beyond is the eternal here. The street-life, the home-life, the business-life, the City-life in all the varied range of its activity, are an apprenticeship for the City of God. There is no other apprenticeship for it. To know how to serve Christ in these is to "practise dying."

To move among the people on the common street; to meet them in the market-place on equal terms; to live among them not as saint or monk, but as brother-man with brother-man; to serve God not with form or ritual, but in the free impulse of a soul; to bear the burdens of society and relieve its needs; to carry on the multitudinous activities of the City—social, commercial, political, philanthropic—in Christ's spirit and for His ends: this is the religion of the Son of Man, and the only meetness for Heaven which has much reality in it.

No; the Church with all its splendid equipment, the cloister with all its holy opportunity, are not the final instruments for fitting men for Heaven. The City, in many of its functions, is a greater Church than the Church. It is amid the whirr of its machinery and in the discipline of its life that the souls of men are really made. How great its opportunity is we are few of us aware. It is such slow work getting better, the daily round is so very common, our ideas of a heavenly life are so unreal and mystical that even when the highest Heaven lies all around us, when we might touch it, and dwell in it every day we live, we almost fail to see that it is there. The Heaven of our childhood, the spectacular Heaven, the Heaven which is a place, so dominates thought even in our maturer years, that we are slow to learn the fuller truth that Heaven is a state. But John, who is responsible before all other teachers for the dramatic view of Heaven, has not failed in this very allegory to proclaim the further lesson. Having brought all his scenery upon the stage and pictured a material Heaven of almost unimaginable splendour, the seer turns aside before he closes for a revelation of a profounder kind. Within the Heavenly City he opens the gate of an inner Heaven. It is the spiritual Heaven—the Heaven of those who serve. With two flashes of his pen he tells the Citizens of God all that they will ever need or care to know as to what Heaven really means. "His servants shall serve Him; and they shall see His Face; and His Character shall be written on their characters."

They shall see His Face. Where? In the City. When? In Eternity? No; to-morrow. Those who serve in any City cannot help continually seeing Christ. He is there with them. He is there before them. They cannot but meet. No gentle word is ever spoken that Christ's voice does not also speak; no meek deed is ever done that the unsummoned Vision does not there and then appear. Whoso, in whatsoever place, receiveth a little child in My name receiveth Me.

This is how men get to know God—by doing His will. And there is no other way. And this is how men become like God; how God's character becomes written upon men's characters. Acts react upon souls. Good acts make good men; just acts, just men; kind acts, kind men; divine acts, divine men. And there is no other way of becoming good, just, kind, divine. And there is no Heaven for those who have not become these. For these are Heaven.

When John's Heaven faded from his sight, and the prophet woke to the desert waste of Patmos, did he grudge to exchange the Heaven of his dream for the common tasks around him? Was he not glad to be alive, and there? And would he not straightway go to the City, to whatever struggling multitude his prison-rock held, if so be that he might prove his dream and among them see His Face? Traveller to God's last City, be glad that you are alive. Be thankful for the City at your door and for the chance to build its walls a little nearer Heaven before you go. Pray for yet a little while to redeem the wasted years. And week by week as you go forth from worship, and day by day as you awake to face this great and needy world, learn to "seek a City" there, and in the service of its neediest citizen find Heaven.

Beautiful Thoughts From Henry Drummond

Arranged by Elizabeth Cureton

The invisible things of God from the creation of the world are clearly seen, being understood by the things that are made.—Rom. I. 20.

Preface

My first thought of writing out this little book of brief selections sprang from the desire to assist a dear friend to enjoy the Author's helpful books.

The epigrammatic style lends itself to quotation. Taste of the spring brings the traveler back to the same fountain on a day of greater leisure. Many times these "Beautiful Thoughts" have enlightened my darkness, and I send them forth with a hope and prayer that they may find echo in other hearts. E. C.

January 1st. Christianity wants nothing so much in the world as sunny people, and the old are hungrier for love than for bread, and the Oil of Joy is very cheap, and if you can help the poor on with a Garment of Praise it will be better for them than blankets. *The Program of Christianity.*

January 2d. No one who knows the content of Christianity, or feels the universal need of a Religion, can stand idly by while the intellect of his age is slowly divorcing itself from it. *Greatest Thing in the World.*

January 3d. A Science without mystery is unknown; a Religion without mystery is absurd. However far the scientific method may penetrate the Spiritual World, there will always remain a region to be explored by a scientific faith. *Greatest Thing in the World, Introduction.*

January 4th. Among the mysteries which compass the world beyond, none is greater than how there can be in store for man a work more wonderful, a life more God-like than this. *The Program of Christianity.*

January 5th. The Spiritual Life is the gift of the Living Spirit. The spiritual man is no mere development of the Natural man. He is a New Creation born from Above. *Greatest Thing in the World.*

January 6th. Love is success, Love is happiness, Love is life. God is Love. Therefore *love.* The *Greatest Thing in the World.*

January 7th. Give me the Charity which delights not in exposing the weakness of others, but "covereth all things." The *Greatest Thing in the World.*

January 8th. There is a sense of solidity about a Law of Nature which belongs to nothing else in the world. Here, at last, amid all that is shifting, is one thing sure; one thing outside ourselves, unbiased, unprejudiced, uninfluenced by like or dislike, by doubt or fear. . . . This more than anything else makes one eager to see the Reign of Law traced in the Spiritual Sphere. *Greatest Thing in the World,* Preface.

January 9th. With Nature as the symbol of all of harmony and beauty that is known to man, must we still talk of the supernatural, not as a convenient word, but as a different order of world, . . . where the Reign of Mystery supersedes the Reign of Law? *Greatest Thing in the World, Introduction.,*

January 10th. The Reign of Law has gradually crept into every department of Nature, transforming knowledge everywhere into Science. The process goes on, and Nature slowly appears to us as one great unity, until the borders of the Spiritual World are reached. *Greatest Thing in the World.*

January 11th. No single fact in Science has ever discredited a fact in Religion. *Greatest Thing in the World.*

January 12th. I shall never rise to the point of view which wishes to "raise" faith to knowledge. To me, the way of truth is to come through the knowledge of my ignorance to the submissiveness of faith, and then, making that my starting-place, to raise my knowledge into faith. *Greatest Thing in the World.*

January 13th. If the purification of Religion comes from Science, the purification of Science, in a deeper sense, shall come from Religion. *Greatest Thing in the World.*

January 14th. With the demonstration of the naturalness of the supernatural, scepticism even may come to be regarded as unscientific. And those who have wrestled long for a few bare truths to ennoble life and rest their souls in thinking of the future will not be left in doubt. *Greatest Thing in the World.*

January 15th. The religion of Jesus has probably always suffered more from those who have misunderstood than from those who have opposed it. *Greatest Thing in the World..*

January 16th. It is impossible to believe that the amazing successions of revelations in the domain of Nature, during the last few centuries, at which the world has all but grown tired wondering, are to yield nothing for the higher life. *Greatest Thing in the World*

January 17th. Is life not full of opportunities for learning love? Every man and woman every day has a thousand of them. *Greatest Thing in the World.*

January 18th. What is Science but what the Natural World has said to natural men? What is Revelation but what the Spiritual World has said to Spiritual men? *Greatest Thing in the World.*

January 19th. Life depends upon contact with Life. It cannot spring up out of itself. It cannot develop out of anything that is not Life. There is no Spontaneous Generation in religion any more than in Nature. Christ is the source of Life in the Spiritual World; and he that hath the Son hath Life, and he that hath not the Son, whatever else he may have, hath not Life. *Greatest Thing in the World.*

January 20th. It is a wonderful thing that here and there in this hard, uncharitable world, there should still be left a few rare souls who think no evil. *Greatest Thing in the World.*

January 21st. The physical Laws may explain the inorganic world; the biological Laws may account for the development of the organic. But of the point where they meet, of that strange borderland between the dead and the living, Science is silent. It is as if God had placed everything in earth and heaven in the hands of Nature, but reserved a point at the genesis of Life for His direct appearing. *Greatest Thing in the World.*

January 22d. Except a mineral be born "from above"—from the Kingdom just *above* it—it cannot enter the Kingdom just above it. And except a man be born "from above," by the same law, he cannot enter the Kingdom just above him. *Greatest Thing in the World.*

January 23d. If we try to influence or elevate others, we shall soon see that success is in proportion to their belief of our belief in them. *Greatest Thing in the World.*

January 24th. The world is not a play-ground; it is a school-room. Life is not a holiday, but an education. And the one eternal lesson for us all is how better we can love. *Greatest Thing in the World.*

January 25th What a noble gift it is, the power of playing upon the souls and wills of men, and rousing them to lofty purposes and holy deeds. *Greatest Thing in the World.*

January 26th. The test of Religion, the final test of Religion, is not Religiousness, but Love. *Greatest Thing in the World.*

January 27th. There are not two laws of *Bio-genesis*, one for the natural, the other for the Spiritual; one law is for both. Where-ever there is Life, Life of any kind, this same law holds. *Greatest Thing in the World.*

January 28th. The first step in peopling these worlds with the appropriate living forms is virtually miracle. Nor in one case is there less of mystery in the act than in the other. The second birth is scarcely less perplexing to the theologian than the first to the embryologist. *Greatest Thing in the World.*

January 29th. There may be cases—they are probably in the majority— where the moment of contact with the Living Spirit, though sudden, has been obscure. But the real moment and the conscious moment are two different things. Science pronounces nothing as to the conscious moment. If it did, it would probably say that that was seldom the real moment— The moment of birth in the natural world is not a conscious moment—we do not know we are born till long afterward. *Greatest Thing in the World.*

January 30th. The stumbling-block to most minds is perhaps less the mere existence of the unseen than the want of definition, the apparently hopeless vagueness, and not least, the delight in this vagueness as mere vagueness by some who look upon this as the mark of quality in Spiritual things. It will be at least something to tell earnest seekers that the Spiritual World is not a castle in the air, of an architecture unknown to earth or heaven, but a fair ordered realm furnished with many familiar things and ruled by well-remembered Laws. *Greatest Thing in the World*

January 31st. Character grows in the stream of the world's life. That chiefly is where men are to learn love. *The Greatest Thing in the World.*

February 1st. If a man does not exercise his arm he develops no biceps muscle; and if a man does not exercise his soul, he acquires no muscle in his soul, no strength of character, no vigor of moral fibre, nor beauty of Spiritual growth. *The Greatest Thing in the World.*

February 2d. A Religion without mystery is an absurdity. Even Science has its mysteries, none more inscrutable than around this Science of Life. It taught us sooner or later to expect mystery, and now we enter its domain. Let it be carefully marked, however, that the cloud does not fall and cover us till we have ascertained the most momentous truth of Religion— that Christ is in the Christian. *Greatest Thing in the World.*

February 3d. Religion in having mystery is in analogy with all around it. Where there is exceptional mystery in the Spiritual World it will generally be found that there is a corresponding mystery in the natural world. *Greatest Thing in the World.*

February 4th. Even to earnest minds the difficulty of grasping the truth at all has always proved extreme. Philosophically, one scarcely sees either the necessity or the possibility of being born again. Why a virtuous man should not simply grow better and better until in his own right he enter the Kingdom of God is what thousands honestly and seriously fail to understand. *Greatest Thing in the World.*

February 5th. Lavish Love upon our equals, where it is very difficult, and for whom perhaps we each do least of all. *The Greatest Thing in the World.*

February 6th. Spiritual Life is not something outside ourselves. The idea is not that Christ is in heaven and that we can stretch out some mysterious faculty and deal with Him there. This is the vague form in which many conceive the truth, but it is contrary to Christ's teaching and to the analogy of nature. Life is definite and resident; and Spiritual Life is not a visit from a force, but a resident tenant in the soul. *Greatest Thing in the World.*

February 7th. If we neglect almost any of the domestic animals, they will rapidly revert to wild and worthless forms. Now, the same thing exactly would happen in the case of you or me. Why should man be an exception to any of the laws of nature? *Greatest Thing in the World, Degeneration.*

February 8th. The law of Reversion to Type runs through all creation. If a man neglect himself for a few years he will change into a worse and a lower man. If it is his body that he neglects, he will deteriorate into a wild and bestial savage. . . . If it is his mind, it will degenerate into imbecility and madness. . . . If he neglect his conscience, it will run off into lawlessness and vice. Or, lastly, if it is his soul, it must inevitably atrophy, drop off in ruin and decay. *Greatest Thing in the World.*

February 9th. Three possibilities of life, according to Science, are open to all living organisms—Balance, Evolution, and Degeneration. *Greatest Thing in the World.*

February 10th. The life of Balance is difficult. It lies on the verge of continual temptation, its perpetual adjustments become fatiguing, its measured virtue is monotonous and uninspiring. *Greatest Thing in the World.*

February 11th. More difficult still, apparently, is the life of ever upward growth. Most men attempt it for a time, but growth is slow; and despair overtakes them while the goal is far away. *Greatest Thing in the World.*

February 12th. Degeneration is easy. Why is it easy? Why but that already in each man's very nature this principle is supreme? He feels within his soul a silent drifting motion impelling him downward with irresistible force. *Greatest Thing in the World.*

February 13th. This is Degeneration—that principle by which the organism, failing to develop itself, failing even to keep what it has got, deteriorates, and becomes more and more adapted to a degraded form of life. *Greatest Thing in the World.*

February 14th. It is a distinct fact by itself, which we can hold and examine separately, that on purely natural principles the soul that is left to itself unwatched, uncultivated, unredeemed, must fall away into death by its own nature. *Greatest Thing in the World.*

February 15th. If a man find the power of sin furiously at work within him, dragging his whole life downward to destruction, there is only one way to escape his fate—to take resolute hold of the upward power, and be borne by it to the opposite goal. *Greatest Thing in the World.*

February 16th. Neglect does more for the soul than make it miss salvation. It despoils it of its capacity for salvation. *Greatest Thing in the World.*

February 17th. Give pleasure. Lose no chance in giving pleasure. For that is the ceaseless and anonymous triumph of a truly loving spirit. *Greatest Thing in the World.*

February 18th. If there were uneasiness there might be hope. If there were, somewhere about our soul, a something which was not gone to sleep like all the rest; if there were a contending force anywhere; if we would let even that work instead of neglecting it, it would gain strength from hour to hour, and waken up, one at a time, each torpid and dishonored faculty, till our whole nature became alive with strivings against self, and every avenue was open wide for God. *Greatest Thing in the World.*

February 19th. Where is the capacity for heaven to come from if it be not developed on earth? Where, indeed, is even the smallest appreciation of God and heaven to come from when so little of spirituality has ever been known or manifested here? *Greatest Thing in the World.*

February 20th. Men tell us sometimes there is no such thing as an atheist. There must be. There are some men to whom it is true that there is no God. They cannot see God because they have no eye. They have only an abortive organ, atrophied by neglect. *Greatest Thing in the World.*

February 21st. Escape means nothing more than the gradual emergence of the higher being from the lower, and nothing less. It means the gradual putting off of all that cannot enter the higher state, or heaven, and simultaneously the putting on of Christ. It involves the slow completing of the soul and the development of the capacity for God. *Greatest Thing in the World.*

February 22d. If, then, escape is to be open to us, it is not to come to us somehow, vaguely. We are not to hope for anything startling or mysterious. It is a definite opening along certain lines which are definitely marked by God, which begin at the Cross of Christ, and lead direct to Him. *Greatest Thing in the World.*

February 23d. Each man, in the silence of his own soul, must work out this salvation for himself with fear and trembling—with fear, realizing the momentous issues of his task; with trembling, lest, before the tardy work be done, the voice of Death should summon him to stop. *Greatest Thing in the World.*

February 24th. So cultivate the soul that all its powers will open out to God, and in beholding God be drawn away from sin. *Greatest Thing in the World.*

February 25th. There is a Sense of Sight in the religious nature. Neglect this, leave it undeveloped, and you never miss it. You simply see nothing. But develop it and you see God. *Greatest Thing in the World.*

February 26th. Become pure in heart. The pure in heart shall see God. Here, then, is one opening for soul-culture—the avenue through purity of heart to the spiritual seeing of God. *Greatest Thing in the World.*

February 27th. There is a Sense of Sound. Neglect this, leave it undeveloped, and you never miss it. Develop it, and you hear God. And the line along which to develop it is known to us. Obey Christ. *Greatest Thing in the World.*

February 28th He who loves will rejoice in the Truth, rejoice not in what he has been taught to believe; not in this Church's doctrine or in that; not in this issue, or in that issue; but "in the Truth." He will accept only what is real; he will strive to get at facts; he will search for Truth with a humble and unbiased mind, and cherish whatever he finds at any sacrifice. *The Greatest Thing in the World.*

March 1st. "Consider the lilies of the field how they grow." Christ made the lilies and He made me—both on the same broad principle. Both together, man and flower . . .; but as men are dull at studying themselves. He points to this companion-phenomenon to teach us how to live a free and natural life, a life which God will unfold for us, without our anxiety, as He unfolds the flower. *The Greatest Thing in the World.*

March 2d. Our efforts after Christian growth seem only a succession of failures, and, instead of rising into the beauty of holiness, our life is a daily heart-break and humiliation. *The Greatest Thing in the World.*

March 3d. The lilies grow, Christ says, of themselves; they toil not, neither do they spin. They grow, that is, automatically, spontaneously, without trying, without fretting, without thinking. *The Greatest Thing in the World.*

March 4th. Violent efforts to grow are right in earnestness, but wholly wrong in principle. There is but one principle of growth both for the natural and spiritual, for animal and plant, for body and soul. For all growth is an organic thing. And the principle of growing in grace is once more this, "Consider the lilies how they grow." *The Greatest Thing in the World.*

March 5th. Earnest souls who are attempting sanctification by struggle, instead of sanctification by faith, might be spared much humiliation by learning the botany of the Sermon on the Mount. *The Greatest Thing in the World.*

March 6th. There is only one thing greater than happiness in the world, and that is holiness; and it is not in our keeping; but what God *has* put in our power is the happiness of those about us, and that is largely to be secured by our being kind to them. *The Greatest Thing in the World.*

March 7th. We have all felt the brazenness of words without emotion, the hollowness, the unaccountable unpersuasiveness of eloquence behind which lies no love. *The Greatest Thing in the World.*

March 8th. Patience; kindness; generosity; humility; courtesy; unselfishness; good-temper; guilelessness; sincerity—these make up the supreme gift, the stature of the perfect man. *The Greatest Thing in the World.*

March 9th. We hear much of love to God; Christ spoke much of love to man. We make a great deal of peace with heaven; Christ spoke much of peace on earth. *The Greatest Thing in the World.*

March 10th. If God is spending work upon a Christian, let him be still and know that it is God. And if he wants work, he will find it there—in the being still. *The Greatest Thing in the World.*

March 11th. If the amount of energy lost in trying to grow were spent in fulfilling rather the conditions of growth, we should have many more cubits to show for our stature. *The Greatest Thing in the World.*

March 12th. The conditions of growth, then, and the inward principle of growth being both supplied by Nature, the thing man has to do, the little junction left for him to complete, is to apply the one to the other. He manufactures nothing; he earns nothing; he need be anxious for nothing; his one duty is to be IN these conditions, to abide in them, to allow grace to play over him, to be still and know that this is God. *The Greatest Thing in the World.*

March 13th. A man will often have to wrestle with his God—but not for growth. The Christian life is a composed life. The Gospel is Peace. Yet the most anxious people in the world are Christians—Christians who misunderstand the nature of growth. Life is a perpetual self-condemning because they are not growing. *The Greatest Thing in the World.*

March 14th. All the work of the world is merely a taking advantage of energies already there. *The Greatest Thing in the World.*

March 15th. Religion is not a strange or added thing; but the inspiration of the secular life, the breathing of an eternal spirit through this temporal world. *The Greatest Thing in the World.*

March 16th. The stature of the Lord Jesus was not itself reached by work, and he who thinks to approach its mystical height by anxious effort is really receding from it. *The Greatest Thing in the World.*

March 17th. For the Life must develop out according to its type; and being a germ of the Christ-life, it must unfold into a Christ. *The Greatest Thing in the World.*

March 18th. The sneer at the godly man for his imperfections is ill-judged. A blade is a small thing. At first it grows very near the earth. It is often soiled and crushed and downtrodden. But it is a living thing,. . . and "it doth not yet appear what it shall be." *The Greatest Thing in the World.*

March 19th. Christ's protest is not against work, but against anxious thought. *The Greatest Thing in the World.*

March 20th. If God is adding to our spiritual stature, unfolding the new nature within us, it is a mistake to keep twitching at the petals with our coarse fingers. We must seek to let the Creative Hand alone. "It is God which giveth the increase." *The Greatest Thing in the World.*

March 21st. Love is *patience*. This is the normal attitude of Love; Love passive, Love waiting to begin; not in a hurry; calm; ready to do its work when the summons comes, but meantime wearing the ornament of a meek and quiet spirit. *The Greatest Thing in the World.*

March 22d. Have you ever noticed how much of Christ's life was spent in doing kind things? *The Greatest Thing in the World.*

March 23d. I wonder why it is we are not all kinder than we are! How much the world needs it. How easily it is done. How instantaneously it acts. How infallibly it is remembered. How superabundantly it pays itself back —for there is no debtor in the world so honorable, so superbly honorable as Love. *The Greatest Thing in the World.*

March 24th. To love abundantly is to live abundantly, and to love forever is to live forever. Hence, eternal life is inextricably bound up with love. *The Greatest Thing in the World.*

March 25th. Man is a mass of correspondences, and because of these, because he is alive to countless objects and influences to which lower organisms are dead, he is the most living of all creatures. *The Greatest Thing in the World.*

March 26th. All organisms are living and dead—living to all within the circumference of their correspondences, dead to all beyond. . . . Until man appears there is no organism to correspond with the whole environment. *The Greatest Thing in the World.*

March 27th. Is man in correspondence with the whole environment or is he not? . . . He is not. Of men generally it cannot be said that they are in living contact with that part of the environment which is called the spiritual world. *The Greatest Thing in the World.*

March 28th. The animal world and the plant world are the same world. They are different parts of one environment. And the natural and spiritual are likewise one. *The Greatest Thing in the World.*

March 29th. What we have correspondence with, that we call natural; what we have little or no correspondence with, that we call Spiritual. *The Greatest Thing in the World.*

March 30th. Those who are in communion with God live, those who are not are dead. *The Greatest Thing in the World.*

March 31st. This earthly mind may be of noble caliber, enriched by culture, high-toned, virtuous, and pure. But if it know not God? What though its correspondences reach to the stars of heaven or grasp the magnitudes of Time and Space? The stars of heaven are not heaven. Space is not God. *The Greatest Thing in the World.*

April 1st. We do not picture the possessor of this carnal mind as in any sense a monster. We have said he may be high-toned, virtuous, and pure. The plant is not a monster because it is dead to the voice of the bird; nor is he a monster who is dead to the voice of God. The contention at present simply is that he is *dead*. *The Greatest Thing in the World.*

April 2d. What is the creed of the Agnostic, but the confession of the spiritual numbness of humanity? *The Greatest Thing in the World.*

April 3d. The nescience of the Agnostic philosophy is the proof from experience that to be carnally minded is Death. *Greatest Thing in the World.*

April 4th. The Christian apologist never further misses the mark than when he refuses the testimony of the Agnostic to himself. When the Agnostic tells me he is blind and deaf, dumb, torpid, and dead to the spiritual world, I must believe him. Jesus tells me that. Paul tells me that. Science tells me that. He knows nothing of this outermost circle; and we are compelled to trust his sincerity as readily when he deplores it as if, being a man without an ear, he professed to know nothing of a musical world, or being without taste, of a world of art. *The Greatest Thing in the World.*

April 5th. It brings no solace to the unspiritual man to be told he is mistaken. To say he is self-deceived is neither to compliment him nor Christianity. He builds in all sincerity who raises his altar to the *unknown* God. He does not know God. With all his marvelous and complex correspondences, he is still one correspondence short. *The Greatest Thing in the World.*

April 6th. Only one thing truly need the Christian envy, the large, rich, generous soul which "envieth not." *The Greatest Thing in the World.*

April 7th. Whenever you attempt a good work you will find other men doing the same kind of work, and probably doing it better. Envy them not. *The Greatest Thing in the World.*

April 8th. I say that man believes in a God, who feels himself in the presence of a Power which is not himself, and is immeasurably above himself, a Power in the contemplation of which he is absorbed, in the knowledge of which he finds safety and happiness. *The Greatest Thing in the World.*

April 9th. What men deny is not a God. It is the correspondence. The very confession of the Unknowable is itself the dull recognition of an Environment beyond themselves, and for which they feel they lack the correspondence. It is this want that makes their God the Unknown God. And it is this that makes them *dead. The Greatest Thing in the World.*

April 10th. God is not confined to the outermost circle of environment, He lives and moves and has His being in the whole. Those who only seek Him in the further zone can only find a part. The Christian who knows not God in Nature, who does not, that is to say, correspond with the whole environment, most certainly is partially dead. *The Greatest Thing in the World.*

April 11th. After you have been kind, after Love has stolen forth into the world and done its beautiful work, go back into the shade again and say nothing about it. *The Greatest Thing in the World.*

April 12th. The absence of the true Light means moral Death. The darkness of the natural world to the intellect is not all. What history testifies to is, first the partial, and then the total eclipse of virtue that always follows the abandonment of belief in a personal God. *The Greatest Thing in the World.*

April 13th. The only greatness is unselfish love . . . a great difference between *trying to please* and *giving pleasure*. *The Greatest Thing in the World.*

April 14th. The conception of a God gives an altogether new color to worldliness and vice. Worldliness it changes into heathenism, vice into blasphemy. The carnal mind, the mind which is turned away from God, which will not correspond with God—this is not moral only but spiritual Death. And Sin, that which separates from God, which disobeys God, which can not in that state correspond with God—this is hell. *The Greatest Thing in the World.*

April 15th. If sin is estrangement from God, this very estrangement is Death. It is a want of correspondence. If sin is selfishness, it is conducted at the expense of life. Its wages are Death—"he that loveth his life," said Christ, "shall lose it." *The Greatest Thing in the World.*

April 16th. Obviously if the mind turns away from one part of the environment it will only do so under some temptation to correspond with another. This temptation, at bottom, can only come from one source—the love of self. The irreligious man's correspondences are concentrated upon himself. He worships himself. Self-gratification rather than self-denial; independence rather than submission—these are the rules of life. And this is at once the poorest and the commonest form of idolatry. *Greatest Thing in the World.*

April 17th. You will find . . . that the people who influence you are people who believe in you. *The Greatest Thing in the World.*

April 18th. The development of any organism in any direction is dependent on its environment. A living cell cut off from air will die. A seed-germ apart from moisture and an appropriate temperature will make the ground its grave for centuries. Human nature, likewise, is subject to similar conditions. It can only develop in presence of its environment. No matter what its possibilities may be, no matter what seeds of thought or virtue, what germs of genius or of art, lie latent in its breast, until the appropriate environment present itself the correspondence is denied, the development discouraged, the most splendid possibilities of life remain unrealized, and thought and virtue, genius and art, are dead. *Greatest Thing in the World.*

April 19th. The true environment of the moral life is God. Here conscience wakes. Here kindles love. Duty here becomes heroic; and that righteousness begins to live which alone is to live forever. But if this Atmosphere is not, the dwarfed soul must perish for mere want of its native air. And its Death is a strictly natural Death. It is not an exceptional judgment upon Atheism. In the same circumstances, in the same averted relation to their environment, the poet, the musician, the artist, would alike perish to poetry, to music, and to art. *Greatest Thing in the World.*

April 20th. Every environment is a cause. Its effect upon me is exactly proportionate to my correspondence with it. If I correspond with part of it, part of myself is influenced. If I correspond with more, more of myself is influenced; if with all, all is influenced. If I correspond with the world, I become worldly; if with God, I become Divine. *The Greatest Thing in the World.*

April 21st. You can dwarf a soul just as you can dwarf a plant, by depriving it of a full environment. Such a soul for a time may have a "name to live." Its character may betray no sign of atrophy. But its very virtue somehow has the pallor of a flower that is grown in darkness, or as the herb which has never seen the sun, no fragrance breathes from its spirit. *Greatest Thing in the World.*

April 22d. I shall pass through this world but once. Any good thing, therefore, that I can do, or any kindness that I can show to any human being, let me do it now. Let me not defer it or neglect it, for I shall not pass this way again. *The Greatest Thing in the World.*

April 23d. There is no happiness in having and getting, but only in giving . . . half the world is on the wrong scent in the pursuit of happiness. *The Greatest Thing in the World.*

April 24th. No form of vice, not worldliness, not greed of gold, not drunkenness itself, does more to un-Christianize society than evil temper. *The Greatest Thing in the World.*

April 25th. How many prodigals are kept out of the Kingdom of God by the unlovely character of those who profess to be inside! *The Greatest Thing in the World.*

April 26th. A want of patience, a want of kindness, a want of generosity, a want of courtesy, a want of unselfishness, are all instantaneously symbolized in one flash of Temper. *The Greatest Thing in the World.*

April 27th. Souls are made sweet not by taking the acid fluids out, but by putting something in—a great Love, a new Spirit—the Spirit of Christ. *The Greatest Thing in the World.*

April 28th. Christ, the Spirit of Christ, interpenetrating ours, sweetens, purifies, transforms all. This only can eradicate what is wrong, work a chemical change, renovate and regenerate, and rehabilitate the inner man. Will-power does not change men. Time does not change men. Christ does. *The Greatest Thing in the World.*

April 29th Guilelessness is the grace for suspicious people. And the possession of it is the great secret of personal influence. You will find, if you think for a moment, that the people who influence you are people who believe in you. In an atmosphere of suspicion men shrivel up; but in that atmosphere they expand, and find encouragement and educative fellowship. *The Greatest Thing in the World.*

April 30th. Do not quarrel . . . with your lot in life. Do not complain of its never-ceasing cares, its petty environment, the vexations you have to stand, the small and sordid souls you have to live and work with. *The Greatest Thing in the World.*

May 1st. The moment the new life is begun there comes a genuine anxiety to break with the old. For the former environment has now become embarrassing. It refuses its dismissal from consciousness. It competes doggedly with the new Environment for a share of the correspondences. And in a hundred ways the former traditions, the memories and passions of the past, the fixed associations and habits of the earlier life, now complicate the new relation. The complex and bewildered soul, in fact, finds itself in correspondence with two environments, each with urgent but yet incompatible claims. It is a dual soul living in a double world, a world whose inhabitants are deadly enemies, and engaged in perpetual civil war. *The Greatest Thing in the World.*

May 2d. How can the New Life deliver itself from the still-persistent past? A ready solution of the difficulty would be *to die*. . . . If we cannot die altogether, . . . the most we can do is to die as much as we can. . . . To die to any environment is to withdraw correspondence with it, to cut ourselves off, so far as possible, from all communication with it. So that the solution of the problem will simply be this, for the spiritual life to reverse continuously the processes of the natural life. *The Greatest Thing in the World.*

May 3d. The spiritual man having passed from Death unto Life, the natural man must next proceed to pass from Life unto Death. Having opened the new set of correspondences, he must deliberately close up the old. Regeneration in short must be accompanied by Degeneration. *The Greatest Thing in the World.*

May 4th. The peculiar feature of Death by Suicide is that it is not only self-inflicted but sudden. And there are many sins which must either be dealt with suddenly or not at all. *The Greatest Thing in the World.*

May 5th. If the Christian is to "live unto God," he must "die unto sin." If he does not kill sin, sin will inevitably kill him. Recognizing this, he must set himself to reduce the number of his correspondences— retaining and developing those which lead to a fuller life, unconditionally withdrawing those which in any way tend in an opposite direction. This stoppage of correspondences is a voluntary act, a crucifixion of the flesh, a suicide. *The Greatest Thing in the World.*

May 6th. Do not resent temptation; do not be perplexed because it seems to thicken round you more and more, and ceases neither for effort nor for agony nor prayer. That is your practice. That is the practice which God appoints you; and it is having its work in making you patient, and humble, and generous, and unselfish, and kind, and courteous. *The Greatest Thing in the World.*

May 7th. It is a peculiarity of the sinful state, that as a general rule men are linked to evil mainly by a single correspondence. Few men break the whole law. Our natures, fortunately, are not large enough to make us guilty of all, and the restraints of circumstances are usually such as to leave a loophole in the life of each individual for only a single habitual sin. But it is very easy to see how this reduction of our intercourse with evil to a single correspondence blinds us to our true position. *The Greatest Thing in the World.*

May 8th. One little weakness, we are apt to fancy, all men must be allowed, and we even claim a certain indulgence for that apparent necessity of nature which we call our besetting sin. Yet to break with the lower environment at all, to many, is to break at this single point. *Greatest Thing in the World.*

May 9th. There may be only one avenue between the new life and the old, it may be but a small and *subterranean passage*, but this is sufficient to keep the old life in. So long as that remains the victim is not "dead unto sin," and therefore he cannot "live unto God." *Greatest Thing in the World.*

May 10th. Do not grudge the hand that is molding the still too shapeless image within you. It is growing more beautiful, though you see it not, and every touch of temptation may add to its perfection. Therefore keep in the midst of life. Do not isolate yourself. Be among men, and among things, and among troubles, and difficulties, and obstacles. *The Greatest Thing in the World.*

May 11th. Contemplate the love of Christ, and you will love. Stand before that mirror, reflect Christ's character, and you will be changed into the same image from tenderness to tenderness. There is no other way. You cannot love to order. You can only look at the lovely object, and fall in love with it, and grow into likeness to it. *The Greatest Thing in the World.*

May 12th. In the natural world it only requires a single vital correspondence of the body to be out of order to ensure Death. It is not necessary to have consumption, diabetes, and an aneurism to bring the body to the grave, if it have heart disease. He who is fatally diseased in one organ necessarily pays the penalty with his life, though all the others be in perfect health. And such, likewise, are the mysterious unity and correlation of functions in the spiritual organism that the disease of one member may involve the ruin of the whole. *The Greatest Thing in the World*, p. 187.

May 13th. To break altogether, and at every point, with the old environment, is a simple impossibility. So long as the regenerate man is kept in this world he must find the old environment at many points a severe temptation. *The Greatest Thing in the World.*

May 14th. Power over very many of the commonest temptations is only to be won by degrees, and however anxious one might be to apply the summary method to every case, he soon finds it impossible in practice. *The Greatest Thing in the World.*

May 15th. The ill-tempered person ... can make very little of his environment. However he may attempt to circumscribe it in certain directions, there will always remain a wide and ever-changing area to stimulate his irascibility. His environment, in short, is an inconstant quantity, and his most elaborate calculations and precautions must often and suddenly fail him. *The Greatest Thing in the World.*

May 16th. What the ill-tempered person has to deal with, ... mainly, is the correspondence, the temper itself. And that, he well knows, involves a long and humiliating discipline. The case is not at all a surgical but a medical one, and the knife is here of no more use than in a fever. A specific irritant has poisoned his veins. And the acrid humors that are breaking out all over the surface of his life are only to be subdued by a gradual sweetening of the inward spirit. *The Greatest Thing in the World.*

May 17th. The man whose blood is pure has nothing to fear. So he whose spirit is purified and sweetened becomes proof against these germs of sin. "Anger, wrath, malice and railing" in such a soil can find no root. *The Greatest Thing in the World.*

May 18th. The Mortification of a member . . .is based on the Law of Degeneration. The useless member here is not cut off, but simply relieved as much as possible of all exercise. This encourages the gradual decay of the parts, and as it is more and more neglected it ceases to be a channel for life at all. So an organism "mortifies" its members. *The Greatest Thing in the World.*

May 19th. Man's spiritual life consists in the number and fulness of his correspondences with God. In order to develop these he may be constrained to insulate them, to enclose them from the other correspondences, to shut himself in with them. In many ways the limitation of the natural life is the necessary condition of the full enjoyment of the spiritual life. *The Greatest Thing in the World.*

May 20th. No man is called to a life of self-denial for its own sake. It is in order to a compensation which, though sometimes difficult to see, is always real and always proportionate. No truth, perhaps, in practical religion is more lost sight of. We cherish somehow a lingering rebellion against the doctrine of self-denial—as if our nature, or our circumstances, or our conscience, dealt with us severely in loading us with the daily cross. But is it not plain after all that the life of self-denial is the more abundant life—more abundant just in proportion to the ampler crucifixion of the narrower life? Is it not a clear case of exchange—an exchange, however, where the advantage is entirely on our side? We give up a correspondence in which there is a little life to enjoy a correspondence in which there is an abundant life. What though we sacrifice a hundred such correspondences? We make but the more room for the great one that is left. *The Greatest Thing in the World.*

May 21st. Do not spoil your life at the outset with unworthy and impoverishing correspondences; and if it is growing truly rich and abundant, be very jealous of ever diluting its high eternal quality with anything of earth. *The Greatest Thing in the World.*

May 22d. To concentrate upon a few great correspondences, to oppose to the death the perpetual petty larceny of our life by trifles—these are the conditions for the highest and happiest life.... The penalty of evading self-denial also is just that we get the lesser instead of the larger good. The punishment of sin is inseparably bound up with itself. *The Greatest Thing in the World.*

May 23d. Each man has only a certain amount of life, of time, of attention—a definite measurable quantity. If he gives any of it to this life solely it is wasted. Therefore Christ says, Hate life, limit life, lest you steal your love for it from something that deserves it more. *The Greatest Thing in the World.*

May 24th. To refuse to deny one's self is just to be left with the self undented. When the balance of life is struck, the self will be found still there. The discipline of life was meant to destroy this self, but that discipline having been evaded—and we all to some extent have opportunities, and too often exercise them, of taking the narrow path by the shortest cuts—its purpose is baulked. But the soul is the loser. In seeking to gain its life it has really lost it. *The Greatest Thing in the World.*

May 25th. Suppose we deliberately made up our minds as to what things we were henceforth to allow to become our life? Suppose we selected a given area of our environment and determined once for all that our correspondences should go to that alone, fencing in this area all round with a morally impassable wall? True, to others, we should seem to live a poorer life; they would see that our environment was circumscribed, and call us narrow because it was narrow. But, well-chosen, this limited life would be really the fullest life; it would be rich in the highest and worthiest, and poor in the smallest and basest, correspondences. *The Greatest Thing in the World.*

May 26th. The well-defined spiritual life is not only the highest life, but it is also the most easily lived. The whole cross is more easily carried than the half. It is the man who tries to make the best of both worlds who makes nothing of either. And he who seeks to serve two masters misses the benediction of both. *The Greatest Thing in the World.*

May 27th. You will find, as you look back upon your life, that the moments that stand out, the moments when you have really lived, are the moments when you have done things in a spirit of love. As memory scans the past, above and beyond all the transitory pleasures of life, there leap forward those supreme hours when you have been enabled to do unnoticed kindnesses to those round about you, things too trifling to speak about, but which you feel have entered into your eternal life. *The Greatest Thing in the World.*

May 28th. No man can become a saint in his sleep; and to fulfil the condition required demands a certain amount of prayer and meditation and time, just as improvement in any direction, bodily or mental, requires preparation and care. Address yourselves to that one thing; at any cost have this transcendent character exchanged for yours. *The Greatest Thing in the World.*

May 29th. He who has taken his stand, who has drawn a boundary line, sharp and deep, about his religious life, who has marked off all beyond as for ever forbidden ground to him, finds the yoke easy and the burden light. For this forbidden environment comes to be as if it were not. His faculties falling out of correspondence, slowly lose their sensibilities. And the balm of Death numbing his lower nature releases him for the scarce disturbed communion of a higher life. So even here to die is gain. *The Greatest Thing in the World.*

May 30th. Remain side by side with Him who loved us, and gave Himself for us, and you too will become a permanent magnet, a permanently attractive force; and like Him you will draw all men unto you, like Him you will be drawn unto all men. That is the inevitable effect of Love. Any man who fulfils that cause must have that effect produced in him. *The Greatest Thing in the World.*

May 31st. Try to give up the idea that religion comes to us by chance, or by mystery, or by caprice. It comes to us by *Greatest Thing in the World*, or by super*Greatest Thing in the World*, for all law is Divine. *The Greatest Thing in the World.*

June 1st. We love others, we love everybody, we love our enemies, because He first loved us. . . . And that is how the love of God melts down the unlovely heart in man, and begets in him the new creature, who is patient and humble and gentle and unselfish. *The Greatest Thing in the World.*

June 2d. The belief in Science as an aid to faith is not yet ripe enough to warrant men in searching there for witnesses to the highest Christian truths. The inspiration of Nature, it is thought, extends to the humbler doctrines alone. And yet the reverent inquirer who guides his steps in the right direction may find even now, in the still dim twilight of the scientific world, much that will illuminate and intensify his sublimest faith. *Greatest Thing in the World.*

June 3d. Life becomes fuller and fuller, richer and richer, more and more sensitive and responsive to an ever-widening Environment as we rise in the chain of being. *The Greatest Thing in the World.*

June 4th. Before we reach an Eternal Life we must pass beyond that point at which all ordinary correspondences inevitably cease. We must find an organism so high and complex, that at some point in its development it shall have added a correspondence which organic death is powerless to arrest. *The Greatest Thing in the World.*

June 5th. Uninterrupted correspondence with a perfect Environment is Eternal Life, according to Science. "This is Life Eternal," said Christ, "that they may know Thee, the only true God, and Jesus Christ whom Thou hast sent." Life Eternal is to know God. To know God is to "correspond" with God. To correspond with God is to correspond with a Perfect Environment. And the organism which attains to this, in the nature of things, must live forever. Here is "eternal existence and eternal knowledge." *The Greatest Thing in the World.*

June 6th. To find a new Environment again and cultivate relation with it is to find a new Life. To live is to correspond, and to correspond is to live. So much is true in Science. But it is also true in Religion. And it is of great importance to observe that to Religion also the conception of Life is a correspondence. No truth of Christianity has been more ignorantly or wilfully travestied than the doctrine of Immortality. The popular idea, in spite of a hundred protests, is that Eternal

Life is to live forever. . . . We are told that Life Eternal is not to live. This is Life Eternal—*to know. The Greatest Thing in the World.*

June 7th. From time to time the taunt is thrown at Religion, not unseldom from lips which Science ought to have taught more caution, that the Future Life of Christianity is simply a prolonged existence, an eternal monotony, a blind and indefinite continuance of being. The Bible never could commit itself to any such empty platitude; nor could Christianity ever offer to the world a hope so colorless. Not that Eternal Life has nothing to do with everlastingness. That is part of the conception. And it is this aspect of the question that first arrests us in the field of Science. *The Greatest Thing in the World.*

June 8th. Science speaks to us indeed of much more than numbers of years. It defines degrees of Life. It explains a widening Environment. It unfolds the relation between a widening Environment and increasing complexity in organisms. And if it has no absolute contribution to the content of Religion, its analogies are not limited to a point. It yields to Immortality, and this is the most that Science can do in any case, the broad framework for a doctrine. *The Greatest Thing in the World.*

June 9th. To correspond with the God of Science, the Eternal Unknowable, would be everlasting existence; to correspond with "the true God and Jesus Christ," is Eternal Life. The quality of the Eternal Life alone makes the heaven; mere everlastingness might be no boon. Even the brief span of the temporal life is too long for those who spend its years in sorrow. *The Greatest Thing in the World.*

June 10th. To Christianity, "he that hath the Son of God hath Life, and he that hath not the Son hath not Life." This, as we take it, defines the correspondence which is to bridge the grave. This is the clue to the nature of the Life that lies at the back of the spiritual organism. And this is the true solution of the mystery of Eternal Life. *The Greatest Thing in the World.*

June 11th. The relation between the spiritual man and his Environment is, in theological language, a filial relation. With the new Spirit, the filial correspondence, he knows the Father—and this is Life Eternal. *The Greatest Thing in the World.*

June 12th. It takes the Divine to know the Divine—but in no more mysterious sense than it takes the human to understand the human. The analogy, indeed, for the whole field here has been finely expressed already by Paul: "What man," he asks, "knoweth the things of a man, save the spirit of man which is in him? Even so the things of God knoweth no man, but the Spirit of God. Now we have received, not the spirit of the world, but the spirit which is of God; that we might know the things that are freely given to us of God."—I. *Cor.* II. 11, 12. *The Greatest Thing in the World.*

June 13th. To go outside what we call Nature is not to go outside Environment. Nature, the natural Environment, is only a part of Environment. There is another large part, which, though some profess to have no correspondence with it, is not on that account unreal, or even unnatural. The mental and moral world is unknown to the plant. But it is real. *The Greatest Thing in the World.*

June 14th. Things are natural or supernatural simply according to where one stands. Man is supernatural to the mineral; God is supernatural to the man. When a mineral is seized upon by the living plant and elevated to the organic kingdom, no trespass against Nature is committed. It merely enters a larger Environment, which before was supernatural to it, but which now is entirely natural. When the heart of a man, again, is seized upon by the quickening Spirit of God, no further violence is done to *Greatest Thing in the World*. It is another case of the inorganic, so to speak, passing into the organic. *The Greatest Thing in the World.*

June 15th. Correspondence in any case is the gift of Environment. The natural Environment gives men their natural faculties; the spiritual affords them their spiritual faculties. It is natural for the spiritual Environment to supply the spiritual faculties; it would be quite unnatural for the natural Environment to do it. *The Greatest Thing in the World* of *Bio-genesis* forbids it; the moral fact that the finite cannot comprehend the Infinite is against it; the spiritual principle that flesh and blood, cannot inherit the Kingdom of God renders it absurd. *The Greatest Thing in the World.*

June 16th. Organisms are not added to by accretion, as in the case of minerals, but by growth. And the spiritual faculties are organized in the spiritual protoplasm of the soul, just as other faculties are organized in the protoplasm of the body. *The Greatest Thing in the World.*

June 17th. It ought to be placed in the forefront of all Christian teaching that Christ's mission on earth was to give men Life. "I am come," He said, "that ye might have Life, and that ye might have it more abundantly." And that He meant literal Life, literal spiritual and Eternal Life, is clear from the whole course of His teaching and acting. *The Greatest Thing in the World.*

June 18th. The effort to detect the living Spirit must be at least as idle as the attempt to subject protoplasm to microscopic examination in the hope of discovering Life. We are warned, also, not to expect too much. "Thou canst not tell whence it cometh or whither it goeth." *The Greatest Thing in the World.*

June 19th. Many men would be religious if they knew where to begin; many would be more religious if they were sure where it would end. It is not indifference that keeps some men from God, but ignorance. "Good Master, what must I do to inherit Eternal Life?" is still the deepest question of the age. *The Greatest Thing in the World.*

June 20th. The voice of God and the voice of Nature. I cannot be wrong if I listen to them. Sometimes, when uncertain of a voice from its very loudness, we catch the missing syllable in the echo. In God and Nature we have Voice and Echo. When I hear both, I am assured. My sense of hearing does not betray me twice. I recognize the Voice in the Echo, the Echo makes me certain of the Voice; I listen and I know. *The Greatest Thing in the World.*

June 21st. The soul is a living organism. And for any question as to the soul's Life we must appeal to Life-science. And what does the Life-science teach? That if I am to inherit Eternal Life, I must cultivate a correspondence with the Eternal. *The Greatest Thing in the World.*

June 22d. All knowledge lies in Environment. When I want to know about minerals I go to minerals. When I want to know about flowers I go to flowers. And they tell me. In their own way they speak to me, each in its own way, and each for itself—not the mineral for the flower, which is impossible, nor the flower for the mineral, which is also impossible. So if I want to know about Man, I go to his part of the Environment. And he tells me about himself, not as the plant or the mineral, for he is neither, but in his own way. And if I want to know about God, I go to His part of the Environment. And He tells me about Himself, not as a Man, for He is not Man, but in His own way. *The Greatest Thing in the World.*

June 23d. Just as naturally as the flower and the mineral and the Man, each in their own way, tell me about themselves, He tells me about Himself. He very strangely condescends indeed in making things plain to me, actually assuming for a time the Form of a Man that I at my poor level may better see Him. This is my opportunity to know Him. This incarnation is God making Himself accessible to human thought—God opening to Man the possibility of correspondence through Jesus Christ. *The Greatest Thing in the World.*

June 24th. Having opened correspondence with the Eternal Environment, the subsequent stages are in the line of all other normal development. We have but to continue, to deepen, to extend, and to enrich the correspondence that has been begun. And we shall soon find to our surprise that this is accompanied by another and parallel process. The action is not all upon our side. The Environment also will be found to correspond. *The Greatest Thing in the World.*

June 25th. Let us look for the influence of Environment on the spiritual nature of him who has opened correspondence with God. Reaching out his eager and quickened faculties to the spiritual world around him, shall he not become spiritual? In vital contact with Holiness, shall he not become holy? Breathing now an atmosphere of ineffable Purity, shall he miss becoming pure? Walking with God from day to day, shall he fail to be taught of God? *The Greatest Thing in the World.*

June 26th. Growth in grace is sometimes described as a strange, mystical, and unintelligible process. It is mystical, but neither strange nor unintelligible. It proceeds according to *Greatest Thing in the World*, and the leading factor in sanctification is Influence of Environment. *The Greatest Thing in the World.*

June 27th. Will the evolutionist who admits the regeneration of the frog under the modifying influence of a continued correspondence with a new environment, care to question the possibility of the soul acquiring such a faculty as that of Prayer, the marvelous breathing-function of the new creature, when in contact with the atmosphere of a besetting God? Is the change from the earthly to the heavenly more mysterious than the change from the aquatic to the terrestrial mode of life? Is Evolution to stop with the organic? If it be objected that it has taken ages to perfect the function in the batrachian, the reply is, that it will take ages to perfect the function in the Christian. *The Greatest Thing in the World.*

June 28th. We have indeed spoken of the spiritual correspondence as already perfect—but it is perfect only as the bud is perfect. "It doth not yet appear what it shall be," any more than it appeared a million years ago what the evolving batrachian would be. *The Greatest Thing in the World.*

June 29th. In a sense, all that belongs to Time belongs also to Eternity; but these lower correspondences are in their nature unfitted for an Eternal Life. Even if they were perfect in their relation to their Environment, they would still not be Eternal. . . . An Eternal Life demands an Eternal Environment. *The Greatest Thing in the World.*

June 30th. The final preparation . . . for the inheriting of Eternal Life must consist in the abandonment of the non-eternal elements. These must be unloosed and dissociated from the higher elements, And this is effected by a closing catastrophe—Death. *The Greatest Thing in the World.*

July 1st. "Perfect correspondence," according to Mr. Herbert Spencer, would be "perfect Life." To abolish Death, therefore, all that would be necessary would be to abolish Imperfection. But it is the claim of Christianity that it can abolish

Death. And it is significant to notice that it does so by meeting this very demand of Science—it abolishes Imperfection. *The Greatest Thing in the World.*

July 2d. The part of the organism which begins to get out of correspondence with the Organic Environment is the only part which is in vital correspondence with it. Though a fatal disadvantage to the natural man to be thrown out of correspondence with this Environment, it is of inestimable importance to the spiritual man. For so long as it is maintained the way is barred for a further Evolution. And hence the condition necessary for the further Evolution is that the spiritual be released from the natural. That is to say, the condition of the further Evolution is Death. *The Greatest Thing in the World.*

July 3d. The sifting of the correspondences is done by Nature. This is its last and greatest contribution to mankind. Over the mouth of the grave the perfect and the imperfect submit to their final separation. Each goes to its own—earth to earth, ashes to ashes, dust to dust, Spirit to Spirit. "The dust shall return to the earth as it was; and the Spirit shall return unto God who gave it." *The Greatest Thing in the World.*

July 4th. Few things are less understood than the conditions of the spiritual life. The distressing incompetence of which most of us are conscious in trying to work out our spiritual experience is due perhaps less to the diseased will which we commonly blame for it than to imperfect knowledge of the right conditions. It does not occur to us how natural the spiritual is. We still strive for some strange transcendent thing; we seek to promote life by methods as unnatural as they prove unsuccessful; and only the utter incomprehensibility of the whole region prevents us seeing fully—what we already half-suspect—how completely we are missing the road. *The Greatest Thing in the World.*

July 5th. Living in the spiritual world . . . is just as simple as living in the natural world; and it is the same kind of simplicity. It is the same kind of simplicity for it is the same kind of world—there are not two kinds of worlds. The conditions of life in the one are the conditions of life in the other. And till these conditions are sensibly grasped, as the conditions of all life, it is impossible that the personal effort after the highest life should be other than a blind struggle carried on in fruitless sorrow and humiliation. *The Greatest Thing in the World.*

July 6th. Heredity and Environment are the master-influences of the organic world. These have made all of us what we are. These forces are still ceaselessly playing upon all our lives. And he who truly understands these influences; he who has decided how much to allow to each; he who can regulate new forces as they arise, or adjust them to the old, so directing them as at one moment to make them cooperate, at another to counteract one another, understands the rationale of personal development. *The Greatest Thing in the World.*

July 7th. To seize continuously the opportunity of more and more perfect adjustment to better and higher conditions, to balance some inward evil with some purer influence acting from without, in a word to make our Environment at the same time that it is making us—these are the secrets of a well-ordered and successful life. *The Greatest Thing in the World.*

July 8th. In the spiritual world . . . the subtle influences which form and transform the soul are Heredity and Environment. And here especially, where all is invisible, where much that we feel to be real is yet so ill defined, it becomes of vital practical moment to clarify the atmosphere as far as possible with conceptions borrowed from the natural life. *The Greatest Thing in the World.*

July 9th. What Heredity has to do for us is determined outside ourselves. No man can select his own parents. But every man to some extent can choose his own Environment. His relation to it, however largely determined by Heredity in the first instance, is always open to alteration. And so great is his control over Environment and so radical its influence over him, that he can so direct it as either to undo, modify, perpetuate, or intensify the earlier hereditary influences within certain limits. *The Greatest Thing in the World.*

July 10th. One might show how the moral man is acted upon and changed continuously by the influences, secret and open, of his surroundings, by the tone of society, by the company he keeps, by his occupation, by the books he reads, by Nature, by all, in short, that constitutes the habitual atmosphere of his thoughts and the little world of his daily choice. Or one might go deeper still and prove how the spiritual life also is modified from outside sources—its health or disease, its growth or decay, all its changes for better or for worse being determined by the varying and successive circumstances in which the religious habits are cultivated. *The Greatest Thing in the World.*

July 11th. In the spiritual world . . . he will be wise who courts acquaintance with the most ordinary and transparent facts of Nature; and in laying the foundations for a religious life he will make no unworthy beginning who carries with him an impressive sense of so obvious a truth as that without Environment there can be no life. *The Greatest Thing in the World.*

July 12th. There is in the spiritual organism a principle of life; but that is not self-existent. It requires a second factor, a something in which to live and move and have its being, an Environment. Without this it cannot live or move or have any being. Without Environment the soul is as the carbon without the oxygen, as the fish without the water, as the animal frame without the extrinsic conditions of vitality. *The Greatest Thing in the World.*

July 13th. What is the Spiritual Environment? It is God. Without this, therefore, there is no life, no thought, no energy, nothing—-"without Me ye can do nothing." *The Greatest Thing in the World.*

July 14th. The cardinal error in the religious life is to attempt to live without an Environment. Spiritual experience occupies itself, not too much, but too exclusively, with one factor—the soul. We delight in dissecting this much-tortured faculty, from time to time, in search of a certain something which we call our faith—forgetting that faith is but an attitude, an empty hand for grasping an environing Presence. *The Greatest Thing in the World.*

July 15th. When we feel the need of a power by which to overcome the world, how often do we not seek to generate it within ourselves by some forced process, some fresh girding of the will, some strained activity which only leaves the soul in further exhaustion? *The Greatest Thing in the World.*

July 16th. To examine ourselves is good; but useless unless we also examine Environment. To bewail our weakness is right, but not remedial. The cause must be investigated as well as the result. And yet, because we never see the other half of the problem, our failures even fail to instruct us. After each new collapse we begin our life anew, but on the old conditions; and the attempt ends as usual in the repetition—in the circumstances the inevitable repetition—of the old disaster. *The Greatest Thing in the World.*

July 17th. After seasons of much discouragement, with the sore sense upon us of our abject feebleness, we do confer with ourselves, insisting for the thousandth time, "My soul, wait thou only upon God." But, the lesson is soon forgotten. The strength supplied we speedily credit to our own achievement; and even the temporary success is mistaken for a symptom of improved inward vitality. Once more we become self-existent. Once more we go on living without an Environment. And once more, after days of wasting without repairing, of spending without replenishing, we begin to perish with hunger, only returning to God again, as a last resort, when we have reached starvation point. *The Greatest Thing in the World.*

July 18th. Why this unscientific attempt to sustain life for weeks at a time without an Environment? It is because we have never truly seen the necessity for an Environment. We have not been working with a principle. We are told to "wait only upon God," but we do not know why. It has never been as clear to us that without God the soul will die as that without food the body will perish. In short, we have never comprehended the doctrine of the Persistence of Force. Instead of being content to transform energy we have tried to create it. *The Greatest Thing in the World.*

July 19th. Whatever energy the soul expends must first be "taken into it from without." We are not Creators, but creatures; God is our refuge *and strength.* Communion with God, therefore, is a scientific necessity; and nothing will more help the defeated spirit which is struggling in the wreck of its religious life than a common-sense hold of this biological principle that without Environment he can do nothing. *The Greatest Thing in the World.*

July 20th. Who has not come to the conclusion that he is but a part, a fraction of some larger whole? Who does not miss, at every turn of his life, an absent God? That man is but a part, he knows, for there is room in him for more. That God is the other part, he feels, because at times He satisfies his need. Who does not tremble often under that sicklier symptom of his incompleteness, his want of spiritual energy, his helplessness with sin? But now he understands both—the void in his life, the powerlessness of his will. He understands that, like all other energy, Spiritual power is contained in Environment. He finds here at last the true root of all human frailty, emptiness, nothingness, sin. This is why "without Me ye can do nothing." Powerlessness is the normal state, not only of this, but of every organism—of every organism apart from its Environment. *Greatest Thing in the World.*

July 21st. Friendship is the nearest thing we know to what religion is. God is love. And to make religion akin to Friendship is simply to give it the highest expression conceivable by man. *The Changed Life.*

July 22d. The entire dependence of the soul upon God is not an exceptional mystery, nor is man's helplessness an arbitrary and unprecedented phenomenon. It is the law of all Nature. The spiritual man is not taxed beyond the natural. He is not purposely handicapped by singular limitations or unusual incapacities. God has not designedly made the religious life as hard as possible. The arrangements for the spiritual life are the same as for the natural life. When, in their hours of unbelief, men challenge their Creator for placing the obstacle of human frailty in the way of their highest development, their protest is against the order of Nature. *Greatest Thing in the World.*

July 23d. The organism must either depend on his environment, or be self-sufficient. But who will not rather approve the arrangement by which man in his creatural life may have unbroken access to an Infinite Power? What soul will seek to remain self-luminous when it knows that "The Lord God is a Sun?"

Who will not willingly exchange his shallow vessel for Christ's well of living water. *Greatest Thing in the World.*

July 24th. The New Testament is nowhere more impressive than where it insists on the fact of man's dependence. In its view the first step in religion is for man to feel his helplessness. Christ's first beatitude is to the poor in spirit. The condition of entrance into the spiritual kingdom is to possess the child-spirit—that state of mind combining at once the profoundest helplessness with the most artless feeling of dependence. *Greatest Thing in the World.*

July 25th. Fruit-bearing without Christ is not an improbability, but an impossibility. As well expect the natural fruit to flourish without air and heat, without soil and sunshine. How thoroughly also Paul grasped this truth is apparent from a hundred pregnant passages in which he echoes his Master's teaching. To him life was hid with Christ in God. And that he embraced this, not as a theory but as an experimental truth, we gather from his constant confession, "When I am weak, then am I strong." *Greatest Thing in the World.*

July 26th. One result of the due apprehension of our personal helplessness will be that we shall no longer waste our time over the impossible task of manufacturing energy for ourselves. Our science will bring to an abrupt end the long series of severe experiments in which we have indulged in the hope of finding a perpetual motion. And having decided upon this once for all, our first step in seeking a more satisfactory state of things must be to find a new source of energy. Following Nature, only one course is open to us. We must refer to Environment. The natural life owes all to Environment, so must the spiritual. Now the Environment of the spiritual life is God. As Nature, therefore, forms the complement of the natural life. God is the complement of the spiritual. *Greatest Thing in the World.*

July 27th. Do not think that nothing is happening because you do not see yourself grow, or hear the whirr of the machinery. All great things grow noiselessly. You can see a mushroom grow, but never a child. Mr. Darwin tells us that Evolution proceeds by "numerous, successive, and slight modifications." *The Changed Life.*

July 28th. We fail to praise the ceaseless ministry of the great inanimate world around us only because its kindness is unobtrusive. Nature is always noiseless. All her greatest gifts are given in secret. And we forget how truly every good and perfect gift comes from without, and from above, because no pause in her changeless beneficence teaches us the sad lessons of deprivation. *Greatest Thing in the World.*

July 29th. It is not a strange thing for the soul to find its life in God. This is its native air. God as the Environment of the soul has been from the remotest age the doctrine of all the deepest thinkers in religion. How profoundly Hebrew poetry is saturated with this high thought will appear when we try to conceive of it with this left out. *Greatest Thing in the World.*

July 30th. The alternatives of the intellectual life are Christianity or Agnosticism. The Agnostic is right when he trumpets his incompleteness. He who is not complete in Him must be for ever incomplete. *Greatest Thing in the World.*

July 31st. The problems of the heart and conscience are infinitely more perplexing than those of the intellect. Has love no future? Has right no triumph? Is the unfinished self to remain unfinished? The alternatives are two, Christianity or Pessimism. But when we ascend the further height of the religious nature, the crisis comes. There, without Environment, the darkness is unutterable. So maddening now becomes the mystery that men are compelled to construct an Environment for themselves. No Environment here is unthinkable. An altar of some sort men must have— God, or Nature, or Law. But the anguish of Atheism is only a negative proof of man's incompleteness. *Greatest Thing in the World.*

August 1st. A photograph prints from the negative only while exposed to the sun. While the artist is looking to see how it is getting on he simply stops the getting on. Whatever of wise supervision the soul may need, it is certain it can never be over-exposed, or that, being exposed, anything else in the world can improve the result or quicken it. *The Changed Life.*

August 2d. What a very strange thing, is it not, for man to pray? It is the symbol at once of his littleness and of his greatness. Here the sense of imperfection, controlled and silenced in the narrower reaches of his being, becomes audible. Now he must utter himself. The sense of need is so real, and the sense of Environment, that he calls out to it, addressing it articulately, and imploring it to satisfy his need. Surely there is nothing more touching in Nature than this? Man could never so expose himself, so break through all constraint, except from a dire necessity. *Greatest Thing in the World.*

August 3d. What is Truth? The natural Environment answers, "Increase of Knowledge increaseth Sorrow," and "much study is a Weariness." Christ replies, "Learn of Me, and ye shall find Rest." Contrast the world's word "Weariness" with Christ's word "Rest." No other teacher since the world began has ever associated "learn" with "Rest." Learn of me, says the philosopher, and you shall find Restlessness. Learn of Me, says Christ, and ye shall find Rest. *Greatest Thing in the World.*

August 4th. Men will have to give up the experiment of attempting to live in half an Environment. Half an Environment will give but half a Life. ... He whose correspondences are with this world alone has only a thousandth part, a fraction, the mere rim and shade of an Environment, and only the fraction of a Life. How long will it take Science to believe its own creed, that the material universe we see around us is only a fragment of the universe we do not see? *Greatest Thing in the World.*

August 5th. The Life of the senses, high and low, may perfect itself in Nature. Even the Life of thought may find a large complement in surrounding things. But the higher thought, and the conscience, and the religious Life, can only perfect themselves in God. *Greatest Thing in the World.*

August 6th. To make the influence of Environment stop with the natural world is to doom the spiritual nature to death. For the soul, like the body, can never perfect itself in isolation. The law for both is to be complete in the appropriate Environment. *Greatest Thing in the World.*

August 7th. Take into your new sphere of labor, where you also mean to lay down your life, that simple charm, Love, and your life-work must succeed. You can take nothing greater, you need take nothing less. It is not worth while going if you take anything less. *The Greatest Thing in the World.*

August 8th. Politeness has been defined as love in trifles. Courtesy is said to be love in little things. And the one secret of politeness is to love. Love *cannot* behave itself unseemly. You can put the most untutored persons into the highest society, and if they have a reservoir of Love in their heart, they will not behave themselves unseemly. They simply cannot do it. *The Greatest Thing in the World.*

August 9th. I believe that Christ's yoke is easy. Christ's "yoke" is just His way of taking life. And I believe it is an easier way than any other. I believe it is a happier way than any other. The most obvious lesson in Christ's teaching is that there is no happiness in having and getting anything, but only in giving. *The Greatest Thing in the World.*

August 10th. Half the world is on the wrong scent in the pursuit of happiness. They think it consists in having and getting, and in being served by others. It consists in giving, and in serving others. He that would be great among you, said Christ, let him serve. He that would be happy, let him remember that there is but one way—it is more blessed, it is more happy, to give than to receive. *The Greatest Thing in the World.*

August 11th. "Love is not easily provoked." . . . We are inclined to look upon bad temper as a very harmless weakness. We speak of it as a mere infirmity of nature, a family failing, a matter of temperament, not a thing to take into very serious account in estimating a man's character. And yet here, right in the heart of this analysis of love, it finds a place; and the Bible again and again returns to condemn it as one of the most destructive elements in human nature. *The Greatest Thing in the World.*

August 12th. The peculiarity of ill-temper is that it is the vice of the virtuous. It is often the one blot on an otherwise noble character. You know men who are all but perfect, and women who would be entirely perfect, but for an easily ruffled, quick-tempered, or "touchy" disposition. This compatibility of ill-temper with high moral character is one of the strangest and saddest problems of ethics. *The Greatest Thing in the World.*

August 13th. What makes a man a good artist, a good sculptor, a good musician? Practice. . . . What makes a man a good man? Practice. Nothing else. There is nothing capricious about religion. We do not get the soul in different ways, under different laws, from those in which we get the body and the mind. *The Greatest Thing in the World.*

August 14th. Love is not a thing of enthusiastic emotion. It is a rich, strong, manly, vigorous expression of the whole round Christian character—the Christ-like nature in its fullest development. And the constituents of this great character are only to be built up by ceaseless practice. *The Greatest Thing in the World.*

August 15th. We know but little now about the conditions of the life that is to come. But what is certain is that Love must last. God, the Eternal God, is Love. Covet, therefore, that everlasting gift. *The Greatest Thing in the World.*

August 16th. To love abundantly is to live abundantly, and to love forever is to live forever. Hence, eternal life is inextricably bound up with love. . . . Love must be eternal. It is what God is. *The Greatest Thing in the World.*

August 17th. When a man becomes a Christian the natural process is this: The Living Christ enters into his soul. Development begins. The quickening Life seizes upon the soul, assimilates surrounding elements, and begins to fashion it. According to the great Law of Conformity to Type this fashioning takes a specific form. It is that of the Artist who fashions. And all through Life this wonderful, mystical, glorious, yet perfectly definite, process, goes on "until Christ be formed" in it. *Greatest Thing in the World.*

August 18th. The Christian Life is not a vague effort after righteousness—an ill-defined, pointless struggle for an ill-defined, pointless end. Religion is no disheveled mass of aspiration, prayer, and faith. There is no more mystery in Religion as to its processes than in Biology. *Greatest Thing in the World.*

August 19th. There is much mystery in Biology. "We know all but nothing of Life" yet, nothing of development. There is the same mystery in the spiritual Life. But the great lines are the same, as decided, as luminous; and the laws of natural and spiritual are the same, as unerring, as simple. Will everything else in the natural world unfold its order, and yield to Science more and more a vision of harmony, and Religion, which should complement and perfect all, remain a chaos? *Greatest Thing in the World.*

August 20th. When one attempts to sanctify himself by effort, he is trying to make his boat go by pushing against the mast. He is like a drowning man trying to lift himself out of the water by pulling at the hair of his own head. Christ held up this method almost to ridicule when He said: "Which of you by taking thought can add a cubit to his stature?" The one redeeming feature of the self-sufficient method is this—that those who try it find out almost at once that it will not gain the goal. *The Changed Life.*

August 21st. The Image of Christ that is forming within us—that is life's one charge. Let every project stand aside for that. "Till Christ be formed," no man's work is finished, no religion crowned, no life has fulfilled its end. *The Changed Life.*

August 22d. Our companionship with Him, like all true companionship, is a spiritual communion. All friendship, all love, human and Divine, is purely spiritual. It was after He was risen that He influenced even the disciples most. *The Changed Life.*

August 23d. Make Christ your most constant companion. Be more under His influence than under any other influence. Ten minutes spent in His society every day, ay, two minutes if it be face to face, and heart to heart, will make the whole day different. Every character has an inward spring, let Christ be it. Every action has a key-note, let Christ set it. *The Changed Life.*

August 24th. Under the right conditions it is as natural for character to become beautiful as for a flower; and if on God's earth there is not some machinery for effecting it, the supreme gift to the world has been forgotten. This is simply what man was made for. With Browning: "I say that Man was made to grow, not stop." *The Changed Life.*

August 25th. How can modern men today make Christ, the absent Christ, their most constant companion still? The answer is that Friendship is a spiritual thing. It is independent of Matter, or Space, or Time. That which I love in my friend is not that which I see. What influences me in my friend is not his body but his spirit. *The Changed Life.*

August 26th. Love should be the supreme thing—because it is going to last; because in the nature of things it is an Eternal Life. It is a thing that we are living now, not that we get when we die; that we shall have a poor chance of getting when we die unless we are living now. *The Greatest Thing in the World.*

August 27th. When will it be seen that the characteristic of the Christian Religion is its Life, that a true theology must begin with a Biology? Theology is the Science of God. Why will men treat God as inorganic? *Greatest Thing in the World.*

August 28th. We should be forsaking the lines of nature were we to imagine for a moment that the new creature was to be formed out of nothing. Nothing can be made out of nothing. Matter is uncreatable and indestructible; Nature and man can only form and transform. Hence when a new animal is made, no new clay is made. Life merely enters into already existing matter, assimilates more of the same sort and rebuilds it. The spiritual Artist works in the same way. He must have a peculiar kind of protoplasm, a basis of life, and that must be already existing. *Greatest Thing in the World.*

August 29th. However active the intellectual or moral life may be, from the point of view of this other Life it is dead. That which is flesh is flesh. It wants, that is to say, the kind of Life which constitutes the difference between the Christian and the not-a-Christian, It has not yet been "born of the Spirit." *Greatest Thing in the World.*

August 30th. The protoplasm in man has a something in addition to its instincts or its habits. It has a capacity for God. In this capacity for God lies its receptivity; it is the very protoplasm that was necessary. The chamber is not only ready to receive the new Life, but the Guest is expected, and, till He comes, is missed. Till then the soul longs and yearns, wastes and pines, waving its tentacles piteously in the empty air, feeling after God if so be that it may find Him. This is not peculiar to the protoplasm of the Christian's soul. In every land and in every age there have been altars to the Known or Unknown God. *Greatest Thing in the World.*

August 31st. It is now agreed as a mere question of anthropology that the universal language of the human soul has always been "I perish with hunger." This is what fits it for Christ. There is a grandeur in this cry from the depths which makes its very unhappiness sublime. *Greatest Thing in the World.*

September 1st. In reflecting the character of Christ, it is no real obstacle that we may never have been in visible contact with Himself. Many men know Dante better than their own fathers. He influences them more. As a spiritual presence he is more near to them, as a spiritual force more real. Is there any reason why a greater than . . . Dante should not also instruct, inspire, and mold the characters of men? *The Changed Life.*

September 2d. Mark this distinction. . . . Imitation is mechanical, reflection organic. The one is occasional, the other habitual. In the one case, man comes to God and imitates Him; in the other, God comes to man and imprints Himself upon him. It is quite true that there is an imitation of Christ which amounts to reflection. But Paul's term includes all that the other holds, and is open to no mistake. "Whom having not seen, I love." *The Changed Life.*

September 3d. In paraphrase: We all reflecting as a mirror the character of Christ are transformed into the same Image from character to character—from a poor character to a better one, from a better one to one a little better still, from that to one still more complete, until by slow degrees the Perfect Image is attained. Here the solution of the problem of sanctification is compressed into a sentence: Reflect the character of Christ and you will become like Christ. *The Changed Life.*

September 4th. Not more certain is it that it is something outside the thermometer that produces a change in the thermometer, than it is something outside the soul of man that produces a moral change upon him. That he must be susceptible to that change, that he must be a party to it, goes without saying; but that neither his aptitude nor his will can produce it is equally certain. *The Changed Life.*

September 5th. Just as in an organism we have these three things— formative matter, formed matter, and the forming principle or life; so in the soul we have the old nature, the renewed nature, and. the transforming Life. *Greatest Thing in the World.*

September 6th. Is it hopeless to point out that one of the most recognizable characteristics of life is its unrecognizableness, and that the very token of its spiritual nature lies in its being beyond the grossness of our eyes? *Greatest Thing in the World.*

September 7th. According to the doctrine of *Bio-genesis*, life can only come from life. It was Christ's additional claim that His function in the world, was to give men Life. "I am come that ye might have Life, and that ye might have it more abundantly." This could, not refer to the natural life, for men had that already. He that hath the Son hath another Life. "Know ye not your own selves how that Jesus Christ is in you." *Greatest Thing in the World.*

September 8th. The recognition of the Ideal is the first step in the direction of Conformity. But let it be clearly observed that it is but a step. There is no vital connection between merely seeing the Ideal and being conformed to it. Thousands admire Christ who never become Christians. *Greatest Thing in the World.*

September 9th. For centuries men have striven to find out ways and means to conform themselves to the Christ Life. Impressive motives have been pictured, the proper circumstances arranged, the direction of effort defined, and men have toiled, struggled, and agonized to conform themselves to the Image of the Son. Can the protoplasm *conform itself* to its type? Can the embryo *fashion itself?* Is Conformity to Type produced by the matter *or by the life*, by the protoplasm or by the Type? Is organization the cause of life or the effect of it? It is the effect of it. Conformity to Type, therefore, is secured by the type. Christ makes the Christian. *Greatest Thing in the World.*

September 10th. O preposterous and vain man, thou who couldest not make a fingernail of thy body, thinkest thou to fashion this wonderful, mysterious, subtle soul of thine after the ineffable Image? Wilt thou ever permit thyself *to be* conformed to the Image of the Son? Wilt thou, who canst not add a cubit to thy stature, submit TO BE raised by the Type-Life within thee to the perfect stature of Christ *Greatest Thing in the World.*

September 11th. Men will still experiment "by works of righteousness which they have done" to earn the Ideal life. The doctrine of Human Inability, as the Church calls it, has always been objectionable to men who do not know themselves. *Greatest Thing in the World.*

September 12th. Let man choose Life; let him daily nourish his soul; let him forever starve the old life; let him abide continuously as a living branch in the Vine, and the True-Vine Life will flow into his soul, assimilating, renewing, conforming to Type, till Christ, pledged by His own law, be formed in him. *Greatest Thing in the World.*

September 13th. The work begun by Nature is finished by the Supernatural —as we are wont to call the higher natural. And as the veil is lifted by Christianity it strikes men dumb with wonder. For the goal of Evolution is Jesus Christ. *Greatest Thing in the World.*

September 14th. The Christian life is the only life that will ever be completed. Apart from Christ the life of man is a broken pillar, the race of men an unfinished pyramid. One by one in sight of Eternity all human Ideals fall short, one by one before the open grave all human hopes dissolve. *Greatest Thing in the World.*

September 15th. I do not think we ourselves are aware how much our religious life is made up of phrases; how much of what we call Christian experience is only a dialect of the Churches, a mere religious phraseology with almost nothing behind it in what we really feel and know. *Pax Vobiscum.*

September 16th. The ceaseless chagrin of a self-centered life can be removed at once by learning Meekness and Lowliness of heart. He who learns them is forever proof against it. He lives henceforth a charmed life. *Pax Vobiscum*.

September 17th. Great trials come at lengthened intervals, and we rise to breast them; but it is the petty friction of our everyday life with one another, the jar of business or of work, the discord of the domestic circle, the collapse of our ambition, the crossing of our will or the taking down of our conceit, which makes inward peace impossible. *Pax Vobiscum*.

September 18th. There are people who go about the world looking out for slights, and they are necessarily miserable, for they find them at every turn—especially the imaginary ones. One has the same pity for such men as for the very poor. They are the morally illiterate. They have had no real education, for they have never learned how to live. *Pax Vobiscum*.

September 19th. Christ never said much in mere words about the Christian graces. He lived them, He was them. Yet we do not merely copy Him. We learn His art by living with Him. *Pax Vobiscum*.

September 20th. Christ's invitation to the weary and heavy-laden is a call to begin life over again upon a new principle—upon His own principle. "Watch My way of doing things," He says. "Follow Me. Take life as I take it. Be meek and lowly, and you will find Rest." *Pax Vobiscum*.

September 21st. If a man could make himself humble to order, it might simplify matters, but we do not find that this happens. Hence we must all go through the mill. Hence death, death to the lower self, is the nearest gate and the quickest road to life. *Pax Vobiscum*.

September 22d. Whatever rest is provided by Christianity for the children of God, it is certainly never contemplated that it should supersede personal effort. And any rest which ministers to indifference is immoral and unreal—it makes parasites and not men. *Greatest Thing in the World*.

September 23d. Just because God worketh in him, as the evidence and triumph of it, the true child of God works out his own salvation—works it out having really received it—not as a light thing, a superfluous labor, but with fear and trembling as a reasonable and indispensable service. *Greatest Thing in the World*.

September 24th. Christianity, as Christ taught, is the truest philosophy of life ever spoken. But let us be quite sure when we speak of Christianity, that we mean Christ's Christianity. *Pax Vobiscum*.

September 25th. So far from ministering to growth, parasitism ministers to decay. So far from ministering to holiness, that is to wholeness, parasitism ministers to exactly the opposite. One by one the spiritual faculties droop and die, one by one from lack of exercise the muscles of the soul grow weak and flaccid, one by one the moral activities cease. So from him that hath not, is taken away that which he hath, and after a few years of parasitism there is nothing left to save. *Greatest Thing in the World*.

September 26th. The natural life, not less than the eternal, is the gift of God. But life in either case is the beginning of growth and not the end of grace. To pause where we should begin, to retrograde where we should advance, to seek a mechanical security that we may cover inertia and find a wholesale salvation in which there is no personal sanctification—this is Parasitism. *Greatest Thing in the World*.

September 27th. Could we investigate the spirit as a living organism, or study the soul of the backslider on principles of comparative anatomy, we should have a revelation of the organic effects of sin, even of the mere sin of carelessness as to growth and work, which must revolutionize our ideas of practical religion. There is no room for the doubt even that what goes on in the body does not with equal certainty take place in the spirit under the corresponding conditions. *Greatest Thing in the World.*

September 28th. It is the beautiful work of Christianity everywhere to adjust the burden of life to those who bear it, and them to it. It has a perfectly miraculous gift of healing. Without doing any violence to human nature it sets it right with life, harmonizing it with all surrounding things, and restoring those who are jaded with the fatigue and dust of the world to a new grace of living. *Pax Vobiscum.*

September 29th. The penalty of backsliding is not something unreal and vague, some unknown quantity which may be measured out to us disproportionately, or which, perchance, since God is good, we may altogether evade. The consequences are already marked within the structure of the soul. So to speak, they are physiological. The thing effected by our in difference or by our indulgence is not the book of final judgment, but the present fabric of the soul. *Greatest Thing in the World.*

September 30th. The punishment of degeneration is simply degeneration— the loss of functions, the decay of organs, the atrophy of the spiritual nature. It is well known that the recovery of the backslider is one of the hardest problems in spiritual work. To reinvigorate an old organ seems more difficult and hopeless than to develop a new one; and the backslider's terrible lot is to have to retrace with enfeebled feet each step of the way along which he strayed; to make up inch by inch the leeway he has lost, carrying with him a dead-weight of acquired reluctance, and scarce knowing whether to be stimulated or discouraged by the oppressive memory of the previous fall. *Greatest Thing in the World.*

October 1st. He who abandons the personal search for truth, under whatever pretext, abandons truth. The very word truth, by becoming the limited possession of a guild, ceases to have any meaning; and faith, which can only be founded on truth, gives way to credulity, resting on mere opinion. *Greatest Thing in the World.*

October 2d. It is more necessary for us to be active than to be orthodox. To be orthodox is what we wish to be, but we can only truly reach it by being honest, by being original, by seeing with our own eyes, by believing with our own heart. *Greatest Thing in the World.*

October 3d. Better a little faith dearly won, better launched alone on the infinite bewilderment of Truth, than perish on the splendid plenty of the richest creeds. Such Doubt is no self-willed presumption. Nor, truly exercised, will it prove itself, as much doubt does, the synonym for sorrow. *Greatest Thing in the World.*

October 4th. Christianity removes the attraction of the earth; and this is one way in which it diminishes men's burden. It makes them citizens of another world. *Pax Vobiscum.*

October 5th. Then the Christian experiences are our own making? In the same sense in which grapes are our own making, and no more. All fruits *grow*—whether they grow in the soil or in the soul; whether they are the fruits of the wild grape or of the True Vine. No man can *make* things grow. He can *get them to grow* by arranging all the circumstances and fulfilling all the conditions. But the growing is done by God. *Pax Vobiscum.*

October 6th. Men may not know how fruits grow, but they do know that they cannot grow in five minutes. Some lives have not even a stalk on which fruits could hang, even if they did grow in five minutes. Some have never planted one sound seed of Joy in all their lives; and others who may have planted a germ or two have lived so little in sunshine that they never could come to maturity. *Pax Vobiscum*.

October 7th. There is no mystery about Happiness whatever. Put in the right ingredients and it must come out. He that abideth in Him will bring forth much fruit; and bringing forth much fruit is Happiness. The infallible receipt for Happiness, then, is to do good; and the infallible receipt for doing good is to abide in Christ. *Pax Vobiscum*.

October 8th. Spend the time you have spent in sighing for fruits in fulfilling the conditions of their growth. The fruits will come, must come. . . . About every other method of living the Christian life there is an uncertainty. About every other method of acquiring the Christian experiences there is a "perhaps." But in so far as this method is the way of nature, it cannot fail. *Pax Vobiscum*.

October 9th. The distinctions drawn between men are commonly based on the outward appearance of goodness or badness, on the ground of moral beauty or moral deformity—is this classification scientific? Or is there a deeper distinction between the Christian and the not-a-Christian as fundamental as that between the organic and the inorganic? *Greatest Thing in the World*.

October 10th What is the essential difference between the Christian and the not-a-Christian, between the spiritual beauty and the moral beauty? It is the distinction between the Organic and the Inorganic. Moral beauty is the product of the natural man, spiritual beauty of the spiritual man. *Greatest Thing in the World*.

October 11th. The first Law of biology is: That which is Mineral is Mineral; that which is Flesh is Flesh; that which is Spirit is Spirit. The mineral remains in the inorganic world until it is seized upon by a something called Life outside the inorganic world; the natural man remains the natural man, until a Spiritual Life from without the natural life seizes upon him, regenerates him, changes him into a spiritual man. *Greatest Thing in the World*.

October 12th Suppose now it be granted for a moment that the character of the not-a-Christian is as beautiful as that of the Christian. This is simply to say that the crystal is as beautiful as the organism. One is quite entitled to hold this; but what he is not entitled to hold is that both in the same sense are living. "He that hath the Son hath Life, and he that hath not the Son of God hath not Life." *Greatest Thing in the World*.

October 13th. Man is a moral animal, and can, and ought to, arrive at great natural beauty of character. But this is simply to obey the law of his nature—the law of his flesh; and no progress along that line can project him into the spiritual sphere. *Greatest Thing in the World*.

October 14th. If any one choose to claim that the mineral beauty, the fleshly beauty, the natural moral beauty, is all he covets, he is entitled to his claim. To be good and true, pure and benevolent in the moral sphere, are high and, so far, legitimate objects in life. If he deliberately stop here, he is at liberty to do so. But what he is not entitled to do is to call himself a Christian, or to claim to discharge the functions peculiar to the Christian life. *Greatest Thing in the World*.

October 15th. In dealing with a man of fine moral character, we are dealing with the highest achievement of the organic kingdom. But in dealing with a spiritual man we are dealing with *the lowest form of life in the spiritual world*. To contrast the two, therefore, and marvel that the one is apparently so little better than the other, is unscientific and unjust. *Greatest Thing in the World*.

October 16th. The spiritual man is a mere unformed embryo, hidden as yet in his earthly chrysalis-case, while the natural man has the breeding and evolution of ages represented in his character. But what are the possibilities of this spiritual organism? What is yet to emerge from this chrysalis-case? The natural character finds its limits within the organic sphere. But who is to define the limits of the spiritual? Even now it is very beautiful. Even as an embryo it contains some prophecy of its future glory. But the point to mark is, that "it doth not yet appear what it shall be." *Greatest Thing in the World*.

October 17th. The best test for Life is just *living*. And living consists, as we have formerly seen, in corresponding with Environment. Those therefore who find within themselves, and regularly exercise, the faculties for corresponding with the Divine Environment, may be said to live the Spiritual Life. *Greatest Thing in the World*.

October 18th. That the Spiritual Life, even in the embryonic organism, ought already to betray itself to others, is certainly what one would expect. Every organism has its own reaction upon Nature, and the reaction of the spiritual organism upon the community must be looked for. In the absence of any such reaction, in the absence of any token that it lived for a higher purpose, or that its real interests were those of the Kingdom to which it professed to belong, we should be entitled to question its being in that Kingdom. *Greatest Thing in the World*.

October 19th. Man's place in Nature, or his position among the Kingdoms, is to be decided by the characteristic functions habitually discharged by him. Now, when the habits of certain individuals are closely observed, when the total effect of their life and work, with regard to the community, is gauged, ... there ought to be no difficulty in deciding whether they are living for the Organic or for the Spiritual; in plainer language, for the world or for God. *Greatest Thing in the World*.

October 20th. No matter what may be the moral uprightness of man's life, the honorableness of his career, or the orthodoxy of his creed, if he exercises the function of loving the world, that defines his world—he belongs to the Organic Kingdom. He cannot in that case belong to the higher Kingdom. "If any man love the world, the love of the Father is not in him." After all, it is by the general bent of a man's life, by his heart-impulses and secret desires, his spontaneous actions and abiding motives, that his generation is declared. *Greatest Thing in the World*.

October 21st. The imperious claim of a Kingdom upon its members is not peculiar to Christianity. It is the law in all departments of Nature that every organism must live for its Kingdom. And in defining living FOR the higher Kingdom as the condition of living in it, Christ enunciates a principle which all Nature has prepared us to expect. *Greatest Thing in the World*.

October 22d. Christianity marks the advent of what is simply a new Kingdom. Its distinctions from the Kingdom below it are fundamental. It demands from its members activities and responses of an altogether novel order. It is, in the conception of its Founder, a Kingdom for which all its adherents must henceforth exclusively live and work, and which opens its gates alone upon those who, having counted the cost, are prepared to follow it if need be to the death. The surrender Christ demanded was absolute. Every aspirant for membership must seek *first* the Kingdom of God. *Greatest Thing in the World*.

October 23d. Until even religious men see the uniqueness of Christ's society, until they acknowledge to the full extent its claim to be nothing less than a new Kingdom, they will continue the hopeless attempt to live for two Kingdoms at once. And hence the value of a more explicit Classification. For probably the most of the difficulties of trying to live the Christian life arise from attempting to half-live it. *Greatest Thing in the World.*

October 24th. Two Kingdoms, at the present time, are known to Science— the Inorganic and the Organic. The spiritual life does not belong to the Inorganic Kingdom, because it lives. It does not belong to the Organic Kingdom, because it is endowed with a kind of Life infinitely removed from either the vegetable or animal. Where, then, shall it be classed? We are left without an alternative. There being no Kingdom known to Science which can contain it, we must construct one. Or, rather, we must include in the Program of Science a Kingdom already constructed, but the place of which in Science has not yet been recognized. That Kingdom is the *kingdom of god. Greatest Thing in the World.*

October 25th. The goal of the organisms of the Spiritual World is nothing less than this—to be "holy as He is holy, and pure as He is pure." And by the Law of Conformity to Type, their final perfection is secured. The inward nature must develop out according to its Type, until the consummation of oneness with God is reached. *Greatest Thing in the World.*

October 26th. Christianity defines the highest conceivable future for mankind. It satisfies the Law of Continuity. It guarantees the necessary conditions for carrying on the organism successfully, from stage to stage. It provides against the tendency to Degeneration. And finally, instead of limiting the yearning hope of final perfection to the organisms of a future age—an age so remote that the hope for thousands of years must still be hopeless—instead of inflicting this cruelty on intelligences mature enough to know perfection and earnest enough to wish it, Christianity puts the prize within immediate reach of man. *Greatest Thing in the World.*

October 27th. No worse fate can befall a man in this world than to live and grow old alone, unloving and unloved. To be lost is to live in an unregenerate condition, loveless and unloved; and to be saved is to love; he that dwelleth in love dwelleth already in God. For God is Love. *The Greatest Thing in the World.*

October 28th. "Love suffereth long, and is kind; love envieth not; love vaunteth not itself." Get these ingredients into your life. Then everything that you do is eternal. It is worth doing. It is worth giving time to. *The Greatest Thing in the World.*

October 29th. The final test of religion at that great Day is not religiousness, but Love; not what I have done, not what I have believed, not what I have achieved, but how I have discharged the common charities of life. *The Greatest Thing in the World.*

October 30th. The words which all of us shall one Day hear sound not of theology but of life, not of churches and saints, but of the hungry and the poor, not of creeds and doctrines, but of shelter and clothing, not of Bibles and prayer-books, but of cups of cold water in the name of Christ. *The Greatest Thing in the World.*

October 31st. The world moves. And each day, each hour, demands a further motion and re-adjustment for the soul. A telescope in an observatory follows a star by clockwork, but the clockwork of the soul is called the Will. Hence, while the soul in passivity reflects the Image of the Lord, the Will in intense activity holds the mirror in position lest the drifting motion of the world bear it beyond the line of vision. To "follow Christ" is largely to keep the soul in such position as will allow for the motion of the earth. And this calculated counteracting of the movements of a world, this holding of the mirror exactly opposite to the Mirrored, this steadying of the faculties unerringly, through cloud and earthquake; fire and sword, is the stupendous cooperating labor of the Will. *The Changed Life.*

November 1st. All around us Christians are wearing themselves out in trying to be better. The amount of spiritual longing in the world—in the hearts of unnumbered thousands of men and women in whom we should never suspect it; among the wise and thoughtful; among the young and gay, who seldom assuage and never betray their thirst—this is one of the most wonderful and touching facts of life. It is not more heat that is needed, but more light; not more force, but a wiser direction to be given to very real energies already there. *Pax Vobiscum.*

November 2d. Men sigh for the wings of a dove, that they may fly away and be at Rest. But flying away will not help us. "The Kingdom of God is *within you.*" We aspire to the top to look for Rest; it lies at the bottom. Water rests only when it gets to the lowest place. So do men. Hence, be lowly. *Pax Vobiscum.*

November 3d. The kingdom of God is righteousness, peace, joy. Righteousness, of course, is just doing what is right. Any boy who does what is right has the kingdom of God within him. Any boy who, instead of being quarrelsome, lives at peace with the other boys, has the kingdom of God within him. Any boy whose heart is filled with joy because he does what is right, has the kingdom of God within him. The kingdom of God is not going to religious meetings, and hearing strange religious experiences: the kingdom of God is doing what is right—living at peace with all men, being filled with joy in the Holy Ghost. *First.*

November 4th. The man who has no opinion of himself at all can never be hurt if others do not acknowledge him. Hence, be meek. He who is without expectation cannot fret if nothing comes to him. It is self-evident that these things are so. The lowly man and the meek man are really above all other men, above all other things. *Pax Vobiscum.*

November 5th. Keep religion in its place, and it will take you straight through life, and straight to your Father in heaven when life is over. But if you do not put it in its place, you may just as well have nothing to do with it. Religion out of its place in a human life is the most miserable thing in the world. There is nothing that requires so much to be kept in its place as religion, and its place is what? second? third? "First." Boys, carry that home with you today—FIRST the kingdom of God. Make it so that it will be natural to you to think about that the very first thing. First, pp. 15, 16.

November 6th. The change we have been striving after is not to be produced by any more striving after. It is to be wrought upon us by the molding of hands beyond our own. As the branch ascends, and the bud bursts, and the fruit reddens under the cooperation of influences from the outside air, so man rises to the higher stature under invisible pressures from without. *The Changed Life.*

November 7th. Every man's character remains as it is, or continues in the direction in which it is going, until it is compelled by *impressed forces* to change that state. Our failure has been the failure to put ourselves in the way of the impressed forces. There is a clay, and there is a Potter; we have tried to get the clay to mold the clay. *The Changed Life.*

November 8th. Character is a unity, and all the virtues must advance together to make the perfect man. This method of sanctification, nevertheless, is in the true direction. It is only in the details of execution that it fails. *The Changed Life.*

November 9th. We all reflecting as a mirror the character of Christ are transformed into the same Image from character to character—from a poor character to a better one, from a better one to one a little better still, from that to one still more complete, until by slow degrees the Perfect Image is attained. Here the solution of the problem of sanctification is compressed into a sentence: Reflect the character of Christ, and you will become like Christ. *The Changed Life.*

November 10th. There are some men and some women in whose company we are always at our best. While with them we cannot think mean thoughts or speak ungenerous words. Their mere presence is elevation, purification, sanctity. All the best stops in our nature are drawn out by their intercourse, and we find a music in our souls that was never there before. *The Changed Life.*

November 11th. Take such a sentence as this: African explorers are subject to fevers which cause restlessness and delirium. Note the expression, "cause restlessness." *restlessness has a cause.* Clearly, then, any one who wished to get rid of restlessness would proceed at once to deal with the cause. *Pax Vobiscum.*

November 12th. What Christian experience wants is *thread*, a vertebral column, method. It is impossible to believe that there is no remedy for its unevenness and dishevelment, or that the remedy is a secret. The idea, also, that some few men, by happy chance or happier temperament, have been given the secret—as if there were some sort of knack or trick of it—is wholly incredible. Religion must ripen fruit for every temperament; and the way even into its highest heights must be by a gateway through which the peoples of the world may pass. *Pax Vobiscum.*

November 13th. Nothing that happens in the world happens by chance. God is a God of order. Everything is arranged upon definite principles, and never at random. The world, even the religious world, is governed by law. Character is governed by law. Happiness is governed by law. The Christian experiences are governed by law. *Pax Vobiscum.*

November 14th. We *are changed*, as the Old Version has it—we do not change ourselves. No man can change himself. Throughout the New Testament you will find that wherever these moral and spiritual transformations are described the verbs are in the passive. Presently it will be pointed out that there is a rationale in this; but meantime do not toss these words aside as if this passivity denied all human effort or ignored intelligible law. What is implied for the soul here is no more than is everywhere claimed for the body. *The Changed Life.*

November 15th. Rain and snow do drop from the air, but not without a long previous history. They are the mature effects of former causes. Equally so are Rest, and Peace, and Joy. They, too, have each a previous history. Storms and winds and calms are not accidents, but are brought about by antecedent circumstances. Rest and Peace are but calms in man's inward nature, and arise through causes as definite and as inevitable. *Pax Vobiscum.*

November 16th. Few men know how to live. We grow up at random, carrying into mature life the merely animal methods and motives which we had as little children. And it does not occur to us that all this must be changed; that much of it must be reversed; that life is the finest of the Fine Arts; that it has to be learned with life-long patience, and that the years of our pilgrimage are all too short to master it triumphantly. *Pax Vobiscum.*

November 17th. Christ's life outwardly was one of the most troubled lives that was ever lived: Tempest and tumult, tumult and tempest, the waves breaking over it all the time till the worn body was laid in the grave. But the inner life was a sea of glass. The great calm was always there. At any moment you might have gone to Him and found Rest. *Pax Vobiscum*, p. 35.

November 18th. The creation of a new heart, the renewing of a right spirit is an omnipotent work of God. Leave it to the Creator. "He which hath begun a good work in you will perfect it unto that day." *The Changed Life.*

November 19th. To become like Christ is the only thing in the world worth caring for, the thing before which every ambition of man is folly, and all lower achievement vain. Those only who make this quest the supreme desire and passion of their lives can even begin to hope to reach it. *The Changed Life.*

November 20th. A religion of effortless adoration may be a religion for an angel but never for a man. Not in the contemplative, but in the active, lies true hope; not in rapture, but in reality, lies true life; not in the realm of ideals, but among tangible things, is man's sanctification wrought. *The Changed Life.*

November 21st. Nothing ever for a moment broke the serenity of Christ's life on earth. Misfortune could not reach Him; He had no fortune. Food, raiment, money—fountain-heads of half the world's weariness—He simply did not care for; they played no part in His life; He "took no thought" for them. It was impossible to affect Him by lowering His reputation; He had already made Himself of no reputation. He was dumb before insult. When He was reviled, He reviled not again. In fact, there was nothing that the world could do to Him that could ruffle the surface of His spirit. *Pax Vobiscum.*

November 22d. Life is the cradle of eternity. As the man is to the animal in the slowness of his evolution, so is the spiritual man to the natural man. Foundations which have to bear the weight of an eternal life must be surely laid. Character is to wear forever; who will wonder or grudge that it cannot be developed in a day? *The Changed Life.*

November 23d. To await the growing of a soul is an almost Divine act of faith. How pardonable, surely, the impatience of deformity with itself, of a consciously despicable character standing before Christ, wondering, yearning, hungering to be like that? Yet must one trust the process fearlessly, and without misgiving. "The Lord the Spirit" will do His part. The tempting expedient is, in haste for abrupt or visible progress, to try some method less spiritual, or to defeat the end by watching for effects instead of keeping the eye on the Cause. *The Changed Life.*

November 24th. The Image of Christ that is forming within us—that is life's one charge. Let every project stand aside for that. "Till Christ be formed," no man's work is finished, no religion crowned, no life has fulfilled its end. Is the infinite task begun? When, how, are we to be different? Time cannot change men. Death cannot change men. Christ can. Wherefore *put on Christ. The Changed Life.*

November 25th. Christ saw that men took life painfully. To some it was a weariness, to others a failure, to many a tragedy, to all a struggle and a pain. How to carry this burden of life had been the whole world's problem. It is still the whole world's problem. And here is Christ's solution. "Carry it as I do. Take life as I take it. Look at it from My point of view. Interpret it upon My principles. Take My yoke and learn of Me, and you will find it easy. For My yoke is easy, works easily, sits right upon the shoulders, and *therefore* My burden is light." *Pax Vobiscum.*

November 26th. There is a disease called "touchiness"—a disease which, in spite of its innocent name, is one of the gravest sources of restlessness in the world. Touchiness, when it becomes chronic, is a morbid condition of the inward disposition. It is self-love inflamed to the acute point. . . The cure is to shift the yoke to some other place; to let men and things touch us through some new and perhaps as yet unused part of our nature; to become meek and lowly in heart while the old nature is becoming numb from want of use. *Pax Vobiscum*.

November 27th. Christ's yoke is simply His secret for the alleviation of human life, His prescription for the best and happiest method of living. Men harness themselves to the work and stress of the world in clumsy and unnatural ways. The harness they put on is antiquated. A rough, ill-fitted collar at the best, they make its strain and friction past enduring, by placing it where the neck is most sensitive; and by mere continuous irritation this sensitiveness increases until the whole nature is quick and sore. *Pax Vobiscum*.

November 28th. No one can get Joy by merely asking for it. It is one of the ripest fruits of the Christian life, and, like all fruits, must be grown. *Pax Vobiscum*.

November 29th Christ is the source of Joy to men in the sense in which He is the source of Rest. His people share His life, and therefore share its consequences, and one of these is Joy. His method of living is one that in the nature of things produces Joy. When He spoke of His Joy remaining with us He meant in part that the causes which produced it should continue to act. His followers, that is to say, by repeating His life would experience its accompaniments. His Joy, His kind of Joy, would remain with them. *Pax Vobiscum*.

November 30th. Think of it, the past is not only focused there, in a man's soul, it IS there. How could it be reflected from there if it were not there? All things that he has ever seen, known, felt, believed of the surrounding world are now within him, have become part of him, in part are him—he has been changed into their image. He may deny it, he may resent it, but they are there. They do not adhere to him, they are transfused through him. He cannot alter or rub them out. They are not in his memory, they are in *him*. His soul is as they have filled it, made it, left it. *The Changed Life*.

December 1st. Temper is significant, not in what it is alone but in what it reveals. . . . It is a test for love, a symptom, a revelation of an unloving nature at bottom. It is the intermittent fever which bespeaks unintermittent disease within; the occasional bubble escaping to the surface which betrays some rottenness underneath; a sample of the most hidden products of the soul dropped involuntarily when off one's guard; *in a word*, the lightning form of a hundred hideous and un-Christian sins. *The Greatest Thing in the World*.

December 2d. You will find, as you look back upon your life, that the moments that stand out, the moments when you have really lived, are the moments when you have done things in a spirit of love. As memory scans the past, above and beyond all the transitory pleasures of life there leap forward those supreme hours when you have been enabled to do unnoticed kindnesses to those round about you, things too trifling to speak about, but which you feel have entered into your eternal life. *The Greatest Thing in the World*.

December 3d. If events change men, much more persons. No man can meet another on the street without making some mark upon him. We say we exchange words when we meet; what we exchange is souls. And when intercourse is very close and very frequent, so complete is this exchange that recognizable bits of the one soul begin to show in the other's nature, and the second is conscious of a similar and growing debt to the first. *The Changed Life*.

December 4th. In the natural world we absorb heat, breathe air, draw on Environment all but automatically for meat and drink, for the nourishment of the senses, for mental stimulus, for all that, penetrating us from without, can prolong, enrich, and elevate life. But in the spiritual world we have all this to learn. We are new creatures, and even the bare living has to be acquired. *Greatest Thing in the World*.

December 5th. The great point in learning to live the spiritual life is to live naturally. As closely as possible we must follow the broad, clear lines of the natural life. And there are three things especially which it is necessary for us to keep continually in view. The first is that the organism contains within itself only one-half of what is essential to life; the second is that the other half is contained in the Environment; the third, that the condition of receptivity is simple union between the organism and the Environment. *Greatest Thing in the World*.

December 6th. To say that the organism contains within itself only one-half of what is essential to life, is to repeat the evangelical confession, so worn and yet so true to universal experience, of the utter helplessness of man. *Greatest Thing in the World*.

December 7th. Who has not come to the conclusion that he is but a part, a fraction of some larger whole? Who does not miss at every turn of his life an absent God? That man is but a part, he knows, for there is room in him for more. That God is the other part, he feels, because at times He satisfies his need. Who does not tremble often under that sicklier symptom of his incompleteness, his want of spiritual energy, his helplessness with sin? But now he understands both—the void in his life, the powerlessness of his will. He understands that, like all other energy, spiritual power is contained in Environment. He finds here at last the true root of all human frailty, emptiness, nothingness, sin. This is why "without Me ye can do nothing." Powerless is the normal state not only of this but of every organism—of every organism apart from its Environment. *Greatest Thing in the World*.

December 8th. To seize continuously the opportunity of more and more perfect adjustment to better and higher conditions, to balance some inward evil with some purer influence acting from without, in a word to make our Environment at the same time that it is making us—these are the secrets of a well-ordered and successful life. *Greatest Thing in the World*.

December 9th. In the spiritual world the subtle influences which form and transform the soul are Heredity and Environment. And here especially, where all is invisible, where much that we feel to be real is yet so ill-defined, it becomes of vital practical moment to clarify the atmosphere as far as possible with conceptions borrowed from the natural life. *Greatest Thing in the World*.

December 10th. These lower correspondences are in their nature unfitted for an Eternal Life. Even if they were perfect in their relation to their Environment, they would still not be Eternal. However opposed, apparently, to the scientific definition of Eternal Life, it is yet true that perfect correspondence with Environment is not Eternal Life. . . . An Eternal Life demands an Eternal Environment. *Greatest Thing in the World*.

December 11th. On what does the Christian argument for Immortality really rest? It stands upon the pedestal on which the theologian rests the whole of historical Christianity—the Resurrection of Jesus Christ. *Greatest Thing in the World*.

December 12th. The soul which has no correspondence with the spiritual environment is spiritually dead. It may be that it never possessed . . . the spiritual ear, or a heart which throbbed in response to the love of God. If so, having never lived, it cannot be said to have died. But not to have these correspondences is to be in the state of Death. To the spiritual world, to the Divine Environment, it is dead—as a stone which has never lived is dead to the environment of the organic world. *Greatest Thing in the World.*

December 13th. The humanity of what is called "sudden conversion" has never been insisted on as it deserves. . . . While growth is a slow and gradual process, the change from Death to Life, alike in the natural and spiritual spheres, is the work of the moment. Whatever the conscious hour of the second birth may be—in the case of an adult it is probably defined by the first real victory over sin—it is certain that on biological principles the real turning-point is literally a moment. *Greatest Thing in the World.*

December 14th. Christ says we must hate life. Now, this does not apply to all life. It is "life in this world" that is to be hated. For life in this world implies conformity to this world. It may not mean pursuing worldly pleasures, or mixing with worldly sets; but a subtler thing than that—a silent deference to worldly opinion; an almost unconscious lowering of religious tone to the level of the worldly-religious world around; a subdued resistance to the soul's delicate promptings to greater consecration, out of deference to "breadth" or fear of ridicule. These, and such things, are what Christ tells us we must hate. For these things are of the very essence of worldliness. "If any man love the world," even in this sense, "the love of the Father is not in him." *Greatest Thing in the World.*

December 15th. To correspond with the God of Science, the Eternal Unknowable, would be everlasting existence; to correspond with "the true God and Jesus Christ," is Eternal Life. The quality of the Eternal Life alone makes the heaven; mere everlastingness might be no boon. Even the brief span of the temporal life is too long for those who spend its years in sorrow. *Greatest Thing in the World.*

December 16th. The relation between the spiritual man and his Environment is, in theological language, a filial relation. With the new Spirit, the filial correspondence, he knows the Father—and this is Life Eternal. This is not only the real relation, but the only possible relation: "Neither knoweth any man the Father save the Son, and he to whomsoever the Son will reveal Him." And this on purely natural grounds. *Greatest Thing in the World.*

December 17th. Communion with God—can it be demonstrated in terms of Science that this is a correspondence which will never break? We do not appeal to Science for such a testimony. We have asked for its conception of an Eternal Life; and we have received for answer that Eternal Life would consist in a correspondence which should never cease, with an Environment which should never pass away. And yet what would Science demand of a perfect correspondence that is not met by this, *the knowing of god*? There is no other correspondence which could satisfy one at least of the conditions. Not one could be named which would not bear on the face of it the mark and pledge of its mortality. But this, to know God, stands alone. *Greatest Thing in the World.*

December 18th. The misgiving which will creep sometimes over the brightest faith has already received its expression and its rebuke: "Who shall separate us from the love of Christ? Shall tribulation, or distress, or persecution, or famine, or nakedness, or peril, or sword?" Shall these "changes in the physical state of the environment" which threaten death to the natural man, destroy the spiritual? Shall death, or life, or angels, or principalities, or powers, arrest or tamper with his eternal correspondences? "Nay, in all these things we are more than conquerors through Him that loved us. For I am persuaded that neither death, nor life, nor angels, nor principalities, nor powers, nor things present, nor things to come, nor height, nor depth, nor any other creature, shall be able to separate us from the love of God, which is in Christ Jesus our Lord." Rom. viii, 35-39. *Greatest Thing in the World*.

December 19th. "We find that man, or the spiritual man, is equipped with two sets of correspondences." One set possesses the quality of everlastingness, the other is temporal. But unless these are separated by some means the temporal will continue to impair and hinder the eternal. The final preparation, therefore, for the inheriting of Eternal Life must consist in the abandonment of the non-eternal elements. These must be unloosed and dissociated from the higher elements. And this is effected by a closing catastrophe—Death. *Greatest Thing in the World*.

December 20th. Heredity and Environment are the master-influences of the organic world. These have made all of us what we are. These forces are still ceaselessly playing upon all our lives. And he who truly understands these influences; he who has decided how much to allow to each; he who can regulate new forces as they arise, or adjust them to the old, so directing them as at one moment to make them cooperate, at another to counter act one another, understands the rationale of personal development. *Greatest Thing in the World*.

December 21st. It is the Law of Influence that *we become like those whom we habitually admire*. Through all the range of literature, of history, and biography this law presides. Men are all mosaics of other men. There was a savor of David about Jonathan and a savor of Jonathan about David. Jean Valjean, in the masterpiece of Victor Hugo, is Bishop Bienvenu risen from the dead. Metempsychosis is a fact. *The Changed Life*.

December 22d. Can we shut our eyes to the fact that the religious opinions of mankind are in a state of flux? And when we regard the uncertainty of current beliefs, the war of creeds, the havoc of inevitable as well as of idle doubt, the reluctant abandonment of early faith by those who would cherish it longer if they could, is it not plain that the one thing thinking men are waiting for is the introduction of Law among the Phenomena of the Spiritual World? When that comes we shall offer to such men a truly scientific theology. And the Reign of Law will transform the whole Spiritual World as it has already transformed the Natural World. *Greatest Thing in the World*.

December 23d. We have Truth in Nature as it came from God. And it has to be read with the same unbiased mind, the same open eye, the same faith, and the same reverence as all other Revelation. All that is found there, whatever its place in Theology, whatever its orthodoxy or heterodoxy, whatever its narrowness or its breadth, we are bound to accept as Doctrine from which on the lines of Science there is no escape. *Greatest Thing in the World*.

December 24th. In Nature generally, we come upon new Laws as we pass from lower to higher kingdoms, the old still remaining in force, the newer Laws which one would expect to meet in the Spiritual World would so transcend and overwhelm the older as to make the analogy or identity, even if traced, of no practical use. The new Laws would represent operations and energies so different, and so much more elevated, that they would afford the true keys to the Spiritual World. *Greatest Thing in the World*.

December 25th. The visible is the ladder up to the invisible; the temporal is but the scaffolding of the eternal. And when the last immaterial souls have climbed through this material to God, the scaffolding shall be taken down, and the earth dissolved with fervent heat—not because it was base, but because its work is done. *Greatest Thing in the World.*

December 26th. The natural man belongs essentially to this present order of things. He is endowed simply with a high quality of the natural animal Life. But it is Life of so poor a quality that it is not Life at all. He that hath not the Son hath not Life; but he that hath the Son hath Life— a new and distinct and supernatural endowment. He is not of this world. He is of the timeless state, of Eternity. *It doth not yet appear what he shall be. Greatest Thing in the World.*

December 27th. The gradualness of growth is a characteristic which strikes the simplest observer. Long before the word Evolution was coined Christ applied it in this very connection—"First the blade, then the ear, then the full corn in the ear." It is well known also to those who study the parables of Nature that there is an ascending scale of slowness as we rise in the scale of Life. Growth is most gradual in the highest forms. Man attains his maturity after a score of years; the monad completes its humble cycle in a day. What wonder if development be tardy in the Creature of Eternity? A Christian's sun has sometimes set, and a critical world has seen as yet no corn in the ear. As yet? "As yet," in this long Life, has not begun. Grant him the years proportionate to his place in the scale of Life. "The time of harvest is *not yet." Greatest Thing in the World.*

December 28th. Salvation is a definite process. If a man refuse to submit himself to that process, clearly he cannot have the benefits of it. "As many as received Him to them gave He power to become the sons of God." He does not avail himself of this power. It may be mere carelessness or apathy. Nevertheless the neglect is fatal. He cannot escape because he will not. *Greatest Thing in the World.*

December 29th. The end of Salvation is perfection, the Christ-like mind, character, and life. Morality is on the way to this perfection; it may go a considerable distance toward it, but it can never reach it. Only Life can do that. . . . Morality can never reach perfection; Life *must.* For the Life must develop out according to its type; and being a germ of the Christ-life, it must unfold into *a Christ. Greatest Thing in the World.*

December 30th. Perfect life is not merely the possessing of perfect functions, but of perfect functions perfectly adjusted to each other, and all conspiring to a single result, the perfect working of the whole organism. It is not said that the character will develop in all its fulness in this life. That were a time too short for an Evolution so magnificent. In this world only the cornless ear is seen: sometimes only the small yet still prophetic blade. *Greatest Thing in the World.*

December 31st. The immortal soul must give itself to something that is immortal. And the only immortal things are these: "Now abideth faith, hope, love, but the greatest of these is love." Some think the time may come when two of these three things will also pass away—faith into sight, hope into fruition. Paul does not say so. We know but little now about the conditions of the life that is to come. But what is certain is that Love must last. God, the Eternal God, is Love. Covet therefore that everlasting gift. *The Greatest Thing in the World.*

The Program of Christianity

Table of Contents

To Preach Good Tidings unto the Meek:
To Bind up the Broken-hearted:
To proclaim Liberty to the Captives and the Opening of the Prison to
Them that are Bound:
To Proclaim the Acceptable Year of the Lord, and the Day of
Vengeance of our God:
To Comfort all that Mourn:
To Appoint unto them that Mourn in Zion:
To Give unto them—
Beauty for Ashes,
The Oil of Joy for Mourning,
The Garment of Praise for the Spirit of Heaviness.

The Program of Christianity

"What does God do all day?" once asked a little boy. One could wish that more
grown-up people would ask so very real a question. Unfortunately, most of us are
not even boys in religious intelligence, but only very unthinking children. It no
more occurs to us that God is engaged in any particular work in the world than
it occurs to a little child that its father does anything except be its father. Its father
may be a Cabinet Minister absorbed in the nation's work, or an inventor deep in
schemes for the world's good; but to this master-egoist he is father, and nothing
more. Childhood, whether in the physical or moral world, is the great self-centered
period of life; and a personal God who satisfies personal ends is all that for a long
time many a Christian understands.

But as clearly as there comes to the growing child a knowledge of its father's
part in the world, and a sense of what real life means, there must come to every
Christian whose growth is true some richer sense of the meaning of Christianity
and a larger view of Christ's purpose for mankind. To miss this is to miss the
whole splendor and glory of Christ's religion. Next to losing the sense of a personal
Christ, the worst evil that can befall a Christian is to have no sense of anything
else. To grow up in complacent belief that God has no business in this great
groaning world of human beings except to attend to a few saved souls is the
negation of all religion. The first great epoch in a Christian's life, after the awe and
wonder of its dawn, is when there breaks into his mind some sense that Christ has
a purpose for mankind, a purpose beyond him and his needs, beyond the churches
and their creeds, beyond Heaven and its saints—a purpose which embraces every
man and woman born, every kindred and nation formed, which regards not their
spiritual good alone but their welfare in every part, their progress, their health,
their work, their wages, their happiness in this present world.

What, then, does Christ do all day? By what further conception shall we
augment the selfish view of why Christ lived and died?

I shall mislead no one, I hope, if I say —for I wish to put the social side of
Christianity in its strongest light—that Christ did not come into the world to give
men religion. He never mentioned the word religion. Religion was in the world
before Christ came, and it lives to-day in a million souls who have never heard His
name. What God does all day is not to sit waiting in churches for people to come
and worship Him. It is true that God is in churches and in all kinds of churches,
and is found by many in churches more immediately than anywhere else. It is also
true that while Christ did not give men religion He gave a new direction to the
religious aspiration bursting forth then and now and always from the whole
world's heart. But it was His purpose to enlist these aspirations on behalf of some
definite practical good. The religious people of those days did nothing with their
religion except attend to its observances. Even the priest, after he had been to the
temple, thought his work was done; when he met the wounded man he passed by
on the other side. Christ reversed all this—tried to reverse it, for He is only now

beginning to succeed. The tendency of the religions of all time has been to care more for religion than for humanity; Christ cared more for humanity than for religion—rather His care for humanity was the chief expression of His religion. He was not indifferent to observances, but the practices of the people bulked in His thoughts before the practices of the Church. It has been pointed out as a blemish on the immortal allegory of Bunyan that the Pilgrim never did anything, anything but save his soul. The remark is scarcely fair, for the allegory is designedly the story of a soul in a single relation; and besides, he did do a little. But the warning may well be weighed. The Pilgrim's one thought, his work by day, his dream by night, was escape. He took little part in the world through which he passed. He was a Pilgrim traveling through it; his business was to get through safe. Whatever this is, it is not Christianity. Christ's conception of Christianity was heavens removed from that of a man setting out from the City of Destruction to save his soul. It was rather that of a man dwelling amidst the Destructions of the City and planning escapes for the souls of others—escapes not to the other world, but to purity and peace and righteousness in this. In reality Christ never said "Save your soul." It is a mistranslation which says that. What He said was, "Save your life." And this not because the first is nothing, but only because it is so very great a thing that only the second can accomplish it. But the new word altruism—the translation of "love thy neighbor as thyself"—is slowly finding its way into current Christian speech. The People's Progress, not less than the Pilgrim's Progress, is daily becoming a graver concern to the Church. A popular theology with unselfishness as part at least of its root, a theology which appeals no longer to fear, but to the generous heart in man, has already dawned, and more clearly than ever men are beginning to see what Christ really came into this world to do.

What Christ came here for was to make a better world. The world in which we live is an unfinished world. It is not wise, it is not happy, it is not pure, it is not good—it is not even sanitary. Humanity is little more than raw material. Almost everything has yet to be done to it. Before the days of Geology people thought the earth was finished. It is by no means finished. The work of Creation is going on. Before the spectroscope, men thought the universe was finished. We know now it is just beginning. And this teeming universe of men in which we live has almost all its finer color and beauty yet to take. Christ came to complete it. The fires of its passions were not yet cool; their heat had to be transformed into finer energies. The ideals for its future were all to shape, the forces to realize them were not yet born. The poison of its sins had met no antidote, the gloom of its doubt no light, the weight of its sorrow no rest. These the Savior of the world, the Light of men, would do and be. This, roughly, was His scheme.

Now this was a prodigious task—to recreate the world. How was it to be done? God's way of making worlds is to make them make themselves. When He made the earth He made a rough ball of matter and supplied it with a multitude of tools to mold it into form—the rain-drop to carve it, the glacier to smooth it, the river to nourish it, the flower to adorn it. God works always with agents, and this is our way when we want any great thing done, and this was Christ's way when He undertook the finishing of Humanity. He had a vast intractable mass of matter to deal with, and He required a multitude of tools. Christ's tools were men. Hence His first business in the world was to make a collection of men. In other words He founded a Society.

The Founding of the Society

It is a somewhat startling thought—it will not be misunderstood—that Christ probably did not save many people while He was here. Many an evangelist, in that direction, has done much more. He never intended to finish the world single-handed, but announced from the first that others would not only take part, but do "greater things" than He. For amazing as was the attention He was able to give to individuals, this was not the whole aim He had in view. His immediate work was to enlist men in His enterprise, to rally them into a great company or Society for the carrying out of His plans.

The name by which this Society was known was The Kingdom of God. Christ did not coin this name; it was an old expression, and good men had always hoped and prayed that some such Society would be born in their midst. But it was never either defined or set agoing in earnest until Christ made its realization the passion of His life.

How keenly He felt regarding His task, how enthusiastically He set about it, every page of His life bears witness. All reformers have one or two great words which they use incessantly, and by mere reiteration embed indelibly in the thought and history of their time. Christ's great word was the Kingdom of God. Of all the words of His that have come down to us this is by far the commonest. One hundred times it occurs in the Gospels. When He preached He had almost always this for a text. His sermons were explanations of the aims of His Society, of the different things it was like, of whom its membership consisted, what they were to do or to be, or not do or not be. And even when He does not actually use the word, it is easy to see that all He said and did had reference to this. Philosophers talk about thinking in categories— the mind living, as it were, in a particular room with its own special furniture, pictures, and viewpoints, these giving a consistent direction and color to all that is there thought or expressed. It was in the category of the Kingdom that Christ's thought moved. Though one time He said He came to save the lost, or at another time to give men life, or to do His Father's will, these were all included among the objects of His Society.

No one can ever know what Christianity is till he has grasped this leading thought in the mind of Christ. Peter and Paul have many wonderful and necessary things to tell us about what Christ was and did; but we are looking now at what Christ's own thought was. Do not think this is a mere modern theory. These are His own life-plans taken from His own lips. Do not allow any isolated text, even though it seem to sum up for you the Christian life, to keep you from trying to understand Christ's Program as a whole. The perspective of Christ's teaching is not everything, but without it everything will be distorted and untrue. There is much good in a verse, but often much evil. To see some small soul pirouetting throughout life on a single text, and judging all the world because it cannot find a partner, is not a Christian sight. Christianity does not grudge such souls their comfort. What it grudges is that they make Christ's Kingdom uninhabitable to thoughtful minds. Be sure that whenever the religion of Christ appears small, or forbidding, or narrow, or inhuman, you are dealing not with the whole —which is a matchless moral symmetry— nor even with an arch or column—for every detail is perfect—but with some cold stone removed from its place and suggesting nothing of the glorious structure from which it came.

Tens of thousands of persons who are familiar with religious truths have not noticed yet that Christ ever founded a Society at all. The reason is partly that people have read texts instead of reading their Bible, partly that they have studied Theology instead of studying Christianity, and partly because of the noiselessness and invisibility of the Kingdom of God itself. Nothing truer was ever said of this Kingdom than that "It cometh without observation." Its first discovery, therefore, comes to the Christian with all the force of a revelation. The sense of belonging to such a Society transforms life. It is the difference between being a solitary knight tilting single-handed, and often defeated, at whatever enemy one chances to meet on one's little acre of life, and the feel of belonging to a mighty army marching throughout all time to a certain victory. This note of universality given to even the humblest work we do, this sense of comradeship, this link with history, this thought of a definite campaign, this promise of success, is the possession of every obscurest unit in the Kingdom of God.

The Program of the Society

Hundreds of years before Christ's Society was formed, its Program had been issued to the world. I cannot think of any scene in history more dramatic than when Jesus entered the church in Nazareth and read it to the people. Not that when He appropriated to Himself that venerable fragment from Isaiah He was uttering a manifesto or announcing His formal Program. Christ never did things formally. We think of the words, as He probably thought of them, not in their old-world historical significance, nor as a full expression of His future aims, but as a summary of great moral facts now and always to be realized in the world since he appeared.

Remember as you read the words to what grim reality they refer. Recall what Christ's problem really was, what His Society was founded for. This Program deals with a real world. Think of it as you read—not of the surface-world, but of the world as it is, as it sins and weeps, and curses and suffers and sends up its long cry to God. Limit it if you like to the world around your door, but think of it— of the city and the hospital and the dungeon and the graveyard, of the sweating-shop and the pawn-shop and the drink-shop; think of the cold, the cruelty, the fever, the famine, the ugliness, the loneliness, the pain. And then try to keep down the lump in your throat as you take up His Program and read—

To Bind up the Broken-hearted:
To Proclaim Liberty to the Captives:
To Comfort All That Mourn:
To Give unto Them—Beauty for Ashes,
The Oil of Joy for Mourning,
The Garment of Praise for the Spirit of Heaviness.

What an exchange—Beauty for Ashes, Joy for Mourning, Liberty for Chains! No marvel "the eyes of all them that were in the synagogue were fastened on Him" as He read; or that they "wondered at the gracious words which proceeded out of His lips." Only one man in that congregation, only one man in the world to-day could hear these accents with dismay—the man, the culprit, who has said hard words of Christ.

We are all familiar with the protest "Of course"—as if there were no other alternative to a person of culture—"Of course I am not a Christian, but I always speak respectfully of Christianity." Respectfully of Christianity! No remark fills one's soul with such sadness. One can understand a man as he reads these words being stricken speechless; one can see the soul within him rise to a white heat as each fresh benediction falls upon his ear and drive him, a half-mad enthusiast, to bear them to the world. But in what school has he learned of Christ who offers the Savior of the world his respect?

Men repudiate Christ's religion because they think it a small and limited thing, a scheme with no large human interests to commend it to this great social age. I ask you to note that there is not one burning interest of the human race which is not represented here. What are the great words of Christianity according to this Program? Take as specimens these:

Liberty,
Comfort,
Beauty,
Joy.

These are among the greatest words of life. Give them their due extension, the significance which Christ undoubtedly saw in them and which Christianity undoubtedly yields, and there is almost no great want or interest of mankind which they do not cover.

These are not only the greatest words of life but they are the best. This Program, to those who have misread Christianity, is a series of surprises. Observe the most prominent note in it. It is gladness. Its first word is "good-tidings," its last is "joy." The saddest words of life are also there—but there as the diseases which Christianity comes to cure. No life that is occupied with such an enterprise could be other than radiant. The contribution of Christianity to the joy of living, perhaps even more to the joy of thinking, is unspeakable. The joyful life is the life of the larger mission, the disinterested life, the life of the overflow from self, the "more abundant life" which comes from following Christ. And the joy of thinking is the larger thinking, the thinking of the man who holds in his hand some Program for Humanity. The Christian is the only man who has any Program at all— any Program either for the world or for himself. Goethe, Byron, Carlyle taught Humanity much, but they had no Program for it. Byron's thinking was suffering; Carlisle's despair. Christianity alone exults. The belief in the universe as moral, the interpretation of history as progress, the faith in good as eternal, in evil as self-consuming, in humanity as evolving—these Christian ideas have transformed the malady of thought into a bounding hope. It was no sentiment but a conviction matured amid calamity and submitted to the tests of life that inspired the great modern poet of optimism to proclaim:—

"Gladness be with thee, Helper of the world!
I think this is the authentic sign and seal
Of Godship, that it ever waxes glad,
And more glad, until gladness blossoms, bursts
Into a rage to suffer for mankind
And recommence at sorrow."

But that is not all. Man's greatest needs are often very homely. And it is almost as much in its fearless recognition of the commonplace woes of life, and its deliberate offerings to minor needs, that the claims of Christianity to be a religion for Humanity stand. Look, for instance, at the closing sentence of this Program. Who would have expected to find among the special objects of Christ's solicitude the Spirit of Heaviness? Supreme needs, many and varied, had been already dealt with on this Program; many applicants had been met; the list is about to close. Suddenly the writer remembers the nameless malady of the poor—that mysterious disease which the rich share but cannot alleviate, which is too subtle for doctors, too incurable for Parliaments, too unpicturesque for philanthropy, too common even for sympathy. Can Christ meet that?

If Christianity could even deal with the world's Depression, could cure mere dull spirits, it would be the Physician of Humanity. But it can. It has the secret, a hundred secrets, for the lifting of the world's gloom. It cannot immediately remove the physiological causes of dulness— though obedience to its principles can do an infinity to prevent them, and its inspirations can do even more to lift the mind above them. But where the causes are moral or mental or social the remedy is in every Christian's hand. Think of any one at this moment whom the Spirit of Heaviness haunts. You think of a certain old woman. But you know for a fact that you can cure her. You did so, perfectly, only a week ago. A mere visit, and a little present, or the visit without any present, set her up for seven long days, and seven long nights. The machinery of the Kingdom is very simple and very silent, and the most silent parts do most, and we all believe so little in the medicines of Christ that we do not know what ripples of healing are set in motion when we simply smile on one another. Christianity wants nothing so much in the world as sunny people, and the old are hungrier for love than for bread, and the Oil of Joy is very cheap, and if you can help the poor on with a Garment of Praise, it will be better for them than blankets.

Or perhaps you know someone else who is dull—not an old woman this time, but a very rich and important man. But you also know perfectly what makes him dull. It is either his riches or his importance. Christianity can cure either of these though you may not be the person to apply the cure—at a single hearing. Or here is a third case, one of your own servants. It is a case of monotony. Prescribe more variety, leisure, recreation—anything to relieve the wearing strain. A fourth case—your most honored guest: Condition—leisure, health, accomplishments, means; Disease—Spiritual Obesity; Treatment—talent to be put out to usury. And so on down the whole range of life's dejection and ennui.

Perhaps you tell me this is not Christianity at all; that everybody could do that. The curious thing is that everybody does not. Good-will to men came into the world with Christ, and wherever that is found, in Christian or heathen land, there Christ is, and there His Spirit works. And if you say that the chief end of Christianity is not the world's happiness, I agree; it was never meant to be; but the strange fact is that, without making it its chief end, it wholly and infallibly, and quite universally, leads to it. Hence the note of Joy, though not the highest on Christ's Program, is a loud and ringing note, and none who serve in His Society can be long without its music. Time was when a Christian used to apologize for being happy. But the day has always been when he ought to apologize for being miserable.

Christianity, you will observe, really works. And it succeeds not only because it is divine, but because it is so very human—because it is common-sense. Why should the Garment of Praise destroy the Spirit of Heaviness? Because an old woman cannot sing and cry at the same moment. The Society of Christ is a sane Society. Its methods are rational. The principle in the old woman's case is simply that one emotion destroys another. Christianity works, as a railway man would say, with points. It switches souls from valley lines to mountain lines, not stemming the currents of life but diverting them. In the rich man's case the principle of cure is different, but it is again principle, not necromancy. His spirit of heaviness is caused, like any other heaviness, by the earth's attraction. Take away the earth and you take away the attraction. But if Christianity can do anything it can take away the earth. By the wider extension of horizon which it gives, by the new standard of values, by the mere setting of life's small pomps and interests and admirations in the light of the Eternal, it dissipates the world with a breath. All that tends to abolish worldliness tends to abolish unrest, and hence, in the rush of modern life, one far-reaching good of all even commonplace Christian preaching, all Christian literature, all which holds the world doggedly to the idea of a God and a future life, and reminds mankind of Infinity and Eternity.

Side by side with these influences, yet taking the world at a wholly different angle, works another great Christian force. How many opponents of religion are aware that one of the specific objects of Christ's society is Beauty? The charge of vulgarity against Christianity is an old one. If it means that Christianity deals with the ruder elements in human nature, it is true, and that is its glory. But if it means that it has no respect for the finer qualities, the charge is baseless. For Christianity not only encourages whatsoever things are lovely, but wars against that whole theory of life which would exclude them. It prescribes aestheticism. It proscribes asceticism. And for those who preach to Christians that in these enlightened days they must raise the masses by giving them noble sculptures and beautiful paintings and music and public parks, the answer is that these things are all already being given, and given daily, and with an increasing sense of their importance, by the Society of Christ. Take away from the world the beautiful things which have not come from Christ and you will make it poorer scarcely at all. Take away from modern cities the paintings, the monuments, the music for the people, the museums and the parks which are not the gifts of Christian men and Christian municipalities, and in ninety cases out of a hundred you will leave them unbereft of so much as a well-shaped lamp-post

It is impossible to doubt that the Decorator of the World shall not continue to serve to His later children, and in ever finer forms, the inspirations of beautiful things. More fearlessly than he has ever done, the Christian of modern life will use the noble spiritual leverages of Art. That this world, the people's world, is a bleak and ugly world, we do not forget; it is ever with us. But we esteem too little the mission of beautiful things in haunting the mind with higher thoughts and begetting the mood which leads to God. Physical beauty makes moral beauty. Loveliness does more than destroy ugliness; it destroys matter. A mere touch of it in a room, in a street, even on a door knocker, is a spiritual force. Ask the working-man's wife, and she will tell you there is a moral effect even in a clean table-cloth. If a barrel-organ in a slum can but drown a curse, let no Christian silence it. The mere light and color of the wall-advertisements are a gift of God to the poor man's somber world.

One Christmas-time a poor drunkard told me that he had gone out the night before to take his usual chance of the temptations of the street. Close to his door, at a shop window, an angel—so he said—arrested him. It was a large Christmas-card, a glorious white thing with tinsel wings, and as it glittered in the gas-light it flashed into his soul a sudden thought of Heaven. It recalled the earlier heaven of his infancy, and he thought of his mother in the distant glen, and how it would please her if she got this Christmas angel from her prodigal. With money already pledged to the devil he bought the angel, and with it a new soul and future for himself. That was a real angel. For that day as I saw its tinsel pinions shine in his squalid room I knew what Christ's angels were. They are all beautiful things, which daily in common homes are bearing up heavy souls to God.

But do not misunderstand me. This angel was made of pasteboard: a pasteboard angel can never save a soul. Tinsel reflects the sun, but warms nothing. Our Program must go deeper. Beauty may arrest the drunkard, but it cannot cure him.

It is here that Christianity asserts itself with a supreme individuality. It is here that it parts company with Civilization, with Politics, with all secular schemes of Social Reform. In its diagnosis of human nature it finds that which most other systems ignore; which, if they see, they cannot cure; which, left undestroyed, makes every reform futile, and every inspiration vain. That thing is Sin. Christianity, of all other philanthropies, recognizes that man's devouring need is Liberty—liberty to stop sinning; to leave the prison of his passions, and shake off the fetters of his past. To surround Captives with statues and pictures, to offer Them-that-are-Bound a higher wage or a cleaner street or a few more cubic feet of air per head, is solemn trifling. It is a cleaner soul they want; a purer air, or any air at all, for their higher selves.

And where the cleaner soul is to come from apart from Christ I cannot tell. "By no political alchemy," Herbert Spencer tells us, "can you get golden conduct out of leaden instincts." The power to set the heart right, to renew the springs of action, comes from Christ. The sense of the infinite worth of the single soul, and the recoverableness of man at his worst, are the gifts of Christ. The freedom from guilt, the forgiveness of sins, come from Christ's Cross; the hope of immortality springs from Christ's grave. We believe in the gospel of better laws and an improved environment; we hold the religion of Christ to be a social religion; we magnify and call Christian the work of reformers, statesmen, philanthropists, educators, inventors, sanitary officers, and all who directly or remotely aid, abet, or further the higher progress of mankind; but in Him alone, in the fulness of that word, do we see the Savior of the world.

There are earnest and gifted lives to-day at work among the poor whose lips at least will not name the name of Christ. I speak of them with respect; their shoe-latchets many of us are not worthy to unloose. But because the creed of the neighboring mission-hall is a travesty of religion they refuse to acknowledge the power of the living Christ to stop man's sin, of the dying Christ to forgive it. O, narrowness of breadth! Because there are ignorant doctors do I yet rail at medicine or start an hospital of my own? Because the poor raw evangelist, or the narrow ecclesiastic, offer their little all to the poor, shall I repudiate all they do not know of Christ because of the little that they do know? Of gospels for the poor which have not some theory, state it how you will, of personal conversion one cannot have much hope. Personal conversion means for life a personal religion, a personal trust in God, a personal debt to Christ, a personal dedication to His cause. These, brought about how you will, are supreme things to aim at, supreme losses if they are missed. Sanctification will come to masses only as it comes to individual men; and to work with Christ's Program and ignore Christ is to utilize the sun's light without its energy.

But this is not the only point at which the uniqueness of this Society appears. There is yet another depth in humanity which no other system even attempts to sound. We live in a world not only of sin but of sorrow—

"There is no flock, however watched and tended,
But one dead lamb is there;
There is no home, howe'er defended,
But has one vacant chair."

When the flock thins, and the chair empties, who is to be near to heal? At that moment the gospels of the world are on trial. In the presence of death how will they act? Act! They are blotted out of existence. Philosophy, Politics, Reforms, are no more. The Picture Galleries close. The sculptures hide. The Committees disperse. There is crape on the door; the world withdraws. Observe, it withdraws. It has no mission.

So awful in its loneliness was this hour that the Romans paid a professional class; to step in with its mummeries and try to fill it. But that is Christ's own hour. Next to Righteousness the greatest word of Christianity is Comfort. Christianity has almost a monopoly of Comfort Renan was never nearer the mark than when he spoke of the Bible as "the great Book of the Consolation of Humanity." Christ's Program is full of Comfort, studded with Comfort: "to bind up the Broken-Hearted, to Comfort all that mourn, to Give unto them that mourn in Zion." Even the "good tidings" to the "meek" are, in the Hebrew, a message to the "afflicted" or "the poor." The word Gospel itself comes down through the Greek from this very passage, so that whatever else Christ's Gospel means it is first an Evangel for suffering men.

One note in this Program jars with all the rest. When Christ read from Isaiah that day He never finished the passage. A terrible word, Vengeance, yawned like a precipice across His path; and in the middle of a sentence "He closed the Book, and gave it again to the minister, and sat down". A Day of Vengeance from our God—these were the words before which Christ paused. When the prophet proclaimed it some great historical fulfilment was in his mind. Had the people to whom Christ read been able to understand its ethical equivalents He would probably have read on. For, so understood, instead of filling the mind with fear, the thought of this dread Day inspires it with a solemn gratitude. The work of the Avenger is a necessity. It is part of God's philanthropy.

For I have but touched the surface in speaking of the sorrow of the world as if it came from people dying. It comes from people living. Before ever the Broken-Hearted can be healed a hundred greater causes of suffering than death must be destroyed. Before the Captive can be free a vaster prison than his own sins must be demolished. There are hells on earth into which no breath of heaven can ever come; these must be swept away. There are social soils in which only unrighteousness can flourish; these must be broken up.

And that is the work of the Day of Vengeance. When is that day? It is now. Who is the Avenger? Law. What Law? Criminal Law, Sanitary Law, Social Law, Natural Law. Wherever the poor are trodden upon or tread upon one another; wherever the air is poison and the water foul; wherever want stares, and vice reigns, and rags rot—there the Avenger takes his stand. Whatever makes it more difficult for the drunkard to reform, for the children to be pure, for the widow to earn a wage, for any of the wheels of progress to revolve—with these he deals. Delay him not. He is the messenger of Christ. Despair of him not, distrust him not. His Day dawns slowly, but his work is sure. Though evil stalks the world, it is on the way to execution; though wrong reigns, it must end in self-combustion. The very nature of things is God's Avenger; the very story of civilization is the history of Christ's Throne.

Anything that prepares the way for a better social state is the fit work of the followers of Christ. Those who work on the more spiritual levels leave too much unhonored the slow toil of multitudes of unchurched souls who prepare the material or moral environments without which these higher labors are in vain. Prevention is Christian as well as cure; and Christianity travels sometimes by the most circuitous paths. It is given to some to work for immediate results, and from year to year they are privileged to reckon up a balance of success. But these are not always the greatest in the Kingdom of God. The men who get no stimulus from any visible reward, whose lives pass while the objects for which they toil are still too far away to comfort them; the men who hold aloof from dazzling schemes and earn the misunderstanding of the crowd because they foresee remoter issues, who even oppose a seeming good because a deeper evil lurks beyond—these are the statesmen of the Kingdom of God.

The Machinery of the Society

Such in dimmest outline is the Program of Christ's Society. Did you know that all this was going on in the world? Did you know that Christianity was such a living and purpose-like thing? Look back to the day when that Program was given, and you will see that it was not merely written on paper. Watch the drama of the moral order rise up, scene after scene, in history. Study the social evolution of humanity, the spread of righteousness, the amelioration of life, the freeing of slaves, the elevation of woman, the purification of religion, and ask what these can be if not the coming of the Kingdom of God on earth. For it is precisely through the movements of nations and the lives of men that this Kingdom comes. Christ might have done all this work Himself, with His own hands. But He did not. The crowning wonder of His scheme is that He entrusted it to men. It is the supreme glory of humanity that the machinery for its redemption should have been placed within itself. I think the saddest thing in Christ's life was that after founding a Society with aims so glorious He had to go away and leave it.

But in reality He did not leave it. The old theory that God made the world, made it as an inventor would make a machine, and then stood looking on to see it work, has passed away. God is no longer a remote spectator of the natural world, but immanent in it, pervading matter by His present Spirit, and ordering it by His Will. So Christ is immanent in men. His work is to move the hearts and inspire the lives of men, and through such hearts to move and reach the world. Men, only men, can carry out this work. This humanness, this inwardness, of the Kingdom is one reason why some scarcely see that it exists at all. We measure great movements by the loudness of their advertisement, or the place their externals fill in the public eye. This Kingdom has no externals. The usual methods of propagating a great cause were entirely discarded by Christ. The sword He declined; money He had none; literature He never used; the Church disowned Him; the State crucified Him. Planting His ideals in the hearts of a few poor men, He started them out unheralded to revolutionize the world. They did it by making friends and by making enemies; they went about, did good, sowed seed, died, and lived again in the lives of those they helped. These in turn, a fraction of them, did the same. They met, they prayed, they talked of Christ, they loved, they went among other men, and by act and word passed on their secret. The machinery of the Kingdom of God is purely social. It acts, not by commandment, but by contagion; not by fiat, but by friendship. "The Kingdom of God is like unto leaven, which a woman took and hid in three measures of meal till the whole was leavened."

After all, like all great discoveries once they are made, this seems absolutely the most feasible method that could have been devised. Men must live among men. Men must influence men. Organizations, institutions, churches, have too much rigidity for a thing that is to flood the world. The only fluid in the world is man. War might have won for Christ's cause a passing victory; wealth might have purchased a superficial triumph; political power might have gained a temporary success. But in these, there is no note of universality, of solidarity, of immortality. To live through the centuries and pervade the uttermost ends of the earth, to stand while kingdoms tottered and civilizations changed, to survive fallen churches and crumbling creeds—there was no soil for the Kingdom of God like the hearts of common men. Some who have written about this Kingdom have emphasized its moral grandeur, others its universality, others its adaptation to man's needs. One great writer speaks of its prodigious originality, another chiefly notices its success. I confess what almost strikes me most is the miracle of its simplicity.

Men, then, are the only means God's Spirit has of accomplishing His purpose. What men? You. Is it worth doing, or is it not? Is it worth while joining Christ's Society or is it not? What do you do all day? What is your personal stake in the coming of the Kingdom of Christ on earth? You are not interested in religion, you tell me; you do not care for your "soul". It was not about your religion I ventured to ask, still less about your soul. That you have no religion, that you do not care for your soul, does not absolve you from caring for the world in which you live. But you do not believe in this church, you reply, or accept this doctrine, or that. Christ does not, in the first instance, ask your thoughts, but your work. No man has a right to postpone his life for the sake of his thoughts. Why? Because this is a real world, not a think world. Treat it as a real world— act. Think by all means, but think also of what is actual, of what like the stern world is, of low much even you, creedless and churchless, could do to make it better. The thing to be anxious about is not to be right with man, but with mankind. And, so far as I know, there is nothing so on all fours with mankind as Christianity.

.

There are versions of Christianity, it is true, which no self-respecting mind can do other than disown—versions so hard, so narrow, so unreal, so super-theological, that practical men can find in them neither outlet for their lives nor resting-place for their thoughts. With these we have nothing to do. With these Christ had nothing to do— except to oppose them with every word and act of His life. It too seldom occurs to those who repudiate Christianity because of its narrowness or its unpracticalness, its sanctimoniousness or its dulness, that these were the very things which Christ strove against and unweariedly condemned. It was the one risk of His religion being given to the common people—an inevitable risk which He took without reserve—that its infinite luster should be tarnished in the fingering of the crowd or have its great truths narrowed into mean and unworthy molds as they passed from lip to lip. But though the crowd is the object of Christianity, it is not its custodian. Deal with the Founder of this great Commonwealth Himself. Any man of honest purpose who will take the trouble to inquire at first hand what Christianity really is, will find it a thing he cannot get away from. Without either argument or pressure, by the mere practicalness of its aims and the pathos of its compassions, it forces its August claim upon every serious life.

He who joins this Society finds himself in a large place. The Kingdom of God is a Society of the best men, working for the best ends, according to the best methods. Its membership is a multitude whom no man can number; its methods are as various as human nature; its field is the world. It is a Commonwealth, yet it honors a King; it is a Social Brotherhood, but it acknowledges the Fatherhood of God. Though not a Philosophy the world turns to it for light; though not Political it is the incubator of all great laws. It is more human than the State, for it deals with deeper needs; more Catholic than the Church, for it includes whom the Church rejects. It is a Propaganda, yet it works not by agitation but by ideals. It is a Religion, yet it holds the worship of God to be mainly the service of man. Though not a Scientific Society its watchword is Evolution; though not an Ethic it possesses the Sermon on the Mount. This mysterious Society owns no wealth but distributes fortunes. It has no minutes for history keeps them; no member's roll for no one could make it. Its entry-money is nothing; its subscription, all you have The Society never meets and it never adjourns. Its law is one word— loyalty; its Gospel one message — love. Verily "Whosoever will lose his life for My sake shall find it."

The Program for the other life is not out yet. For this world, for these faculties, for his one short life, I know nothing that is offered to man to compare with membership in the Kingdom of God. Among the mysteries which compass the world beyond, none is greater than how there can be in store for man a work more wonderful, a life more God-like than this. If you know anything better, live for it; if not, in the name of God and of Humanity, carry out Christ's plan.

Made in the USA
Lexington, KY
05 July 2011